NICHOLAS BORNOFF

Pink Samurai

The Pursuit and Politics of Sex in Japan

Grafton

An Imprint of HarperCollins*Publishers*

Grafton
An Imprint of HarperCollins*Publishers*
77–85 Fulham Palace Road,
Hammersmith, London W6 8JB

Special overseas edition 1992
This edition published by Grafton 1992
9 8 7 6 5 4 3 2

First published in Great Britain by
GraftonBooks 1991

ISBN 0 586 20576 4

Set in Palatino

Printed in Great Britain by
HarperCollinsManufacturing Glasgow

Born in London of Anglo-French parentage, Nicholas Bornoff was schooled both in England and France. After a year of graphic design at Hornsey College of Art, he went to a film school in Paris, where he lived for a decade. In 1979 a two-year job as a European language translator prompted him to move to Tokyo which subsequently became his home for eleven years. While in Japan, Bornoff worked as an advertising copywriter, was film critic for the *Japan Times* newspaper, and contributed many articles about society, culture, business and travel in a wide variety of publications. A freelance journalist, Bornoff now lives in London with his Japanese wife.

Christianity gave Eros poison to drink – he did not die of it, to be sure, but degenerated into vice.

Friedrich Nietzsche, *Beyond Good and Evil*

The temple, the teahouses and the shops, as well as the *kashi-zashiki* are decorated with banners and gay paper lanterns in which lighted candles are placed at night, and most of them are an appropriate scarlet, though I read that scientists have recently discovered that the colour of sin is pink.

W. E. Curtis, remarking on the Yoshiwara in 1896

Camellia, plum,
Once these were white –
I find in peach
Colour
That does not blame my sin.

Akiko Yosano, from *Midaregami* (1901)

Contents

Part II: The Rites of Spring

Part IV: Heatwaves in the Water Trade

Part VI: A New Era

Foreword

The English-speaking world must be colour-blind: its sexual manifestations are 'blue'. In Japan, where erotic horizons are unclouded by notions of sin, these things are *'pinkku'* – pink. Despite the demographic decline common to most industrial societies, the Japanese obviously continue to beget Japanese. In the process, they face the universal dilemmas between procreative urges and love, between the pleasure principle and propriety. Although such things are common to all humanity, the way they are perceived can vary a great deal. In the world of the pink samurai, procreative sex and licentious passion are equally acceptable, but strict Confucian codes of conduct keep them rigorously apart.

Where many marriages are still arranged and a woman's place is the home, Love Hotels are dotted about the landscape and late night TV is notoriously unchaste. While imported Victorian values decree stringent censorship, violent erotic comics are read on trains and the striptease theatre is a temple for amateur gynaecologists. Ancient Shinto fertility festivals survive, yet sex education lags sorely behind. Spartan machismo sees sex as sissy, yet there's a national cult for mawkish young female singing stars. Homosexuality has a long and venerable history of tolerance, but an office worker – gay or not – may forego promotion if he does not marry.

Japan has swamped most of its visible Asian attributes beneath a sea of ferroconcrete, yet archaic stringencies survive at the helm. Hence the western imagination supplants cherry blossoms and geisha with high-tech and workaholic robots. The cliché holds true, but the blossoms and the geisha (just) remain, and the faceless corporate and industrial armies endure all as individual human beings. The warriors still have their rest and recreation. High on the list of options, with obsessive fantasies often far overshadowing the realities, is sex. Arousing, mercantile, straightforward and/or bizarre, sex swamps the media, including those targeting women. Abroad one hears as much about Japan's sexual frankness as one does about its puritanism: this book is an attempt to shed light on the paradoxes and their precedents.

Notwithstanding a rich cultural heritage emerging from the pleasure quarters and an enduring degree of sexual innocence, Japan is a far cry from Eden. Due to the rigidity of the social structure, the escape routes are apt to go to extremes. Most of these are to be found in the *mizu shobai*, the water trade, where bar hostesses massage egos and Soapland massages the rest. Covering all things from *bona-fide* bars to overt – yet illegal – prostitution, the *mizu shobai* has evolved directly from the dazzling floating world of yore – an island of tolerance in an ocean of dictatorial austerity. Then, as now, if many facets of the world of Japanese sex can be absurd, hilarious, seductive and charming, they can be as exploitative and sordid as anywhere.

In Japan sexual pleasure has long been entirely a male preserve. The momentary stars of some of the world's most expensive weddings, women are buried in the home for a lifetime. When not a family icon, the Japanese woman has been either a mistress or a prostitute. Notwithstanding the emergence of a vast female labour force during the last century, emancipation only began from the postwar period. Never has the Japanese woman risen as far as she has during the 1980s. The corruption

and sex scandals tainting a tenacious ruling party gave
her resentment a voice. She has been instrumental in
ousting politicians but, even though the officially buttressed fortress of male supremacy is under siege,
change has a way to go. This also applies to both
inter-sexual relationships and perceptions of sex in the
broadest sense. Sex is the one area in which Japan's
dichotomy between archaic values and a post-industrial
society is most painfully apparent.

My bias is admittedly towards individual freedom,
and some will argue that such freedom is purely a
western concept. But in eleven years in Japan, I have
never seen a people striving more to adopt it than the
Japanese. I would not have written *Pink Samurai*
otherwise.

Acknowledgements

(**NB** The opinions expressed in this book are my own, and not necessarily shared by those who were gracious enough to offer me their assistance.)

My thanks are due first to William Miller, whose good agency and initiatives made this project a reality. A long-standing thank you to Ian Buruma, who helped orient my disorientation when I arrived in Japan in 1979 and whose insights I greatly value, as I do those of Donald Richie, to whom I am deeply indebted for his encouragement and sagacious advice. I am very grateful to Ronald Bell, both for generous assistance and for imparting his knowledge of Japanese fertility worship. Many thanks are due in this area, too, to Hirohiko Nakamura, high priest of the Kanamyama shrine in Kawasaki, to Noboru Tsukamoto and Koichi Mori.

I can never thank Bruce Osborn enough for his wealth of introductions, and my gratitude for these goes, too, to Tomoko Ura, Hiroko Horiguchi, Diane Diele and Hiroshi Ishikawa. I am very grateful to Rumi Kanesaka for her help with interviews, and likewise to Tamako Hamaguchi, who also greatly assisted with organization. I am also much indebted to Joseph Cali for his invaluable comments on earlier drafts, as I am to Gregory Starr. My heartfelt thanks to all those who offered their advice during the course of the project, including Corinne Bret, Jean-Michel Bugnot, Elizabeth Bumiller, Peter Cove, Deborah Fiedler, Jean-Luc Gaudin, Kazuko Kawakita, Leonard Koren, Kuro, Jean-François Lepez, Kiyoharu

Masuda, Don Morton, Bertrand Renaudineau, Tomoaki Tsushima and Karel Van Wolferen.

My deepest thanks for interviews are due to the writer Oniroku Dan, artist Numata Genqui, Ken Ikuta of *Brutus* Magazine, dancer Hoshi Kirara, adult video star Kaoru Kuroki, publisher Shoji Suei, Tamio Suenaga and Yasuko Ezaki (editors of the *More Report* on Japanese sexuality), journalist Kazue Suzuki and to Noboru Yamada of 'Bird'. I am also specially grateful to the writer Komimasa Tanaka for his on-the-spot reminiscences of Shinjuku and Asakusa, as well as for taking me to meet Jun Sayama, manager of the Fransu-za theatre, to whom I am also very thankful. I also owe a deep debt of gratitude to those who would rather I kept to their pseudonyms: I could never have written this book without them.

Finally, I would like to convey my deepest gratitude to my parents for their great encouragement and assistance and, most of all, to my wife, who toiled long and mightily to offer me her devoted support – while I merely sat and wrote.

To Masami, with love

Prologue

Hiroshi Murakami and Mayumi Yamashita were in a car stuck in one of those holiday traffic jams. Although it was winter, they were hot, flustered and fidgeting in their seats. They had been in Nagoya for the afternoon, out on a date, and they had been to the movies. Out of several choices, one film had had to be ruled out, for Mayumi had heard gossipy Mrs Takeda announcing plans to see it the same afternoon. It wouldn't really do, Mayumi thought, if she were seen in the company of a young man; tongues would wag in the whole neighbourhood. So they had finally gone to see Mickey Rourke doing some extraordinary things to Kim Basinger in *9½ Weeks*, and some of these things had even involved food.

In between these bizarre erotico-culinary diversions, it had all been as 'yuppie' and elegantly minimalist as the trendy magazines had promised, but neither Hiroshi nor Mayumi had particularly liked it. It was about a love affair going on the rocks, because the man imposed his sexual eccentricities upon the lady and the lady ultimately wasn't having it.

Mayumi thought that their fierce individualism was a bit much. They were both very selfish, not a bit like the Japanese. Hiroshi mused that the couple attached too much importance to sex to seal a permanent relationship and that the girl, who was career-orientated, would have gained much from being more domestically minded. Besides, if the rich young man had such weird tastes, he could always go out and fulfil them in the *mizu shobai* – the water trade – the world of brothels and bars. Perhaps

America didn't have one or didn't see these things the same way. Hiroshi and Mayumi turned these thoughts over in their minds and didn't talk about the film at all. They were not quite sure whether they wholly agreed with the traditional precepts which made such ideas occur to them in the first place.

Still, it had all been rather sexy. Although they had kept their heads decorously facing the screen, Hiroshi had discreetly squeezed her hand in the darkness of the cinema. Now they were sitting rigidly at the traffic lights, darting surreptitious glances at the faces in the cars surrounding them. Knowing that her normally pale, porcelain-pure complexion had by now acquired a rosy flush, Mayumi hoped that her predicament would go undetected by the occupants of other cars. If they didn't put it down to the setting sun, they might even think that she had been drinking, which was about as bad as the truth. One driver looked like one of Hiroshi's old high-school teachers, so his heart almost skipped a beat.

Ah, how different things are in the city. In Tokyo, these days, to the alarm of conservatives, girls go out drinking and even high-school kids hardly give currying favour with teachers a passing thought. Every now and then Hiroshi's eyes dropped to the hem of Mayumi's pink skirt, to her lap, where her hands were clasped over the apparent focal point of her demure gaze, but his mind was wandering around and taking considerable liberties in places underneath. Last night, incidentally, he had been out with the boys and they had gone to a striptease theatre in which, after doing even more outrageous things in which one of his companions had even been invited to participate, the strippers struck poses making it almost possible to see what their tonsils looked like from underneath. That was last night, however, and although certain associations came to mind with painful intensity, Hiroshi was convinced that they were too outlandish to entertain. Those girls were only prostitutes.

Hiroshi and Mayumi were speechless, overcome with desire. He wondered whether she would or she wouldn't. As the lights changed to green, he dithered painfully for the right moment to ask her, but his mouth was too dry to utter a word.

This was their fourth date and, since they were obviously warming to each other, the time seemed ripe to bring their affair on to the next stage: the love hotel. Electrified with neon signs, painted in garish 1950s pastels and graced with florid wrought-iron baroque balconies entwined with green metal ivy, Hiroshi's and Mayumi's love nest might evoke a set for some improbable post-modern operetta. Hiroshi could hardly bring himself to suggest it.

It was almost dark as the flustered lovebirds were approaching the vicinity of Mayumi's home, which lies about halfway between Nagoya and Toyohashi, in a village called Goyu. It is a flat, semi-industrial wasteland, but just behind the road and train tracks, in places like Goyu, you can still see rows of tall, gnarled pine trees and a few venerable wooden houses – small fragments of the old Tokaido road linking Tokyo and Kyoto existing in a virtually pristine state. This is Aichi prefecture, birthplace of Tokugawa Ieyasu, the mightiest of the shoguns and the man who unified a samurai Japan, which was shortly afterwards to go into isolation from the rest of the world for more than two hundred and sixty years.

Huge chromed trucks emblazoned with firecracker Chinese characters thundered along on the long haul between Tokyo and the south-west through the traffic beside them. They were passing a bleak landscape boasting American fast-food drive-ins, noodle stops, used car lots, garishly neoned *pachinko* pinball parlours and, as Hiroshi was by now very painfully aware, ubiquitous love hotels fancifully architectured like Cinderella castles or Japanese fortresses.

Rising above the forest of TV aerials, palatial love hotels virtually dominated the skyline outside the confines of the villages they passed. Built with convenience uppermost in mind, love hotels lie strategically along the highway, particularly in spots close to interchanges. As it happened, they were coming up to an interchange now. Hiroshi thought of mentioning the Dandy a few yards further on, an inspired architectural cross between a Las Vegas casino and the Arabian Nights outlined in brilliant red and green neon, but they passed it. The words formed again in the back of his throat as they neared the Shogun's Castle, an air-conditioned and illuminated replica of the real thing. What about turning off up the mountainside a bit further on, where plenty more romantic little love hotels lie tucked discreetly away in the woods? You can see the neon signs winking invitingly through the trees, but he missed that one too.

He could always use the old line about going to the love hotel 'just to find a quiet place to talk', but they were anyway alone together in the car. The trouble, Hiroshi thought, was that one always had to say something. Mayumi and he had quite spontaneously made their mutual attraction clear before parting company on a previous date, but they had never gone all the way and they never mentioned sex. Now they were stopping at some traffic lights, not far from the last opportunity before they reached Mayumi's home. Many people much younger than 26-year-old Hiroshi would make their overtures with hardly a moment's hesitation but, again, that was in the big city. The lights turned green.

As he gulped and pressed his foot down on the accelerator, he darted a longing, nervous glance at Mayumi to find her looking at him out of the corners of her eyes. '*Neeehhh* … ' she began, her voice rising with an interrogatory note as coy as it was suggestive, 'Why don't we go to a love hotel?'

PART I

New Year

1

Hotels and Legends

THE CREATION MYTHS

> The whole pathos and weirdness of the myth, the vague
> monstrosity of the fancies, the formal use of terms of
> endearment in the moment of uttermost loathing and fear
> – all impress one as unmistakably Japanese.

> Lafcadio Hearn, *Japan: An Interpretation* (1894)

Among the increasing numbers of foreigners coming
over to Japan in the 1880s, the majority were only too
happy to be walled off from the natives in gilded ghettos;
and the growing numbers of Christian missionaries
found in Japanese culture as much to appal them as
scholars did to enthral them. Among the greatest of the
latter was Professor Basil Hall Chamberlain, who read
his translation of the *Kojiki* (*Records of Ancient Matters*)
before the Asiatic Society of Japan in 1882. First presented to the emperor in 720 A.D., it is a compilation
melding myth and fact so inextricably that it has been the
object of heated scholarly debate ever since. At first the
venerable book might seem to be to the Shinto religion as
the Bible is to Judaeo-Christianity, but the *Kojiki* is
devoid of doctrine and has never been consulted as a
basis for ritual. Presenting history and Shinto myth in
the same perspective, it begins with the Emperor Jimmu
on the more factual side and with the creation myths on
the other.

Missionaries or not, most of the expats in Chamberlain's time looked out at the world through the narrow

glasses of nineteenth-century morality. They had been horrified to find that Japan was 'a country in which all the women dressed from the waist down and all the men from the waist upwards' and that, in general, it was 'a country of nudity, lewdity and crudity'. Comments such as these stung a Japan eager to modernize into measures such as segregating the bath-houses, and the adoption of Western prudery has everything to do with why the country came to know less and less about its own mythology.

Although enlightened scholarship overruled whatever prudish inclinations he may have had, Chamberlain nevertheless had to comply with contemporary mores and was soon moved to resort to antiseptic passages of Latin. Wasting no time, the seminal god and goddess resolve to join their august private parts on about the second page. Whether it pleased Victorians or not, the myths frankly underscored the primordial progenitive fusion that the Book of Genesis had been pleased to bury in the flower-beds of Eden. The first Japanese man and woman are subordinate coital accessories to a creative principle based on the fusion of opposites.

How much the myths can vary shows in the *Nihon Shoki* (or *Nihongi*), *The Chronicles of Japan*, which, written some eighty years after the *Kojiki*, is considered just a shade more historically accurate. The narrative is peppered with variants exhaustively listed in frequently contradictory paragraphs preceded by the words 'In one writing it is said'. Hinting at a hidden chronology, some divergences suggest later Confucian or Buddhist attempts to reorientate and/or bowdlerize the primitive myths. Nobody knows how old they are; handed down orally for centuries, they had anyway been embroidered and altered for as long as a millennium before either book was written. Indeed, by the time they were, they had been swayed by a Chinese influence which had by then taken root in Japan for centuries.

In all versions, the Master-of-the-August-Centre-of-Heaven and the High-Producing-Wondrous-Deity precede a whole gamut of others spontaneously populating the Plain of High Heaven. A reed shoot sprouts up to transform itself into more deities, among them the Luxuriant-Integrating-Master-Deity and the Deity-Oh-Awful-Lady. Figures from myths long lost, some of these 'awful' deities remain obscure; well over fourteen centuries old, their names are not only awkward to translate, but have ambiguous meanings to the modern Japanese. Modern translations leave proper names in the original language, so that Chamberlain's rigorously literal English renditions appear extremely quaint by present standards. Nevertheless, for 'awful', he conceded in a footnote, read 'venerable'.

THE COITAL GENESIS

In the beginning, there was chaos. Perhaps because chaos makes the Japanese unhappy, unlike the one in the Book of Genesis, this one had form. It floated like a jellyfish on water; it was egg-shaped. For aeons, the primeval amalgam inside had been populated with the six generations of invisible gods and goddesses who had emerged from a reed stalk. At last came the visible seventh: the siblings Izanagi-no-Mikoto and Izanami-no-Mikoto, the Male-Who-Invites and the Female-Who-Invites, respectively.

The ancestral gods bestowed upon them a gift of a mighty lance studded with jewels. Not so much a weapon as a gigantic organ of generation, it is believed to have been shaped like an *obashira*, which means 'male post' and signifies the end-posts decorating the balustrades around Shinto shrines. Consisting of an onion-shaped brass dome set atop a red wooden column, the *obashira* is clearly a phallic symbol. As they stood upon a celestial bridge spanning the swirling maelstrom of the universe, following their instructions, Izanami and Izanagi hoisted the all-powerful tool up in their arms. Plunging it deep inside the convoluted void until the tip sank into a vast ocean, they stirred it around 'until it went curdle-curdle'. As they pulled it out again, the gobs of foaming brine dripping from the end formed the island of Onogoro-Jima: 'the island spontaneously congealed'. Then they lodged the lance right into the island's centre and came down to solid ground. To this Japanese Adam and Eve, the island dominated by a huge phallic pillar was Eden. Their task was not only to populate it but also, since animistic Shinto regards all things as being possessed with spirits and deities, to beget the environment too.

Knowing that they were to procreate, they began ritually circling in opposite directions around the primordial maypole. Rather like adolescents in modern Japan, having been told nothing about the process by their parental gods, they were left to work it out themselves. As they met during the first turn, it was the woman Izanami who made the first move. Then Izanagi began by asking her how her body was shaped. 'Oh, mine is pretty much the same as yours,' she said, 'except in one place, which is the source of womanhood. What about yours?' Izanagi said that his was much the same too, except for that salient point which is the root of masculinity. After inspecting each other's parts, *vive la différence*: they figured that the one ought to go inside the other.

During what was an eternity before the advent of the

erotic woodblock print, let alone 'How to Sex' magazines, Izanami and Izanagi were increasingly moved but
quite at a loss as to how to respond to the procreative
urge. Just then they saw a wagtail. Watching the bird's
tail moving suggestively up and down, Izanami and
Izanagi were getting ideas. Interestingly, aeons later in
the real world, this information still applies more to birds
than people in the curriculum of most Japanese schools.
Somehow, they had gone wrong. Izanami gave birth to
an island called Aha which, despite such an encouraging
name, they disowned. Then she gave birth to a hideous
leech-child, which they placed in a boat made of reeds
and set adrift. Subsequent legends have it that this child
made his way back to Japan later as the vastly grinning
and pot-bellied Ebisu, the god of marine abundance who
still sits atop shelves in taverns, fishmongeries and
restaurants today.

Sorely perplexed, Izanami and Izanagi consulted their
ancestral deities and discovered the mistake: the woman
had made the first move. So returning to the ground,
they circled around the pillar again, until Izanagi finally
took some initiative: 'How wonderful', he said to her
admiringly, 'to have met such a beautiful maiden.' And
'How wonderful', she replied in kind, 'to have met such
a handsome youth.'

Having at last learned how to do it, the celestial lovers
did so diligently indeed. Izanami successively gave birth
to the Japanese archipelago, the winds and the elements,
trees, plants and the mountains and plains, as well as the
gods inhabiting all of these. But alas, calamity struck her
when she gave birth at last to Kagu-Tsuchi, the god of
fire. Making his way into the new world, the flaming
babe seared her vagina so badly that she howled and
writhed in agony. During her death throes, Izanami
vomited up the god and goddess of the mountains of

metal, the faeces pouring from her bowels materialized as the goddess of clay and other deities emerged from her streams of urine. These immediately engendered others in turn, but Izanami was dead.

'Oh, that I should have given my beloved sister in exchange for a single child!' wailed heartbroken Izanagi, as more deities materialized from his tears. Maddened with rage and grief, he dismembered his fiery offspring with his sword. Like the gouts of blood spattering from the blade, the bits and pieces he scattered over the earth turned into more deities joining others to form the vanguard of the Shinto pantheon. In one way and another, Izanagi and Izanami produced the eight thousand ancestors of the eighty thousand and then eight million and more Shinto gods. Some went to dwell in the blue Plain of High Heaven; others remained on earth to become the ancestors of the Japanese race.

DEATH AND POLLUTION

The bereaved Izanagi went to the dark and dreadful land of Yami to seek his spouse. Receiving him as her beauteous former self, Izanami was all smiles in the palace of the dead but, having already partaken of the tainted food prepared in its kitchens, she was to stay there for eternity. She would, however, try to implore the lords of the underworld to allow him to take her back. Just as Orpheus was forbidden to look upon Eurydice and just as surely as disobedient Lot turned around to find his wife transformed to salt, so the Japanese myth finds a man blindly relinquishing reason to passion.

Imploring Izanagi not to look upon her again until she had consulted the lords of Yami, Izanami disappeared into the darkness behind a curtain. As time passed, Izanagi grew impatient. Snapping off one of the teeth of the comb he wore in his hair and setting alight to it, he strode boldly into the realm of death to find her. Glistening in the light of this small flame, the horror that had once been Izanami stood before him and the rotting flesh falling away from her bones was crawling with maggots. Among the eight thunder deities affixed to various parts of her body, the great thunder god sat like a crown atop her leering skull and the god of cleaving thunder had taken up residence in her genitals.

Hell hath no fury like a woman scorned, and Izanagi's Hades has its Furies too. When he turned to flee, the mortified and enraged Izanami sent the ugly hags of hell in hot pursuit. Removing his comb as he ran, Izanagi distracted them by tearing out the teeth and scattering them on the ground, where they turned into bamboo shoots which the hags eagerly devoured. When Izanami unleashed the eight thunders, Izanagi only just managed to escape by feeding them peaches (an old Taoist vulvar symbol) from an enchanted tree. As his putrescent spouse ran tottering after him, threatening to follow him out of death's domain, Izanagi rolled a vast stone over the gate of hell, and finally held her at bay. As she trembled with rage behind the boulder, Izanagi pronounced her divorced.

'My dear lord and master,' Izanami cried, 'if you do so, each day I shall strangle a thousand of your people!' And Izanagi answered her: 'My beloved sister, do that and in one day I shall cause fifteen hundred more to be born.' What Izanami had to say to that is not recorded, for at least one version has it that a goddess called Kukurihime intervened with placating words which finally caused Izanami to vanish.

In all versions, Izanagi has the last word and the

statement implies a phallo-generative principle essential to a patrilineal and patriarchal society. The seed-dispensing male is a giver of life; the female is an accessory, an incubator. In informal male speech today, *oyaji* is 'my august Dad', but Mum is the frankly amniotic *ofukuro* – 'the honourable bag'. Izanagi rids himself of Izanami in just a few words, divorcing her just as easily as could any man until only very recently in Japan. A mediating third party, Kukurihime restores the proper order by settling the dispute in favour of the male and, brought to her senses, the female principle Izanami defers.

IMPURITY AND THE FEMALE

During the course of this creation myth, the female principle Izanami progresses from unsullied virgin to sacred mother – incest notwithstanding – before degenerating into the demonic alter ego deeply ingrained in the Japanese cultural concept of womanhood. Japanese ghosts, for instance, especially the most feared and vengeful kind, are overwhelmingly female. 'These myths', suggested French Japanologist Théo Lésoualc'h, 'perhaps express woman's real status in the Japanese mind: Izanagi's exalted love when he pursues her shows man confronted with the terrible reality of death.'

Although Izanagi escapes, he has been doubly defiled: first through contact with woman in a polluted state, secondly through contact with death. In addition to the polluting emissions – especially blood – Izanami's death agony involves, her wounded vagina symbolizes the universal taboo of menstruation. Like many other of the world's religions, Shintoism prohibits menstruating women from entering hallowed ground, but it also regards her as being in a polluted state for several weeks following and including parturition.

Having been tainted with blood, the same applies to a newborn baby. Once virtually shunned by other villagers until a pre- to post-natal term had elapsed, women were confined to a parturition hut called *ubu-ya*. Mentioned several times in the *Kojiki*, it was specially erected outside the village and always rigorously out-of-bounds to men. The custom of sending a woman to spend time alone with her child in the *ubu-ya*, which was moreover often on a mountainside, contributed much to the drastically high infant mortality rate of former times. Later, the *ubu-ya* became a dark cubbyhole inside the house itself and, although the custom died out earlier this century, they are still sometimes to be seen in ancient farmhouses left standing in remote areas.

PURIFICATION

In mid-July, before they ascend sacred Mount Ontake, a volcano in Nagano prefecture, some hundred thousand white-clad pilgrims line up to purify themselves beneath the famous Kyotaki waterfall. Before a wedding ceremony, the bride, groom and guests must likewise wash their hands before entering the shrine. In secular contexts too, the Japanese are renowned for their cleanliness. The bath is a daily ritual; many people spend their scant holidays contentedly immersed in hot springs. Given customers in restaurants and coffee shops, *oshibori* wet towels are said to be kept in ample supply in *yakuza* gangster headquarters. Although these are for wiping hands and mopping brows during 'board' meetings, traditionalist *yakuza* are well aware of the

Shinto connection. Because water not only washes away dirt but also cleanses the spirit from contact with impurity, lustration forms an essential part of the Shinto ritual.

When Izanagi returned from Yami and back to the world, he immersed himself in the Tachibana river and stripped off his clothes and washed them. As the water he wrung from his garments splashed down, the droplets turned into myriad other deities; the goddess of the moon materialized from the water running from his right eye and the most important deity in the Shinto pantheon was born from his left: Amatarasu-no-Omikami. Rising up over the other deities, the sun goddess brought light into the world and shed her life-giving rays over the rice paddies of what was to remain until only very recently a predominantly agricultural land.

CHILDREN OF CHILD-LIKE GODS

As repugnant as she becomes as a demoness, Izanami is irreproachable – a victim of fate. Izanagi, although he has violated a Shinto taboo by venturing into the land of the dead at all, is defiled through no fault of his own. Recognizing neither good nor evil, Shinto is free from blame; none of its deities is truly bad. Essentially a folk religion, deeply rooted in primitive animism and devoid of doctrine, Shinto lacks the sophistication needed to develop a code of ethics.

Regarded as part of the community, the gods who are not part of the higher pantheon are none other than the forebears of the ordinary Japanese. In what gradually became an ancestor cult, the dead go on to become *kami* in the afterlife and the duty incumbent on the living is to honour them both as gods and as members of the family. Having left the cares of the world behind them for better or worse, the family *kami* are naturally exempted from the obligations and responsibilities controlling the lives of everyone else. Although the wrath of the *kami* is to be feared, unlike most gods in this world, they enjoy privileges akin to children and the old.

As the *omikoshi* palanquins containing higher deities and paraded through Shinto festivals today might suggest, the gods are not so much worshipped as indulged. They are symbolically treated to an outing; as with mischievous children, good behaviour is coaxed from them by showing them a good time. Neither meditative, nor for spiritual guidance nor a gesture of contrition, prayer is merely to augur good fortune or for making a material request. Under the circumstances, offerings are *de rigueur*. One drops coins into the box before the shrine altar, or leaves fruit, vegetables or sake bottles to please the gods further. Just as the Japanese still curry favour with, bestow obligations on and give thanks to each other through offering gifts, so Shinto believers hope to be repaid in kind through propitiating divinities.

Japanese culture is often regarded as the triumph of form over content, an inclination which is not only reflected in Shinto religion, but which may well also be rooted in it. Unlike in meditative Buddhism, where ritual is generally subordinate to piousness, Shinto ritual places more emphasis on pomp than prayer. Thus, one wonders, how religious are the Japanese? To Kurt Singer, writing in the thirties in *Mirror, Sword and Jewel*, the answer seemed clear:

The very life of Shinto is to be found not in a set of beliefs but in a definite way of acting: bowing quietly, reverently calling the gods by clapping the hands and silent prayer after having purified one's hands, one's mouth and one's thoughts. Theologians speak of an act of communion between the soul of the worshipper and the god. But do gods exist in any form other than in such acts of reverence? The monk Saigyo professed not to know whether gods were or were not present behind the curtain of the Shrines of Ise. But he admitted that a reverential awe made tears well forth ('although I do not know at all whether anything honourably deigns to be there'). This is Japanese piety, agnostic and reverential, full of awe and lucidity.

Hardly to be bettered for pomp is Tokyo's largest festival, the three-day Sanja *matsuri* (festival), which draws crowds some 800,000 strong to Asakusa and reaches a frenzy as hefty portable *omikoshi* shrines are borne on the shoulders of exaltedly chanting bearers. Once the last of the largest three of these juggernauts has been carried through the streets to its final destination at the third of the Sanja shrines, a grand procession holding coloured lanterns aloft stands before the regal figure of the high priest. The *matsuri* is about to reach its finish, and the air is electric with expectancy. One waits in awe for some kind of mystical revelation, but the priest merely picks up a microphone. 'Quite a good turnout this year,' he announces offhandedly, 'despite the weather. Thank you very much and we're looking forward to seeing you again next time!'

The awe Singer described is with the Japanese still. While many attend festivals for the sheer fun of it, they will always clasp their hands and bow heads before the altar to be on the safe side, and enduring superstition may well dictate the purchase of a talisman to increase the odds.

When crossed, the gods can be sulky and troublesome. Izanagi's lustration in the Tachibana river produced one more deity, born from the water streaming from his nose. A storm god, the impetuous Susano-o's initial misbehaviour almost belies his fierce bearded aspect and suggests a very naughty child. Enraged by his older sister Amaterasu's decision to give him dominion only over the sea, the sorely vexed Susano-o was suddenly seized with a desire for wrongdoing. First, he committed the terrible sacrilege of blocking up all the irrigation ditches of the celestial rice fields and trampling down the banks of earth dividing them. Gaining no attention from his motherly sister or the other gods, he carried his mischief a step further. Bursting into a temple during a sacrosanct rice-offering ceremony, he defecated beneath Amaterasu's throne and horrified the attendant deities by tossing faeces in all directions, but the radiant Amaterasu indulged her brat brother and uttered not a word of reproach.

So Susano-o did something really and truly awful. As Amaterasu sat making sacred garments among the Celestial Weavers, he smashed a hole in the roof of the hall and hurled down the dismembered remains of a piebald horse of heaven. Worse still, the *Kojiki* tells us, he had flayed the divine steed 'with a backward flaying'. So blasphemous and ghastly was this that one of the weaving maidens, beside herself with horror, accidentally pricked her genitals with her shuttle and expired. This time, Susano-o had gone too far. So enraged was Amaterasu over the tragedy that she stormed from the palace, ran all the way into the mountains and hid in a cave. As she rolled a huge stone across the entrance, the world was plunged into darkness.

THE CELESTIAL STRIP-SHOW

In order to placate Amaterasu and bring back the light, the myriad other deities convened an extraordinary meeting with the various gods of sorcery and lengthy consultations, they finally reached a consensus. Amatsumara, the blacksmith god, would take iron from the Heavenly Metal Mountains and forge a mirror. Other gods would mine the fabled jewels to hang together with the mirror in a tree outside Amaterasu's cave and, finally, they would avail themselves of the services of Ama-no-Uzume, the Heavenly Alarming Female.

Having built fires in the darkness around the sealed entrance to Amaterasu's cave, the gods sat in a vast semicircle and awaited Ama-no-Uzume's arrival as eagerly as an audience for some gigantic outdoor burlesque theatre. Appearing at last, Ama-no-Uzume wore garlands of flowers in her hair, clasping sacred plants in one hand and a lance in the other. Fixed by myriad divine pairs of eyes, she leapt up onto a boat-shaped *ukefune* tub in front of the cave and began dancing. Stamping her feet and pounding the lance in an ever more frenzied rhythm, she was gradually possessed by a divine spirit. As her hair flailed wildly atop her ecstatically tossing head, she caused the top half of her dress to slide from her shoulders and revealed her breasts. The gods ogled Ama-no-Uzume loosening the waistband of her skirt, which at last fell to the ground. Then to everyone's great delight, as she contorted herself about in the nude, the Heavenly Alarming Female explicitly revealed her genitals, and the entire pantheon filled the firmament with riotous roars of laughter.

Wondering at the merriment outside, Amaterasu pushed the stone back a crack from the cave mouth, sending sunbeams darting out into the darkness as she peeped outside. Ama-no-Uzume brazenly informed her that since she'd apparently gone into retirement, another goddess was going to replace her. Leaning out further to hear this shattering news, Amaterasu caught sight of her blazing reflection in the mirror outside and heaved the boulder a little too far. Tajikarao, the macho god of strength, grabbed her gently but firmly by the arm and pulled her outside. In so doing, he caused the sun to rise once more over the world of men.

RED AND WHITE

> Still yearning
> After the good,
> The true, the beautiful?
> Oh, my love, this flower in my hand
> Is dazzling red!

Akiko Yosano, *Midaregami* (1901)

Yin-Yang (male and female, black and white, light and dark, dry and wet) has been adopted in Japan from ancient times, but the red and white symbolizing female and male respectively were no doubt adopted long before the introduction of Chinese culture. This is the predominant colour scheme of Shinto. The *Kohaku* (Red-White) year-end TV song contest is a competition between male and female. Consider the mouths of the bride or the geisha: mere petals of vermilion adorning an immaculately blank face. Or the dish of white rice and red beans cooked to mark a girl's first monthly period and her passage to womanhood. On the Japanese flag, the *Hinomaru* – the Circle of the Sun – the red and white live together in perpetual harmony. While the design also evokes the splendid sun goddess Amaterasu as an orb rising against an immaculate sky, the 'cinnabar cleft' is the ancient Chinese term for the female genitals and the colour of carnal passion in Japan. As at least one irreverent Japanese satirical cartoon has implied, the flag also seems to suggest polluting woman soaking into a background of pristine male purity like a menstrual stain.

LOVE HOTELS

When the popular songstress Midori Satsuki opened a love hotel in Tokyo during the mid-seventies, the press went to town. Near Shibuya station, it was simply called Hoteru Japan and praised for its interiors in the 'Italian style'. On a more indigenous note, however, red and white compounded the dominant colour scheme in the rooms, some of which contained a decorative pair of stones of the kind associated with ancient phallicism and fertility worship. Ms Satsuki was in earnest about the benefits of her hotel. 'I wanted to make it a dreamland for the night,' she told the press, 'where the dreams of young lovers will come true. And even if they are not lovers,' she concluded less romantically, 'they should think of themselves as such in my hotel.'

Featured in magazine pictorials overseas, outrageous architecture and kitsch interiors have made the Japanese love hotel internationally famous; but too often the assumption is that it is a brothel – which it isn't. Even though used by many professionals to entertain their customers and only incidentally or consequentially for sleeping in, like the restaurant, the coffee shop or the public toilet, the love hotel is a purely pragmatic answer to a basic physical need. When neither studying nor working in towns away from home, young Japanese like Hiroshi and Mayumi tend to live with their parents until they marry. Even then, since the chances are that their new home will be minute, the love hotel will loom large again after the production of progeny. With little privacy from growing children and/or the husband's widowed mother, the love hotel is for many Japanese virtually the only haven of sexual intimacy there is.

In 1984 there were some 35,000 nationwide, and nearly 4,000 in Tokyo, where some new ones go up and more come down, as the *rentaru rumu* (rental room), offering no more than a large couch, a TV set and a box of tissues, becomes a cheaper option for growing hordes of young people enjoying a more liberal lifestyle. During the sixties, they had to resort to the upper floors of some of the broader-minded coffee shops, which provided high-backed booths and unobtrusive waiters. Dating couples are sometimes known as being *abekku*, from the French *avec*: a handy loan-word for implying that they are 'with' each other. Although the *abekku kissa* (*avec* coffee shop) provided a private haven for necking and sometimes more, only a small handful remains.

The claimants for the honour of being the originator are many, but the first love hotels were born simply from a more lucrative transformation of the bona fide hotel. Not a few old ryokan, the traditional inns, have similarly reorientated their business to serve as love hotels, without refurbishing classic interiors to compete with their newer and more garish counterparts. Like these, such ryokan proliferate most on the fringes of amusement districts and thus have a fairly long-standing function as *hôtels de passe*. During the Occupation, many new ones are said to have been built specially to cater for American soldiers and local *pan-pan* girls; others were destitute bona fide hotels welcoming an alternative to bankruptcy. Coined during the early postwar years, the term *Rabu Hoteru* – love hotel – properly designates the facility's function and sets it apart.

The love hotel's interior reflects a deep-rooted love of the artificial. Where constant conformity reduces the scope for individual fantasy, it must be provided from outside. The love hotel is thus a theatre set. The foyer might find the Venus de Milo in gilt or silvered splendour against a royal red velveteen backdrop. There could be coloured spotlights and twinkling chrome and glass chandeliers. The discretion is legendary: the reception desk is a mere pigeonhole, behind which one sometimes glimpses a moonlighting old lady. Some love hotels even provide electronic members' credit cards: the key is delivered when the card is put in a slot. Guests choose rooms from a showcase displaying large back-lit transparencies; the dark ones signify occupancy. Along with the room number, a blurb underneath boasts the merits of each. These include revolving and vibrating beds, water beds and beds that massage and/or rock like cradles. There might be ionized air, plush chairs with leg-rests instead of armrests, SM paraphernalia, sing-along *karaoke* tape decks, jacuzzis, palatial sunken baths and more. Love hotels also proliferate around hot-spring resorts, boasting bathrooms fed by curative and piping-hot water welling up from the bowels of the volcanic earth.

You takes your choice and you pays your money. The average rate for *sabisu taimu* (service time – or a couple of hours) is 3,000 to 4,000 yen and it doubles for an overnight stay. No breakfast and, in most, an extra sum will be exacted for every hour slept over the 10 A.M. check-out time. During the mid-eighties, collective annual love hotel earnings were between three and four trillion yen annually, much of which is unreported to the revenue authorities.

In some of the plusher love hotels, the scope of fantasy is large: tatami matting and plastic cherry trees for a classic Japanese touch, Hawaiian tropicana, medieval Western torture chambers, heated swimming pools complete with chutes to send the lovers sliding into each other's arms. In one instance, the bed is like an island anchored in the middle of the pool, in another the bed suggests a 1950s Cadillac sitting complete with chrome fins and tail-lights in the middle of what looks like an ornate Chinese restaurant. One finds beds modelled like Venetian gondolas, hearts, pineapples, jet planes and assorted spacecraft, including the space shuttle Columbus.

Some rooms claim to provide sound-sensitive coloured lighting that brightens, dims and changes colour in rheostatic response to the action of their occupants. Invariably flanking the bed and often gracing the ceiling, mirrors are often arrayed to produce a kaleidoscopic image of the proceedings. The latest developments in love hoteldom are not infrequently reported on late-night TV programmes, which find nubile female models coyly giggling their way behind their hands through strip routines as brash male compères in baseball caps extol the ins and outs of the bedrooms. The constant flux of gimmickry yields beds arranged around a disco floor complete with strobes and laser beams for 'parties', or rooms with twin double beds for *swizinggu capuru* – swinging couples.

In addition to standard hoteldom's vacuum flask of hot water and green tea bags, a refrigerator stocked with drinks and a pay TV, in any love hotel worthy of the name the screen is flanked by a library of porn videos. There is usually a small vending machine selling *otona-no-omocha* (adult toys) in the form of assorted dildos and ticklers and, invariably, another selling condoms which, prophylactic considerations aside, happen to be the preferred method of birth control for 70 per cent of the population.

No relevant article published abroad fails to mention the Queen Mary roadside love hotel near Yokohama, which is shaped like an ocean liner, in which the bed in one room is said to replicate Queen Elizabeth II's coronation coach. Hundreds have ornate façades artistically festooned with friezes of nude statuary. One is built like a house upside-down with the roof buried in the ground; another is surmounted by a vast Statue of Liberty; not a few evoke the palace of Versailles and in the countryside one sees some that, from the steeple to the stained-glass windows, look so like churches as to invite embarrassing confusion.

Renowned for its outlandish Disneyland castle architecture and hailed universally as the ultimate Japanese love hotel, Tokyo's Meguro Emperor is the proud creation of architect Kurosaka Yasuhisa and the brain-child of a wealthy family fallen on hard times. Built in 1973, it offered de luxe service throughout some thirty rooms appointed with the last word in advanced bedroom gadgetry. Indeed, room service could be prevailed upon to send up fancy meals, doctors, hairdressers and bona fide masseurs and the refrigerators were stocked with expensive French brandies, wines and champagne. By the end of 1973, estimates showed that the Meguro Emperor's electronic fantasies cost about a million yen a month to run, a figure which would have by now more than tripled. Moving with the times, however, it has recently been renovated within, divided into smaller rooms reflecting a more austere aura of ersatz European sophistication and renamed the Gallery Hotel.

While the better love hotels strive to maintain standards, the picture can be different in the cheaper mainstream. The rooms are almost invariably smaller than in the wide-angle photographs advertising them downstairs. The revolving beds don't revolve, the dimmers don't work and a flickering half-hour porno video in amazing greens and magentas can wreak havoc with the eyesight. No one complains. It may well be that patrons have other things on their minds, but the Japanese aversion to any sort of confrontation is legendary. On a more macabre note, after all, the body of a murdered woman was discovered some years ago under the bed in a love hotel in the Tokyo suburb of Kamata, but only once the smell had become quite overpowering. It had been there for about a month.

Recently, among the welter of magazines extolling *raifustairu* – lifestyle – for the younger set, there are several fashionable city guides presenting young women with a blueprint for a *deeto* – a date. Such idealizations begin with fashionable restaurants, progress to sipping florid cocktails in trendy café-bars and culminate in a love hotel chosen from a select, detailed and illustrated list set out like a catalogue. The party choosing the setting for the evening's conclusion is not the gentleman, but the lady. Spurned by dedicated urban followers of fashion as the trappings of bumpkinland and too close to the massage parlour besides, rococo vinyl, pinball gothic and automotive chinoiserie are on the way out, swept away by the new wave of minimalism and high-tech. Still, if the edge has been taken off the fantasy in Tokyo, the facility thrives ubiquitously in the wake of a pressing demand.

'On Friday and Saturday nights,' drily remarked one Tokyo rake of the back streets of Shibuya, 'the love hotels are like *gokiburi hoi-hoi*' – a cockroach trap with a sticky floor. The rate of occupancy can be daunting. Couples beetle in and out of the hotels, while others wander the streets like souls in purgatory, desperately waiting for those glued together inside to come unstuck and emerge.

With bicycles in the hallway and washing on the balcony, the average Japanese home looks cluttered from its sheer exiguity. There may be the odd *objet* atop the TV set, a vase of flowers and a couple of pussy-cat calendars, but there is room only for the functional. It is rarely used for receiving guests and is hardly a setting conducive to romance. Had he seen it, Le Corbusier may well have thought twice before he made his famous statement that 'a house should be a machine for living in'; the ordinary Japanese home carries it to an extreme.

As a machine for sensual pleasure, the love hotel pulls out all the architectural stops. Exempt from having to conform to the norms determining the relentless sameness of the average Japanese home, it is an antidote to humdrum lives. Hence the outlandishness which has earned it so many pictorials in western magazines. In addition to being titillated, the West is amused: the love hotel is the ultimate in kitsch. Appreciation of kitsch requires a rather haughty sense of irony, and the Japanese are not much given to irony. Such as it is, their snobbery points more to a desire to signify membership of a certain group than to the western ideal of being better than everyone else. The love hotel is seen as kitsch only by the more urbane and educated; some of its clientele would call it beautiful. The oft-heard analogy with Disneyland is more than superficially apt: the primary function of the décor is escapist. Like Disneyland, the love hotel has about it an air of childishness, of innocence, which not even a strong undercurrent of rapacious commercialism can wholly belie.

If the West finds it kitsch, it is also because it sees its sexual function as vaguely indecent. Although most of us like to imagine that we have transcended it, centuries of conditioning still taint our sexual outlook with shades of guilt. Thus, if no longer sinful, the love hotel is slightly improper. To the Japanese it is a haven for something perfectly natural and as completely deserving of celebration as its outrageously fanciful architecture suggests. The Tinseltown rococo palaces do, however, express one of Japan's great reservations: if the love hotel's design is too far-fetched to have much to do with real life, it is because, ideally, the same should apply to sex.

2

In the Middle of the Road

FIGURES IN A LANDSCAPE

Renovated, draught-proofed and yet still traditionally styled, the Yamashita family home stands on a street flanked with tall pine trees: recognizably a section of the Tokaido road. As a former post town, Goyu was even more reputed than neighbouring Akasaka for the charm of its travellers' inns. The print from Hiroshige's famous *Fifty-three Stations of the Tokaido Road*, after all, depicts two rapacious little trollops hauling a couple of reluctant wayfarers into a roadside bordello by the scruff of their necks. Hiroshige's Edo now lies buried beneath the ferroconcrete high-rises and traceries of overhead highways of modern Tokyo, and most of the more picturesque former features of the fifty-three stations have long gone.

As in most villages in Japan, rice fields lie beside residential streets of houses old and new, testifying to the rapid evolution from the farming to the dormitory community. Most of the working population is employed in nearby towns or the city of Nagoya, and villages such as Goyu merge into what might be described as rural suburbia, complete with mammoth supermarkets with trading stamps and free-insides, not forgetting *pachinko* parlours a-dazzle with blinking, cybernetic bagatelle. In every sense but the strictly geographical, Goyu is in central Japan – the middle of the road. Neither wholly rural nor wholly industrial, it is the kind of place that comes to mind as archetypically average.

Frowned upon in the West, generalization comes easily where the majority aspires to be *futsu* – ordinary. Conformity means harmony, uniformity reassures and there are no mediocre connotations in the word *heibon* (average). The leading teenage magazine for four decades after all was simply called *Heibon* too, and it had found avid readership among the younger Yamashitas until it finally folded in 1988: a sign of an era blitzing away old group values with media slogans such as *mai hausu, mai kaa, mai raifustairu* – my house, my car and my lifestyle. As indubitable as the trend towards greater individualism may be, it nevertheless makes itself felt more in Tokyo or Osaka. Lying midway between them, Aichi prefecture has a reputation for being conservative. Although their grip is relaxing, many patterns of the past still prevail.

Modern Japan is often described as a classless society, and one sees opulent and modest households side by side. Between these two extremes of rich and poor, according to surveys conducted during the early eighties, over 80 per cent describe themselves as 'middle class'. Notwithstanding more recent polls indicating that this blissful stratum is shrinking, class in the western sense is a vague notion in a society controlled fundamentally through a rigorous hierarchy operating in a series of closed circles which, simultaneously or successively, involve everyone at some point during their lives. As hubs of activity and the only source of social relationships, such circles might be devoted to sports, leisure or culture and abide by the same rules as the most cogent of all, namely, the school and university, the workplace and the immediate community. Standing absolutely paramount over them all, however, is the family. Constituting the very core of existence, so powerful is its influence that its hierarchical structure and distribution of responsibilities is reflected in almost all group activities and institutions in Japan. In middle-of-the-road Goyu, the 'Yamashitas' are your ordinary middle-class family – the Japanese Joneses.

During Oshogatsu, the New Year holidays, everything grinds to a halt in Goyu as it does in all Japan. It is 1 January 1988, or the sixty-third year of Showa, the Year of the Dragon according to the Chinese calendar. In the Yamashita home, four generations are seated on the tatami floor before a low table spread with a traditional festive lunch of morsels of raw fish, sundry meats and vegetables daintily arranged in gleaming lacquered boxes. Mayumi's father, 54-year-old Shigeru Yamashita, *kachō* – a section chief – in the sales department of a local branch of a major electronics firm, dressed today in a dark blue kimono, beams beneath a framed portrait of the imperial family. The Emperor, it must be remembered, is the symbolic father of the Japanese. In recent times, Yamashita considers, the family institution has been buffeted on the tides of change. His brother Tsuneo, for instance, has joined the family New Year celebrations along with his wife Etsuko; but their teenage children have gone away on a skiing trip. On Shigeru's left sits his wife Kimiko; on his right is his eldest son Keisuke, a 32-year-old executive in a Nagoya department store, together with his wife and children. Next to them is 30-year-old Takashi, Keisuke's brother, who was yesterday one of the hundreds of thousands to leave Tokyo's grey business districts eerie and deserted behind him as he made the jam-packed trip home on the Shinkansen bullet train.

Eroded first by the waves of modernization during the Meiji period between 1868 and 1912, the institution of the family has been undermined by war, then by a reconstruction process with its corollaries of all-out industrialization, a draconian work ethic and rampant materialism. Indeed, as sociologists are forever pointing out, it has gone from an extended to a predominantly nuclear structure in less than a century, especially during the past four decades. Like many rural families, the Yamashitas remain more closely knit than their urban counterparts. Surrounded by her sons, most of her grandchildren and her two great-grandchildren, Shigeru's mother Sumiko is *Obāsan*, honourable Grandma, and she has been living with them ever since her husband died in 1969.

NEW YEAR, TRADITIONAL AND TELEVISED

Just past midnight on 31 December, when the TV hails the New Year with the ritual number of 108 deeply booming bells relayed live from Buddhist temples throughout Japan, families consume bowls of steaming soup and *soba* noodles and exchange congratulations.

As always when the Yamashitas are at home, the TV had been on all day. Like in the majority of Japanese households, it is more or less a radio with a picture on the front and seldom actually watched. Around New Year, however, since most TV stations programme annual roundups of the best of certain popular shows, all eyes are riveted to the set. In between watching annual sports rundowns, Shigeru and his sons got a good laugh from highlights of a programme dealing with freaks and oddities. The swimming race between thin and fat circus men was almost as much of a riot as the young American lady wobbling around with those absolutely gigantic, record-busting tits. It was still not quite as amusing, Shigeru recalled inwardly, as those Beautiful Bottom competitions one saw on late-night TV before the

Government clamped down in 1985. In those days there was also 'Tissue Time', a five-minute striptease building up to a final climax accompanied with the vocal ejaculation of the programme name in a rambunctious female voice. Despite having its style cramped, *11p.m. – The Wide Show*, a phenomenally popular magazine programme with topics mostly targeting men, still lives up to its name with detailed and often hilarious rundowns on the highspots of the *demi-monde*.

On New Year's Eve, NHK's *Kohaku* (*The Red and White*) is pretty well mandatory watching for everyone in Japan. In the West, we would call a similar mammoth year-end popular-song contest 'The Pink and Blue', for it pits the boys against the girls. As the star-spangled extravaganza unfolds in a post-Hollywood décor of grand staircases and rainbow arches of coloured lights, the audience give points to each alternately male and female singer and a grand total is totted up for each side.

At 11.45 P.M. on 31 December 1987, the Reds finally won. Much to the edification of misty eyes all over Japan, many of the women contestants broke down and cried buckets from the sheer joy and sadness of victory. Presiding over the Reds was the enduringly popular Akiko Wada, a short-haired songstress with a booming voice and a powerful build, who was now struggling to hold back the tears as they tumbled down her cheeks. Whilst her colleagues looked on dabbing their eyes, Seiko Matsuda, elfin queen of the Kawaii-ko-chan (Cute Little Girls) singing stars cried so much that she choked and faltered through the repeat of her winning song. Then again, Seiko's popularity owes more to performances such as this than to her ability to sing.

The younger Yamashitas braved the sub-zero darkness outside and drove to a Shinto shrine in the nearby hills. With a week before them for *Shogatsu* devotions anyway, the older generation remained behind, glad to stay in the warm – snoozing before a perennial old favourite samurai film being rerun on the TV, perhaps *Chushingura* or *The Tale of the Forty-seven Loyal Retainers*, all slashing swords and virtuous bravado. Despite the late hour, the little shrine in the pine woods was crowded with celebrants of all ages standing with their faces glowing orange around a huge bonfire and chewing roasted rice cakes, eating tangerines and sipping a thick, sweetened, opaque rice wine with the alcohol boiled out of it. The brew was served free at nearby red-and-white canvas stalls, which also purveyed noodles, traditional snacks and New Year good-luck charms for warding off evil during the year.

People mounted the wooden stairs of the shrine and stood to pray to the deity for good auspices during the coming year. As others queued behind, devotees took turns in yanking a mammoth cable of plaited red-and-white cloth hanging over the central door before the altar, thereby jangling two large globular bells. After having thus called the god, they clapped their hands twice before joining them in front of faces bowed low in prayer – for some five seconds.

Once the young Yamashitas had paid their respects, one of two old priests, their faces visibly reddened with alcohol even in the rosy half-light, handed them tangerines as the other distributed glasses of sake to those old enough to drink it. As Takashi, Mayumi and Shoji took theirs, they overheard the wizened cleric bantering with a recently married local couple. Mischief gleamed in the fire reflected in his spectacles. 'What, still no children?' Pouring them each a glass of sake, he triggered much general merriment when he said, 'Here, drink enough of this – and you'll be back on the job until daybreak!'

Shrines throughout Japan were meanwhile presenting

a similar scene. People gathered in their hundreds of thousands at the Meiji Jingu shrine in Tokyo, jostling each other before the TV cameras in vast queues waiting for hours to pull the bell rope. At a shrine in the Tokyo amusement district of Shinjuku, denizens of the bar world were similarly rubbing shoulders with the *demimonde*, drinking sake proffered for the occasion by cropped-headed members of local *yakuza* gangs. Other members of the *mizu shobai* joined merchants and farmers in lining up for annual good auspices at countless shrines devoted to the fox god Inari, the alternately male and female deity of gain and grain.

On this same very early New Year morning, perhaps a handful of others will have queued before shrines devoted to more obscure Shinto deities still dotted about the country – those deploying rampant phalli of wood and stone upon their altars. Indeed, some of the most prominent of these shrines, such as Tagata, are to be found right here in Aichi prefecture. At home, other people were no doubt indulging – most probably unaware of the tradition – in the old custom of *Hime Hajime* or 'starting princess', which was formerly set aside as the first and particularly auspicious coital act of the year. Although city dwellers and many urbanized country people today are hardly even aware of the mythologies of the faith at all, phallic worship and fertility rites still colour Shinto, a religion whose primitive animist origins reach far back into the dark forests of prehistory.

WHO ARE THE JAPANESE?

It has been customary to speak of Japanese history as beginning with the accession of Jimmu Tenno, alleged to have reigned from 660 to 585 BC and to have lived for 127 years. Before the time of the Emperor Jimmu was the Age of the Gods – the period of mythology. But trustworthy history does not begin for a thousand years after the accession of Jimmu Tenno, and the chronicles of those thousand years must be regarded as little better than fairy tales.

Lafcadio Hearn, *Japan: An Interpretation* (1903)

In summer 1988, there was an exhibition at the National Science Museum in Tokyo entitled: 'Where Do the Japanese Come From? – The Origins of the Japanese'. Hordes of out-of-town families travelled up to queue before the museum entrance beneath a forest of umbrellas as they braved the torrential rains of the worst summer in decades. One has difficulty in imagining an 'origins' exhibition triggering quite such enthusiasm in Paris or London but, in Japan, an obsession with roots betrays an enduring national identity crisis. Even relatively minor archaeological discoveries, such as the unearthing of some unrecognizably corroded Yayoi period sword, can make front-page news and spawn a spate of learned TV documentaries. Primitive origins almost as mixed as Europe's have been swept under the carpet of nationalism and, with such a very recent swing away from myth to fact, the question becomes something of a national preoccupation.

The Japanese tend to see themselves more comfortably as a gigantic, exclusive and homogenous tribe. Even if it is no longer taken at face value, the notion of common ancestry established in Shinto myth was formalized as a nationalist ideology by Meiji politicians, and inculcated by the wartime militarists. With the emperor so strongly revered as a father figure, a symbolic patriarch heading one vast family, it takes comparatively simple ideological manipulation to turn a spiritual figurehead into a goad for physical belligerence.

Incredibly, the opening chapters of standard school history text books made no distinction between mythology and history until the introduction of the new constitution in October 1946. A science little known until the Meiji period, archaeology continued to be viewed with suspicion and even disbelief until after the Second World War, when efforts to uncover the prehistoric past at last began in earnest. Until then, if the more enlightened viewed their ostensibly divine descent with scepticism, the arguments for keeping their views to themselves were highly persuasive and archaeologists safely confined their opinions to scholarly tomes.

Meaning 'straw rope pattern', the word 'Jomon' refers both to the people of neolithic Japan and the technique they used to decorate their pottery. Spanning very roughly from 10,000 to 200 B.C., the long Jomon period saw the march from the stone age to the dawn of civilization. In the Science Museum, beyond the cases of hominid remains indicating South-East Asian and Siberian connections in the remote past, there was a lifesize replica of a typical mid-Jomon dwelling specially built for the exhibition. Round and thatched, it was cut away on one side all the way from the earthen floor to its pointed roof. Inside there were animal skins hanging with other neolithic paraphernalia from wooden beams. Every now and again girls dressed in very skimpy sackcloth mini-tunics pretended to busy themselves over a cooking pot suspended over glowing red electric light bulbs covered with ash-grey plastic.

Composed of students on a summer job, the Jomonette sisterhood graciously explained whom they were portraying, responding with sweet smiles as children pointed and fathers ogled them out of the corners of their eyes. 'Although we are Jomon people,' a small boy read aloud from a notice flanking the exhibit, 'we can speak Japanese.' When the Jomonette congratulated him effusively on his reading abilities, the little boy cried out *'Yappari, Nihonjin-da!'* with a mixture of surprise and relief: 'I thought so – she's Japanese!' The thought that Jomon people might have been otherwise, even to a small boy, is disturbing.

Outside the hut meanwhile, two well-scrubbed male students in sackcloth tunics worked lumps of clay through dexterous demonstrations of Jomon pottery techniques. As the contents of the nearby glass cases testified, Jomon pottery came in an astonishing variety of inventive shapes and decorations. Allotted a case to herself, a celebrated Jomon Venus stood some 30 centimetres high and surrounded with mirrors to show her assets off from all sides. Her enormous pelvic girth showed that, as in most neolithic cultures, beauty resided most in fertility. She was no lumpy, dumpy Venus of Willendorf, but then she was a good deal more recent. From her tiny pointed breasts to a face with eyes made with just the merest nick of a blade point, the Jomon Venus rises up over her outsize bottom with an oriental charm all her own. Lending a whimsical touch to her nudity in modern eyes, her helmet no doubt denoted her as a goddess. Magical and ritual, such figurines are overwhelmingly female, which implies that Jomon was a matriarchal society and, like most neolithic cultures, as such it was probably egalitarian. The changes in role definition in Japan were a long time coming. Narrowing first with the introduction of Confucianism from China, woman's social standing declined as the country lapsed into centuries of war after a 300-year idyll during the Heian era, until her lowly status became firmly established during the dictatorial reign of the Tokugawa shoguns.

Some scholars believe that early Japanese mythology

has been influenced by that of the Ainu, whose proto-Caucasoid characteristics combine a heavier distribution of body hair with more prominent noses and chins, as well as thinner lips – implying an early European origin. Most anthropologists agree that there are no Ainu of pure descent surviving; the Japanese generally tend to be hairier than other sino-mongolians. Scattering like Amerindians before European conquerors, the Ainu were gradually driven northwards to Hokkaido, but not before there was some interbreeding with other peoples in Japan. Although there is little doubt that they are the country's oldest natives, like other minorities, the Ainu have long been the victims of discrimination. The real national origins lie mostly on the Asian mainland, in successive waves of Koreans, Mongolians, Chinese and, to a lesser degree, South-East Asians. Isolated and degenerating in remote Japan, these invaders and settlers were in turn conquered and absorbed over the centuries by others – especially by the increasingly sophisticated Koreans. Melding into larger and more powerful tribes, they gradually drove the Ainu northwards. In time they evolved to become the great clans instrumental in shaping Japan.

A predominantly agricultural country until very recently, Japan's history virtually begins with rice. Originating in China, rice farming is thought to have arrived fully developed, introduced by Koreans migrating to northern Kyushu, the cradle of Yayoi (Early Spring) culture. Beginning with rice and agriculture, the 'Korean connection' pattern was to be repeated in innumerable other fields and was decisive in shaping the country's religion, society and culture.

THE FIRST TRUE RULERS

Corroborated by references in old Chinese records, credible references to envoys sent from the mainland to the emperor of Japan are mentioned fairly early on in the historical portion of the *Kojiki*. These indicate that the first documented Japanese emperor is not the mythical Jimmu, but Nintoku, who reigned sometime between the fourth and fifth centuries. It is known that he did a great deal in introducing culture and technology from Korea: enough for many scholars to believe that he may well have been Korean himself. His time, the late Yayoi, is known as the Tomb Period, named after a large number of tumuli which follow a Korean model, the largest one found to date being Nintoku's own. Lying near Osaka, the tomb contained no less than 20,000 terracotta *haniwa* figurines representing men, women, horses and sometimes houses. Buried in the tombs of emperors and dignitaries, the funerary *haniwa* figurines were probably offerings left to curry favour with the deified deceased, as well as (as in Chinese tombs) for providing for the latter in the hereafter. On a grimmer note, they are believed to be symbolic substitutes for earlier human sacrifice. Nothing much is known about Yayoi culture, but the primitive Shinto myths must have been orally transmitted down through the period. There is little doubt Yayoi religion was coloured with phallicism and fertility, for the *haniwa* were sometimes unabashedly endowed or carved with the attributes of their sex, the male figurines displaying impressive erections.

Preceding Nintoku by some 200 years is an important though even hazier figure standing against the horizon of Japan's sunrise: the witch-queen Himiko. She is known to have ruled a country called Yamatai-koku, whose frontiers have yet to be defined. That she existed at all is known from ancient Chinese historical records which, even if they tended to be cursory in their references to what their writers then considered to be a benighted land, are generally fairly reliable. Himiko's tomb has nonetheless never been found; nothing verifiable is known about her at all. Transmitted orally for many centuries, however, the Himiko legends have been absorbed into Shinto and, like some others, may well hold a kernel of truth.

Revered as a deity, Himiko lived in a heavily guarded 'palace' (an outsize thatched hut) and not even her family members were allowed to set eyes on her. Folk legends dress her in the white robe and red sash of the Shinto priestess, which is not so far-fetched, for the queen would have been essentially a shamaness. She is said to have delivered oracles after a frenzied ritual dance, during which she held a sprig of sacred *kisaki* leaves in one hand. Equating Himiko with the *Kojiki* legends dealing with the sun goddess and Ama-no-Uzume's erotic dance, some scholars contend that the role of Ama-no-Uzume in the myth about Amaterasu the sun goddess might be based on historical fact. Circular assemblages of monoliths found at various sites imply that the early Japanese worshipped the sun; the Heavenly Alarming Female could well have been a shamaness ruling, like Himiko, over some ancient matriarchal society. One can well imagine runaway panic during a solar eclipse, and the elders gathering around a witch-queen whose erotic gyrations appeared to restore light to the world.

BUDDHISM – THE GENTLE ART OF PERSUASION

Chinese scholars probably first visited Japan in the first century; by the third, studying Chinese literature was all the rage among the ruling classes. By the time Japan became the country called Yamato in the fifth century, it had been steadily absorbing elements of Chinese culture for some 400 years. Shinto remained the dominant religious force but its principles, such as they were, had become ordered and codified as a result of the Confucian influence, which is also thought to have reorientated it into an ancestor cult. Along with the introduction of the doctrine of filial piety and the fact that it complemented an indigenous hierarchical structure, Confucianism introduced systems of administration, government and education. By the Nara period (710–84), Japan had virtually become a clone of T'ang dynasty China.

Buddhism made a first if rather cautious entry into Japan in 525, via the Korean connection. Up against what was by now a conservative religious and ethical system combining animistic Shinto, the ancestor cult and Confucianism together, the first Buddhist mission met with little success. Abiding by the virtue of patience at least as strongly as the Confucians, its sages were nonetheless past masters of compromise. During the long Buddhist march from India, Mongolia and Tibet, then on into China and Korea, experience had shown its missionaries that animism and ancestor cults could not be supplanted. To take root successfully, they had to adapt to local beliefs.

Although it had yet to be recognized as an official religion in Japan, Buddhism gradually built more monasteries over the next 300 years and found increasing numbers of adherents among the ruling class. The doctrines it introduced were absent from Shinto: notions of good and evil, compassion and reincarnation, the bliss of Nirvana and the torment of the Buddhist hells. Buddhism was moreover an even greater educational and cultural spearhead than the Confucian learning; it brought a rich heritage of painting, sculpture and literature into Japan. Championed by the aristocracy and the emperor during the Heian era (793–1185), the paramount Buddhist Tendai sect had the status of a state religion.

The lower orders meanwhile adhered strongly to Shinto, many practising it in its primitive and phallic pre-Confucian form. A learned aristocracy immersed itself in the intellectual pursuits inwrought with Buddhism, but the religion's rarefied, elevated essence wafted too high for the common nose. If the great seventh-century churchman and statesman Shotoku had prepared the ground, the one really bringing Buddhism to the people was Kūkai (774–835), the founder of the still-prominent Shingon sect. Having studied esoteric Buddhism for years in China, the astute Kūkai sought to endow an élitist religion with more appeal for commoners, which he achieved simply by announcing that the higher gods of Shinto were incarnations of various Buddhas. The result was Ryobu-Shinto, a double religion earning imperial approval and support. The Japanese have lived comfortably with the two dissimilar religions ever since.

3

The Family Mainstays

THE OLDER GENERATION

> Twenty, jealous,
> Wilting this summer
> In the village heat,
> I listen to my husband
> Taunt me with Kyoto pleasures!
>
> Akiko Yosano, *Midaregami* (1901)

Looking like a wizened sparrow in her sombre brown kimono, Obāsan is a spritely and quick-witted eighty-four. This is the first day of 1988 and Hirohito, the emperor Showa, four years her senior, is still alive. She still believes him to be a god, even though she had heard him deny it over the radio in his own surrendering speech on 15 August 1945. It had been almost as devastating as the atom bombing of Hiroshima and Nagasaki which had prompted it. It wasn't true, of course. That Japan had to 'endure the unendurable and suffer the insufferable' was one thing, but once a god, always a god. Besides, given the circumstances, whatever else could His Majesty say?

In the street as at home, these days everyone calls her Obāsan, but her given name is Sumiko. She regularly honours the dead before the family shrine here in the living room; they watch over the Yamashitas from the beyond. She prays for them along with other gods she visits in Shinto shrines, and makes sure she never misses observances on their behalf in Buddhist temples. When she needs advice, she consults I-Ching diviners or palmists and draws *Mikuji* fortune leaflets in shrines. In times of sadness or disappointment, she seeks solutions to her problems from the Shinto gods. Presenting the world only with a charming smile, she would consider it rude to mention them to anyone else. Her husband had been a doctor, and his practices had been a meld of western and traditional Chinese medicine. Whenever Obāsan ails, the herbal remedies come first; so far, they work.

Her wrinkled countenance is wreathed in smiles but she hardly utters a word. Not because she is senile, but because she believes silence becomes a virtuous woman. When Sumiko was born, Japan had just defeated the Russians at Port Arthur in 1904 and surprised a condescending West by becoming Asia's first major power. Her late husband's photograph scowls from a frame before the family shrine in the alcove just behind her.

Masaoka Yamashita, eighteen years her senior, had been taciturn and aloof, but he commanded a great deal of respect. Decorated by the Meiji emperor for services rendered as a young army doctor during the Russo-Japanese War, he eventually left a practice in his native Kobe to take up a more important one here in Aichi prefecture. Along with the silver pocket watch also presented to him on that occasion, Obāsan keeps the medal with other memorabilia in a drawer of the *tansu* chest in her room. She had been his third wife. In 1929, when she was twenty-five, her more modestly born parents had found it expedient to give her hand to the doctor, Masaoka Yamashita, who had employed her as a nurse, and so it was. Oh, he'd had a temper all right, but he'd been a handsome man and given her two fine sons.

Masaoka had first come to Aichi in 1923 and left a past behind him. He had divorced his first wife because she was barren; in 1910, anyone would. Despite the overthrow of feudalism during the Meiji reformation of 1868, like many, Masaoka inwardly upheld the kind of ideals advocated by Confucian sage Kaibara Ekiken (1631–1714) in *Onna Daigaku – The Great Learning of Women*. It would seem curious to occidentals but not in the least incongruous to the Japanese that Kaibara's other claim to fame was in penning a highly explicit sex manual, which he probably saw in the same light as his well-known extolments of the virtue of feminine obedience. In keeping with the neo-Confucian principles which he strongly advocated, Kaibara had it that divorce was dishonourable and that the divorcee 'carries lifelong shame with her'. He justified it, however, by the reiteration of a Confucian precept over twenty centuries old, the 'Seven Rules for Sending a Woman Away': if she disobeys her in-laws, is barren, morally lax, jealous or steals, if she is diseased or too outspoken, for such a woman causes discord among relatives and breaks the harmony of the family.

Masaoka married again in 1913, during the first year of the Taisho emperor's reign. His second wife was a former geisha who bore him a son. She may well have been a geisha, but her career had been a decorous matter of singing, playing the shamisen and eventually imparting her art to others. Even if it had been otherwise, any possible moral laxities past could always be absolved by a respectable marriage. If marrying a geisha was good enough for Prime Minister Katsura, who headed the government during the Russo-Japanese War, it was good enough for Masaoka too. But perhaps his spouse talked too much or disobeyed her in-laws, for the couple didn't get along.

Three years later, she wound up being summarily dismissed as a servant. It had taken only a *mikudari-han* or three-and-a-half-line letter to divorce her, which was common practice in Japan until the new constitution in 1946. Custom automatically gave the father custody of the child, whom he packed off to be brought up in his brother's family. Meanwhile, outside surgery hours he indulged freely in his favourite pastime: haunting the amusement quarters in Kobe and Kyoto. The odd medical conference in Tokyo also took him to the licensed quarter of the Yoshiwara which, lost and lamented, thrives today in disguise. In the final analysis, his unfortunate former wife is most likely to have been jealous.

Philandering Masaoka devoted part of his appreciable wealth to keeping mistresses and rumour had it that the Yamashita family, as it is among some of today's prominent tycoons, was rather larger than officially registered. Masaoka's deeds and habits were in keeping with the times. Until the Meiji period, concubines were common among the wealthier samurai, the norm among the daimio feudal lords and the rule for the shogun. Since there were no scandals over disgruntled mistresses and/or natural offspring, Masaoka's rumoured extramarital dependants were properly provided for, as custom dictated. During his youth, a *mekake* or concubine was sometimes still taken to live beneath the same roof as the first wife, in which her status was akin to a glorified servant. The same ethics governing the keeping of a *nigo* (number two or mistress) still often apply today. No longer able to keep her in the family home, a man with another woman in his life has to commute between two households.

Whether he dumped a wife and deprived her of a son, kept mistresses or visited brothels were neither here nor there; that he was unfaithful was perfectly natural. Not that divorce could be pronounced out of hand: if considered unjustified, it might have drawn the ire of the community. On the other hand, if you were as well-to-do as Masaoka had been before his invested Manchurian fortune vanished with the war, you were as good as your word. The important thing was that both his esteemed career and his fulfilment of duties and obligations were not only blemishless, but exemplary.

Japan's wartime campaigns in the Philippines saw the systematic rapine and wholesale slaughter of entire villages; during one of these battles, Masaoka's thirty-year-old son died of shrapnel wounds and left behind a young widow and two children. The militarists had it that a sacrifice of that kind was a great honour for the family but Masaoka, who had anyway hardly ever seen his son and only heard about his grandchildren, never mentioned him again. The Yamashitas' Kobe relatives are still extant. A part of the dim past, they dutifully emerge every now and again during larger family functions such as funerals and weddings.

MOTHER AND FATHER

Kimiko and Shigeru Yamashita consider themselves lucky. The son and daughter of neighbouring families and attracted to one another, they were allowed to marry with parental blessings on both sides. Kimiko's parents had been artisans, a social caste beneath the ruling samurai in feudal times. They were well-to-do, but perhaps not quite up to the aura of samurai ancestry and medicine surrounding the Yamashitas. Abandoned during the last century, the old social ranks survive in some ways in people's desire to stick to their own kind. In the poverty-stricken chaos of the postwar years, however, social standing became meaningless to all but a few. Shigeru's father was anyway remote, an ageing, crusty man locked away in a world of his own and who apparently took no interest in family affairs. They married in 1955, when Shigeru and Kimiko were twenty-two and twenty-one respectively; their first son Keisuke was born soon enough to provide a choice topic for neighbourhood gossips and Takashi was born two years later.

Women account for over 40 per cent of today's work force, out of which over two-thirds of them are married. When their youngest son, Shoji, at eighteen entered junior high school some eight years ago, Shigeru's wife Kimiko began her current job with an accounting firm – at first on a part-time basis. Like most local womenfolk, she used to devote some of her free afternoons to various community activities before she began working again, and also attended classes in flower arrangement, playing a traditional instrument such as the koto and versing herself in the ritualized art of the tea ceremony. Entreated to do likewise, Mayumi did so rather reluctantly; modern dancing was more fun. Such cultural pastimes are frequently practised by unmarried women by way of adding accomplishments to increase their marital chances in much the same way as girls from the European bourgeoisie are expected to play the piano.

Each morning Kimiko is the first to rise to prepare breakfast and the second to last to take the evening bath, coming in between her mother-in-law and her daughter. The latter two frequently help with household chores and preparing meals. Owing to their various professional and scholastic schedules, however, family members often dine at different times. The male contingent expect meals whenever they ask for them; on days when they get home before Kimiko, Obāsan will oblige. Whenever Shigeru asks for tea, Kimiko will drop whatever she is doing to make it. Even when they dine alone, male family members stack dishes in the sink;

they would never wash up so much as a glass themselves. Forever returning late from work, men are said to function at home according to a monosyllabic routine ironically referred to as '*Meshi-Furo-Neru*' – Food! Bath! Bed! Mild-mannered Shigeru would never use such terse wording and nor would he have to – his wife's ministrations are automatic.

The home, on the other hand, is always the wife's domain. Her husband hands over his monthly pay either in an envelope or has it credited to a joint bank account. She manages every side of running the home, including purchasing clothes for the menfolk, the children's schooling and any expenses incurred through repairs, new household appliances and even new houses. Her book-keeping commonly goes as far as handling stocks and shares. Every month she gives her husband his *kozukai* or pocket money. On average this is 15 per cent of his salary and it has to cover fares, petrol, meals and the minimum incidental expenses. The hefty tabs a man like Shigeru might be presented with in hostess bars after work are paid in fact with corporate money. Any holes a wife might discover in the bank account may well require a good excuse; if particularly large, they may point to the existence of a mistress.

If Japanese society opens few doors to the career woman, the degree of power the housewife enjoys around the home is something almost inconceivable to her western counterparts. Superficially apparent, the traditions of female compliance, subservience and delicatesse are often belied, not least by the prevalence of the hen-pecked husband as a stock-in-trade in popular culture, as typified from the seventies by TV's *Hisatsu* samurai drama series focusing on the exploits of a middle-aged swordsman. In between bouts of derring-do, he spends most of his time at home cringing before a shrill wife and a nagging mother-in-law. For many unemployed housewives, domestic power, a great deal of leisure time and a steady cash flow provide few reasons to challenge the status quo. To the consternation of Japanese feminists, many of the staunchest opponents of socio-sexual change are women.

This rosy picture, however, is disfigured by boredom. These days the media gives blitz coverage to stories about idle and neglected housewives with absentee and/or workaholic husbands. Tired of sitting slumped all day before the TV set, some turn to adultery and the bottle, to prostitution and even stimulant drugs. Mrs Yamashita may have little time to herself, but hers is a quiet, contented life with no room for extremes. Shigeru may have occasionally returned home in his cups and, for all she knows, he may once or twice have wandered some of the sleazier avenues of the *mizu shobai*. Most men do. She might not like the idea, but jealousy is enough of a sin in the eyes of Confucianism to make her unlikely to voice her opinion, unless her husband has a real affair. Shigeru never has. He has always found time to play an active family role and neither drink nor adultery – let alone drugs or prostitution – have ever entered her mind.

THE WORKAHOLICS

Like himself, Shigeru Yamashita's sons are each a *sarari-man* – in Japlish, a *salaryman* – a white-collar worker. Takashi wears his grey everyday business suit, but then it's of a more fashionable cut, and no longer the mandatory dark blue which many still wear and which he wore too for the first two years from the '*nyusha shiki*' ceremony welcoming the hundreds of other new recruits into the great corporate family. The *shacho* – the president – had personally welcomed each of them as they mounted the podium in turn to bow before him. Then everyone endured his lecture on corporate philosophy before rising to sing the company song to the strains of an Electone soaring majestically over the assembly hall. This family will be theirs for the rest of their working lives.

Although numbering thousands of employees and spread out over many different departments, even overseas, worker interrelationships are ruled by a hierarchical structure which follows what is called the *oyabun-kobun* (father-child) pattern. From the largest corporations to the smallest shops, the *oyabun-kobun* system holds sway and is even more strictly applied in the underworld – the domain of the *yakuza* gangs. Working in Tokyo and not in the provinces, where the pace is generally more relaxed, Takashi's life might be more hectic than his brother's and father's. Once he marries, the chances are that he will only be able to afford to live in a neighbouring prefecture, and he will have to commute. An essential prerequisite of corporate life is company loyalty, and many employees will stay on until 10 P.M. or even later, merely to impress theirs upon the few who might actually still be working. Shigeru's is the generation that fought hardest to shape the postwar economic miracle; many of them feel resentful towards rising generations whom they see as taking everything for granted. The baby-boom generation of *salarymen* draw scathing mutterings from their older colleagues for wanting to spend more time with their families. Whether they manage to or not, a different picture generally awaits them when they reach their forties. The Japan Travel Bureau recently published an unusually frank and humorously illustrated little book simply called *Salaryman in Japan*. It makes for enlightening reading.

At forty, the *salaryman* climbs further up the hierarchy and his workload and responsibilities increase accordingly. Those in their forties are the workaholics, the JTB book tells us, the *mooretsu shain*. 'Without so much as a glance back at their families,' it explains, 'they live for their work only. The company is the battlefield for them, for which they will use any means available to achieve their goals.' In their fifties, some *salarymen* might suffer from *moetsuki shookoogun* – the burnout syndrome. After having worked for years to fan the fires of the economic miracle, they burn out. The JTB book proves the point with an illustration showing a suited skeleton slumped over a desk.

Many *salarymen* are sent to work away from their homes and families with callous disregard for their personal lives. This is known as *tanshin funin* – solo assignment – and means that a *salaryman*, typically in his forties, is transferred to a responsible position in another province for an average period of three years. According to a survey conducted by the Institute of Labour Administration in 1988, there are 175,000 *tanshin funin* workers and the number grows yearly by about 10 per cent. It also transpired that 70 per cent of the companies surveyed gave transfer orders without even a passing thought for the transferee's family circumstances.

Upon retiring, many a *salaryman* comes home to live with a complete stranger – his wife. For the past thirty years, apart from the odd wedding or funeral, he has had no social life outside of a corporate context whatsoever. He has been on company trips, to sports meetings, to annual office parties and, of course, out drinking with his colleagues after hours. He hardly knows his children, who will by now have left home. He has been involved neither in their education nor in their upbringing and would hold his wife responsible for their failures. He has seen no films, never been to the theatre and has watched sport only on Sunday's TV out of eyes bleared from corporate drinking the night before. Sundays may also dictate a round of company golf, whether he likes it or not; or he would be flat out on the tatami floor, yawning, belching, dead-tired and dishevelled in his nightclothes, looking up from his sports paper only to bellow to his wife to bring him tea or beer. When he retires, this monster becomes what a spouse might call *sodai gomi* – big garbage. Her husband, the father of her children, is home at last.

She meanwhile may still hold a job. Over the years since her children started high school, job or not, she has had time to pursue activities and hobbies, to socialize with other women and, especially while her husband suffered himself to be posted to a distant province for five years, she may even have had affairs. So when her corporate samurai comes marching home, she suddenly finds herself expected to tend to a creature as helpless around the house as a baby, with whom she has nothing in common and whom she married only as an arrangement suiting their respective families. Her predicament underlies the currently rising divorce statistics among the middle-aged, the suits being overwhelmingly filed by wives. If anything, his lot is even worse: he put everything he had into the big corporate family. Too blinded by loyalty to feel that it betrayed him and forced him to betray his own, he has nothing to look forward to except for an average of twenty more years of existence.

This, of course, is a 'worst case' scenario. Many men, when they retire, return to more congenial surroundings, find time to pursue a wealth of hobbies and interests and not a few use their pensions to travel the countryside and sometimes abroad with their wives. Notwithstanding, sooner or later, all *salarymen* have to endure more than one aspect of the bleaker picture. As a poignant letter from a distraught woman to the *Mainichi Shimbun* put it in mid-November 1987:

> I've been married for ten years but my husband has never made it home for supper once! For the past year, he has worked every weekend because his firm has been hit by a slump caused by the rising yen, and he simply couldn't take a day off. The company's official policy dictates a five-day working week and long summer and winter holidays, but my husband has never taken all the days he's entitled to.
>
> He has been overworked and still hasn't recovered from a cold he caught this summer. He blew his nose so often that it finally began bleeding. I was shocked to see the bloodstains on his shirt when he came home from work early one evening. I have learned that *pokkuribyoo* [drop-dead-sickness] is increasing among middle-aged men because of overwork. They work so hard and are repaid by an early death. Something is very wrong.

Wrong or not, Takashi is travelling the same road. With his trading company currently expanding and fighting hard against the high yen, Takashi has suffered his New Year holiday to be cut short by two days without a murmur. His sacrifice might be taken into account in his biannual bonuses, but it will earn him no *overtime*. Tomorrow morning he will be boarding the Shinkansen back to the Marunouchi corporate ghost town in Tokyo to assist his department in preparing new business for the coming year. His case is not unique. The lights in the office buildings are never out for very long; there are legions of other *salarymen* apparently only too eager to curtail their holidays in their zeal to impress the company with their loyalty. Japanese workers are also entitled to two weeks paid holiday in the summer but, where the histrionics of loyalty are unwritten rules, most reduce this time to some three days. One in ten can expect to succumb to stress and go off the wall and some will work themselves to death. Most will simply grey gently and uncomplainingly over the years as they make their preordained climb up the corporate ladder.

THE BACHELOR LIFE

Takashi is still a bachelor. If he hasn't already eaten take-out fare delivered to the office with the others before he finally reaches his twenty-square-foot apartment in a Tokyo suburb, he subsists on a diet of packaged instant foods and Japanese TV dinners. As tiny as his apartment is, one wall is entirely occupied by a barrage of audio-visual equipment. Slurping one-cup *ramen* soup noodles purchased from a nearby 24-hour convenience store, he contemplates porno fare hired from one of the several video rental outlets in his neighbourhood. The strategically concealed hard-core exploits of video porn queen Kaoru Kuroki, renowned for her defiant crop of underarm hair, might be the unmarried *salaryman*'s sexual heroin, but once the fantasy comes to rest in a wad of tissue paper, it's a lonely life. For some of his younger colleagues it's even worse; they live in remote company dormitories and are locked in or out at 10 P.M.

Six years ago, during a student party, Takashi took to a classmate's sister and the feeling was mutual. He was lucky; in most universities, men outnumber women by about five to one. She moved into his tiny apartment but, when they graduated and started work, the time they had left for each other was not much. Soon they met only in bed, which exhaustion reduced to an appliance only for sleeping in. Their passion was drowned in an ocean of professional commitments and they drifted apart.

These days, Takashi fancies some of his female colleagues, but he has no girlfriend. He might be the recipient of a Valentine's Day token, but it could hardly presage a love affair. The Japanese observation of Valentine's Day finds only women expressing their admiration for men and constitutes a bonanza for confectioners. To put themselves in good stead with male colleagues, women customarily offer them what they call '*giri choco*' or 'obligation chocolate', often spending some twenty thousand yen each. In Takashi's office, the boys outnumber the marriageable girls, who are called '*shokuba no hana*' ('workplace flowers'), several to one. Most of them are anyway engaged. There may be the odd office flirt: she might be a good sport if and when you get her, but her round-heeled disposition precludes more serious prospects.

The *Oeru* or OL – the Office Lady – is a favourite subject of sexual fantasy. A group of women lawyers handling cases of sexual discrimination in the workplace recently revealed that one in five of the cases they deal with stems from sexual abuse including unwelcome overtures, promotional seduction ploys and rape. This is a far cry from the general rule. Office love between dominating male staffer and dominated OL is a common theme in films, videos, magazines and comics, especially those of the pornographic persuasion. But while men entertain themselves with such illusory distractions, the reality is rather different. Office affairs are usually frowned upon, although everyone knows them to be extremely common. This is because they have to be discreet: as long as everyone knows about them but the evidence is low-key enough for them to pretend they don't, corporate affairs are fine. Enhancing the image of the company as family, office marriages on the other hand are encouraged – usually on the understanding that the woman resigns immediately to assume her proper duties as wife and mother.

As a younger employee in a gradually changing working climate and a rapidly changing social environment, however, Takashi and his younger office colleagues would, according to the image attributed to them in the media, be going out in mixed company more frequently than ever before. Takashi moreover gets every other Saturday off, belonging as he does to a middling-sized firm able to afford this relative luxury. In fact, however, female employees have far shorter office hours than their male counterparts and the boozing stopover on the way home is almost exclusively an all-male pursuit. This makes socializing between the sexes the exception rather than the rule. On the rare weekends and holidays when Takashi goes home, his relatives take pains to introduce him to local girls. Being thirty years old, he'll have to get married fairly soon; in a conservative company such as his, his promotion may depend on it.

In November 1988, an NHK TV programme called *Anata nara doo suru?* (*What would you do?*) focused on the problem of workers being too busy to mingle with the opposite sex. Middle-aged and married himself, Mr Watanabe, a genial *kachō* in an Osaka computer company, lamented the fact that the employees in his firm, 90 per cent of whom were male, had absolutely no opportunities to meet women. So, since his own company dealt often with a nearby computer software research and development firm with an overwhelming majority of female employees, he hit upon an idea. He organized weekend parties and sports meetings, inviting the women from the other firm. His idea was that the younger set could meet what he hoped would be *pichi-pichi gyaru* – spry or lively girls.

Neither NHK nor Watanabe seemed to be promoting socializing between the sexes for its own sake; indeed, it seemed very far from their minds. The motive here was for the young *salarymen* to land themselves not a girl-friend but an *oyome-san* – a bride – a word repeated on the programme with obsessive regularity. When the twain finally met, they seemed tellingly shy and awkward. The girls, interviewed during the course of afternoon parties and tennis competitions, giggled behind their hands; scratching nervously at the backs of their heads, the boys evasively greeted the interviewer's questions with polite monosyllabic replies. In their twenties and early thirties, they all looked about as relaxed in each other's company as fourteen-year-olds from sexually segregated schools. At the time of the NHK programme, Watanabe's initia-tive had not been adopted long enough to show whether it brought any results, but despite their initial awkward-ness, many of the interviewees were enthusiastic about what was undoubtedly a very good idea.

OFFICE BLOSSOMS

When a labour union official heard that some women had complained about having to serve tea, he said he saw nothing wrong with the rule. His wife served tea; why should Office Ladies not serve tea? Higher positions open to the men are not available to these Office Ladies; in fact, they are expected to perform 'womanly' duties, such as serving tea, to make working conditions more pleasant for the men.

James Trager, *Letters from Sachiko* (1980)

The remark perfectly sums up a status quo which, at the close of the decade, was just beginning to show signs of change. Employed between the ages of eighteen and twenty-two, most OLs will marry as soon as their four- to six-year stint as secretaries and tea brewers is over. Many will join the work force again when their children are old enough to cope on their own. Day-care facilities are still sorely lacking in Japan, where a working mother is often frowned upon for callously shirking the traditional duties of motherhood.

When recruiting young OLs, conservative companies favour those living at home with their parents. This not only reinforces the desired quality of primness but, since they pay no rent, justifies lower salaries. OLs are often expressly forbidden to wear make-up or jewellery. Many wear uniforms, even in companies in which their male counterparts do not. The lucky ones wear discreet clothing of their choice. Living at home, they are able to spend more of their income on clothes and it shows; designer-brand apparel is a must, and the Louis Vuitton handbag is virtually *de rigueur*. Leaving the office earlier than their male colleagues, those not obliged to return home have plenty of time and money for dining out, which explains why gourmet restaurants, apart from the fact that real Japanese men don't eat quiche, are overwhelmingly frequented by women.

Paying lip service to the United Nations' Decade for Women, the Equal Employment Opportunity Law was adopted during the very last year of the decade, showing just how eager the Government was to improve conditions for the female labour force. In fact, not very much has changed. In that the law leaves plenty of scope for its detractors with the word 'opportunity' and provides no punishment for them, this is hardly surprising. A survey conducted in 1987 revealed that discriminatory hiring and salary practices are still the norm in many companies based in Tokyo. Fifteen per cent of the companies surveyed continue to hire female employees on different terms from males, paid them less for doing the same jobs and forced them to retire at an earlier age. When asked whether they 'understood' the provisions of the law, 84 per cent of the larger firms (i.e. with over a thousand employees) replied affirmatively. When it came to the smaller ones with thirty to forty employees, however, 64 per cent gave a negative response. Significant, too, is the fact that, out of the 2,500 firms covered by the survey, only 40 per cent bothered to respond at all.

Nevertheless, if legions of women in white blouses and blue sleeveless uniforms – even holders of university degrees – may continue to brew tea, an emerging breed of Japanese career women is working longer, marrying later, and seeking greener pastures elsewhere.

PLAYTIME

Many fashionably minded young women are fond of telling foreigners of either sex that *salarymen* are boring. Notwithstanding, a recent poll revealed that 40 per cent of women put money first when considering a husband. Thus with a secure future for the most part, *salarymen* are still Japan's most eligible bachelors. *Salarymen* are also stock-in-trade figures of fun. A popular comic-book hero for well-nigh two decades, little Furiten-kun is a fellow with a face drawn with as many lines as it takes to alternate between blank resignation and disappointed surprise. His four-frame misadventures are avidly read in newspapers, sell briskly in book anthologies and have found their way into feature-length cartoon films. Like scores more, imitators and otherwise, downtrodden Furiten-kun's antics consist of devices to peer up the skirts of female employees, unsuccessful seduction ploys, shirking, pub-crawling and getting into trouble with the boss.

Self-sacrificing and subservient, *salarymen* have been poignantly depicted in films such as Ozu's even before the Second World War. They have just as often spawned dozens of screen comedies translating their subservience into terms of irresponsibility, bumbling incompetence and ludicrous efforts to save face. In a host of recent TV soap operas, they have been depicted as anything from insensitive, drunken and adulterous workaholic brutes to intimidated, tragic victims of overwork, adultery and worse. Either way, the primordial common factor underlying all these depictions is frustration and the most alluring escape route, predictably, is sex. For too many, home is the one place they are least likely to get it.

While *salarymen* are exploited by their own firms, so they are also indulged. The same is true of society at large, where the tacitly tolerated theatre of indulgence is the *mizu shobai*. A sawdust and tinsel world of erotic artifice, it is populated by actors and – above all – actresses playing roles according to codes just as rigorous as those governing their patrons. In here they can let off steam, getting blind drunk in small bars presided over by a woman significantly called *mama-san*, who will lend a sympathetic ear to their inebriated and tearful tales of woe and perhaps admonish them gently when reversions to childhood or adolescent prurience go over the top. Meanwhile, bar hostesses will charm them, sing along with them, generally inflate their battered egos and, in many places, encourage them to part with extraordinarily large sums of corporate money for this and nothing more.

Apart from the more decorous hostess bars and dwindling geisha activities, however, the brunt of the business going on barely beneath the surface of the water trade is, strictly speaking, illegal. Notwithstanding a ban on prostitution in 1956, Soapland massage parlours thrive alongside a host of other more or less inventive outlets in the vast field of Japanese sex for sale. These are in fact the direct descendants of an ancient, ambivalent heritage combining repression and tolerance. Designed by the samurai rulers to keep family duty and amorous passion rigorously apart, licensed quarters were off limits to the samurai themselves, but they went there anyway. In seeking the sexual contentment he is still in all probability unable to obtain at home, the *salaryman*, the archetypal pink samurai, seeks illusory freedom in a world set aside as the economic soldier's rest and recreation, a world governed by ambiguous, loop-holed laws in which fantasy reigns supreme.

4

The Marriage-go-round

THE HONOURABLE ONCE-OVER

> The fact that two families generally lived in widely separated areas and had no knowledge of each other prompted the use of a go-between initiating the marriage. Needless to say, the marriage partners themselves had little or no previous acquaintance with one another until the day of the wedding.
>
> Harumi Befu, *Japan – An Anthropological Introduction* (1971)

The son and heir of the prosperous owner of a large local supermarket, Hiroshi Murakami formally asked his prospective father-in-law for his daughter's hand only days ago. Although he may have lost some sleep over the prospect, there was little chance that Yamashita would refuse him. Such a proposal is nothing more than a ritual involving participants from families who have already agreed on the outcome. Besides, Mayumi had undergone *omiai* (honourable seeing-meetings) or arranged-marriage introductions no less than twenty-three times, so that Shigeru – who likes Hiroshi anyway – was more than relieved at her choice.

Obāsan's one and only *omiai* had been for the benefit of her parents and that was that. With her mother and grandmother, it had merely been a pact sealed between families; until fairly recently, that used to set the more educated families apart from the peasants and the poor, who rarely bothered with formal marriage at all. According to ancient custom, too, a family with no sons can 'adopt' their daughter's husband. Assuming the role of first son and their family name, he becomes a *yōshi* – a substitute heir assuring the transmission of the patriarchal line. In effect, the formula has also frequently formed a basis for male *mariages de convenance*, since a husband of lower status can thus take a step up the social ladder or enter a lucrative business partnership.

Omiai still determines roughly half of all marriages today, although the outcome is generally up to the couple concerned. Rather than choosiness, Mayumi's spurning of scores of bachelors might have had more to do with a former sweetheart. That the Yamashitas and his parents did not see eye to eye eventually prompted her to end the affair, which had been permissible as long as all traces of sexuality were concealed and it showed no signs of becoming serious. Shigeru always prides himself on his open mind and progressive spirit. Mayumi, after all, has been an office employee since she left school. She earns her own income, drives her own car and after office hours her time has largely been her own. There was one point, however, about which both her parents had been quite adamant: Mayumi was to be home by ten. A young lady of twenty-five has no business being out too late after dark – the dire consequences of which are stressed in a great many frightening posters hanging outside the country's plentiful police boxes.

That the proliferation of love hotels might allow Mayumi to do what she cannot do at night during the day is neither here nor there to her parents. What really matters is to keep up appearances. Like everyone else in most other contexts too, provided she upholds her own and the family's *tatemae* (front) and keeps her *honne* (true situation) strictly to herself, Mayumi can reasonably do as she pleases. But when it comes to father, he may well remain remote and aloof as a patriarchal figurehead but, when he puts in a word, reverence for filial piety commands obedience.

The defiance underlying the passionate and unconventionally feminist verses of the poet Akiko Yosano (1878–1942) was perhaps instigated by her own past. Infuriated that his first-born was not a son, her father dumped her with an aunt, until her brilliance prompted him to take her back home. While she was made to manage the family shop when her mother died, at twenty she was expressly forbidden to walk abroad during the day and locked in her bedroom at night. Yosano's leaving home to marry a noted poet marked the beginning of a career; notwithstanding ostensible servitude to a husband, many women see greater freedom in marriage than in protracted spinsterhood.

Even when they have passed *tekireiki* – marriageable age – many single women live at home and their parents' words are law. It is not unusual to see a spinster in her thirties hastening home to honour a curfew before the end of a dinner with friends. I recall a 25-year-old office employee living alone who, faced with opposition over a fiancé, found that a noted Tokyo bank had complied with her father's demand to block her account. A painter of the same age was ordered back to the country by her parents in a bid to end her liaison with a noted avant-garde artist. Since they wanted an adoptive *yōshi* to help out on the farm, in 1988 this university graduate did as she was bidden as dutifully as a Sicilian peasant daughter of thirty years ago.

When Mayumi was still unmarried at the advanced age of twenty-five, however, the family began to share her mounting anxieties. The successive meetings came to nothing, the round of eligible bachelors began to deplete itself; Mayumi lived in such a state of panic that the strain showed on her face, and she soon feared that the *omiai* photographs sent round to prospects were too flattering. *Omiai* portraiture is one of the mainstays of the photographer's studios found in all but the smallest villages. It keeps them especially busy on 15 January during *Seijin no hi* or Adults Day, a national holiday observed by all young people who have turned twenty during the preceding year. Often displayed in their shop windows, the portraits find the young ladies in traditional attire and the gentlemen in business suits, seated in a chair in the Louis XV style or posed rigidly against a cloudy silvan backdrop. Nineteenth-century photography – albeit in colour – is charmingly alive and well in Japan.

Relatives or trusted parental friends, who are generally female and can expect a cash contribution for their services, act as *nakodo* (go-between) and present subsequent prints of snapshot size to the prospective family. Informal snapshots are often offered too and, if the girl concerned should have hobbies such as ballet or jazz dancing, skating or aerobics, pictures in accordingly skimpy attire and showing her to her best advantage might work further in her favour. Beach photographs, however, particularly in this age of shrinking swimwear, are out.

If expressing interest, the parties will be brought together during an excruciating meeting process, which finds the two families lunching together in a restaurant in a climate of strained conviviality. Both in immaculate tailored suits, the young man and woman in question stare unwaveringly at the tablecloth, hardly daring to exchange a glance – let alone a word. The girl eats practically nothing. The parents talk over their heads. The boy's father reels off his son's academic achievements and his prospects; the girl's father will extol her virtuous nature, schooling, hobbies, housekeeping abilities and fondness of children. At some point, the two will be expected to say something, generally a tremulous and extremely modest version of the already very reticent paternal summary.

During the following week, if he doesn't like her, the boy will back out with a range of polite excuses. If he does, he will wipe his sweating palms on the back of his trousers, find his voice and at last grab the telephone to ask her out on a date. If shyness is common among young men in similar circumstances everywhere, its prevalence in Japan is betrayed by the fact that *omiai*, a practice widespread among the rural and the diffident, would otherwise have died out long ago. If mutually impressed, the couple will go out on what might well be a rather painful first date. It may be on a Saturday evening but, where the notion of night holds improper connotations, it might more properly occur on a Sunday afternoon. The scope of activities is pretty much universal, with movies and perhaps amusement parks high on the list, but the culminating meal or cup of coffee is discernible as an *omiai* date at a glance. Facing each other across the table, they are only nominally more comfortable than with their parents the previous week. Their eyes remain glued to their banana sundaes to avoid contact; they are only animated by the sheer relief of a waiter arriving to break the spell. After about a quarter of an hour of awkward silence, one often sees the boy look up with a sudden flash of inspiration, which culminates in his rather over-loudly blurting out something such as 'Do you like tennis?'

If the girl stares with blank embarrassment and gently shakes her head, their future as a couple may well be uncertain. If she happens to like tennis and they warm to each other, they will go from date to date, from restaurant to disco and from hotel to the Shinto altar.

The pious might opt for the more austere and less popular Buddhist ceremony and, today, the Christian wedding sometimes offers an exotic and romantic alternative to non-Christians. The staggering proliferation of posters throughout Japan's trains and subways present a wide range of wedding alternatives, as do TV commercials and newspaper and magazine advertisements. Some might offer bizarre fantasies such as parading the couple around the wedding hall in a white and gold Venetian gondola on wheels amidst clouds of dry ice and whisking them off to their honeymoon aboard a helicopter. There are underwater weddings for diving enthusiasts and even schemes to have Christian weddings staged in small, mercenary-minded churches in Europe. The underlying message is clear: Thou Shalt Get Married. Being considered as 'un-adult' at the very least, detractors are viewed with the gravest suspicion. An eccentric couple of my acquaintance, living in separate cities but regularly meeting at weekends and spending holidays together, felt that their life was fine just as it was. Both being thirty, however, and pressured by their families, they simply staged a grand wedding and carried on exactly as before.

With the pull to get married as strong as it is, marriage agencies are a lucrative business. A cheaper alternative for lonely hearts is even to be found in local government offices, in which matchmaking is conducted by civil servants entering the names and particulars of interested parties in ledgers for a nominal fee. Founded in 1967, the Beauty Life Association for one had some 6,000 hopefuls on its books by the mid-seventies, when there were nearly 300 other private agencies catering to all ages and persuasions in Tokyo alone, not a few of which specialize in companions for the widowed and divorced. One might be forgiven for assuming that those who drop out of the *omiai* routine in favour of agencies might be more romantically than practically inclined, but this is far from being the general rule. Well-advertised on posters throughout the Tokyo transport system is an agency aptly called the Magpie Association, which not untypically targets young ladies with an eye to the main chance: 'You can trust us. We arrange introductions only to the élite: doctors, lawyers, dentists.'

Fully computerized, today's thousands of marriage agencies boast of their ability to match data and preferences to come up with perfect partnerships. Prim middle-aged ladies in business suits aim video cameras at prospects, providing them with what is only just a more animated alternative to the *omiai* photograph. Individuals pay a flat fee of 150,000 yen to join, couples confront each other over a table on the premises and if the romance – or progenitive business partnership – doesn't work out, they shell out 10,000 yen for next time. One Tokyo agency calling itself Rodin and unabashedly targeting the élite demands a ten million yen registration fee, degrees and moneyed backgrounds and stages matchmaking procedures including chaste separate-room weekends in plush resorts, culminating with a grand wedding in New York.

If some women still throw away their lives by respecting their parents' wishes rather than their own feelings, the majority of people welcome *omiai* as a means of meeting members of the opposite sex – whether the outcome is marriage or not. Nevertheless, a grimly humorous phrase for marriage, especially among women, is *jinsei no hakaba* – the cemetery of life. The alternative to an *omiai* wedding procedure is *renai kekkon* – a love marriage. If the new trend still tends to be more of an urban fantasy concocted by the media than a reality, the fact is that girls and boys are nevertheless going out more together and more freely; the *renai* pattern is becoming more common.

When Mayumi Yamashita started to pine away reading wedding-wear and honeymoon magazines among the serried ranks of fluffy animals festooning her room, her parents found it difficult to get her out of the house at all. On the rare occasions when she did go out, other than to go to work, she not infrequently drove to Shinto shrines and prayed to the deities most likely to augur a good matrimonial future. Finally, Shigeru resorted to a truly desperate measure: he relaxed the 10 P.M. curfew.

So for the few months before Mayumi and Hiroshi were introduced, she went to discos in Nagoya on Saturday nights. She sometimes even came home at two or three in the morning and, in the meantime, she saw a whole lot of boys. But since wherever she went she was invariably with the same three girlfriends, the operative word here is 'saw'. The four girls would dance together on the dance floor and giggle as they tippled discreetly in the deco-tech interiors of fashionable café-bars, taking turns in being the teetotal and driving fourth. In one disco, a couple of boys sauntered up to ask them to dance, which found them raising their hands in front of their faces and giggling all the more as they shook their heads. Crestfallen and sheepishly grinning, the boys soon went back to join their comrades at another table.

Mayumi's aunt Etsuko had acted as the *nakodo* or go-between in the *omiai* process; Hiroshi's aunt was one of her colleagues in the administrative office of a neighbouring town hall. Before Hiroshi, there had been the son of that Nagoya hotelier whom Mayumi had thought too fat, the young chartered accountant who had talked only of cars and golf in a whiny voice and the boy from the electronics store who suffered from acne. There had been that Yamaguchi boy, too, the one who owned three beauty salons and drove a Porsche. The Yamashitas didn't like him; he had a hairstyle like a gangster and Mayumi's mother pointed out that the signs outside his salons were *purple*. The family hardly needed the sort of fellow who puts up purple signs.

In one way or another, everyone agreed. To use purple was presumptuous – for it had once been the colour of the mighty Tokugawa shogunate; mauve is precious for having been the dominant colour of the effete Heian age. Worse still, as a marriage between red and blue, the colour is ambiguous, risqué and thus so very *mizu shobai*.

TYING THE KNOT

Statistics weren't available on those who decided to remarry. Could there really be people out there who would be willing to go through it all again? Irish wakes are much more fun.

Gail Nakada, *The Tokyo Journal* (June 1984)

A legacy of rich merchant ostentatiousness from the late Edo period, weddings are elaborate and expensive. From the exchange of relatively inexpensive symbolic tokens of good luck, the bride's parents have become increasingly saddled with items such as ruinously expensive suites of furniture and a supply of kimonos considered proper (though seldom worn) for the married woman's wardrobe. Wedding expenses thus cover far more than just the ceremony, the cost of which is shared with the groom's parents. In the Nagoya area, ever a bastion of conservatism, the parents of one couple of my acquaintance indulged in a curious and ruinous game of one-upmanship in which the bride's parents, although far less well-off than the groom's, felt obliged to go all-out to contribute as much as they could to the most ostentatious wedding either could afford. That all this is a venerable custom is widely believed, although even a cursory glance at history would prove the notion to be fallacious; the high cost of weddings is upheld by peer pressure buttressed by the sacrosanct commerce sector, in the form of companies specializing only in weddings, furniture stores, clothiers, and the hotel and catering trade.

As 'tradition' dictates, Mayumi's and Hiroshi's wedding will be a grand affair. The Yamashitas are comfortably off, but far from wealthy; it will take ten million yen out of their savings, even if Hiroshi's parents make substantial contributions. That's life. Besides, all relatives and wedding guests will place a white envelope on a silver tray at the entrance to the wedding hall. Along with their wishes of goodwill, it will contain a minimum of 10,000 yen in cash for a more casual guest, and substantially more for members of the family. In many cases the roster of guests includes business associates; the cash contributions from those wishing to curry favour with the groom or his father will be commensurate with their involvement or expectations. As with wedding presents, the exact value of each contribution will be carefully totted up afterwards, not through stinginess, but to gauge the effusiveness of subsequent thanks, the degree of favours owed in return and the value of presents marking similar occasions later on.

Arriving in a black Nissan limousine of the genus 'Cedric' hired for the day, Mayumi will be presented to the groom at a large local Shinto shrine. She will be wearing majestic bridal finery, which is so astronomically expensive today that all but the wealthiest brides hire it. Red and white or plain white and for rent at about

100,000 yen, a wedding kimono is intricately embroidered with floral and bird motifs enhanced with gold and
silver thread. On her head, the bride wears a traditional
wig made of real human hair spiked with decorative
hairpins and combs. A large starched crown in a plain
white fabric completes a picture that will have taken a
professional dresser almost an hour to prepare.
Although she will undoubtedly be lovely, the new wife,
with her whitened face and tiny, beestung red lips, will
look totally unlike Mayumi Yamashita and very like a
standard Japanese bride. Decked out in a black formal
kimono and wide *hakama* striped trousers, the groom will
meanwhile be processed in only a few minutes.

Then there is the Shinto ceremony. As the priest
officiates, a *miko* shrine maiden will guide the couple
through the proceedings; there is no rehearsal. As a
robed *gagaku* ensemble plays instruments imported from
China some twelve hundred years ago, the bride and
groom ritually exchange cups of sake three times. The
groom then reads a document aloud, the gist of which is
that he expects his wife to honour and obey. He will
complete this by announcing his full name, while his
wife announces her forename only, for she has now been
adopted by her husband's family.

After the ceremony, a photographer freezes the stiffly
posing newlyweds in front of their families and principal
guests on film for eternity, and then there will be a
reception held in one of the capacious wedding halls of a
large hotel. Guests will file in over a plush red and
yellow carpet in the rococo style beneath a ceiling dripping with shimmering crystal chandeliers. Before entering, Mayumi will have changed into her second kimono
(again unlikely to be her own) and enter the room with
the groom to the strains of Mendelssohn's Wedding
March piped out at deafening volume. Carefully placed

around the banqueting hall according to their station, guests sit before round tables impeccably set with flower-pieces and a dazzling array of beautifully presented cold delicacies. The bride and groom preside almost invisibly at one end behind a jungle of flowers. Staring rigidly ahead, they might just exchange a few words together out of the corners of their mouths. In the process of becoming bride and groom, they relinquish their identities.

Guests and family members are specially allotted functional roles essential to the event: one or two masters or mistresses of ceremony and a best man, and many will take turns in playing musical instruments and/or singing songs. Nearly all will rise in turn to deliver lengthy speeches, some extolling the background of the bride and others the groom's. We know what schools they went to, what their work and hobbies are and the names of their best friends who, being present, will soon be delivering speeches of their own. Nothing said will come as any kind of surprise, for had everyone not known all there was to know about the newlyweds, they could hardly be assembled here. One also commonly hears someone reading out a farewell letter from the bride to her parents, thanking them poignantly and profusely for her happy childhood years. Some wedding concerns enhance this with a syrupy musical backing and even a retrospective slide-show; either way, there is hardly a dry eye in the hall.

Many wedding halls offer all-inclusive package deals. A newly built hotel in Okazaki, Aichi prefecture, for instance, typically owes its vastness less to its room capacity than to the fact that it caters overwhelmingly for weddings. The capacious third and fourth floors are devoted to the entire process, which is conducted with conveyor-belt efficiency. The betrothed are encouraged to make plans months beforehand. Some shops on the third floor deploy selections of appropriate gifts, others offer wedding attire for hire or purchase; another handles all the announcements, invitations and banquet place cards and the honeymoon can be organized in an adjacent travel agency. On the day, the bride can be processed in an all-inclusive beauty parlour providing everything from a sauna, through facials and make-up to dressing; a barber shop offers similar facilities for the groom. On the fourth floor are dressing rooms for each, on either side of an antechamber in which the guests of both families sit facing each other before the ceremony, which is held in a specially consecrated Shinto shrine a few doors down the corridor. Then everyone troops into the elevators to go down to the capacious banquet halls. Coming as part of the package is a professional wedding supervisor, who steers the couple firmly through their duties like a strict nanny. As does the shrine maiden or priestess during the Shinto ceremony, she will instruct them on how and when to move or speak. Under her guidance, they will ritually hammer open a keg of sake, which is ladled out to guests.

Then the bride sometimes dons a third wedding dress. These days it would generally be lacy, expensive and of western design. While she is away changing, the speeches drone on as the groom's male friends and relatives might treat him to a quick toast; to avoid offending anyone, he will refuse none of the proffered glasses. Although he might find himself downing quite a formidable amount of sake, beer and whisky, this will be one of the very rare occasions when he will be expected to keep his composure when tipsy.

During the course of the reception, the bride will have no time to eat; but the sight of one eating would be untoward anyway. A demure doll, she might poke daintily at the delicacies before her with her chopsticks, perhaps daring to nibble at a shrimp. She will anyway soon be grabbed by the wedding supervisor and posed alongside the groom to allow guests to take photographs. These days there will be much amusement when he is even entreated to kiss the bride. The entire event is formalized and rigorously timed to last some three hours, not one second of which will be left to spontaneity or allow anyone time to themselves. Where timing could have left a gap, it will be filled with *Candoru Sabisu* (Candle Service), a ritual which finds the room plunged in darkness and the newlyweds passing from table to table, lighting candles with a gas taper and bowing low to each guest to express their thanks. These days, urban couples might throw a more informal party for their friends later on, but the practice is rarer in the country.

The couple will finally change into street clothes which, befitting the occasion, should in the bride's case be of a recognizable and expensive designer brand. Guests start wending their way home bearing huge white carrier bags and silk *furoshiki* bundles full of presents offered by the bride's family. These presents are often fantastically expensive: at the recent wedding of a renowned kabuki actor, for instance, some 2,000 guests were each presented with a pair of small gilt silver chalices, each set with a ruby and a diamond in the bottom.

Glad that the exalting if agonizing ceremony is over, the exhausted couple will finally sink into the back of the limousine which carries them symbolically off to their conjugal life. Next, they will board a train for the nearest airport and on to their honeymoon, which may well take the form of a five-day package tour shuttling dozens of bewildered newlyweds to overcrowded tourist hotels in Hawaii, Guam and – recently capping the list – Australia.

In tune with the more intrepid new breed, however, Hiroshi and Mayumi will be going to Europe. She has always wanted to go to Paris, which has the Champs-Élysées, and to London, which has Harrods. Wherever they go, this will be the first and probably the last trip they will make abroad until future progeny, the first of which should ideally be born within the first year of their marriage, grows up.

That the bride's parents wave tearfully at the departing car is virtually a universal phenomenon. A cherished bird has flown from the nest, leaving the progenitors facing their declining years. In Japan, however, the wedding was once far more poignant – a girl given into marriage became the property of her husband and his family. A custom observed from early times allowed a pregnant wife to go back to her parents' home to give birth, but among the spartan samurai she often never saw her family again.

5
High-school Confidential

BOYS WILL BE BOYS

> You young men!
> Don't you think about love, want love?
> Are you blind to these red lips?
>
> Akiko Yosano, *Midaregami* (1901)

Mayumi's brother, Shoji, is eighteen. It seems hard at first to imagine that he is destined to lead much the same life as his father and his elder brother; he sports a moderately spiky hairstyle and, decked out in Sunday's fashion uniform, he wears stonewashed jeans and a sweatshirt boldly emblazoned with the words 'Nice Music, Good Sounds and Right Now We are Busy Engaged in Sexy Rock 'n' Roll and Motorcycle'. Soon he will be going to university, where he could turn this trendy slogan in purely decorative English into a reality. With fewer demands than in the working world and a less taxing curriculum than at high school, university is widely seen as little more than four halcyon years of comparative freedom.

Shoji studies desperately hard at school. Like all his peers, he attends a *juku* crammer after class until 9 P.M., five days a week. He is going through a period they call *shiken jigoku* – examination hell. If he fails to enter a good university next year among the hundreds of thousands of candidates, he will jeopardize his future career and bring shame upon his parents. Pandemonium reigns each year when the results are posted outside the major universities. Alongside the wild cheering of successful graduates, failure finds loss of face met by unrestrained and hysterical outbursts of parental and filial grief. In what is a ruthlessly competitive society, academic achievement is a sine qua non for success, and children feel the pressure from schools and parents alike. Shoji Yamashita must be lucky; merely doing what everyone else does, he accepts his lot. His is a conservative family in which you make and do for the best; adversity is endured in silence. *Shoganai* – there's nothing to be done about it; overwork is just a fact of life.

During the week he will probably have to smooth down his trendy hairstyle and certainly wear a high-collared black uniform with brass buttons, modelled after German naval academies of the nineteenth century. Outside the school itself, he will have to make sure that he neither drinks, smokes nor enters a restaurant or coffee shop. Teachers are often on the lookout for transgressors; some schools even employ special snoops to lurk around and report them. Despite the fact that most high schools are coeducational, many absolutely forbid classmates of opposite sexes from socializing after school.

Confucianism dictates the segregation of the sexes at seven years old. 'At school the girls were taught in special classrooms, and we could not even play together. If a boy said anything to a girl, his friends immediately ridiculed him. And so we had no girl friends.' The shape of things may have changed since Ogai Mori wrote this in his *Vita Sexualis* in 1909, but not the essence. Akiko Yosano's poem quoted above, an entreaty to young men of the Meiji period hardening to an increasingly spartan official outlook, fell on deaf ears. Sexual segregation exists everywhere as a state of mind – and dies hard. If increasing numbers of young mixed groups do go out on the town, the concept is new enough to warrant the term *konpa* which, a contraction of loan words denoting mixed company, generally finds the men at one end of the table and the women at the other.

Despite postwar educational reforms, girls are still versed in domestic sciences and womanly duties to make them good wives and mothers. Their enduring image of prim subservience is emulated by the popular *Kawaii-ko-chan*, the cute little girl singing stars whose success lies in their very inability to sing. Confucianism teaches that ingenuousness is becoming in a girl; everyone is more touched by the one who evokes the faltering efforts of the girl next door than by a professional who has the brazen assertiveness to pursue a career. Times are changing, however, and the little stars simpering on-stage in flared pink party dresses with mutton-chop sleeves ubiquitous a decade ago have almost gone. It is said that elderly record producers used to like looking up their skirts from the front row; as sexy as they are, perhaps the torn denim miniskirts of the tougher Madonna emulators and the new 'career girl' image have taken the edge off their paedophiliac fantasies.

Most women are still confined to subordinate roles in the home and the workplace. Like the *Kawaii-ko-chan*, lift girls, receptionists and tour-bus guides still announce everything in high-pitched, stilted voices. Careful training results in the human equivalent to the bonsai tree with its limbs wired to cramp its growth. Serried ranks of shop girls are trained to bow at exactly the right forty-five degree angle; in April 1989 a Mainichi newspaper photograph showed shop girls flanked by a male instructor wielding a cardboard triangle cut to appropriate bowing measurements. Young people are the first to refute antiquated sexual stereotypes, yet the youth scene comprises the *burikko*, the 'pretend' girls who, embellishing a baby-doll image with frilly clothing, outsize hair ribbons and squeaky voices, consciously affect ingenuous posturings to lure the male. Much revered too among the older generation is the demure young woman of high breeding, as epitomized by Setsuko Hara in the films of Yasujiro Ozu during the fifties. She still finds her equivalent in the unattainable *ojō-sama*, the august daughter of the gilded suburbs. Equanimous and austere, her frigid pose is the very antithesis of sexiness in western eyes.

Meanwhile, the stuff of male camaraderie and stoicism is impressed less in the classroom and more through sports, to a degree rendering the toughest British public school positively effete. Still popular and widely practised in schools, by both sexes, martial arts are seen more as means of training the spirit, for practitioners are on their own or in opposing twos. Since they thus do not foster the quintessential team spirit, they pale before *yakyu*, a veritable cult which other countries simply call baseball.

In summer, high-school finals are blared throughout the land over radio and TV in homes, restaurants, bars and banks. Players march into Osaka's Koshien stadium with all the trappings of similar events in the USA – the cheerleaders wielding coloured pompoms, the parades, the spectators chanting rallying cries. It's fun, of course, and, as is universally the case, from the preliminary martial music onwards, the sporting event itself is combat in pantomime. Assembling in their teams and standing rigidly to attention for a preliminary pep talk delivered by the coach, the young players are motionless and emotionless, their faces set in righteous scowls beneath close-cropped heads. Their egos blown away by team spirit, they look like soldiers and Buddhist monks. They have undergone arduous day and night training with bellowing coaches in extra-curricular bas⌐b⌐⌐

camps, catching and swatting balls until they drop from exhaustion. Underlings wash the club's floors, scrub the toilets and wash senior players' underwear.

To conservative sports critics exalting them like kamikaze pilots, the young players are paragons of discipline: baseball is 'the shrine to the fighting spirit', 'the ultimate crucible of youth' and 'the temple of purity'. If a young male TV idol's preprogrammed career can be damaged by an amorous affair, for a young baseball star, it simply means the end. In July 1986, a scandal erupted when a student manager of the Keio High baseball squad, manifestly overcome with acute frustration, was caught stealing panties off a clothesline. Mortified, the school's headmaster sought atonement by withdrawing the team from the season's games.

In a man's world, associating with women is for *nampu*, sissies. Instilled at school, the ideal is bolstered with the qualities of the macho heroes of history, legend, stage and screen. Typical among these is the sixteenth-century writer, painter and swordsman Miyamoto Musashi, who is the author of *The Book of Five Rings*, a celebrated treatise on the spiritual prerequisites of the martial arts. Although precious few documented facts have come down about him at all, he is enshrined in the popular imagination as a super-swordsman, rugged ascetic and misogynist. Gleaned from a monumental novel popularly serialized during the 1930s, many of Musashi's exploits are familiar to every schoolchild today, especially the one finding him standing for hours beneath a freezing waterfall to chill his feelings towards an admirer of the opposite sex. A paragon of *gaman* (endurance), that most noble of qualities, this also explains why the tough guys now fading from the screen gauchely greet feminine overtures by embarrassedly scratching the backs of their heads.

Called *tateyaku*, such heroes are the main or standing leads, a term harking back to the kabuki. Usually samurai, the *tateyaku* later became exaltations of the virile commoner and finally of an even more unrealistically idealized *yakuza*. The opposite is *nimaime* – the second lead – and the main one in pictures for women, since the *nimaime* is actually weak enough to fall in love. From John Wayne to Sylvester Stallone, that western hunks almost invariably get their girl largely explains why foreign films fare roughly three times better at the box office. Because the majority of today's film audience is female, the *nimaime* is superseding his macho counterpart and, as dwindling audience figures show, the *tateyaku* holds little appeal for the young. Based on rigorous old codes of obligation, the ethics they uphold are as antiquated and boring to the rising generation on screen as they are in life. As the older generation sees it, however, nothing has come to replace them.

BLACKBOARD JUNGLE

> The shrewd observer of the modern scene will note that sons are altogether inferior to their fathers, and that the grandson rarely offers hope for improvement.
>
> Ejima Kiseki, *Characters of Worldly Young Men* (1715)

Real-life equivalents to the *tateyaku*, men fanatically exalting the male mystique, are said to be *koha*, the stalwarts, the hard school. When not puritanical sportsmen, they are usually rightists, gangsters, delinquents and members of *bosozoku* (thunder clan) biker gangs. Revving up and roaring around the city streets at night and noisome as they are, the *bosozoku* are still fairly innocuous compared to their western equivalents. Described as *koha furyo shonen*, the hard-school bad boys, such delinquents run errands for virulent ultra-rightist factions and *yakuza* gangs, and indulge in their fair share of violence, petty crime and speed of both the stimulant and wheeled varieties. Like the *Be-Bop Highschool* gang serialized in a comic book and thrice filmed, high-school rebels set themselves apart with uniforms especially tailored to an outsize fifties-cut matching greaser hairstyles or close-cropped 'punch' perms. Wearing long skirts and fluorescent socks, girls bleach their hair and/or streak it with gaudy colours. Publishing posters and pamphlets depicting this as a sign of delinquency, the police have prompted many schools to tighten restrictions on dress. While these bar incorrectly dressed kids from school photographs or weed them out altogether, the tighter the restrictions, the more the kids go to extremes. James Dean has long been a youth idol of a purely superficial kind; thirty years later, Japan has belatedly entered the era of *Rebel Without a Cause*.

So far, it is still the land with the lowest crime rate in the industrialized world. Whatever a handful of delinquents may do, drug abuse is negligible and the city streets are relatively safe at night. Yet although serious crime constituted only a third of the total, juvenile offences accounted for almost half of all crimes committed in recent years. The eighties have shown record crime figures and the trend oscillates up and down along a slowly rising curve. Violence, however, is not necessarily confined to the street. High schools are plagued by bullying, and some victims have committed suicide. The trend subsided slightly after peaking in 1986, when parent-teacher associations and education authorities intervened and police introduced a telephone hot-line for the benefit of the victims and their parents. The cases reported, however, are said to be only the tip of the iceberg; like rape victims, the bullied prefer to keep silent. Not just out of personal fear, but to avoid embarrassing social exposure which might cause both them and their parents loss of face.

Spanning from playground extortion rackets to gratuitous classroom humiliation, bullying is often tinged with sadism; a favoured torture chamber is the school toilet. Nor are bullies always boys. Now accounting for some 20 per cent of juvenile crime, females can be quite as vicious as their male counterparts. Girl bullies have been known to order their henchwomen to strip victims, push their heads down the bowl and flush the toilet, apply cigarettes to buttocks and genitals and finally leave them with their skirts tied up over their heads.

The *sukeban* (a word coined from the gangster words *suke* meaning moll and *bancho*, boss) who might lead such exploits are not necessarily all bad. The word is often used to denote tomboys and girls of a rebellious disposition. Populating comic books and teen-screen vehicles, the more righteous *sukeban* rule a realm akin to the paper and celluloid fantasies of the caricatural delinquents in *Be-Bop Highschool*, in which good classroom gangs wax victorious over the bad. Reflecting changes in feminine aspirations, if not real roles, fictional *sukeban* are sometimes invocations of wish-fulfilment and rule improbably over gangs with a majority male membership. With swinging baseball bats and wooden kendo swords, these pugnacious sagas can be pretty violent stuff. Despite having the wicked *sukeban* slapping faces with a gloveful of razor-blades, the popular teen-screen vehicle '*V-Madonna Senso*' (The V-Madonna War) finally had the good gunning down the bad with weapons firing soft bullets containing symbolically satisfying blood-red paint.

Blitzed by aspirations of individualism from fashion and the media, many youngsters find themselves constrained in circumstances in which there is little hope of turning even the mildest of these fantasies into reality. Some face a continual paradox between inflexible discipline at school and uninterested, weak and neglectful parents at home. Crippled by a draconian curriculum and confined to uniforms, their acute frustration not surprisingly sends some out on the wild side.

In a society characterized by rampant consumerism, the message is 'buy'. The latest compact disc player, the latest bike, the latest watch, the latest clothing – all are trotted out in the media to the strident tune of *'shin hatsu bai'* – newly on sale. And all are insistently plugged as juvenile status symbols and the quintessentials of individualism. In his pleasant *petit bourgeois* heaven, Shoji Yamashita may well own several of these things, but others who could never buy them resent their inaccessibility; without them they have no identity.

Delinquent gangs supplement parental pocket-money, if any, with theft and classroom extortion. The females – the subordinate *suke* – often keep the cash supply flowing with shoplifting and prostitution. Running away from home and into the arms of pimping punks, classroom *suke* find lucrative careers both in the oldest profession and in newer porno video rackets. In many cases, the pimps are superfluous. The 'Thou Shalt Buy' media message is highly persuasive; legions of young girls eager for the good things in life have few qualms about taking meretricious initiatives on their own.

EDUCATION MAMA

Smouldering under the constraints of the education system, some children lead lives with no freedom at all;

their parents merely add fat to the fire. Delinquency may be the product of indifferent or broken homes, but many much worse teenage sociopathies can be triggered by smothering parents and blind emphasis on academic achievement. Invariably peaking around the start of the autumn term, every year of the last decade has brought a sad crop of about 500 juvenile suicides. The notes they leave behind or their final conversations all cite depression over an inability to keep up with curricular obligations and join in sports, hobby and play activities at the same time. Some suicides have been as young as nine years old.

Academic pressure has been known to unhinge shy teenagers sufficiently for them violently to assault and occasionally even murder parents chiding them for their poor performances at school. Isolated cases representing odds of one in scores of millions, child murderers and suicides are extremely rare. Nonetheless, the factors they share with the much more common absentees and those inflicting lesser violence on parents, teachers or classmates, tend to be the same.

The *Kiyoiku-mama* – education mama – is at once one of the great bugbears and victims of society. Inculcating their children with 'future-shock' long before the future rolls around, these women avidly attend parent-teacher meetings and take draconian measures to ensure that even the smallest noses are pressed tightly to the grindstone. *Kiyoiku-mama*'s concern starts with kindergarten: only the best will do. Then she will pressure her offspring to qualify for the finest possible elementary school. To ensure that their children enter the best senior high schools and prestigious universities, *Kiyoiku-mamas* not only compete feverishly with one another in entering their progeny in the best cram schools, but also supervise hours of extra work at home. Around examination time, some present teachers with cash gifts, in the hope that it might earn them a good word in the desired senior high school or university. Many *kiyoiku-mamas* are concerned less with their children's personal welfare than in making sure that they keep up with or better the achievements of the young Yamashitas next door.

It is not entirely their fault. Large firms, after all, will only recruit graduates from a chosen university and to qualify for university entrance at all candidates must have attended a given high school. Parents wanting to see their children embark on a brilliant career are thus forced to map out their entire academic track record so far in advance that now entrance examinations are set by some élite kindergartens. Falling as they do into that favourite old category of blind self-sacrifice, *Kiyoiku-mamas* are the subject of searing TV soap operas. Such *homu doramas* are often inspired from case histories, and not a few have dealt with the problem of incest. The press got a lot of mileage during the mid-eighties from the confessions of *kiyoiku-mamas* who had anonymously admitted having sex with their teenage sons. Some stopped short at masturbation and fellatio, others went the whole way. In all cases, the gist was that it was more desirable to provide their progeny with relief than to encourage them to chase girls. A surfeit of sex on the mind would distract them from their homework.

Some high schools are beginning to relax antiquated school rules in the wake of widespread criticism, but none can make a dent in the national curriculum. To the consternation of Nikkyoso, the Japanese Teachers' Union, the recent moves towards reform from the Ministry of Education have proved too reactionary to make any alleviation of the problem likely. Spawned by the remnants of their nationalist prewar equivalent, the Ministry of Education takes a dim view of left-leaning Nikkyoso, which finds its meetings constantly harassed by rightist thugs while the police stand by looking on.

Proposed by the Ministry of Education in June 1988 and ostensibly biased towards the curtailment of juvenile crime, a draft of an education revision for primary and junior high schools conceded a need for 'greater flexibility', but the emphasis was on morality and called for 'instilling more nationalism and patriotism'. All countries have a generation gap, but Japan has a canyon. Faced with growing youth problems, the gerontocratic authorities typically lumped the separate issues of lack of communication between the generations and the shortcomings of the education system in a single package. Exalting filial piety, their countermeasures ultimately bring Neo-Confucianism of the Tokugawa period to the rescue in modern dress. For the time being, the uniforms stay.

MULTIPLICATION – THE NAME OF THE GAME

'Although many teachers stress the necessity for sex education, deep in their minds they still worry about its effects on children.' Following a Japan Teachers' Union meeting in Sapporo in October 1988, this was the conclusion reached by a high-school teacher after conducting a survey among fifty-five of her colleagues. Nearly two-thirds omitted the subject from the curriculum and, when asked why, the unanimous reply was: 'I don't know how to talk about it in class.'

The stuff of the birds and bees – and frequently left at that – sex education lags behind in Japan. The Education Ministry leaves the delicate matter to the discretion of individual schools, although it did issue some classroom guidelines for teachers in 1984. These typically rather fudged the issue, conceding discussions of anatomical changes in a purely scientific context. Guidelines are merely guidelines, besides, and school authorities are quite free to leave their students floundering in the dark. Avoided in too many schools, the subject is rarely discussed in the home. Mothers traditionally allay their daughters' panic over a first menstrual period by cooking a dish of white rice and red beans as a prelude to discussion, but the utilitarian attitudes to the human body do not necessarily extend to details involving its sexual functions.

The custom is fading in the city, but according to one 28-year-old Tokyoite recalling her rice and beans, 'My mother told me that menstruation marked the passage to womanhood. That was all. She said nothing at all about boys and having babies. She should have done.'

Notwithstanding the large number of schools dodging the sex education issue altogether, the majority do in fact include it in their curriculum. *Hoken taiiku* (health and physical education) is part of all school programmes. Having been introduced through Chinese medical manuals as long as thirteen centuries ago, the equation between health and sex is a very ancient one in Japan. How much information is divulged about sex during *hoken taiiku* is entirely up to individual school policy. The health side of the information is generally imparted to ten-year-olds. Boys and girls are led to separate classrooms for the momentous occasion and the teacher is usually a physical education instructor. All too often, the lecture cautiously focuses on those busy little birds and bees. By the fifth grade, however, many eleven-year-olds already know, especially those from more enlightened backgrounds and from the streetwise underbelly of the monolithic middle class. Having witnessed animal behaviour firsthand, farm children have noted the mathematical paradox that one plus one can produce more than two.

Talk around the playground among twelve-year-olds, particularly girls, frequently focuses on the riveting subject of *Dareka to dareka kissu shiteiru* – who's kissing who. Inevitably, this leads to discussions about sex. Kissing couples are still a comparatively rare sight in Japan, where the kiss, until recently defused through foreign films, was part of sexual foreplay and relegated to the bedroom. As pupils graduate to senior high school, approved or not, *deeto* or dates are quite the done thing. Until a comparatively late age, however, chances are that a *deeto* will never go very much further than a furtive *kissu*.

As in most places, Japanese junior high schools have a naughty-boy contingent fond of teasing girls and sexual braggadocio. One sometimes hears these described as *Onnanoko no oshiri o oi kakeru grupu* – the group running after girls' bottoms. The female reaction to attentions of this kind would be a shriek of '*Yadaaaa!*' which, if not always sincerely, properly suggests surprise and disgust. Such boys grow up to be *sukebe* (lechers) and girls are not supposed to like them. As they both grow older, however, the boys' approaches might be a little more subtle and the girls a little more responsive. Having sex, however, is a different matter.

The scope is rather limited. Being compelled to wear uniforms rules out love hotels, for all sex-orientated businesses are officially prohibited from servicing high-school pupils by law. Many private schools, especially the conservative kind who staunchly emphasize *shitsuke* – discipline – tend to keep an even stricter eye on students, even outside the school building. A government survey conducted in 1980 revealed that 40 per cent of young people aged between fifteen and nineteen never associated socially with members of the opposite sex at all, and that only 7 per cent were going steady. Although increasing, the likelihood of sexual hanky-panky is still not very great. A survey conducted in the US in 1978 revealed that 80 per cent of males and 70 per cent of females had had sexual intercourse by the age of nineteen. A similar survey taken by the Japan Sex Education Association among the same age group in colleges in 1981, on the other hand, showed that this applied to only 17 per cent of girls and 30 per cent of boys. The results of another survey taken by the same association in 1987 shows that things are hotting up: the male percentage had increased to 47 and the female to 26.

At senior high school level, however, to everyone's surprise, the statistics were down. Akira Fukushima, a psychiatry professor at Tokyo's Sophia University, gave his own interpretations in *Voice* magazine: 'A stable environment where parents provide material and psychological support acts as a damper on sexual activity.' Noting that the 1987 survey contradicted earlier indications that the age for sexual initiation was dropping, he extrapolated that young people were less interested in intimate sexual relationships, erotic stimulation, masturbation and dating:

Raised in an affluent society and exposed from an early age to a wide variety of information about sex, adolescents nowadays do not have the burning curiosity of earlier generations about the topic. Ignorance and taboos once whetted sexual desire; incited by neither, today's teenagers are less preoccupied with sex. Young people seem to lack the drive to obtain sexual gratification and cope with complicated human relationships. The sexual impulse and desire for heterosexual love are no longer as urgent as they used to be. Nor is sex the only way to achieve emotional satisfaction.

The fact that young people lack the drive for 'complicated human relationships' sounds ominous and may be true. The arduous Japanese high school curriculum undoubtedly leaves as little scope for it as it does for sexual experimentation. Fukushima's conclusion is highly revealing about the conservative, official attitude to sexuality, especially as it begins by attacking the West: 'In the US sex remains a high priority. Many young people, starved for affection because of divorced parents, become sexually promiscuous or homosexual in a desperate search for fulfilment.'

How much healthier the Professor's rosy picture of Japan: 'To Japanese youth, sex is just one of many concerns and diversions. It competes with TV and movies, games, schoolwork, jobs, fashion and sports. Despite Coke and McDonald's hamburgers, our teenagers have their own priorities and lifestyles.'

Meanwhile, the incidence of abortion among teenage girls has not only doubled during the past decade, but it is also rising steadily despite an overall decline in other age groups. Surveying abortion internationally in 1980, New York City's Population Council found that the rate in Japan, at 84.2 per thousand women, was the third highest among the twenty-eight countries surveyed. In fact the figure is roughly only half what it was three decades ago.

The precedents lie in the overall matter-of-factness about organic functions, which means that an abortion is not usually seen with the opprobrium of the West. It is often said that medical officialdom's obstinate refusal to prescribe the pill except as a drug to regulate ovulation has much to do with the fact that abortion is a highly lucrative business in Japan. The high abortion rate is also a matter of ignorance. As many gynaecologists and obstetricians lament in Japan, among their pregnant patients even married women are surprisingly unaware of their own bodily functions and younger ones often know nothing about reproduction at all.

HAU TSU SEKKUSU – HOW TO SEX

Shoji Yamashita's room, naturally, is a shambles. The walls are postered with pictures of Bruce Springsteen, baseball stars, motorbikes, and a rock group with spiky heads and big suits called the Checkers, as well as a wealth of leotarded singing stars with frail pubescent bodies and weak, insipid smiles. The floor is littered with luridly colourful *manga* comic books, including those featuring *Be-Bop Highschool*, in which violent comical adventures serve to allay fears about the juvenile delinquents in real life. In a drawer, deep beneath his underclothes, is an array of rather more startling magazines, which are freely purchasable from bookshops, newsagents and convenience stores where riveted young gentlemen browse before shelves sagging beneath the weight of them.

In a country in which early evening TV cartoon programmes include fare about little boys' strivings to peer up the skirts of simpering and acquiescent lady teachers, perhaps this is not surprising. Looking at these magazines, one would be quite correct in assuming that Japan has a schoolgirl fixation similar to the uniform-and-knickers obsession still fairly common in Britain. Foreigners sometimes decry what they see as moppet cheesecake all over Japan's news-stands, but its natives are fortunate in generally looking years younger than their Caucasian counterparts. In western eyes, many Japanese pin-ups look like jail-bait, including the singing stars in their late teens decorating Shoji's wall.

Roricon (short for 'Lolita complex') is, however, a quirk so widespread as to constitute a national trend. Outlawed as a practice as it is almost universally, paedophilia is nevertheless tolerated in Japan, like other more harmful deviations, provided it confines itself to fantasy. Psychology generally sees it in terms of ageing, immature, sexually insecure and/or impotent males longing for girls too naive to challenge their virility. Amply catered to in *ero-manga* (erotic comics), *roricon* moreover fuels the mass-production of a welter of kiddy-porn magazines, books and videos.

Shoji's secret library, however, focuses less on true *roricon* than sex fantasies vehicling girls only slightly younger than himself. Shoji Suei, a publisher specializing in this particular genre, showed me one of his magazines, called *Supaa Shashin Juku* (Super Photo Cram School). Here a pictorial feature with the Japlish title 'High Schoolgirls *Doki-Doki* [pit-a-pat or palpitating] Afternoon' discovers sweetly smiling young things in sailor collars raising pleated navy-blue skirts over frankly spread vistas of pristine white panties. Another, '*Gaba-gaba-Hey!*', shows high-school baseball cheerleaders in jumping (*gaba-gaba*) action taken with floor-level cameras trained up their skirts. As their titles generally suggest, Suei explained, such magazines are not aimed at ageing voyeurs and paedophiles, but at adolescent boys.

In the West, the concept of pornography for adolescents would be almost as outrageous as child pornography. In Japan, however, where basic attitudes towards sex are down-to-earth despite the paradoxical formalities and official injunctions curtailing them, such magazines raise only the eyebrows of the more puritanical. In the absence of adequate programmes in schools and reticence to bring such matters up in the home, they are seen by many as a substitute for sex education. In a magazine called *Otanko High School Girls*, for example, there was a feature entitled (in English) 'HOW TO SEX – Miss Manami's Sex Lecture'. Miss Manami, a lascivious little wench of the porn video persuasion, gives instruction in words and step-by-step photographs. Donning lensless black-rimmed spectacles, she points to the blackboard before bending over to reveal her panties as she picks up the chalk. The lesson goes on with a photo series on 'The skills of taking it in the mouth' using a banana, followed by 'Do you understand tampons and sanitary pads?' – all explained with copiously captioned photographs of the requisites in question, as Miss Manami dispels any doubts about their function by pressing them against the crotch of her panties. The gist of the text? 'There is that one tough time of the month that men don't have. So that's why you can't have sex.' Miss Manami's lesson proceeds with an anatomical description of the female genitalia, and she points to the clinical details in a diagram painted on the front of her panties.

Panties and more panties. Those worn by peepshow girls are sometimes auctioned after the show; some magazines advertise panties 'actually worn' by video porno stars available on a mail-order basis. Candid pantie shots irk feminists as blatant and arrogant invasions of feminine privacy, as indeed they are. Women are probed with hidden cameras on trains and in baseball stadiums; one video artiste even invented a special mini-dolly which could allow an upward-pointing camera to be moved along the ground by remote control. The quirky predilection for peeking beneath skirts is a fetishistic trait occurring among men of all ages in Japan. Paralleling *roricon* as a symptom of widespread immaturity, it finds expression not only in publications exclusively devoted to panties, but even in mass-circulation magazines. During a lull in a rehearsal for a TV show, a vigilant photographer's shots of an inadvertent pantie flash from singing star Seiko Matsuda yielded a cover story in a lurid and popular mass-circulation weekly magazine.

In their context, teen sex magazines compare favourably with more adult porn which can be violent, sadistic and degrading. For all their bizarre and blatant boys' talk, candid cheerleader squat-shots and almost-nudie pictorials, most of these magazines are not only comparatively wholesome, but almost mawkish. In the absence of true sex education, they inform young males about the female anatomy and their own, which prompts many to find much to be said in their favour. And indeed, why should sex education be grim? If there is no harm in their titillation, the more is the pity that such magazines tend to be puerile and irresponsible, ignoring issues such as prophylactics and birth control.

Apart from the argument over their contents, however, can the fact that these masturbatory magazines proliferate to such a staggering degree for the young and not-so-young be said to be a wholesome phenomenon at all? The magazine editor Shoji Suei thinks not: 'In actual fact, many young men are not having sex any more. The fault is not theirs but society's. They're too used to being alone – their childhood has really been marked by years of studying and not playing. They're totally introverted. One hears a lot about greater mingling between the sexes, but those who do are in fact only a minority.'

Suei, a former political activist who moved into carnal mercantilism out of defiance, is a staunch advocate of sexual freedom. Siding with the freer attitudes towards sex once so typical of the Japanese people, his lament is that modern, workaday Japan has become cold, colourless and alienated! 'The authorities might well talk of sexual morals, but they're avoiding the real issues. Japan is excessively materialistic. With too little contact between parents and children these days, the young receive no ethical guidance at home. They have no sense of morality at all. I don't know where we're going, but it looks like it's going to be a hell of a mess.'

OF BABIES ...

The cast of characters in the imperial picture on the wall is replicated in the Yamashitas' living-dining room, albeit on a smaller and rather more unruly scale. Shigeru's little grandson Shintaro, six and squealing with glee, is bullying his four-year-old sister, Emiko. As the adults converse oblivious to the din, Shintaro pins her to the tatami floor and merrily begins tickling her just where he is always intrigued to note just what makes her different. His mother, Sachiko, merely widens her eyes in mock anger and – '*Kora!*' – chides him gently when Emiko begins to howl with rage. If necessary, Shin-chan (dear little Shintaro) can always be induced to behave with a handful of sweets from an ample supply in Sachiko's handbag.

When his little son errs, Yamashita's son Keisuke never says a word. Like many East-Asian peoples, the Japanese seldom smack a child. Raising children is a woman's job and boys will be boys, so that the juvenile macho is privileged to do as he pleases. In what is commonly regarded as a paradise for children, so too will the little princess Emi-chan. Pretty soon, however, she will learn to obey her older brother and to take second place in the world of men, although the pattern is by now a great deal less stringent than in the past. For all the apparent parental laxity, discipline and responsibilities will be impressed upon them both at school and in the world outside, as social obligations gradually and relentlessly increase their grip on them as they grow up.

Until they can walk, children are strapped to their mother's back in a sling and, whether she is at home or out shopping, they look out at the world from a snug marsupial pocket. Thus when the mother converses with neighbours and shopkeepers, the child learns the rules of etiquette such as bowing and the correct vocal inflections from the vibrations emanating from the warmth of her back. When she bows, the child attached to her back goes down there with her, and she will gently pressure its head to bring the message home. When the child can stand, he or she is taught to sit the proper way, the mother always manipulating the body with her hands, rather like a Balinese dancing teacher pulling a small pupil's arms and legs through choreographic routines. The gestural process is repeated, with demonstrations, until the child masters the technique. Indeed, this process of physical learning by rote in unison with the teacher forms the basis of the *kata*, the way-to-do, which finds application in cultural fields as far apart as martial arts, dancing, pottery and even in the erotic techniques practised in the *demi-monde*.

Despite a steely exterior cultivated to belie it, the Japanese are intensely physical and unabashedly sentimental. The protagonist of many a tear-drenched soap opera, mother – *okāsan* – is a source of constant physical contact, of reassuring warmth. Clinging to her back most of the day, small children bathe with her before bedtime and sleep with her at night. Until only shortly after the

Second World War, they were still sometimes not weaned until long after they could walk. That suckling should preferably go unremembered is rather typically Anglo-Saxon, but Japan's mother-worshipping outlook is closer to the Mediterranean. In *The Bridge of Dreams*, a curious oedipal fantasy echoing his own, author Junichiro Tanizaki's hero is distraught and unbalanced after his beautiful mother dies during his early childhood. When his father marries a look-alike, the sixteen-year-old hero's infatuation with his surrogate mother is exaltingly fulfilled as he suckles her breast.

Until recently, a mother would not hesitate to check a tantrum in a four-year-old by proffering her nipple as a pacifier. If Sachiko would no longer follow this pattern, she nevertheless knows that the physical closeness she has cultivated has cemented an emotional bond so powerful that it provides her with a deterrent rendering spankings quite unnecessary. 'If you don't behave, I will send you away' presents the dire threat of abandonment. By extension later on, exclusion from the tribe sufficiently discourages anti-social behaviour to keep Japan's crime rate enviably low. Mother also commands, consciously and unconsciously, by instilling guilt: she has completely sacrificed herself to her child and any deviation from her wishes is tantamount to spurning her love.

Of very ancient origin, this mother fixation has been amplified in the change from the extended to the nuclear family. Mothers have been celebrated in Japan for at least as long as certain poems over a millennium old imply, but never were they such obsessive figures as they have become since they began devoting their undivided and sometimes suffocating attention to a smaller number of offspring.

The Chinese character for the Japanese *ama* means

sweet, from whence the verb *amaeru*. Among the definitions commonly given in English one finds 'to behave like a spoilt child', 'play the baby to' and 'to avail oneself of another's kindness'. To psychologist Takeo Doi, it is one of the key components of the Japanese psyche. Analysing it in terms of reciprocation of passive love, feelings of indulgence and the ability to presume on others, he sees it as the result of the closeness to their mother during childhood. Expressed in a wide variety of figures of speech, *amae* extends into all areas of social conduct. Company men find additional incentive for work by being rewarded with indulgence by the great corporate parent, leading them into a state of child-like dependence.

Until two years ago, Shin-chan slept alongside his mother, as Emiko-chan still does. Being a little man now, he sometimes sleeps on a futon mattress of his own, or with his father. He will still sometimes snuggle up under the covers with Sachiko, although her softly voiced 'You are not a baby any more' remonstrances are, however reluctantly, beginning to sink in. In all probability, the yearning to be close to her will remain with him always. It is as though the process of growing up were a long ordeal of gradual deprivation. The West grows up out of the constraints of childhood into the comparative freedom of adulthood; Japan grows up the other way round. Seeking maternal reassurance from his firm, his girlfriends, his wife, a mistress and even his fleeting encounters with prostitutes, the grown-up Shin-chan will, when he gets drunk enough, also revert to childish behaviour together with his inebriated colleagues.

In three years time, both children will sleep in bunks in a bedroom of their own. For the time being, the one-room sleeping arrangements are interchangeable. When the futons are taken out of the cupboard and placed on the parental bedroom floor, the boy sprawls spread-eagled on his while the mother carefully places her daughter on her back and arranges her as decorously as a figure on a gothic tomb. She makes sure that the little girl's head rests squarely on the pillow, that her arms are by her sides or folded on her breast and – above all – that her legs are firmly together. This is good training for later: Confucianism holds that virtuous women are not even to suggest inviting sex, let alone enjoy it. This is a male privilege to be gratified only in its proper place: among the denizens of the *mizu shobai*. The proper destiny for a virtuous woman is that of a wife and mother. Even if she moves later in her sleep, a small girl should ideally adopt this initial sleeping position for the rest of her life. In all probability, however, a young woman such as Sachiko, one of the last generation to have been taught the Proper Way to Sleep, would, like her sisters in the big cities, allow her little girl to sleep as she pleases.

... AND BIRTHDAY SUITS

That water is purifying is one of the principles of the Shinto faith; the daily bath is a ritual the Japanese indulge in from cradle to grave. The spas of Europe mostly draw droves of rheumatics, but Japanese of all ages spend entire holidays wallowing in their volcanic homeland's abundant *onsen* – hot springs. The bath is a source of pleasure and togetherness; womb-like and mollifying, it is also one of the most common preludes adopted in the realm of prostitution. At home, depending on the size of their bathroom, pre-pubescent children bathe together with one or both of their parents. Until western prudery caught on in the deceitful guise of modernism, the country's ubiquitous *sento*, the public baths, were mixed. Neighbourhood families busied themselves in the steam, the younger members outside the tub soaping up and rubbing down the older ones in preparation for the long, alternately meditative and gossipy final soak together in piping hot water.

Nudity is entirely natural to the Japanese; it is traditionally considered neither aesthetic nor titillating. Perhaps this is why the figures in old erotic prints were invariably partially clothed and genital-display artistes in the modern striptease parlour often keep the upper half of their bodies clad. There is also evidence suggesting an ancient taboo: that long ago the entirely naked human form had been regarded with magical dread. In the diary she wrote during the tenth-century Heian period, Murasaki Shikibu mentions a household thrown into total confusion when a couple of distraught ladies-in-waiting are robbed of their clothes during the night. 'Unforgettably horrible is the naked body,' she concludes. 'It really does not have the slightest charm.'

Far from living in an age of prudishness, Murasaki, the author of the monumental *Tale of Genji*, a romance about a seducer *extraordinaire*, lived in one of the most promiscuous periods in Japanese history. Today, the celebration of the nude has made inroads into Japanese culture as a western import. That it is not seen in the same erotic light as in the West may also be rooted in extreme pragmatism: the human body is merely an assemblage of different functional parts; eroticism and arousal are more relevantly and intrinsically to be derived from the genitals.

For small children, provided they confine such indulgences to private contexts, playing with these is no big deal. They can play 'doctors' with comparative impunity; they naturally tire of this just as rapidly as they do a game with Transformer robots or electronic talking dolls. Adults, after all, have to devote time to other things too. Women bathing baby boys often flick nascent appurtenances with a finger, laughing about the lady-killer its proud owner will grow up to be. 'I don't know,' I heard one woman say to unruffled visitors as she explicitly displayed a baby boy pink and steaming from the bath, 'but just look at the size of his balls. Don't you think he might have three in there?'

THE GENITAL VOCABULARY

As in most languages, the Japanese vocabulary offers more words to describe the genitals than the act of putting them together. There are so many Japanese words for the genitals that, in the seventies, sexologist Nakano Eizo compiled and published a popular *Genital Glossary*. Biology tends to make the female a passive sexual partner and the male an active predator; social conditioning everywhere has subsequently ensured that sexual terminologies are more likely to roll off the male than the female tongue. Hence the existence of about twice as many words to describe the female genitals than the male. In Japanese, the assortment of cavities and tumescences begin as in most languages with *ana* (hole) and *tsue* (stick). Of these primeval and universal terms, which are more likely to be found as metaphors in erotic prose than in practical parlance, the second is rarer than the first.

Words to describe the penis call upon mushrooms and assorted vegetables, eels and snakes, swords, spears and arrows. It includes the flute (*shakuhachi* – which is also a term for fellatio) and, as in other East-Asian countries in which this aggressive and grotesquely phallic-headed creature is common, the snapping turtle. For resembling a well-loved animal renowned for its attributes, the well-hung gentleman might find both himself and his appendage described as *uma* – a horse. Like the British, the Japanese occasionally use the term 'middle leg' – *mannaka no ashi* – and *doogu*, tool. More intrinsically Japanese is *nagachochin* – long lantern – as well as words referring to indigenous folklore: the *tenggu no hana*, a reference to the mythical goblin Tenggu and its outsize nose. Reflecting Confucian patriarchy is the fairly commonly used word *musuko* which, in ordinary non-penile parlance, simply means 'son'.

Evoking the usual nooks, crannies and declivities, the vocabulary for the female genitals includes a variety of topographical features such as dells, caves, valleys, forests and ponds. 'Pussy', similarly if rarely, makes its presence felt as *nekko* and suffers the indignity of finding its metaphorical function shared with creatures as far apart as the hedgehog, the octopus and the wild boar. A famous Japanese fairy tale finds the boy hero Momotaro born from a peach; in a sense all other children are too, for *momo* (peach) is another allusion to the female genitals, a notion harking back to Taoist China.

Reflecting the woman's traditional place, the vagina comes into its own in the kitchen and is paralleled with dozens of miscellaneous pots, pans, bowls, teapots and even cooking stoves. Words referring to boxes, purses and bags are legion, as well as many more romantic metaphors of Chinese origin evoking jewels and flowers. Some words can be frankly anatomical: *shita-kuchi* (lower mouth) and specific (*mame*, bean, meaning clitoris). Others with primary meanings such as shrine, shrine gateway, temple hall and goddess evoke a degree of awe and reverence.

Just as *moule* is one of the most widespread of the

many French slang words denoting the vulva (as well as the less common English 'clam'), shellfish occupy the paramount position among all Japanese terms for the female genitalia. The word *kai* (shell) is thus often evoked in sexual contexts. Among several varieties serving this application, the most common are *hotategai* (scallop) and *hamaguri* (clam). Such widely consumed denizens of the deep are frequently used as votive symbols in Shinto shrines devoted to fertility cults. The power of this metaphor was once amply illustrated in the Yoshiwara licensed quarters of old Edo during New Year celebrations, when itinerant fishmongers customarily sold auspicious clams.

The words most commonly used to mention genitalia in polite or family contexts are *are* or *asoko*, 'that' or 'there', as well as *odaiji-no-tokoro* for girls and *odaiji-no-mono* for boys – the august important place and thing, respectively. Unlike little girls, however, small boys are honoured as the proud possessors of the *ochinchin*. At once meaning 'honourable tinkle-tinkle' and a polite abbreviation of the more taboo *ochimbo* (honourable rare jewel), the word has no female equivalent. Condemning this as a symptom of the inculcation of male specialness at an early age, some Japanese feminists took exception during the early eighties and attempted to balance things out by introducing the word *wareme-chan* (dear little slit) but, so far, they have met with little success.

Unlike the most common *ochimbo* and *omanko* (honourable absolute place), considered just as vulgar as cock and cunt are in English, these are euphemisms. Notwithstanding, their perception as such is very different from the West. To the Japanese, the genitals are not objects of fear and loathing to be debased to oaths and personal insults. Whether they are slang, formal or euphemistic, the terms are respectfully preceded by honorifics and duly emphasize the importance of the organs in question. According to convention, however, very few of these words may properly be uttered by women.

As the nineteenth-century meld of Neo-Confucian propriety and Victorian morality becomes increasingly archaic, women rise in social status and sexual freedom increases. The older Japanese sexual terms were decreed taboo for females and banned from polite society. Where an ingrained aversion to causing offence makes people perpetually wary of challenging old rules directly, English sexual terms make a congenial compromise.

WHAT'S IN A WORD?

As children learn to talk, language gradually determines their sexual roles and the places they will occupy in society. If feminist objections to the use of 'man' as a generic term has left us with the dreadful 'person', that insipid creature with neither gender nor genitals, current English usage at least reflects greater equality between the sexes. In Japan, however, where feminine subservience is ingrained in the language to a deeper and more subtle degree than in English, philological feminists have a hard time, especially as gender differentiation tends to be more clearly defined in the ideogrammatic writing of languages using Chinese characters. In Japanese, a language already prizing the vague over the assertive, women are moreover constrained to use politer, softer and often even vaguer figures of speech.

Humility, the quintessence of good manners for both sexes, begins (as it does in other Asian languages) with how you say 'I' or 'me'. Men are entitled to use much more informal, even slangy forms of 'me', but no such linguistic concessions are granted women. Language makes a woman's proper place apparent as soon as she becomes a bride: the word is *yome* and it is written with a Chinese character compounded of the ideograms for woman and house. And once she is married, terminology sends her deeper into the recesses of the home. To the consternation of Japanese feminists, the term *tsuma*, wife, is written with a single character topping the ideogram for woman with the one for brush, as if the feminine lot is to be eternally overshadowed by a broom. The formal word men use when denoting their own wife is *kanai* – in-the-house. Figures of speech are designed to express the correct and polite degree of self-effacement. *Gusai*, a very humble way of saying 'my wife' in formal contexts, is at last rapidly disappearing. It may seem fine to the old codgers who still use it, but it bothers young Japan. Literally, *gusai* means 'foolish wife'.

The generic word referring to other people's wives is *okusan* or 'honourable person in the house', the word *oku* actually referring to the innermost recess of the feudal castle in former times. *Danna*, *shujin* et al., the words women use to mention their husbands, on the other hand, are all variants of the terms 'lord' and 'master'. A word men use to refer at once humbly and informally to their own wives is *nyobo*, which combines two characters again denoting the women's quarters in feudal households. Incorrectly assuming the word to be an informal term I could use to denote my own wife, I hastily abandoned it when it triggered some merriment as a *faux pas* among younger Japanese friends. It was old-fashioned and sounded funny coming from a foreigner; the proper word is *waifu* (from the English 'wife'). To the Japanese the selection of the word depends also on the rank of the person addressed. Small wonder that *waifu* is by now becoming so widespread that I once heard a middle-aged man using it exclusively to denote his wife in the formal setting of a Tokyo commercial court.

Struck both by the words denoting and used by women, feminist American writer Kittredge Cherry published some highly trenchant and amusing analyses of them in specialized and general-interest magazines in Japan during the mid-eighties. As she put it in the preface of a book compiling such words in glossary form, 'Even Japanese women said my approach awoke them to the gender-based assumptions built into their language. Their enthusiasm propelled me beyond my main reservation: shouldn't Japanese women, like all people, be speaking for themselves?'

The fact that most don't, of course, stems from the 'seen and not heard' Confucian feminine ideal. Since there are nevertheless times when they must be heard, their language accordingly reflects the modesty and reserve of *onnarashiisa* or femininity. Few women would care to detract from striving to live up to the paradigm; it would be a mark of non-conformity and it would be rude. Today, however, a current trend finds high-school tomboys and some females of the *demi-monde* boosting their self-assertiveness in the defiant use of informal male figures of speech.

With terms of address proper to respect or expressing distance, warmth or intimacy, the many subtle nuances of the Japanese language reflect a rigorous code of social etiquette. Required to convey the appropriate degree of politeness, the right word can be crucial and the choice difficult. Like the French, many conservative Japanese lament the onslaught of English loan-words tainting the language. If most countries have found it convenient to import words in the absence of domestic equivalents in specialized areas, the Japanese have been moved to adopt a large number of everyday English terms merely for their neutrality. Coming from abroad, they waive the complexities of hierarchy. Often having the same meaning as several Japanese words which must be carefully chosen according to the context, they make a handy substitute.

One area in which imported words are beginning to dominate is sex. Having neither lewd nor lofty medical connotations, English words increasingly pepper everyday Japanese sexual terminology. As writer Yasuko Ezaki, joint editor with psychologist Tamio Suenaga of the celebrated 1984 *More Report* on Japan's sexuality, once told me: 'The Japanese don't feel comfortable with domestic sexual words. The slangier ones are taboo for women and the medical words sound too hard and remote. Sex was something one didn't discuss anyway.'

Nowadays, of course, people do. Thus one finds *onanie* and *masutabeshan* denoting masturbation, *resu* or *resubian* meaning lesbian and *reepu* is now commonly replacing *gokan* as the word for rape in the newspapers. There are many other instances too, but just how difficult talking about sex used to be is perhaps best illustrated by the fact that today's most common word for it is simply *sekkusu*. In its practical application, it becomes *sekkusu-suru* – to 'do' sex.

PART II

The Rites of Spring

6

Phallicism and Fertility

THE METAL PHALLUS SHRINE

A grey industrial wasteland steeped in some of the most polluted air in Japan, Kawasaki is an unprepossessing suburb sprawling between Tokyo and Yokohama. Like most districts with a history of industrial exploitation in Japan, its population comprises the descendants of former social outcasts, as well as people of Korean origins. A sea of functional grey concrete with small, featureless houses clustered here and there around factories like huts around a feudal castle and new housing projects presenting a relentless Orwellian sameness, the treeless Kawasaki hinterland is terminally dull. Nevertheless, light came recently to Kawasaki in the form of better pollution control, improved housing and a vast, futuristic new urban centre.

Kawasaki is ebullient. Its famed amusement quarter boasts an inordinate number of restaurants and *nomiya* drinking spots festooned with lanterns outside, and clattering *pachinko* parlours vie for supremacy alongside sleek new stage and screen complexes announcing the advent of a more sophisticated urban culture. Nearby it boasts a venerable red-light district which, once a first stop out of Edo on the old Tokaido road, survives in 'Soapland' disguise. As the only means of subsistence for many women during the bleak postwar years, prostitution began thriving in Kawasaki on a scale as industrial as its factories. The oldest facet of Kawasaki's carnality, however, goes much further back than its history of sex-for-sale.

A couple of outward-bound suburban train stops from the tomorrowland of Kawasaki station is Daishi, the home of a modest Shinto shrine holding the distinction of being the last in the urban Tokyo-Yokohama area primarily devoted to a phallic deity. Kanamara-sama jinja, the Metal Phallus Deity Shrine, holds an annual fertility festival in mid-March. If the actual casting of an iron phallus sets it apart, the festival is conducted according to much the same rituals as the forty-odd better-known Shinto shrines devoted to sexual deities remaining in Japan. The voyeur or aspiring participant seeking a tangible correlation between Kawasaki's myriad fleshpots and Kanamara-sama's bizarre Jibeta festival will be disappointed for, aspiring purely to material gain, most of the denizens of the *demi-monde* would be as misplaced in the context as stockbrokers in a farm commune.

If the two notions coexist, it is solely insofar as red-light districts proliferate in *shitamachi* (low city) areas in which conservatism, as in the overwhelmingly rural districts in which fertility rituals are still practised, perpetuates customs which have vanished elsewhere. The correlation, such as it is, shows a parallel rather than a connection between two different facets of Japanese sexuality, whereby prostitution and fertility are pointedly unrelated. Although shrine maidens occasionally practised the oldest profession in some of the old post towns, there has never been a tradition for temple prostitutes as clearly defined as in ancient Greece, Rome or India. Although prostitution is a lucrative and recreational rather than a procreative pursuit among people everywhere, the Japanese draw a more rigid line of distinction between these inclinations than most. Like all extant vestiges of phallicism, today's Jibeta festival is about fertility worship and not an occasion for hanky-panky.

Not that this has always been the case. Far from it. Since the dawn of civilization in Japan, religion and sex were as closely interrelated as the creation myths imply. Although subject to sporadic suppression ever since Buddhism increased its clout during the ninth century, not to mention from intermittent Confucian purges, fertility festivals were ubiquitous and frequently culminated in a sexual free-for-all. Mentioned several times in the *Kojiki* and evidenced by prehistoric statuary, phallic worship is no doubt one of the oldest aspects of religion in Japan. Kawasaki's Kanamara-sama, along with a hardy handful of survivors, keeps the flag flying.

Considering the shrine's history, this is no mean achievement. During the last century, Kanamara-sama stood deep in the woods covering much of this part of Kawasaki, and its collection of stone, iron and wooden phalli is said to have been prodigious. The urban-industrialization process began with the building of a railway in 1900, which happened to pass so close to the shrine that passengers would often bow devotedly from the train. The Meiji authorities, in their wonted zeal for bleaching Japan to emulate the West, opined that the Kanamara shrine (like others) would have to go. Their enthusiasm for modern virtue, however, appears to have been unshared by local residents.

Among those who had prayed to the phallic deities for generations were infertile women, newlyweds, bachelors and spinsters seeking a mate and sufferers of venereal diseases, not to mention well-wishers seeking divine intervention on their behalf. Not that train passengers would have been assailed by any embarrassing or bizarre rituals. Outside of festival time, most devotees, especially those ashamed of their afflictions, visited the shrine at night. Following years of controversy, in 1920 Kanamara was finally moved and rebuilt nearby by way of a compromise, its new site being immediately alongside a larger Shinto shrine dedicated to the fourth-century Emperor Nintoku, the Wakamiya Hachiman-Gu.

As militarism raised its ugly head, a further clamp-down on phallic worship was inevitable. If the repression of things sexual during the Meiji period had relaxed a bit during the Taisho era, in the wake of the ultra-nationalist fervour galvanizing the country in the 1930s, Shinto was given a fanatical imperialist facelift and shrines such as Kanamara had to put their pants on. At last the militarists' virtuous designs on the priapic shrine were fulfilled, but not quite in the manner they had expected. Ironically and sadly, this came about during an air raid towards the end of the Second World War, which left Hachiman-Gu severely damaged and burned Kanamara-sama to the ground. Its forest of phalli went in the blaze, as did a very large collection of *ema* (painted votive plaques) which had been left by generations of devotees who, in various devotional, preventative and curative capacities, had drawn divine attention to their nether regions. What was left of Kanamara-sama was amalgamated with the remains of the Hachiman-Gu in 1945. It wasn't much, but the religion that had survived repression now defiantly reared up against adversity with a stout wooden phallus standing proudly again on the altar. That no one seemed to object to the penile presence in the new surrounds was a sign of the times in devastated Japan: Hachiman is in fact a god of war.

As though making amends for having moved the shrine some three decades before, the Keihin Express Railway Company backed construction of a new one in

1952. Over the years since, the little shrine has accumulated a large collection of votive phalli and *ema* plaques again. However, like the artifacts displayed in a small adjacent museum of recent construction, many of these have been donated or loaned by collectors rather than devotees. Barren women and the sexually lonely or afflicted nonetheless still pay their respects at the Kanamara shrine. During its annual Jibeta festival, a young working-class couple recently presented their tiny baby at the altar; they may well have produced it through the good auspices of the gods. Exhorting fertility, local parents and grandparents pointedly place toddlers of either sex atop two monster phalli set on wooden frames like cannons. In 1989, when one old woman set her four-year-old granddaughter astride a massive wooden phallus, a gaping young American nudged his friends. 'Tell me this is real,' he whooped. 'No way, but absolutely no way could you ever see this back home!' It may not be for long in Japan either yet, although undeniably dwindling, the old beliefs tend to persist beneath the surface and modern notions of propriety have not altogether managed to suppress phallic worship.

KANAMARA-SAMA, THE LEGENDS

With a history not traceable beyond the mid-Edo period, the phallic shrine of Kanamara-sama may not be as old as some. Still officially called Kanayama and not Kana*mara*, the shrine had formerly been dedicated only to the Kanayama-sama deities. The *Kojiki* has it that these, the Metal Mountain Prince and Princess, were rather unceremoniously born from the expiring Izanami's vomit as she gave birth to the god of fire. Elevating the two above their emetic origin, a later folk legend concedes that it was the Kanayama deities who tried to nurse Izanami after the tragedy. The patrons of blacksmiths, these deities are thus also considered to be particularly good at healing genital disorders. Smiths were once common in the Daishi area of Kawasaki, and prior to the Meiji era the Kanayama gods had probably only rarely been invoked in their phallic capacity.

According to one devotee, a local carpenter, the story goes that the Kanayama shrine's newer orientation all began with a dream. During the early days of Meiji, the high priest (reportedly an ancestor of the current one) was distraught to find that his new wife was barren. He must have been fond of her, for rather than divorcing her after several years of infertile marriage, he prayed ardently each day to the patron Kanayama deities. Finally, they appeared to the priest in a dream. 'Forge us a phallus of iron,' they told him, 'and your wife will become fertile.'

Wasting no time, the priest beat out the iron phallus on an anvil and set it on the altar, some months after which his wife gave birth to the first of several children. News of the miracle spread far and wide. To give thanks, the high priest decreed a fertility festival – Kawasaki's first and only Jibeta – and in days when fertility festivals were still (just) fertility festivals, no doubt the local populace was more than eager to attend. The shrine became more generally known as Kanamara-sama (Metal Phallus Deity), and barren women came from all over Japan along with other people with sexual aspirations and afflictions to conjure the good auspices of the metal mountain deities. As blacksmiths gradually disappeared from the area, the sexual aspect of the shrine remained – as it does today.

THE PHALLUS AND THE SWORD

To Hirohiko Nakamura, an effusive and affable man of athletic build in his early forties, the most important aspect of the Kanamara shrine is not the part occupied by the phallic Kanamara deities, but the *Kanayama* deities formerly revered by the local blacksmiths. Sex, he insisted, was only incidental in Shinto as in life. Nakamura ought to know. A former veterinary surgeon and currently director of a local kindergarten, he assumed his duties as high priest of the shrine in question upon his father's demise.

It seemed a surprising argument coming from one officiating over a cult renowned for a fertility festival, but he stuck to his guns. In one sense, quite literally. The old Daishi smiths had turned to making gun barrels during the late Edo period, but long ago their skills had been in forging swords. This of course was something of a degeneration, as *yakuza* gangster films set in the Meiji period testify, for the good guys all use swords and the bad use guns, a corrupt and cowardly weapon imported from overseas.

'Shinto is essentially a sword cult,' Nakamura explained. 'The sword is a symbol of purity.' In the latter part of the myth about the unruly storm god Susano-o, as it happens, after all his misdeeds and subsequent banishment, he was redeemed by slaying a monstrous eight-headed serpent and extracting a gleaming sword from its severed tail. The ancestor of the Japanese sword, this is the one joining the mirror and jewel to form the emperor's crest.

The sword is so deeply rooted in Japanese culture, Nakamura believes, that it even influences the traditional sitting posture. Sitting back on his heels on the tatami matting and straightening his torso to prove the point, Nakamura – a former kendo instructor besides – showed how easy the position made it to make a grab for your sword. This may be true, but which came first is debatable. Unlike Buddhism or Christianity, more flexible Shinto is less a religion apt to shape people's lives than it is one adapting to the reverse. The samurai and later the militarists could bend it in the direction of the sword, but surely a sword cult found little relevance among rural communities preoccupied only with generation and crops.

'The Kanamara blacksmiths were not celebrating war,' Nakamura points out. 'They only made the tools. The cult was based only on the principle of worshipping blacksmiths' deities, rather like Odin or Vulcan.' So, if Kanamara is not about sex and fertility, is it about blacksmiths and swords? In point of fact, both. Epitomizing the flexibility of Shinto, phallic Kanamara and blacksmiths' Kanayama are one and the same shrine. Kanayama in fact embraced phallicism after being devotionally orientated in another direction. The pattern of most Shinto shrine histories is the reverse, but a blacksmiths' shrine in a community in which there were no longer any blacksmiths made no sense. The myths shifted with the change. Although the story in which the priest dreams about a metal phallus sounds comparatively plausible, it has been overshadowed by a more recently adopted tale borrowed from a much older folk legend, which tells of a hapless princess suffering from a vagina dentata affliction which would have delighted Sigmund Freud.

Following a delightful wedding consummation, a demon appears in the sleeping couple's bedchamber and kills the prince by tearing off his genitals with its frightful fangs. The distraught princess goes through several more weddings, but each husband suffers a similar castratory fate. The area's eligible bachelors are either gelded and dead or hastily turning their attentions elsewhere and the princess looks very much like being without a husband. At his wits' end, her father eventually decrees that any man who can slay the demon, regardless of his station, can have her.

The next suitor may be poor, ugly and a hunchback, but he happens to be a blacksmith. Telling her father that he has a plan and managing to win the princess's heart with his great kindness (the princess, being twenty-five and unmarried, is by now probably ready to marry anyone), her father gives him her hand. Now having forged an iron phallus only nominally sturdier than his own, the wily smith takes it with him into the nuptial chamber. The demon soon appears after the consummation, but the crafty blacksmith holds the iron member ready in his groin. Crunching into the wrong rod, the demon disappears for good with a howl of agony, leaving the bed littered with broken fangs. The blacksmith and the princess, of course, beget legions of children and live happily ever after.

THE JIBETA FESTIVAL

Like all Shinto festivals, Kanamara's Jibeta *matsuri* is characterized by bearing *omikoshi* shrines, drinking, merrymaking and a bare minimum of prayer. This is anyway a duty incumbent on the priest. Just as it is unseemly to meet members of a large Japanese corporation without prior introduction, so the priest addresses the gods on behalf of the participants behind him. What most visibly sets the Jibeta apart from run-of-the-mill Shinto festivals is that the portable *omikoshi* contain wooden phalli and that devotional objects displayed on the shrine altar are graphically phallic and vulvar in shape.

The pattern is pretty much the same as in other fertility festivals surviving in Japan. Many of the revellers joining the street parade affix outsize papier mâché penises to the front of their carnival costumes. Some wear traditional masks representing the more frankly sexual and comical denizens of Shinto myth, such as Okame the insatiable fat girl, the octopus-faced buffoon Hyotoko (often a kind of sexual incompetent) and the irascible Tenggu, a bawdy, benign ogre with a scowling red face and an enormous nose forming the butt of a great many ribald manifestations elsewhere – both jocular and literal.

Later on, some of these grotesques may be featured during a shrine dance called *kagura* which revolves around a mythological repertoire and has been performed since time immemorial in Shinto festivals. A theatrical form of exorcism and a sacred ancestor of the Noh play, *kagura* is only given to ribaldry where appropriate. In the country, it often was. In fertility festivals, which are anyway generally of rural origin, *kagura* subject matter is often comical, derived from folk myths and leaning predictably towards seduction, procreation and parturition.

As the phallic festival parade wends its way through the streets, participants typically prod passing women with the tips of their wooden phalli. Five years ago, the revellers at the Jibeta did likewise but now no longer. As the parade passes, one sees several women casting a wary eye on it behind the safety of their window panes. In other fertility festivals, the pattern is still much the same, with women being 'chased' along the street. Unlike those so frequently and tiresomely molested by sex-starved *salarymen* on Japan's crowded commuter trains, women at many fertility festivals welcome bottom-pinching from sacred celebrants with gales of laughter: theirs will be a happy and perhaps productive sex-life during the coming year.

The focus of many a fertility parade is a formidable penis, a kind of granddaddy of 'em all. As is the case with the burning super-giant tossed into the sea in Nishimachi in Hakata, phalli are often made of straw and torched at the end of the festival. At the climax of the Yamagami *matsuri* in Chiba, a neighbouring prefecture to Tokyo, a vast wooden member is plunged into a giant straw vulva as participants symbolically spatter the connected organs with milk-white *doboroku* raw sake. Sadly, many of these festivals, which were described only twenty years ago in the present tense in Donald Richie's and the late Kenkichi Ito's *The Erotic Gods*, are gone.

Others are in the process of disappearing. The Kamiyamada Natsu Matsuri, for instance, a summer solstice festival held in Nagano, paraded a mighty stone phallus weighing over two tons. Until less than a decade ago, it was loaded onto a palanquin and borne by hundreds of bearers through a torchlight parade down a mountainside, before making a triumphant entry into the town. Symptomizing the fertility festival's decline, the giant organ is made of wood and trundled rather less ceremoniously down aboard a truck.

Although the phallus has long and virtually everywhere, both literally and figuratively, lorded it over the vulva, the female organ does have its place in Japanese folk religion. In olden times, the vulva was often regarded as handy for repelling a variety of demons, but the penis was acclaimed for its altogether more powerful capacity to ward off evil in general. Regarded as the source of fertility, it was thought to be the embodiment of the life force, while the vulva, although revered for its procreational, exorcistic and of course pleasurable charm, took second place – more or less as the entrance to an incubator.

Much the same applied in ancient Greece where as one specialist noted: 'the amulet in the form of the female sexual organ was far less common than the male, but this can readily be explained. The Greeks ascribed greater power to the man, and therefore his genitals would have the greater effect in averting the evil eye.'

Nevertheless, in Inuyama in Aichi prefecture, a shrine called Ogata jinja leaves one in little doubt about its devotion to a female deity. On every 15 March, her rites of spring are celebrated with a rousing *matsuri*, the climax of which is a parade of *mikoshi* shrines and bizarre carnival floats on phallo-vulvar themes. The *pièce de résistance* of the pageant is a large model clamshell which opens and closes as it is paraded through the streets. Meanwhile, a small girl seated in its pink inside tosses out propitious rice cakes to the crowds.

Another more famous *matsuri* is held on the same day at nearby Tagata jinja, no doubt the most celebrated phallic shrine in Japan. Progressing before crowds of tens of thousands and eyed by grim-faced policemen prowling in land-cruisers surmounted with speakers, the parade is festooned with banners bearing phallic calligraphies and focuses predictably on a monster organ which, painted vermilion, stands out majestically from a long train of barely competitive counterparts. Every five years, Tagata and Ogata shrines traditionally stage a particularly auspicious phallo-vulvar rendezvous which must have been quite a lively bash in former times.

At some fertility festivals, including until quite recently the Jibeta, participants wielding phalli used to knock on doors and enter houses to prod the female contingent of child-bearing age within. Today, even if the idea is still that the household will be bathed in good auspices and that its younger women will bear many children, the festival is observed as much as anything for fun. In the good old days, the fun was rather more intense; in many places, the 'prodding' was not only perpetrated with the real thing but also quite welcome.

While fashion-conscious young Japanese anyway turn their backs, foreign faces at the Jibeta festival by now outnumber the natives four to one. Jibeta, it seems, is an event finding little relevance in a country immersed in the grey workaday ocean of high-tech and which has been moreover gradually acquiring the sexual outlook of the West. Firstly, and for worse, in terms of nineteenth-century sexual puritanism; secondly, and for better, in more relaxed intermingling between the sexes. Either way, as Japan grows yearly more agnostic – if not frankly atheist – despite continuing formal observance of ritual, Jibeta is little more than a quaint vestige of the past.

The reason for their disappearance in the countryside, meanwhile, has less to do with changing social patterns than it has with simple demographics. The majority of the population in many areas once abounding with fertility festivals are predominantly senior citizens; the young people supposed to benefit from them have moved to the towns.

Children at the Jibeta festival lick away at phallic lollipops or munch bananas topped with a circular blob of pink chocolate. There are phallic cakes, phallic signs and pictures, phallic toys and phallic *objets d'art*. Eager to cash in on that quaint occidental predilection for bric-à-brac and antiques, flea-market dealers display their wares around the shrine compound during the festival. As per the delicate official mores of modern Japan, however, some of their more interesting items are shown only on request. In most Shinto festivals today, in both their protective and repressive capacities, the police are never very far away.

In recent years, the highlight at the Jibeta festival has come with the members of the Elizabeth Club. A celebrated transvestites' association, the Elizabethans turn up *en masse* and in full drag and pose for eager snapshooters before a gigantic polystyrene penis sprayed fluorescent pink. Mincing around the shrine compound in fishnet stockings, they display wiry male muscles beneath sequinned microskirts and are subordinate to sweet 'Candy', a squat fellow of sumo wrestler proportions and with features like a seasoned truck driver. Simpering behind layers of make-up and fluttering his false eyelashes, Candy is swathed in pink down to his lacy bobby socks to evoke a famous character from a comic book for little girls. By now dominating the Jibeta parade, the improbable Elizabethans bear a mammoth phallus erect atop a palanquin, and cavort through Kawasaki-Daishi streets in a colourful admixture of traditional Japanese and western camp. On a more ominous note, Jibeta runs the risk of becoming something of an *in*fertility festival in the 1990s.

Meanwhile back at the shrine, unlike in former times, the majority of participants only throw casual glances in the direction of the priests. Regally robed in sumptuous brocades and topped with tall black wicker hats, they are engaged in lighting a fire with flints. Later, fanning the coals with box-shaped bellows operated with a horizontal piston pulled back and forth with a copulatory rhythm, they heat a thick rod of iron and forge it into a phallic shape on an anvil. Notwithstanding the apparent lack of interest, a hush falls over the shrine compound when the glowing red phallus is placed on a special stand beneath a canopy and the priest waves sacred *kisaki* boughs over the assembly. No one cares to make light of this invocation for divine auspices for a happy and – more importantly – a fertile sex life.

PHALLIC BUDDHISM

During the ninth and tenth centuries, unlike rudimentary and simple Shinto, more sophisticated Buddhism offered a philosophical doctrine appealing to the more educated mind. With its elaborate and splendid rituals, gorgeous costumes and resplendent temples, it soon won over the aristocracy as a whole but was still beyond the grasp of the populace. Perhaps seeking a way of making compromises with Shinto phallicism and fertility worship, the Shingon sect looked to Tantric Buddhism. It is thus rather ironic that a religion ostensibly preaching the vanity of the world and the transience of life, which practised asceticism and condemned the pleasures of the flesh, should have been indirectly instrumental in opening up new horizons of fertility worship applied in various other contexts for well over a thousand years.

No doubt involving only decorous rituals stopping at symbolism, the Tantric influence focused on the double-headed deity Shōten, said to be the progeny of two of the Buddha's elephants. In fact, like other gods introduced into Japanese Buddhism, Shōten is of Hindu origin. An adaptation of the god Ganesha, the elephant-headed son of Lord Shiva and his consort Parvati, Shōten's two heads suggest male and female forms so closely entwined in a seated or standing coital embrace that they form a single body. Represented as a statue and tightly juxtaposed at the top of their single stem, the bulbous twin elephant heads predictably form the glans topping what is an impressively proportioned phallus.

The old line about 'achieving oneness with the universe', often used today as a seduction ploy by many a wily Indian guru, was promulgated on a grand scale during the twelfth century by a resourceful Shingon priest named Ninkan, who was well versed in Tantric doctrines. Creation was the great law of the universe, one could tune in to the awesome principle directly – simply through copulation. It is easy to be cynical today, but officiating at a time when orgiastic fertility worship was still commonplace despite ostensible bans, Ninkan is likely to have been perfectly serious. To an illiterate majority unable to grasp the simplest doctrine, Ninkan's pious celebrations presented the added advantage of requiring neither study nor prayer. There were no sutras, no sages and no learned texts. All the more attractive, in fact, for being so very like Shinto.

In 1114, Ninkan founded a sect called Tachikawa Ryu in the Heian capital. At first recognized as a sub-sect by the Shingon church, Ninkan's phallic cult saw a popular and successful beginning. Revolving around a ritual calendar based on an eroticized interpretation of the Chinese zodiac, the cult apparently indulged in all manner of sensual rituals focusing on a double-headed deity of its own. Instead of Shōten's two elephant heads, the ritual core was a mandala consisting of stylized male and female heads and torsos joined at the waist.

After flourishing for some two hundred years, it seems that the pious sex-cult degenerated into a form of prostitution run by pimping priests. Worse, rumour had it that they had found a lucrative sideline in selling aphrodisiacs concocted from grinding up human skulls. After long casting a baleful eye on Tachikawa Ryu, the powerful and austere Shingon sect eventually decreed that putting the principle of cosmic unity into practice as fornication was blasphemy, and the ritualized fun and games were over. It seems more probable that the skull story is the spawn of biased propaganda, for getting people anyway obsessed with death and defilement to boost flagging sexual energies with a cannibalistic tonic sounds a tall story. Very few writings or votive objects of Tachikawa Ryu have survived. Experts nevertheless believe that manuscripts are still kept in monasteries in Mount Koya, near Osaka, but they are locked away like so many skeletons and monks adamantly turn down any requests to consult them even today.

As it happens, Tachikawa Ryu was to resurface later in a different form. This was typically in a meld with Shinto, always the more powerful influence over the ordinary Japanese psyche, which orientates itself more happily towards celebrating life than asceticism and death.

Emerging during the sixteenth century, a religious association calling itself Fuji-Kō substituted the double-headed elephant principle with male and female deities said to dwell in the crater of Mount Fuji. Fuji-Kō itself was based on a ninth-century Shinto predecessor called Asama Shinko, which it eventually replaced. Asama Shinko celebrated the union between a volcanic Venus called Toyodasu-Hime and her god lover Sumeminami-Nigi. The cult held its copulatory celebrations in a cave dominated by a six-foot stone phallus. Back in the days when Mount Fuji was still active, periods of eruption were considered to be particularly auspicious. The lava ejaculating from the mountain was hailed as a divine orgasm between the fiery lovers, although Asama Shinko cultists rather wisely opted for relinquishing their cave during eruptions and holding rituals a safe distance away.

Archaic Asama Shinko dwindled as Fuji-Kō replaced

it. Although Fuji-Kō is likely to have been a lot less wild than its ancient predecessor, it nevertheless soon went into hiding in the wake of persecution by the Shogunate, and its phallo-vulvar hanging scrolls cleverly – and typically – disguised their subject matter. The perceptive observer can still see that the Mount Fuji depicted in the background is a female pubis upside-down, that the two peculiar deities on either side wear phallic hats and that the Chinese characters on one votive hanging are decoratively calligraphed so as to form a phallus. One might thus assume that the Japanese authorities were extraordinarily dense. Disobedience could be viciously punished but, as long as some kind of lip-service was paid to the ban, they were satisfied; neither party lost face. Today's censorship and official curtailments of licentiousness tend often to abide by the same rules.

A country with an overwhelmingly rural population obviously leaned more towards folk religion. Thus as Buddhism spread into the countryside, it was inevitably the phallic aspect that struck the most familiar chord in people habitually worshipping fertility. Inevitable too were curious religious hybrids, which found deities of Buddhist origin closely adjoining if not frankly confused with the pantheon of Shinto gods. The sea-goddess Benten, for instance, an openly erotic lady much revered by her male devotees for her insatiable sexual appetite, made her way into Japan from India and through China via a rather obscure Buddhist connection. Once upon a time she had been Sarasvati, Hindu muse of music and a goddess of the sea.

Somehow or other she found herself sailing into Japan with six shipmates who, with Benten herself, altogether came to form a variant of the seven Chinese gods of good fortune – *Shichi-fuku-jin* in Japanese. The others were Daikoku, a god of wealth also of probable Indian origin;

bewhiskered old Fukurokuju, of Taoist origin and a phallic-headed god of longevity; Jurojin, originally a corpulent Chinese god of happiness; the obese Hotei, a personification of goodness said to be a deification of a tenth-century Chinese monk; Bishamon (originally the Hindu Visravan), a god of wealth and, in less happy times, war. Then there is Ebisu, another very obese fellow who, in this land of raw fish, is popular as a god assuring plenty from the sea. According to Shintoist folklore, the latter is regarded as the leech-child whom Izanami and Izanagi disowned.

BENTEN AND KANNON – WANTON AND SISTER OF MERCY

Legend has it that Benten, being the only lady aboard, was more than generous to her male companions during the long trip over. Bishamon, although extremely ugly, had certain attributes finally earning him the position of Benten's favourite consort and certain explicit statues make the nature of this (generally seated) position quite clear. Being gods of happiness and plenty and first appearing at a time when sex was very much part of the religious package, these gods are inextricably connected with phallicism. Statues of Daikoku and Ebisu stand frequently beside the *dosojin* roadside deities connected with fertility worship, the former being seated on cylindrical rice bales which when viewed from behind often become the testicles at the base of a frankly phallic symbol.

Benten is said to have landed at the island of Enoshima, near Yokohama, where the Shinto shrine (and not a Buddhist temple) houses a famous wooden statue of her in the nude. The pose, which is more rather than less elegant for the revealing extended leg, is very similar to that of Indian bronzes of Sarasvati. Where her Indian counterpart holds a sitar even now, Benten plays a *biwa* lute. Next to Tokyo's Ueno park is Shinobazu pond, to one side of which lies a temple dedicated to Benten. A favourite place for strolling lovers, the tiny temple compound boasts a statue of a Buddhist monk said to have been one of Benten's consorts. When viewed from behind, the bald-headed fellow standing atop a pedestal is in fact a monumental stone phallus.

Apt to frown on couples, Benten is sometimes said to wreak mischief to break them apart. Although jealousy makes her not overly fond of members of her own sex either, she might nevertheless fulfil the amorous wishes of a single woman. That the Benten shrine in Ueno should have become something of a trysting place is not so much a sign of waning superstitions as an indication of the contradictions characterizing Japanese beliefs. The gods are very human; they have their moods. Whatever hers might be, capricious Benten is still a favourite motif decorating the dildoes used in Japanese striptease parlours, and her sacred form is a favourite motif gracing the backs of prostitutes sporting elaborate tattoos.

Depicted in a manner not unlike a western Madonna and cuddling a baby is the very popular Kannon-sama, who is at once goddess of mercy and childbirth. Brought from India into China with Buddhism, she was once the male deity Avalokitesvara, 'he who looks down from on high', a divine incarnation of the Amida Buddha. Just as folk religion often caused him to undergo a sex-change by popular demand in China, so did he in Japan. Although devouter Buddhists still maintain that the god is male, popular devotional practice acknowledges only the goddess. Revered by those calling upon her auspices for progeny, gentle Kannon has been closely connected with fertility cults since ancient times. Not her own, the baby she sometimes carries is widely believed to be a crying child she descended from heaven to bear up in her arms.

Although the Orient hardly sees her in the same euphemistic light, the goddess of mercy's other function is comparable to that of the western stork. In the Fuki museum in Yamanashi prefecture, a rare nude statue shows her without a child, holding a symbolic vulvar flower aloft and clearly exposing her own. A goddess eroticized to some extent in the popular imagination even now, it seems likely that Kannon-sama's celebration with explicit statuary was once common. A small temple in Tatebayashi boasts a detailed Edo period stone figurine showing her squatting with parted legs; another in a temple called Miyojin Kannon in Atami is made of wood and said to date from the seventh century. In both cases, the privates have been worn and patinated from centuries of caresses from supplicants seeking lovers and progeniture. In these ostensibly enlightened times, as is the case with the Benten figure in Enoshima, such statues are only put on view with their more indubitably feminine attributes hidden, if at all.

Old Buddhist sects such as Shingon and Nichiren still count millions of followers. Once considered just as heretical, if not quite as colourful as Tachikawa Ryu, various austere Zen sects find plenty of adherents too. In some areas, the cult dominates. There are other forms of Buddhism of much more recent origin, such as the modernistic and materialistic Soka Gakkai, which counts millions of followers all over the world. Nevertheless, the average Japanese is born and married Shinto and reserves Buddhist ritual for funerals. He will pray for material success at a Shinto shrine, structure his life according to the dictates of Confucianism, attribute luck to the good offices of Shinto and interpret misfortunes according to the Buddhist concept of karma.

Buddhist temples and Shinto shrines often stand on the same compound, as Sensoji temple (dedicated to Kannon) and the adjacent shrines dedicated to the Sanja deities in Tokyo's Asakusa testify. The Japanese equivalent to All Souls' Day, the Bon festival was originally introduced with Buddhism, but is also honoured in Shinto. After paying their respects to the dead in the temple and the graveyard, people go and party at the Shinto shrine. This festival is still nationally observed, although the date was shifted from mid-July to mid-August when the old Chinese calendar was abandoned during the last century. Anything but sombre, Bon is an occasion for drinking, dancing and merrymaking – until only recently in the broadest possible sense.

In the end, despite its important position over the centuries, not to mention the twelfth-century Ninkan's novel detraction from more characteristic restraint, Buddhism managed neither to become the principal Japanese religion nor to create a single, definitive hybrid with Shinto. In most respects, Buddhism and Shinto only coexist. Commenting during the Meiji era, Lafcadio Hearn neatly summed up the final outcome:

> It was not until the ninth century that Buddhism really began to spread through the country. Eventually it overshadowed the national life and coloured all the national thought. Yet the extraordinary conservatism of the ancient ancestor-cult – its inherent power of resisting fusion – was exemplified by the readiness with which the two religions fell apart on the disestablishment of Buddhism in 1871. After having been literally overlaid by Buddhism for nearly a thousand years, Shinto immediately resumed its archaic simplicity and reestablished the unaltered forms of its earliest rites.

In fact, the religious changes the Meiji restoration had brought about by turning Shinto into a state religion were superficial. The Japanese populace and officialdom are two very different entities and worlds apart. Despite the ostensible Buddhist leanings of the Tokugawa shogunate and its strict reinforcement of Confucian ethics in parallel, peasants living for better or worse in remoter areas were barely aware of change. Like officialdom, history is generally the stuff of the city. Parts of the Japanese countryside remained extremely remote until as recently as forty years ago. Thus the populace did not exactly resume or re-establish the practices of archaic Shinto. It merely went on practising them as it had for thousands of years.

RURAL FERTILITY WORSHIP VERSUS URBAN LAW

The wider fertility festivals were known as *utagaki*. The word *uta* means singing, and what fanned the ardours between the young male and female celebrants was sung repartee, which was humorously spiced with plenty of innuendo. Staid and confined strictly to the singing, *utagaki* sometimes still occurs in Japan. A courtship custom of probable south Chinese origin, it is also still fairly common in countries in South-East Asia. Like the Dionysian revels of ancient Greece and the Bacchanalia of Rome, however, the *utagaki* of former times climaxed as inebriated participants either copulated on the spot or paired off and went out into the woods or fields. Out of these options, the rice-field was of course strongly advocated as a particularly auspicious spot for sexual intercourse.

Like folk religions in other East-Asian countries,

Shinto discovers deities everywhere, in trees and rocks, in towns, teapots and toilets. Before the Second World War, the Japanese Tennis Players' Association seriously discussed naming an appropriate deity: Ame-no-Hayadame-no-Mikoto – the Heavenly God of Speedy Ball. Typically animistic, rural Japan drew only a physical line of distinction between human and vegetal fertility but, in the invisible world of the gods, the human, animal and vegetable fertility principle was one and the same. Thus while the couples frolicked in the fields, it was widely believed that when the male semen ejaculated into the female, the gods auguring human fertility would be simultaneously moved to cause germination in the crops. In some places copulation was also considered essential to the successful culture of the silk-worm; some say that couples still spend the night next to the trays of spinning grubs in attics in Akita, but the custom may by now have disappeared with the rapid decline of silk culture in Japan.

Auspicious days still dominate the calendar in remote rural life to some extent today; some farming couples reportedly make a point of engaging in propitious coitus at planting time, although if the custom is observed at all it is in the privacy of the home rather than in a rite in the surrounding fields. Until recently, life in the countryside could be very harsh; copulation was at least as vital as crop germination to survival. The family and tribe were virtually synonymous, which meant that individuals belonging to neither were doomed or at best outcasts. It took a whole family to cultivate crops; the individual without the one was deprived of the other and consequently was bound to starve.

It is well known that religions with their primitive roots in animism universally share preoccupations with phallicism, fertility worship and ancestor cults. The similarities between them can be remarkable, but perhaps none so striking as those between Japanese phallicism and those of ancient Rome. In his *De Civitate Dei*, St Augustine summed it all up admirably by quoting from Roman man of letters Marcus Terentius Varro (116–27 B.C.), while adding some pretty fiery deprecations of his own. Indeed, this passage could hardly come closer to the manifestations of phallicism in Japan:

> Varro says among other things that the rites of Liber were celebrated at the crossroads in Italy so immodestly and licentiously that the male genitals were worshipped in honour of the god – and this not with any modest secrecy but with open and exulting depravity. That shameful part of the body was, during the festival of Liber, placed with great pomp on wagons and carried about to the crossroads in the country and at last into the city.
>
> In the town of Lanuvium, a whole month was dedicated to Liber. During it, all the citizens used the most disgraceful words until the Phallus had been carried across the market place and put to rest again. It was necessary that the most honourable of the matrons should publicly place a wreath on that disgraceful effigy. The god Liber had to be propitiated to ensure the future of the crops and the evil eye had to be repelled from the fields by compelling a married woman to do in public that which not even a harlot might do under the eyes of married women in the theatre.

Since the roots of Shinto are compounded of so many elements of ancient folk religion, so they came to colour court religion too. Among the many grand and glittering occasions featured in the Heian (794–1185) Court Calendar, for instance, was the Festival of the Holy Light. Held in the third month of the lunar calendar, or April, this great vernal celebration was of primordial importance: 'To protect the country and avoid calamities, His Majesty dedicates a light to the Deity of the North Star. At night tapers are lit in honour of the Great Bear and a feast is held during which young men and women dance and disport themselves.'

As poetic as it sounds, the 'disporting' climax to the event was little different from its rural *utagaki* counterpart. The goings-on in the dark during the Holy Light amounted to an orgy on such a grand scale that it was subsequently banned. Another, if less bombastic, festival with phallic overtones on the Heian calendar was called the Full Moon Gruel. The rice gruel specially served to mark the occasion was stirred with sticks of elder, which women used afterwards to whack each other around the loins in the belief that it would augur the birth of male progeny. Little is known about the shape of the culinary implements in question, but the fact that similar customs probably preceded and certainly outlived them in the franker countryside for more than a millennium leaves little doubt as to their phallic origin. The festival, being held on the fifteenth day of the first month on the old lunar calendar, was moreover devoted to male Shinto deities. A mid-January festival in Akita, meanwhile, still finds children building snow houses from which they rush out to wallop passing women with twigs as they chant out an entreaty to give birth to more boys.

As Confucianism and Buddhism tightened their grip on morals during the eighth century, many of the quainter religious customs began their decline first among the aristocracy and then, however reluctantly or merely apparently, among the urban commoners. As is so typical in Japan, as repressive as subsequent moral rearmament campaigns were, they were ambivalent. They were first enforced with meticulous zeal, tended to weaken in time and could be revised, dropped or reinstated according to the social swing of the pendulum.

The peasant orgies which invariably followed rice-planting festivals were banned during the eighth century. According to a governmental edict, 'During Shinto festivals held at night, men and women become inebriated and commit licentious acts harmful to public morals. Henceforth, Shinto festivals shall be performed during the daytime and not at night.' They still are. Whether proscribed then or surviving on until as recently as the 1950s, the trick among fertility cults was to get the Shinto ceremony over and done with early in the afternoon so that when the real festivities took off afterwards and things really warmed up the sun just happened to be setting. The disobedience of the rule occurred not as part of the ceremony, but as a kind of aftermath. To everyone's satisfaction, the letter of the law had been obeyed.

In Fuchu, near modern Tokyo, a festival ostensibly banned as long ago as 789 survived for more than a thousand years. Held at the Rokusho Myojin shrine, the Yami (Hell) Matsuri (also later called Nareai Matsuri or misconduct festival) honoured a six-fold representation of a deity called Jizo, who is of Buddhist origin. Originally from India (Khitigarbha) and travelling with Buddhist belief to China, the deity was a minor Bodhisattva revered as the guardian of the souls of infants. Represented as a small stone statue in Japan and being placed by the roadside, Jizo gradually became a relative of the *dosojin* and in some cases assumed a more phallic form. Jizo statues, like those in Fuchu, often stand in rows of six called *rokubozo*.

The little fellow's bald head and narrow body frequently look distinctly and intentionally phallic when viewed from behind. As is the case with a great many other Buddhist statues with erotic overtones, if the Jizo wears a halo, it takes the traditionally broad-based and tapering petal shape, but with various embellishments leaving the observer in no doubt as to its vulvar symbolism. Jizo is also the patron of women who have suffered still-births or had abortions, and *rokubozo* festooned with a sad and colourful array of bibs, toys and dummies are a common sight in specialized shrines around modern Japan. Although the Japanese attach little importance to abortion and count relatively few anti-abortion 'pro-life' crusaders, they acknowledge the existence of the infant soul. Jizo ensures that the *Mizu-go*, the water-child, will not wreak vengeance on their infanticidal mother from the beyond.

Honouring *rokubozo* of an altogether different calibre, the Yami Matsuri first used to stage a rousing parade of phallic *omikoshi* around the town, during which young revellers of both sexes would drink and carouse with rare abandon. Afterwards, they would make for the Rokusho shrine compound, just as the main switches of the municipal electricity supply were thrown to plunge the town in darkness. According to Richie's and Ito's *The Erotic Gods*, the six-fold deity 'was fond of darkness and encouraged all kinds of excess. Eventually the streets were filled with screaming boys and girls more possessed than drunk, all making for the temple grounds. These, although already large enough, soon became packed as the youth of the entire city forced its way in and milled about singing, dancing and pleasing the gods in other ways until dawn.'

That the authorities, and not for want of trying, only finally banned the Yami Matsuri in 1953 says much for the power of fertility cults in Japan. Another famous night festival in Uji, near Kyoto, found revellers wandering around naked and copulating in the fields. This, similarly the last of the *utagaki*, met the same fate as its counterpart in Fuchu at about the same time.

In the aftermath of bans in the olden days, more decorous behaviour was conspicuously observed until things typically began to revert to their bawdy old former selves. For better or worse, this is most unlikely to happen today. Not only because transport and communications make it simple for the authorities to keep an eye on even the remotest villages, but more importantly because the celebration of fertility no longer has its place in modern Japan. Back in the Heian era, however, when the focus on the capital was so tight that it was tantamount to exile for court officials to be posted a mere thirty miles away, the amount of control the government could exert over the countryside was limited to say the least.

Sometimes, the authorities relented anyway – especially where it served their best interests. In 810, for instance, a worried court dignitary presented a document to the Emperor Saga which humbly entreated the reinstatement of certain events in the Chinese almanac, which was widely adopted during Heian times and tied to Shinto to govern a broad range of activities.

'The union between youths and girls on auspicious days is of primordial importance in human law' states part of the document, and in virtually the same breath, 'Agricultural sowing and reaping constitutes the very basis of the state.' Nevertheless, it was neither pragmatism nor broad-mindedness but superstition that brought the fertility festival back into the proper, if not entirely moral, order of things during the Heian era.

Banning it outright might only mean that people would do what they formerly only did on auspicious occasions at other times – a sure way of inviting calamity. Heaven forbid that people should turn from doing it propitiously on New Year's *Hime Hajime*, to name but one, and romping on *ki no e ne* – the baleful day of conjunction between wood and rat, when intercourse was proscribed. Phallic worship was to suffer a great many subsequent clampdowns, but it was to be a very long time before it vanished from the countryside, particularly considering that some fertility festivals – albeit in a castrated form – still survive.

THE PHALLIC STONES

Primitive cultures often both endowed and incised the male and female nude with the same degree of detail but, as a different moral climate evolved with the gradual progression from matriarchal or egalitarian prehistory to patriarchal urban societies, the change came to be reflected in representations of the human form. Provided it is not shown standing to its best advantage, the male appendage is almost universally acceptable; below the navel, the female nude displays all the realism of an unclad store-window mannikin. Just as this has remained true of much western statuary even from before the Graeco-Roman era, so Japanese stone phalli continued to proliferate as their vulvar counterparts were buried along with any representations of interconnection between the two. In Japan as in other countries, the fact that the penis was always a life principle and the vulva at once its subordinate accessory and a mysterious object of ritual awe may have as much to do with this development as morals.

In any event, decency, which is so often decreed by those who resent others enjoying what they do not enjoy themselves, strictly limited the scope of erotic statuary. Officially, that is. While officials acting according to a rigid meld of Confucianism and Buddhism kept a stern eye on the urban scene from the eighth century onwards, life in the remoter countryside, as some of the old stones tell us, went on as usual. The swing between periods of tolerance and repression over the centuries has nevertheless left few ritual objects behind likely to cause offence. The more guarded representational trend became less a conscious form of compliance than a habit and, moreover, disguise added sophistication by lending the statues a note of symbolism where none had been before. Surviving the more zealous and comparatively recent clampdowns during the eighteenth and nineteenth centuries, a very rare few that might offend delicate sensibilities still stand in obscurer shrines and in the countryside, notably in parts of Nagano, Gumma and Yamanashi prefectures. These are overwhelmingly of a kind known as *dosojin*, or roadside deities.

Dosojin is by now something of a generic term covering an entire petrified pantheon going by a variety of different names. Perhaps first there were the aptly termed phallic *tategami* (standing deities) with roots deep in prehistory, followed by road-fork gods, preventative deities, the *Sei no Kami* or sex gods and many more. References to the *dosojin* are to be found in the *Fuso Ryakki*, a book written in the middle of the tenth century which describes their prolific emplacement along roads and the benefits to be gleaned from passing them by. Few of the oldest *dosojin* remain, although one near Masuda in Sendai and another in Kamikyoku in Kyoto were also both mentioned in writing almost a thousand years ago. The extant majority mostly date from not much before the early eighteenth century and are in fact substitutes for the older, franker erotic monuments that had been proscribed.

The most primitive type of *dosojin* consists of a pair of forked tree branches, each suggesting the human form and topped with a naively painted face. The male fork had a shorter third branch emerging from the crotch and, during the course of a ceremony enacted in a clearing in the woods, was placed atop the female and left in a coital position to ensure vegetal and human fertility throughout the coming year. Although the ritual may no longer be performed today, it was still an important part of the annual calendar in a village in the Kyoto country-side to honour mountain deities during the 1960s.

Not much is known about the origin of the custom but, for what it's worth, identical copulative tree branches can be seen at the entrance to Akha tribal villages in the mountainous Golden Triangle area of northern Thailand. A tribe of south Chinese origin, the Akha seem to share much in common in the configuration of their dwelling places and in some of their customs with the rural Japan of centuries ago.

Another early and die-hard type of *dosojin* was just a rudimentary stone phallus by the wayside on the village confines, a life-principle with the power to ward off evil and ensure fertility. Elsewhere, the petrified penis (or sometimes a male figure) might find itself tantalized by a stone vulva (or an inviting female figure) placed on the opposite side of the road.

The frustrated conjunction between the two estranged objects or entities was thought to imbue the passer-by with a powerful connective and protective aura. It was also thought to deter rogues and thieves. Other *dosojin* depicted male and female deities copulating in bas-relief on a single stone. Succumbing to waves of repression over the years, the vast majority of these have dis-appeared.

The most prevalent form of *dosojin*, likewise a single stone, depicts a couple standing side by side and fully clad. These are still fairly common, notably in the countryside around the town of Hotake, in Nagano. Reflecting the newer aversion to graphic copulation, these show a female deity pouring sake for a male deity proffering a cup. The sexual symbolism, mandatorily hidden, is no less obvious for being in reverse. Besides, according to the time-honoured Japanese tradition of gentlemen first, mixed drinking etiquette dictates that women pour sake for men. To emphasize the point, some rural sculptors gave the flask and cup phallic and vulvar shapes respectively; others set a globular hat on the man's head leaving the shrewd observer in little doubt about the symbolism.

One also frequently notes that the lady's arm emerges from a sleeve with folds strongly reminiscent of what in earlier times would have been carved between her legs. In other *dosojin* bas-reliefs, the couple hold hands, often with the woman clutching the man's arm above his clenched fist in a highly evocative grasp. Some of these figures, which can be very charming examples of folk art, are gaily repainted each year: the man's kimono is white or blue and the woman's, of course, red. Although the *dosojin* one sees today are mostly of unpainted stone, in many cases the typically rather garish colours have merely worn away over the years.

The reason for cladding the *dosojin*, however, was not entirely a matter of priggishness. Some fertility cults may well have believed that the genitals generated such awesome power that they were best left covered until the most propitious or pressing moment. In the countryside, moreover, where clothing was little more than extremely ragged hand-me-downs, complete or semi-nudity was commonplace. Just as the opulence of the Christian church was seen as the poor man's glimpse of heaven, so it seemed more seemly for deities to be gorgeously attired in aristocratic trappings. This is also one reason why the nude, which tends to generate an aversion having less to do with morals than aesthetics, has never been celebrated in Japanese art. The quirk is rather amusingly corroborated by a few extant *dosojin* (especially the rarer 'face-to-face' type) which, not unlike the protagonists of erotic *shunga* woodblock prints, are manifestly engaging in coitus partially or fully clothed.

Placed by the wayside or in small shrines, *dosojin* were almost invariably erected in close proximity to the rice fields, often in between them. They were not only a source of protection, warning or inspiration to the passer-by, but were also the object of the celebration of fertility festivals. A Shinto ceremony would be performed at dusk, followed by music and dancing. As the sake flowed freely, carousers would gradually lose whatever inhibitions they may have had, especially the young and fertile. Such festivals were after all essentially theirs and on certain auspicious days the *dosojin* shrines served as trysting places. Beside one pretty little couple of brightly painted *dosojin* near Hotake, another large stone of discreetly phallic shape is inscribed with characters meaning '23rd Day', thought to be the most propitious time for insemination.

Built on a rather larger than standard scale, some *dosojin* were supposed to provide lovers with a screen. Among some examples of these to be seen in Nagano, they still seem, at only some four feet high, too small to afford much privacy. Then again, the lovers would not just be sitting behind them coyly holding hands; in all probability, according to one local connoisseur in Hotake, they would have been lying behind the dais supporting their symbolically copulating divine counterparts. Being a man in his mid-sixties, chances are he knew exactly what he was talking about.

Such *dosojin* were frequently placed beneath a sloping

roof, which turned the ensemble into a miniature Shinto shrine and incidentally made the trysts a little more private. Although privacy may have been a low priority during a Japanese festive orgy as in similar contexts in ancient Greece, intimacy is a condition for coition preferred by most of humanity. Notwithstanding, if the tryst could well be private and romantic, it is perhaps rather delicate a term to describe what was, in the early days, when such customs were most widespread, probably little given to preliminaries or subtle foreplay. In fact the *dosojin* added a typically Japanese ritual touch to what was the equivalent to the old European rustic roll in the hay.

DOSOJIN TODAY

An inauguration ceremony for a *dosojin* statue was held in the town of Hotake, Nagano prefecture, in August 1988. Such an event being a great rarity, it seemed a good idea to take a look. The local tourist organization, generally given to shuttling winter holidaymakers to and from the ski slopes in the nearby mountains, had moreover organized a two-day '*Dosojin* Tour', including pertinent lectures by experts to be held at a prominent local Shinto shrine. The group comprised some seventy men and women who had come from all over Japan and, as they began assembling outside Hotake station, it became apparent that its average age was about sixty and its demeanour ominously scholarly.

The new *dosojin* stone, carved by a prominent sculptor in a charming traditional style, graced a traffic island in the middle of the square outside the station in between a row of souvenir shops and a bus terminal. Wooden stands topped with votive trays stood before it, but among the fruit and vegetables perennially placed on these as offerings, only a few carrots forlornly echoed the dominant phallic varieties of yore. Indeed, fertility cults generally opt for the giant *daikon* white radish and to make sure it pleases the gods even more, the vegetable is often carved in the shape of a phallus.

Rarer and better still is when the *daikon* is forked, looking as though it ended in a pair of human legs. Rather like the mandrake of Europe and the ginseng root of China and Korea, such anthropomorphic root vegetables are considered magical and specially auspicious. Forked *daikon* are thus often offered up as a female counterpart to the more ordinary single male. There were none of these. Neither were there any other vegetables favoured by rural fertility cults. There were no turnips, no mushrooms and neither were there any phalli, either made of wood, stone or fashioned out of rice straw. The unexpected presence of the imported and irrelevant pineapple, however, was perhaps a safely sterile sign of the times.

A ceremony was conducted by a Shinto priest in purple robes but, hardly daring even to be a pageant, it was a pale imitation of its former self. In the background, meanwhile, a man stood up a ladder and solidly painted a large sign for a local hotel, three hikers conceded a cursory glance on their way to the station and a portly matron in a smock and wellingtons obliviously washed taxis in an adjacent garage. The mayor and various local dignitaries made long and edifying speeches about how much progress and prosperity the town of Hotake had seen since 1945 and, altogether, not a word was mentioned about the *dosojin* themselves.

The talks at the shrine lecture hall were given by a succession of venerable *sensei* (professors) as the *dosojin* enthusiasts sat on the tatami floor and diligently took notes on the low tables before them. It was a hot afternoon, the sliding doors of the wooden lecture hall were opened out onto a sun-soaked garden of dwarf pines and the continual drone of the lecturers was almost drowned by the crickets outside. Several elderly men in the audience were slumped over their tables, fast asleep. The *sensei* covered the etymology of the characters inscribed upon the stones, their probable origin, their dates, dimensions, shapes and the deities they represented. Not one stone featured either in the illustrations in the lecture pamphlet or during the slide show in an adjacent hall afterwards was anything but very remotely phallic in shape. In no less than three and a half hours of solid lecturing, the *sensei* had managed the astonishing feat of entirely omitting to mention what exactly the *dosojin* were for.

The next day, travelling around the countryside from one *dosojin* to the next aboard a bus, we chanced upon another small festival devoted to the roadside deities. The orientation here had shifted from fertility to progeny. The *daikon* radishes were still offered before the deities, but those attending the mid-morning event were schoolchildren in the company of their parents, teachers and a host of local dignitaries. Evolving from cause to effect, history has progressed from sacred orgy to school outing. The male and female *dosojin*, the children had been told, were deities representing their parents. Hardly surprising, then, that a large poster of a *dosojin* couple was even used recently in a campaign to boost savings accounts in a large Tokyo bank. Exercising a wholly different function as little as forty years ago, the *dosojin* look like keeping their pants on for all time.

During the Hotake *dosojin* tour, our stopping place for the night (I was travelling with my wife) was a bona fide inn which happened to double as a love hotel. Believing us to be romantically inclined, the proprietors saw fit to put us in a room that would turn the most extreme Osaka love hotel green with envy – and green was the operative colour. A garish viridian bedspread of acetate satin matched the Op-Art-cum-Art-Deco ceramic tiling of fluorescent leaf-green all over the walls, and a fierce strip light in a chromium chandelier cast a baleful glow over the dizzying geometric pattern on the green and yellow carpet. Behind the big round bed was an illuminated stained glass window. Depicting greasy-haired and ponytailed teenagers in a 1950s Cadillac convertible parked outside a diner called Graffiti Romansu, the overall effect hit you in the eyes like a Gottlieb pinball machine of the same vintage. At the foot of the bed was a 25-inch coin-operated TV flanked by a large cabinet absolutely crammed with porno videos which, inexplicably if aptly, also included a cassette of *The Wizard of Oz*. The entire room, this shattering plastic pastoral symphony of horror green, was filled with the subtly matching and pervasive reek of mildew. How much more dignified the olden days, when one made love in the amiable shadow of the *dosojin*, alongside rice fields soft and green in the orange glow of the setting summer sun.

YOBAI

The next time you visit, come around behind the house.
The sliding doors in front make too much noise.
. . . To the gentleness of one whom I love not
I prefer the hardness of the man I love!

From an old rustic *dodoitsu* poem

In resort souvenir shops, among the popular illustrated compilations of ribald local folk tales about maidens and priapic gods and men deluded by fox goddesses, one also frequently finds a series called *Yobai Stories*.

Closely associated with the fertility cult, *yobai* (night creeping) is a custom which died out so very recently that whether or not it actually survives in very remote villages is still being discussed. An acquaintance, a 34-year-old Tokyo designer, who was born in a mountain village in Nara, remembers his elder brother's excitement over 'going *yobai*' (*yobai iku*). 'Until years afterwards,' he told me, 'I had no idea what it was all about.'

Occurring after Shinto rice-planting ceremonies or on certain auspicious days, *yobai* may have originated as a means of getting round the old bans on the sacred orgy. The archetypal *yobai* reunited all the village bachelors at a party, often held in the house of the headman. In some villages, the actual 'creeping' became superfluous for young people of both sexes partied and paired off in the rooms of a house known as *Wakamono-yado* – the inn for young people. On the confines of a mountain village in Yamagata prefecture, I'm told, one of these still stands. A Mr Mori, its elderly proprietor, laments better days about which he reminisces to travellers with voyeuristic sparkle. Today it is mostly empty, although it is still sometimes used as an inn by urban trekkers and, more rarely, by surreptitious rural couples.

As the bibulous stag party ended in the more traditional *yobai* celebrations, the youths would leave and cruise silently around the village in groups. Standing outside a house inhabited by a local girl, they would play *janken-pon* (scissors-paper-stone) and the lucky winner would sleep with her.

The average farmhouse generally had only one floor, although some were raised on high stilts, the area underneath being used as a woodpile and for housing the bath and latrine. Rooms generally gave out onto a veranda or outdoors, which no doubt greatly facilitated the custom. With the tacit sanction of parents who had no doubt found their lifelong mate in the same way, girls simply left the doors of their rooms open for the occasion. The other boys, meanwhile, would make their way to the next house.

Reflecting the archetypal Japanese pattern of *honne* (true conditions) and *tatemae* (the front), *yobai* was common knowledge but it had to be discreet. The youths did not carouse around the village; they crept. Parents knew exactly when it was scheduled to occur, but they feigned ignorance. Rooms were separated by thin wooden partitions, so it seems very unlikely that anyone could sleep very well through all that humping on a creaking wooden floor. Nevertheless, in some places, before entering the maiden's room, the young Lothario urinated against the base of the sliding door to prevent any noise when it was drawn open against the saturated groove. Rather as with the spraying of a tom cat, the reek informed any other *yobai* aspirants that the house had already been visited.

Not that all the young women necessarily ended their evening with a single postulant. Many a bawdy *yobai* tale tells of ladies of a generous disposition, and these no doubt hold a kernel of truth. In many instances, the process was spiced with voyeurism. As some erotic prints show and the modern striptease parlour implies, voyeurism is seen not as a perversion but as a perfectly normal sexual stimulus in Japan. Glueing their ears to the wall of the love nest or even holding aloft a candle to watch the ecstatic undulations of their winning comrade, many night-creepers must have been worked up into a frenzy considerably curtailing their staying power when their turn came.

Although arranged marriages were usual in more populous areas, they were not the general rule in the more remote spots in which *yobai* was common. Until the Meiji period, many peasants, like the urban poor, never bothered with marriage anyway. Nor was *yobai* necessarily a determinant in the selection of a mate; if the affair had not gone to the satisfaction of the parties concerned, there was always next time. Fulfilling their purpose, such nocturnal adventures often resulted in offspring and, if they didn't, the young lady made herself available for more *yobai*. Abortion was often a grim consequence: performed with a rice stem by a local hag, it was widely practised and a serious hazard to the woman's life. In those days childbirth was not without risk either; if the mother survived, it was quite likely that her progeny would not. This was not just due to the high rate of infant mortality. As it was in China, where another child meant another mouth to feed, infanticide was common in old Japan.

Many country people lived in absolute wretchedness until well after the turn of the last century. At the mercy of the elements in a disaster-prone country in which floods, earthquakes and volcanic eruptions can come as an unwelcome complement to a four-season pattern itself often presenting extremes, Japanese peasants had lived with the threat of famine since prehistoric times. During the Heian era, peasants were regarded as little more than animals by the ruling class, as epitomized by Sei Shonagon who, in her *Pillow Book*, expresses disgust at their stunted appearance and repulsive eating habits. They were tossed around on the tides of civil war for five hundred years afterwards. Until the Tokugawa shoguns began to lose their grip, Japanese peasants were every bit as harshly exploited as the villeins of medieval Europe.

In what was almost entirely an agricultural nation until Meiji times, 'peasant' meant the majority of the population.

In the old days when the fertility festivals were most common, their lives were at best dull beyond description. Caught in a perpetual routine of subsistence farming, they lived in thatched hovels in featureless hamlets or villages in which life was without quality. There were no taverns and no entertainments for months on end, and they lived under the constant shadow of superstition and disease. Small wonder that fertility festivals, which tended to lump eating, drinking, merrymaking and sex together in one big bash came to be the only notable form of enjoyment there was.

So rare were these opportunities, at most only four times a year, that they must have gone desperately overboard. It is easy to see all this in terms of liberalism, but it was quite the reverse. During years of plenty, there must have been blissful incidences of what advocates of free love anywhere and at any time might see as an ideal. Unfortunately, in lean years, fertility festivals must have been more like the sexual equivalent of turning starving prisoners loose in a restaurant, and the frenzied and inebriated collective copulations between ragged and wretched bodies were probably anything but a pretty sight.

Writing about the orgy in general, erotologist Georges Bataille had this to say:

> The orgy is the sacred aspect of eroticism, where human generation progresses beyond isolation to attain its fullest expression. But only in one sense. In the orgy, generation is intangible. Ultimately, the participants are lost in a confusing mass. The orgy is inevitably disappointing. It is in fact a complete denial of the individual; it dictates

equivalence between its participants. If it appears to present the utter obliteration of restrictions, it can only occur when no differences – moreover an intrinsic part of sexual attraction – remain between the protagonists. The final significance of eroticism is fusion, the abolition of restrictions. In the first place, the meaning of eroticism is signified to a high degree by the position of an object of desire. In the orgy, this object becomes indistinguishable: sexual excitement herein is triggered by an exacerbated movement running contrary to habitual reserve.

This could hardly apply more to Japan, where the individual is anyway obliterated by the group. Villages were – and still are – extremely tight communities. True, there were instances of villages with too few males in which women dolled themselves up as best they could to walk up to the road crossings, in the hope of enticing a passing stranger for a roll in the rice fields. To all intents and purposes, however, peasants were even more wary of strangers than now and forbidden to travel; Japanese rural communities were as close knit as a single family.

Just as incestuous marriage was permissible among the Heian emperors provided the partners did not share the same mother, so *yobai* and the orgies of small farming communities must have involved no small degree of interbreeding. Everyone knew everyone else, they lived according to codes of superstition rather than ethics or morals and the choice of mates was limited. Confusion over paternity hardly mattered. Even today, there are many middle-aged Japanese in the countryside who neither know nor, since they grew up in the warmth of an entire community like an extended family, care who their real fathers might be.

Insofar as the group patterns inherent in most Japanese institutions are closely modelled on the family, it may not be unreasonable to assume that those close-knit, exclusive communities profoundly influenced the thinking of the great Japanese tribe. Hence a rural matter-of-factness about sexual matters still runs deep in the Japanese psyche, while it suffers constant frustration from having to restrain itself beneath the veneer of propriety urban officialdom dictates.

More recently, in a better-fed Japan, surviving incidences of sacred orgies and customs such as *yobai* may indeed have presented the titillating kind of picture that nostalgic pink eyeglasses can conjure. But what about the women? Although chances are the boy was not a stranger, could a girl really enjoy a one-night stand with an unchosen partner? To one woman journalist often covering feminist issues in the *Asahi Shimbun*, the answer, surprisingly, was yes. 'Unlike their city counterparts, country women were not especially demure,' she says, 'and the scope of their enjoyments was extremely limited.' It is after all statistically proven that the introduction of TV in many rural areas in Japan caused a marked drop in demographic growth.

When occurring at a time constituting a peculiar limbo between the ancient orient and modern Japan, such sexual phenomena involved young people who were neither as religious, ignorant nor as destitute as they had been in the past. For some, *yobai* and the old sacred orgies no longer made any sense; for others they had been fun. And it is precisely because they were fun that they were on the way out: in the eyes of the 'modern' authorities, fertility observances no longer had an excuse.

7

Heian Idyll

LIFE IN HEIAN

Nearly nine hundred years gone, the Heian era casts a nostalgic spell over the Japanese. The style has been celebrated in paintings and woodblocks, echoed in poetry and drama and continues to permeate the media of the twentieth century. Prized by the catering industry and the *mizu shobai*, the Heian yields grand and romantic names for restaurants, hotel banqueting halls, massage parlours and love hotels. The most evocative treasure trove of things Heian is *The Tale of Genji*, one of the world's earliest novels and a source of names and themes for *demi-mondaines*, gay revues, a current rock group and animated cartoons. The Heian period is a kind of long-lost utopia, an elegant and rarefied cloud-cuckoo-land capturing the Japanese imagination in much the same way as classical Greece or Camelot inspire Europe.

It was grand and voluptuous and it was sedate and melancholic. Grand rather than gaudy and fonder of the oblique than the obvious, it was an age as vague and tranquil as a cloud of incense and coloured with subdued seasonal hues discreetly dominated by the pastel mauve of wistaria blossom. Like the modern Japanese, the Heian people were at once stoics and melancholics, hedonists and sybarites. Eulogizing endlessly over the vagaries of love and fate and the tears soaking sleeves, the Heian era was in many ways mournful and even austere, but it was also one of the most sensual Japan has ever seen; an early cultural morning glory regretted ever since.

The Heian period is really all about a single city. Replacing nearby Nara as the capital in 794, Heian-kyo – the city of peace and tranquillity – lay on the site of what later became Kyoto. Like Nara, it was planned as a downscaled emulation of China's T'ang dynasty capital of Chang'an; the population comprised some one hundred thousand souls when the city reached its zenith. The original Chinese bureaucratic government model functioned according to a system of merit, but the ranks of the petrified Japanese equivalent were entered and ascended on a purely hereditary basis, for birth was the sole criterion for being a member of the élite. The civil service, a cornucopia of sinecures, and the aristocracy were synonymous; Heian aristocrats were the navel of the world and what they were pleased to call *Yoki no Shito* – the Good People – a distinction that was qualitative, not moral. Basking in the tranquil shade of Buddhism and obsessed with aesthetics even to the point of absurdity, the refined Heian was an era of prolonged peace, during which the ultimate punishment was banishment rather than execution. Something of a quirk in the whole of human history, it lasted for three hundred years.

Control was exercised quietly and, for most of the era at least, efficiently by the Fujiwara family – one of the most powerful in Japanese history. *Fuji* means wistaria, and it was they who gave the age the pastel mauve colouring forever associated with Heian. They ruled over a network of mansions spread out over the country, fiefdoms usually owned by the powerful metropolitan aristocracy and supervised by provincial governors. No matter how wealthy and powerful some of them became, they were always looked down upon as country bumpkins by the haughty élite in the capital.

Embracing less than 10 per cent of the population, the world of the Good People was as uneventful as a pond swimming with a languid school of rare and decorative fish. As long ago as it was, however, a great deal about them has come down through literature, for many Heianese wrote exhaustive diaries and romances. Before waxing too lyrical, one should realize that the age was golden only for aristocrats. Focusing on the nobility and the imperial court, the literary horizons of the Good People went no further than their own, for the lives of others were beneath their consideration. The lower part of the city was probably a maze of insalubrious alleyways and rickety huts, but the kind of life they enclosed is as much a matter of conjecture as the lives of Heian peasants, which were likely to have been anything but idyllic.

As they had been and would be for centuries, fortunes were measured in rice, the currency of a bartering system. Peasants owned precious little of the land they worked and lived in poverty, but at least some legislation had been introduced to ensure their minimal welfare. The rustics of Heian were by no means as abused or repressed as they would be later; they were simply ignored. In Heian days, if you weren't Good People, you were nobody.

Urban planning followed the Chinese pattern, but the wooden architecture had been adapted to less grandiose local taste; the Heian palaces and capacious aristocratic dwellings presented a simple, fragile elegance more typically Japanese. Luxuriating in idle splendour, the Good People were partial to exquisitely crafted furnishings and *objets d'art*, but their spacious homes were sparse. Only a few cushions and woven straw mats adorned an uncluttered floor of dark polished wood. In the shadowy vastness of the interior, rooms and bedrooms were often only partitioned off by screens and curtains.

They were passionately fond of the arts. The smallest gathering was tinged with ceremony, and they competed heatedly in composing poems and *belles-lettres*, in painting, music and dancing. Grand imperial competitions were frequently held in all these spheres – especially poetry – involving over a thousand participants. Like religious festivals, such imposing occasions found the Heianese taking to the road in splendidly decorated ox-carriages with outsize wheels and flanked by retinues of gorgeously liveried attendants. Traffic could be a serious problem in Heian-kyo. Some accounts mention huge jams with over five hundred ox-carts vying for space in the city's wide avenues; *kuruma arasoi*, the collisions and spats between carriage attendants, often came to blows.

The Heianese were obsessed with fashion and, like buildings, their clothes were of T'ang inspiration. Noblewomen donned brocaded or embroidered Chinese jackets, beneath which they commonly wore some twelve robes of unlined silk designed in decreasing order of size so that the successive layers of carefully matched colours of appropriate seasonal hue would be visible at the neck and sleeves.

'Now the Empress's hair had been dressed, and she was ready to be robed. Over a three-layered scarlet dress of beaten silk she wore two plum-red robes, one of heavily embroidered material and the other more lightly worked. "Tell me," she said, "do you think the plum red really goes with dark scarlet? I know this isn't the season for plum red, but I hate colours like light green."

'Unusual though the combination was, Her Majesty looked beautiful.'

The passage comes from the celebrated diary of Sei Shonagon, lady-in-waiting to the Empress Sadako over a thousand years ago. Later on in the same entry, she describes the attire of a Chancellor, who wore a court cloak of pale violet, a scarlet under-robe and trousers of light green. This would have been topped with a tall, light cap of lacquered wicker. Men were as fastidious about their clothing as women.

The predominant Buddhist sect was the Tendai, which made its headquarters in the temples and monasteries to the north-east of the city in the hills around Mount Hiei. Both before and after Heian times, the north-east has always been the most unlucky of directions, the province of demons and evil spirits. Protected from all these by the sacred presence of the monks on the Mount, however, Heian-kyo broke with tradition and the north-eastern quarters of the city blossomed to the detriment of the western side.

The love of pomp and circumstance found ready outlets not only in the arts, but also in a wealth of colourful Shinto and Buddhist festivals, the importance and frequency of which also betrayed the shadow of superstition darkening the whole of the era. Issued partly from the Chinese cosmological injunction to harmonize yin and yang, these beliefs complemented others rooted in Buddhist karma, Shinto taboos and ancient folk religion. Notwithstanding good vibrations from Mount Hiei, the Heianese lived in constant terror of ghosts, demons, evil spirits and goblins. Life was influenced by the interpretation of dreams, which inspired fear and trembling. Should a soothsayer announce an unlucky day, the victim would stay indoors quaking behind the curtains. If the horoscope announced a temporary unlucky direction, travel plans were cancelled; if the unlucky direction was permanent and involved a home, many Heianese simply moved.

Superstition also heavily influenced politics. The pronouncements of the Department of Astronomy and Divination were awaited with bated breath; fires, floods, earthquakes and other catastrophes were given occult interpretations. Like the army in general, the imperial guards were not renowned for their martial proficiency. Parading up and down in grandiose silks, they were most diligent of all in defending the palace against the unknown. Every hour or so, they loudly twanged their bowstrings to complement the efforts of gong-beating and chanting clerics to frighten away *momonoke*, the evil spirits which, like bad omens of cosmological origin, were seen as the cause of misfortune and disease.

The Heian passion for incense elevated its preparation and appreciation into a unique art form still practised by the rarefied adepts of *Kodō* – the Way of Incense – today. It perfumed their temples and their clothing; it wafted through their elegant homes. Brought over as an accessory for Buddhist ritual, the habit perhaps originally turned secular out of pragmatism. Sewerage in Heian was at best a matter of gathering fertilizer; the garden parties during which Heian dandies languidly floated cups of sake to each other along the streams that passed beneath the houses, and hence the latrines, were perhaps not quite as elegant as they sound. Every summer brought its share of lethal epidemics, and malaria was a common complaint among people who considered themselves lucky to live to be forty-five.

The Good People were fastidious and performed perfunctory daily ablutions, but they were not as immaculate as latter-day idealizations like to believe. Although they would have scorned the foulness pervading European courts until the eighteenth century, the measure for cleanliness still lay more in the frequency of changing clothes than it did in soap and water. Bathing was more popular during the sweltering summer, but during the winter water held about as much appeal as in rural Tibet, and women went months without washing their floor-length hair. Their layered clothing too was due to more than just fashion. Ensconced behind the curtains in bitterly cold homes, everyone shivered around inadequate braziers of a more aesthetic than practical function.

Not a few slept at night in the clothes they wore in the daytime. Some of the grander members of the community had Chinese-style beds, but these were a matter of prestige, not comfort. A four-poster dais with no mattress, it was covered only with layers of the same thin matting of woven reeds laid upon a wooden floor, which was the sleeping arrangement for everyone else. If it hardly deterred them from ardently practising the arts of the bedchamber, theirs, for all its elegant pursuit of aesthetics and pleasure, was in many ways a Spartan age. Although a civilization of Chinese inspiration, it was already very Japanese. Quite at home with contradictions and paradoxes, it was promiscuous and polygamous, but also rigid and austere. Although its women enjoyed a considerable degree of freedom, they were seldom permitted to walk abroad.

FEMALE LINES

The Fujiwara clan's ascent was fired by shrewd political strategy and, from the outset of the Heian era, their position was so secure that the sword had virtually become superfluous. Although Japan had by now adopted patrilinear Confucianism for centuries, the Fujiwara power tactic battened on the female line. By marrying their daughters to puppet emperors, the Fujiwara patriarchs could pull the strings from the confines of the family. As it was for most of Japanese history, the system closely resembled a Chinese prototype in which emperors were divine figureheads carefully groomed to be aloof and detached from matters of state. Ascending the throne during childhood, they could be persuaded to abdicate at an average age of thirty-one. Whether they subsequently entered the priesthood or simply went into elegant retirement, the powers of state were passed between the Fujiwara regents, the most prominent being Fujiwara no Michinaga (966–1027), during whose 21-year regency the Heian reached its glittering zenith. Michinaga's matrilinear strategy spanned three generations. He got his first and second daughters to marry the emperors Ichijo and Sanjo respectively, and with rules about intermarriage being loose, he married his third daughter to the Emperor Goichijo – his own grandson.

Although it was due more to calculating Fujiwara policies than any stirrings of feminism, women in Heian enjoyed an enviable status compared to their sisters of later centuries. Custom kept them hidden and secluded, but legislation not only forbade common barbarisms such as wife-beating, but also entitled women to inherit, to own property and to an education. Nevertheless, no amount of money could buy a woman more than a subordinate position and an education hampered by limitations.

All official, administrative and clerical posts in Heian were exclusively held by men and their business was entirely put on paper in Chinese. Universities and colleges focused on Chinese classical learning and women were debarred from both. Being a male preserve, the Chinese script was called *otokomoji* – characters for men; women were taught to write in a phonetic script called *kana*, the invention of which is popularly attributed to the Buddhist priest Kukai during the early ninth century. Many literary ladies nevertheless widened their horizons by learning Chinese on their own. Used in conjunction with Chinese characters, the *kana* syllabary forms an integral part of the Japanese script today, but in Heian days it was *onnade* – characters for women.

Men had by now been composing poems in the Chinese classical style for centuries, and a few had recently been writing *monogatari*, or tales. The adoption of rigid Chinese conventions had tended to fossilize their literary output, however, so that there was as little scope for freedom of expression as originality. Confined to using the more colloquially adaptable *kana* script, women turned an educational impediment into a literary asset. *Kana* allowed them to describe their world in everyday language, and many kept diaries before turning to *monogatari*, and overwhelmingly excelling men at the genre.

The greatest of all Heian women writers were Murasaki Shikibu (c.980–c.1014), who wrote *The Tale of Genji*, and Sei Shonagon (c.966–c.1025), the writer of the famous diary known as *The Pillow Book*. Handsome and charming beyond compare, the 'shining prince' Genji meanders slowly from one seduction to another through a life some thousand pages long and amounting to fifty-four separate books. A telling and magnificent evocation of Heian court life, the work is something of a rake's progress Heian style. Genji is by turns seducer and husband, father and widower. Admired, disgraced, exiled and reinstated, he travels through life as the supreme example of Heian chic and winds up a victim of the vagaries of karma, ending his days as a disillusioned monk. Concerned with the sexual conquests of its hero and expressed in the vaguest terms, the work is hauntingly beautiful and edifyingly sombre in tone.

The prim Murasaki Shikibu was not a bit like her elder contemporary Sei Shonagon, whose *Pillow Book* hints freely at her own promiscuity and casts a refreshingly cynical eye on a great variety of curious, telling and colourful aspects and goings-on at court. She had her strong likes and dislikes and aired them freely with the corrosive tip of her brush. Unlike the introverted Murasaki, flamboyant Sei was arrogant, haughty and not one to suffer fools gladly. Legend has it that she was also more dazzling than the plain Murasaki Shikibu; the two women loathed each other. Making disparaging remarks about her rival in her diary, Murasaki Shikibu cites Sei Shonagon's arrogance and predicts that she would come to a sticky end. She was right. Falling out of favour upon the demise of her patron empress, Sei Shonagon is said to have died in obscure poverty.

Among the tiny flock of élite literary ladies in a tiny world, Sei Shonagon must have stuck out like a black sheep. Despite her brilliance, ultimately her outspokenness caused her to fall into disfavour. Then as now, conspicuousness has never been a virtue in self-effacing Japan.

THE INVISIBLE WOMAN

As appropriate as it is in defining the amorous pursuits of the Heianese, the term 'Courtly Love' is far removed from its western equivalent. Here was a cult of good manners, not chivalry. Men wooed not with derring-do but with love letters and poems, and women responded in kind. The Lady was as dissimilar to the Mariolatrous object of unfulfilled desire besotting medieval European knights as Shinto is to Christianity. A Byzantine fantasy spreading westwards for centuries, the fabled Lady of the occident was a hybrid between the Christian ideal of virginity and the Muslim ideal of woman secluded in the seraglio. A paragon of manners and deportment, the aristocratic damsel of Heian was every inch a lady, but she hardly needed to be chaste to qualify.

She did, however, live in seclusion. By and large, she was invisible. Venturing outside only for the grander festivals, she lived most of her languid life in scented semi-darkness indoors. Surrounded by retinues of female servants, she was ensconced behind blinds and curtains, speaking to male visitors from behind finely latticed or elaborately decorated opaque *kichoo* – screens of state. Even if she ventured out during the course of a festival, on the journey only the sleeves she left conspicuously trailing from beneath the window-blinds of her ox-carriage for the admiration of passers-by betrayed her presence at all.

Seclusion did nothing to deter an obsession with fashion and finery. Starting at the top, Heian women viewed the hair on their heads with almost the same degree of fetishism as their admirers. The standard Heian beauty's sleek cascade of jet-black hair spilled over her shoulders and reached the floor. Ideally, according to Chinese T'ang dynasty canons of beauty, she was plump and also wore make-up. She powdered her face an immaculate full-moon white, rouged her chubby cheeks and coloured her lips with a paste made from the brilliant red safflower. With two large round dots of charcoal grey just above where her eyebrows would have been had she not plucked them out, the rotund and diminutive Heian belle would fare none too well as a modern contestant for Miss Japan.

Like spouses and courtesans until the end of the nineteenth century, Heian women also blackened their teeth with *haguro*, a dye compounded of vinegar, gall-nut and powdered iron. Some South-East Asian peoples blacken their teeth too, or, as is still common in Bali, file down the points of the canines. The Balinese idea is that upon reaching heaven the departed will not be mistaken for demons and turned away. In Japan, where women are sometimes regarded as having demonic leanings, perhaps the practice derives from a similar superstition.

Heian purdah was not so much a product of Confucianism as a concept rooted in religion and superstition. It was partly due to the Shintoist concept of female impurity and partly her second-class status according to Buddhism, which taught that, if virtuous enough, a woman could hope to be reincarnated as a man. As secluded as they were, Heian ladies would have been the last to see themselves as victims of a social system. The rules of social behaviour were so inextricably interwoven with superstition that to challenge them was to invoke calamity. Despite their limitations, women regarded their status quo as a fact of life and enjoyed more freedom than they would for many hundreds of years.

Persuasive too were the aesthetic and existential dictates of *mono no aware*, a notion largely formulated during the Heian era and its most distinctive characteristic. Rooted in Buddhist concepts of the fleeting world and finding no true equivalent in English, the word *aware* at once suggests pathos and beauty and thoroughly permeates the bases of Japanese aesthetics. During the 1930s, literary historian Hisamatsu Senichi summed it up thus: 'The spirit of *aware* pervades all Heian literature. It is discovered in the feelings inspired by a bright spring morning and also in the sense of sadness that overcomes us on an autumn evening. Its primary mood, however, is one of gentle melancholy, from which it can develop into real grief.'

Fashion made Heian women gently melancholic as they languished alone behind their curtains, but the real grief sometimes came in with the men who stole their hearts behind the screens.

POLYGAMY: MORE BUT NOT MERRIER

With a quintessential facet of beauty being a wistful acceptance of fate and the way of things, resignation came easy in fashion-conscious Heian. Prince Genji was no gay blade; most of his many conquests are tinged with sadness and some with dire tragedy; the mood enveloping the work as a whole is one of sadness. Where the notion of a lovelorn lady pining indoors was such a popular literary theme, it was easy to turn the adversity of female seclusion into the asset of affectation. Whereas the beauty might not languish too long before some shining suitor stole behind her screen, as some *monogatari* suggest, the lot of the less alluring, the more ordinary and the luckless was bleak. If most women were hardly even aware of the shortcomings of the social system to challenge them, some prolifically aired amatory and other grievances in their diaries.

The oldest and in fact the earliest surviving woman's diary of all is *Kagero Nikki* (*The Gossamer Diary*), in which a wife chronicled her unhappy marriage to Fujiwara no Kaneie between 954 and 974. Her predicament, like that of many Heian women, resided in the fact that she was one of the more neglected of eight wives, all of whom were lower in status than Kaneie's number one. In polygamous Heian, emperors and noblemen had one principal wife, who was married to them by arrangement. Until their fathers died, noblemen took up residence in the family home of the principal wife, although this was more in theory than practice. Like Prince Genji, many a man hardly spent any time in his wife's house at all. Once she moved in to his own family abode, however, she became the *Kita no Kata* – the Northern Person – and assumed the role of matriarch. She was so called because she inhabited, and in many cases utterly dominated, the crucial northern family quarters in the house.

As with the old Chinese model, secondary wives had the same status as concubines, who were to keep their socio-sexual place in Japanese society until the Meiji period and beyond. Unlike concubines, second wives became such in Heian days with a modest ceremony. If a first wife could be dumped in later times according to the draconian tenets of Neo-Confucianism, a *Kita no Kata* was not easily got rid of in Heian Japan. If she was barren, she merely adopted a child from a concubine just as she might for centuries to come, regardless of how hard giving up progeny could be on the latter. If concubines and the principal wife resided under the same roof, it was generally in the case of a man wealthy enough to afford the space to house several families. A man often kept his wife and concubines in their own respective family homes, and when the disposition came upon him, he went visiting.

Far from being seen as a sign of licentiousness, polygamy was a mark of distinction. It showed that one was a man of consequence, one of the Good People. Ostensibly, monogamy was for those who could not afford otherwise. According to Confucian ethics, polygamy was also a duty. With a painfully short average life span and a high infant mortality rate, producing a large number of offspring was a practical imperative assuring continuation of the line.

Heian Japan was prodigiously promiscuous. Custom obviously made this a male prerogative, but an unmarried woman or a neglected concubine could and indeed did receive lovers into her screened and curtained inner sanctum. Although much larger, one can well imagine that the *kichō* screen was in many cases just a grander version of the fan an eighteenth-century western *horizontale* held before her face as she seductively fluttered her eyes; sensuous court ladies enjoyed even more freedom than most. Prince Genji's affair with the emperor's favourite concubine earns him temporary exile, but the gentle potentate's reaction is poignant and pathetic: '"I know that there is someone you have long preferred to me; but it has been a way of mine to concentrate only on one object, and I have thought only of you. Even if the man you prefer does as you wish him to, I doubt that his affection can match my own. The thought is too much for me."' The emperor was in tears.

Unlike later in Japan, where adultery could be cruelly punished, including crucifixion for both parties, Heian law conceded that it might be excusable for a cuckold to kill his wife provided he caught her *in flagrante delicto*. In other words, if it was a crime of passion.

Promiscuity is everywhere and always a fine game when played casually enough by both partners, until the pleasure is marred by emotional involvement on only one side. The happiest outcome is of course a lasting relationship, but when this occurred in Heian, where promiscuity was the basis of courtship, it meant that the woman entered into a polygamous hierarchy. The practice took a lot of the gold out of the golden age.

Many men found themselves burdened emotionally and financially with other women and other families and, as the romances and diaries testify, in a world in which only the first wife was secure, concubines faced an uncertain future and lived in constant fear of rejection, neglect and bitter rivalry.

Written in about 970, *Ochikubo Monogatari – The Tale of the Lady Ochikubo –* is the first realistic novel to appear anywhere in the world. It is also a first in heralding a later stock-in-trade, the cruel stepmother, who in turn foreshadows the mother-in-law, the archetypal bugbear for latter-day Japanese brides. Here the cruel *Kita no Kata* confines the beautiful daughter of her husband's former wife to a tiny room, scathingly calls her Ochikubo (lower-room lady) and treats her as a servant. Always seeking ways to torment and humiliate her stepdaughter, she even goes as far as to push a disgusting old man into bed with her. A remote figure in the background, rather than being the aloof patriarch tradition supposed him to be, the girl's father is merely hen-pecked and ineffectual. Eventually Ochikubo is wooed, won and rescued by a powerful nobleman.

When Ochikubo is still only a concubine, her husband is pressured by his mother to take an emperor's daughter as a first wife. Defying convention for the sake of his beloved (that she is in fact of noble birth helps, of course), the nobleman refuses. Ochikubo eventually gives him sons and daughters, becomes his true *Kita no Kata* and, after forgiving her stepmother, the two live happily ever after. What makes the tale particularly interesting is that between the lines of vengeance on the stepmother and a happy end, one reads what is a highly wishful and idealized celebration of monogamy – something that Cinderella would have taken for granted.

THE RELUCTANT VIRGIN

*C'est une des superstitions de l'esprit humain d'avoir imaginé
que la virginité pouvait être une vertu.* (One of the superstitions of the human mind is to have imagined that
virginity could be a virtue.)

Voltaire

Secluded and ladylike, the Heian woman's similarities
with her western counterpart end at the beginning:
with her virginity. Unless she was destined to be a
nobleman's first wife, a Heian girl normally lost her
virginity when biology swayed her and as soon as the
opportunity presented itself. As in most societies with a
short life expectancy, men and women married in their
early teens. In rural contexts always, if more rarely
among the aristocracy, women were on the marriage
market very soon after they began menstruating and
produced offspring as soon as they were able. In Heian,
women who remained virgins for too long were thought
to be possessed by an evil spirit. Ono no Komachi, for
instance, was an early ninth-century poetess renowned
for her extraordinary beauty. Enamoured ranks of
esteemed noblemen vainly sought her favours and one
of the most eligible of all is said to have pined outside her
house for one hundred consecutive nights like a stricken
tom cat, but to no avail.

According to legend, Ono no Komachi lived virgo
intacta to a very great age and has been regarded with
ambivalent feelings ever since. From the sedate
Buddhist angle, she was a sage and ascetic renouncing
her personal attributes along with the vanities of the
physical world. But far more popular are the horror
stories of folk legend, in which Ono no Komachi returns

either as a pathetic phantom pining on the sites once haunted by her unrequited lovers, or as a vengeful demoness.

Until it was glorified by Tokugawa Neo-Confucianism as just another restriction slapped on women to cement their status as property, virginity was granted a low priority in old Japan, especially among the populace. As in most places, however, there was a ritual correlation between virginity and purity. In many Shinto rice harvesting ceremonies even today, the first stalk is plucked by a young girl. Devoted to the sun goddess Amaterasu, the Ise shrine is the most sacred in all Shinto and virginity is a mandatory prerequisite for its nubile high priestess, who moreover had to be a princess in Heian times. In *The Tale of Genji*, the beautiful daughter of one of the hero's former flames is on her way to Ise to take up her sacred office. As soon as he sets eyes on the fourteen-year-old, Genji is moved to make a pass at her by sending an amorous poem. The high priestess's rejoinder is a sharply worded poetic rebuttal, and dejected Genji spends a day in gloomy seclusion.

'He had to smile, however,' Murasaki wrote, 'at the priestess's rather knowing poem. She was clever for her age, and she interested him. Difficult and unconventional relationships always interested him.' This one would have been difficult and unconventional to say the very least; it would have involved the violation of a religious taboo. One such incident actually occurred. When it was discovered that the Ise high priestess Saiko-jo had been seduced by a shrine guard in the late tenth century, the scandal rocked Heian.

For all its permissiveness and emphasis on fertility worship, the Shinto religion regards those who have just had sexual relations as ritually impure. It is not that they are defiled or unclean according to the 'sinful' connotations of the West, it simply means that the parties are taboo. During the twenty-four hours the effect lasted, if the parties in fact seldom troubled to refrain from ordinary social contact as they ideally should, they scrupulously kept away from shrines. Again, this is not the stuff of morality, but magic. The copulators were still immersed in a powerful occult aura and, unlike during the fertility festival, it followed a personal rather than a divine celebration. To waive the taboo would be the spiritual equivalent to failing to wear a tie to a tuxedo dinner, or being intoxicated in a courtroom. But unlike with a social *faux pas*, the occult retribution incurred as a result might be too awful to contemplate. Having never known coitus at all, virgins are as ritually pure as anyone can be. As instruments of communication between humanity and the gods, they represent all the difference between new and used.

There is no record of anything of the kind in Heian-kyo, but there is evidence that ritual defloration was widely practised in ancient and not so ancient rural Japan. Writing in the mid-1960s, French Japanologist Théo Lésoualc'h mentions a village near Nagasaki where a young woman was still taken to the shrine and symbolically deflowered on the eve of her wedding. The priest held a phallic wand over the strategic spot between her parted legs, but in olden times it is likely that the defloration was really performed, either with the same wooden phallus or the one anatomically affixed to the priest. The country custom of *yobai* (night-creeping) was also frequently a form of ritual defloration. Following their first menstrual period, girls often roamed their villages to offer themselves to local youths.

In several instances she ran through a kind of gauntlet with a piece of silk hanging from her sash, which the village boys would try to grab as she dashed past, and the one who succeeded was rewarded with the debatable privilege of the awkward first time. Lésoualc'h also mentions a rustic custom until quite recently reserved for girls who had still not lost their virginity by the ripe old age of seventeen. Grabbing hold of a post in the family home and gritting their teeth, they bent over and spread their legs as they were summarily deflowered by a specially appointed youth whose face they never saw.

Today Japan is as ambivalent about virginity as it is about sexual matters in general, but old rustic earthiness still glimmers faintly beneath the hard lacquer of social propriety. It would seem that the graphic contents of modern Japan's ubiquitous carnal publications would finally erode the veneer, and that, generally, the media's obsessive coverage of freer sexual lifestyles would sway archaic macho expectations of female chastity. But a poll taken during the mid-eighties by a leading women's magazine revealed that this is not necessarily the case. Half of the young men surveyed tenaciously asserted that they expected their future wives to be virgins. In a country obsessed with marriage, renewed virginity can be bought. Plastic surgeons make tidy profits from expanding breasts and enlarging eyes, but others find repairing and restoring broken hymens an even more lucrative business. Notwithstanding, another recent government survey revealed that unmarried women were losing their virginity younger, so the chances are that the young men entertaining fantasies about bona fide virgin brides will find them increasingly difficult to fulfil.

THE BLIND DATE AS A FINE ART

A political move on the part of the families concerned, the first marriage was prearranged without the consent of either party. As was the case with Genji, who was married at twelve, early weddings were often considered expedient, the partners could be absurdly young, and the bride was usually slightly older than her tender-aged spouse. Murasaki's tale makes the discomfiture of both quite clear. As Genji matured so he typically became more estranged from her, spending less time in her family home. By now infatuated with his beautiful step-mother anyway, Genji admitted that although his wife was no less a beauty, 'he was not at all sure that they were meant for each other'. As in later centuries, neither sexual attraction nor basic compatibility were criteria in an arranged marriage. However cool their mutual feelings were, the couple would eventually do their Confucian duty, which was to produce offspring.

The quest for a subsequent wife is what made the Heian era as promiscuous as it was. Provided the object of his affections was of a rank considered compatible with his, a man was free to follow his personal incli-nations in choosing a wife. Marriage to women of much lower rank was impossible, but dalliance, although officially frowned upon, was frequent. In *The Tale of Genji*, one emperor is described as keeping a large number of very pretty servant girls and seamstresses in addition to his concubines. Like aristocrats everywhere, Heian noblemen were probably fond of chasing petti-coats below stairs.

An important consideration in determining a lady's marriageability, or even her powers of sexual attraction, lay in her skill with a writing brush. Her accom-plishments had to include the ability to write subtle, elegant letters and poems. So secluded was she that the chances are that literary exchanges were often the only prelude to a sexual relationship there was. The aspirant sent his poem first as an opening gambit; unless he chanced to be a particularly brilliant prospect, if the lady considered his efforts substandard, her reply made her lack of enthusiasm clear. Similarly, if the phrasing and subtlety of the lady's reply failed to pass muster, or if her calligraphy was poor, the affair could simply be a nonstarter.

Since women seldom walked abroad, encounters were difficult. Looking at *The Tale of Genji*, one finds that even a man of high rank had to go through elaborate ploys and intrigues to get his woman. Chancing to pass by an auspicious-looking house, for instance, the interested party would attempt to peer discreetly through the lattices. With luck he would be rewarded with the silvery sound of female voices or even a glimpse of brilliant silk and the gloss of long hair in the shadows within. Standing outside in the moonlight, perhaps he might hear the elegant strains of a koto being plucked by dainty feminine fingers. If aroused, he would despatch a trusted servant to make discreet enquiries about the household. In one instance, Genji is told that the new occupant of a very humble but promising-looking house was very beautiful. His manservant actually glimpsed her sitting forlornly before a writing desk as her ladies-in-waiting gathered around her in tears.

'Genji,' the text tells us, 'suspected something of the sort.' Short of crediting him with exceptional powers of intuition, how he arrived at this conclusion is left unsaid but, then again, the world of Heian aristocrats was very small and rumours flew swiftly; changes in tenancy would be as obvious as in a small village. Anything at all unusual about the household or perhaps the arrangement of a garden fired neighbourly curiosity and said much about the occupants. In this case, the sight of a despondent woman in an unprepossessing house surrounded by lacrimose maids obviously pointed to an aristocratic lady who had fallen on hard times.

Next, the affair called for a messenger to deliver a poem. If she had spotted an admirer's attempts to spy on her and was interested, it was not unusual for the woman to take the first step. One of Genji's many women has a little girl deliver him a heavily scented fan bearing the words:

> I think I need not ask whose face it is,
> So bright, this evening face, in the shining dew.

To which Genji composes a reply:

> Come a bit nearer, please. Then you might know
> Whose was the evening face so dim in the twilight.

And then he has his messenger bring it to the lady without delay. If the poems triggered mutual interest between the parties, the affair was on.

Gaining access into the house after nightfall and creeping along the veranda, suitors wasted no time in making their conquest. For all the apparent romance and elaborate formality cloaking the exchange of poems, the seduction itself was perfunctory in the extreme. It was the hurried and promiscuous conclusion to a blind date, an aristocratic medieval answer to making out in the back of a parked car. Stealing behind the curtains and into the scented darkness of the waiting lady's bedchamber, the gentleman simply removed his clothing and got into bed with her. During these encounters the couple only rarely saw each other's face, and more than one Heian tale mentions cases of mistaken identity. After spending the night with the lover of their dreams, not a few found them rudely shattered afterwards upon finding that they had in fact spent the night with someone else.

204   *Pink Samurai*

The suitor's presence may well have been perfectly obvious to the entire household, but servants and the girl's parents alike went to elaborate lengths to feign ignorance. Custom dictated that the Lothario was to rise and depart at the crack of dawn. Donning his wide silk trousers and robes and placing his hat of thin, black-lacquered wicker on his head, he would slip silently out of the house. Before he left, however, there would have been a touching exchange of whispered farewells which, along with the events of the night, determined how ardently the young man would transmit his customary respects upon returning home. Taking ink and brush, he would sit down to compose a poem and letter on paper of the highest quality and of seasonal hue, in the most eloquent terms he could muster.

The poetry accompanying these morning-after letters often alluded to other, older verses which were not infrequently Chinese. Most of the time, these compositions made florid parallels between the early morning dew and the tears soaking sleeves at the sorrow of parting. One can well imagine that leaving a warm bed and its charming occupant behind on a chilly dawn did much to lend a touch of heartfelt poignancy to the poem. After selecting a seasonal flower or sprig of leaves with which the colour of the paper would have been carefully matched, the lover would then roll the letter and send it back to his girlfriend via messenger.

The girl would meanwhile have been awaiting it with fluttering heart and bated breath. Having pondered the content, she would busy herself writing a reply. The morning-after literary routine obeyed strict rules of etiquette and was little more than a formal ritual; the more favourable letters were frequently seen, admired and commented upon by members of the household. Instances in *Genji* find aristocratic young female recipients eagerly expecting the message in the company of their ladies-in-waiting, who moreover often lent their assistance in the composition of the rejoinder. If he had brought good tidings, the messenger was showered with presents. Whether or not he was sent away with an unceremonious footprint on his rump if he didn't, the delicate romances do not say.

When the poems and letters were to the mutual satisfaction of both parties, they amounted to an invitation for a replay, which was formally designated the Second Night. The rules were exactly the same, but the game generally portended matrimony. The Third Night required more elaborate preparation. Although they maintained their low profile during the proceedings, the girl's parents would have servants leave rice cakes and flasks of sake ceremonially arranged on a low table in the bedchamber, which would on this occasion be lit with oil lamps and tapers. The affair was now official: it had come out of the dark. According to Shinto, sake has the property of ritual purification and sharing cups between bride and groom is still a vital part of a Japanese wedding ceremony today. If there was no grand ceremony as in the case of a first wife, the Third Night was tantamount to tying the knot and there would still be an exchange of cups. The gentleman stole into the bedchamber on the eve just as he had done on the first and second nights, but he was not required to leave again at dawn after the third. On what was called the Fourth Morning, husband and wife could stay in bed and enjoy connubial bliss to their hearts' content.

GOING BY THE BOOK

Of all the ten thousand things created by Heaven, man is the most precious. Of all the things that make man prosper none can be compared to sexual intercourse. It is modelled after Heaven and takes its pattern by Earth; it regulates yin and rules yang. Those who understand its significance can nurture their nature and prolong their years; those who miss its true meaning will harm themselves and die before their time.

Li Tung-Hsuan, *Ars Amatoria* (mid-seventh century)

With such a short lifespan, the Heianese naturally did all they could to prolong it. Most of all, they depended upon the proper balance of yin (female, water, moon, north, winter, etc.) and yang (male, fire, sun, south, summer, et al.). The quintessence of cosmology and medicine in China, the concept of yin-yang had already been adopted by then in Japan for centuries and governed daily life. The bedchamber was only one of the many places in which people sedulously applied themselves to its harmonization, but since yin-yang is about the melding of male and female, it was nevertheless as vital as the Tung-Hsuan quotation above implies. Yin-yang thoroughly permeated the ancient Chinese medical manuals which reached their apogee during the Sui and T'ang dynasties, and they were the gospels of good health in Heian Japan.

The quotation, actually the opening paragraph of the medical scholar Tung-Hsuan's *Art of the Bedchamber*, sums up a Chinese equation between health and sex heartily shared by the Japanese. In addition to general health, physiognomy and child-care, the old Chinese medical manuals devoted much space to sex; equally famous handbooks were devoted to nothing else. History's sporadic waves of priggery and repression, however, were obviously not confined only to Japan. In China, notably during the fourteenth-century Yuan or Mongol era and again during the long Manchu dynasty between 1644 and 1912, moral clampdowns hit the old good-health guides very hard, especially below the belt. Some bowdlerized versions are still extant but, with the exception of those unearthed fairly recently by archaeologists in Dun Huang, all but the tiniest and most innocuous fragments of the grand old Sui and T'ang sexual handbooks vanished ages ago in China.

References in other texts had long made Chinese and other scholars aware of their former existence. Searching for these bygone treatises during the late nineteenth century, they at last discovered that some of the greatest were still extant: not on the mainland, but in that great lost-property department for things Chinese – Japan. What was found was the *I-Shin-Po*, a weighty compilation by Tamba Yasunori, a tenth-century court physician and scholar of Chinese descent. Availing himself of some of the most famous Sui and T'ang dynasty manuals, such as the combined *Secret Recipes of the Plain Girl* and *Handbook of Sex of the Dark Girl*, not to mention *Secret Prescriptions of the Bedchamber*, Tamba quoted wholly or extensively from the originals.

Tamba began his task in 982, and it took him two years. Chinese scholars are agreed that although he annotated and commented on the texts, he had scrupulously refrained from tampering with them; his wholly unaltered copies formed the basis of Japanese medical and sexual knowledge for centuries. In 1854, a physician in the service of the shogun's harem had Tamba's ancient *I-Shin-Po* manuscripts beautifully printed on new scrolls, and it is mostly this version that Chinese scholars used to reconstruct the lost Sui and T'ang dynasty originals.

Through Tamba's good offices, the Heianese conscientiously followed the manuals, among others which have since vanished without trace. Notwithstanding, there were many differences between the cultures of T'ang

China and the Heian. Except in the case of the highest and mightiest such as the regent and the emperor, for instance, polygamy was practised more sparingly in Japan and generally precluded the harems full of concubines that were the norm among the Chinese aristocracy. With good health and longevity uppermost in mind, it seems, the Chinese advocated copulation several times with at least ten women in a single night. According to one celebrated bedside vade-mecum: 'The Yellow Emperor had intercourse with twelve hundred women and thereby became an Immortal. Ordinary men have but one woman and that one suffices to make them perish.'

Heian men overawed by a ferocious *Kita no Kata* may have found the remark especially apt, but it was not in fact the hen-pecked husband's lament it sounds. Constant intercourse with only one woman was believed to decrease her vital yin essence, causing her to waste away. Deprived of life-giving yin as a result, the man would weaken too and both would eventually die. Yin was believed to turn into yang essence in the male stomach and, if there was no yin, the essential chemical change was neutralized. Without yang, he would wither and die just as surely as he would if he was to leave his Jade Stalk inactive. Having it off repeatedly with ten women in a single night sounds like a daunting prospect for even the most energetic sexual athlete, but there was a catch: one should as far as possible refrain from emitting semen.

The more times one had sex without ejaculating, the greater the benefits to the health. Once, and the vital essence was strengthened; twice improved sight and hearing, thrice cured all diseases and so on, until the diligent practitioner, even if he was crawling up the wall, was that much closer to immortality. How closely he followed the prescriptions for this was left to his personal aspirations, not to say staying power, for one or two male orgasms in ten copulative sessions was the generally accepted allowance. Semen was primarily thought to nourish the brain; by grinning and bearing his way through coitus, a man could reverse the flow of vital essence and send it to his head. Obviously this did not apply to procreation, and in all cases the manuals generously emphasized female orgasm as an essential prerequisite for healthy sex, and advocated staving off the surge to await the explosive abandon of a mutual climax.

To check himself, Tung-Hsuan advised, the man squares his shoulders, opens his nostrils wide and holds his breath. Other manuals give more detailed and arduous prescriptions for withholding ejaculation, which hardly presented the lady with a sight conducive to orgasm. In all probability her partner was alternating between flapping his arms, glaring angrily and rolling his eyes, prodding himself between anus and scrotum and constantly inhaling and exhaling deeply, all the while gnashing his teeth. In addition to sending the vital essence from the testicles to the brain, such measures singly or collectively helped to cure a man of what ailed him, for they could remedy the seven aches and the hundred diseases.

Blocking ejaculation conserved the man's yang, even as his penis swam to and fro in the source of yin. Since there was every advantage in his obtaining even more yin than this, the sex handbooks strongly recommended a man's replenishing his supply by inhaling his partner's breath as she gasped her way through their exertions. Kissing too is greatly emphasized as part of foreplay, for yin could be sucked from the woman's saliva as the couple's tongues met or when the man nibbled her lower lip.

There were many details about rubbing and caressing the lady's organs to get her yin essence flowing, for as the Taoist sage Liu Ching is quoted in the *Records of the Bedchamber*: 'the man must always first engage her in protracted gentle play to harmonize her mood with his and make her feelings respond.'

A more esoteric complement to the Sui and T'ang period sex handbooks was Taoist sexual magic. Preponderantly concerned with the quest for immortality, it similarly called for unions at times and intervals prescribed according to cosmology. It was if anything even more biased towards accumulating vital yin, and strongly recommended taking it straight from the source. Cunnilingus was considered particularly beneficial. Later on, erotic Japanese prints celebrated this invigorating tonic by graphically depicting male tongues slithering through female founts of yin. While this is common in pornography everywhere, such prints fairly frequently referred to the quest for immortality in their accompanying texts. A recurring theme shows a man lapping assiduously away at his mistress's source of femininity, as the excess vital elixir drips down to collect in a flask or sake cup placed beneath her parted thighs.

Then there were Tung-Hsuan's Six Ways of Penetration. To mention three:

> One: pushing the Jade Stalk down and letting it move to and fro over the Lute Strings like a saw, as if one were prying open an oyster to obtain the precious pearl shining inside. Two: hitting the Golden Gully over the Jade Veins, as if one were cleaving a stone to discover the Jade Kernel. Three: letting the Positive Peak hit against the Jewel Terrace, like an iron pestle descending into the medicine bowl.

The couple would follow further prescriptions once they were on the job. Tung-Hsuan was a stickler for doing things properly. 'Deep and shallow, slow and quick, straight and slanting thrusts,' he warned, 'all these are by no means uniform, each has its own characteristics.' These are duly enumerated, and their various healthful and healing benefits described.

Once it was in, there were the Nine Styles of Moving the Jade Stalk. One involved flailing out to right and left like a brave general breaking up enemy ranks, another moving up and down like a wild horse bucking through a stream. Number four called for 'swiftly alternating deep and shallow strokes, like a sparrow picking rice grains from the bottom of a mortar', and five, 'deep and shallow strokes in steady succession, like large stones sinking into the sea'.

As quaint as they seem, it is likely that their whimsy escaped the notice neither of the Chinese nor the Japanese. As perfectly sedate and serious as they were, both Chinese and Japanese sexual sages were also quite well aware that their prescriptions were not only medical, but guidelines for attaining ecstasy. The florid imagery and metaphors they employ not only clearly illustrate the techniques involved, but some no doubt struck a chord in the hearts of anyone as passionately fond of poetry as the Heianese.

There were different views on the number of 'main' positions, but most manuals listed some thirty. How the Heianese managed some of these in pitch darkness is anyone's guess. To name but a few of the positions in Master Tung-Hsuan's *Ars Amatoria*, promulgated in Japan through Tamba Yasunori, there was the more standard and missionary 'Close Union' for starters, followed by the more advanced 'Pair-Eyed Fish', 'Wailing Monkey Embracing a Tree', the 'Bamboos Near the Altar', the 'Cat and Mouse in One Hole' or the 'Hounds of the Ninth Day of Autumn'. As their fanciful names imply, some of these involved sexual acrobatics of the kind depicted later in a great many Japanese woodblock prints. One often finds curios and handkerchiefs printed with stylized diagrams of the thirty positions in the souvenir shops of hot-spring resorts today.

At once precious and frankly clinical, the metaphors eminently suited a people as fond of dressing up their very nonchalant and cursory sexual activities in rarefied mannerisms and pompous charades as those of Heian. The Lute Strings referred to the female pubic hairs and the Jade Gate to the vulva; the Golden Gully denoted the upper part of the same and the Jewel Terrace was the clitoris. The Jade Veins meant the place where the labia meet beneath the vulva and the vagina was the Cinnabar Cleft. The Jade Stalk and Positive Peak denote the penis, which is characteristically treated in less detail than the female organs. Referring to the inner right and left sides of the parted vulva, the term 'Examination Hall' is in every sense revealing, for it implies a marked and uninhibited predilection for admiring scrutiny of the female genitalia, which is nowhere so exalted as in Japan. In modern striptease parlours, after all, thighs are not only spread to reveal all, but rapt spectators are often handed a magnifying glass.

The handbooks were undoubtedly always in the possession of Heian physicians, but how widely read they were otherwise is a matter of conjecture. Obviously the fact that they were written in Chinese makes it that much more improbable that they were read by women, but such medico-erotic scrolls were likely to join tales and poetry in the nobleman's library. They were essentially medical books, and their florid Chinese terminology finds a ready equivalent in the Latin names in European medicine. Later sex manuals, such as the *Zoku Gunsho-ruijuu*, condensed from Tamba's Sino-Japanese

I-Shin-Po and presented to the court by a physician in the late thirteenth century, retranslated Chinese terms into more prosaic Japanese equivalents.

The sex handbooks comprehensively covered various complaints and their prevention and cure. The indiscriminate emission of semen was considered to do grievous harm to the blood vessels and finally obliterate the brain; so many strokes of the penis would be beneficial to this and that disease. Prescriptions were cosmological and directional too – depending on the season, the couple would have to perform with their heads facing given cardinal points. Apart from the obvious taboo period of menstruation, the horoscope proscribed sexual intercourse on other days too. Extreme age differences were frowned upon as a gross imbalance of yin-yang, and older men were advised to refrain from intercourse altogether, for it might constitute the final flare of the oil lamp before it goes out. Nevertheless, taking the proper medicines, some wily old codgers could hope to be rewarded with rejuvenated vigour.

The Chinese herbal pharmacopoeia was used to treat every kind of ailment both before and after the Heian era. Among the many purported cures for general complaints, there were also medicines and unguents for shrinking over-large vaginas and others for exalting diminutive penes. Paramount among medical preparations are those which were used for boosting flagging or collapsed male sexual energies. The Bald Chicken Medicine was not only especially recommended for impotence, but had the additional benefit of curing a man's five sufferings and seven aches. The *Art of the Bedchamber* tells the story of Lu Ta-Chin, Prefect of Shuh, who took this potion and sired three sons when seventy years old. His renewed vigour was hard on his wife, for 'she came to suffer from a vaginal disease so that she could neither sit nor lie down', and the old man had second thoughts. 'Then the Prefect threw the potion into the courtyard where a cock ate it. This cock jumped on a hen and continued copulating for several days without interruption, pecking the hen's head until it was completely bald.'

Extract of white dog liver, powdered dried lizard et al.; some medicines and penile ointments shared unsavoury animal ingredients in common with medieval western witchcraft and primitive folk remedies everywhere – and sometimes still do. By and large, the prescriptions for potency consisted mainly of plants. In Japan, as in most of East Asia, morphological beliefs still assume that peniform mushrooms and hard deer antlers, powdered along with other herbs, can produce untold vigour and splendid, bone-hard erections.

Sold in pharmacies and vending machines and advertised by the media, for example, Japan's ubiquitous *dorinkku* (drink) frequently claim to have remarkable properties especially for what ails gentlemen, and some of their ostensible ingredients are the same as they were all those centuries ago. In Tokyo station there is a kind of stand-up bar specializing in these, which finds commuting *salarymen* quaffing small bottles purporting to cure more than just a hangover. Commonly touted as containing Korean ginseng root, 'snake essence' and assorted priapic plants, the cheaper versions of these preparations consist of no more than sugar, the odd vitamin and a galvanizing emphasis on caffeine. In pharmacies, especially homeopathic ones stocking items from the Chinese pharmacopoeia, some élite forms of these potions might contain powdered stag antlers and rhinoceros horn and cost 5,000 yen for a tiny bottle. The only visible effect they have over their vegetal counterparts is to turn the depletion of certain endangered animal species into a lucrative business.

It is known that some of the old sex handbooks contained illustrations, but these are long gone. The same applies to graphic erotica, which has gone the way of everything else, for sadly only precious little painting from the Heian period of any kind survives. The *monogatari* often mention painting competitions, in which courtiers composed elegantly worded critiques of each other's work. Some of these paintings were *onnae* (paintings of women) and *otokoe* (pictures of men). These are thought to have depicted frank sexual themes for, as one old *monogatari* has it, they made their genteel contemplators blush. In *The Tale of Genji*, one of the characters on the point of leaving his beloved behind paints her a picture by way of a keepsake, which depicts a beautiful man and woman 'lying side by side'.

Of Heian erotic art only one example remains. Although painted in the thirteenth century, it is said to be an exact copy of a lost tenth-century original. This is the *Koshibagaki-zoshi*, a scroll of sixteen pictures graphically depicting the erotic exertions of a couple of Heian courtiers. Rather than dalliance between courtiers, some experts believe, the work actually shows the illicit affair between high priestess Saiko-jo and a guard at the Ise shrine. If this is true, then it would seem that the Japanese propensity for using sexual themes as a gesture of provocation and defiance already existed in Heian-kyo.

THE WISTERIA WITHERS

As the exaltation of monogamy in *The Tale of the Lady Ochikubo* suggests, faithfulness towards one's lover was something about which a society both as socially stratified and as promiscuous as Heian could only dream. The patterns of polygamy persisted a long time in Japan but, unlike during the Heian era, later officialdom saw love in the same light as erotic passion. Consequently it was relegated to the realm of the licensed quarters, where it was transmogrified into an enduring obsession with prostitutes which would have horrified the Heianese.

The Heian era had its courtesans, but it was perhaps its sheer promiscuity that forestalled anything like the licensed quarters of later days. It is known that among Fujiwara no Michinaga's legions of concubines and mistresses, he was especially fond of Kokannon, the Little Goddess of Mercy who had been an *asobime* – a woman for play. Although the *monogatari* make almost no mention of an *asobime* courtesan class, there is nevertheless just one single and revealing reference to it in *The Tale of Genji*. The setting is a magnificent festival and the Shining Prince's musings on a group of *asobime* seems to sum up the prevailing Heian attitude towards prostitutes:

> Women of pleasure were in evidence. It would seem that there were susceptible young men even among the highest ranks. Genji looked resolutely away. It was his view that one should be moved only by adequate forces, and that frivolous claims were to be rejected even in the most ordinary affairs. Their most seductive and studied poses had no effect upon him.

Genji is the ultimate gallant and prostitutes, who require none of the elaborate courtship games at which he excelled, are beneath him.

Yet for all the mannered façades and elevated courtships of the Good People, the culmination was exactly the same as *yobai* – the peasant custom of 'night-creeping' – which some maintain is an emulative and rustic degeneration of the aristocratic courtship tradition. Nonetheless, since rural Japanese amatory mores and sexual mysticism extend far back into the proto-historic past, others support the reverse. In all probability arriving with early migrations from the mainland, Japanese ritual springtime romps bear remarkable similarities to Yin dynasty country festivals recorded as early as 1500 B.C. Rural fertility rituals, including *yobai*, may well have been around long before the appearance of any civilization as sophisticated as the Heian. Although they went through periods of prohibition and reinstatement even then, their existence during the Heian period (e.g. the orgiastic Festival of the Holy Light) implies that the ancient, licentious practices of the countryside merely came to be dressed in elaborate aristocratic finery.

One might wonder why, as freely acceptable as they were, pre- and extra-marital love affairs were ideally consummated in complete darkness. The paradox seems rooted both in Confucianism and the balancing of yin and yang. Being considered properly as a nocturnal (yin) activity, sexual intercourse should not be allowed to interfere with the activities of the daytime (yang). Like the pretence of keeping affairs secret from parents, which precluded the lighting of lamps and candles, it was also in keeping with Confucian conventions.

Although love and sexual passion had yet to be repressed as they would be later on, in Heian days they nevertheless belonged to the same realm as the later Japanese *honne*, the true conditions. *Tatemae* accordingly made it more seemly for the protagonists to dress up their real feelings in a polite courtship ritual that was artificial, theatrical and standardized. This is true of the exchange of poems. There were great literary exceptions, but the poetic run of the mill was not much more than the pat, one-size-fits-all equivalent to a modern valentine card and betrayed none of the writer's true emotions.

The ladies' screens and curtains were in all probability often an equally empty gesture: men were forever parting them and peeking behind them; on some, the lattices were so thin that they were virtually transparent. No doubt the Heian era was as much a paradise for voyeurs as the Edo period brothels. Even if the exertions of lovers could not always be seen, there is little doubt that they could be overheard. Even in daytime, when a woman could perhaps receive a male guest provided she remained behind her screen, the fact that one could sometimes see through it did not matter; what was important was that it was there, and that the gesture of concealment and Confucian sexual segregation had been ritually observed.

Many western scholars have compared the Heian pursuit of seduction to eighteenth-century Europe, and imply that Heian love affairs were to true feelings as birds in flight are to taxidermy. To Ivan Morris, for one, they were 'mere exercises in seduction'. Yet if the consequences of the game were to break hearts and ruin lives, as love always can, the liaisons of the Heian period nevertheless lacked the premeditated perversity to make them as dangerous as the eighteenth-century western equivalent. If the vague phrasing of the romances can be interpreted as nonchalance, the protagonists are forever unabashedly swayed by powerful emotions. Admittedly some of their sentiments are affected, for even the beauty of a painting, a piece of music or a dance occasioned ostentatious outpourings of tears. Nevertheless, romantic languishing hardly seems to have been alien to the Heianese, and their romances were full of it.

Art, love, grief: all are quintessentials in the *mono no aware* permeating Heian aesthetics, literature and life in general. Perhaps, then, the *monogatari* are less reflections of reality than mannered works of art. But the broken hearts, tears and sentimental outpourings reflected an emotional freedom which would not be permitted again in Japan, where love was soon to be trampled beneath warriors' feet. One could argue that Heian courtships were all pomp and circumstance and no substance, but this ultimately applies less to love affairs and more to the era as a whole, for it was this that led to its downfall.

History shows us that great civilizations can bloom and wither like so many potted plants, and that yesterday's wisteria can be tomorrow's thorn bush. The Fujiwaras had shrewdly fuelled their glittering ascent with political marriages and manipulated a fairy-tale imperial court, but the delicate serenity of the world they had so carefully nurtured was to be its undoing. Notwithstanding the splendour described by Sei Shonagon and Murasaki Shikibu, whole districts of Heian-kyo were already in squalid ruin by the end of the tenth century. The presence of the Tendai monks on Mount Hiei may have assuaged the terror the Heianese harboured for the inauspicious and demonic north-east, but the south and west of the city went into an early decline. In Murasaki's day, parts of it already presented derelict houses overgrown with weeds and sordid hovels inhabited by diseased wretches and thieves. Travel outside the city itself was very dangerous, but wandering these forlorn quarters after dark was not much safer. No longer the sedate ascetics they once were, many of the Buddhist monks on Mount Hiei eventually degenerated into unruly warriors and brigands. Periodically terrorizing parts of the city with their raids, they burnt houses and subjected the aristocratic and defenceless occupants to pillage and rape.

The imperial police were notoriously ineffectual.

Towards the end of the eleventh century, burglaries were not only common in broad daylight but perpetrated even in the palace. The military and bureaucracy were fonder of dancing than the martial arts and the captains of the imperial guard taught elegant Bugaku dance routines of T'ang dynasty inspiration. Administrators too were expected to show some skill at dancing, and their duties degenerated into a hopelessly unproductive series of ceremonies that were as highly bibulous as they were ostensibly refined. The equestrian abilities of high-ranking Fujiwara army officers had become such that subordinate soldiery greeted them with gales of derisive laughter. Such a manifest lack of respect and discipline hardly escaped the notice of the predatory warrior clans in the outlying provinces – especially the Taira and Minamoto, who were meanwhile honing their swords.

Although the Heian era went on officially until 1192, Armageddon really came with the civil wars of Hogen and Heiji in 1156 and 1159, respectively. Shortly after his Minamoto rivals had overrun the Heian court and seized power, Kyomori, the commander of the Taira clan, finally wrested it from them. Feeble and disorganized Heian resistance was no match for fire and sword, and the delicate severed heads of Kyomori's rivals were displayed on pikes, announcing a norm that was to remain in force for centuries.

PART III

The Venereal Equinox

8

The Edo Period

THE DAWN OF THE SAMURAI

Bringing carnage and rapine in their wake, men in ornate armour torched castles, obliterated villages and slashed each other to ribbons. As their horses' hooves thundered over the countryside, they complemented the natural cycles of famine and disaster, for peasants were now dragged into a vicious circle of bellicose feudalism as their sons were recruited to swell the ranks of the troops that wolfed their crops. Among women, even the high-born became chattels tossed about on the tides of raging macho heroics; the aesthetes who had wooed them in verse were long gone. With the Heian period only a memory, the country was torn apart by rival military potentates. Akin to the warlords of China, they were the shoguns – a word finding an apt modern equivalent in 'generalissimo'.

The imperial court was to remain in Kyoto until 1868, but after defeating the Taira clan towards the end of the twelfth century, Minamoto Yoritomo installed a military government in Kamakura, south-west of present-day Tokyo. Called *bakufu* or camp-office, his system was to govern the country from 1192 for nearly seven hundred years. The architect behind the shogun's victory, which culminated in the legendary naval battle of Shimonoseki in 1185, was his brother Yoshitsune. Although Yoritomo mistrusted him and hounded him until he took his own life, he lived on in a grand legend which found him escaping to China to become none other than Genghis

Khan, as well as in an incongruously effeminate incarnation of youth and beauty in the popular imagination.

Continually marred by bloodshed, the Kamakura period lasted under two centuries and is regarded by admirers of chivalry as the fountainhead of the samurai mystique. The era also saw the seminal apogee of the revered samurai custom of *seppuku* or belly-slitting, better known in the West as hara-kiri. Defeated in 1331 and further disgraced for having exiled the emperor, the proud Hojo family that had once ousted the Minamoto had no alternative to save face but to subject themselves to a gruesome ritual which, involving some thousand retainers, called for successive self-eviscerations and decapitations down to the last man, who was left to cut his own throat. This was to be considered a particularly ennobling and honourable death for many centuries to come.

As violent as it was, the Kamakara period was paradoxically also an age during which Buddhism came to the fore, notably with Zen, a sect of ancient Indian origin and introduced from China. As strange as it seems that this most meditative and serene doctrine (which moreover brought with it an important ancillary cultivation of the arts) should have come to be so revered by the warrior class, Zen is of an extremely stoic mould, and Japan was already quite comfortable with paradoxes. During the long centuries marred by military brutality, lulls in the storm saw the blossoming of other cultures. A typically Japanese trait, chrysanthemum-and-the-sword fashion, even the fiercest warriors and draconian dictators could be lulled by delicate aesthetic refinements. The contradiction was to appear again with a vengeance shortly after the great shogun Ashikaga Takauji transferred the seat of power to the Muromachi district of Kyoto in 1339. Despite the direst strife everywhere else, in quieter Kyoto the era proved to be another heyday for Japanese culture.

Towards the end of the fourteenth century, increased trade with Ming-dynasty China brought over a fresh supply of various cultural raw materials for further refinement in Japan. Following in the wake of tea and Zen, the Neo-Confucian reforms enforced in China during the 1370s gradually caught the attention of Japanese scholars and made their way into the country. Homebound and having the virtues of subservience and motherhood ardently impressed upon them, Chinese women were increasingly finding their freedom curtailed. The years of war in Japan hastened the depreciation of women and the glorification of manhood, which spawned a widespread exaltation of pederasty on the one hand and prepared highly fertile ground for the seeds of Neo-Confucianism on the other.

Meanwhile, forever leaning more towards religion and culture than bellicosity, Kyoto's effect upon the spartan shoguns was mollifying. Like clouds of incense, ghostly vestiges of the refined Heian era lingered to intoxicate them and, melding Chinese cultural concepts with aesthetics and ingenuity of its own, the shogun's court in Kyoto soon shone with a splendour comparable to that of its elegant predecessor. The Ashikaga shoguns Yoshimitsu (1358–1408) and Yoshimasa (1436–90) were avid patrons and practitioners of the arts, ruling over splendid courts which developed the tea ceremony, flower arranging, landscape gardening, painting and the Noh theatre to bring Japanese culture to a new apogee.

Alas, the luxury of the effete Ashikaga shogunate was swiftly depleting the coffers of a divided nation and the strife of centuries came to a head. The refined urban élite put away their paintbrushes and suffered the rude interruption of their tea ceremonies, for war raged in and around Kyoto for eleven years. Rival shoguns battled with each other and mobs of starving peasants rioted; in one way and another, Japan remained in a permanent state of civil war until the end of the sixteenth century.

During the late 1540s, visiting Portuguese merchants introduced Christianity and the musket. Praising the Lord soon proved unwise for foreign missionaries and Japanese converts alike, but passing the ammunition did much to speed up the unification process and bring the centuries of strife to an end. Oda Nobunaga (1534–82), Toyotomi Hideyoshi (1536–98) and Tokugawa Ieyasu (1542–1616) are the triumvirate shogun élite who fought together and successively towards unifying Japan. The ultimate showdown came in 1600 at the battle of Sekigahara, where the super-shogun Ieyasu's hundred thousand warriors defeated Ishida Mitsunari's army of eighty thousand. Japan was at last one nation. Dying in 1616, Ieyasu was the first and greatest in the long Tokugawa line, which was not only to rule the country for the next 268 years, but also to sever it from the outside world.

The early Tokugawa era was marked by the persecution of Christians, whom the shoguns had viewed with mixed feelings ever since Francis Xavier landed in Japan in 1549. Fearing political intrigues between Japanese Christians and the Portuguese, Ieyasu had already ordered the destruction of churches and all missionaries out of the country, but his son's and grandson's persecution programmes were far more virulent and notoriously cruel. Once the last of the missionaries had departed or been murdered, Japanese Christians refusing apostasy could expect to be crucified, beheaded, boiled in oil or burned at the stake in exactly the same way as the heretics of Europe.

With the exception of a handful of Dutch traders

allowed to operate on the tiny island of Deshima in Nagasaki harbour, there were no foreigners left. In 1637 the shogunate declared that any Japanese going abroad and returning did so on pain of death. A popular uprising crushed east of Nagasaki in the following year involved so many followers of the faith that it went down in history as the apocalypse for Christianity in Japan, and tens of thousands of men, women and children were savagely massacred.

Despite and because of the notorious exception of the persecution of Christians which had served to convince others of the ruthlessness of the Edo dictatorship, the Tokugawa regime was peaceful almost from the start. By making his headquarters in the city of Edo and turning it into the seat of government, Ieyasu not only availed himself of a strategically sound central position, but also consolidated the separation between religion and state initiated during the Kamakura period. With the emperor safely ensconced in the spiritual capital of Kyoto like a religious icon, the Tokugawa shogunate busied itself with matters in the real world. From the inception of the dictatorship in 1600, the warrior class attained its apogee and within thirty years the country was hermetically sealed and oppressively governed through the samurai. They were the links in a chain at last cohesively binding a system which had for centuries found the country ruled but divided by provincial feudal lords: the daimio (literally, the 'big names').

With all due respect to popular myth, especially in the West, the word samurai does not in fact mean warrior at all. Applying to those in the service of the shogun and the daimio, it means 'retainer'. Apart from the persecution of Christians, the quelling of a few ill-fated popular uprisings or the odd slash at an uppity commoner, for most of the Tokugawa era, the majority of retainers wore their swords as accessories signifying their class. By the end of the seventeenth century, the samurai were already on the way to becoming an anachronism. When it comes to institutions, however, anachronism does not necessarily portend a speedy end in conservative Japan. Like the aristocracy of Heian, the samurai class was a social élite which was bureaucratic, conservative and accessible only on a hereditary basis, but far more intractably Confucian and resolutely spartan. Even as some of the shoguns themselves degenerated into milk-sops, samurai officialdom continued to hold the country in a grip of iron.

During the fifteenth century, bartering on the basis of rice gradually became obsolete with the appearance of coinage, but trading was strictly for commoners. Merchants or *chonin* came beneath farmers and artisans as the lowest class beneath the samurai, whose strict code debarred them from anything so crass as business. The Tokugawa government maintained its solvency through the exactions of the daimio, but the orientation of the rice trade changed as farmers sold their crops to city merchants. For all their prestige, many samurai were soon in dire financial straits. Despite the unbending rule of the *bakufu*, from the early seventeenth century Kyoto, Osaka and Edo were in practice the realm of the merchant prince. The Edo period was the era of the townsman.

TROUBLE WITH BATH-HOUSES AND BROTHELS

More is known about the artistic and cultural accomplishments of the various courts during the ages of war than about their erotic pleasures. As women came to be regarded with increasing contempt, the warrior's rest narrowed increasingly on an ultra-masculine exaltation of homosexuality. In fact, it had been a time of extreme licentiousness on all fronts. Explicit erotic scrolls in the *Yamato-e*, or Japanese picture tradition, survive from the fifteenth century, as do a number of prurient toys and artifacts implying that people did sometimes have time for things other than war. Notwithstanding the *asobime* – the 'playing' courtesans – mentioned in *Genji* whatever brothel activity there may have been otherwise was scarcely mentioned before 1193, when Minamoto Yoritomo's administration decreed guidelines regulating the earliest red-light districts.

As feudalism took hold, the powerful daimio had kept well-appointed harems and, following a pattern identical to a very ancient rural custom, they sometimes offered concubines to their more distinguished house guests. These women were called *uneme* and their history is thought to go back at least to the seventh century. The ranks of *uneme* at first comprised the daughters of aristocratic provincial families who were sent to the court to find a husband. In promiscuous olden times, many of these girls drifted from one affair to the next without making a permanent match and consoled themselves by setting a price upon their favours. It seems that the *asobime* were expected to excel in accomplishments such as dancing, but the line distinguishing them from *uneme* was hazy indeed in Heian times. In the countryside until quite recently, village headmen extended generous hospitality to their more important male visitors, who were not only wined and dined, but offered wives, daughters and perhaps girls from neighbouring farms as impromptu *uneme* to sweeten their stay.

The words 'stew' and 'bagnio' have come to refer to

brothels, but their origins are respectively in the French *estuve* and the same Italian word, which referred in medieval times to bath-houses run in a free and easy manner. Proliferating in Japan as in medieval Europe, similar establishments were reserved exclusively for gentlemen who, after wallowing in the water, could feast and carouse with courtesans. The practice of regular bathing had gradually spread, and towards the end of the sixteenth century public bath-houses proliferated in the larger centres of population throughout the country. Many employed female attendants called *yuna*, who diligently scrubbed the customers and savantly massaged them.

Although all but a handful of rural hot springs are segregated today, the *yuna* tradition survives in many modern saunas, in which bona fide female bath attendants separately service both sexes. The core of the sauna in Japan is less the steam room than a tiled bathtub of swimming-pool proportions, around the sides of which the role of the *yuna* survives virtually unchanged. In Kobe, for instance, there is a sauna complex including plush salons and restaurants, in which hot water splashes from beneath the feet of a gold effigy of Mickey Mouse, as bath-girls decorously soap and massage male customers. Their uniforms are skimpy, but it's hanky-panky no-how. In Tokyo, some such establishments are open all night, offering a convenient haven and a relaxing couch for inebriated *salarymen* who miss the last train home.

Until western opprobrium persuaded bewildered Japanese authorities to pry the sexes apart in Edo in the early 1860s, the city's bath-houses were mixed. Whilst most of them were just good clean fun for the whole family, the attendants' ministrations in others were of a more private and liberal nature. Some, as one Edo-period woodblock print suggests, could fall between two stools: as a woman leads her companion into the hot water by his penis, a nearby child points enquiringly at the erect member of a male bather who is eagerly ogling a bevy of nubile naked women.

In the wake of the mounting emphasis on Neo-Confucian morality during the late sixteenth century, brothels were increasingly frowned upon, and many hastily dressed themselves up as bath-houses. At the outset of the Edo period, the *yuna* were popular in establishments operating along very similar lines to their medieval European counterparts. In some places the attendants were male and reserved for gentlemen of the other persuasion, not to mention also for servicing lonely ladies. Nearly four hundred years later, these characteristics are still extant in many of today's hot-spring resorts; the hedonistic equation between licentiousness and the bath survives.

In many resort hotels, guests sit up to their necks in hot water, sipping sake and selecting choice morsels served to them on floating trays. Afterwards, they can engage an *onsen-geisha*, whose services not infrequently offer a great deal more variety than their more artistic and conversational urban counterparts. In some of the broader-minded *onsen* hotels, the traditional trappings and customs of true geishadom have almost become superfluous. *Onsen-geisha*, who these days often hail from South-East Asia, provide services beginning right in the bath, as did the dexterous and liberal ministrations of the *yuna* nearly four hundred years ago.

Notwithstanding the tough stance the samurai affected towards women, they were only human. Knowing this full well, Ieyasu's administrators adopted a novel tactic for ensuring the loyalty of his subjects, which virtually amounted to hostage taking. Rotating and posting samurai and daimio between Edo and the provinces for extended periods, the system forced them to leave their wives and families behind, a practice which in some ways finds itself echoed today in the *tanshin-funin* routine endured by *salarymen*. Since the legions of *bakufu* administrators in the capital had left their families behind, small wonder that the late seventeenth-century satirist Ihara Saikaku dubbed Edo the 'City of Bachelors'.

With main population centres now controlled from a central government, the post roads became the country's vital arteries. The samurai could travel with few questions asked, but lesser mortals not showing their official permits at the checkposts at the entrances to every town could expect to be arrested, and many came to sticky ends. Notwithstanding, the post roads galvanized inter-urban trade and communications, especially along the famous Tokaido connecting Edo, Kyoto and Osaka together. Brothels mushroomed in the major cities, and no post town worthy of the name was without its inns and taverns well-staffed with *meishimori*, the 'rice-serving' waitresses allotted to individual male customers. After bathing them on arrival, they served them food and banter at dinner and sex at bedtime.

Like the shoguns and the daimio, Tokugawa Ieyasu kept legions of concubines, just as others preferred flurries of pretty page boys. But what was good for the shogun was not necessarily good for the *chonin*, and even less for the samurai. So with stews here, 'rice-servers' there and brothels sprouting up hither and thither all over the towns, Ieyasu and his Neo-Confucian advisers were not amused. Not because it was immoral but because, being disorderly, it encouraged dissipation rather than the more dutiful things in life. It was high time to do something about it.

9

The Great Indoors

THE SHOGUN AT HOME

Japanese harems were never appointed on the same scale as their Chinese equivalents, and nor were they staffed with legions of supervising eunuchs. Nevertheless, there is no doubt that the harems of some Japanese emperors were well stocked. The larger a family, the greater the likelihood of prolonging the male line. Where polygamy and monogamy ostensibly set the upper and lower orders apart, there was an equation between high breeding (both hereditarily and progenitively speaking) and safety in numbers. But here there were neither the excesses of King Solomon, nor those of the sated sitters on the Dragon Throne across the sea.

Heian romances and diaries can be remarkably revealing about imperial love affairs; the courtiers who wrote them seemed to enjoy a kind of intimacy with their sovereigns as unthinkable in latter-day Japan as anywhere. Be this as it may, the polygamous imperial portrait one gains from Murasaki Shikibu, for one, is tinged more with restraint and amorousness than uncaring profligacy. Either way, ritual reverence and latter-day nationalism keep later Japanese history rather sparing about the details.

Old romances imply a great deal about the emperor's love affairs, but almost nothing about his dalliances. With the shoguns, the situation is almost the reverse. It seems that their love affairs were shrouded in much greater secrecy, perhaps because of politics and certainly because love was increasingly proscribed by the stoic Neo-Confucian code of the samurai. The shoguns modelled their amorous habits along lines similar to the old Chinese imperial pattern and could be as profligate as they pleased. As one often hears when today's bibulous bar-room conversations take a historical turn, they were *onnadarake* – covered with women. Tokugawa Ieyasu was partial to sex and the story goes that he had a peculiar fascination with *miboojin* or widows. On the other hand Toyotomi Hideyoshi, his earlier rival, had a marked preference for women of aristocratic origin, especially the daughters of high-ranking samurai. Although the fascination the low-born Hideyoshi harboured for these was undoubtedly that of a *nouveau riche*, like all the shrewder shoguns, his criteria for selecting concubines were also political.

Edo castle was divided into two rigorously separate parts. One was the *omotte* (front) for state business, and the other was the *Oku* – the Indoors. The pattern is similar to shops in all Asian countries in the Chinese sphere of influence, whereby business is conducted in front and the family resides in the back. The shogun's castle replicated the pattern on rather a grander scale; the *Oku* comprised no less than 200 rooms. These were further subdivided into two parts: the *nakaoku* (middle) and the *O-oku* (great). With the exception of some 280 male guards and servants quartered elsewhere and working in the *Oku* in shifts, men were expressly prohibited from entry. It was exclusively inhabited by some 600 women falling into innumerable different ranks and categories and who, in one way and another, were all in the service of one single man.

Forever capturing the Japanese popular imagination as a harem to end all harems, *Shogun no Oku*, the shogun's indoors, is a preponderant source for pulp fiction, popular films and TV series, not to mention an inordinate number of soft-porn spin-offs. Small wonder. Intriguing historians, the juicy rumours that leaked from the castle walls provide plentiful inspiration for lurid popular culture. Comprising quarters for the shogun's children, the kitchen and legions of maids, however, the *Oku* was not just the home of carnal extravagance. Out of the many hundreds of women, those who provided services of a sexual nature resided exclusively in the *O-oku*, the Great Indoors or the harem itself. Never officially numbering more than about a score in the case of the most energetic shoguns, these women were really only a small fraction of the total. Still, with some twenty to be getting on with, the shogun could afford to be a creature of shifting whims. Rivalry for his favour was fierce; it sometimes went as far as murder. Concubines not only cast decorum to the wind to fight like cats, but as many a film has depicted, they strangled and poisoned or conspired to have their rivals tossed down wells.

If she was not the object of a tactical move of his own during adulthood, the shogun's first wife would have been selected while both were of a tender age by his father. Again, such a marriage was never a matter of love and pleasure, but politics and progeneration. The wife's position was similar to the *Kita no Kata* of Heian days but, even if her authority may well have been greater than the chauvinism of the Tokugawa period would admit, her clout was probably less than her earlier counterpart. The *midaidokoro*, or *midai-sama* for short, could nevertheless not be divorced. The shogun was of course free to have as many affairs as he pleased, but he could not get rid of the *midai-sama*. For all its long history of abject feminine subjugation, Japan has never produced a Henry VIII.

The shogun's life was strictly regulated by ritual pomp

and circumstance. At ten o'clock at night, he customarily retired to his own bedroom, which was just a short walk away from his wife's. Instead of being able to spend the night with her if the mood took him, he had to announce his intention formally in advance. Upon reaching his spouse's bedroom, he waited first in a small adjoining antechamber in which he would be served tea or, occasionally, sake. As the regal couple engaged in rather artificial conversation, they were ministered to by the wife's ladies-in-waiting, the *midaisama-no-kerai* (*midai's* retainers). The custom was generally that the *kerai* were to be two in number and always that they should be virgins. Again, this prerequisite had more to do with ritual purity and superstition than morals. The *kerai's* duties after all included taking away the shogun's swords, always symbols of purity in the eyes of Shinto, and placing them on a rack in the bedroom. Samurai films and TV dramas sometimes find a *kerai* attempting to take murderous advantage of the privilege but, notwithstanding the cloak-and-dagger intrigues haunting the later shoguns, the premise is purely fanciful.

After setting out thick and sumptuous bedding, the *kerai* would assist the regal pair to don their sleepwear, put screens up around the bed and retire into an adjacent room called the *otsugi no ma*. Leaving the shogun and his wife to it, they remained on tap to be summoned by a bell to bring water or sleeping potions or to accompany either the *midai* or the shogun to the toilet, in which case they would afterwards wash their august employer's hands. Until very recently in the *mizu shobai*, when a patron communed with nature, a hostess or geisha waited outside the toilet with a bowl of hot water and a towel. In bars today, as one emerges from a toilet equipped with its own washbasin and paper towels, *mama-san* or one of her hostesses still often proffers a moistened towel.

At thirty years old and still in her prime, the shogun's wife was traditionally past it and suffered becoming '*otoko gommen*': 'honourable bed, sorry'. As is commonly the case with arranged marriages, the husband was anyway as unimpassioned over his conjugal obligations as his spouse. The shogun no doubt sometimes lamented that the *O-oku* was less conveniently located than his wife's bedroom, for he had to negotiate a labyrinth of lengthy corridors to reach it.

The formal ceremony and ritualized bureaucracy governing the shogun's gallantry was in many ways like some oriental and sexual equivalent to the cobwebby routines of Gormenghast. His amours in the *O-oku* were naturally designated by a proper name, which was *otawamure* – the august dalliance. Like most activities in here, it required documented advance notice and left little room for spontaneity. Having been formally notified, the chosen concubine in the *O-oku* was dressed in a ceremonial kimono of white silk like a wedding gown, and was led down the corridor to the master bedroom by a chaperone as the other concubines stood enviously by on either side. Taken to a special antechamber near the lord's bedroom, she awaited him for about an hour, during which ladies-in-waiting removed all her clothing and searched her. They undid her hair, which was tied back in a sleeping style with a long jet-black ponytail loosely cascading down her back. Hairpins being expressly forbidden, it was secured with a comb, and even this was subject to scrutiny to ensure that it concealed no cutting edge. Having fastidiously restored her hairstyle and dressed, maidservants brought her a pillow, boxes of cosmetics and a day kimono for the morning.

The shogun customarily arrived at ten o'clock, and all

the servants knelt upon the floor and bowed low, pressing foreheads to the tatami matting in formal greeting. The exquisitely decorated sliding paper door from the antechamber to the shogun's bedroom was drawn open. At once luxurious and sparse, the master bedchamber contained carefully devised, minimal furnishings. The concubine shared the shogun's bed, but not for sleeping. His consisted of several layers of mattresses and splendid silken covers and was much larger than hers, which was always set to the right of it.

As high and mighty as he was, the shogun could enjoy a degree of privacy with his principal wife, but not during his amorous encounters with concubines. As though referring to their lower status, concubines were less ceremoniously known as *sokushitsu* – side-rooms. On the far side of the shogun's bed was a mattress laid out for a maidservant, whose duty it was to spend the night in the same room. She was called the *ojōrō* – the upper court lady. Somewhat paradoxically, the girl the shogun actually slept with had the lower-sounding rank of *ochurō* or middle court lady. Folding screens placed around the *ojōrō's* bed provided token privacy, and although she was obliged to face away from the performing shogun, that she could still hear everything was quite the idea. Forbidden to sleep, the *ojōrō* had to report what she had overheard in exhaustive detail on the following morning to the *otoshiyori* (honourable aged), an old woman who had meanwhile similarly spent a sleepless night in an adjacent room.

The object of this curious arrangement was to keep track of all the shogun's sexual encounters, for this was ostensibly the only way of making sure whether or not any subsequent progeny was his. For despite rigorous surveillance and seclusion, it was not unusual for members of the shogun's harem to meet lovers old and new during their brief excursions into the outside world. There was also the danger of a man taking the opportunity to conspire with a girl, get her to coax favours from the shogun or perhaps have him sign politically compromising documents. The fears were not unfounded, especially when some of the later shoguns became decadent to the point of degeneracy. The women near and inside the master bedchamber were thus bidden to keep their ears open, and woe betide them if the reports from the concubine, *ojōrō* and *otoshiyori* failed to tally the next day.

During the early nineteenth century, the eleventh Tokugawa shogun Ienari broke all records with twenty-one official concubines and sired fifty-four children between them. When they grew up, the plentiful offspring of the shoguns were traditionally farmed out to marry the sons and daughters of provincial daimio, whether these and their progeny liked it or not. By Ienari's time, meanwhile, the merchant classes outside the castle walls had grown richer and more powerful than ever. It is not surprising that the shoguns were in financial decline. According to a calculation by Kiyoyuki Higuchi, a social historian specializing in the Edo period, running the *Oku* cost a staggering sum of two thousand million modern yen per year.

Being the potentate he was, the shogun's scope for sexual relationships was not restricted to his wife and concubines; out of the many hundreds of women in the *Oku*, he had the pick of the crop, provided they were of suitable class. The cleaning and cooking staff were beneath his dignity and consideration, but the ladies-in-waiting were recruited only from good families. When he had his eye on a maidservant on his wife's side rather than in his designated hunting ground in the *O-oku*, he would appoint one of his own servants as a go-between.

Theoretically, the *midai-sama*'s maidservant was free to refuse, a stance known as *'oshitone gommen'* – 'august mattress, sorry'. Unless founded on a monthly indisposition, such a refusal would be an affront earning her prompt dismissal, and those who demurred were few and far between. Sleeping with the shogun was a great privilege, and carried ample financial rewards for the girl's family.

Confucian notions of filial piety meant that the honour and its ancillary material benefits were less for the girl than for her parents. Neither attracted to nor in love with the shogun, the average concubine merely put her parents first and did as she was told. Arranged marriages followed a similar pattern and, at the other end of the social scale, much the same applied to prostitution.

A WORLD WITHOUT MEN

Military households have strict rules. The ladies of the inner apartments seldom even see a man, much less catch the scent of a loincloth. When they look at those delightful erotic pictures by Moronobu, they suddenly begin to feel rather skittish and amorous. They cannot help drawing up their heels and curling their middle fingers. But solitary pleasure does not satisfy them, since they want real love.

The Woman Who Spent Her Life in Love Ihara Saikaku, 1686

Concubines were confined exclusively to the *O-oku* for their first three years, after which they were entitled to an annual holiday and the occasional day off. These were ostensibly for visiting parents, paying religious respects or admiring seasonal blossoms. The shogun no doubt found it as hard to live up to the recommendations of the old Sino-Japanese sex manuals as anyone else; the life many women in the *O-oku* endured was one of sexual deprivation, and their 'excursions' to temples and shrines were not quite as pious as they seemed. Much the same applies to the religious institutions in question. In Heian times, after all, some of the monasteries on Mount Hiei had formed convenient trysting places for illicit couples. Marriage has always been a duty for a Shinto priest but, though Buddhist sects have since conceded wedlock for theirs, in the Edo period monks were sworn to celibacy. Transgressors could theoretically even lose their lives, but documented instances of this are very few and far between. As in most countries, one of Japanese folk irony's great stock-in-trades is the randy monk, and the frustrated women visiting monasteries on their rare days off had things other than religion on their minds. The dalliances between these elegant ladies and handsome young monks provided favourite subject matter for titillating pulp fiction and pornographic woodblock prints; it was a scandalous state of affairs for both parties but, as is so frequently the case in Japan, provided things were kept at a safely dispassionate level and a pretence of discretion was rigorously observed, both the secular and temporal authorities turned a blind eye.

In the *O-oku*, sexual frustration led to goings-on that have fanned the imaginations behind the more scabrous and pornographic celluloid celebrations of the shogun's harem. Nowadays lesbianism is naturally high on the list, and it often takes sadistic overtones. A typical scenario finds a harem neophyte framed for some misdemeanour by her jealous, older and/or uglier sisters. The ire of the rivals may not always have resulted from the shogun's roving eye, but from competition over the neophyte's favours. The alleged crime would be reported to a fearsome harem chaperone, an elderly termagant who supervised the *O-oku* with an efficiency rendering the most draconian Chinese eunuch superfluous. Such films might go on to have the neophyte stripped of her silken finery and thoroughly flogged. Although '*Shogun no Oku*' films take considerable liberties, the repression and cruelty one reads between the lines of fantasy undoubtedly hold a kernel of truth. Plotlines in fact read the same way as lurid American B-movies set in women's prisons, for the *O-oku*, for all its gilt-edged finery, was in practice very similar.

LONELY HEARTS COLUMNS – THE WAY OF DO-IT-YOURSELF

'When I use this thing,' said the maid, 'I feel quite dead. Since it's one of my life's enemies, I beg you to help me take my revenge on it. Ah, dear sir, how slow you are!' At last understanding, the samurai embraced her, laid her down and mounted her before she could even remove her obi.

From the *Kōshoku Koshiba-gaki* by Suikyōan, 1696

'The Japanese are not moralistic about auto-erotic pleasures,' remarked anthropologist Ruth Benedict. 'No people ever had such paraphernalia for the purpose.' In the Edo period, as evidenced in erotic prints of lonely ladies or nuns, the perennial *harigata* (dildo) reached an apogee. Made of wood or porcelain, the *harigata* was frequently decorated, carved or moulded. Sometimes representing Otafuku, folk religion's patron of feminine sexual appetite, or the popular erotic goddess Benten, it was also often sculpted with painstaking anatomical realism, ferociously veined and in sizes with which the real thing could never compete. When made of leather, buffalo horn or occasionally tortoiseshell, it could be soaked in warm water prior to use and was reputed to have exactly the right, subtle blend of hardness and flexibility. And whatever it was made of, it also presented the added advantage of never failing to rise to the occasion.

The common *harigata* was held by hand, but there were other models which could be affixed to the heel and which had indubitable merits in a country in which heels are traditionally sat upon. Moreover, with the *harigata* thus attached, a lady might also loop a cord around her foot and place the other end behind her neck, so that the toy could move around according to the sway of her torso and the ecstatic nodding of her head. Some Edo-period erotic prints show elaborate variants. In one, for instance, a solitary female protagonist lies on her back, having affixed the *harigata* to a bolster which she suspended from the ceiling with an elaborate system of cords and pulleys, thus enabling her to move it up and down between her legs by pulling a string.

That the Japanese have devoted a great deal of ingenuity to onanistic pursuits for centuries there can be no doubt. The same applies to a variety of sexual aids, including ticklers and penile sheaths, some of which have been catalogued in woodblock prints. A popular device known as *higo zuiki* consisted only of long strands from the dried fibres of a certain plant. When soaked in warm water, they became soft and slippery, and men used them to truss up their members like a salami sausage. Once wet, the *higo zuiki* greatly expanded and was regarded as having the double advantage of increasing the size of the penis and prolonging erection. In view of the obvious discomfort – not to say danger – the device must have presented to the wearer, such assets amount to a rather generous concession to the recipient. Other Edo-period sexual aids consisted of leather sheaths used by solitary men as an ersatz vulva, while other variants were primitive condoms.

Rin-no-tama (bell-balls) were popular items too and they still are. Like most of these sex devices, the tiny balls were common in China, although perhaps not of Chinese origin. Van Gulik suggests rather drily that the Chinese were fond of ascribing foreign origin to their mechanical sexual playthings, in much the same way as the French are pleased to call the condom *capote anglaise* and the British to call it a French letter. Either way, *rin-no-tama* probably made their way into Japan during the late fifteenth century, for they were known and used in China during the Ming dynasty. They were also known to female libertines in eighteenth-century Europe, where they were literally translated from the original Chinese as 'Burmese Bells'. Alleged by the Chinese to be filled with blobs of saliva from a mythical Burmese bird, the little silver balls were thought to contain an aphrodisiac so powerful that it reached boiling point even from the heat in the palm of the hand, which set the bells vibrating.

Rin-no-tama were ingeniously fashioned from different metals. Both balls were made of silver, one containing a blob of mercury and the other a tiny tongue of copper. The balls do indeed vibrate even on the palm of the hand, and it is claimed that they emit a tiny sound like a high-pitched tuning fork – hence the idea of bells. Inserted into the vulva, as the woman swayed her body to and fro, the vibrations produced as they knocked together procured a whole gamut of sensations from pleasurable to ecstatic. In the *O-oku*, perhaps they amply compensated for sufferings endured as a result of the shogun's neglect.

The Japanese also found the bells fun for both partners when inserted prior to sexual intercourse, for they could tickle the tip of the penis. No doubt influenced by the old Chinese idea that they were aphrodisiac, some men thought that *rin-no-tama* increased potency. The notion survives rather curiously among the Japanese today. Pearls are thought to have a similar effect on potency, no doubt also because they are the product of the vulviform oyster. Some men have one or more pearls surgically inserted under the skin and down the length of their penes. Unlike *rin-no-tama*, of course, pearls do not vibrate. Perhaps fortunately. A Tokyo taxi driver highly loquacious about the pursuit of pleasure once proudly boasted to me that he had had this operation performed. As excruciating as it sounds, he assured me that it not only enhanced erections, but also rubbed his companion in the most wonderful ways.

In the Japanese sex shop today, nearly all of these items – even the cumbersome *higo zuiki* – are still on sale. This workaday age turns solitary pleasure into a convenient last resort and finds the ranks of masturbatory toys augmented with a comprehensive range of Dutch Wives complete with grotesquely gaping, serviceable mouths, carefully textured flesh and optional pubic hair, as well as with a range of elaborate artificial vaginas squeezing the lonely male in folds of silicone and blood-pressure meter technology. Disembodied vulvas can be purchased too: a monstrous rubber sausage with a gaping vertical mouth at one end.

Some years ago the celebrated 11 *p.m.* late-night TV show interviewed a small machine-shop operator in Asakusa with a lucrative new sideline: teddy bears. Not quite Winnie-the-Pooh, however, for these were four feet tall and came with a large, electrically-operated rubber penis that could go in and out at four different speeds. A rather haughty panel of ladies including a cutie-pie actress and a crusty middle-aged *mama-san* from a Ginza bar was asked for its opinion. Despite the maker's assurances that he made them to order in black, white or yellow plush or, optionally, with real fur, the ladies were not impressed. Notwithstanding, the manufacturer claimed that he sold about ten a month at 150,000 yen each.

Innovations are sometimes imported and some years ago many Japanese sex magazines were advertising amazing penis-enlarging underpants from Korea. Elaborate scientific diagrams explained the principle: the briefs kept the wearer's member in a state of permanent erection. Today's dildos come complete with the same old sculptural attention to detail, but the preferred material is rubber. Electronics have also afforded remarkable progress in masturbatory science, evidenced both in dildos and in the *rin-no-tama*. Equipped with minute and dauntingly powerful buzzers, the bells sell for about 30,000 yen a pair. I once examined some of these items, including a remarkably varied selection of dildos, in a shop in Shinjuku managed by a couple of elderly ladies, who were prodding me to take home a souvenir.

Not wanting to be rude, I ostentatiously admired models in fanciful colours, even fluorescent greens and pinks, with coloured feathers and that lit up, but I declined. My wife would probably not greet them with much enthusiasm; I could get along fine on my own. 'That's because you're still young,' warned one saleslady, and placed another formidable example on the counter. 'That', announced the other one proudly, as it twitched grotesquely about like an agonized electric slug, 'can vibrate and turn round and round. I'll bet your august tinkle-tinkle can't do that.'

LAUNCHING THE FLOATING WORLD

Virtuous men have said both in poetry and classic works that houses of debauch for women of pleasure and for streetwalkers are the worm-eaten spots of cities and towns. But these are necessary evils and, if they be forcibly abolished, men of unrighteous principles will become like ravelled thread.

The Legacy of Tokugawa Ieyasu, quoted in *Nightless City*,
J. E. DeBecker

The august dalliances of the shoguns and the excesses behind the castle walls were one thing, but the licentiousness of the townsmen was quite another. As it was to be again in the late twentieth century, when irate inhabitants of Tokyo's Shinjuku reacted to the unbridled proliferation of commercial sleaze in their neighbourhood, officials were not the only ones to frown upon the brothels sprouting up in clusters of twos and threes all over Edo. In 1605, the older brothel quarter of Yanagimachi had been razed to make way for the construction of the shogun's castle and, as they had done before and always would under similar circumstances, its denizens wasted no time in setting up shop elsewhere. Between citizens infuriated with rowdy bordellos keeping them awake until all hours and a spartan shogunate turning increasingly to rigorous Neo-Confucian reforms, there was little doubt that a clampdown was under consideration.

Although protecting his own interests, Shoji Jinyemon was shrewd enough to mask them in a petition carefully devised to promote the common good and presented it to the authorities in 1612. After lamenting that the haphazard spread of houses of ill-fame was 'to the detriment of public morality and welfare', Jinyemon, himself a wealthy pimp, suggested that Edo's venal businesses should be concentrated into a closely supervised licensed quarter. As he was quick to point out, following administrative measures under former shoguns, Kyoto had its quarter in Shimabara and Osaka had Shinmachi.

Fully aware of the shogunate's true preoccupations, Jinyemon knew better than just to present his petition as a moral masquerade. By this time, samurai who had either been fired by their feudal lords or in the service of those who had fallen into disgrace were known as *ronin* or 'wave' men. *Ronin* having no other means of survival were not above resorting to a life of highway robbery and professional gambling similar to that of the American Wild West. Allying themselves with other outcasts, some *ronin* formed roaming bands of ruffians, the ancestors of today's *yakuza* gangs.

What worried the shogunate even more than common-or-garden crime was the possibility that the *ronin*, especially those who had once served feudal lords deposed during the recent civil wars, were engaged in political intrigue against the government. Drifting *ronin* not only found the brothels a convenient place of temporary residence, but conspiratorial elements were apt to use them as their headquarters. If the authorities granted his petition and confined houses of tolerance to one place, argued the shrewd Jinyemon, 'the brothel-keepers will pay special attention to this matter and will cause searching enquiries to be made about persons who may be found loitering in the prostitute quarters: should they discover any suspicious characters they will not fail to report the same to the authorities forthwith.'

After four years of administrative dithering, the shogunate at last gave Jinyemon its formal consent. The licensed quarter would be walled and surrounded by a moat. The brothel buildings were to be entirely functional, of predetermined size and devoid of decoration; their inmates were to be strictly prohibited from wearing showy finery. Heeding Jinyemon's guidelines and using morality as a weapon against political subversion, the shogunate decreed that all patrons would have their names entered in a register kept by the brothel and regularly examined by the authorities. Patrons were also to be barred from remaining in the quarter for longer than twenty-four hours, and the gates of the Yoshiwara would only remain open during the day.

Notable only for its *yoshi* rushes, mephitic marshland outside Edo's northern boundary thus came to be designated as the new home for the *demi-monde* in 1617. Although construction was not fully completed until November 1626, the Yoshiwara, 'Rush Field', was open for business early in 1618. Whores from the former unofficial red-light districts moved *en masse* to fill the new brothels and the five streets were named after their original districts. It was boomtown, and bawds from as far away as the southern capital of Kyoto moved to the grand *yukaku*, the pleasure quarter, in sufficient numbers for one of the streets to be named Kyo-machi, or Western Town.

Substituting the former *yoshi* with a homophonous character meaning 'auspicious' brought little luck to the Yoshiwara. Further urban planning during the mid-seventeenth century provided for moving the quarter to a new location further to the north-east. By now the Yoshiwara was thriving and among its inhabitants were many conducting ancillary trades. Although the government granted Yoshiwarians a few months' grace to move elsewhere, in 1657 it rejected their appeal to spare the quarter. In March the same year, much of Edo was anyway destroyed in one of many deadly and regular great fires. Since the *Moto* (original) Yoshiwara had burned to the ground, the government reluctantly tolerated another haphazard proliferation of bordello shanties, before setting aside a plot of land to the north-east of Asakusa, about half a mile behind the Kannon temple. In addition to financial compensation, the government was fairly generous with other concessions: the buildings could be slightly larger and, more importantly, in view of the *Shin* (New) Yoshiwara's greater distance from the walled city centre, the *yukaku* was to be allowed to operate during the night. Started in May, the construction of the Shin Yoshiwara, also known as the Fuyajo, the Nightless Castle, was completed in September 1657.

Again, there were the same five streets. At first they comprised only brothels, but the elegant *ageya* houses for arranging introductions gave enterprising local shopkeepers a new business more lucrative than sundry goods. Later, the *ageya* came to be called *machiya* (meeting houses) and *chaya* or tea houses, although throughout their long subsequent history, none of these was ever known to serve tea.

Wealthy townsmen eager to circumvent the austerities of the regime did so with a characteristic step-by-step escalation towards sybaritic ostentatiousness. Despite sumptuary laws and a great many sporadic and arbitrary clampdowns, the Yoshiwara was the one place in which they could enjoy with impunity a freedom forbidden elsewhere. Surpassing even Kyoto's Shimabara, the Yoshiwara became much more than just the haunt of harlotry. A splendid cultural microcosm, it was to become the home of restaurants and fancy shops, high fashion and the kabuki theatre, of music and dance, of literature and the visual arts. In this unique setting, there blossomed a culture which, for the first time, issued not from the aristocracy but from the people. The *ukiyo*, the fabled floating world celebrated in woodblock print masterpieces by now familiar everywhere, was afloat.

10

The Culture of Desire

In the days before the creation of the *ukiyo*, amusements for the townsmen were few and, if anything, fewer still for the sedate samurai. Although the commoners were exempt from abiding by the rigorous codes of the élite, the Tokugawa regime watched them closely to ensure that they never went too far. The samurai's cultural pastime included poetry, calligraphy, the tea ceremony, painting that had mostly by now become like so much mildewed chinoiserie, and a Noh theatre that had been petrified for two hundred years. Like country folk, the townspeople enjoyed Shinto festivals and votive theatre performances such as *kagura*, but their cultural diversions were otherwise virtually none. From early Tokugawa times, plebeians found attending the Noh were liable to a daunting fine.

In those days, the higher orders frowned upon frivolity and lumped together its various manifestations with the word *kabu*, which implied dissipation and ruin and covered a variety of sins. To commoners, the verb *kabuku* merely came to denote a popular and frequently *risqué* kind of dance. During the late sixteenth century, however, a woman named Okuni was to give the word *kabuki* new meaning. Contradictory legends make it hard to tell who she really was, but the gist is that she was a blacksmith's daughter and endowed less with beauty than brilliance. Okuni began her career as a *miko*, one of the shrine maidens whose ritual dances in those days sometimes preluded the prostitution filling the coffers of the more commercial Shinto shrines. Staging a performance with a small troupe of sister seductresses in the fairground on the dry bed of the Kamo river in Kyoto in 1586, Okuni began with conventional votive dancing and chanting but, as the routine progressed, it wound up as a form of dance drama which no one had seen before.

Although such events were scathingly dismissed as 'riverbed things' by upright citizens, Okuni's *onna-kabuki*, the women's kabuki, enjoyed phenomenal success: for, as Faubion Bowers remarked in his book *The Japanese Theater*, 'At the conclusion of Okuni's programmes, she held a "general dance" (*so-odori*), in effect a kind of lively curtain call for the entire troupe, but one in which spectators could participate in whatever manner they saw fit. Such abandon was the essence of the word *kabuku* in the Japanese mind.'

At first not so much art as an artful front for prostitution, Okuni's performances developed into a phenomenally popular form of theatre enjoyed by both sexes, and came to be called *Okuni kabuki* in contradistinction to *onna kabuki*, which scores of emulators continued as a bawdy masquerade. Rising above her riverbed origins, she performed on the exclusive Noh stage before the samurai and toured around the country's main cities in the wake of her growing fame. None of this great drama pioneer's plays survive, but there can be no doubt that she put plotlines and characterization where there had hitherto been little more than mime. Okuni's ordinary dancing girls gradually grew as actresses, and many assumed male roles.

Okuni's seminal troupe was given the distinction of command performances before the Edo shoguns and, reportedly, even before the emperor in Kyoto. Elsewhere, hundreds of bogus *Okuni* continued to disport themselves before inebriated male patrons sprawling on the grass for, like the contemporary Shakespearian equivalent, kabuki theatres were still in the open air with a roof only over the stage. The real Okuni is thought to have died in about 1610, the year Monteverdi wrote his famous *Vespers* in a Europe which, even if not altogether unfamiliar with licence masquerading as piety among some dubious offshoots of the Commedia del' Arte, would have found a theatre form marrying itself happily and openly to the oldest profession unthinkable.

The shogunate was having second thoughts. Increasingly troubled with urban licentiousness, it looked upon the kabuki phenomenon with wary disapproval. As it came to tighten its control over the brothels, it noted that the kabuki similarly encouraged what it saw as dissipation and disorder and turned its attentions to cleaning it up. In 1629 the *bakufu* expressly barred women from the stage. By the end of the first decade of the seventeenth century, however, the popularity of kabuki with the townsfolk was such that not even the shogunate could wipe it out altogether. A new urban culture had taken root and found its voice in a form of theatre, and it had blossomed at an unforeseen and stupendous rate. Once again, since blatantly to flout officialdom was unthinkable, the answer lay in adaptation and compromise.

If the ban was a blow to those who had looked forward to selecting bedmates from among the participants, no one else seemed to mind. There was always the *wakashu* or young men's kabuki, a trend already in existence for some years prior to its official inception in Edo in 1624. Inspired by the *onna* kabuki, the *wakashu* were a dramatic offshoot of the catamites catering to the warrior followers of *shudo*, the Way of Youth. When actresses were outlawed, they took centre stage.

To the delight of the townsfolk, actors donned costumes more realistically if outlandishly representing contemporary society and the ruling samurai. The kabuki playlets took a satirical turn, and female impersonators of unsurpassed beauty began to be called *onnagata* – woman-forms. In many early theatres, cross-sexual pantomime triggered much hilarity among the groundlings, while other more licentious ones apparently staged plays with ribald *double entendre* revolving around matters such as sodomy. Afterwards, actors offered themselves to those in the audience who fancied them. Even the samurai were known to let composure slip as they drew swords to fight for the favours of a beauteous *wakashu*.

Alongside the visual dazzle and ribald indulgences, the *wakashu* kabuki increasingly acted out slices of life with which the commoners could readily identify. It was thus not just the licentiousness in some of the less refined theatres that worried the government, but that the kabuki was becoming dangerously tainted by a creeping hint of satire. Faced with subversion, they cast an increasingly baleful eye upon the theatres. The widespread popularity of kabuki aroused the shogun's curiosity, but a command performance staged for his benefit was to no avail. The *wakashu* kabuki was finally banned in 1652.

The *bakufu* thought that by prohibiting gorgeous costumes, effeminate hairstyles, music and dance they would be fatally cramping the kabuki style. By decreeing that the only permissible form of drama thenceforth was mime, they thought they would deal it a mortal blow below the belt. And as usual, they were wrong. Abiding by the proscription on pretty boys, *yaro* kabuki (*yaro* =

guy, fellow) appeared almost immediately with all the music, dance and splendid trappings of its predecessor but, by deploying a cast of more seasoned actors, it safely separated the men from the boys. Eventually, the word *yaro* was dropped and the kabuki grew up to become a sophisticated all-male form of theatre which still exists in Japan today.

To the prolonged consternation of the authorities, however, kabuki continued to be licentious and subversive. Sheer ability sometimes made even very old men into outstanding *onnagata* as it does even now, but female roles were still more popularly the domain of the pretty youth, even though they were no longer the blatant catamites they once were. Becoming some of the greatest public faces of the Edo period, actors soon had to depend upon thespian skill alone for their success. From the great actor-playwright Ichikawa Danjuro I (1660–1717), the kabuki stage became the province only of those who had been trained by recognized masters and, like today, the profession was usually handed down from father to son. Homosexuality was still as common as it is sempiternally in the theatre everywhere, but women too fell heavily for the kabuki élite in whom they often aroused like feelings. Among the many and increasingly ineffectual Tokugawa clampdowns of the kabuki, one famous one was triggered by the illicit love affair between a woman from the aristocratic Ejima samurai family and the famous actor Ikushima in 1711.

What riled the authorities most was that plays openly reflected and commented upon their time. One kabuki ploy consisted of sending contemporary incidents and scandals into the distant past. 'It was the tenth year of such-and-such a reign,' the narrator's *joruri* chant would announce to a samisen accompaniment, 'seven hundred years ago.' But all the costumes would be contemporary and, apart from the characters having ancient-sounding names, the situation might be readily identifiable as a scandal not six months old. Another ploy was to retell recent history with characters merely given anagrammatic or sound-alike versions of their real names.

Despite drastically dwindling financial means, the Tokugawa dictatorship maintained power, arguably only on the strength of time-honoured conservatism. The virtue of endurance was as thoroughly inculcated as the dread of confrontation. Officially spanning only from 1688 to 1704, the era named Genroku is popularly seen as covering the latter half of the seventeenth to the mid-eighteenth century. Despite an earthquake and consequent fire destroying much of Edo in 1704 and the adoption of a new era name, Edo attained a mercantile and cultural zenith which was to last for about another fifty years. Forever associated with the apogee of the Edo period, the name Genroku is synonymous with Edo style.

Townsmen were largely at peace with a system which had after all allowed them to grow rich and powerful; lip-service to sumptuary laws on attire and lifestyle was a small price to pay for a congenial status quo. The class division, i.e. samurai, farmers, artisans and tradesmen, as well as the classless *Eta* or *Hinin* pariahs, was not as clear cut in practice as it was in theory. As low down on the list as the merchant *chonin* were, from the Genroku era onwards some merchant princes were powerful enough to pull strings behind the scenes. Destitute or discredited, many samurai and *ronin*, on the other hand, dropped down to live among lower social castes such as artists and the *demi-monde*.

Yet even the most prosperous of merchants had to tread extremely carefully. The fabulously wealthy Kinokuniya Bunzeimon, who made his fortune through judicious food imports in times of shortage, has entered folk legend among other things for offering the entire Yoshiwara a day off and closing it down just to throw a party for his friends, and families such as the banking Mitsui survived over the centuries to become one of today's corporate supergiants. Perhaps all of these were more public-spirited or had better political connections than poor Yoyoda Tatsugoro, whose arrogant ostentatiousness went too far. His had been a palatial home blatantly displaying priceless furnishings, fittings, screens and fabrics, not to mention a solid gold board for playing the game of Go. The *bakufu* showed its displeasure by prohibiting his business and confiscating everything he owned.

A *chonin* was free to accumulate wealth, but he could only enjoy its power by abiding by the rules, which he could also bend and circumvent by dressing up his aspirations with compromises in much the same way as the kabuki theatres did theirs. Flouting authority was extremely dangerous, carrying ruinous fines and sanctions at the very least. Then there was Kotsukappara, Edo's notorious execution ground. Conspicuously placed near the northern post roads on the confines of the city for the edification of passing travellers, the display of severed heads hardly had time to attract flies before being replaced with a fresh daily crop. Most had belonged to thieves and murderers, but political and antisocial elements, not to mention the occasional adulteress and her paramour, went the same way. At the beginning of the Meiji period when it was happily abandoned, it was estimated that over some three centuries, Kotsukappara had been the site of various kinds of public execution for some 200,000 men and women. Kotsukappara was not the only execution ground in Edo; there was one or more in every town in Japan.

Why, one might wonder, if it so disapproved of the kabuki, would such a draconian regime have any compunction about wiping it out altogether? The answer lies in the advocations of Neo-Confucian sages who saw it in the same light as the brothels, close to which the theatres were significantly situated. The kabuki was deplorable, but to be maintained as a necessary evil. Officialdom advocated a parsimonious kind of 'all things in moderation'. And the things, be they brothels, theatres or even the lifestyles of the townsmen, were allowed to continue until they showed excessive symptoms of immoderation. As the government concerted efforts to repress them together, the townsmen made them progress together. In the licensed quarters, the home of amusements of every kind, social class and restrictions tended to fade along with the tolerated pursuit of pleasure. The licensed quarters of the Genroku era thus managed to become a cultural crucible from which fashion, theatre, literature and other arts evolved in symbiosis.

Edo's theatres burned down during the great fire of 1657, sending all their greatest exponents with their props and costumes rolling down the Tokaido road to seek fortunes in Kyoto and Osaka. Although it soon resumed, theatrical activity was not to attain the refinement of its newer southern counterparts for decades. Edo liked flash and flamboyance and the kabuki was most popular in the bombastic *Aragato* style, which was created and epitomized by the great Danjuro I. Actors incarnating macho super-swordsmen sported fantastical make-up and swaggered about the stage in outlandish brocaded costumes, freezing at climactic moments and posturing with their eyes crossed like Siamese cats to thunderous applause. *Aragato* is epitomized by Benkei, the formidable fighting monk and retainer to military hero Minamoto Yoshitsune, who the Edo stage turned into an effeminate youth customarily portrayed by the fairest of *onnagata*.

This was in no way considered degrading; it provided a more effective foil to the strutting Benkei. Yoshitsune's great beauty was an extreme stylization serving to make the ill-fated youthful hero's demise all the more tragic. Overall it was a matter of style rather than content, for in the Edo kabuki and the city in general, style was everything.

By the early days of the nineteenth century, Edo's kabuki had become a theatre of blood and thunder; the plays of the 'decadent' period epitomized by Tsuruya Nanboku were the stuff of murder most foul and ghostly revenge, featuring marvellously sinister stylizations and sadistic erotic overtones. First performed in 1817, Nanboku's *Sakurahime Azuma Bunsho* (*The Eastern Document and the Cherry Blossom Princess*) tells the perverse tale of an unfortunate princess exploited by a villainous lover. Always played by the most beautiful of *onnagata*, Sakurahime is the reincarnation of a *chigo*, one of the pretty boys kept in temples to palliate the physical frustrations of Buddhist monks.

This particular *chigo* died during a suicide pact he held with his lover, the priest Seigen. Demurring, Seigen survives to fall in love with Sakurahime. Sakurahime gives birth to a child, the fruit of an earlier love affair with a ruffian she does not realize murdered her father and brothers at the orders of a devious samurai. Winding through gruesome avenues of cruelty and horror, a convoluted plot eventually finds Sakurahime sold as a Yoshiwara prostitute. Pragmatically turning her adversity into an asset, she wastes no time in becoming a member of the courtesan élite. The baddies eventually beat Seigen to death, but only after horribly mutilating his face with acid. When his vengeful ghost tells

Sakurahime that her baby is the progeny of the man who murdered her family, she stabs the child to death. After a grand finale featuring the recovery of a stolen scroll (the 'Eastern Document' of the title) revealing Sakurahime's true aristocratic identity, everyone lives happily ever after. Pulling out all the stops, Namboku treated virtually every stratum of society with corrosive cynicism. Even his 'good' characters are sorely lacking in moral fibre. Such sociopathic excesses hardly endeared the kabuki to the *bakufu* government.

Along with other restrictions following the Ejima-Ikushima scandal in 1711, a good century before Namboku's time, the *bakufu* decreed that the roofs recently built over the kabuki theatres were to be removed. During the long period in which the *bakufu* was weakening, roofs had quietly reappeared over the playhouses again and boxes had been sprouting surreptitiously back around the walls. As in the European opera houses in Mozart's time, the kabuki theatre's private boxes afforded frolics of all kinds. Nowhere was the chasm between the Japanese authorities and the people as clearly illustrated as in the kabuki. Try as it might, officialdom could no more silence the earthy and expressive voice of the urban street than squash its inclinations.

The *bakufu* continued to take minor stabs at the kabuki until the end of the Edo period, but the final onslaught came with a virulent Neo-Confucian last gasp. Between 1841 and 1843, the draconian Tempo reforms decreed that all theatres not located in the vicinity of the pleasure quarters would have to go. The kabuki theatres dwindled from some five hundred to about fifteen. This time there were no ploys to disguise or restructure the genre. Not because of the law, but because it was too late. Like the *bakufu* government trying so hard to curtail it, the kabuki had entered its twilight. In just over twenty years' time, feudalism would be gone and Japan would be changed almost beyond recognition. By then the kabuki had at last become respectable but, in so doing, it had lost the patronage of the groundlings so eager for novelty and had become fossilized. As spectacular as it still is, the kabuki survives today as museum culture.

LOVE VERSUS DUTY

Born into a poor samurai family in Kyoto in 1653, Chikamatsu Monzaemon is still hailed as a Japanese equivalent to Shakespeare. His perceptive dramatic output reflects his familiarity with different walks of life and his greatest plays revolved around contemporary characters with whom city folk could most readily identify – the samurai, merchants, the little people and the courtesans. Heartily sick of the prima-donna whims of stars who tampered freely with plays to suit their inflated egos, Chikamatsu in fact wrote most of his for the *joruri* (or *bunraku*) puppet theatre rather than the kabuki stage. A pioneering realist, his greatest plays underscore society's relentless pressure on the individual; many were inspired by true occurrences and nearly all are tragic – especially those involving the *shinju* or double suicide.

Committed by lovers transgressing social rules, double suicides were as common in real life as they were popular on the stage. Chikamatsu wrote several plays on this theme, including *Sonezaki Shinju*, one of the most enduring favourites of the kabuki repertoire. The tragedy focuses on the humble Tokubei, a clerk in the employ of his merchant uncle, and the lovely courtesan Ohatsu. The two hope ardently that he will one day save enough to buy her out of the brothel. In the meantime,

Tokubei's aunt arranges to marry him off to a wealthy bride in order to wheedle a large dowry. This Tokubei eventually manages to retrieve from his aunt in order to return it to the parents of the girl he does not love.

Running into a needy friend, however, Tokubei lends him the money in the belief that it will be repaid the next day. Denying ever having been lent the money, the man publicly denounces Tokubei to discredit him. The only way out for Tokubei is to agree to go through with his aunt's and uncle's wedding plans, but his love for Ohatsu is too strong. The two commit suicide together in Sonezaki forest. Since their love was officially considered illicit, the *shinju* was the only way out.

Neo-Confucian dogma allowed a man to dally in the pleasure quarters, but not to fall in love. Given away to men they had never seen to suit their parents' material designs, women were even more strictly debarred from love than men. As Chikamatsu and many other playwrights suggested, however, love loomed large in the frustrated hearts of the Edo-period Japanese, and his most popular plays were those in which he never failed to bring home the inhumanity of such a situation. Chikamatsu also showed that honour was not just the preserve of the samurai but to be found among ordinary people, for they too abided by the concepts of *giri-ninjo*. The very basis of samurai loyalty, *giri* implies an uncompromising obligation towards employers, the family and the group. It is often in agonizing opposition to *ninjo*, which has been variously translated as 'humanity', 'sympathy', and summed up as 'personal inclination'. The world of *ninjo* is soft – the stuff of love, emotion, affections and, of course, sex. To the hard school, these things are trivial compared to the dutiful concept of *giri*, which still affects the daily run of things in a great many contexts in modern Japan. Torn between his corporate obligations and the desire to spend more time with his family, for instance, today's *salaryman* is still caught in the same predicament.

One can hardly deal with *giri* or the Japanese concept of loyalty without mentioning the *Tale of the Forty-Seven Ronin*, which was retold and glamorized in *Chushingura* – still one of the perennial favourites of the kabuki stage today. Emulated in this and many other plays from very shortly after the occurrence of actual events, the theme has been celebrated as many as a hundred times on film in the twentieth century. A saga invariably perplexing the western mind, it was banned from screen and stage by Occupation authorities bent on eradicating feudalism after the Second World War.

In 1701, during the course of an official meeting between daimio in the shogun's castle in Edo, the younger lord Asano questioned the elderly lord Kira on a point of etiquette. Laced with insulting sarcasm, old Kira's reply so infuriated the impetuous Asano that he drew his sword. Others intervened but not before Asano had taken a swing at Kira and slightly injured him. As much for this breach of conduct as for the outrage of drawing a sword in Edo castle, Asano was forced afterwards to commit *seppuku* at the shogun's orders. With their feudal lord dead and disgraced and his estate confiscated, Asano's vassals were now *ronin* – masterless samurai. Having plotted together for a full year to avenge their master, forty-seven of these at last murdered Kira one winter night. After presenting his severed head before Asano's grave, they quietly gave themselves up to the authorities.

To the Japanese, the rights and wrongs of Asano's behaviour are irrelevant. Although the truth is unknown, the plays and films invariably depict Kira as an irredeemable scoundrel. What really matters is that the forty-seven admirably fulfilled *giri*, sacrificing themselves blindly and utterly to defend the honour of their employer. Instead of executing the forty-seven *ronin* as common criminals, the shogun was greatly touched by their loyal zeal and conceded them the privilege of dying honourably. The forty-seven disembowelled themselves.

Being unattainable to all but a very fortunate few, love too was rigorously governed by *giri-ninjo*. Most of the characters in Chikamatsu's tragedies come to grief through nothing else. Tokubei cannot, as he might in the West, talk the whole thing over with his aunt and uncle and explain that he was cheated. Nor, having lost face, can he take any action against the wrongdoer except perhaps by killing him. Nor, in the Tokugawa police state, could Tokubei even think of eloping with Ohatsu to sunnier climes. His *giri* is towards his aunt and uncle, and all the greater since they are also his employers.

The unwritten rules in the contract binding Ohatsu to the brothel stipulate *giri* both towards her employers and her parents. It is easy to see why the prostitute made a great tragic heroine on-stage, for so she did in real life. What has saved prostitutes in Japan from the same social stigma as in the West is not just a matter of the fortunate lack of Christian morals. While looked down upon for exercising a profession running against the grain of Confucian virtue, girls sold into the licensed quarters by destitute parents were ennobled in the eyes of the public as poignant symbols of filial piety. They had sacrificed themselves.

THE FLOATING WORLD IN WORDS

> How cruel the floating world
> Its solaces how few –

And soon my unmourned life
Will vanish with the dew.

Ihara Saikaku, *The Woman Who Spent
Her Life in Love* (1642–93)

Education was no longer exclusive nor prohibitively expensive; quite early in the Edo period, some 40 per cent of the people had become literate and the majority of these evidently lived in the towns. Dynamic urban growth widened plebeian horizons, and it inevitably brought mass-production in its wake. Publishing houses thrived and popularization swept through the visual arts. With the notable exception of its various folk manifestations, Japanese art had by now long been an aristocratic preserve, but the Edo period saw the emergence of a variety of new genres. The potential of the woodblock print, a medium known since Heian times but uncommon, was ripe for exploitation on an unprecedented scale.

With its famous actors and courtesans and its sights, festivals, events and fast-changing fashions, the *ukiyo* was fertile ground for the cultivation of a popular culture. Given its main focus, it is hardly surprising that so much of the subject matter for books and pictures produced and sold in the *ukiyo* was erotic. Among the first popular woodblock prints to appear was a series illustrating a book published in 1660, which was evocatively entitled *Yoshiwara Makura* – *The Yoshiwara Pillow Book*.

Sensing the potential over the next few years, many painters working in both the classic Kano and Tosa styles gradually turned to designing woodblock prints. The single print was to come later; for the time being their talent found a highly lucrative outlet in illustrations for popular novels. Concentrating almost exclusively on the pleasure quarters, the literary genre coming rapidly to the fore was consequently called *ukiyo-zoshi* – novels of the floating world. Ribald and satirical in tone, the corrosive brushtip of Ihara Saikaku brought it to its zenith in 1686.

The prominent book illustrator Hishikawa Moronobu (1618–94) pioneered designing woodblock prints on single sheets. The Tosa and Kano schools had long depicted scenes from daily life and Moronobu, who had studied both, applied genre painting to the woodblock medium. The focus was again overwhelmingly on the sights and scenes in the streets, tea houses, brothels and theatres of the pleasure quarters, so it was hardly surprising that the style initiated by Moronobu and sweeping urban Japan became known as ukiyo-e – the pictures of the floating world.

Meanwhile, the Neo-Confucian sages in the employ of the *bakufu* had recently been distinguished with the title of 'Lords of Learning'. Aware that doctrineless Shinto left plenty of scope for loose behaviour and dissipation among the people, the learned lords managed a feat of ideological acrobatics by decreeing that Shinto and Confucianism were identical. Setting a precedent that was to be upheld long after the Tokugawa shoguns' decline, they succeeded in sending the currents of Neo-Confucianism flooding deeper into ordinary lives.

However much they prated about didactic and edifying literature and for all the published reams of tedious Neo-Confucian treatises, the books riveting the people in the streets were rather different; most were swashbuckling romances variously tinged with violence, comedy, the macabre and sex – with the odd ethical parable thrown in to give respectability. Containing few pages, Edo-period pulp fiction emphasized the picture, with *kana* script arranged decoratively around the figures and features it depicted. As in modern *manga* comic books, dialogue in the *e-hon* picture books sometimes consisted of clusters of words around the characters uttering them. Between lurid printed covers depicting the grimacing facial expressions of the kabuki, were facile tales akin to the Victorian penny dreadful.

During the Edo period, literature presented a great deal of variety, including poetry and history, and ranging between the extremes of learned tomes and pictorial pulp. Popular too were straight-faced guides and treatises on the pleasure quarters, brothel lore and sundry courtesans, such as Fujimoto Kizan's *Great Mirror of the Yoshiwara*. However florid the prose devoted to the floating world in these, for the most part it was bland, uncritical and uninspired. Yet here was a world of superficial dazzle and ritualized pleasure populated with rogues and hypocrites of all descriptions. There were devious merchants, scheming courtesans, fallen or slumming samurai, slimy sycophants, lecherous monks, horny nuns, vainglorious actors, ludicrous fops and fey spendthrifts. Of merchant birth, steeped deep in the floating world and prodigiously lucid, the writer Ihara Saikaku was well placed to scoff at the absurdities of the floating world, in which hordes of samurai and monks donned commoners' clothing to enter the quarters forbidden to their class and cloth. And when he did, he launched a genre known as *ukiyo-zoshi*, the novel of the floating world.

Blessed with great versatility, Saikaku was also an eminent and prolific haiku poet, and very capably designed woodblock prints to accompany his own tales. Published in 1682, his *Life of an Amorous Man* was fifty-four chapters long: so was Murasaki Shikibu's *Tale of Genji*. Trenchant satirist and literary parodist that he was, Saikaku was irreverently recasting the great

Shining Prince, the seducer at odds with fate and his own conscience, as a drifting rake tumbling some four thousand women through the pleasure quarters up and down the country. The last word in *ukiyo-zoshi*, the book was phenomenally popular. Within two years, it had not only been re-edited with illustrations by the great Suzuki Moronobu and pirated, but had also spawned innumerable imitators.

Inspired by Saikaku's travesty of *Genji*, other writers merrily sent prominent pieces of literature and weighty Confucian and Buddhist didactic works and parables into the realm of the brothels. Nothing was sacred. Like kabuki plays, some novels disguised factual scandals and, for those fond of things more purely pornographic, there were always titles such as *The Lascivious Little Tangled Bush*. A compendium in 1778 included *The History of the Famous Courtesan Who Plucked Out Her Pubic Hair*, defused with the sub-heading, *And the Korean Kokeishi Saved by His Father's Foresight*. Writers often cautiously redeemed volleys of parody with Confucian ethics, their profligates coming to edifying, if not always convincing, sticky ends. The stories could, however, reflect the tragedy haunting the Ukiyo like a shadow, often winding up with lacrimose love-suicides or melodramatic executions. For all his caricatures and merry social satire, Saikaku's tragedies were genuinely poignant; his vision was less uncritically fatalistic than the majority of his peers. Several of his tales were based on true events involving those falling foul of edicts such as these:

> Persons such as those who have engaged in illicit intercourse with their master's daughter or who have attempted such: Death.
> Persons such as those who commit adultery with their master's wife or with their teacher's wife: Death for both the man and the woman.

Those who propose adultery or who send love letters to their master's wife: Death or banishment.

A pardon could nevertheless be conceded to a servant bearing letters between the lovers, but not in the case of 'Persons accessory to adultery with a master's wife' who, naturally, were rewarded with 'Death'.

If the adulterer was his equal, however, the woman's husband or father was free to draw his sword and execute him or both of them on the spot, but such cases were often not pursued. A high-ranking samurai finding his wife dallying with a commoner, on the other hand, could have them both crucified. If a father or husband was moved to prosecute a man of lower rank, it was also because social pressures were such that he had to. The conventions of duty overruled any compassion or capacity for forgiveness. To let the seducer or guilty wife go free was to lose face; a matter of falling into complete dishonour and disrepute dragging one's family down also.

Like Chikamatsu's plays, Saikaku's novellas made one oppressively aware of social restrictions and the dispro-portionate savagery of sentences for minor offences. Saikaku's characters leave the reader in little doubt that their crime resided solely in falling in love. One of his most famous tales, for instance, concerns fifteen-year-old Oshichi who, having temporarily moved to a mon-astery with her parents after their house has burned down, has a passionate first affair with a young monk. Driven to distraction when her parents veto this socially prohibited liaison, she unsuccessfully attempts to burn down their newly constructed home. Arrested as an arsonist, she is burned at the stake. Oshichi's story was based on a real tragedy.

Similarly from a wealthy merchant background and a

great admirer of his elder contemporary Saikaku, Ejima Kiseki was born in 1667. A profligate living above his means and consuming the family fortune after his father's death, he profitably turned his corrosive wit to fiction about wastrels who had followed paths similar to his own. Less given to telling stories, Kiseki's popular works amounted more to ironical, perceptive portraits of *ukiyo* stock-in-trades in prose. Focusing on disloyal sons and daughters, his witty observations are sparked very often by disapproval of those who fail to live up to orthodox standards of Confucian behaviour. Yet, focusing on prigs or bigots, some of his tales could be rather rude about Confucianists too. As Howard Hibbett explained, 'Kiseki implies that most Confucianists are tireless, supercilious bores – Sinophiles who disdain not only Buddhism and the businessman's point of view, but indeed all opinions except their own.'

Although he set many of his male profligates' adventures in rousing rather than critical brothel settings, Kiseki seems a far more convinced Confucian in his *Characters of Worldly Young Women* than in *Characters of Worldly Young Men*. 'Few women of former times – courtesans excepted – used oil of aloes-wood, but now young ladies smear it down to their navels,' he lamented caustically. A few paragraphs later on he sums it all up: 'In general it may be said that a woman's morals nowadays are as changeable as a cat's eyes.'

If Saikaku shared such opinions, he conceded, ever the realist, that a woman's beauty was an asset that she could not unreasonably turn to her advantage. More of a humanist than a moralist, Saikaku's accounts of the floating world are vividly nuanced tragi-comedies. Where his wit and perception were at their most acute was in the realm of prostitution. *The Woman Who Spent Her Life in Love* is a picaresque account given by a destitute, eccentric old Buddhist nun reminiscing over a life running the whole gamut of the profession. Her listeners are two young rakes, who note that the scent of the incense filling her hermit's hut is more proper to the whore-house than the temple. Hers has been a long journey from noble birth and early ruin, up to the top rank in the pleasure quarters of Kyoto and a marriage to a nobleman, then down again into the pits.

She's a crafty old bird, to be sure, and she brags rather than confesses to her rapt audience about the many tricks and wiles she used during her long horizontal career. The fact is, she was simply crazy about sex. Even during the brief episodes when she marries and goes off the game, she can never overcome her hot response to male overtures. Ultimately, she is rendered pathetic not so much through misfortune coming as the karmic retribution for sin, but from the ravages of time. Her rank as a prostitute decreases commensurate with her advancing years. For all his merry cynicism, however, Saikaku was hardly blind to the seamier side of the profession. He knew well that although poverty had driven almost all the frail sisters into the floating world, for every tragic waif there were several vixens who were not quite as uncomfortable in the brothels as latter-day moralists would like to believe. In Edo-period Japan, many girls were much better off in the pleasure quarters than they could ever be at home.

In *The Life of an Amorous Man*, the rake's progress graced with Moronobu's prints, one of Saikaku's characters looks at ragged, squalid streetwalkers in a north-western fishing town, and launches into a poignant lament. On a more cynical note, the man making this remark is a wholesaler who just happens to run a rather neat and cheery little brothel as a sideline himself. But there were whore-houses and whore-houses, so perhaps his lament is perfectly sincere:

> 'Some of them earn money in this way to help out aged parents, others with no other means of family livelihood are forced into the clandestine trade. Mothers leave their babies with grandma. Older sisters sacrifice younger sisters. Uncles, aunts, nieces, all exploit one another just to keep body and soul together … They know nothing of the pleasures of moon viewing, nothing of the beauty of the snow, nothing of the happiness of the new year. Oh, the ignominy, the misery, the pity of it all!'

SPRING IN PICTURES

From the late 1680s, publishing and book illustration were booming industries. After Moronobu's death in 1694, Nishikawa Sukenobu acquired renown for his illustrations of Ejima Kiseki's novels and scores of contemporaries were jumping on the bandwagon. Art was affordable for the first time; prints of popular kabuki actors found avid buyers as soon as they were off the press. Like most artists in the *ukiyo*, Moronobu's subject matter for 'scenes from daily life' was inspired both from the sights of the city in general and straight from the brothels. There was a brisk market for varyingly pornographic *warai-bon* (laughing books) and *sharebon* (joke books), as well as for the explicit *makura-e* 'pillow pictures' ostensibly devised to inspire newlyweds unfamiliar with their conjugal duties. The more explicit prints soon required a proper generic name setting them apart, and since the pictures concentrated so graphically on the intrinsics of a business known as *baishun* (selling spring) the obvious choice was *shunga* – Spring Pictures.

Reflecting idealizations of beauty rather than reality,

Moronobu's appealingly plump characters tended to come in twos and were shown engaged in some highly private activities, but his *shunga* were genteel and refined despite their blatancy. His was a delicate world in which a handsome young samurai might be explicitly shown dallying with a delicate belle, very much in the Chinese Ming dynasty style, in a garden of flowers and willow trees. Depicting other sides of life too, Moronobu and his peers did not confine themselves solely to the erotic side of the pleasure quarters. Popular too were the *bijinga*, or pictures of beautiful women, which were idealized portraits of celebrated courtesans. Moronobu and other artists depicted a wealth of scenes and sights in the streets and shops of Edo in general, but the *shunga* and *bijinga* were probably more lucrative. In what Saikaku called the City of Bachelors, pornography no doubt furnished solitary pleasures and the *bijinga* were moreover a means of advertising the brothels in which the beauties worked.

Japan has never been too preoccupied with realism. For the next two hundred years, the *ukiyo* artists reduced their subject matter to graphic icons and ciphers; within the scope of the different styles and formulae they learned from their masters or occasionally set themselves, all their subjects looked the same. An additional attraction to love-starved Edoites was that the early *shunga*, although similarly ciphers of femininity and sexuality, were sweetened with a note of romanticism, which was to sour with cynicism and lurid exaggeration towards the end of the era. Although there was much repetition and stylistic convention, *ukiyo-e* showed a great deal of variety and their bold and subtle concepts of design would one day change the course of western painting.

The earlier *ukiyo-e* had been printed entirely in black

ink but Masanobu, another prolific illustrator with considerable skill in *shunga* subjects, introduced two-colour printing in the early eighteenth century. Suzuki Harunobu (1725–70), however, introduced true polychrome printing with what was called *nishiki* or brocade pictures. Clothing was an aspect vital to the genre, and the term implies that the pictures were as beautifully hued as fabrics. Representing their real-life counterparts only in name, Harunobu's more elaborately illustrated courtesans prompted coinage of the expression *Harunobu-bijinga* in contradistinction to the *bijinga* by everyone else. Compared to Harunobu's more sophisticated stylizations, work by many of his contemporaries still looked naive and primitive. Frequently printed with pigments mixing real gold and silver, Harunobu's expensive *ukiyo-e* held considerable appeal to merchants, for the precious metals added a touch of class.

However great the emphasis on clothing, it was often partially, strategically, explicitly but never entirely removed. Reflecting Ming influences and often daintily disporting themselves in a prettified outdoors, Harunobu's winsome *femmes enfants* are exquisite little things looking only slightly more cherubic than their male partners. Japanese refinement has a way of fostering the epicene; in the real world outside the prints, many *tsu* dandies cultivating a studied androgynous look were quite as obsessively preoccupied with style and attire as women. Many habitually bragged of their intimacy with courtesans and their affairs with kabuki actors in the same breath. There were brothels for homosexuals called *hage mazaya*, and *ukiyo-e* print masters such as Masanobu and Harunobu catered to the persuasion with prints featuring the merry sodomization of young *chigo*. Despite circumspection regarding lesbianism, it was not uncommonly treated among *shunga* artists easy to please everyone. By the early nineteenth century, pictures inspired from ribald folk legend even found the odd wanton tumbling with a dog or a horse.

Shunga themes were self-explanatory, but many enhanced their content with texts. For all its wealth of Chinese influence, Japan never produced anything approaching the prolixity of the erotic sagas of the Ming dynasty. Japanese erotic literature was given more to innuendo than anatomical details and explicitness resided mostly in the illustration. Using captions, the single prints often told jokes. A charming couple by Harunobu, for instance, stand in the snow making love propped up against a tree. 'Ah, this is so much better than the usual way,' says the young man. 'Surely,' replies his charming companion, 'you must be joking!'

Reflecting their beginnings in books, other *shunga* employed dialogues placing their contorted protagonists in a context revealing who, what and where they were. A late eighteenth-century example finds an old husband with his ear pressed to the floorboards. His curiosity has been aroused by sounds coming from below, but he does not realize that their source is in fornication between his nubile wife and a lusty young neighbour in the space beneath the house.

'Whatever can those strange sucking noises be?' the old man wonders. 'I must ask my wife.'

'I wish I could do this only with you,' murmurs the wife to her lover meanwhile. 'Just make the old codger do it as often as you can,' he replies, 'and send him to an early grave.'

A universal favourite, the cuckold is frequently represented in *shunga* both as a dotard and as the perennial absentee. Several prints, for example, show a man attentively fondling his lover's exposed genitalia after a long separation: 'Someone else has been in here. It feels wider.' In one eighteenth-century instance the recurring theme involves a geisha reunited with a patron, and in an early nineteenth-century print by Kunyoshi, the man making exactly the same remark is perhaps a samurai official returning home: 'Why would anyone want to waste their time with me?' his wife protests, adding rather huffily: 'Stop looking at it like that, you're putting me off.'

Of samurai birth but an artist by inclination, Isoda Koryusai was a close friend and pupil of Harunobu. Before turning full time to painting, he further refined the art of *shunga* during the 1760s and seventies. Notwithstanding its explicitness, Harunobu's work had been rather aloof, but Koryusai excelled at subtle hints at spontaneity and a more intimate atmosphere. Considering that not a shadow of emotion clouds the blank expressions on the lovers' faces, this is no mean feat. Koryusai's bettered mere stylization with a wealth of evocative details and visual allusions making the prints more realistic. One, for example, shows lovers elegantly entwined on a balcony. Behind them lies a snowscape; their passion is such that they don't even feel the cold. The action subtly suggests a lapse of time: he is on the point of penetrating her and she, languidly spreading her legs and quite overcome with desire, seems to be loosening her grip on the samisen she had no doubt just been playing. Koryusai was also partial to depictions of intercourse with adolescent girls. Neither rape scenes nor the equally common theme of an Edo-period Lolita paired off with an ageing roué, they usually portrayed the union between a young girl and a lover barely older than herself.

Like most *ukiyo-e* artists, Kitagawa Utamaro (1753–1806) first rose to prominence by churning out pictures of actors and scenes from the *kabuki*. Becoming the ultimate painter and innovator in the *bijinga* line, Utamaro immortalized the courtesan aristocracy and the newly emerging geisha élite for all time; their exquisite 'melon-seed' faces launched a thousand emulators in Japan, and his style came to be greatly revered in Europe. Whether it was *The Twelve Hours of a Brothel*, showing the girls' activities outside of their bedrooms, or whether a portrait depicted Komurasaki of the house called Tamaya or Hanatsuma of the Hyogoya, Utamaro's courtesans were basically indistinguishable. Yet the degree of variety in their expressions is astonishing. It is suggested with even greater subtlety than Koryusai, in composition and settings, colours, body positions or the direction of a glance, by the way a dainty hand holds an accessory such as a mirror, a comb or a pipe and by the vigorous flow of clothing. As regal and aloof as they are winsome and sexy, Utamaro's foxy courtesans seem animated by sly duplicity. He not only introduced the head-and-shoulders portrait but also used dauntingly difficult transparency to consummate effect: a girl's face seen through the tulle fabric she holds up to admire, a couple graphically making love behind a mosquito net on a torrid summer night. Deference to Utamaro's genius is reflected in today's *mizu shobai*, in which dozens of brothels and massage parlours carry his name.

Naturally, the artistic merits of *ukiyo-e* were lost on the government. When sporadic clampdowns loomed, *shunga* exponents were always careful to redeem their reputations with other subjects. Yet sex was generally tolerated in the areas allotted it and, with the notable exception of Sukenobu, whose *shunga* suffered an official ban in 1722, those who kept their work strictly below the belt and devoid of open criticism seldom came to grief until government reforms tightened later on. It is probably no coincidence that versatile Kuniyoshi, as famous for his ghost and warrior prints as his *shunga*, should have designed an atypical *Twenty-Four Chinese Paragons of Filial Piety* during the 1840s, shortly after the notorious Tempo reforms.

Stringent reforms nevertheless came during the eighteenth century too. Underlying the bigotry of the Kyoho reforms drawn up between 1716 and 1736 and the Kansei reforms between 1787 and 1793 were austerity measures to boost the flagging shogunate's income. The idea was also to curb the power of the townsmen and show them who was boss, and the reforms carried sumptuary laws and various restrictions on clothing, books, theatres, etc. in their wake. While heads could fall literally and figuratively elsewhere, the *ukiyo* soon slipped back into its old sybaritic ways after a cursory observation of the new rulings. Samurai haunted the pleasure quarters increasingly; they had long ceased to bother with disguises.

Lulled by the hedonism of the floating world, Utamaro trod less carefully. Nothing more than an illustration to a historical work, his depiction of the sixteenth-century shogun Toyotomi Hideyoshi with five concubines was not in the least indecent but, to the *bakufu*, it held political overtones. Seen as a slur on samurai prestige, Utamaro's offence was tantamount to *lèse-majesté* and in 1804 he was thrown in jail. Although he was imprisoned for only a few days, his sentence included the humiliation of being manacled for two months, and the incident broke his spirit. Following a long period of acute depression, Utamaro died in 1806.

A recluse, an eccentric who could never sit still and something of a profligate, the great Hokusai was a prodigiously hard worker; he called himself the Madman of Painting. Born in 1760 and the adopted son of a mirror-maker, Hokusai is said to have moved house ninety-three times in his ninety years. Much of his work represented a triumph of individual artistry over stylized conventions and, to western impressionists, it was of a quality comparable to that of Rembrandt. Hokusai, revered everywhere today for his great artistic genius, greatly influenced their style. In his time, the very versatile 'madman' was renowned as much for fine landscapes such as the famed *Thirty-six Views of Mount Fuji* series as he was for prints with birds and flowers, genre themes, ghosts and *shunga*. Quite naturally, he excelled in erotica too; to Hokusai, who was equally moved to draw most aspects of the world about him, sex was as perfectly natural as anything else.

'Hokusai' is his most frequent and best remembered name, but he signed his works with different ones almost as frequently as he changed places of residence. 'Shishoku Ganko', an allusion to a rampant penis, was the one he fondly reserved for signing his many *shunga*. Some of these, like the ecstatic woman in the slippery cunnilingual embrace of a giant octopus, which is often hailed as a subtle metaphor for female orgasm, are world famous. Less widely circulated are items such as Hokusai's detailed vulvar close-ups, for the master's *shunga* could be clinical in the extreme. The model he used for some of his erotic subjects is thought by many to have been his daughter Oei, with whom he lived alone until his death. It is widely believed that he found the energy to have an incestuous relationship with Oei despite his advanced age.

Given to wild exaggeration, the prints of the early nineteenth-century 'decadents' are mirror reflections of kabuki plays like Tsuruya Namboku's. They similarly featured costumes almost stifling in their ornateness, stylization bordering on the sinister and a marked predilection for the macabre. The tendency to enlarge the genitals had been typical of Japanese erotica at least since *yamato-e* erotic scrolls of the early sixteenth century, but the 'decadent' *shunga* blew them up out of all proportion. Utagawa Kuniyoshi (1797–1861), an illustrator of fantasy and warrior themes who turned to *shunga* in 1828, favoured prurient illustrations of scandals between famous actors and ladies of high breeding. Unlike their more aesthetically minded predecessors, Kuniyoshi, his pupils and their many imitators seemed to darken their *shunga* with a foreboding note of morbidity.

Their clothing in wild disarray and contorted into exaggeratedly tortuous coital positions, the men and women portrayed look like the slaves of their own grossly enlarged and gluttonously interconnected genitals. Crumpled tissue paper litters the mattress and floor and the couple are gushing with effluvia, their jaws have dropped open and, in faces suggesting agony, dementia and death, their eyes are revolved to show only the whites. During the 1840s, perhaps due as much to the repressive Tempo reforms as to the economic crisis, the pleasure seemed to be waning from the pleasure quarters. The pursuit of erotic love had become something desperate, excessive, violent and deadly serious.

Utagawa Kunisada (1786–1864), who often signed himself Toyokuni III as a tribute to his master, was an all-rounder excelling in *kabuki* prints. He was renowned as an eroticist, and his *shunga* so frequently focused on rape and sadism that he was sometimes called the Master of Forceful Love. Sex and the macabre made fine bedfellows. A famous phantasmagorical *shunga* by Kunisada shows an eerie highlight from *The Peony Lantern*, a popular old tale about a young man who receives nightly visits from his beloved, without realizing that she has been dead for months. Kunisada's lover ejaculates between the empty ribs of a skeleton lying on top of him.

By the end of the nineteenth century, when *shunga* had been banned for more than twenty years and styles began to westernize, artists such as Yoshitoshi designed prints melding classic *bijinga* beauties with fantasy and horror themes. Best known for his subtle illustrations for ghost stories, Yoshitoshi was irreproachable. A genre popular during Meiji and Taisho and early Showa, however, revelled in the pornography of violence. Blood-spattered, often depicting torture and spilled entrails in loving detail, these prints never disturbed the government in the least. Like the direct equivalent in modern *manga* comic-books, they showed no genital organs, so they weren't about sex.

SHUNGA MESSAGES

Few examples of erotica in the world tell us as much about the sex fantasies and practices of a people as do the *shunga* of Japan. The common presence of children, for instance, shows just how very uninhibited and frank about sex the Japanese were. Until children reached puberty, there was precious little '*pas devant les enfants*' among the populace. The *shunga* show couples copulating before their small and occasionally not-so-small children, although these pictures are usually coloured with humour arising from evasive and fanciful answers to the child's question: 'What are you doing?' Then as now, it seems that talk of sex elicited more reluctance than its pursuit.

The prevalence of third parties evidences a conscious vehicle for the viewer's vicarious voyeurism, and sometimes these are animals. Hokusai, for instance, lent a charming note of humour to one famous *shunga* by depicting mice mating alongside a couple similarly engaged. Just as it can be a child gazing enquiringly at his parents' amours, so the witness can frequently be a *kamuro* spying upon her courtesan mistress's erotic embraces in the bedroom. As it was in John Cleland's *Fanny Hill*, so this too was an intrinsic part of the brothel novice's training. The pleasure quarters were a paradise for voyeurs. Sliding screen doors dividing rooms could always be opened a crack, and the flimsy *shoji* doors of latticed wood giving out onto the corridor often had spyholes torn in their thin white paper covering. This was as much for the benefit of the *kamuro*'s education as to cater for the Peeping Tom, another stalwart in the *shunga* repertory.

A famous variant is the lilliputian Mamesuke. A lubricious Tom Thumb found tucked away in a panoramic corner in a great many *shunga*, the 'bean man' spends his entire life creeping around rooms in the gay quarters to ogle couples on the job. One phantasmagorical diptych of the decadent period shrinks him down far enough to show him emerging triumphant from an enormous vulva in the first, only to find himself confronted by a rampant, towering penis in the next.

The number of scraps of crumpled tissue paper littering the floor in most *shunga* prints not only betrays the ardour of the couple on the mattress but also points to their extravagance, for paper was an expensive commodity. We discover also that the courtesans plucked and trimmed their pubic hair, leaving only a pretty little wisp to adorn the top of the mons Veneris. With themes such as 'Preliminary Inspection' or 'The *Shunga* Artist at Work', not to mention big, anatomically detailed close-ups and even entire catalogues devoted solely and clinically to the different varieties of vulvae, erotic prints point to Japan's uninhibited male adulation of the female genitalia. The *shunga* also tell us all about dildos and sex-aids. They depict open promiscuity in public baths and reveal that some brothels consisted of latticed cubicles hardly even suggesting privacy. We know at a glance that monks and kabuki actors liked youths and little boys and vice versa, that nuns liked each other or were given to solitary pleasures.

One suspects a partiality for group sex too. Although orgies on a grand scale were common in the countryside and by no means unheard of in brothels, depictions of these are inexplicably rare. Perhaps it was dismissed as the practice of country bumpkins, and not recherché enough for the floating world. Nevertheless, many *shunga* focus on three or more protagonists and they are often bizarre. Here, for instance, a single profligate's little brothel game: blindfolded, he takes pot luck as he follows his erection while he gropes his way towards four nude prostitutes lying offered before him. There, a print of a dandy sodomizing a youth having intercourse with a young girl. Heterosexual threesomes were more common, but one man with two women seems to have been rarer than the reverse. Frequently used by men today, the term *mara-kyodai* (penis brothers) reflects a peculiar macho predilection, which some psychologists see as homosexuality by proxy, in the idea of a woman shared.

Shunga often show one waiting his turn as his comrade finishes his business, and this is not infrequently a rape theme with the unfortunate woman elaborately trussed up with her legs forced apart with a wooden pole behind her knees. Over and above sadistic fantasy, we gather too that travel was dangerous, especially for women. Borne along the post roads in palanquins, they could be raped by bandits or even by their two bearers, and some wanton hussies even gave themselves quite willingly to one or both of them.

Burlesque humour in the *shunga*, like that of Rabelais, is not infrequently without an underlying streak of cruelty. Yet one should be wary of passing hasty judgements. As callous as the young man's comment about getting his girlfriend to fuck her old husband to death mentioned earlier seems, the intended implication is of a young woman forced into a wholly unsuitable match with a crusty old dotard. For all the bizarre and sadistic subject matter and whether or not the settings were brothel rooms, boats or homes, the pictures and the smattering of text most often bring home that the couple in question, with their outsize interconnected genitals and eyes upturned like kitsch Italian saints, are much more likely to be in the passionate throes of love than of a casual carnal encounter. The impact of the print lies as much in titillation as in the allusion to love, the true forbidden fruit.

One particularly violent and macabre print of the decadent period shows the aftermath of a double suicide. Scraps of tissue paper litter the blood-spattered floor and the semi-nude couple lie together in a stiff embrace. The man sprawls over his lover's body with a sword-point sticking out of his back and the woman's throat is cut from ear to ear. Beneath her upturned, dead eyes, exaltation and triumph seem frozen together in a hideous smile. The scene is redolent with grim humour and powerful social protest lurks behind it. It finds a parallel in the macabre expressionist cartoons of George Grosz or Otto Dix, who were similarly working in a period of grey depression and oppression, during which the desperate quest for libertarianism was not always such a successful antidote to despair.

11

Spring for Sale

LA VIE EN ROSE – EDO STYLE

> Being scarce nowadays, Tayu may be compared to the
> cherry blossom, for as no other flowers can equal the
> cherry in point of colour and fragrance, in like manner
> the beauty and loveliness of the Tayu surpasses all
> courtesans.
>
> From an early eighteenth-century commentary on
> the ranks of courtesans in the Yoshiwara

Ah, spring. Nowhere is this most auspicious of seasons
more celebrated than in Japan, where its herald is the most
exalted of trees, the *sakura*. Not just a tree, the cherry
is an institution. The delicate pink flowers perfectly
blend the Shinto red and white, blossom during the
season of the old fertility rites and, fading fast after their
ephemeral glory, epitomize the poignant Buddhist
concept of the transitoriness of the world. Blessed with a
cherry tree, even the greyest corner of modern Tokyo
can look beautiful beyond compare. 'If only we might fall
like cherry blossoms' goes a famous verse written by a
young kamikaze pilot on the eve of his death. The
flowers of the cherry tree were also a favourite metaphor
for the prostitutes of the Yoshiwara. What the latter had
in common with the airborne suicide was that after their
brief flowering, they were exalted through self-sacrifice
and often similarly doomed.

Even when constrained to arm themselves with
umbrellas, untold hordes take to the parks in late March
and early April for the ancient custom of *hanami* – flower

watching. Rugs, plastic sheeting or flattened cardboard boxes are laid out on the ground for a mass picnic. Groups of office workers, students, families and people from every conceivable walk of life sit in their hundreds of thousands beneath the blushing blossoms, especially in places such as Ueno park. Munching through *bento* packed lunches and drinking until dusk and sometimes beyond, many will hardly be able to see their way home, let alone admire the flowers.

Bibulous *hanami* is still a time-honoured activity and certainly a lot of fun, but it withers before the resplendent Genroku equivalent. Merchant princes, rakish *tsu* dandies, kabuki actors, geisha and ladies of wealth and leisure partied beneath the soft snowfall of pale pink, picking at expensive delicacies from fine lacquered boxes as they were tended by cowed retinues of servants. Having stretched wind curtains of fine printed cloth between the trees, fashionable ladies competed in vying for attention by changing kimonos several times behind them during the course of a single extravagant afternoon. Their finery was always hued to match the hazy canopy of pale pink, and their elaborate *shimada* coiffures were spiked with combs and long bodkins of lacquer and tortoiseshell. 'It was once believed that excessive virtue is typical of young ladies,' remarked the satirist Ejima Kiseki. 'Now, however, mother and daughter alike behave immodestly: they ape the manner of harlots and courtesans.'

Indeed, these ladies' kimonos were inspired from the styles worn by the *tayu*, who were the harbingers of fashion in early Edo-period Japan. The same goes for their exquisitely embroidered brocade *obi* sashes, of course, but with one notable difference. Ordinary women wore theirs tied in a large bow at the back, but those called *jorō* or *yujō* were ladies of the evening and they denoted their calling by tying theirs in front. Among their ranks precious few were *tayu*; that was a title bestowed only upon the harlots of the highest order, the queens of the profession. Their elaborately fashioned chignon was widely adopted at the time and, even today, is replicated in the wigs worn by geisha and set upon the head of the Japanese bride.

During *hanami* parties, the *tayu* and other members of the Yoshiwara courtesan élite staged glittering dancing spectaculars in pastel silks and satins beneath the clouds of blossoms in nearby Ueno. Perhaps indulging a necessary evil in the eyes of the shogunate and certainly 'living on immoral earnings' in the view of many later foreign visitors, these nymphs were engaged in a profession more daintily known to the ordinary Japanese then as now as *baishun* – selling spring. A similar ranking system crowned by *tayu* had existed in the old brothel quarter of Yanagimachi, but from the earliest Yoshiwara days their number had never been more than about a score. Meeting a *tayu* was a very expensive privilege and, by the middle of the eighteenth century, there were only about three or four in all Edo. It was no doubt to give them an aura of greater accessibility that the Yoshiwara courtesan élite was subsequently called Yobidashi, meaning the coming-out-when-called.

If she could come out when called, a prostitute could never go very far. A girl was commonly sold to a brothel during childhood under a contract, which often stipulated that she was to remain there for twenty years, and she was absolutely forbidden to leave until it came to term. There were two notable exceptions: one, viewing the cherry blossoms in groups under strict surveillance and, two, visiting dying parents or attending the funeral of the same.

Like their inmates, the brothels in the licensed quarter

fell into ranks and categories clearly demarcated both by the government and the trade. Forever changing, the classification of brothels and their inhabitants alike evolved through complex histories and etymologies, often indicating migrations from the pleasure quarters of Kyoto and Osaka. The nomenclature in the floating world was thus as much subject to the vagaries of dialect as it was to pricing systems, and classifications were further liable to change whenever the government decreed reforms.

Courtesans throughout the pleasure quarters always addressed their seniors as *oiran*, which originally meant 'rare flower'. In the late eighteenth century, the term came to be used as a general name for the cream of the crop. If the Meiji-era whore could hope to work her way up the hierarchy of the entire profession until she became an *oiran*, the *tayu* of yore rose only within the context of a single brothel of the top class. In the eighteenth century, one did not simply walk off the street into one of the better brothels for a spot of the other; that sort of thing was available among the *tsubone-jorō* who, as one Genroku period commentator put it, were 'an exceedingly low class of women and their houses were frequented by the riff-raff and scum of the neighbourhood exclusively'.

Ranks went down through the middling *Sancha* (unsifted tea, i.e. indiscriminate) and *heya-mochi* (the have-rooms) to the *teppo*, the 'guns' who, as the name suggests, were the summary purveyors of wham-bam-thank-you-ma'am. In a class of their own were the *yakko*, solely comprising of samurai adulteresses who, if lucky to be spared their lives, were sent into the brothels as a punishment. Then there were the *jigoku* – the 'hell' prostitutes who were unlicensed. Some of these might be beauties working in the illegal brothels and bogus bath-houses which continued to exist elsewhere in spite of official repression, not to mention those who plied their trade in gaily lanterned little boats on the nearby Sumida river. Once caught, they were dealt with rather leniently, for they were mostly picked up and parked in brothels in the Yoshiwara itself. There were some *jigoku* practising clandestinely even there, but their appeal was debatable. Frequently diseased crones with layers of macabre white make-up cracking over their syphilitic sores, the *jigoku* plied their trade with a rolled quilt under one arm, perhaps enticing some hapless drunk down a dark alleyway near the fetid Yoshiwara moat.

When nightfall was announced by a nearby temple bell, the *yujo* entered brightly illuminated cages faced with vertical bars of crimson wood. Their elaborate hairstyles were adorned with a halo of spiky bodkins so that each looked like some pagan madonna; their lips framed darkness as deep as the night outside. Until Meiji times, the majority of *yujo* blackened their teeth with metallic *haguro* lacquer like married women. With their whitened necks and faces emerging from silken brocades, they pursed little scarlet mouths as they posed according to rank, looking for all the world like dolls arrayed on shelves for Hina matsuri – the national girls' festival. Some puffed seductively on tiny brass tobacco pipes with long stems and cooed at passing prospects, others made little toys of folded paper which they handed over to the admirers to whom they whispered enticingly through the bars. The height of the lattices determined the class of the establishment; set low down enough to cause the passer-by to stoop, the long narrow windows of the sordid lowest class were faced with horizontal bars.

It was well-nigh impossible for a girl starting life in one of the lowlier bordellos to cross the threshold of the Seiro

– the Green Houses, the opulent domain of the *taiyu*, let alone to become one herself. Purchased very young, likely fodder for the Green Houses had to show signs of becoming both remarkably pretty and exceptionally accomplished. All higher ranking courtesans were expected to offer a great deal more than sexual satisfaction. From as young as six years old, girls started their calling as a *kamuro*, a female page in the service of a courtesan, whom they were to address as *ane-jorō* – elder-sister whore. If the brothel-keepers found a particularly promising child, they would exempt her from some of her duties as a servant, and have her educated at their own expense. The gifted *kamuro* was not only taught to read and write but also to play the samisen or the koto, to sing, dance and to compose poetry.

Whether she qualified for grooming and finishing or not, the *kamuro* eventually became a *shinzo* – an apprentice courtesan. The debatable honour befell her shortly after her first menstrual period which, as in the home, was customarily marked by the ritual preparation of a dish of rice and red beans. During the ensuing merry-making, this was shared among the brothel inmates and portions were also sent around to the teahouses, along with other guileful presents such as sake cups inscribed with the newcomer's name. Whether or not the *shinzo* shared in the general gaiety is conjectural; she would shortly be summarily deflowered by a brothel proprietor or a privileged customer.

The daughter of an impoverished former samurai and the Meiji era's most promising woman author, consumptive young Higuchi Ichiyō lived towards the end of her short life on the confines of the Yoshiwara. Most famous among her vivid depictions of life in the quarter during the 1890s is the tragi-comic tale *Takekurabe* (*Growing Up*), which evokes the predicament of a future brothel inmate. Made into a popular film by Heinosuke Gosho in 1955, it concerns pretty young Midori, whose sister is a celebrated *oiran* in a prominent Yoshiwara brothel. As the haughty, pampered little girl grows up taking the fact that the local brothel-keepers spoil her for granted, her blissful ignorance is gradually marred by despondent misgivings she never quite understands. Subtle hints, however, leave the reader in no doubt. One is made poignantly aware that Midori's carefree childhood is over: she will soon inexorably be forced to follow in her sister's footsteps.

Singly or severally, the *shinzo* spent a week or so parading the five streets of the Yoshiwara in the company of their *ane-jorō*, being introduced around the teahouses and distributing promotional gifts. Back in the brothel, they would have been given congratulatory presents by the other inmates, which would have to be repaid in kind. The fledgling courtesans would now have been assigned rooms of their own, the '*kashikiki-zashiki*' or 'loan-rooms', and provided with gorgeous bedding and gaudy silken finery – all of which would be deducted from their wages. Regardless of her eventual success and unless she was lucky enough to find a patron who redeemed and married her, ensuring that a courtesan worked on to the end of her contract simply meant keeping a *yujo* in perpetual debt from her first day.

She had to allow for New Year and midsummer gift-giving, and substantial tips had to be given to members of the brothel staff, especially to the draconian and ubiquitous chaperones called *yarite*, the brothel hags, who were usually retired *jorō* themselves. Like the whores, the *yarite* came under the ultimate command of the madam, who was addressed as *obasan*: 'auntie'.

Facing declining years with nowhere else to go, the *yarite* could be embittered and vindictive. Then there were the *wakaimono* – the 'youths'. Wearing blue denim tunics printed with the brothel crest over torsos given to copious tattoos, they acted as messengers, servants and bouncers. Whether actually young or not, they were in most cases seasoned toughs fervently dedicated to the proper enforcement of brothel regulations. How kindly disposed all these people were towards the *yujo* could often be reckoned in cash.

Yujo were also forever forced to spend their earnings on large, resplendent wardrobes, for their popularity with patrons resided as much in their natural attributes as in their attire. To offset the beauty of her white flesh, the *yujo*'s quilts and futon mattresses were made of deep red or purple silks and satins, as well as dauntingly expensive dark velvets. During the course of the special *tsumi-yagu* annual festival, the *yujo* would display their luxurious bedding from the Yoshiwara balconies for the admiration of passing crowds. Cash could buy a man a night with a *yujo*, but the girls were highly skilled at wheedling something more. Many men aspired to becoming favoured patrons, a privilege bought generally with additional gifts of expensive quilts and kimonos. High-ranking Edo period courtesans sometimes sold these afterwards to their lowlier sisters, but the latter had to be careful where they put their money: the *bakufu*'s sumptuary laws equating rank and bedding were just as stringent as those governing clothes. Theoretically, a *yujo* could save up her money to buy herself out of the Yoshiwara but, since the higher she rose in rank the greater her expenditure became, relatively few managed to redeem themselves before their contracts came to term.

DECORUM IN DREAMLAND

The greatest authority on brothel lore was the prolific and profligate Fujimoto Kizan (1626–1704), who took some twenty years to complete his monumental *Yoshiwara no Okagami* (*The Great Mirror of the Yoshiwara*). Kizan devoted his life to what he called his Way, and took his research very seriously. 'I have been a devotee of this Way ever since that long-ago autumn of my thirteenth year, when I first squeezed a hand under a trailing sleeve.' So he wrote at thirty, adding that, for eighteen years, he had 'cultivated the art unremittingly, day and night, forgetting food and sleep, and I have mastered its supreme doctrines'.

The Great Mirror, however, is not as titillating as it sounds. Expressed in terms becoming a Confucian sage and deploying flowery prose, it is a far cry from the memoirs of a Casanova endlessly boasting about his own conquests. A book of etiquette divulging the proper behaviour for courtesans, brothels and their patrons, it is the Edo period bordello's equivalent to Mrs Beeton's *Book of Household Management*. Both its contents and success speak eloquently of the mores of the times: 'It is a mistake to assume that only crude, ignorant men buy prostitutes,' Kizan wrote. 'If a woman can converse adequately with a cultivated customer, why should he ever look elsewhere?'

Looking for the finest was not accessible to every pocket. Appointments with the gracious occupants of the Green Houses had to be arranged. This was formerly the business of the *age-ya*, which Victorian Japanologists translated not inaptly as 'houses of assignation'. During the eighteenth century the *age-ya* gradually gave way to *hikite-jaya*, the teahouses, for arranging introductions, which were soon better known by the shorter word *cha-ya*. Houses of assignation nevertheless survived as *machi-ya*, or meeting houses, although the difference between a *cha-ya* serving invisible tea and a *machi-ya*, which called a spade a spade, is a moot point. The courtesans are long gone, but some of these venerable establishments still exist, occasionally as a ramshackle and squalid vestige of the past, but mostly as a stage for dwindling and exclusive geisha parties commanding astronomical expenditures and precious little licentiousness.

Not that carousing in the *cha-ya* was invariably a prelude to more intimate activities. The Tokugawa period's wealthier male urbanites generally visited the Yoshiwara in groups; sex was certainly a likely conclusion, but by no means essential to a night on the town. The possibility of bringing an evening's merrymaking to an unforgettable climax with a charming new acquaintance holds a strong appeal everywhere (and for both sexes), but societies in which women are rigidly subordinate are those in which this is least likely to happen. In Tokugawa Japan, which additionally squashed anything which might ignite real amorous passion, it was impossible. Rural people might find permanent and/or temporary mates during freewheeling rustic frolics and Shinto festivals, but such spontaneity was inconceivable to those in the towns.

Few men could hope for love and passion at home, outside of which female companionship of any kind amounted only to a purchasable commodity. An antidote to its real counterpart, the floating world was a stage on which artificiality reigned supreme. The kabuki turned female impersonation into a fine art in its own right; far from being regretted, real actresses could never hope to compete with their more popular impersonators.

Similarly in the Yoshiwara, the geisha carefully rehearsed a repertory of artificial ciphers standing for female companionship and the courtesans presented the facets of love and passion as a studied charade. The Yoshiwara was thus not just purveying sexual gratification, but selling dreams. Wined, dined and surrounded by pretty girls in the *cha-ya* or stylish brothels such as the Green Houses, the customer and his friends were offered an illusion of gracious living and spontaneous socio-sexual contact. Bantering with courtesans who played roles as skilfully as actresses, they were flattered with simulated responses to their overtures. The gay paper lanterns, gorgeous attire, music, dancing and the sumptuous spread on the table – all were props on a stage for an elaborate masquerade.

'It is unfortunate for anyone not to be able to write, but for a courtesan it is a disaster. They say that playing the samisen is the most important of the artistic accomplishments of a courtesan, but in fact writing comes first ... even for a samisen virtuoso, it would be unfortunate if people said she wrote a bad hand or that her grammar was shaky.' Fujimoto Kizan's remark shows just how much was expected from a high-ranking courtesan. Like a hetaera of ancient Greece, she was constrained to excel in a great many accomplishments in addition to the obvious. Custom had it that she was to fan the ardours of her admirers in writing and, like those of a Heian period belle, her florid love letters had to reveal her talents as a poetess.

The courtesans' game of amorous intrigue involved emulating the courtship of the Heian era, to which their very professional pseudonyms so often alluded. As the many still-extant Edo-period pictures in the tenth-century style imply, the Heian era was very much in vogue. In Genroku society, *nouveau riche* merchants eager for refinement dabbled not only in more recent aristocratic pursuits such as the tea ceremony, but also in Heian style incense-guessing games, archery and a revival of the pompous football game of *kemari*. The *tsu*, the dedicated followers of fashion in the floating world, adopted the superficial trappings of aristocracy as conspicuously as they dared.

To get a wealthy patron truly hooked, a *yujō's* stylish love letters had to convince him of her sincerity. The greater her popularity, the lower the volume of her correspondence. During her struggles to join the ranks of the élite, chances are that her amorous correspondence bordered on mass-production. Accompanying a letter with a lock of hair stressed the point and, if a particularly cherished patron should show signs of indifference, there was nothing like composing searing poems in blood or enclosing a torn-off fingernail. In *The Life of an Amorous Man*, Ihara Saikaku quipped that grave-robbers did a roaring trade in hair and fingernails for courtesans shy of giving up their own. As the many graves of double suicides in nearby Minowa cemetery testified, for all the extreme artificiality of the *ukiyo*, real love affairs were far from unknown. Courtesans not only genuinely fell in love, but thousands dreamed of marrying a patron able to buy them back from their life of bondage.

THE GREAT HARLOT QUEENS

Sleeping only with the men they chose and making regular patrons solely of the very rich, high-ranking courtesans such as the *tayu* could be haughty and capricious. The envy of the entire sisterhood, they enjoyed private favour on a par with *les belles horizontales* of nineteenth-century France and public fame akin to sex goddesses of the Hollywood screen. A great *tayu*'s name would be passed on: there were several Ko- and Waka-Murasakis (little and young purple) and no less than eleven successive Takaos. Such names are still attributed to some of the less exalted denizens of Soapland today. Superstars in their time, some even lived on in legend. They owed their fame to a variety of reasons which, strangely enough, rarely included their sexual expertise.

The Genroku favourite Usugumo (Thin Clouds) was renowned for her wit, as well as for a curious legend about the loyalty of her pet cat, which died in a desperate attempt to save her from the visitations of a viper in the lavatory. A great favourite with patrons and the sisterhood alike, Tamagiku's untimely death in 1726 continued to be commemorated with a lantern festival held during the midsummer Bon festival for the dead until the end of the Meiji era. Confucianism extols ingenuousness as a feminine virtue, and beautiful Kaoru (Fragrance) was celebrated above all for her peerless stupidity. The story goes that she once bade her servants extract goldfish from their bowl and place them side by side upon a plank. 'They looked so tired swimming around all day,' she said, 'I thought I'd let them lie down awhile.'

Far from being considered incongruous, the fair Katsuyama's reputation as a devout Buddhist greatly enhanced her success as a *tayu*. She was also remembered for the verses she dedicated to a rare pet bird presented to her by an admirer:

Sweet little bird, there may be those who envy your position in a gold and silver cage and being petted by people ... But I have resided in the Yoshiwara many years and I sympathize. I too have lived in a golden cage and am arrayed in gorgeous robes but, like the captive Chinese

Princess Chao Chun to whom jewels and flowers meant nothing, I am deprived of freedom.

Needless to say, she opened the cage and cast a wistful eye upon the bird as it took wing into the tent of blue.

Apocryphal or not, many of these stories show that few entertained any doubts about the harsh realities behind the Yoshiwara's gaudily painted face. Confucianism made women into creatures of subordination and subservience at the best of times, and a *yujō*'s fate was accepted along with everything else as a fact of life. Their scant ecstasies and prolonged and varied agonies made engrossing topics of conversation and exciting dramas on-stage. As for their real hardships, well – such is the way of this fleeting world.

So famous was the late eighteenth-century *tayu* Hana-ogi that she received ardent love letters from a visiting Chinese scholar who left without setting eyes on her. In every way a paragon of Japanese prostitution, Hana-ogi was the epitome of the Confucian ideal. Complying dutifully with *giri* professional obligations, she saved all her earnings to care lavishly for her ageing mother, which greatly moved her Chinese admirer. Once, however, she eloped with a lover. Recaptured by the brothel, at first she had the effrontery to refuse any further customers. A degree of capriciousness was her privilege as a *tayu*, but her manager seems to have been more lenient than most and did no more than send her a delicate poem of reproach:

Despite the careful attention given the plum-tree by its caretaker to protect its flowers from injury, the wind increases in violence.

Reading this, Hana-ogi burst into tears. 'The plum blossoms that tightly closed themselves to avoid being shaken by the merciless wind,' she wrote back, 'may be found in bloom again next spring.' To everyone's satisfaction and edification, the exemplary Hana-ogi, a model of filial piety and *giri* towards her employer, fervently reopened for business as the perfect whore.

Even now the story has a familiar ring to it. Some years ago there was a prime-time TV drama called *Pinkku Onnatachi* (*Pink Women*) on a remarkably similar theme. A typically lacrimose, though by no means humourless, plot concerned a penniless young widow reduced to working as a hostess in a 'pink salon' to support her small son. Although not strictly prostitutes, such hostesses generally orchestrate manoeuvres in the dark to provide patrons with manual relief. Balking at going as far as fellating favoured clients, however, the heroine in question gets a rocket from her boss.

Despite her tearful promises to 'put her whole life into doing her best' thenceforth, she is forced to miss work when her undernourished little boy falls ill. Sent around from the salon to bully her, a managerial punk stops in his tracks as soon as he sees the sick child. 'Oh, why didn't you tell us?' he gushes, and dashing off to buy some prime steaks, he even troubles to cook up a slap-up dinner himself. The little boy recovers and the woman is moved no end. The punk from the salon becomes her lover and the last, elevating frame of the drama finds order restored. She is dutifully back at work in her skimpy tunic with boundless zeal, happily greeting clients with the rousing traditional welcome: '*Irasshaimase!*'

Far from being devised for male titillation, like most evening TV fare, this drama was primarily aimed at women. The prostitute, an icon of passion to men and a poignant symbol of servitude to women, is often celebrated today just as she was all those years ago. While twentieth-century Japan may no longer view the profession in the same light, it nevertheless still tends to exalt the prostitute entering the profession to support a relative or a child. A pale legacy of olden days, prostitutes today are hailed in bi-weekly men's magazines, but fame is an ephemeral matter of one issue and usually a promotional ploy by Soapland and pink-salon operators to put their here-today, gone-tomorrow charges in the limelight. The prima donnas of Japanese prostitution today are found among some of the 'idol' striptease superstars, as well as the actresses in the burgeoning porno video trade. The difference is that a famous prostitute of old was also a figure of high fashion. From the 1670s onwards, when culture concentrated increasingly in the floating world, women such as the *tayu* were celebrated by the greatest artists of the day.

THE FLOURISH OF STRUMPETS

Steep and sometimes vicious, the competition between the *yujō* included out-doing each other in terms of gorgeous finery. The greatest courtesans made it a habit never to wear the same kimono twice. At regular intervals, all the ranks from the *tayu* down to the *shinzo* and the ladies in cages donned their best and emerged to stage processions through the five streets. These ritual parades mimicked the formal progress of courtesans in the Moto (original) Yoshiwara as they made their way to answer summons in the houses of assignation. Until it died out at the beginning of the eighteenth century, perhaps in the wake of such a wealth of other processions on a smaller scale, the greatest single annual event in the Yoshiwara had been the *Dochu*, the courtesans' grand procession.

At the end of the Edo period, no doubt to boost the courtesan's waning prestige, the custom was revived as the *Oiran Dochu*. With towering hairstyles spiked with a tracery of foot-long combs and pedestalled on special *pokkuri* – black-lacquered sandals ten inches high – each *tayu* regally headed a gorgeous procession of new inmates and servants from her own particular house. Beneath a large paper umbrella held high above her by a manservant, she advanced at a slow, awkward gait that traced a figure-of-eight pattern while *kamuro* pages and young *shinzo* delicately held her fingertips to assist her balance. Every now and again there was a pause, during which they fanned her or stooped to straighten ruffles in some twenty pounds of layered, fabulously embroidered silks and brocades.

One of the few westerners to record the Dochu in early Meiji was the writer Henry Norman:

> ... the *oiran*'s pyramidal coiffure, the face as white as snow, the eyelashes black, the lips vermilion and even the toenails stained pink ... her stony gaze straight before her, half contemptuous and half timid; the dense and silent crowd; the religious aspect of the vicious ceremony – all these go to make a spectacle apart from anything one has ever seen – an event outside all one's standard of comparison – a reminiscence of phallic ceremonial – a persistence of Priapus.

Every autumn, in modern Tokyo's old north-eastern district of Asakusa, a curious procession begins from the old Yoshiwara shrine and still commands a crowd as it wends its way from the site of the lamented but not-quite-lost pleasure quarter. A revival not two decades old, the current Asakusa pageant is staged with history and the tourist in mind. These days the bogus *oiran* is usually selected from among the daughters of local shopkeepers. Two years ago she was the daughter of a rice merchant; last year the *oiran* was a voluminous matron who, tottering improbably along an Asakusa street with her substantial girth swaddled in brocades, looked for all the world like an Aubrey Beardsley grotesque. In her wake came a retinue of Asakusa geisha, most of whom were over the hill, and a chorus of old ladies ululated tremulously during the pauses in the parade. Oddly enough, however tenuous this ghostly revival of history's grand old flourish of strumpets might be, it still draws substantial crowds. Even as the old Yoshiwara dims further into the past, it continues to capture the popular imagination.

STRIPPING OFF THE FINERY

> The ninth hour is closing time,
> So why do I now hear
> The wooden clappers strike four?
> In the Yoshiwara,
> Even rhythm sticks
> Tell lies.

From *Miyako Furyu* (*Scenes from the Capital*), a collection of eighteenth-century geisha songs

Courtesans would provide extensive and varied tableside entertainments, and it was only at the end of protracted merrymaking that the august guests would eventually be led upstairs. *Tayu* were wined and dined by wealthy aspirants on two separate nights before they could be expected to dispense their physical favours on the third. In the better houses, bedtime could be a long way off and in the Green Houses, an overt display of lecherous impatience was not the done thing. There was anyway no hurry. Except in the 'quickie' establishments, a *yujo* was usually on hire for a period of twenty-four hours. One may well wonder how decorous or even sexually active brothel habitués really were, for the flow of alcohol was prodigious. After leaving a substantial party in the *cha-ya*, guests would carry on carousing in the brothel until the small hours of the morning.

The courtesans used endless wiles to create the illusion of love to fan a client's ardours and augment the frequency of his visits. As the verses from the old geisha song quoted above imply, the pleasure quarters constituted a world of lies. One of them was of course about the time: a *yujo* always tried to convince a guest that the night was young. By deferring bedtime with feasting and entertainment, they were not only procrastinating a duty they frequently viewed with scant relish but were also prompting guests to build up a very hefty tab.

By the middle of the seventeenth century, the Yoshiwara abounded with entertainers who complemented the courtesans' melodic and choreographic routines with performances of all descriptions. The life and soul of the brothel or teahouse party were the female musicians, dancing girls and male jesters called *hokan*. During the eighteenth century, the jesters and the dancing girls became collectively known as 'geisha'.

According to a famous contemporary literary parody: 'The pale faces under the cherry blossom show the truth that all who drink must stagger'; so much for flower watching seventeenth-century style. Given the copious flow of alcohol breaking down inhibitions among people who already had few about sexual matters, one wonders how decorous the parties in the teahouses and brothels really were. As anyone who has attended a geisha party today would know, although the whole affair begins with polite rituals and exquisite manners, composures soon slip as faces begin glowing a boozy red around the table.

If the very top houses of the Yoshiwara maintained decorum, the same is hardly true of the majority. The *hokan* told extremely off-colour jokes, sang the equivalent to rugby songs and staged ribald comical dances. The round of party games entered the realm of burlesque. Ihara Saikaku mentions the game of 'Naked Islanders', which discovered courtesans gradually peeling off to reveal all, which according to him was not always an inspiring sight. Then there was *'Chonkina'*. An onomatopoeic evocation of the rhythmic strumming accompaniment of a samisen, it found the *yujo* dancing round in a circle as they sang *'Chonkina-chonkina – Hai!'* in unison. The final expletive was a signal to freeze in their tracks; the last to do so was out and unwound her *obi* sash. The dance resumed. The rounds of *'Chonkina-hai!'* continued with the gradual removal of kimono, underkimono and the red silk underskirt until the girls finally danced lasciviously around their impassioned patrons in the nude. From Meiji times, *'Fukagawa-Asagawa'* (Shallow River-Deep River) was a well-known variant not only among *yujo* but also among the less reputable geisha. This dance, during which the girls gradually raised the hems of their kimonos as though crossing a river, resulted in a genital display intermittently concealed with an open fan. Other variants of the meld between nursery games and striptease are similarly played by broader-minded geisha today, particularly among the steamier species in hot-spring resorts.

Naturally, all this was a very far cry from the decorous directives of Fujimoto Kizan, who would have deplored the overall climate of crapulence. The ruffianly *wakaimono* were not just employed to drag back escapees; drunken and frequently violent quarrels were an intrinsic part of brothel life. Once the booze had blown away all the rituals of courtship and the pretences of delicatesse, a rousing dance by nude courtesans often triggered a Bacchanalian romp, *sans façon*, upon the tatami floor.

In his novel *The Woman Who Spent Her Life in Love*, written in 1686, Saikaku wryly described life in a low, but by no means the lowest, brothel in the pleasure quarters of Kyoto. Social decorum seems very far from the minds of the august patrons:

> Two prostitutes might entertain five guests, who drew lots for their turns as they sat down. They also gobbled up salted clams before the sake arrived, threw kaya-nut shells into the tobacco tray instead of the receptacle close at hand, wet their combs in the water of a flower vase and when they were passed the sake cup, carefully returned it, in the way one does at the New Year.

Saikaku's heroine goes on to describe the course of her duties, which were not only performed in the uncouth atmosphere implied above, but also with only a modicum of privacy:

> 'Indeed, pleasure can keep you busy! ... I dragged a cheap print screen over to hide one corner of the room, arranged two wooden pillows behind it and, still standing, took off my sash and threw it aside. Chanting a snatch of a ballad about a "painful duty", I pulled my partner down by his ear and said rather affectedly, "Do wash a bit around there, it won't cost you anything. Come a little closer. Oh, how awful! Your hands and feet are like ice!" And I wriggled my body violently.
>
> 'When that man got up and left, there was someone else. But almost before I finished saying "Come on, whoever you are!" I was half-asleep and snoring. Then I was tickled awake again, and let this man do as he pleased with me. Afterwards, no sooner had I washed than I was hustled out to another waiting guest. And when I finished him off, I was summoned to a second-floor party with an impatient burst of clapping.'

MODERNIZING JAPAN

The four American vessels that came sailing into Edo bay one day in 1853 looked futuristic and ominous. As awed as they were with what they called the 'Black Ships', the Japanese ignored the demand for a port of call on the China route, which Commodore Matthew Perry, the squadron's commander, made on President Fillmore's behalf. When Perry returned with an ultimatum the following year, however, the rusty dictatorship realized that antiquated muskets and samurai swords would be no match for steamships and artillery, and signed a concession opening the door a crack to the outside world. Within a decade there were foreign treaty ports around the country. Riddled with debt and losing its authority, the *bakufu* dictatorship was plummeting fast during the 1850s. Joining forces with powerful merchant families, dissident samurai clans plotted to overthrow the Tokugawa regime and restore the emperor as head of state. Defeated during several skirmishes, the grizzled government was still holding Edo, but it was wobbling on its last legs.

During the mid-1860s, meanwhile, an extraordinary cult danced its way up and down the Tokaido road between Edo and the sacrosanct Ise Shrine. Motley drifters and drop-outs united under the banners of poverty and provocation, the ragged *Eejyanai-ka* ostensibly worshipped the sun goddess and wore gaudy hand-me-downs matching fanciful make-up often making it hard to tell the sexes apart. Given to carousing drunkenly through city streets, they staged orgies in back alleys, taverns and around Shinto shrines. Cavorting through the towns, the late Edo-period hippie throng chanted '*Eejyanai-ka, eejyanai-ka?*' – Why not? – in unison along its merry way.

The *bakufu* was not overly fond of the *Eejyanai-ka*; they were heralds of decadence. Prostitutes, unemployed actors, *ronin* and various outcasts, they were unruly and, moreover, some cult members were political dissidents. For all their defiance, at first the ragged crew romped around the country with apparent impunity. Once offering a haven from sterile austerity, the licentious *ukiyo* was vanishing. Yet its spirit lived on in frenzied, grotesque synthesis in the *Eejyanai-ka*, the last gasp of Edo-period hedonism. A reaction against oppression, theirs was a freak-show typically substituting provocative sexual mockery for rebellion and, though declining, the *bakufu* was not about to tolerate subversive effrontery. Infiltrated by government *agents provocateurs*, the revels of the *Eejyanai-ka* degenerated into a riot in Edo one day in 1867, and the troops opened fire on the mob.

The frail and sickly successor to a long line of inconsequential figureheads, the young shogun Iemochi had died the year before. Tokugawa Keiki, an older relative hitherto acting as regent, took office as shogun, moved down to Kyoto but, facing armies massed by the dissenting clans, resigned. Though his more zealous supporters persuaded him to take up arms, during the ensuing confrontation, his warriors defected to the other side in droves. The Emperor Komei died in 1867, and Keiki relinquished power to his son, the fifteen-year-old Emperor Meiji, who was to be revered by the Japanese as an icon of modernization.

The very last of the Tokugawa shoguns, Keiki was to live to a ripe old age in princely retirement. Although pockets of fanatics skirmished for months after the shogun's débâcle, on the whole the Meiji Restoration, so called for the temporal role it ostensibly granted the Emperor, was marred by little bloodshed. Leaving Kyoto in the autumn of 1868, the young sovereign moved into the shogun's castle in Edo with unrivalled pomp and show, including a rousing rendition of 'The British Grenadiers' from the band of a British regiment stationed in Japan. The former dictator's castle became the imperial palace, and the city of Edo was renamed the 'Eastern Capital': Tokyo.

Although the shoguns were gone, the new government counted more members from the samurai aristocracy than from the merchant élite. Nonetheless, before its dynamism soured with martial conservatism and ultra-patriotism, its youthful structure was more flexible. The doors were open to the outside world and the boom was on. Americans, British, Dutch, French and Germans arrived to teach economics, medicine and law. They built railways, devised an educational system, and modernized the army, navy and agriculture. Fired by unbridled zeal for learning, educated young Japanese were meanwhile flocking to Europe and America to bring back the know-how of modernization. As H. G. Wells was to reflect earlier this century: 'Never in all history did a nation take such a stride as Japan did ... she completely dispelled the persuasion that Asia was in some irrevocable way hopelessly behind Europe. She made all European progress seem sluggish and tentative by comparison.'

In the turbulent context of such momentous events, the *Eejyanai-ka* dwindle down to a very small detail, but a significant one nonetheless. If they were the only group to do so quite so brazenly, they were the last to flout the Tokugawa dictatorship with their licentious behaviour, and the last it would ever put down. The *bakufu*'s guns sent the survivors of this spirited if bedraggled vestige of the floating world scattering into the oblivion of history. Its former cultural glitter had dimmed during the repressive years of the late 1840s, and the *ukiyo* was now only a memory. With the assistance of adopted western proscriptions, it had become only the realm of pimps and prostitutes and was no better for it.

THE YOSHIWARA WHITEWASHED

The Japanese viewed the foreign settlements flourishing in Kobe, Yokohama and Tokyo during the late nineteenth century with mixed feelings. Some saw foreigners as the emissaries of a superior culture, many were eager to learn from them and nearly all were intrigued by them. Others saw them, like prostitution, as a necessary evil, fanatical ultra-patriots occasionally murdered them and a small number actually liked them. By now there had already been trouble from hooligan sailors in portside taverns and brothels in a land in which even the degeneration of decorum abided by certain rules. Unfortunately, too, the scholars, writers and aesthetes falling heavily in love with aspects of culture and fuelling the western vogue for Japonisme, the Chamberlains, Hearns and Fenellosas, were a tiny minority.

Strait-laced diplomats and traders, the majority met their bewildered hosts with haughty condescension and confined their contacts to business. Still, while many deplored Japan's moral laxities, others were irresistibly charmed by the petite and acquiescent Japanese belles. 'There is not a good friend with some experience here,' wrote the French doctor Tresmain-Tremollieres in the 1900s, 'who would not advise a newcomer to enter a free relationship with a Nipponese girl. She can simply be hired for around 200 francs monthly from an office, kept and dismissed. She will moreover prove an intelligent and economical interpreter rendering a long exile much easier to bear.' Bonjour, Mme Butterfly.

From the 1860s, foreigners beleaguered the Japanese with righteous indignation rising each summer with the temperature. Appalled in town by mixed public baths or workmen in only loin-cloths and by naked swimmers and shapely pearl-divers by the sea, they averted eyes wide with horror at the sight of women dropping kimonos to fan bared torsos in the sultry theatres.

Business acumen often overcame aversion around the treaty ports but the genus *ketto*, or hairy barbarian, was not generally welcome in Japan's brothels. Racism has never been entirely the white man's preserve. Committing suicide after being given to a foreigner, for example, one unfortunate wench is enshrined still as a patriotic folk heroine. To the more upright foreigners, of course, the very existence of licensed quarters was an outrage. That the cruelty, squalor and scope of European brothel life could hardly be rivalled did not deter them from enjoining the Japanese to repent and reform. In Victorian London alone, prostitutes were estimated to number between 80,000 and as many as 120,000, but from the 'prima donna' élite to sordid slumland 'motts', they were quite forgotten; it was a case of taking motes from brothers' eyes before removing the beams from one's own.

The Japanese authorities were no longer samurai in name, but the dogma of the Lords of Learning was alive and well. The overwhelming desire to be considered modern commanded the adoption of western propriety, which coincided perfectly with conservative Neo-Confucian designs. With Christian prudery henceforth happily married to traditional priggery, the government turned to weeding out the country's 'uncivilized' little indelicacies. Arriving in heathen Japan in untold hordes, the missionaries whined louder about them than everyone else. Still, to the more perceptive foreigner and objective missionary alike, the contention over the brothels was sparked less by sin than slavery. Sold or kidnapped, girls were still held on stringent extended contracts, often under appalling conditions. Having been given the Confucian stamp of approval for centuries, however, the Yoshiwara was to stay. Prompted by foreign reproof, the Meiji authorities nevertheless took initiatives to remedy the situation, but their efforts amounted to no more than a temporary respite and new cosmetics on the face of a very old whore.

The city bath-houses had already been segregated during the late Edo period, and the shadow of so-called Meiji enlightenment fell over the more visible vestiges of former licence. As the pictures of early ex-pat photographers imply, a country in which severed heads were commonly left mouldering on city confines until 1868 was hardly Eden, but Japan was nevertheless about to lose its innocence.

Side by side with venerable Yoshiwara brothels, grand new western-style bordellos soon displayed the turrets and spires of Victorian gothic and the girls within adopted the bustle and the crinoline. Even as Japan was elegantly waltzing in western dress beneath the chandeliers of the majestic new Rokumeikan palace, learning all about the knife and fork and the steam locomotive, the factory, the office and the three-piece suit, it was nevertheless to be quite some years before western trends became widespread in brothel land. Many simply never have. Before the droves of Yoshiwara visitors had even had time to flirt with the erotica of black silk stockings and the ornate brass bed, the Meiji administration decreed sweeping reforms.

He had nothing to do with the reforms himself, but as an Englishman dedicated to the introduction of western law in Japan, Joseph E. DeBecker had a great deal to say about them. Having anonymously published several scrupulously updated editions of his book on the Yoshiwara between 1899 and 1905, he knew what he was talking about. A remarkable work exhaustively covering Yoshiwara laws, history, culture, festivals and customs, for all its *succès de scandale*, *The Nightless City* managed the uniquely Victorian feat of never mentioning exactly what it was that anyone did there. DeBecker's moralizing tone left the reader in no doubt that his book was also an indictment of social evil. Nevertheless, for all its many pages of edifying reprobative prose, the authoritative insights still make one wonder about how far the good lawyer's familiarity went with the locale and the nature of his diligent studies. DeBecker was no bigot. 'You cannot afford to criticize this country too closely,' he warned his own kind, 'for you certainly dare not lay the flattering unction to your souls that you, as a race, have any monopoly of virtue.'

The adoption of western medicine brought measures to prevent venereal disease. There were mandatory weekly medical inspections and the Yoshiwara had its own hospital. DeBecker provided documented medical statistics with contemporary charts; the number of places of examination throughout Japan grew from none before the end of the 1880s to over 500 by 1900. In 1903, however, the Japanese author of a book about the Yoshiwara, quoted by DeBecker, denounced the conditions in the hospital: it was sordid, overcrowded, understaffed and the patients were treated like prisoners. Sleeping two to a bed, even tuberculosis patients had to pay for much of their treatment and all their own food. Brothel managers kept an eye on them, ditching them if they were hopeless cases and striving to maintain hospital costs below levels a girl would not someday be able to refund from the travails upon her back.

If most of the Yoshiwara doctors were, as this writer put it, 'miserable quacks', medical inspections did keep the incidence of disease down. Out of all the prostitutes examined during those years, an average of only just over 3 per cent had syphilis, a figure which compared very favourably with Europe, in which the likes of Guy de Maupassant, Friedrich Nietzsche and Randolph Churchill succumbed to what was a commonplace disease.

Ostensibly outlawing both the *zegen* pimps and the confinement of unwilling women in brothels, new legislation in 1872 also pronounced a general amnesty in licensed quarters throughout Japan. With new-found freedom, tens of thousands of women hitherto stringently bound to protracted contracts flew from their cages. It meant hard times for the trade, but not for long. Although now restricted to three years, the contracts still existed. Girls were now employable only of their own free will, i.e. if they 'agreed' to be sold to the brothel. In 1888, it was reported that brothel-owners had bribed an official to devise a petition extending the term of contract, as well as to reduce the brothel tax, which was eight times higher than for any other business. Although the government refuted the role of the bribe, the tax was reduced but the contractual stipulations remained. Not that they made much difference. Getting girls to sign a contract prior to its ratification by the police was anyway simplicity itself. She was also still bound on the basis of a loan to her parents from the brothel-keeper, and the latter could always ensure that there were debts outstanding when it came to term, so that he could simply extend it another three years.

Lotharios planning trips inspired by the stylish demeanour of the willowy beauties of Utamaro were in for a rude awakening. As Victorian newspaper correspondents were apt to reiterate in heart-rending treatises about the pathetic fates of 'caged doves', there was no doubt: the majority of the brothel inmates were country girls who, stunted by generations of meagre diets, had coarse, washer-women's hands. For all its hardships, the life nevertheless attracted large numbers of women who entered it of their own accord. DeBecker and other westerners, as well as many Japanese, were long on opprobrium and short on the lighter side: was life in the brothels invariably so bad? After all, if it was not exactly respectable, prostitution was an officially recognized and common profession. Working within the context of an albeit questionable but accepted system, many brothel-owners could be perfectly fair, and some could no doubt be generous and compassionate towards their employees.

With industrialization, thousands of country girls were brought wholesale into Tokyo to work in the burgeoning factories, especially those weaving textiles. Their lot was not only not much better than the prostitute's, but remarkably similar. Contractors purchased them from poor parents initially for a period of one year, during which their wages went towards paying off parental debt. The contract was often extended for several more and the girls were legally prohibited from leaving the factories until it expired. At best it meant only very hard work in fairly clean conditions, but life in the ubiquitous sweat-shops was akin to an industrial concentration camp – a state of affairs that was to remain common until 1945. Poorly paid and stacked in tiers in bunks in cramped, squalid rooms, they put on shapeless black smocks at dawn, and stood in serried ranks before their looms for as many as sixteen hours a day. Apart from a break for a niggardly lunch, the girls were forbidden to sit down.

Like those working in the dark satanic mills during the industrial revolution in England, many girls from impoverished rural backgrounds found a profession keeping them pointedly off their feet more attractive – and in the long run, more lucrative. Bright lights, big city: the Yoshiwara was the paramount in-spot and the prospect of becoming a great *oiran* held the lure of fame and fortune. It was largely a matter of the triumph of hope over experience, but a girl could always hope to accumulate a dowry, move out and get married. With the prostitute less socially stigmatized than in the West, she could be and indeed sometimes was redeemed by a customer who made her into a wife or at least a mistress. Although by no means the rule, such success stories occurred fairly frequently during the long history of the *yukaku*. Either way, there was no shortage of brothel fodder. In nearly three centuries, the Yoshiwara housed an average of 3,000 women at any one time. According to DeBecker's statistics, between 1892 and the turn of the century, it received some two million visitors annually.

TWILIGHT ON THE YOSHIWARA

Hideo Gosha's popular 1986 *Yoshiwara Enjo* (*The Great Fire of the Yoshiwara*) stands out among a host of Japanese films focusing on prostitution as a good depiction of standard brothel life at the beginning of the century. Notwithstanding a touch of lurid dramatization, it strikes a fair enough balance between the mundane and the appalling and states its case convincingly. The heroine is one Hisano Uchida, an eighteen-year-old sold to a brothel in 1900 after being legally purchased from destitute parents by a *zegen* procurer. Gosha's account of

'Hisa-chan's' first day in the Yoshiwara is rigorously factual. She has her contract registered by the police, suffers cold and cursory inspection by a doctor, is handed over to the brothel hags and introduced to the haughty *oiran* sisterhood.

As impassive as it is, Hisa-chan's face sometimes betrays her predicament. Offered first to an elderly lecher, she attempts to run away. Recaptured by the *wakaimono* and dragged back to the brothel, she is treated rather more leniently than she might have been some fifty years earlier, when she might have been viciously flogged by the *yarite*, confined to a dark, insalubrious cell below stairs and fed meagre left-overs until she mended her ways.

After a good lecture from the brothel staff, Hisa-chan gets into the swing of things and resigns herself uncomplainingly to Yoshiwara life. She observes the scrupulously depicted customs, rituals and routines. It was a matter of the correct bowing and scraping to adopt before customers, familiarizing herself with the pecking order and, more prosaically, also involved learning how to brew *agar-agar* jelly to use as a vaginal lubricant. This was also thought to have prophylactic properties, and Gosha shows his prostitutes routinely toing and froing to a potful in the kitchen and raising their kimonos to jam it up between their thighs before and after entertaining clients.

Hisa-chan keeps a sympathetic, sometimes horrified eye on the archetypical fates of some of her sisters: the *jorō* beside herself with despair who goes berserk with a razor; the foul-mouthed rebel who finds herself relegated to one of the sordid brothels of the lowest class; the *oiran* who, as so many people did in Japan until very recent times, agonizingly dies of consumption. Japanese audiences are particularly fond of these; the pthisic geisha or courtesan is a recurring stock-in-trade in countless tear-jerkers in the popular cinema.

Although a would-be lover attempts to buy her out of the brothel, it has become a way of life she is used to. To Hisa-chan, money is only a means of paying her way to the top. Under the shadow of a vast paper umbrella proudly upheld by a *wakaimano* and accompanied by a retinue of servants, she graduates to the courtesan élite and at last progresses regally through her *Oiran Dochu* procession. Her resplendent outfit for this scene alone cost over ten million yen, a price which gives an idea of how much an *oiran* worthy of the name had to spend on clothes. Her 'state' costume was lavishly embroidered with a tracery of real gold and silver thread and, although she wore no jewellery, the tortoiseshell, lacquer or ivory combs and pins adorning her elaborate coiffure were inlaid with jewels, pearl and precious metals.

Men, although responsible for perpetuating the Yoshiwara's very existence, dwindle in the wake of the sartorial and other attentions the film, which targets a female audience, lavishes on the courtesan core. Regarded as victims, the courtesans were also creatures of iron resolve playing the game of prostitution to the rules of ruthless competition. Deceiving their customers with vows of undying love and squeezing their pockets not only represents a possible path to freedom, but also an indirect way of getting back at their captors and the male sex in general.

The Great Fire of the Yoshiwara in fact evokes the work of Saito Shinichi, an artist currently highly regarded for his melancholic, obsessive and often beautiful depictions of the pleasure quarters, and is based on a true story. The heroine, Hisano Uchida, had been Saito's elderly childhood nanny and was the posthumous muse for a best-selling biography he wrote and illustrated in 1985. With no special tragedies apart from being a Yoshiwara inmate, Uchida's story was a comparatively banal series of ups and downs in every sense of the term. Her contract expired when she reached the age of twenty-eight; she moved out and got married.

'A dream of spring-tide when the streets are full of cherry blossoms; tidings of autumn when the streets are lined with paper lanterns.' So ran the inscription on the last of the Yoshiwara's several great gates. A hackneyed metaphor for the courtesans, the blossoms also referred literally to the rows of cherry trees planted down the quarter's central Naka-no-Cho avenue. It was a pretty place. Near the Great Gate was a famous willow tree celebrated by many of the artists and littérateurs who haunted the five streets, near to where rickshaw men vied to grab departing guests or deposited those arriving, who were too eager for their forays into the Nightless Castle to worry about being fleeced.

Drawing crowds of all ages and both sexes during its festivals, the Yoshiwara also contained fancy shops and plush restaurants. Innumerable hawkers wandered the five streets, which were lined with lanterned food stalls with gaily printed awnings as bright as those on the many *yatai* snack-sellers' carts. The air was permeated with the twang of the samisen and singing from the brothels, while men ogled the courtesans through the bars and bragging youths attempted to engage them in conversation. Eyeing them meanwhile with a mixture of contempt and awe, passing women paid particular attention to what they wore. The home of fashion and entertainment of every kind, the Yoshiwara had theatres nearby and something for everyone, but not for much longer. The West had introduced Christian prudery, but it had also awakened a conscience in many Japanese no longer comfortable with the harsher realities of the *demi-monde*.

Just a stone's throw away was Asakusa, which would soon rise as the last word in amusement districts in a modern Japan. As such it portended the quarter's decline: with the gradual rise of more commendable pleasures in Asakusa from the beginning of this century, the horizons of the *fuyajo* narrowed down to the carnal. In her famous and often quoted opening lines to *Child's Play*, her poignant tale of urchins and future brothel fodder in 1895, Higuchi Ichiyō beautifully evokes the twilight atmosphere: 'It's a long way to the front of the quarter, where the trailing branches of the willow tree bid farewell to the night-time revellers and the bawdy-house lights flicker in the moat, dark as the dye that blackens the teeth of the Yoshiwara beauties.' In fact, what had been built as an elegant moat in 1657 had gradually dwindled into what was now a stinking ditch some three feet wide.

Coincidentally, Hisano Uchida's career came to an end at a dramatic turning point in Yoshiwara history. After having its spirits seriously dampened by severe flooding in 1910, it was burned to the ground in the conflagration of 1911 which inspired the title of Gosha's film. It had happened some twenty times before and the brothels were rebuilt with the same alacrity, but this time was different. The venerable buildings and teahouses found no true replacement in a rapidly westernizing Japan. The Yoshiwara would never be the same.

In his celebrated *Vita Sexualis*, which caused a furore in 1909 despite its great restraint, writer Ogai Mori (1862–1922) evokes (autobiographically) his rather priggish young hero's first sexual encounter, which occurs in a Yoshiwara brothel. Over and above the young man's reticence, there is something dark and gloomy about the account, a kind of spookiness that not even a touch of humour allays. Greeted politely but cursorily by the *oiran*'s middle-aged assistant, the young man is left waiting in an antechamber lit by a single lantern. As he takes a gulp of an aphrodisiac he mistakes for tea from a nearby kettle, the *oiran*, her finery glittering in the gloom, noiselessly enters through the sliding door. She is certainly beautiful and the tea mishap prompts her to break into a dazzling smile. Silence falls over the introductory meeting like a pall, which one feels is not just due to the male virgin's shyness. The assistant eventually relieves the *oiran* of her combs and bodkins and loosens her hair, then hands her a gorgeous silk gown. Mori emphasizes the weight of the silence by hinting at an underlying professional impatience:

> Without a word the latter slipped her arms through the sleeves of the garment. Her hands were extraordinarily thin, extraordinarily white. 'My dear, it's already quite late,' the assistant said to me, 'so please move over here a bit.'
> 'Are you asking me to go to bed?'
> 'Yes.'
> 'I don't need any sleep.'
> For the third time the women exchanged glances. And for the third time the *oiran* came out with her radiant smile. And for the third time those teeth glittered.

He is then led to the *oiran*'s room, tersely if still ceremoniously undressed by the assistant, and summarily hurried into bed. Conceding that he was made to lie down with gentleness impossible to resist, the writer feels compelled to confess that 'her skill was a tremendous feat'. Depriving the act of spontaneity and revealingly cold, the very word 'skill' relegates sex to the realm of *kata* – the time-honoured and routine 'way to do'. Manifestly, the sparkle of the Yoshiwara was tarnished by the rust of archaic ritual.

It is not surprising, therefore, that wealthier men spurned it altogether, especially as there were geisha all over Tokyo. During the early twentieth century, the combination of a dwindling number of high-class prostitutes and a surfeit of geisha persuaded no small number of the latter to go on the game. After dining and entertainment elsewhere, if they failed to bed their geisha or could simply not afford to, men merely went along to the Yoshiwara as they would to any other red-light district on earth.

Despite the stringency of the Edo-period regime, unlicensed red-light districts had in fact thrived; neither the Tokugawas nor the Meiji Government ever managed to stamp them out. From the late sixteenth century, for instance, the taverns and inns of Shinagawa had been populated with the wanton *meishimori* rice-servers who had partly prompted the creation of the Yoshiwara in the first place. Shinagawa was just far enough outside the southern city limits for the *bakufu* to turn a blind eye; entertaining not the slightest doubt about the *meishimori*'s real services, they officially permitted a given quota to operate. With the marked decline of the Yoshiwara on the eve of the twentieth century, long-standing and less reputable geisha districts such as Fukagawa, and unlicensed prostitute quarters like remoter Funabashi, came to the fore and were complemented with new additions.

Although its cultural assets had faded long ago, droves of hedonistic writers and intellectuals continued to haunt the Yoshiwara during the Taisho period (1912–26) until the eve of the Second World War. In between the booze and purely carnal pleasure, there lingered nostalgia and an attempt to savour something irrevocably lost. It showed in the work of many, but most of all in the writings of Nagai Kafu (1879–1959), renowned for his eccentricity and revered for his literary brilliance.

As influenced by the Japanese classics as he was by French writers such as Zola, Gide and Maupassant, Kafu had frequented the Yoshiwara since his youth and was generally inspired by the *demi-monde*. Returning after a stay in Europe and America, he eloquently berated the changes in the quarters which were soon to be complete with the Yoshiwara's subsequent destruction and rebuilding. Nonetheless, he was known to shut himself up in the brothels for days at a time. A recluse and an inveterate nostalgic, he was also given to visiting the graves of celebrated courtesans in the nearby cemetery in Minowa and those of famous writers elsewhere. In works unsurpassed for a hazy, melancholic atmosphere, geisha, prostitutes and wistful, virtually autobiographical hedonists witness the passage of time in quiet conversations in a world of decaying urban landscapes steeped in a gentle mist in which even the sordid becomes sublime.

For all his acrimonious laments about the quarter's decline, Kafu was soon lured by the more modern alternatives. The twenties roared in Tokyo and in the cafés now proliferating on the Ginza, and loudly in his own favourite 'Tiger', which was typically staffed by young waitresses with bobbed hair, many of whom were really unlicensed prostitutes with very liberal ideas about serving at table. Across the Sumida river there was also the new quarter of Tamanoi, the Yoshiwara's poorer sister. Sprouting up in the twenties and never truly reviving after the Second World War, it amounted to some 700 two-storey semi-detached bordellos housing about 1,600 inmates. Wasting no time in making exploratory forays, Kafu finally spent days in the dingy little houses of a couple of favourite prostitutes, who were the muses for the composite heroine of one of his finest stories.

Obsessed with *demi-mondaines*, whom he called 'flowers in the shade' in the title of one of his more famous novels, Kafu embarked on an unsuccessful second marriage with a geisha, whom he later callously pushed into prostitution. For all his literary merits, Kafu was not quite the champion of female emancipation. Buying prostitutes out of bondage and keeping several fallen ladies in succession, he kept a diary obliquely describing his major affairs. The last entry concerns his persistent patronage of a Miss Watanabe, a trollop performing habitually before him with a male partner: as he grew older, Kafu became an avid voyeur. During the thirties, he sometimes sat for hours in a house in Tamanoi drinking tea and smoking alone while the girls turned tricks elsewhere. Lost in nostalgic reveries about the old licensed quarters, he occasionally pressed an ear to the thin wall to hear the goings-on in bedrooms in the brothel next door.

ARMAGEDDON

According to the swing of the moral pendulum, the West has always regarded prostitution as a more or less legitimate relaxation for the warrior. In Japan of the Edo period, it had been the despised preserve of the townsman and theoretically forbidden to the samurai. In a new age in which the emulation of things western was taking a colonialist turn, the warriors at last had wars to fight. They were soon not only permitted carnal R & R, but also actively supplied with it, visiting brothels abroad as routinely as they frequented them at home.

If they were not always quite so fired with patriotism, the sisters of the *demi-monde* had a sense of occasion. From the days of the Russo-Japanese War to the altogether less gentlemanly one in China, soldiers returning victorious from the Manchurian fronts were hailed by Yoshiwara good-time girls and geisha waving rising-sun banners and treated to wild bibulous celebrations. Austere beyond any of their predecessors, however, the authorities began curtailing such recreations for all but the warrior élite. Indeed, after a lull during the 'golden' Taisho period from 1912 to 1926, the rise of militarism portended a period known as *Kurai Tanima*: the Dark Valley.

While Japanese military offensives intensified ruthlessly during the thirties, the civilian government was gradually ousted in the wake of political intrigue and assassinations. Confucian ethics were back with a vengeance. The militarists reiterated the old warrior code of bushido even more cogently than their Meiji counterparts and further rehashed Shinto to blow along with the divine winds of belligerence. The resulting mish-mash was served up as historical and ethical disinformation in a booklet called *Kokutai Hongi* (*The Chronicles of National Polity*). Devised to drum up martial fanaticism and fan the fires of xenophobia, it was relentlessly drilled into the mind of every schoolchild in Japan.

As the political climate degenerated into something even worse than the most draconian Tokugawa dictatorship, the police became ubiquitous. An equivalent to the Nazi Gestapo, the sinister Kempetai were notorious for exacting confessions using the hitherto abandoned methods of the Tokugawa regime. Joining forces with the ordinary urban police, the insidious Kotto, the thought-police in charge of 'political' affairs, created a harsh totalitarian environment in which citizens came to eye one another with growing fear and suspicion.

Like former Neo-Confucianists the militarists were moved to tighten the reins on sexual activity. Ostensible concern over 'spies' in 1939 gave xenophobic police an excuse to forbid Japanese women from entertaining relations with aliens, although prostitutes were tacitly allowed to remain open to foreign trade. Some years before this and prompted by a desire to project a spartan image abroad, the government had abandoned its patent if shadowy support of *karayuki* (outside-bound) flesh-trading overseas. Outlawed in 1920, the practice survived under a different name. The militarists had no qualms about providing soldiers in the war theatres overseas with *ianfu* (*ian* a word aptly meaning at once comfort, solace and recreation and *fu*: lady), who were typically Koreans, Chinese and Japanese outcasts. Usually of very tender age, they were shipped out in much the same way as the *karayuki* women ten years earlier. Imposing strict austerity measures at home meanwhile, the government again banned alcohol in the brothels. For the geisha, tolerated for being dolled up with ornamental respectability, this was at first a windfall, especially to those with broad ideas about the scope of their profession.

The unrelenting militarist grip on power became absolute in October 1941, when Prince Konoye, the prime minister, was overthrown along with his cabinet. The figurehead ruling the roost was the shaven-headed General Hideki Tojo, a gaunt Fascist caricature with thin horn-rimmed spectacles and a narrow toothbrush moustache framing a mouth as grim as a dagger cut. With the sudden attack on Pearl Harbor on the morning of 7 December 1941, Japanese militarism reached the height of madness. It hurled the country into a war rivalling the entire history of western colonialism for sheer brutality, and which it had in fact neither the technology nor manpower to win.

Meeting fiery and largely ineffectual ends, the young kamikaze pilots were hailed as 'falling like cherry blossoms'. There was nothing very pink either about the spring of 1944, when Tojo's government not only decreed the closure of brothels and swept away the fallen blossoms of the other kind, but also prohibited the geisha from operating. As usual, this was less a matter of moral zeal than pragmatism. Despite the triumphant trumpetings the population heard over the radio, the war was by now clearly a disaster. Draconian rationing found everyone toiling on a meagre subsistence diet, women were swept into the all-out war effort and children sent to work in the fields. Abandoning their finery, geisha and prostitutes alike donned drab smocks and baggy *mompe* trousers to work in ammunition factories or sew uniforms and parachutes around the clock. Detained in Japan during the war, French journalist Robert Guillain recalls a geisha of his acquaintance who admitted joining some of her sisters in a geisha black market set aside for none other than Tojo and his cronies, who had proscribed such luxuries for everyone else.

Be it ever so humble, not a few of the *demi-mondaines* found there was no place like their rural homes, especially when some two million bombs poured from the B29s during the course of over one hundred raids on Tokyo. Beginning during the freezing outset of 1945, firebombing turned snowflakes red in the glare, took some 100,000 lives on the nights of 9 and 10 March alone and altogether destroyed about a million homes. As formidable as it was in terms of destruction and

casualties, however, the firebombing of Tokyo was soon
eclipsed by a novelty in the American arsenal itching for
a practical application. On 6 and 8 August respectively,
the world entered the nuclear age as two devices
facetiously named 'Little Boy' and 'Fat Man' fell on
Hiroshima and Nagasaki to dematerialize and flay
hundreds of thousands in a single blinding flash. 'We
must suffer the insufferable and bear the unbearable,'
Hirohito, the Emperor Showa, said in his broadcast of
surrender some three weeks later but, although handfuls
of hysterical fanatics unable to suffer defeat staged
abortive coups or promptly disembowelled themselves,
the worst was already over.

PAN-PAN AND UNCLE SAM

In September Emperor Hirohito signed the official surrender before General Douglas MacArthur aboard the
USS *Missouri*, and the Occupation began in earnest.
Many of the Americans and other allies arriving in Japan
from mid-1945 were shaken by the omnipresent vision of
utter desolation. There was none of the violent resistance some of the allies anticipated, just a lot of shabby,
half-starved people staring vacantly at the arriving
troops. Some even greeted them effusively. Finding that
the allies neither slaughtered them nor raped their
women as the militarists who had made the practice a
rule over all East Asia had warned, the Japanese directed
whatever animosity they had towards a government that
had marched them into a lost cause. Reassured, droves
of city women who had fled before the conquerors into
the countryside returned to Tokyo.

Mount Fuji was now visible again from central Tokyo
as in the Edo period: save for a few solid stone buildings

and miles of charred, twisted structural frames still standing in a sea of ash and rubble, there was nothing in the way. Shacks of salvaged wood and corrugated iron were clustered around any solid stone walls left standing. Huddling under the overhead girder bridges carrying the train tracks, people ate potato-peel stews cooked over bucket fires.

The initial guidelines of SCAP, the Supreme Command of the Allied Powers, were very strict. During the first phase of the Occupation, there was to be absolutely no fraternizing with the natives and that included prostitutes. Later, dancing was rather grudgingly permitted between GIs and local women, but American puritanism added a curious footnote to the ruling: couples had to remain at least six inches apart. Recalling Occupation days, when he was a journalist with *The Stars and Stripes*, Japanese-film historian Donald Richie relates how stauncher MPs enforced abidance by surveying the dance floor and placing a ruler between couples getting too carried away.

In 1946, SCAP even ordered the abolition of licensed prostitution. Ambivalence is not exclusively a Japanese preserve, however, and no one, neither the occupying forces nor the occupied, took the slightest notice. The six-inch ruling was soon laughed out of existence and MPs joined GIs to drive up to Funabashi's thriving brothels by the Jeep-load. Asakusa was a heap of rubble; the Yoshiwara was obliterated. In a bid to dissuade Americans from polluting respectable native women, the Japanese police had taken the initiative of rounding up the remaining inhabitants of the *demi-monde* to sate Yankee appetites. The ranks of prostitutes had grown way beyond the scope of the former professionals; they were everywhere. Many were destitute women waiting for husbands out of the hundreds of thousands of men still to be repatriated from China and East Asia, and many waited in vain. Prostitutes walked the streets of Yurakucho near the Ginza, only yards away from SCAP headquarters, pulling GIs along for a quickie in some hut alongside the railway tracks in exchange for PX goodies such as cigarettes, chewing gum, silk stockings and, more pathetically, anything edible.

Obviously, the postwar prostitutes – *pan-pan* girls – were by no means solely reserved for the GIs. In a climate of chaos and destruction, the promiscuity was such that for many Japanese, resorting to prostitutes was all but unnecessary. Here was hedonism of the more desperate kind, perhaps, and poverty is the best aphrodisiac no doubt. Still, once the stunned and devastated Japanese came to their senses, the townsmen were back to their unruly old ways even as a new merchant/bureaucrat oligarchy sat at the table with MacArthur's minions to work out the new constitution and hammer out the future. As the ragged townsfolk scavenged to survive, they drowned their sorrows with near-lethal bathtub brews in squalid little corrugated iron shebeens, trying and often succeeding in letting the good times roll.

A staunch contingent of ultranationalists still swears vociferously otherwise, but there is no doubt that the US Occupation helped make the country a brighter place. Having come out of the Dark Valley, Japan was now to abide by the rules of universal suffrage and democracy. Even if true sexual equality has still some way to go, women were given the right to vote and granted emancipation. Naturally, prostitutes and geisha benefited from reforms and their days of bondage were theoretically over. Notwithstanding rulings drawn up on paper, however, the old ways died hard.

Pre-eminent survivors and unrivalled in their expertise at overcoming disaster, the Japanese were soon busily rebuilding their devastated cities. They made the best of substantial US aid and available materials, and with sheer hard work they dotted Tokyo about with clean, if very cheaply constructed, one- and two-storey houses in less than eighteen months. Electric signs and neon lights were up outside the simple new bordellos of a Yoshiwara reborn for the nth time. The tone was very different. The strains of Glenn Miller emanated from countless tawdry little bars with bedrooms upstairs and names like 'Las Vegas' and 'Hollywood'. Emulating Betty Grable, the girls lounging in the doorways wore garish décolleté blouses and had stocking seams painted up the backs of legs emerging from flared skirts. The old shogun Tokugawa Ieyasu had pronounced the brothels off-limits to the samurai who went anyway; the new shogun Douglas MacArthur (the 'Macardo') pronounced them off-limits to the GIs who went there likewise.

In 1947, the noble whore was back again in top form in a play by Masafusa Ozaka called *Gates of Flesh* (*Nikutai no Mon*), the tale of a group of self-sacrificing *pan-pan* girls who plied their trade with devotion beyond the call of duty in order to build a community dance hall. With a highlight focusing on a traitor stripped and flogged on-stage by her outraged sisters, the play, based on a best-selling novel by Taijiro Tamura, enjoyed a tremendous *succès de scandale* and triggered so many offshoots that it spawned a genre known as *Nikutai Bungaku* – flesh culture. It gave rise to several films, the most recent of which was made in 1987.

Commenting on this version, film critic Toshio Kanai remarked that back in 1947, 'Men in Japan were weakened from defeat and destitute women such as these *pan-pan* heroines grabbed hold of their hapless independence to fight for survival on their own. They only had their bodies to believe in.' Indeed, the implications of *Nikutai no Mon* are that the country took its first steps towards reconstruction by strutting through the gates of flesh on high heels.

Having fallen from being an industrial nation to the bottom of the Asian third world, Japan lacked just about everything. With such a scarcity of basic commodities, the *yami ichi*, the black market, was a bonanza for the *yakuza* gangs. As the people gradually managed to feed themselves, the *yakuza* relaxed their hold on the food and vegetable trade and turned to more lucrative businesses such as booze, bars, morphine and, naturally, prostitution. Replacing the prewar *zegen*, their business of pimping and procuring flourished in parallel to the black market.

Like their medieval predecessors, these scavenging flesh-traders exploited the adversities of others; poverty and disaster provided them with plenty of fodder for the brothels. By the time the American Occupation ended in 1951, the black market had gone white and, as such, is still active under the train tracks in many places today. Notwithstanding the Constitution of 1946, universal suffrage and all that, young girls were sold, kidnapped and pushed into the red-light districts that emerged jerry-built from the ashes. Among others focusing on the plight of prostitutes during the postwar period, the films of Kenji Mizoguchi stirred the national conscience, especially *Street of Shame*.

Some women wasted no time in marching down the avenues opened to them by the new Constitution. Fixing the brothels with baleful eyes, the Japanese Women's Christian Movement and other crusading groups lobbied in the Diet to have them outlawed. Among them were the usual prudes but, like the maligned and actually libertarian Marthe Richard who brought down the brothels in France, others were crusading only against slavery. The Prostitution Prevention Law was passed in 1956. The country's red-light districts were granted a year's grace, after which the estimated 260,000 ladies of the night engaged in 50,000 hitherto licensed brothels nationwide would have to find employment elsewhere. While many took wing just as they had done some eighty years before, it seemed that there were plenty of slaves in no hurry to leave.

As the clock hands in brothel parlours moved just past twelve one spring night in 1957, that old Japanese song *Hotaru no Hikari*, 'The Light of the Firefly' – better known in the West as 'Auld Lang Syne' – filled the air, rising lustily if wistfully from the throats of prostitutes and clients alike. After 340 years of existence, the cherry blossoms had fallen and the Yoshiwara was to close forever. As no English-speaking foreigner familiar with Japan ever fails to point out with an eyebrow raised in irony, however, this momentous occasion occurred in the wee hours of the morning of the first day of April.

PART IV

Heatwaves in the Water Trade

Left: Red on white: the Shinto colours of male and female, as on the flag. The patriotic apron hints at a monthly indisposition, and the sign upheld by the brothel maid in the Meiji-period satirist Miyatake Gaikotsu's irreverent cartoon reads: 'Today we are closed for a holiday'.

Below: Panties and more panties. Some magazines are devoted to nothing else. Pantied high-school girls pander to *roricon* – the Lolita complex – a widespread men's fixation in a culture worshipping the *ingénue*, but these come from one of many magazines for adolescent boys.

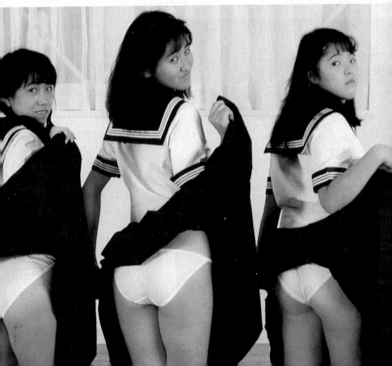

Above: Erotic magazines and comic books weigh down the shelves of bookshops and newsagents in Japan. For those returning late from work, the porno vending machine, like the video rental outlet, provides a handy substitute. (*© Ace Photo Agency*)

Left: Kanayama in Kawasaki is one of the few Shinto shrines still devoted to ancient fertility gods. During its annual Jibeta festival, grandma proudly sets a toddler astride a giant wooden phallus to augur the little girl's fertility as a future bride. (*Photo by the author*)

Right: Dating from the early nineteenth century, these *dosojin* roadside deities in Nagano prefecture once joined thousands of others as the harbingers of fertility festivals. Nearby there is typically a stone inscribed with the words '23rd Day' – the one once considered auspicious for love among the haystacks. *(Photo by the author)*

Left: The court life of the elegant, languid and sensual Heian age (794–1185) has come down from some of the world's oldest novels. Paramount among them is the monumental *Tale of Genji* by the great authoress Murasaki Shikibu, which describes the life of a prodigiously promiscuous prince. *(An eighteenth-century* Genji *illustration by Hironao. Courtesy of the British Museum)*

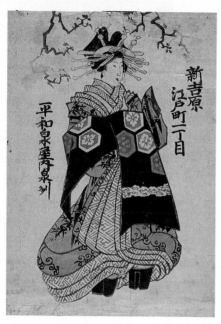

Left: A woodblock advertisement for a Yoshiwara brothel depicting an *Oiran* – a high-class courtesan. For all their fame, most were only privileged slaves sold to procurers by destitute parents and bound by protracted contracts.
(Anon., mid-nineteenth century. Author's collection)

新吉原
江戸町二丁目

平和泉屋今泉列

Below: Strict Edo society vetoed love, but set aside a male sexual preserve in the floating world. For many, all there was to do was dream. Like today's erotic comic books, prolific *shunga* prints offered flights of sexual fantasy. (Shunga *by Harunobu (1724–70). Courtesy of the British Museum)*

Left: Celebrated courtesans in a top Yoshiwara brothel. From the *tayu* of the sixteenth century on, the élite were also appraised for their artistry.
By the time the quarter closed in 1957, they had been rivalled by generations of geisha, and their accomplishments had long narrowed down to the carnal.
(From a Toyokuni tryptich, c. 1850. Author's collection)

Above: Makurabashi shinju: the 'Pillow Bridge Love Suicide', once a common tragedy among 'illicit' couples. Artist Shinichi Saito illustrates a sad tale of a courtesan and a lover who cannot afford to pay her debt; ultimately togetherness means only drowning in the Sumida river.
(Shinichi Saito, 1985. Courtesy Kawaide Shobo Shinsha)

Left: Formally trained from childhood, geisha or 'arts people' are still essentially tableside entertainers. The profession has nevertheless always covered all categories from great artists and conversationalists to those who please patrons in other ways. *(Geisha postcard, 1900s. Author's collection)*

Centre left: Geisha in Asakusa, Tokyo, sharing a joke during a modern revival of the *Oiran Dochu* – the courtesans' parade. Today this is only a pageant. The courtesans are gone and the Asakusa geisha, who never joined such parades during their heyday, have dwindled from legions down to a small handful. *(Photo by the author)*

Below left: Another female demon is the impure temptress seducing the immaculate male. Typical of popular eroticism, this siren's elaborate body tattoo hints at gangsterdom, prostitution and sado-masochism. Evoking a famous old ghost story, her lantern makes her all the more sinister. *(Courtesy N. Tsukamoto)*

Right: Exalting polygamy, Confucianism proscribes female jealousy. The *Hannya* shown here is a demoness – the jealous woman transmogrified as in the Noh theatre. Japanese phantasmagoria prefers a female ghost; her victim is invariably male. *(Hannya mask, eighteenth to nineteenth century. Courtesy of the British Museum)*

Above: Kaoru Kuroki, adult video's superstar from the mid-1980s, and Toru Muranishi, a director triggering a new boom for video erotica. Deriding official censorship with a crop of underarm hair, the articulate and defiant Kuroki is an icon for female sexual liberation, and popular on TV chat shows. *(Courtesy of Byakuyosha)*

Left: The *moga* – the modern girl – combined the flapper and the emancipated woman during the 1920s. Emancipation only came about during the postwar period, but as a sudden and aggressive female social and political rise has recently shown, the march towards true equality goes on.
(Author's collection)

Right: Transvestism was exalted on the kabuki stage, and homosexuality was extolled by samurai warriors. Neither much fazes Japan, but today's gays are nonetheless expected to keep a straight face. Coming out of the closet here, a drag-queen poses jubilantly during a phallic festival parade.
(Photo by the author)

12

Mizu Shobai – *The Water Business*

THE WATER

I quench my thirst by a hot liquid of amber-coloured.
The ice in the rock-glass ticked away with a crash.
I get drunk on my favourite liquor with my congenial friends.
The home world only for men.

Anonymous, *Japlish advertising copy from a catalogue
for bar and club furniture* (1988)

Try telling an upright British publican or respectable
French café proprietor that he is in the same boat as
bawds and pimps, SM clubs, gay bars, trollops and
striptease. You wouldn't be picking yourself up off the
floor if you put this to Noboru Yamada; he is completely
unfazed. To the Japanese, all the provinces of pleasure
are part of a single world: the sphere of human feelings,
the realm of *ninjo*. Although everyone would acknowledge the nuances between the different kinds, whenever
one is purveyed as a business it enters a category
officialdom terms the Businesses Affecting Public
Morals.

Epitomizing the freewheeling spirit of the *mizu shobai*
and now in his late fifties, Yamada has in his time been a
drifter, a stand-up comedian and an interior designer
and has extensively travelled the world. Here in his bar
in Asakusa he is *masutaa* (master). From Japanese standards to Sonny Boy Williamson, a tape deck plays
whatever he or his barmaid believe appeals to customers. She looks a trifle young to qualify as *mama-san*, but

she serves pick-me-ups and sympathy for a habitual male microcosm in which this is how she is traditionally addressed. The house speciality happens to be Bourbon whiskey; bottles of scores of different brands line the bar, behind which shelves bear serried rows of the same make – each label being marked with a customer's name according to the custom of 'bottle keep'. Once purchased, his personal potion awaits him on his next visit, and gives him the essential feeling of belonging.

Softly illuminated in glass display cabinets alongside the bar is a collection of American and Japanese memorabilia and plush wine-coloured sofas surround a low coffee table in the background. The place is cosy, friendly and intimate. Take away the bar and quite so many bottles, and Bird, which Yamada named after Charlie Parker, would look exactly like a private home. Dotted about the country are tens of thousands of similar, and yet all different, small bars; to customers in the neighbourhood, these places are virtually a second home.

Add a couple of hostesses, perhaps a rather more complex and mercenary charging system and a *karaoke* (*kara*: empty; *oke*: orchestra – a sing-along playback deck) and the place would be what is known either as a *pabu* (pub), a *sunakku* (snack) or both. Whatever it is, unless properly introduced by someone else, one would no more barge into a bar of this kind off the street than into a private house.

However Japanized it may have become, the bar concept is of western origin. From plush high-rise 'sky lounges' and cocktail bars to hostess bars and café-bars and more, the scope for bars is pretty vast. They can be theme conceived: there are retro rock 'n' roll bars, a rickety bar designed to evoke an obscure old Russian film and one in which leotarded hostesses drive pudgy executives through taxing fitness workouts in between glasses.

The most classic Japanese watering hole, however, is not strictly speaking a bar at all. The big red paper lantern hanging outside signifies that it is a *nomiya* (drinking shop), a traditional tavern also serving food. More freely open to the street, *nomiya* usually require none of the introductions more proper in small bars. The larger ones are like a rowdy Japanese equivalent to the French brasserie – with the emphasis almost as much on food as on drink. Some of Asakusa's tinier *nomiya* are open very late and offer locals returning from jobs in clubland or binges elsewhere a haven for a cosy nightcap on the way home. Rustic artifacts and shrine souvenirs hang from wooden beams and rafters; behind the counter, kimonoed *mama-san* – perhaps a retired geisha – goes over reminiscences and neighbourhood gossip as she prepares traditional down-home cooking. The omnipresent TV is placed as in the family parlour for everyone to see without actually watching.

In places like these, *mama-san* lives up to her name. Counterside conversations can be surprisingly candid. Hanging his head in shame, a crew-cut tough who might be an off-duty bouncer for a pink salon will be shrilly taken to task for walking out on his wife and kids. The *shitamachi* neighbourhood is as close-knit as a farm community and its smaller *nomiya* are barely part of the no-questions-asked universe for men alone; the rules governing the hostess bar and the rest of the *mizu shobai* often do not apply. Asakusa's little bars sometimes hold other surprises, too. Every amusement district has its share of bars – by no means necessarily gay bars – run by transvestites. Non-conformism is one of the privileges of the *mizu shobai*; in their avid search for fantasy to enliven a colourless routine, men not only forgive its eccentricities but actively dote on them.

Where does the term *mizu shobai* come from? Like the old word *ukiyo*, the floating world, it is also a poetic metaphor for impermanence. Literally, it means 'water business', but as firmly as the proudest hang-outs seem rooted in the stream, they are soon worn away with the currents of time. Some say the word came about as an allusion to the trade plied by unlicensed prostitutes aboard little pleasure boats on the rivers in the Edo period; others contend that it owes its name more prosaically to drinking, rather like the English term 'watering hole'. To Yamada, whose bar lies a stone's throw away from the site of the former Yoshiwara, the expression emerged partly from the pendulation between banning and permitting alcohol in the brothels; it was a convenient way of grouping drinking and the pursuit of other pleasures together.

'It's a strange world,' says Shoji Suei, a writer who specializes in it. 'Lying out on the fringe, it looks freer from the outside, but in fact it is just as tightly bound both by the same social conventions and different ones of its own.' If it has its own obligations and hierarchy behind the scenes, like the old floating world it is nonetheless a haven of tolerance and also the one area – and virtually the only one – where the average man can loosen up. And this he can never do without drinking. Thus what flows along the riverbed of the *mizu shobai* is alcohol – the water upon which all the other businesses float.

THE WAY OF DRINKING

> This sacred sake
> Is not my sacred sake:

'Tis sacred sake brewed
By Oho-mono-nushi of Yamato,
How long ago!
How long ago!

Nihon Shoki (c. A.D. 720)

The origin of sake, rice wine, is in the dim past. Korea prefers the lactescent semi-refined *makali*, which is the same brew as the *doboroku* ever popular in rural Japan. Sake is thus thought to have made its way to Japan thousands of years ago from the mainland with the cultivation of rice. Cold sake is an intrinsic part of all Shinto rituals and festivals; in taverns, restaurants and homes it can be served either heated in small *tokkuri* flasks or straight from the bottle. It is rarely consumed in bars. Nowadays it faces increasingly steep competition not only from beer and whisky, both produced domestically since the Meiji period, but also from a kind of vodka called *shochu*. Not that it is about to disappear. The Japan Sake Brewers' Association markets 6,000 brands produced by some 3,000 regional makers, and stores data concerning no less than 35,000 altogether.

Being hidebound by rigorous codes of social behaviour, the Japanese often find unwinding difficult; the ice is broken only when the cubes start dropping into a glass. Alcohol is virtually the only pretext for spontaneous behaviour there is; it is a frequent seduction ploy and a love potion *par excellence*. During a drinking party, an inebriated underling can let out his pent-up grudges and yell insultingly at his boss. All will be forgotten on the morrow and a hangover can be the employee's only reasonable excuse for lateness or even absenteeism. The *salaryman*'s homeward session around a bottle of Suntory whisky with colleagues is the final duty for the working day. For most this is a moderate affair, but a fixture commonly found in offices is a resident alcoholic basking in the clemency of the life-employment system. Widely seen as unmanly, refusing to drink can sometimes even be indelicate, particularly when one clinks glasses with future business associates who might be fond of tippling themselves.

For better and worse, there are no moral proscriptions against drunkenness in Japan. Late at night in amusement districts such as Shinjuku, perfectly respectable businessmen prop each other up as they totter about the streets. They wobble through the train stations like ants sprayed with insecticide, and the last trains are pervaded with the reek of booze. Alas, it is even possible to study the Japanese diet from looking at it lying in pools on the station platform or outside on the pavement.

Statistics in 1983 showed that Japan's annual per-capita alcohol intake stood at 5.07 litres, just over half the amount in the US and way under half of the amount in France. Not a lot, perhaps, but considering that women are traditionally not supposed to drink, the figures imply that men do a rather substantial amount of drinking. As more women now drink alcohol, the traditional pattern is undergoing rapid change; the phenomenon is already boosting consumption statistics and is readily visible in the city.

With increased acceptance of drinking by women during the past decade, a hitherto very narrow range of social intercourse has widened a great deal. Few younger women, in the cities at any rate, would think twice about going out on the town. Indeed, the trendy 'café-bars' proliferating in the cities are designed with women and the young in mind. Liquor manufacturers compete frenziedly to turn out new brands aimed at the same targets, plugging them relentlessly through glitzy media campaigns. Although Japan may take pride in being comparatively free from drugs, the incidence of alcohol abuse has markedly increased in recent years, particularly among the young. Late in the amusement districts, alongside the welter of older male drunks, one not only sees youths, but also sometimes young women sprawled in doorways as their inebriated and embarrassed companions try to revive them. The ranks of female tipplers include bored housewives, recently denoted by the Anglo-Japanese expression *kichin dorinkaa* – kitchen drinker.

The traditional Japanese drinking method is to tank up before eating, the first mouthful of rice being a signal to stop the flow. The custom may be quaint, but imbibing on an empty stomach has a lot to do with why the Japanese have come to view and accept exaggerated drunkenness and even vomiting as inevitable side effects. Liquor soon turns the sino-mongolian complexion red, which prompts many western visitors to assume rather smugly that the Japanese can't take it. Anyone trying to keep up with the hardier members of a *Hashigonomi* (ladder-drinking) pub-crawl, which mixes drinks as haphazardly as drinking dives, might find this preconception rather drastically belied. All-night saunas in places such as Shinjuku offer inebriated night-owls who have missed last trains a haven for the night; after sweating out the toxic wastes, they can sleep off the effects on plush reclining chairs. The popularity of the new 'capsule hotel' too, in which guests sleep in bunks or 'capsules' with all mod-cons but not much larger than the sleeping berth on a train, has everything to do with drinking.

As anthropologist Harumi Befu has pointed out, however, the difference between real drunkenness and drunken behaviour can be considerable:

... Japanese derive security through interaction with others. Moreover their facility for 'emotional inter-penetration' enables them, in drinking situations, with very little alcohol to reach a level of euphoria where they loosen up and start talking in loud voices, singing, and generally manifesting 'drunk' though not drunken behaviour patterns. That it is not the amount of alcohol alone which causes euphoria is obvious from the fact that the same person, drinking the same amount of alcohol alone, would remain quite sober.

Perhaps this propensity for a 'contact high' explains why Japanese bars and taverns are quite as merrily raucous as they are. In addition to the interaction Befu describes, ritual etiquette dictates that a drink poured from a companion's bottle should be drunk, a fact which points to peer pressure as a commanding incentive to drink.

Whereas the drunk sprawled in the gutter in the West can expect to be thrown unceremoniously in the slammer, in Japan the police thoughtfully provide four centres known as *Tora Bako* (tiger boxes). The 'tiger' is gently loaded on to a stretcher by white-coated attend-ants and taken to one of these, in which he will be placed in a room with soft padded walls, lest alcoholic fury should cause him to come to grief. Based on police records, the weekly *Shukan Gendai* stated in 1980 that 182,000 drunks had benefited from the service in two decades, an average of 750 per month. Police issue them with clean clothes on entry, and those too drunk to control themselves have their underwear graciously washed.

Until very recently drunks in Japan were given lenient sentences for the crimes they committed, almost as though alcohol came under some unwritten *force majeure* clause. Although alcoholism has yet to be officially acknowledged as the national problem it has become, the laws concerning drinking and driving have been drastically tightened. Transgressors can not only expect to lose their licences immediately but to wash their own underwear in jail.

The sum total of boxed tigers represents only a small fraction of the population, but statistics in 1980 revealed that whereas they were once overwhelmingly blue-collar workers and derelicts, there are increasing numbers of white-collar workers and students. In the same magazine article, one police inspector said that mothers informed that their soused sons had been boxed dashed frantically off to retrieve them, but women were surprisingly offhand about their husbands. When notified about a spouse in the tiger box, some said only: 'Please leave him there.'

SHINJUKU – THE POSTWAR PLEASURELAND

During the Occupation, Tokyo's black market thrived largely under the rule of Kinosuke Ozu, a crime lord who had reigned since prewar days over the *tekiya* – the barrow boys or itinerant pedlars – in his native district of Shinjuku. Despite the bitterness of defeat, the postwar years were times for rejoicing. With a democratic new constitution, the pursuit of happiness seemed on the cards and the mood soon became festive. Catering to the zeitgeist in Shinjuku, Ozu wasted no time in building a series of speak-easies of wood and corrugated iron. Dubbed Harmonica Yokocho (Harmonica Alley) and looking like its namesake with rows of tiny bars perforating low parallel buildings, it was a runaway success.

Among the many thousands of soldiers repatriated from Manchuria in 1946 was Komimasa Tanaka, the 22-year-old son of a Christian minister. Born and brought up in Shinjuku, his studies had been interrupted by the war, but on his return, his fluency in English earned him an interpreter's job in the navy town of Kure. After six months, having saved some money, he quit the job and headed back home. With time on his hands before term started at Tokyo University in April 1947, Tanaka got a job as a theatre comedian. His extracurricular endeavours soon interfered with his studies and, alas, were no more befitting to a student at a prestigious university than a minister's son, for Tanaka's theatre was one embracing a new genre: striptease. That this caused his father despair Tanaka cheerfully denies: 'We had rather different ideas, but we got along just fine.'

A diminutive man with large sad eyes set in a face which might belong to an ageing street tough, Tanaka wears a small skull cap, scruffy jeans and a perpetual stubble. A hard drinker, he gazes about him with the surprise of a waking sleepwalker and is wont to quip with a deadpan expression as his melancholy features light up with a grin like a delighted urchin's. A kind of Charles Bukowski but given neither to nihilism nor squalor, he is a pub-crawling sage who records the *mizu shobai* with ironic humour and a great deal of warmth. While the Western Beat generation was versing itself in Zen and the wisdom of the East, Tanaka preferred his hedonism without metaphysics or political overtones. Having found life in the street more inspiring than in the groves of academe, he dropped out of sporadic years of reading philosophy to wander the fringes of the Tokyo bohemian scene. Between the burlesque theatre and the university, Tanaka was broadening his scope. 'I'd liked Shinjuku *tekiya* since I was a child,' he explains. 'To me they were like *rakugo* comedians. They used to tell great stories from the stalls they operated during *matsuri*, and in the postwar black market they made every day seem like a festival too.'

Selling wares on the black market, Tanaka became a *tekiya* himself. Tanaka's subsequent career embraced an incongruous variety of professions including bartender and palmist, but it began taking a literary turn when he contributed essays to magazines, became a film critic, occasionally wrote crime fiction and translated Raymond Chandler novels. However, he became most famous of all for his wry looks at the *mizu shobai*, especially his best-selling *Shinjuku Fura Fura Zoku – The Reeling Tribe of Shinjuku*. An intrinsic part of the Shinjuku scene, he sees himself as a man of the streets, a role which is part fact and part myth and which he has perfected for decades.

'I am a *yakuza*,' he insists, for he is an honoured guest among his former street comrades, some of whom have become bigwigs in the gangs today. Sometimes he boards the Shinkansen to go on a drinking spree with an old friend, who is the *oyabun* of a crime syndicate ruling the *mizu shobai* in a prominent provincial town. Punks standing outside the doors of dives in Shinjuku's Kabuki-cho bow politely to him as he pads unobtrusively past in his worn sneakers, and reverently address him as *sensei*.

Published in a recent book about the *demi-monde*, an old photograph of the *sensei* sitting in a bath with a giggling bevy of nude strippers is striking: it is difficult to imagine anyone looking more miserable. On the other hand, when and wherever cameras are levelled at Tanaka, he freezes in his tracks and, by way of a subtle private joke, poses as stiffly as in an old corporate group portrait. 'Strippers and whores don't turn me on just because they're strippers and whores,' he says when you ask him about the possible fringe benefits during his strip theatre days. 'They're really just like other people.

Gangsters, bar girls, you name it, we're all in the same boat.' Just after the war, the name of the game was also survival, and Tanaka has remained staunchly loyal to the ties he sealed with companions as they floated together on the tides of the *mizu shobai*.

Although Kinosuke Ozu's Harmonica Yokocho became a favoured haunt for artists and intellectuals during the fifties, like many other makeshift postwar ventures, it was buried a decade later under tons of ferroconcrete when urban development determined a more affluent and fashionable Shinjuku. Once official-dom had swept away most of the city's ramshackle jungles of booze and sex for the benefit of the Tokyo Olympics, gangland's focus narrowed on Kabuki-cho, an area so called for plans to build a kabuki theatre which never actually materialized.

As Shinjuku moved upmarket, Kabuki-cho emerged as the greatest entertainment district in Tokyo. It may no longer be the haunt of an intellectual élite and of guitar-toting students, but it still proliferates with cinemas, playhouses and every conceivable kind of bar, and is still home to the *demi-monde*. One old drinking enclave to survive Olympic cleansing was the more cut-throat *Daisan Sōko*, which had been notorious for the streetwalkers flocking there to fleece drunken clients. Not all of its bars had been shady, however, and the streetwalkers had largely been banished during the 1970s. When developers eyeing some of the world's most valuable land squeezed out the tenants in 1987, there were scores of intellectuals and corporate executives once fond of slumming in *Daisan Sōko* to mourn its passing.

A more reputable survivor is Goruden Gai – Golden Town. The former site of jerry-built brothels for *pan-pan* girls and little bars run by women known disparagingly as *onri* (only) for being the mistresses of US servicemen, the area was cast in the doldrums when the Occupation ended. If there had nonetheless still been plenty of Americans around during the Korean War, the Yankee went home with the armistice in 1953 and the area met a sudden demise. A hardy handful of whores remained, but the bars emptied and the plots went up for sale. Among those wise enough to purchase, not a few gave the place a new start with a fanciful touch perennially popular in Japan: they were transvestites. Today Golden Gai survives precariously, but it is still a kaleidoscope of over a hundred tiny bars. Some are moribund and dingy, others festive and colourful; all have character and are accessible only through an introduction. A regular since the beginning, when he actually lived there with his mistress, Komimasa Tanaka harbours a special fondness for it and is welcome everywhere.

Golden Gai is four narrow little alleys flanked by bedraggled one-storey houses of cement and wood. Time was when some of the upper floors were for consummating the business negotiated with the girls downstairs, but now the two floors are just separate bars. If sometimes a bit peculiar, the majority of the mamas are blemishless. Unlike most of nearby Kabuki-cho, Golden Gai is not owned by gangsters and has been kept relatively free of their influence. It is said that the plots were sold by the Wada Gumi gang in the Ozu heyday, but once the purchases had been made, apart from some initial protection racketeering, Golden Gai was left alone.

During the sixties, Golden Gai was a hangout for students and the likes of writer Akiyuki Nozaka, theatre exponents Kara Juro and the late Shuji Terayama, and film director Nagisa Oshima. As the pointedly anti-war décor in one bar implies, with its scorched mannikins and melted plastic models of ships and planes suspended in fishnets hanging from the ceiling, the sixties live on. Many bars still collect writers, journalists and artists and people from screen and stage, most of whom are long-haired die-hards in jeans and anoraks on the other side of middle age.

La Jetée, so called after renowned French fringe documentarist Chris Marker's film classic of the same name, is still a haunt for Japanese film folk and popular with foreign film exponents who like to drop in when in Japan, including Marker, Daniel Schmidt, Wim Wenders and Francis Ford Coppola. Another Golden Gai stalwarts' bar is run by an unpredictable transvestite: the ordinary middle-aged man you see one night looks like a gaudy harridan straying from the set of some orientalist Fellini film on the next. Late on some nights, the balding man with a thin moustache sitting at one of the two tables and peering into the gloom from dark glasses as round as the cavities in a skull would be Araki, a photographer who fills pages with social-realist porno fantasies in countless lurid magazines.

Like most mamas in Golden Gai, Kuro is not one to adopt the soothing maternal role: inebriated *salarymen* reverting to childhood and talking smut are ordered outside. Her customers are journalists, writers and artists of the conceptual kind and the bar is frequented by members of both sexes and from different countries. A conceptual sculptor herself and a second generation Goldenite, Kuro saw the bar as a way of pursuing her artistic career; when she started up in the early seventies, little did she know how taxing six hours a night behind the counter can be. It is not a job, but a way of life. In a country with little scope for socializing outside the family and corporate circles, the bar offers a substitute and the relationship between customers, bar masters and *mama-sans* quickly becomes a close-knit circle of friends, especially in Golden Gai. Until her weekends became devoted to her small son, Kuro, for instance, would organize lively Sunday parties – perhaps sailing in Yokohama bay or a special bash in a hot-spring resort.

There is obviously no better guide to Shinjuku drinking spots than Komimasa Tanaka. An upstairs bar in a nondescript concrete building nearby might be owned by an old friend; it is just another comfy living room in which customers might join in learned historical arguments about the origins of striptease over omelettes and *gin-tonic*. Another old friend is the formidable Maeda-san, the *oyabun* of Golden Gai, the one who makes the rules and the one whose word is law. The Goldenite community is strictly regulated; association meetings may not be shirked without a good excuse. No one takes pictures in the alleyways, not even of each other. Not even, as I discovered, of a fat tabby sprawled asleep atop an illuminated sign. 'Maeda-san says not to,' sniffs an ageing mama in a kimono, 'that's who.'

Maeda-san is a woman in her early sixties with cropped steel grey hair and the stern spectacles of a schoolmarm. Stolichnaya vodka bottles and Russian peasant dolls echo the Soviet affinities of the Golden Gai *vieille garde*; she makes James Bond's nemesis Rosa Klebb seem like a pussycat. Her bar draws a steady contingent of middle-aged writers and journalists. As the area's heaviest mama, she laid down most of the rules in Golden Gai from the outset, which is no mean achievement for a very young woman in the early 1950s. The authoritarian look is appropriate; it may even have intimidated the gangs. It does, however, appear to be the armour around a big heart. As Tanaka sings one of the lusty solos for which he is justly renowned, Maeda cuts him short. Too much drink is not good for Tanaka. 'That's enough,' she snaps, taking our glasses away.

'You,' she barks at me, but not unkindly, 'get out and go home. I'm putting the *sensei* in a taxi.' In Maeda's bar we are all her children, and we can but very meekly do as we're told.

Golden Gai is currently under siege from developers eager to get the mamas and masters off the land they would have more lucratively piled high with glass and ferroconcrete. Some of the old haunts are boarded up and ready to go, but resistance is strong. Some of the second generation Goldenite mamas in early middle age join the indomitable Maeda-san; they are not about to leave without putting up a fight. Notwithstanding the Japanese propensity for shunning things antiquated, the recent exposure of some bars in the press has drawn a younger crowd, many of whom belong to the same walks of life as their middle-aged counterparts. Perhaps a bit too late.

Some Goldenites have found developers' offers tempting enough to sell out, but Kuro was one who dug in her heels. 'When the controversy first erupted, we formed a Golden Gai watch committee and took turns staying up all night. We had to make sure no one tried to torch it.' As is usual in Japan, the legal wrangles are highly intricate, for many people purchased the bars but not the land they stand on. The rumour is that Golden Gai has five years' grace. 'Nonsense,' growls Maeda-san. 'We're still negotiating. Either way as I see it, we're staying.' Sad as it is, however, according to the all-powerful developers, they're going.

Improbably, little alleys of far more ramshackle bars still stand precariously on the other side of the station in Shinjuku, as well as in Shibuya – all shunned by the more conventional majority, who do not relish the picturesque. Sweeping the traumatic postwar period under the carpet is such a tradition that even the good times are pointedly ignored. *Shomben yokocho* (piss alley – because the walls made convenient substitutes in the pre-toilet postwar days) is a term applied specifically to one of these places in Shinjuku and generically to the others. With the exception of a tiny renegade intellectual contingent, the young live in a world in which artistic movements have succumbed to the flood of commercialism and prefer the impersonal interiors and canned music of the café-bar.

This is also why recent attempts to reanimate Asakusa have failed. The same applies increasingly to nearby Ueno, in which the rowdy and garish, if admittedly often seedy, bars and cabarets were until recently very much alive. After the last trains nowadays, drunks lie slumped on the floor beneath the greenish strip lighting of the ranks of glass telephone booths outside the station like foetuses in specimen jars. Not exactly bar revellers, the majority are *rumpen* or derelicts. A combination of the 1985 amendments to the morals law and sheer old age steeps Ueno's water business in neglect.

Asakusa Ueno: the great contiguous northern amusement districts have fallen into decline in that order. In addition to Bird, Noboru Yamada owns a *nomiya* complete with antique furnishings in a back room popular with some uptown *retro* addicts eager for old Asakusa's *shitamachi* (low city) atmosphere. He was also one of those most active and influential in the recent 'Asakusa–Ueno Retropolis' drive to bring young Japanese back to the area in the wake of the *retro* boom. They staged Old Time jazz festivals, and they projected silent films on a screen put up in front of Asakusa's Kannon temple. Apart from sending flea-market prices through the roof, *retro* never really boomed in Japan; once an amusement district is dead it can never be revived.

As vibrant and lusty as it still is, Shinjuku shows signs

of going the same way. The weekend onslaught of rustics has typically driven the trendy urban vanguard to other areas, notably to Shibuya and Roppongi. Rather than stamping out the bar and sex businesses, the 1985 clampdown cramped their style and shortened their hours of operation. Some Shinjuku bars face hard times and its sex-for-sale is currently becoming the carnal equivalent to fast food. A combination of the search for novelty and authoritarian repression is precisely what turned the crowds away from the great amusement quarters of the north-east, but the decline of one merely guarantees the emergence of another. Moving in parallel if never hand in hand, fashion marches first and vice slithers along in its wake to other parts of the city. Following the tide, the police and the law come next, but the unruly current of the people always flows ahead.

13

The Ladies Upstream

THE GEISHA

> ... the great monks who have left this world and the great
> courtesans and geisha who are living beyond the pale ...
> in each case life means surrender, not fulfilment. It is in
> the style of their self-abandonment that they are granted a
> degree of self-determination denied to ordinary members
> of the human hive.
>
> Kurt Singer, *Mirror, Sword and Jewel*

The young woman sitting with us in an Akasaka restaurant is very pretty to be sure and, elegantly coordinated in light grey, she almost could be just another local OL (Office Lady). But Yukari Matsuyama has about her an indefinable quality that makes her particularly striking. She looks the very model of poise. The mouth is sensuous and the smile winning but discreet, the softly tapering eyes sparkle not so much with coquettishness, which would be narcissistic, but with a kind of electricity lighting up the company. She wears her lustrous jet-black hair loose on her shoulders; this being the weekend, she is off duty and does not have to spend hours piling it up on her pretty head or donning an elaborate wig before sallying forth.

Even in mixed company and among friends, Yukari insists on serving others and graciously refills any empty glasses. In a country renowned for its elaborate social etiquette, she has been carefully trained to have better manners than anyone else. The charm is undeniable, if just a trifle artificial. She is not just hiding behind a screen of affectation; she can speak her mind much more candidly than the feminine norm allows. Her laughter is engaging and frequent, her manner is laced with a barely perceptible hint of flirtatiousness.

Neither a tease nor a temptress, she is merely acting the part of the Perfect Woman, an accepted icon of femininity in the eyes of Japanese men for centuries. Not a wifely woman of course, but rather one who embodies the ideal of female companionship – amenable, sociable, talkative and covertly erotic – in an artificial world in marked contradistinction to the home, in which it would not be proper for a wife to meet such colourful standards at all. Yukari, who has just turned thirty, has in fact long and carefully rehearsed a role for a difficult career. It dominates her bearing even when she is off duty; she has been an Akasaka geisha for twelve years.

The daughter of a middle-class company employee, Yukari was born and brought up in Sendai in the north-east. When illness forced her father into premature retirement when she was seventeen, the privilege of further education went to her brothers. Yukari left school. She was too young to get married, but she had to find a job. Working as a shop assistant was a grim prospect, and the *mizu shobai* was unthinkable. Nevertheless, it did offer one highly distinguished alternative. Yukari, who had always been made aware of the arts and traditions of old Japan at home, was strongly sold on the idea of becoming a geisha. Her family was not exactly keen at first, but the geisha mystique as custodians of traditional culture, their daughter's determination and sheer pragmatism won them over.

When just eighteen, Yukari travelled down to enter an *okiya* (geisha house) in Tokyo and became a geisha apprentice. These are called *maiko*, but although often loosely used, the expression exists officially today only in Kyoto. In the past, by the time she was Yukari's age, a girl's training period would have been long completed. Having started during childhood, she would be a professional geisha by the time she was sixteen. Even though it is irrevocably dwindling, the profession is still attractive.

'Many more girls than one would imagine think they'd like to be geisha,' says Yukari, 'but when they've understood what being a *maiko* involves, they give up halfway through.' Indeed, only three out of ten aspirants survive the ordeal. For all the changes and setbacks it has undergone in the last fifty years, aspects of Yukari's calling still remain much as they were over two hundred years ago.

During a seventeenth-century frolic in the brothels of the floating world, the singing and dancing of the courtesans was complemented with diversions from professional entertainers. Often collectively called *taiko-mochi* or drum-holders, they were jesters, musicians, comic storytellers and they were overwhelmingly male. Brothel kingpin Shoji Jinyemon, the founding father of the Yoshiwara, was himself very fond of a *taiko-mochi* in his own employ, whose talents quickly made him into a precursor for a genre which became popular in the floating world throughout Japan. The percussion was only an accessory to a variety of other skills, and some say Jinyemon was also the first to dub these men *otoko geisha* – male arts people. Have drum, will travel. Before they came to be called such or disappeared altogether, many *taiko-mochi* formed itinerant troupes including dancing girls. They were often professional actors and achieved a great deal of fame, but they faded as the status of the male entertainers fell in the teahouses.

Confined later to the brothels, they came to be known collectively as *hokan*.

The vogue for *hokan* lasted until the close of the Meiji era. Commenting in the 1890s, J. E. DeBecker, the ultimate, if ostentatiously righteous and disparaging foreign authority on Japanese brothel lore, noted that the art had degenerated. 'The disgusting and highly suggestive antics of the *hokan*,' he fumed, 'far from scandalizing guests, are received with great applause and appear to afford much amusement to all present.'

Female entertainers on the other hand, after making their way along the same road as the men, either in parallel or with them in itinerant troupes, began soaring off at a more dignified tangent. Having gradually honed their talents to attain a high degree of proficiency, *odoriko* – dancing girls – came to be called *geiko* (arts-children) from the early eighteenth century. In Kyoto and some of the provinces, the word is often used even now. While some danced, others excelled at singing short *ko-uta* and long *naga-uta*, poetic songs derived from the narrative chanting of the theatre, which they accompanied with great virtuosity on the strings of the koto and the long-necked samisen. Exceeding those of the courtesans, the artistic accomplishments of these women earned them a high reputation, above all in Kyoto where they were most popular. From the mid-eighteenth century they gradually came to be known collectively as geisha throughout Japan.

Literally meaning 'arts person', the geisha initially included men in their ranks, among them those eager to be distinguished from the less elegant *hokan*. Similarly accomplished, some haunted the gayer side of the gay quarters as homosexual equivalents to their female counterparts and others worked solely as practitioners of musical and performing arts. Already fairly small, their number declined during the Meiji era, although television programmes sometimes dig up a few very old *otoko* geisha who were active as recently as the postwar years.

The early geisha shared very broad ideas about the scope of their profession in common with the dancing girls. Offering themselves freely to patrons, they presented the blossoms in the floating world with sufficient competition to make their delicate countenances flush red with ire. Nipping unwelcome rivalry in the bud, spring traders all over Japan soon prompted the government to prohibit geisha from sleeping with customers in the brothels. Although there was no way of preventing them from doing this elsewhere, the calling was to be confined to more edifying entertainments and the geisha assigned to parties by official bureaux called *kemban*, which often still manage their appointments today.

The traditional geisha make-up turns the eyes into black brushstrokes and the mouth a couple of petal-shaped daubs of brilliant red, reducing features into a cipher for femininity as stark as a Chinese character on white paper. Today's geisha is powdered rather than painted, however, and the thicker white make-up is reserved for the stage. The perfect geisha party should never comprise a mere bevy of beauties, but should include one or more women who, sometimes even advanced in years, are revered for their brilliance as exponents of traditional music, song and dance, as well as for their wit and powers of conversation.

The geisha's every measured, dainty gesture complements the meticulous stylization of her utterances. She shines at the dinner table, she dazzles with her performances and her mere presence makes men feel good. The human work of art is sexual sublimation personified and its function is to be a living sculpture depicting a feminine ideal. Nevertheless, the effigy is not there solely to be admired, for beneath her immaculate face and gorgeous silks eroticism radiates like a magnetic field and, besides, the banter and repartee around the table can grow *risqué* and sometimes frankly raunchy. The geisha is emphatically not a prostitute, and this is as far as it is meant to go.

In practice, however, the line dividing geisha and prostitutes can be a very fine one, drawn mostly from social standing. Geisha tended to be better educated than prostitutes, for schooling was never a prerequisite for harlotry except among those aspiring to become great courtesans in former times. Notwithstanding, many geisha were desperately poor and less reputable *okiya* (geisha houses) were no more than rough fronts for some pretty harsh unlicensed prostitution. Whether it culminated in bed or not, an evening with a geisha was in all cases a good deal more expensive than walking off the street into a Yoshiwara knocking shop. It was often said that richer men dallied with geisha and poorer ones with prostitutes and today this holds truer than ever.

Cherry blossoms, Mount Fuji, the geisha – the old western cliché of Japan, but nevertheless one until only very recently too dear to the Japanese themselves to have prompted them overmuch to debunk it. The revered mountain and the cherries remain, but the geisha are precious few. Apart from on their TV screens, plenty of Japanese have never actually seen one in their lives. Driven up to Asakusa by the busload, participants in 'Tokyo by Night' tours are presented accordingly with dinner-time revues featuring one or two of the genuine article flanked by actresses depicting 'Yoshiwara *oiran*' and waitresses in old-time fancy dress. Today there are some 17,000 geisha, only about one-fifth of the number before the war. Like wildlife squeezed by urbanization, they continue to dwindle as their territory shrinks, but a small surviving core will in all probability find itself preserved as a museum culture in much the same way as the Noh and the kabuki theatre.

Be this as it may, the weeklies sporadically churn out geisha scandals. Some mercenary geisha behave like courtesans; conspicuously younger ones, it seems, are sometimes offered between favour-seeking corporate and political tycoons, a little doll coming gift-wrapped in her finery, her obi sash neatly knotted like a ribbon just dying to be untied. Elsewhere one hears of the venerable and genuine exponents of a dying art too; one sees them deployed in traditional festival parades and in theatrical geisha dance spectaculars. Involving chaste artistic accomplishment and conversational dazzle on the one hand and eroticism implied or supplied on the other, the geisha concept, like many things Japanese, is itself ambivalent and ambivalently perceived.

Tonight Yukari Maruyama is just herself, but on any other she is Oborozuki – Misty Moon. Inspired from *The Tale of Genji*, the name was given to her by her *okāsan*, which means 'mother' and refers to the woman who runs the *okiya* and who took her on for training. Geisha used to live in the *okiya* itself, and life in it could be harsh and only nominally better than for the courtesans of old. Since the postwar Occupation and the comparative emancipation of women, geisha generally live outside it and tend to turn up at scheduled times like office employees. These days they also have the All Japan Geisha and Geisha House Operators' Union to protect them, although about a third of the profession are not members.

Yukari lives conveniently close to her *okiya*, in a modest but expensive apartment on the Akasaka hill.

Having been contacted in advance by the customer, either directly or through the *kenban*, the *okiya* will send her off to her appointment. Although the demands of professional commitment and capriciousness still don't go too well together, a geisha is free to refuse it. If her engagement is in the Akasaka district, she will be wheeled there through the streets, boxed as invisibly as a Heian belle in an ox-carriage beneath a flap on the front of a hooded rickshaw drawn by a liveried runner. A hallmark of Japan between the Meiji era and the twenties, the rickshaw exists today only in the geisha world. In Tokyo, the districts of Akasaka and Shimbashi – playgrounds of the nation's big wheels – are the only places still boasting small fleets.

Excelling at several traditional accomplishments and beautiful into the bargain, Yukari comes close to the geisha ideal. Painted and powdered each night Monday to Friday as Oborozuki, her slender nape will emerge from the broad neckline of a very costly, but discreet, kimono. Except on-stage, the geisha costume should never be gaudy. Delicately serving sake from fragile hands emerging from wide silken sleeves and offering cajoling, stylized conversation, Oborozuki will kneel decorously and decoratively back on feet clad in split-toed *tabi* socks of immaculate white. For all the artifice, however, she is expected to speak with spontaneity and frankness. She may never have finished her schooling, but her house mother, unlike some these days, properly saw to it that she was well versed in the traditional arts and culture. Yukari, as an exceptional geisha invariably must be, is moreover of above average intelligence. She is well read and thoroughly aware of current affairs and the world around her. After all, her job consists of following and making conversation with the *kaizai* business élite and influential politicians in Tokyo's top class *ryotei*, which are among the most expensive restaurants on earth.

Astronomical prices have made both the *ryotei* and the company of geisha less into diversions and more into matters of prestige, a sure-fire way for a host to impress his guests. The former flatters the latter even as he flatters himself, and the guest knows that in all probability something will be expected of him in return. Once in a while, however, the mask of corporate and traditional good practice slips to reveal the human frailty behind it.

GEISHA POLITICS

Geisha can earn a lot of money. Yukari, for instance, is paid a flat hourly fee of 5,000 yen, which she receives from the *okiya* on the basis of five working days per week. She is paid not only for the hours worked in the evening, but for the time she spends at music and dance practice organized by her employers. On average, Yukari earns about 800,000 yen a month. This includes handsome tips, not for doing anything untoward, but just as a customary matter of course.

Like *salarymen*, geisha sacrifice their weekends to professional obligations. A wealthy company director might invite her to rounds of corporate golf at his club, often more for the edification of his co-workers and customers than for himself. Donning golfing apparel and sometimes expected to join in the game (which also requires expensive training in the rudiments of play), 'golf geisha' are becoming a staple in top management circles. Invited also to a variety of corporate functions calling either for traditional regalia or designer civvies, many geisha find themselves becoming select mascots greatly enhancing corporate prestige.

They thus become Mitsubishi, Mitsui or whatever geisha and remain exclusively in the service of one company and receive substantial fringe benefits to foster their loyalty. Nevertheless, since they are still left to fund much of their costly professional expenditure out of their own pockets, geisha often have trouble getting by and most seek salvation in the form of a more or less permanent sponsor. Unlike ordinary womenfolk and common prostitutes, high-class geisha have long enjoyed the privilege of picking their own partners. The élite, many of whom are wily predators in doll's clothing, can not only afford to choose but sometimes also make fine catches. A top geisha is considered quite acceptable not just as a concubine but as a wife; regardless of the wobbly morals inherent in the profession, her refinements endow her with standing rendering her more marriageable than her less accomplished sisters. Geisha have even married national leaders. Prime Minister Katsura married one in the Meiji period; more recently, the widower Shigeru Yoshida, who headed Japan during the postwar years, chose one as a blemishless second bride.

'If any of the geisha in Akasaka indulged in idle talk about what we see and hear among our guests,' said Yukari only half-facetiously one evening in November 1988, 'there would be chaos; it would bring down the government.' She wasn't referring to drunken misbehaviour or unseemly propositions; geisha are taught to take such things in their stride. She meant politics: the Lockheed bribery scandal that brought down Prime Minister Kakuei Tanaka and, although she didn't yet know it at the time, the Recruit scandal that was to oust

Prime Minister Takeshita only months later. Everyone knows that key sequences in the plots were enacted within the elegant walls of *ryotei* in Shimbashi and Akasaka.

Untold legions of high-ranking Japanese politicians have kept geisha as mistresses. Extra-marital affairs often bring down politicians in the West but the Japanese do (or did) not consider a man's sex life to be relevant in assessing his political abilities and, although Japan is a country with little respect for privacy as understood in the West, men are entitled to indulge in sexual recreation provided they neither allow it to interfere with their duties nor fail to mask it with a respectable façade. There is no sin in the sex, but there is loss of face in getting caught. Not only are the politician's carnal peccadilloes not seen as such, but they are an accepted tradition. Heading a party deeply tainted with corruption and beleaguered by the opposition in 1989, Prime Minister Noboru Takeshita resigned. It was not merely political corruption that floored his successor Sousuke Uno less than two months later, however; it was his dalliance with a geisha from the Kagurazaka district, another of Tokyo's last bastions of entertainment in the classic tradition.

Being in fact a hostess and entertainer, the geisha is beset with as many temptations and pitfalls as the politicians she entertains. Like ladies are wont to do (and the geisha stands out as such in the *mizu shobai*), some say yes and some say no but the really skilled geisha is past mistress of the protracted 'maybe'. If some are motivated by profit rather than love, it is with an eye to the long rather than the short term. No self-respecting geisha would slight her career by doing it at the drop of a hat. Perhaps this is truer today than it was from the late nineteenth century to the 1930s, when a glut of geisha commonly forced the lower echelons of the profession into prostitution in order to survive. In a more affluent Japan in which she is part of a tiny élite, the true geisha wears a halo of respectability. Even if it occasionally slips a little, it continues to hover over her sleek coiffure.

GEISHA PARTY

Echoing the old *ukiyo*, some of the geisha haunts are still called *machiai* (houses of assignation) and *cha-ya* or tea-houses. The only difference between the equally bibulous two is that the latter serves no food, whereas the former occasionally still has rooms discreetly tucked away upstairs for overnight stopovers. The most common site of geisha entertainment in Tokyo today is the *ryotei*, which functions to all intents and purposes solely as a highly refined restaurant. Naturally, even the *ryotei* fall into different classes, the top being the exclusive domain of a privileged few. I once had the good fortune to be invited to a party in what was admittedly nowhere near the top of the Akasaka *ryotei*, but the experience may be taken as fairly representative of the average geisha party.

A room of twelve tatami mats (i.e. measuring some 15 square metres) was devoid of decoration except for a hanging scroll calligraphed with a poem and a tastefully sober ikebana flower arrangement of sprigs of plum blossom – both in the *tokonma* alcove. Next to it was a gilded paper folding screen, in front of which were several low tables combined and set to accommodate twelve. There were four geisha assigned to the party. Attired in elegant, rather sombre kimonos, their faces were powdered to pallor rather than creamed lily-white and all were at least on the threshold of middle age. They were gracious and exquisitely mannered and, individually assigned to groups of three guests and intermittently relaying each other, they managed to make each guest feel that they were devoted heart, soul and perhaps even body only to him. The affair began as decorously as may be imagined. Delicate and tiny *kaiseki* dishes, subtly arranged and decorated on judiciously chosen tableware, succeeded one another as the culinary equivalent to miniature paintings. Notwithstanding the feast, everyone was apparently on their best behaviour, the geisha conversation largely comprised well-worn platitudes and only sheer good manners seemed to prevent the company from dying of boredom.

So delicately did Kimiryu or Umechyo pour sake for my neighbours and myself that we hardly even had the impression of drinking at all. The contents of the tiny cups had a magical way of evaporating and reappearing, as the hot *tokkuri* flasks came and went in endless succession on the table. One was in fact being subtly persuaded to drink. Both the semblance of socializing and traditional etiquette demanded pouring cupfuls for the geisha too, and faces were flushing an ominous deep red around the table. The *tokkuri* on the table were now flanked by bottles of beer, whisky and French brandy; over a dessert of fresh fruits daintily cut into floral shapes, the party was becoming raucous.

There now entered the only absolutely whiter than white face, and it belonged to a truly beautiful dancing geisha in a gorgeous black formal kimono trimmed with exquisite embroideries of flowers and birds. Moving regally before the gilded folding screen to the haunting twang of the samisen, she dexterously manipulated a golden paper fan which was a prop to offset the poses she struck at strategic intervals. The effect was spellbinding; save for the music, there was an awed silence.

For all the delicacy of the dance, the other geisha bade the guests rise to their feet almost before the spell was broken. Tottering grotesquely through traditional dance routines in a general display of self-mockery apparently prompted by the star dancer herself, everyone was soon floored with gales of laughter and more to drink. In between further outbreaks of riotous dancing to classical comic songs, the geisha played rounds of party games, with chanted rhymes accompanying something very like pat-a-cake. As childish as it seemed, the chants between guest and geisha involved a degree of innuendo triggering a great deal of merriment.

One of the more illustrious guests was the septuagenarian Taro Okamoto, a famous surrealist painter whose renowned eccentricities are much cherished and who wasted no time in becoming the life and soul of the party. Despite her mask of good manners, the shock showed somewhat on the face of the geisha next to him when, snatching her samisen, Okamoto proceeded to crown the event with inebriated delirium by strumming away at the strings with his chopsticks. The party, perhaps mercifully for the geisha, was nearly over. Given by a noted independent film company, it had gone on for exactly three hours and, at a conservative estimate, may have cost them altogether some 700,000 yen. In the *karyukai* – the geisha 'world of flowers and willows' – a mere trifle.

FIGHTS, FINERY AND AFFAIRS

The image of the geisha was formed during Japan's feudal past, and this is now the image they must keep in order to remain geisha. A fully decked out geisha in 1975 looked much the way a formally dressed geisha did in 1875 – but this very fact means that the social import of the geisha

has changed considerably. They are no longer innovators,
they are curators.

Liza Dalby, *Geisha*

Yukari is shocked. 'Fancy playing the samisen with
chopsticks!' she gasps. 'Good samisen strings are made
of real cat gut!' Being a consummate player, she ought to
know. Dancing, singing, playing the samisen and/or the
koto, as well as classical cultural pursuits such as the tea
ceremony and even the odd bit of incense guessing – all
are part of the geisha training. After attending parties
until late at night, Yukari rises early in the morning to
practise the samisen, which is her own particular forte.

The pursuit of feminine perfection is a lifelong one;
when they do not retire to open bars or run an *okiya*,
many ageing geisha go on to impart their art to others
and some, often of advanced age, are officially designated 'living national treasures'. In the old days, following a pattern very similar to prostitutes, girls were sold
into geishadom by their parents. In recent times and
within families owning *okiya* especially, the geisha profession is often handed down from mother to daughter.
Some nationally revered old geisha are the exacting
mistresses behind such dazzling and televised annual
dance spectaculars as the Azuma Odori which, staged in
Tokyo's Shimbashi Embujo theatre in spring, involves a
cast of geisha stalwarts from the Shimbashi district.
Tickets for such grand annual events in Tokyo and Kyoto
sell out months in advance, many being handed out to
corporate patrons by the *okiya* concerned. Nonetheless,
the majority of the audience for geisha stage performances today is female.

For all the carnality a venerable silken exterior conceals, there is something almost monastic about the
geisha profession. In the old days many girls remained

in it virtually from cradle to grave. Although they were bought, sold and bound to the *okiya* by a contract, their lot was much better than the prostitute's, for they could always hope to rely upon their talents alone and had a much better chance of being redeemed by a patron. Even today, when emancipation has rendered the geisha more like employees and freelancers, backing out too soon goes in some ways against the grain of a professional commitment. Having responded to the calling, the tradition was and sometimes still is that there should be no turning back. Ideally, fading looks should in no way herald the end of a career, especially for a geisha excelling as the exponent of an art. Yukari's tone when she speaks of the *maiko* who drop out during training is delicately and revealingly scathing. Unlike most women in Japan, she pushes family life into the background and puts her calling first, almost with the dedication of a nun. 'I never even think of getting married,' she proclaims. 'I enjoy life without children. Besides, once you get married, your life as a geisha is over.'

Statistics show that as many as 40 per cent of Japanese women put money first when considering a husband, and the geisha would be among those most likely to make their dreams come true. The traditional geisha ethic, however, makes marriage something of a taboo. A dedicated geisha might live with a man and often produces offspring, but as soon as she ties the knot officially, her days as a geisha are over. Besides, the overwhelming majority of men able to afford geisha company are not only already husbands but also very often grandfathers. Geisha are thus most likely to become the mistress of a man in his declining years, which for some is a highly lucrative prospect.

The geisha stands at the crest of the wave of the *mizu shobai*, but she is nevertheless just a star performer in exactly the same theatre. Spinsters and bachelors in the West have always been comparatively freer to pursue each other than in Confucian Japan, which traditionally has no pond in which the fish can swim around to find a mate. With no sanctioned social whirl, the singles pool finds itself reproduced artificially in the *mizu shobai*, an aquarium reserved for men, rather like those Japanese anglers' reserves in which fish are bred specially for release in teeming tanks to be hooked at the drop of a line. Out of all the females floating around in the water trade, the geisha stand out as the prime catch – the women coming closest to eligible spinsters.

Qualifying for the geisha élite is not only a matter of acquired skills or even natural good looks, it also calls for splendid trappings which the geisha will have to purchase herself. It is highly unseemly for a geisha to be seen in the same gown too often by the same guests, and the styles, colours, patterns of kimono and the thickness of silks are rigorously determined by seasonal fashion. Consequently they must have an extensive wardrobe in which well over a hundred kimonos would not be unusual. Every year, a geisha buys a sumptuous new kimono specially for seasonal events, such as the New Year parties which are held 4–14 January, when corporate life resumes after the holidays. A kimono purchased for this, Yukari informs me, is good only for that particular year; alluding subtly to the Chinese zodiac, the design and colour for the following New Year will be different. When Emperor Hirohito fell terminally ill in 1988, the pall falling over the country's night life presented Yukari with a professional disaster. All the New Year parties were cancelled.

This said goodbye to a sum ranging between 500,000 and 2,000,000 yen, the price for the kind of kimono worn by the geisha élite. In addition to purely practical considerations, the high cost of kimonos in general is one of the main reasons why the majority of ordinary women now only own one or two. A hand-dyed and embroidered silk kimono fashioned by a renowned artisan is unique, astronomically expensive, and fragile.

'It costs a fortune to keep yourself in clothes,' Yukari laments. 'A kimono costs 15,000 yen to clean.' And 5,000 per blotch when it comes to removing stains. Even her generous salary falls short. 'Sooner or later,' she concludes, 'a geisha has to get herself a *danna*.'

Though less wealthy lovers are by no means unheard of among geisha today, the *danna*, lord, master and a term used outside the geisha world to denote a husband, is more commonly a man with money: an industrial or trading company tycoon, a banker, a real estate baron or a politician. The *danna* is the geisha's regular patron and, once she enters such a relationship, it usually becomes an exclusive concubinage which is tantamount to marriage. At forty years old and heir to a huge family business, Yukari's *danna* is young. One need not be overly cynical about the allure of his financial background; everyone in their circle of acquaintances agrees that the couple, who have been together for five years, are admirably matched.

Yet geisha ethic or not, there can be no wedding bells and happy end. Her *danna* is not only typically already married and a father, but his is a marriage arranged between venerable families of industrial-political tycoons and there is no way out. He is perfectly free to spend much time with Yukari, for he and his wife have nothing in common and lead separate lives. He can keep the *honne* of his affair to himself but, since his father is a member of the Diet, the obligatory *tatemae* rules out the scandal involved with divorce. Looking at Yukari, a completely contemporary-looking young woman, and her perfectly ordinary, if married, boyfriend – both of whom spend their free weekends in jeans and T-shirts, freely socializing together among friends – it seems fantastic that they should be geisha and *danna*. Despite all appearances to the contrary and their own true aspirations, they are confined to roles hundreds of years old.

Thinking about Hideo Gosha's lurid and glossy 1983 film *Yokiroh*, a tale of fierce rivalry between geisha in the early twenties, one wonders. The pursuit of a *danna* is a deadly serious business, and the legendary geisha rivalry is all too real. Nagai Kafu's classic novel *Udeku-rabe*, the tale of a pathetic Shimbashi geisha buffeted around on the mercenary and cynical tides of her profession, is translated as just that: *Geisha in Rivalry*. Gosha of course focuses on sordid cat-fights: hair-pulling, scratching, biting and kimono-ripping as screaming geisha writhe on the floor of the ladies' toilet in a plush, jazzy Taisho-period dance hall. First of all Yukari's eyes open in dismay. 'Oh, no. My goodness, not these days!'

On second thoughts, she suddenly remembers witnessing a spat at the dinner table involving two inebriated geisha. Having steadily watched her rival pouring sake for her lover and making goo-goo eyes at him, the jealous one finally got up to pour sake all over the other's lustrous black chignon. After relating this, Yukari hesitates a moment and comes clean with a mischievous smile. 'As a matter of fact, I once had a fight with a girl myself. I just grabbed hold of her kimono collar and slapped her face.' She falls shy of giving the details of the contention, but she does glee-fully affirm that she won. It was pragmatism that really won the day however, for: 'Neither of us really dared to fight to the finish. We were too afraid to mess up our kimonos.'

Drunkenness, of course, is as much the norm in the geisha party as it is in the local bar. Nor is it entirely confined to the patrons. Drinking and the geisha life go together. Until her doctor proscribed it, slight and elegant Yukari says she downed between ten and fifteen *tokkuri* flasks of sake on an average night. Amounting to almost two litres, this is enough to send most ordinary mortals into a coma. At thirty, Yukari looks far younger and as fresh as a daisy, but after a period of serious illness last year, she was warned that alcohol had aged her beyond her years. No one really minds if she only drinks orange juice; a geisha who is both pretty and accomplished is now too hard to come by for anyone to quibble. Knowing Yukari's health to be fragile, her *danna* has other ideas. He wants her to quit the profession; he is more than wealthy enough to provide for her. But she won't hear of it. She wouldn't leave her life as a geisha behind for the world.

Time was when the geisha party could be tailored to taste. The *kemban* could be prevailed upon to supply the kind suited to lecherous sybarites, literati or genteel civil servants and everything in between. For all today's emphasis on traditionalism, however, yesterday's refinements are often wasted on today's patrons. I recently heard one retired Asakusa geisha lament: 'A geisha used to be judged more on her accomplishments; nowadays the majority are popular for their looks alone. In any case, customers don't appreciate samisen music and they don't even know how to play the traditional party games any more, even if the geisha do.'

Yukari, although a dedicated traditional performer herself, takes this in her stride. 'It doesn't really matter much to us what the guests do. Sometimes they just get drunk and fall asleep. We wake them up when it's time to go.' It seems a shame to go to such elaborate and expensive lengths to wind up snoring on the floor, but in a country boasting eight of *Fortune* magazine's top-twenty world tycoons, some have money to burn.

Yukari thinks back on the tragi-comical and indecorous geisha-in-rivalry scene mentioned earlier, which she witnessed some eight years ago. 'As a matter of fact you used to be able to get away with things like that, but now the grey workaday world is making clients lose their sense of humour. Time was when you could get drunk and forget about it all the next day, but these days they're *majime* [grave] all the time – and vindictive too. A geisha with a character fiery enough to do something like that might even have amused people before, now they would never call her again.'

Robert Guillain, an eminent French journalist who remained in Japan for many years from the early thirties and is one of the West's few true geisha connoisseurs, recently wrote a book about his experiences in the world of flowers and willows. He mentions a geisha party in the 1950s, when one of the guests confided that, without the urbane geisha to prompt them, their evening of conversation was doomed. 'If it wasn't for us,' one geisha added, 'they would only be familiar with Hollywood and Marilyn Monroe. Luckily we're there to keep them in Japan. Not only to entertain them with chatter, but to cultivate them – to bring them our art and all the arts of Japanese culture.'

The geisha party was once an affair cherished by intellectuals and artists of all persuasions too, but these days it is a luxury to be enjoyed only by an ageing and privileged few who are rarely from the more modest cultural walks of life. The astronomical expenses lavished on geisha socializing are just part and parcel of corporate expenses; very few of the politicians, industrial representatives, real estate barons, élite gangsters, etc. are paying for it out of their own pockets.

The geisha's art and artifices were once a product of their time, but the world she reflects has vanished. Japan has changed a great deal; the geisha, at least ideally, has changed not at all or too little. Outside of the geisha world, classical singing, dancing and musical instruments join flower arrangement and the tea ceremony either as revered and petrified arts, or as occupational therapy for housewives. Technopolitan Japan is the land of the symphony orchestra, TV, aerobics and the rock video clip. Sad as it is, the geisha's rigorously structured make-believe is superannuated; no longer understood, their stylizations and artistry lose out as the contemporary curtain falls on all but the prettiest. Pretty girls simply never go out of fashion.

It's getting late; tomorrow is Monday and Yukari has to rise at seven for samisen and singing practice; in the evening there will be a *ryotei* party with guests from a large corporation entertaining a couple of important foreign clients. As we make our way to the train station and Yukari heads for home, we pass some of urban Japan's currently ubiquitous construction sites and vacant lots along the way, upon many of which there stood *ryotei* and *machiai* only months ago. *Ryotei* are traditionally built of wood, but these days some have been incongruously moved upstairs behind the cold façades of purely functional new buildings and, naturally, many have simply gone for good.

'I don't think this is going to last,' one of the 180 remaining geisha in Akasaka reflects a little sadly. 'It can't.' I almost ask her what she'll do if – when – it doesn't, but on second thoughts I swallow the question and bid her goodnight.

THE GEISHA CLIMATE

> In those days, when he hadn't really known anything at all, geisha had seemed to him the most beautiful and enchanting of creatures. When a geisha spoke to him, it made him so unspeakably happy that he hardly knew what to do. Today, even if he wanted to, he could never return to such an innocent state of mind.
>
> Nagai Kafu, *Geisha in Rivalry*

Out of 17,000 geisha remaining, most are of the altogether less dainty *onsen*, hot-spring, persuasion. The *onsen* geisha's reputation is not of the most refined. At a hot-spring resort in Nagano prefecture in 1982, no less than 230 of them stormed the local police station and government offices in high dudgeon. The contention was that foreign *Japayuki* prostitutes had invaded their turf. The geisha also appealed to the All Japan Geisha and Geisha House Operators' Union and the reluctant authorities were forced to take action; prostitutes are illegal and geisha are not.

Having conspicuously deported a handful of the foreign invaders, the authorities typically turned their backs as fresh batches of South-East Asians were merely headquartered thenceforth in a neighbouring town. The local geisha business continued to decline. In a weekly magazine, one hotel manager explained that the geisha could be haughty with clients, especially 'farmer types' lacking in *savoir-vivre*, and that the younger, prettier and more compliant *Japayuki* were more popular items anyway. True or not, the *onsen* geisha have always had the reputation for being shorter on the cultural and longer on the carnal, which has earned them the disdain of their urban sisters. These days more and more *onsen* geisha will join the customer in the curative waters of the bath and please him in other ways. An increasing number are from abroad, and fewer and fewer are the genuine article.

One should not dismiss the *onsen* geisha out of hand. I remember one party in which the carnal and the cultural were perfectly balanced between Chidori, who was a spry lady of seventy, and Pinko, who was opulent, seductive and not quite so much a lady in early middle age. Chidori was a consummate singer and samisen player and, although no one knew the songs, like her highly entertaining conversation, they were by turns poetic, evocative and ribald enough in content to arouse an enthusiastic response. The old lady was indeed the life and soul of a party which, after ending in the hotel banquet hall, moved into a large bedroom upstairs. The table was set with food again around armies of bottles standing to attention; the party went on.

Meanwhile, Pinko not only kept all glasses full with even greater assiduity than is usual even among geisha, but flirted openly and extremely promisingly with everyone. There were ten men present, and all ten were made to feel that they were each to be the sole and exclusive beneficiary of her charms when the evening drew to a close. Since all ten were sharing the room, this, of course, was not to be. As drink flowed freely, plump Pinko suffered the most indiscreet attentions with peals and squeals of merriment. It seemed that everybody had one hand beneath the folds of her kimono and wherever one moved one's own someone else's was already there.

Looking like the party sequence in Kurosawa's film *The Lower Depths*, others were carousing through classic dance routines in their dishevelled cotton *yukata* kimonos as Chidori worked up a storm on the samisen. I have a polaroid picture commemorating the occasion, which shows one bespectacled celebrant perched on top of the TV set leering as beatifically as a small boy with a prawn protruding from the fly of his underpants. At two o'clock in the morning the party was over. The old lady put her samisen away in its case and her younger companion smoothed her kimono and assumed a belated mask of dignity. As I watched them walk away into the night to a waiting taxi from the hotel window, they seemed like femininity's and Japonisme's answer to Laurel and Hardy. Comical perhaps, but a dying species nevertheless. When lean old Chidori retires (as she no doubt has by now) or is no more, the plump, amiable Pinko, who has none of her accomplishments, will never be able to replace her.

In Niigata, a regional capital in the north-west of Honshu, there were 500 geisha active two decades ago; in 1987 there were only sixty. The situation was so drastic that local corporate moguls intervened to form the Niigata Geisha Company to protect the remainder and to attract new recruits. According to an article in the magazine *Shukan Sankei*, the company geisha are paid a rather unremarkable monthly salary of 250,000 yen. Still, a few hopefuls presented themselves and seven were accepted for training by seasoned professionals. As the advertisement the company placed in the press implied, there are still fringe benefits, although one of these was highly unorthodox in true geisha terms: 'Become a Niigata star, enhance your culture and find a good husband!'

With a history going back to the Heian period, Kyoto remains Japan's pre-eminent repository of traditional culture. Once upon a time some of the narrow streets sloping steeply from Kyomizu temple were lined with teahouses and brothels, especially towards the foot of the hill where they began to concentrate in earnest in a quarter called Gion. The brothels were moved long ago of course, but sedate teahouses, *ryotei* and *machiai* of old wood still stand in the streets of Gion, which is not only one of the very rare old districts to be preserved and protected in Japan but also with nearby Pontocho along the Kamo river makes Kyoto the nation's geisha heartland.

Beautiful Gion is a prime tourist destination, but the street is as far as the tour guide dares or the intrepid individual can afford to go. Gion is expensive and exclusive. The *maiko*, gaudy little dolls with tiny mouths and big black eyes in heavily painted white faces, bustle awkwardly along the sedate streets of wood, pigeon-toed on their high sandals, while the geisha, haughty and svelte in their more streamlined lengths of sumptuous silk, glide with studied, regal nonchalance.

A trifle over-ornate and blanched according to bygone canons of beauty, the Kyoto geisha are saved only from looking like the kind of dolls that gather dust beneath glass bells by a scintillating vivacity which concrete modernism has not altogether succeeded in crushing. Both disappear from sight into doorways leading to a secret world of the past accessible only to a select few. Summer finds Pontocho geisha parties in the open air along the riverside; the multicoloured butterfly women hover between seated rows of ageing and high-ranking corporate penguins in white shirts. Such parties are virtually to be enjoyed by no one else. In nearby Gion are more *ryotei*, *cha-ya* and *machiai*, where elegant but blank wooden façades mask rooms in which glittering geisha officiate in décors of sumptuous antique fittings looking out onto tiny landscape gardens with dwarf pines and flickering stone lanterns.

It is a secret world that no ordinary tourist, whether Japanese or foreign, can ever hope to see. Not even money can buy a man into the élite haunts of geishadom, for he must first be invited or introduced. The money, the secrecy and the élitism are also precisely what has contributed to the geisha's decline. It is often and correctly said that it is cheaper to live according to western patterns in Japan. A fine wooden Japanese house costs more to build than one made of ferroconcrete; plastic is cheaper than lacquerware; refined Japanese cuisine is far more costly than the costliest western fare; even a top western designer's dress comes much cheaper than a good kimono. Traditional Japan is prohibitive. The geisha, an intrinsic part of it, have priced themselves out of the market.

Kyoto seems to survive as the geisha capital, but appearances are deceptive: there are only about twenty-two maiko and 500 fully fledged geisha left. With 2,000 distributed in other small enclaves but concentrated mainly in Shimbashi, Akasaka and Kagurazaka, Tokyo still has the greatest number in Japan. In Okazaki, an important town in Aichi prefecture, the proprietress of a *ryotei* which has a long tradition of geisha parties told me that elderly performing *geiko* (they use the Kyoto term here too) still turn up to sing and play the samisen like cultural relics, but the younger ones are no more. Instead, as the *geiko* go through the old routines, the business of making conversation with the guests at table has been taken over by young women in modern designer clothing calling themselves 'companions'. Many of them are in fact recruited from the by-now long and well-established ranks of what is the geisha's single greatest rival: the bar hostess.

Only a very young man would 'be so unspeakably happy that he wouldn't know what to do' when addressed by a geisha. As a middle-aged man circa 1912, Nagai Kafu's jaded protagonist was thinking nostalgically back on his youth. Nowadays a young man is as unlikely to know 'what to do' as he is to encounter a geisha at all. Older men scarcely know much better. The correct form involved an appreciation of the geisha's company at face value, of the little games and the ritualized reversions to childhood, as well as a celebration of the ultimate *femme-objet*. Whether it was sublimated or physical, it did indeed require an innocent frame of mind, of a kind all but lost in modern Japan.

'In just a few years,' as Junichi Mita, a writer focusing often on the geisha world, drily remarked a few years ago, 'the profession will go the way of the American Indian, with dancing staged only for tourists.' In Asakusa, where bus-loads of foreigners and rural Japanese on package tours line up outside bogus geisha and *oiran* restaurants, this dire prophecy has already been fulfilled.

THE BAR HOSTESS

On the plump side and fifty years old, the handsome woman with the necklace of pink pearls and dressed in an immaculate and expensive white blouse and long black velvet skirt could easily be mistaken for a first violin in an orchestra. Or so it at first seems. On the nights she wears a kimono, she almost has the bearing of high breeding. Her raven hair has just been permed, artistically teased by flattering hands and finally sprayed to taxidermic rigidity in her usual beauty parlour in a Ginza back street, and her foundation cream is just a fraction too thick. Studded with tiny diamonds, the Cartier watch is solid gold, and the wearer is shrouded in an aura of Chanel No. 5. *Mama-san* has come a long way.

Kyoko remembers all too well how thirty years ago, barely educated and coming up to Tokyo from Kyushu, she started out as a hostess in a none too respectable club in Shinjuku. Not that she had been a prostitute or anything, for Kyoko was exceptionally pretty and there are plenty of ways for a girl to use her charms without actually selling them. Even if once in a blue moon there were those favoured customers to whom one did have to be especially nice. From these humble beginnings Kyoko moved up in the world to Akasaka. Being near to the Diet and the administrative hubs of industry and trading, the area had class.

Kyoko was no fool. She had no house mother like a geisha to prompt her, but in her spare time she read a great deal. She devoured anything from Dostoevsky to Albert Camus, and from Natsume Soseki to Junichiro Tanizaki. She just adored Françoise Sagan's *Bonjour Tristesse*, she saw all the right films and she went to the theatre. She listened to music: classical and popular, Japanese and western. She educated herself. At the time, she was hostessing in Akasaka's Mikado, which joined the Copacabana in the cabaret élite, billing glittering revues from Las Vegas and Mexico City, from Brazil and the Folies of Paris.

During its heyday in the sixties, the garish and cavernous Mikado (a safely archaic word for 'emperor') was reputed to have some 2,000 hostesses. It was a kind of railway station pullulating with pretty passengers bound for the bright lights, but despite being oft and loudly trumpeted, their incredible numbers diminished year by year. The armies of girls were organized in smaller platoons headed by one of a copious contingent of mamas – the sergeant majors to the handmaidens of thirsty corporate samurai battling to boost the rising economy of the sixties.

The Mikado was right in front of my office when I arrived in Japan in 1979, and rumour had it that the hostesses numbered a thousand. By then no one even suggested that I go there and, indeed, its glitzy posters of feather-and-sequin showgirls of the genus Japonica made it just old-fashioned enough to be quaint, but not enough to be interesting. It was also expensive. Two years later the hostess contingent had dropped by half again and by 1985 both the Mikado and the Copacabana, relics from another time, had closed their doors for good.

One night at the Mikado in 1963, Kyoko was called to the table of one Saito-san, a senior business executive who subsequently made his ardour clear by coming again, and again, and again. The father of two children who were the fruit of an otherwise sterile *omiai* marriage, Saito was typically eager to spend as much time as he possibly could outside his home. Taking care not to rebuff him during the year he wooed her several nights a week at the Mikado, Kyoko merely held out an evasive but promising 'next time'. It's extraordinary what one can get on the strength of such a painless promise. A gold bracelet, perhaps a mink stole. One had to be careful, though. Too many expensive presents and a girl finds herself having to give in. Kyoko trod very carefully. Saito was not the only admirer she had, for there was Suzuki who sent her orchids and huge boxes of caviar on her birthday and Murano who lavished expensive *oseibo* seasonal gifts on her every summer and New Year. Saito was more cultivated; he was an avid reader. A top executive in an expanding medium-sized trading company moving Japanese products abroad, Saito was the eldest son in a family owning a lot of land. He had dabbled in writing in his youth, which Kyoko found attractive, but he was now dabbling more profitably in real estate, which she found irresistible.

To Kyoko meanwhile, the trouble was that with all those hostesses at the Mikado, one wound up being just another face in the crowd. Having done her homework besides, she felt that she had educated herself out of it.

Saito meanwhile sometimes frequented another, smaller and more opulent hostess club with an old university chum, who was similarly employed in a trading company in Akasaka. One of the hostesses had apparently left the club and the *mama-san* was looking for someone else. Would Kyoko be interested?

The comely Kyoko landed the job and Saito never went back to the Mikado. Although he was fifty-five, 26-year-old Kyoko found Saito increasingly elegant and dapper, assets which were greatly enhanced as their intimacy and her familiarity with his business increased. She gradually accepted to go out with him on dates. He took her to exorbitantly expensive little restaurants and on Sundays she sometimes accompanied him to his renowned and very expensive golf club. The inevitable happened when Saito took her off to the plush Fujiya Hotel in Hakone for the weekend. The romantic escapade had been a great success; Saito and Kyoko habitually trysted thenceforth in Tokyo, but only in hotels, about which Kyoko had reservations. To Saito's regret, Kyoko often found excuses to leave shortly after their lovemaking, just when he was looking forward to breakfast tête-à-tête. She never allowed him back to her apartment; she 'lived with her elder sister' who was in fact married to a plumber in Hakata and had never left Kyushu. Sometimes, for no apparent reason, Kyoko would rebuff him gently at the club, and there was no taking her out afterwards.

Saito wanted something more. During one of their hotel dates, he made a proposition that was partly love and, for her benefit at least, partly business. Would it not be more convenient for both of them if she had an apartment in the neighbourhood? Kyoko would think about it. Perhaps she'd like him to rent her a bar which she could run on her own? By 1967, Kyoko had not only been Saito's mistress for three years, managed a posh little hostess bar at his expense, but also occupied an apartment purchased in her name, which he visited regularly. That year she announced that she was pregnant and had no intention of being otherwise. No one was more pleased than Kyoko that their child, Sayuri, was a girl.

Poor Saito-san. It was pathetic really. He'd always seemed to find time for her but he'd been a busy man – too busy. Against medical advice, he had presided too energetically over his company instead of retiring; a massive stroke took him out of this world in 1977 in his sixty-eighth year. He'd provided very generously for Kyoko; Sayuri had attended the best schools. So generously in fact, that in 1978, Kyoko dropped the Akasaka bar she had merely been renting and purchased a place standing on what was even then some of the most expensive land on God's earth, here in the Ginza.

Finding an eye moistening as she thinks back on Saito, Kyoko dabs discreetly at it with the corner of a lace handkerchief: a mote of mascara has fallen into the corner. Now she casts both shrewd eyes over a large room of silken plush and thick woollen pile in an art deco symphony of warm beige, pinky greys and rich mellow lighting. A fountain representing the zodiacal sign Aquarius stands surrounded by potted plants at one end of the room, with perfumed water trickling from a gold-plated bronze nude also in the art deco style. Dressed in white tuxedos with silver lamé lapels over salmon-pink shirts, a small combo congregates around a piano Kyoko had custom-lacquered in light chestnut brown. Many hostess bars go with the trends, and Kyoko believes in keeping up with them. Out of the options, she found high-tech a bit cold but found in *retro* a particular appeal. The band leader, tanned, in his late forties and sporting a thin trimmed moustache, wears his hair slicked back in the fashion of the fifties and has a penchant for the Platters. More often, however, his guitar work is confined to requests for Enka standards in deference to the guests. Even in the Ginza, clients totter up to sing through the microphone *karaoke*-fashion, with the added asset of a live band behind them.

This is the court over which Kyoko reigns as queen. She knows every regular client's name, the founding day of his company and his birthday. She needs no Dunn and Bradstreet for all the details of corporate history, the annual turnover and everyone's rank. She knows that Watanabe-san likes playing golf and Otard cognac and that Eguchi-san is a sumo fan who drinks Jack Daniels on the rocks. She spends a fortune on expensive gifts for her favoured clients at appropriate times of the year. Out of ten pretty girls attired in seductive and expensive designer clothing, including her pretty 22-year-old daughter Sayuri, several coo, twitter, fawn over and agree with everything uttered by middle-aged business-men sitting before low tables of dark rosewood and polished brown marble around the walls. Others have taken to the floor to dance with them.

In a really top-class bar, however, twittering at the tables and using nubile charms to flatter greying egos is not enough. This club might not be the *crème de la crème*, but in view of her own experience, a mama like Kyoko would still favour girls who keep track of current events, know something about the stock exchange, politics, sport, showbusiness and, albeit to a much lesser degree these days, culture. Their opinions will neither be taken seriously nor appreciated. As a truly fine art, however, agreeing is more than just a matter of nodding a pretty head, it requires knowing what the honourable guests are talking about. Like the geisha, the hostess catering for the élite will be bound sometimes to silence. Those exchanging pleasantries on plush sofas might find their tongues sufficiently loosened to spice their talk with high-flying corporate matters, not to mention politics. Like those holding sake cups in the *ryotei*, some of the hands holding glasses of whisky and VSOP in the top hostess bars also hold the nation's future.

Although some would be uncomfortable in the alien presence, overseas clients are often brought to hostess bars by Japanese businessmen, but those frequenting hostess bars on their own are few. Mixed company is so much part of life in the West that the average westerner greets with little enthusiasm the idea of what are in fact actresses professionally providing an illusion of socializing that he takes for granted at home. At least not when he knows that the chances of pursuing the matter after hours are meagre indeed. More importantly, unless he happens to be a millionaire, not even the well-heeled foreign executive in Tokyo would think of paying the prices incurred in top-notch hostess clubs.

The tariffs in hostess bars are not just a consequence of the high yen but, as in the geisha world, simply because a customer's outlay is almost never his own. In Japanese firms, 'entertainment' expenses are considered part of the costs of running a company. Indeed they are. In 1988, the aggregate sum for corporate wining, dining, gift-giving and political donations amounted to over four and a half trillion yen. The top Ginza clubs are the haunts of the élite of Japan's giant corporations. Their fabulous cost enhances the firm's prestige and executives pay unhesitatingly when eager to impress the clients they treat to a night on the town.

According to one executive, there is a long-standing joke about the Ginza bar pricing formula: 'Just for starters it's 10,000 yen to cross the threshold, 10,000 to sit

down; ten for a glass and 10,000 each for the ice cubes.'
An exaggeration perhaps, but with drinks, exorbitantly
priced snacks not too appropriately known as *charm*, a
daunting table charge and hostess fees, 100,000 yen per
head is by no means unusual in the top clubs.

Aware that they are beyond the reach of foreign
clients, some hostess bars in need of more customers
have dropped their charges from the astronomical to the
merely expensive. Knowing that the Japanese tend to
spend corporate money and that foreigners shell out of
their own pockets, one hostess bar in Roppongi has
introduced a dual pricing system. If Ginza hostess clubs
still draw the corporate élite, there are signs that the only
slightly less expensive run-of-the-mill clubs are declining. The younger executives once frequenting these have
taken to the fashionable bars of Aoyama and Roppongi.
Rather than having female company provided, they
sometimes bring their own.

Ichi ban, niban otokui, number one, number two clients:
Japanese corporations categorize their business relations
according to their importance. The *ichi-ban* client, or one
that the firm hopes will become such, is taken to geisha
parties or to Ginza hostess bars; the third class qualifies
only for an expensive restaurant. The same applies
largely to office personnel; the élite clubs are reserved for
executives at *kacho* (president) and *bucho* (section chief)
levels and many companies subscribe to lesser clubs for
the benefit of staff further down the corporate scale.
Hierarchy extends to the world of pleasure too.

Every month, the hostess bar sends the bill to the
company. In the case of large firms, it might work out at
millions of yen. For smaller clubs dealing with smaller
firms, the system can sometimes be a source of trouble:
finding itself negotiating heavy waters, the firm might be
unable to pay. Hostess clubs owned by gangsters (and,

from the plushest to the sleaziest, many are) can obviously be very resourceful in recouping their losses, but the others have to grin and bear it. Loss can sometimes fall heavily on the shoulders of the hostesses, especially in less prestigious clubs. She is the one who makes sure that the customer and his guests imbibe and orders the rounds of drinks. Customers sometimes fall in arrears with their monthly bills or disappear without paying them, and hostesses can find themselves responsible for debts amounting to several million yen. For these, Soapland is often the only way out.

Pink-tinted mirrors around the walls reproduce the girls in myriad images; when lovely Sayuri opens her petal mouth to laugh, just before she covers it with a dainty hand, she is multiplied as many times over as an angelic choir in some heavenly Hollywood mural. Another beauty, a few years her senior and wearing a tight black cocktail dress and matching lace tights, finds her table warming to the occasion. The bespectacled faces around it glow bright red even in the half-light. The time is ripe for her to lace her conversation with innuendo, not unprompted of course, which she delivers with a studied balance of raucousness and charm. 'I wish I had mirrors like that on my bedroom walls,' she remarks slyly. 'Where do you think I could find a room like that?'

The allusion to the mural arrangement of the love hotel is in no way an invitation; it is a goad. The name of the game is arousing interest, gradually firing passion as the evening wears on and gently extinguishing it when the customer is not drinking any more. The hostess will thus leave an impression on him; the idea is that he will come back to try his luck at seduction next time – and time and time again. If many of the more sleazy counterparts abroad, such as the notorious bar girls in Paris's

Pigalle, are consummate experts at ordering pricey champagne, a good Japanese hostess will always know far more subtle ways of conjuring not champagne, but expensive snacks to appear on the table.

In the legitimate hostess club, sleeping with a customer is the exception rather than the rule. The hostess ethic is that if she allows a guest to seduce her, he feels that he's achieved a goal and won't come back. The ambitious hostess might plot her life out before her, and proceed according to exactly the same methods as Kyoko. Like the majority of women in Japan, most hostesses dream of getting married. Except for those who become someone's *nigo*, they usually do. Nevertheless, scores of hostess bars are in fact fronts for prostitution, setting themselves apart from more frankly sleazy pink salons and cabarets only by such considerations as price, manners and the quality of service.

If some Japanese are put off by the outspokenness of western women, many are fascinated by the exoticism of the blonde, to the extent that foreign hostesses can sometimes be paid higher wages than their Japanese colleagues for the same job. One Frenchwoman for instance, although no longer in her prime, had peroxided herself sufficiently to be the stuff of dreams and worked as a hostess for six months in order to retreat afterwards into a Zen Buddhist temple. Another, an English girl fonder of travelling than a desk job in London, spent some four months of the year hostessing in order to spend the rest on the beaches of South-East Asia. Others, Japanophiles eager to stay put, use hostess money for such mundane enterprises as opening English language schools.

'It's pretty boring work,' lamented an American woman. 'You just sit there looking dumb, pour out the drinks and agree with everything they say.' There's a tendency with some to think that all foreign women are pushovers, but familiarity can breed respect, and most foreign hostesses concede that regular customers are the best behaved.

Many Japanese girls work as hostesses on a part-time basis, complementing an office job with moonlighting two or three nights a week. Not a few are students. Salaries are high, uniforms (usually evening dresses or kimono) are often provided and, as long as the club or the hostess can find a suitable replacement, holidays are usually more flexible than the Japanese norm. Hostesses travel a great deal too. The reverence for a pale, aristocratic complexion has waned with the health and fitness boom, and these days many hostesses are tanned from holidays in Hawaii and Guam, Bali, Phuket or the Philippines.

Some of these forays, however, are not just for pleasure. As the Japanese overseas investment portfolio expands, so the number of executives posted abroad increases. In Thailand, for instance, where the number-one foreign investor is Japan, Ginza hostesses look up favoured customers who lavished large amounts of cash on their clubs before being posted abroad. '*Yoroshiku onegaishimasu*' – please be good to us – is a Japanese *formule de politesse* used as a mere greeting upon introduction, but which can also urge its recipient to continue dispensing favours. To bring the point home and secure their continued patronage on their return to Japan, such hostesses also bring their expatriate customers expensive gifts. Hostesses normally earn substantial perks from the clubs for every extra yen they can squeeze from a patron. One tries to imagine a London barmaid cruising the Costa Brava to entice expat regulars back to the Bull and Bush, but then the pub-crawler in Britain is worth only a few beers.

According to a former tour guide who used to specialize in expensive customized overseas tours for small groups: 'Hostesses are a lively, unpredictable lot. You fix up a sightseeing programme for them in Bangkok only to find that they're off doing business around the Japanese corporations when they get there.' Pointedly keeping out of bed with customers can take its toll too. 'I've seen them ask for interpreters to chat up men they ogle in the hotels and they're not against investing in the services of local gigolos.'

The girls make sure that the honourable guest's glass is always full, pouring the whisky and dropping in the ice cubes in a series of dainty gestures culminating in a dexterous twiddle with a stirrer. Then they play parlour games such as suddenly dropping pencils or banknotes and having guests attempt to catch them, as well as a number of little tricks involving coins, matchsticks and handkerchiefs. Such diversions are obviously a legacy of the geisha. They inevitably trigger gales of perfectly timed silvery laughter and provide excuses for touching fingertips and brushing hands together. They might even give rise to the squeeze of a thigh, until the male hand is gently but firmly pressured away if it appears to be trespassing in earnest. In the better club, a jokingly reproachful pout from the hostess generally suffices to halt lapses in behaviour. If the offending party is more obnoxiously drunk, *Mama-san* may have to intervene, which she will do by addressing him firmly and cajolingly, as though he were a little boy.

Among foreign executives entertained by Japanese clients, many do not stay long enough to be familiar with the ways of Japan. Surrounded by giggling girls, John and Joe look much like ecstatic castaways overwhelmed by exotic islanders, but their dreams will soon end at closing time. Discovering that the compliance, the innuendo, the flattery and the body-language from the hostesses amount only to this and nothing more, they might feel conned. Their Japanese hosts, who in any case are footing the bill, will be back here in a couple of days' time. The play acting is part of the pleasure. The final ritual is enacted on the street at closing time: as the fleets of taxis and black limousines splashed with neon signs line up outside the clubs, serried ranks of dressy mamas and hostesses bow low. With profuse thanks ringing in their ears, the cherished customers hiccup contentedly behind imperturbable white-gloved chauffeurs on their way home to the distant, gilded suburbs.

14

Sirens in the Silt

TURKISH DELIGHTS

'And,' he concluded, 'remember that there is nothing
wrong with using the bodies you got from your parents in
a careful and proper way. Just like the baseball stars Oh
and Nagashima, so all of you too make your living with
your bodies.'

Akiyuki Nozaka, *The Pornographers*

Up to the north of Tokyo's Asakusa is a district marked
on street maps as Senzoku 4-Chome. Here the visitor
might not only be struck with the great profusion of
establishments of the genus Soapland but, having read
about the Yoshiwara and its demise, he will also be
surprised to learn that Senzoku 4-Chome *is* the Yoshiwara. And while the area goes down as Senzoku in all
official metropolitan contexts, he may be delighted to
find that its numerous *demi-mondaines* go down on their
customers just as they have done – with only sporadic
interruptions – since 1657. The elegance and pageantry
are long gone, but the ancient red-light district is still
called the Yoshiwara by Soapland employees and devotees, as well as in scores of magazines promoting the
trade. It is ironical, not to say rather ominously
regressive, that the new façade for the old tricks should
consist once again of a bath-house disguise. In staging
the charade of the assisted bath, the venerable Yoshiwara has put the clock back more than 370 years and
returned to its primitive roots.

Ferroconcrete architectural extravaganzas in the love hotel style reflect the samurai fortress, Las Vegas and the Moulin Rouge. In the interests of mandatory discretion, the showy façades completely conceal the executrixes within. Upon crossing the threshold, it becomes apparent that Soapland ladies join the employees of cabarets and pink salons in a great variety of fancy dress: old-time courtesans in florid kimono, nurses, airline flight attendants, bunny girls, Suzy Wongs in high-necked mini cheongsams slit up the sides, SM leather goddesses and Buddhist and Catholic nuns.

It looks gaudy enough when the neon lights go up and reveal a good turnout on Saturday nights, but save for the touts in loud suits or tuxedos, the streets are virtually deserted on weekday afternoons. Signs on the houses bear enticing, exotic names: Scarlet, Versailles, the immodest-sounding Grand Canyon and with a *retro* touch reflecting one of the greatest foreign movie hits in Japan during the thirties, Pépé le Moko. Alongside all of these, Continental Club Coty defines continentalism with an additional and increasingly common note of welcome: 'No admittance of people from abroad.'

The facelifted Yoshiwara shares the same problems as Soapland as a whole: although far from dead, it struggles in the wake of the great variety of newer, cheaper and quicker forms of prostitution. The more recent decline of the Yoshiwara is due also to competition from a cheaper red-light district in Kawasaki, an industrial suburb on the way to Yokohama.

In 1964, Shirahama (White Harbour) lived in her native village near Niigata up in the north-west and was probably about nine years old. She was no doubt aware that Japan was by now the third largest steel producer in the world. Whether she saw this as just one of the many facts and figures she learned at school or not, like her classmates, she would have been far more excited over the imminent inauguration of the Shinkansen, the bullet train, and the fastest on the planet. But what she and all her schoolchums awaited in an agony of anticipation was a momentous occasion planned for October of the same year: the opening of the Tokyo Olympic Games. To the Japanese the Games stood for hard and well-earned pride; in under twenty years, the country had risen from utter desolation to be a dynamic and still rising member of the international community.

In those days, Shirahama was both too far away and too young to know that the government and the police were meanwhile frantically rushing around Tokyo's prospering red-light districts, taking measures to ensure that foreign Olympic visitors would leave Japan under the firm conviction that there weren't any – a fatuous process that was to be repeated again in Seoul for the Olympics in 1988. Some of the jerry-built amusement areas were being hastily bulldozed away to make way for skyscrapers planned to fill the visiting world with awe. For the remaining survivors it was not so much a matter of making massive arrests or closing everything down as admonishments and warnings to provide a chaste *tatemae*, as the time-honoured carnal *honne* was swept under the metropolitan carpet.

Nevertheless, the various Christian women's movements were on the warpath. A powerful influence behind moral rearmament, they had been steadily and shrilly condemning the laxity of the status quo before the Diet. Although the Prostitution Prevention Law rather sensibly put the squeeze more on pimps than prostitutes, it was as full of holes as the profession it sought to control. Indeed, a survey conducted in 1966 revealed that, ten years after its implementation, the law had only reduced prostitution by a largely conjectural 30 per cent.

If the pre-Olympic cleanup cosmetically focused on the more conspicuous red-light districts in Tokyo, especially Shinjuku, it nevertheless portended bad news for the nation's plentiful bath-and-massage parlours, which were then known as *Toruko-buro*, a euphemism coined from the term 'Turkish bath'.

At the time, the little girl in Niigata was as blissfully ignorant of all this as she was about the profession she would adopt later on as Shirahama and which, by 1988, she had been pursuing for over a decade. Perhaps the greatest single change she has seen in all that time is that her particular kind of establishment, which was known as *Toruko* almost from the day the brothels officially closed down, was abruptly renamed Soapland in 1985. Whether Shirahama basked in more dignity as a *Toruko-jo* (*Toruko*-female) or as a *Sopu-reedi* – Soap-Lady – is a question she dismisses with a derisive smile and a noncommittal shrug.

As an outraged Turkish diplomat pointed out, there was of course nothing, but absolutely nothing in the least bit Turkish about *Toruko*. His vociferous letters to the Japanese press came at a most opportune time: barely six months before Japan's sex businesses were due to come yet again under the axe of propriety and the revisions to the Law on Businesses Affecting Public Morals in February 1985. Fearing the worst and abiding by the old golden rule of change as a means of survival, the Japan Bath Association held a competition to select a new name. After much ponderous deliberation by a panel of judges, the word 'Soapland' won the day.

If the practice of selling daughters into brothels had been wiped out in 1956, slavery survived to some degree as per the universal tendency for the strong to prey upon the weak. It still does. As in most countries attempting to curtail rather than control prostitution, the dividing line between women entering and leaving the profession of their own accord and the *ingénue* kept there by bullying pimps can be extremely difficult to define. In a profession relegated to the shadows by the league of decency and exercised by employees who are consequently denied a union to protect them, such a line is easy to hide. In the event of ill-treatment, the harlot has nowhere to turn. By and large, however, today's Soapland business is run in all senses on the basis of easy come, easy go.

Either way, proper legislation and the fact that some women have no qualms about answering such a calling is always very far from the minds of moral crusaders. Typically galvanized rather than deterred by the prospect of challenging a phenomenon as old as humanity, those crusading again in 1964 made their battlefield in the baths. At their insistence, amendments to existing laws were passed in the Diet, and these made the steamy *toruko* people break out in a cold sweat. From now on, girls were to be decently clothed at all times and to confine their professional activities solely to massage. Under no circumstances were any services to be provided behind a locked door. These rules also explain why the door of the room occupied by Shirahama twenty-five years later should be provided with a window. Strangely enough, it has remained covered with a dusty curtain for just as long, during which time legions of masseuses have never failed to remove their scant clothing to perform services which, needless to say, have only very rarely been other than those occasioning the amendments to the law.

Nevertheless, time was when the *toruko* provided a bona fide bath and massage by a female attendant for a basic fee. For starters, that is. On top of this and properly itemized and priced, there was invariably *sabisu* (service), *supeshiaru* (special) or *daburu* (double service) – more widely known as *furu kōsu* (full course). While the full-course menu included all the masturbatory and oral hors-d'oeuvre, the scope of the favours dispensed depended upon the guest's budget. For a mere *sabisu*, the man could find himself bathing on his own and the cursorily massaging *toruko-jo* rarely bothered to remove her clothes. This breakdown has largely vanished from Soapland today, where the full course is the norm by definition, although detailed and itemized tariff systems are widely used in other fields of the business.

According to Boye DeMente in his *Bachelors' Japan*, the Bath Association pulled wool over the eyes of the Olympics-crazed authorities by 'passing regulations which were even more binding than those passed by the Government. Of course, this latter action was just a smoke screen and none of the regulations were ever carried out.' This peculiar system of smoke-screen self-censorship, which the authorities imposing it like to term 'voluntary' restraint, prevails in the film and video industries too.

Shirahama operates in a house which, like others not under *yakuza* control, is run like a family business. As in the Yoshiwara, some places have been owned for generations by local inhabitants who have moved with the tides to adapt, disguise and remodel their establishments according to the vagaries of morality. Shirahama's Kawasaki Soapland parlour is one of these. It is a three-storey concrete building painted a dull orange and festooned with pots of plastic flowers on sills before geometric stained-glass windows bricked up behind. Standing in front is a genial young fat man with thick black-rimmed glasses. Looking more like a respectable *salaryman*, he wears a spotless white shirt and a tie set awry not by sloppiness but by the thickness of his neck.

As you pass, he hails you amiably, soliciting with neither a dirty word nor a trace of vulgarity. If you show interest, he apologetically enquires, 'You don't mind wearing a condom, do you?' On the contrary. As little as two years ago, the remark made by this man, whom the denizens of the house refer to as the 'boy', would have been unthinkable, but with the gradual advance of Aids in Japan, the necessity for industrial overalls is sinking in.

'This is your first time here, isn't it?' asks the fat man, establishing that you do not have a *shimei* – a nominated girl, a favourite. Going behind the desk in the hotel-style foyer, he turns to an array of rectangular wooden tablets hanging on a rack behind him, each calligraphed with a girl's name. Several of the plaques, a survival from earlier brothel days, are missing: the girls are out or engaged. Ah, how about Shirahama? She's young and fresh, you understand, quite a *bijin* – a beauty. In fact, he adds proudly, she is the house's 'Numba Wan'.

He ushers you politely into a waiting room dominated by a large aquarium in the centre containing three angelfish moping around in water in need of changing. Presumably this is so that the customers sitting on either side of it would not have to look at each other. Beneath a TV set, which is on and unwatched, a plentiful supply of lurid *Eromanga* comic books is neatly displayed as a further deterrent to any conversation. Take away the garishness, and you have an exact equivalent to a doctor's waiting room.

When she arrives, Shirahama bows politely, proffers traditional words of welcome and graciously introduces herself. A rather thickset doll of a woman in her early thirties, dressed in a bright purple silk kimono, she is not exactly a beauty, but hers is a pretty, round face framed by a bobbed, *retro* perm and her winsomeness is enhanced with a hint of provocative irony denoting the seasoned whore. You are led upstairs following a rump tightly sheathed in silken purple, but the edge is taken off any carnal musings by orthodox remarks about the weather.

As in the houses in the old days, Shirahama rents her room on a fluctuating monthly basis, meaning that she gives the management 40 per cent of her earnings. The difference is that she is free to enter or leave as she pleases. Although not connected to the crime syndicates, the owners of such premises usually shell out substantial sums as protection money. Many girls find working for a *yakuza* outfit more profitable, for in the smaller independent places the exorbitant demands the gangs make on the proprietors tend to cut additionally into the girls' earnings.

That this is Shirahama's room there can be no doubt. The window is covered by a canvas awning which catches the sun to shine with fluorescent magenta brilliance offsetting the green potted plant on the sill. Her substantial collection of small plush animals, shrine trinkets, souvenir dolls and glass animals adorns tables and shelves at both ends of a brown naugahyde couch like a psychiatrist's covered with a clean white sheet. In front of this is a tiny miniature TV, placed to be seen lying down. White Harbour naturally does a lot of lying down, but the TV is strictly for when she lies alone.

The couch area opens directly on to a large pink and black tiled bathroom, on one side of which is a matching semi-sunken bath about six feet square and on the other a bulky, antiquated sweat-cabinet looking like a *retro*-futurist fixture from Terry Gilliam's movie *Brazil*. Shirahama disrobes. She stands, or rather poses, in traditional *déshabillé* with a scarlet underskirt moulding her generous hips and bound by a white sash tightly wrapped high up over a slim waist, beneath a bust rather riper than the Japanese norm. Stripping down to her panties and revealing legs rather too short in the shin, she busies herself running the bath, chatting gaily about this and that, without even a hint of seductiveness. The guest is manifestly in the company of a sort of nurse in a spa providing sexual physiotherapy.

Upon being invited to undress, he hands each item over to her, which she folds neatly and places in a shallow rectangular plastic basket. Then the guest is bidden to sit on a plastic stool. The seat is specially divided to facilitate sudsy, ticklish and intimate ministrations before his back is entirely covered with foam copiously squeezed from a sponge. Shirahama's fairy fingers massage tired shoulders and awaken other things, while she rubs a body as firm as an athlete's and soft as a baby's against the guest's back. Rinsing off the soap, she invites him to get into the bath and steps in herself, caressing, rubbing and wriggling like a porpoise.

After the bath, the *awa-odori*: the lather dance. Thai harlotry is popularly seen abroad as the originator of body-body massage, but the Japanese claim that the invention is theirs. The therapy is provided on a king-size inflatable rubber mattress as, assisted by a film of creamy soap suds, the naked girl massages every part of the male anatomy with every part of hers, including that softest and most arousing of natural scrubbing brushes. Following a general rinse-down, the session continues with a skilful display of what is called *shakuhachi*, a poetic metaphor alluding to the classic bamboo flute, and culminates with coitus.

Out of the programmed ninety minutes, some sixty remain. Shirahama makes quite sure that the guest gets every yen worth, beckoning to him to join her over on the psychiatrist's couch. Intermittently resorting to amazingly skilled oral and manual sexual massage techniques for the best part of an hour, Shirahama will coax renewed vigour and repeated encores from even the most flagging and recalcitrant member. The performance is completely ritualized, particularly at the soap stage, and the subsequent sex is provided with curious single-minded determination: the guest must take his pleasure. While there is absolutely no pretence of emotional involvement to keep the client coming back for more, there is none of the terse French '*Dépêche-toi mon chéri*,' or the whining US/British, 'I ain't got all day.' If a job is worth doing to the Japanese, it's worth doing properly; Shirahama wouldn't even think of counting the cracks on the ceiling.

Over a can of beer afterwards, Shirahama says that she came to Kawasaki ten years ago, although she has been in this particular place for five. Bored with life in Niigata, when she was eighteen, she had come down to Tokyo to look for excitement. Her mother owned a small bar; she never mentions her father. She worked first of all and quite willingly as a hostess in a pink salon in the sleazy entertainment district of Ikebukuro, in Tokyo's northwest. Noting a help-wanted sign outside, she merely walked in off the street. The salon was kind of *urusai* – irksome and noisy – and Shirahama was eager for more money.

That she is businesslike is implied by the Filofax diary she keeps by the telephone; it shows too on a calendar on an adjacent wall which has appointments marked on most of her working days. She never fails to hand over her visiting card, which is printed with the same information. Her holiday system is enviable by most working standards, another reason why she found the profession attractive. 'I guess I'm kind of lazy,' she admits with a little smile. Taking the weeks set out horizontally on the calendar, she has drawn three red parallel diagonal lines through them to denote her ten days off. Between the appointments and the guests wandering off the street, especially on busy Saturday nights, she entertains an average of 60 men a month.

'I'm not as rich as people like to think,' she says wistfully, although she probably takes home between 700,000 and 1,000,000 yen a month, out of which only the sum total of the nominal 'bath' fees would be declared to the revenue authorities. She says she has a large apartment in Tokyo's Omori, just a few convenient stops away from Kawasaki on the suburban Keihin express line, and lives alone with her Persian cat. One of these days she might go back to Niigata and open a bar; she hasn't decided. 'I'm no longer so young and Soapland is anyway not as popular as it was. These days we have to compete with *deeto kurabu*, *mantoru* and all the rest.'

From the acrobatic soap dancing to coital expertise calling upon skilled contractions of muscles many women are apparently unaware of possessing, the abilities of the Soapland lady are among the precious few warranting the term 'art', when applied to matters of carnal love and the bedchamber. How, one wonders, did she acquire her skill?

'Oh, the manager in the place I first worked as a *toruko-jo* taught me just about everything himself,' she claims. 'I didn't know anything much before.' In other words, Shirahama was trained.

I recall seeing a soft porn movie in Osaka some years ago, which went into some detail about what this training might entail. The plot was the corny old Japanese porno chestnut of the abducted wife of a *salaryman* being repeatedly raped and forced into prostitution and loving every minute of it and it seemed as far-fetched then as now. What seemed far more outlandish at the time was the hapless woman's training, which involved absorbing an egg into her privates and breaking it when told to. But now I wonder. Having such a question put to her point-blank, Shirahama breaks out in gales of laughter. 'Go on with you – my, what a dirty talker you are!'

LULLABY OF SOAPLAND

Kobe's venerable red-light district of Fukuhara still presents a picture more like the heyday of the *toruko* and even of the prewar brothels. The area leaves nothing to be desired in terms of local colour, and works up a merry throng on Saturday nights. In Fukuhara's unimaginably gaudy streets, the predominant bordello architecture would put even the most fanciful love hotels to shame. The usual shoguns' castles are dwarfed by edifices with stucco baroque façades arrayed with colourful *son et lumière*, and the odd rickety little old Japanese brothel is eclipsed by adjacent chrome-and-smoked-glass pleasure domes and sci-fantasy ferroconcrete extravaganzas from some Babylonian lunatic fringe. Here and there touts in proper *yakuza* uniform lounge in front of the doorways, all short-cropped frizzy hair and neon lights winking kaleidoscopically in their dark glasses. Otherwise pandering seems undertaken entirely by the descendants of the old *yarite*, ageing women sitting on chairs and hailing passers-by.

Fukuhara's Soapland foyer interiors have to be seen to be believed. Sprayed fluorescent pink, statuary modelled after Botticelli's Venus rising from the waves stands blushing outlandishly beneath a red roof evoking a Shinto shrine; traditional Japanese cranes in chromium wing their way across a backlit diorama of the Château de Chenonceaux. Choosing a Soapland parlour at random around the corner from Fukuhara's main drag, the interested visitor might be introduced to a Miss Kiko.

Until you settle for a *shimei*, Soapland is run on a pig-in-a-poke basis and, not infrequently when the management are pretty sure you won't be coming back anyway, you end up finding things the other way around. Miss Kiko is past her prime. Her short hair is dyed carrot red and she is wearing a cobalt blue and orange happi tunic emblazoned with the house initials, giving her the appearance of a fishwife on a market stall. Put a cigarette in her mouth and she would look like a dowdy, if not altogether unattractive, matron one might see mesmerized before a machine in a *pachinko* parlour. Any port in a storm.

Once she has led the guest upstairs, Miss Kiko wastes absolutely no time. He would still be sipping at his beer when he finds his pants down with an alacrity leaving him stunned. He is also likely to be under the impression of being babied by a nanny. 'There now,' she would say, busily folding his clothes, 'Kiko's going to run the bath!' After giving the gentleman's uninterested thing a wag and squeezing him reassuringly on the shoulder, she prances off to the large adjacent bathroom. The guest notes that she is already in her birthday suit and that she still has a figure as surprisingly youthful as her skin. Then she puts her fingers to the organ, cooing and deftly manipulating it until it at last rises to the occasion. 'What a terrible plane crash that was the other day,' she prattles conversationally, handling it all the while. 'All those people left burned and bleeding to death!' At the mention of some recent disaster, the fruit of her professional dexterity goes down as though felled by a firing squad. Kiko is dismayed. 'You've had too much to drink!'

The guest reaches defiantly for his beer glass, which is naughty, and Kiko covers it with her hand. '*Dame!*' It won't do! A skilfully administered kiss of life saves the day, however, and then it's bath time. After a rather perfunctory sudsy massage interspersed with childish interjections and maternal cajolery, she at last delivers everything else. Everything else is provided by nannie as she straddles her supine, passive charge.

Some men might struggle with their imagination to conjure erotic fantasies more likely to bring her ministrations to their proper conclusion, but others will be quite satisfied. Legions of whores in Japan, just like Miss Kiko, have carefully rehearsed their acts over the years to cater to a predilection shared by armies of men eager to be babied even in the arms of prostitutes. The oedipal overtones are strongly reminiscent of Akiyuki Nozaka's hilarious novel, *The Pornographers*, notably the sequence in which the two heroes visit a lowly, conveyor-belt type of *toruko*. 'The man's the one that's supposed to be on the receiving end, not the woman,' one character remarks. 'Why ... you ought to feel that you're getting it from your mother.'

NAMI-CHAN: THE NEW WAVE

> 'I could buy that kimono if I had thirty yen. Come on, I'll take it from you with the cards,' she'd say by way of a challenge. Occasionally she lost, but when she did she knew other 'moves' to get the money she wanted. When she was determined, she would do whatever was necessary.
>
> Junichiro Tanizaki, *Naomi*

There is a hooker élite commanding higher fees but, having no categories like the brothels of yore, Soapland measures prestige entirely within a price range extending from 15,000 to 50,000 yen. Accepted practice allows the management to take 40 per cent, but some girls have to work especially hard, and the sum can be eroded by inflated extras. There are laundry fees for towels, and the cost of customers' drinks and additional sums are slapped on the rent for 'maintenance' and utilities. According to one of countless magazine reports on Soapland, one house exorbitantly charged the girls for the mandatory fresh flower arrangements decorating their rooms. If it is neither so widespread nor taxing, in some ways the old ploy of firing assiduity by keeping girls short of cash still exists.

On duty six days a week, ten hours a day, 22-year-old Nami-chan (Dear Little Wave) diligently plies her trade in an industrial Soapland palace located very conspicuously in the middle of Kabuki-cho in Shinjuku, not a hundred yards from the police box. Charging 25,000 yen, she doesn't take the highest rate, but this being a district crowded any night of the week and wandered by men in their tens of thousands over the weekend, her pitch is a lot better than Kawasaki. Wearing an immaculate, starched and very reduced version of a nurse's uniform and as curvaceous and tiny as Tinkerbelle, Nami-chan is the epitome of *kawaii* (cute) and set to rub away the haggard *salaryman*'s cares with china-white skin as soft and smooth as a baby's. Being younger and prettier than the ladies mentioned so far helps, of course, but Nami's main preoccupation is to go all out to make as much money as possible in the shortest possible time. To Nami, this is not a calling (if indeed it really is to anyone) but a high-paying temporary job. A survey in 1981 revealed that younger prostitutes of all persuasions remained on the game for between three and four years; another one conducted at random on one hundred hookers in the Senzoku-Yoshiwara area in 1988 showed that their average age was twenty-six and that their careers lasted sixteen months.

'My boyfriend and I want to get married and open a restaurant,' Nami-chan says. 'He's still only a trainee cook, though, and we could never afford it.' By going on the game, Nami-chan could save as much as 50,000,000 yen in less than two years. What does her boyfriend say to this?

'Oh, if he minds, he doesn't say so. It wasn't his idea, anyway, it was mine. I don't know if he really even knows. We never talk about it.' All he does know, it seems, is that Nami-chan is a club hostess. Like most forms of prostitution today, Soapland attracts part-timers, many being students and frustrated housewives secretly and lucratively whiling away the afternoon. Unlike in other places, girls work out their own regular timetables and, if they still sometimes have to cope with a drunken guest, they are infinitely better off than those farmed out willy-nilly to clients in the sleazier bars.

In affluent Japan, dutiful consumerism keeps the wheels of industry turning and opens the sluices of the domestic cashflow with the unwritten command: 'Thou shalt spend.' Media advertising relentlessly brings the point home, and hire-purchase schemes buy anything from houses and cars through mink coats to humble electric appliances. Blitzed into keeping up with the Yamamotos, many people, especially women, often because they manage the family budget, find themselves buying more than they can afford. Greed motivates prostitution almost as powerfully as necessity, and necessity is often the result of debt. Loan-sharks swim the waters of the *mizu shobai* and many other areas of society, in the lower strata of which there are women who have run up debts through gambling or sometimes amphetamine drug addiction, either themselves or through being married to a man who has. A woman in debt will soon find opportunity knocking to meet her obligations. Like speed pushers, loan-sharks are preponderantly affiliated to *yakuza* gangs and thus well placed to find her a job on the shadier side of the *mizu shobai*. Bar hostesses running up debts with insolvent clients find prostitution looms large as a means of settling their accounts.

Before aspiring to any kind of profession at all, Nami-chan's boyfriend belonged to a teenage *bosozoku* biker gang, which often have *yakuza* connections. Typically working in a ramification of the sex trade, a chum of her boyfriend was only too happy to help out. One might surmise that she was the traditional exploited paramour of a male parasite, but Nami-chan, with her imperious little chin and vixenish features fired with steely resolve, spoke with a determination making it quite clear that the initiative was hers. Unlike their predecessors who secured customers with pretences of love, the business-like Soap-ladies do no more than purvey pleasure with various acquired skills, acting out a carefully rehearsed role scripted to last only a couple of hours. Precious few care to fish around to become the mistress of a wealthy patron, for today's prostitutes seek financial independence and, like Nami, they aspire to starting up businesses of their own, especially bars and boutiques. Quoted in an article in the magazine *Shukan Shincho* in 1981, a 'morals officer' reported that out of some 800 prostitutes arrested, 80 per cent said prostitution was an easy way to make the money to lead a gay life.

Still, there is a dark side. If the majority of East-Asian *Japayuki* (Japan-bound) girls are knowingly engaged as prostitutes in much the same way as the 'French models' formerly plying the streets of London's Soho, some are lured into Japan on false pretences. The country's runaways, too, make easy targets for pimps. Upon raiding several Tokyo 'cabarets' in one fell swoop in 1975, police nabbed hundreds of people including dozens of members of *yakuza* gangs and 936 teenage girls, who had reportedly been forced on the game. In the Tokyo amusement district of Ikebukuro during the same year, the notorious Sumiyoshi-Rengo gang was busted for luring teenage girls with innocuous 'help wanted' ads in the press and forcing them to provide services in local love hotels.

Two crooks running a cram school for female high-school students in 1983 promised film stardom and TV fame as a sideline. Out of the seventeen falling for the bait, it seems that the 'auditions' had not altogether been to their liking and that none were too keen on this novel way of reducing tuition fees. The ploy lasted only a month, but not before earning its managers profits of three million yen. Gangsters in the flesh trade are partial to recruiting molls from teenage gangs, who are that much less likely to want to go and whine to the police. Newspaper and police reports, however, are often given to moral hyperbole: out of the 900-odd girls mentioned earlier, is it really plausible that all of them were 'forced' into prostitution? Plenty, after all, seem quite capable of selling themselves on their own initiative.

On Sundays in Tokyo's teen fashion heaven of Hara-juku, the scene is set for dancing in the park. Wearing garish acetate satin gowns and weird make-up, the *takenoko*, the bamboo kids, have been prancing around to ghetto-blasters for a decade, alongside the *Amerigura-zokku*, the American graffiti tribe, who emulate a fifties image as they rock and roll to Eddie Cochran and Jerry Lee Lewis. They have since been joined by other fringe groups such as young rightists attired like retro *yakuza* punks, as well as by punks of the other kind with cockatoo hairstyles and studded and studied designer rags. The female contingents bring their outlandish Sunday-best in carrier bags, and for years the weeklies have been getting mileage out of the many voyeurs flocking to the park to watch them changing in the bushes.

The gawking *sukebe* (lechers) gave some girls novel ideas for making extra pocket money; these days it is widely reported that teenage hookers hang around the area to provide the oglers of the shrubbery with something more substantial. Titillating or deprecatory, it's in the press all the time: hookers aged between sixteen and eighteen wander Harajuku and trendy nearby Shibuya to accost anything with a wallet and three legs. A police report in 1986 confirmed the trend in Shinjuku, where a young breed of independents proliferates in discos and video-game halls.

Notwithstanding the official and Confucian ideal of femininity, innocence and youth do not necessarily go hand in hand. In 1975, there was a rollicking scandal involving a group of no less than a hundred schoolgirls in Kofu, a town in Yamanashi prefecture, to the west of Tokyo. The incidence of pregnancies and venereal disease implied the usual ignorance about the mechanics of sex, but it was also partly instrumental in revealing these young ladies' freewheeling and mercenary approach to its practice. All were pupils from two local high schools and the majority were second-year students from middle-class homes. Over a period of about a year, they had been merrily turning tricks in local apartments and hotels. The majority said that they did it out of curiosity, but a few admitted to putting money first. Either way, 'Through police interrogations,' a newspaper report announced with dismay, 'it was discovered that none of the girls expressed any guilt feelings about their actions.'

THE SOFT SELL

When prostitutes began moving out of their cages and away from the eyes of passers-by during the late nineteenth century, the alternative was to present the prospect with a photograph album to assist his selection. Today they advertise. In addition to ads in the daily 'sports' newspapers, rundowns on the practitioners of various kinds of sex businesses are featured in a very large number of weekly and monthly magazines. Less modestly than in the nineteenth-century albums, most of these print rows of photographs of semi-nude Soap Ladies with an enticing little blurb beneath.

Mi-chan, for instance, appearing with some of her sisters under the heading 'Soap Angels – Best Ten', works in a house in Osaka. Beneath a photograph of her standing in front of a bathtub and clad only in a broad grin and the teeniest panties, we are told that she is eighteen, 152cm tall, has vital statistics of 83-58-85cm and, as per the current craze for predicting character from blood groups, that hers is type A. We have her telephone number and price, which is 25,000 yen for ninety minutes.

'This month's number one *pikaichi* [dazzler] girl, Michan, is a *pichi-pichi* [lively] new face not yet 18 years old. So very *kawaii* [cute], isn't she? And in addition to being cute, she says she gets hot so easily that when she's doing 69 she sometimes forgets it's work – so hurry up and go to her shop!'

Miyuki of Tokyo, 22 years old, on the other hand, says in the currently popular 'interview' style: 'I like talking about smutty things with a guest. I always sleep in the nude and usually go around without a bra. I lost my virginity when I was seventeen. I did it with a nice student I met at a party. The kind of body I like is the normal kind.'

A reflection of the reverence for uniformity, this last statement also implies that Miyuki's favours are available to a very broad section of the male public. In the eyes of the very average male, the fact that she lost her virginity at seventeen, although by no means an uncommon occurrence, would, like sleeping in the nude, enticingly imply that Miyuki is the perfect little slut. Azusa's line is very similar, if slightly more daring: 'My first time was during my first year at high school. I did it with a friend of my elder brother. I think I get turned on pretty easily. My *kuri-chan* [little clit] is ever so sensitive! What's more, [laughs] when I find a nice clean cock that stands up straighter than straight, even sucking it without a condom is OK by me!'

Words such as *kawaii*, *pichi-pichi* and *pikaichi* are long-standing clichés in the repertoire of what turns on the male, and they point overwhelmingly to a preference for ingenuous girlishness over experienced womanhood. Between the titillating reference to the loss of virginity and the intimate details, one often comes across the word *yasashii*, meaning nice or gentle. The word works both ways: the men are reassuringly told that the girl is *yasashii*, and to show just how much so, other shrewd little foxes add *yasashiku-shite, ne!* – do it gently, won't you – to their promotional blurbs.

BLIND DATES AND PINK CARDS

'Why don't we do it in the road?' In Tokyo, a novelty reported in 1984 almost made the words of the old Beatles song into a reality. A van service calling itself *Pinkku Shiataru* plied the city streets within a

15-kilometre radius centred on the plush business and entertainment district of Akasaka. Following a phone call to the Pink Shuttle Centre, the tired businessman could sneak off for an hour and spend it in the back of a van linked to the call-girl ring via radio. He was braced with the ministrations of a 'masseuse' on a bed in the back, as the van optionally kept moving or, for those suffering from car sickness, parked in a quiet street.

Perhaps this is as close to the street as prostitution can get. Many of the younger hookers are loosely described as streetwalkers but this is not strictly true. A few high-class whores are said to resort to the streetside technique in areas such as Akasaka, but the prospect is judiciously chosen and more likely to be approached in a bar, and there is simply never any of the old slouching around and propping oneself on one leg in doorways. Ubiquitous during the postwar period, streetwalkers have overwhelmingly been forced indoors; provincial cities may still yield a few, but in Tokyo the *péripatéti-cienne* is a dying breed.

Late at night on the fringes of metropolitan amusement areas such as Ikebukuro and Kabuki-cho, however, one sees the occasional old dear mincing around in the hope of enticing stragglers in their cups. Upon closer and more sober scrutiny, however, it often becomes apparent that these shop-worn ladies have rather large feet and that the excessive layers of make-up conceal not only the inclemencies of time but a bluish tint around the chin. Like the streetwalkers remaining in Parisian Pigalle, not a few are transvestites looking for trade of the other persuasion.

Just as unlicensed quarters thrived illegally throughout the Edo period, so new businesses have sprouted up alongside the tacitly accepted Soapland.

The *man-toru* is so called because it moves the sudsy business of the *toruko* within the confines of a 'mansion', meaning an apartment in a ferroconcrete building of recent construction. Such operations are usually managed by a madam, who may or may not be a *yakuza* employee. Plush and dauntingly expensive, *man-toru* often operate discreetly in residential areas outside of the accepted red-light districts. According to one Japanese informant, however, the more modest variety can be exiguous and sordid 'clap-traps' populated with inexperienced part-timers with very rudimentary ideas about personal hygiene. As the name *hotetoru* (*hotel-toruko*) implies, here the bath-massage-sex pattern is performed in a love hotel. Although a few hotels have recycled themselves to cater exclusively to this kind of business in recent years, the *hotetoru* is generally an itinerant operation made by appointment over the telephone.

Indeed, the call girl is a widely popular alternative to other forms of prostitution. The number of call girls has increased commensurate with the rising proliferation of telephone lines from the postwar years, and there has been a spectacular rise during the last decade. In 1982 *pinkku bira* (pink leaflets) appeared, a new phenomenon in the form of small, garish stickers decorating countless public call boxes standing in amusement districts. In addition to a picture and a telephone number, a pink card typically runs lines such as the following: 'VIP Club. Only beautiful girls: Office Ladies, Students. 70 minutes, 20,000 yen.' The enticing photographs of pretty young models on the pink cards are very seldom the ones prompting interested parties to call the numbers on the cards.

Naturally, the *pinkku bira* outraged moralists and triggered a furore, during which employees of the call-girl rings would patiently wait for members of concerned citizens' groups to finish tearing them all down before sticking up a fresh batch. It was a riveting process which said much for Japanese assiduity: between the late afternoon and midnight, the crusaders taking the cards away and the devil's advocates replacing them relayed each other at fifteen-minute intervals. To the annoyance of moralists, posting the cards warranted such a small fine that the telephone-date club operators counted it among their running costs. In some places the Japanese propensity for harmony resulted in a compromise. Instead of sticking the labels directly onto the phone and walls, many call-girl rings obligingly began leaving piles of small, glossy help-yourself pamphlets binding some twenty pink cards together atop the directory cabinet. Very convenient they are, too. Two blank pages headed with the word 'Memo' help the customer to scribble down any directions unclear in the area maps provided on other pages.

The caller is answered by a silky female voice unctuously informing him that 'Aya-chan' is very young and fresh and fits the bill. The client leaves his name and is instructed to go to a certain coffee shop, where the operators will call him back to reduce the likelihood of practical jokes. Aya-chan will appear within the next half-hour and the two make their way to one of the many love hotels dotted about the area map in the pamphlet along with the coffee shops.

Pink card catalogues cater to a broad variety of tastes. *Rori-chan-tachi* (All the dear little Lolitas) and *shojo* (young girls) await the caller at the Highschool, the Tomato or the Poppins Club. On the page for Harenchi Gakuen (Shameless School) a comic-book balloon rises over a group photograph of tender teenies: 'It's the summer holidays, won't you come and play with us?' Models often appear in high-school uniform but, for those after the less underdone, there are many clubs calling themselves Slim dealing with universally popular, slender girls in their early twenties. Euphemistically referred to as *kompanion*, the women promised by most date clubs are ostensibly OLs (Office Ladies) and university students. As in most Japanese sex businesses, simulations of gauche amateurishness are overwhelmingly preferred to the threat of professionalism; it means all the difference between the guileless maiden and the shop-worn whore.

Like Soapland, telephone clubs strive for images of class and luxury with foreign brand names like Dupont, Chanel and Dior, while others get more to the point with Secret, Lovekiss and Touch. There are scores called Madonna, reflecting the rock sex symbol's popularity in Japan, where American song hits have done the strangest things. For example, inspired less by connotations of youthful piety than by the popularity of the song by the Village People (the gay innuendo in the lyrics was entirely lost in Japan) some ten years ago, there are several call-girl rings called YMCA.

Mrs-no-Heya (The Mrs Room) promises to farm out bored housewives, another popular and readily available item endlessly cited on pink cards. If mother doesn't like it, perhaps a near relative will: Obasan Kurabu (Auntie Club) offers more mature women. Scores of call-girl rings call themselves Mibojin Club which, as the meaning of the word implies, specialize in widows. Even if bereaved in her prime, the *mibojin*, the not-yet-dead-person, tends to be left out in the cold. In the pantheon of Japanese male sexual phantasmagoria, the widow is thus not only sex-starved and insatiable, but slightly sinister. Like the black spider which takes her name in the West, she is similarly seen as a man-eater *extraordinaire*.

One call does it all. Pink-card girls will sometimes service at home and can be had with the ease of home-delivery pizza. Indeed, many date clubs also slip cards into private letterboxes. As the uniformity of the prefixes on the numbers on the pink cards suggests, date clubs with widely differing names and promising all kinds of different delights are in fact one and the same. In most cases, the 'club' is fictitious; its fleeting members and operators are connected outside bedrooms only over the urban network of cables and wires. Hence many pink cards don't bother with the word 'club' at all. Date clubs buy lines from NTT (Nippon Telephone and Tele-communications), sell them off again when things get hot, and buy up another batch.

Always eager to let the pleasure businesses know that they are still around, the police crack down on date clubs too. In the city of Sendai in 1987, for example, a boom in area tourism prompted by a popular and sedate TV samurai drama series set in the Tohoku region presented local date clubs with a bonanza. Local police investigations sparked a row with NTT which, when ordered to cut date club circuits, refused. Citing the subscriber's constitutional rights to privacy, they argued that there was nothing wrong with selling telephone contracts. The National Police Agency's ideas about the Constitution are not always quite so constitutional, however, and ten date club telephone circuits were forcibly withdrawn.

Requiring a membership fee and providing subscribers with regular playmates, some telephone date clubs become what they call a 'lovers' bank'. More elaborate than pink-card set-ups, the banks keep computer data on customers and 'girlfriends', who are mostly prostitutes of the *Belle de Jour* variety, turning tricks in the afternoon once or twice a week and going back to respectable homes at night. Charging membership fees of around 300,000 yen and 50,000 and more for each introduction, lovers' banks are also a good source for wealthy men seeking regular mistresses. Such places generally operate as a kind of agency, in which prospects are provided with data, including photographs, descriptions of sexual tastes and sometimes even highly revealing video recordings of their eventual paramours.

Not a few lovers' banks are also patronized by females who, rather than prostituting themselves, are mainly frustrated married women seeking a more satisfying alternative to TV during the afternoon. Naturally, not a few *tsubame* (swallows) or gigolos find lovers' banks a convenient source of introductions. The sort of services many lovers' banks provide are very much the same as in the broader-minded, user-friendly enterprises arranging introductions much more cheaply through computer-telephone linkup systems common in the West.

In Osaka in 1987, a magnanimous and enterprising 49-year-old housewife opened up a business called Family Aoyama with some forty or fifty caring sister-souls of middle age. She dropped fliers in private mail boxes and advertised her 30- to 50-year-old ladies as 'companions' on the wink-wink pages of sports newspapers. Having told their husbands that they were working at part-time jobs, the date-club employees gleaned tidy profits for themselves and earned madam 9,000,000 yen in under six months. Among these charitable souls was a divorcee, who went on the game in order to put her son through college.

Notwithstanding arrests, for once the police took a rather more sympathetic view. The sisters of mercy had in fact specialized in serving men between the ages of fifty and eighty. Noting that most of the club's members were ageing pensioners, a police spokesman rather wistfully remarked that one 77-year-old was a retired executive widowed four years ago who 'enjoyed the service four times a month'.

Sharing common ancestry in some respects with the pink salon, the *deeto kissa*, or date coffee shops, are run according to a tradition launched in some of the less reputable Ginza cafés during the twenties. As the customer sits sipping his brew, one of a bevy of 'companions' decorating the shop comes and sits with him, making herself available on a take-out basis. The fee he pays the coffee shop (similar to the 'bar fine' system in the Philippines) for the privilege, plus the hotel and the girl's fee, generally adds up to around 40,000 yen. A 1986 survey conducted by the Prime Minister's Office revealed that the 'dating' forms of prostitution, including telephone clubs, lovers' banks and *deeto kissa*, now account for nearly half of all harlotry in Japan.

LOVE AND PROSTITUTION

'Being twenty and still a virgin, I was in a hurry to become a man and wasted no time in going to a *toruko*. I was a bit nervous, but the girl was very kind and gentle. She was also really beautiful. Just before I left she said, "I hope you get to meet a nice girl soon," and she gave me a kiss that I have never forgotten. Why ever, I wondered, would wonderful girls like this work in a *toruko*?'

More Report on Male Sexuality (1984)

Once upon a time Japanese men overwhelmingly had their first sexual encounter with prostitutes. Asking respondents when and where they had had theirs, the *More Report on Male Sexuality* found that the majority aged over thirty said that they had ceased to be *dotei* (chaste: an expression for male virginity) through the good offices of a prostitute, whereas those in their twenties tended to have their first encounters with their *garufurendo*. When they have no girlfriend, however, students and professional trainees living in the same dormitory apartment-house often keep communal Soapland savings in a piggy bank. They drop their loose change in the slot when they come home, and when the bank is full, they hold a lottery to see who gets to enjoy the spoils. The next time around, the lottery is held between the losers.

Regardless of the saponaceous intimacies on the mattress, the girl's farewell to the departing guest is resolutely formal, and a polite goodbye with a studied bow shatters any illusions the more romantic might have entertained about what was no more than a highly skilled performance. Notwithstanding the delightful reminiscences of the 28-year-old man quoted above, the Japanese attitude to the *kisu* should be borne in mind. Even though the kiss is equally intrinsic to erotic foreplay in the West, most professionals consider it too affectionate and personal to extend to a mere customer. In recent years the kiss has been similarly elevated as a gesture of love in Japan, but since it is still seen as belonging more to the realm of erotic skill, many whores no more baulk at kissing than other physical intimacies. If it looks that much more like love during the allotted time, then so much the better. How doubly fortunate was the *More Report*'s respondent: he got his kiss on the way home.

Girls today are said to be less shy about having sex, and some never were. The Confucian proscription of betraying feelings is more cogent for a man; a woman can be rather more candid. She wears a mask of modesty but, like the mythical Izanami, she often makes the first move. Ideally, however, the green light should be curtained with discreet behavioural signals. Many a screen heroine strives to pierce the hero's armour of stoic indifference with chaste – and utter – devotion. Her sexual desire sublimated, her intentions are pure. Perhaps this is why the majority of women surveyed in the *More Report on Female Sexuality* in 1983 said that they did not initiate sex. The area is fraught with contradictions. Between the diffident male and the abstemious super-macho there is still room for gallants and those merely taking it in stride. Between the Ojōsama, the demure daughter of the well-to-do, and the foxy lady is a whole gamut of possibilities. Many girls sow wild oats until a suitable prospect for marriage comes along, when they will drop an erstwhile lover like a hot brick.

Nevertheless the enduring dictates of feminine modesty still deter many women from being anything but passive and unadventurous sexual partners. In Junichiro Tanizaki's famous novel, *The Key*, for instance, the main protagonists are a middle-aged married couple. Despite her primness, the wife's sexual appetite outweighs her husband's, notwithstanding his kinky predilections. Written three decades ago, in many cases her lament still holds true: 'It's my nature to cling forever to the old customs, to want to perform the act blindly, in silence, buried beneath thick quilts in a dark, secluded bedroom. It's a terrible misfortune for a married couple's tastes to conflict so bitterly on this point. Is there no way we can come to an understanding?'

If the husband is supposed to take the dominant role at home, in the world of prostitution the pattern is reversed. On the other hand, just as men seek mother-substitutes in Soapland, so many men look upon their wives in the same light. Soapland hype forever underscores 'kindness' and 'gentleness', and the reassuring maternal pose is often adopted by women improbably young for the role. For many men, especially of the older generation, prostitutes offer greater sexual satisfaction than they can ever expect at home. There is another side of the coin. Surveying nearly 6,000 women between the ages of thirteen and sixty, the *More Report* of 1983 revealed that seven out of ten were not only sexually unsatisfied but, not so unlike their fallen sisters in Soapland, tended to fake orgasm to flatter their partners.

As the coins accumulate in his piggy bank, the budding rake might decide that a Nami-chan provides services too good to overlook. Returning to Soapland, he may well find her gone. Perhaps by now she is married, and ordering her lackadaisical spouse around a brand new restaurant in a provincial town. The man at the Soapland desk will send him 'Haru' instead. She might be a housewife whose *salaryman* husband is out of the house sixteen hours a day and firmly convinced she has a part-time job. Haru was pretty good too, so a month later he goes back to Soapland for seconds. The man behind the Soapland desk laughs politely, 'Haru? Which Haru?'

Adopting names from a limited repertoire for the benefit of one of the highest-paid part-time jobs in the world, the Soap Ladies come and go. These days, the customers do likewise. Even though they are dutifully handed the girl's calling card on their first visit, few have the time or even the inclination for a regular *shimei* and the avid pursuit of novelty soon sends them elsewhere. Unlike in the old floating world where everyone had time, the water in the *mizu shobai* flows on like a river in flood. Going temporarily on the game to save money, many girls bury the past and get married to men who haven't a clue about the few hours a day their wives once spent horizontally in parentheses. As *demi-mondaines* interviewed on late-night TV forever repeat, the motives prompting their harlotry are 'to pay for fashionable clothes and a nice apartment'. This kind of prostitution is known as *arubaishun*, a contraction of the German word *arbeit*, used in Japan to cover a part-time job for students, and *baishun*, the time-honoured practice of selling spring.

The once inviolable privilege of keeping mistresses is currently under siege, and modern *mizu-shobai* women tend to be very independently minded. The extramarital woman in Japan is beginning to emerge from backgrounds as varied as anywhere, but the tendency among older big-shots after mistresses of the traditional kind is still to recruit them either from the *mizu shobai* or the world of entertainment. An overwhelming number are bar mamas and hostesses, geisha, struggling actresses, dancers and singers. In all cases, prostitutes only seldom fit in the picture today.

Comprising as it does of droves of women entering prostitution for a variety of reasons and men from all walks of life frequenting them mainly for one, the scene would seem to leave plenty of room for real love affairs. In 1982, Yoshimitsu Morita's *Noyōnamono* (*Something Like That*) was a popular youth comedy about a gauche apprentice *rakugo* comedian having a romantic affair with a delightful young *toruko-jo*. That the hero should ultimately have opted to become engaged to an insipid, prim student instead would seem disappointing to a western audience, but it was almost a foregone conclusion in Japan.

The icon of whore as a model for self-sacrifice still survives in popular culture to be sure, but the sympathetic if flippant light Morita shed on his bright and lovely demi-rep and her subsequent disappointment clearly indicates changing mores. She is there for use by the hero and ultimately to be felt sorry for but, whereas she could still hope to be redeemed through marriage as little as thirty years ago, in a more affluent society she can no longer be such a tragic figure. Having entered the profession of her own accord, she is neither morally nor nuptially redeemable. Unlike in the old *ukiyo*, where love blossomed illicitly from its dearth elsewhere, not even ersatz love is given much room among the carnal businesses of the *mizu shobai*, where sex confines itself to sex.

Ideally, if still not always in practice, love and sex constitute the bonds between bona fide lovers – at least until the honeymoon is over and society splits the parties into their time-honoured roles of corporate absentee and exalted housekeeper. In Morita's film, the middle-class boy spurns the whore to marry the middle-class girl. In a social context in which young people are marrying more out of personal inclination, the choice is his, but one wonders whether the old sense of duty is now so deeply inculcated that it has become unconscious. Would the hero not in fact have found a happier match with the whore? The film's uplifting happy end still presupposes that the hero's happiness depends less upon his own inclinations than the demands of the community.

THE CAFÉS AND CABARETS GO PINK

The Metropolitan Police Board, which has been enforcing strict control over cafés, bars and other special eating and drinking houses, has made arrangements to enforce similar positive measures for tea halls, bar stands, *odenya*, etc., which have so far been left outside of the scope of such measures, but which have of late markedly increased in number and have been showing less regard for public morality in their ways of business.

Among other measures, the regulations provide that the number of waitresses for such public houses shall not exceed one per *tsubo* of space and a house of less than three *tsubo* shall be permitted to employ a maximum of two waitresses, that the waitresses shall be prohibited from appearing outdoors and touting, that dancing shall be prohibited within the shop, that phonograph play shall be forbidden after 10 P.M. and that after 11 P.M., in specially busy quarters, that the waitress shall be prohibited from going out with a customer.

The Japan Times (December 1935)

A popular last stopover for a late-night drink with noodles or *oden* stew, the picturesque *yatai* is a two-wheeled itinerant vendor's cart complete with roof and red paper lantern. Not all of the *yatai* were quite so innocent as they are today, even though many vendors are still *tekiya* pedlars affiliated with *yakuza* gangs. The *yakuza* do, after all, handle a large number of perfectly legitimate businesses. Until not so long ago, however, the *yatai* vendors were also panderers for unlicensed prostitutes. If the customer had a glass in his hand, he was a legitimate customer of the stall; as far as the police were concerned, any negotiations underway on behalf of a nearby brothel were well-nigh impossible to prove. One of several phenomena to be restricted in 1935, the cart subterfuge emerged briefly after the banning of the brothels in 1957, and survived until the sixties when the touts dispensed with the *yatai* altogether. Thenceforth, attired in the *happi* tunics of the Edo-period tradesman emblazoned with corporate initials over their garish red and black shirts, they would hail a prospect loudly outside the shop: '*Shacho! Shacho!*' and badger the 'company director' to go inside, flattering some down-trodden *salaryman* on his way into yet another world of erotic illusion.

If the stricter public morals laws cramped his style in 1985, he merely began calling out from deeper within the recesses of the doorway, or cruising the streets to target *shachos* in more discreet clothing, ready to disappear into the crowd at the approach of the law. Of all the touts in amusement districts, the most common are those standing in the doorways of the *kyabare* and *pinku saron* (cabarets and pink salons). Time was when the cabaret was, like the Mikado, staffed with armies of hostesses and offering glitzy revues but, as the Japanese economy rose, so began its decline. Hostesses found more lucrative pastures elsewhere, bona fide shows were being staged in theatres and, since land was at an ever higher premium, the huge and genuine cabarets no longer had the income to justify the space they occupied.

Always raunchier, the cheaper cabaret survives on the strength of more compliant hostesses and floor shows given less to chorus lines and more to bump and grind. As in many other haunts of sexual fantasy, the hostess's skimpy attire is often theme-conceived. Schoolgirl uniforms top a list of fantasy options known to include baseball cheerleaders, Red-Indian squaws and Catholic nuns. During the seventies, one cabaret even deployed mini-uniforms evoking those of the wartime Imperial army, but the standard favourite is a short flared tunic made of garish acetate satin, often in a particularly organic and trashy shade of salmon pink.

The newer cabarets may be glittering spot-lit palaces of plush staffed with leggy young beauties and galaxies of lovelies leaping about in leotards, often available on a take-out basis, but elegance is not much of a priority in the seedier run-of-the-mill ones. These have grimy wallpaper of floral psychedelic design and vintage, and threadbare bench seats of scarlet naugahyde flank small tables with marbled formica tops amply stained with cigarette burns. Music screams at deafening volume over rattling, tinny PA systems. The women, many of whom are the dumpy possessors of rococo legs, are often pathetic and ageing cast-offs from Soapland predatorily snuggling up to dishevelled small-time *salarymen* and inebriated blue-collar workers. As they ply their customers with drink, they concede varying degrees of mutual fondling in the dark.

Chains of cabarets such as Hawaii, Monroe and Hi no Maru (Circle of the Sun) used to advertise not only on hoardings in amusement districts, but also on subway posters and in TV commercials. The London chain commercial had high-kicking imported blondes and local talent in micro-skirted uniforms and busbies chanting 'Rondon! Rondon!' Such commercials disappeared during the TV clean-up occurring in parallel with the amendments to the morals laws in 1985, but posters advertising cabarets are still common in suburban train carriages for the benefit of straphangers eager for stop-offs to spice the commuter routine. 'If the *pachinko* parlour has a pink salon next to it,' it is said, 'then both are run by *yakuza*.' Indeed, in most amusement districts, the *pachinko* parlours and pink salons often stand side by side.

Like prostitution and pornography, some cabaret and pink-salon operations are run by far-right factions garnering campaign expenses. Militant rightists and *yakuza* gangs are in many cases synonymous; the two not only collaborate together on a variety of unsavoury enterprises but often look the same. Like those muscling in on the sleazier side of the sex trade, the thugs bellowing ultra-nationalist slogans from speaker trucks sport punch-perms and sunglasses. The traditional view of things, which relegates women to a subservient role, is obviously perfectly suited to their designs. The cabaret and pink-salon scene is in fact one of the most mercenary in the sex trade and many of the sordid little dives it embraces, particularly in the provinces, turn out to be slavery rackets involving *Japayuki* (Japan-bound) girls from South-East Asia.

The pink salon, or *pinsaro* for short, is said to have made its appearance during the early seventies in the Tokyo suburb of Kichijoji, which boasts a lively entertainment district then especially popular with students. A dive incongruously calling itself Vietnam had made drinking in the company of understanding female companions accessible to students and workmen; costing only a tiny fraction of the hostess bar, the pink salon was even cheaper than the cabaret. The Kichijoji area has since moved upmarket and only a comparatively small amount of its former raunchy entertainments remains. Whether the area ever really did score a first in anything other than the name 'pink salon' is a moot point. Like the cabaret, of which it is an offshoot, the *pinsaro*'s distant ancestor is the 'café', which made its appearance in the Ginza at the beginning of the twenties.

The writer Nagai Kafu (1879–1959), who was familiar with the cafés of Europe, found inspiration in the Japanese ones for his famous novels about the *demi-monde*. What he had to say about them in the mid-twenties still applies to the modern *kyabare* and *pinsaro*:

> The cafés that are so popular throughout the city are to all appearances like Parisian cafés. The reality is much different. We try to imitate everything Western, and we always make a botch of it. The girls go to work every day and yet they do not receive salaries, and they must depend on gifts from customers for their livelihood. It is quite evident, therefore, that they actually live by prostitution.

The *kyabare* is to all appearances a cabaret, but the Parisian connotations are long gone. That it is in reality very different these days surprises no one, least of all the police. Although the girls are paid, their salaries vary enormously according to the place. The cream of the cabaret and *pinsaro* hostesses, the kind featured in magazines alongside other *numba-wans* (number ones) in the *demi-monde*, can earn small fortunes; others are paid a mere pittance they would be more than reluctant to complain about. The basic wage between the two extremes is just a little more than for the average female office worker. Whether prompted by greed or necessity, most pink hostesses are obviously moved to find ways of supplementing their income.

Although ostensibly prohibited in the old cafés, prostitution was practised in them much as Edward Seidensticker describes in his biography of Nagai Kafu, where there were 'jerry-built cafés whose young ladies will, for a few yen, go upstairs, disrobe and do whatever the customer wants them to do'. No one goes upstairs in today's equivalent, but arrangements whereby hostesses dispense favours in nearby love hotels are common. From the thirties too, 'salons' were beginning to sprout up alongside the 'cafés'. They had romantic names like Rheingold and were staffed with young ladies with exotic pseudonyms like Paula. Nowadays many salons and cabarets have names like Cats, Venice or Blue Moon, and when their names are not simply Japanese, the hostesses go for Alice, June or Rabu (Love). The fascination for things foreign, without getting too close that is, is strongly reminiscent of the old British habit of insinuating raciness with the adjective 'continental'.

Struck by the spiel which one of these salons had printed out both for the edification of its female employees and the reassurance of its customers, Kafu copied it out in his diary:

> Let us show warm affection in each detail of our everyday life. Let us be fair and selfless in our work. Let us be modest and unassuming with everyone. Let us pass our days clean and upright in mind and spirit. Let us save money for one another, for our house, for our nation.

The patriotic conclusion reflects the rising tides of militarism during the thirties, although banner-waving was by then a time-honoured practice in the brothels. Until as recently as a decade ago, however, such pietistic, self-sacrificing resolutions extolling a meretricious work ethic was unlikely to strike too many Japanese as the nonsense it would appear to the western reader. After all, the *Pink Salon Women* TV drama mentioned earlier ended happily with the heroine ardently swearing to her boss that she would try her utmost to do credit to the company.

'... modest and unassuming ... clean and upright in mind and spirit': the Neo-Confucian ideal of femininity still exists in the ubiquitous *yasashii* (gentle) and contemporary anglicisms such as *fureshu gyaru* (fresh girl) which are loaded with similar implications and seen everywhere on the come-on billboards outside the cabarets and salons. Recently, one dive advertising for employees in a women's *manga* comic-book insisted on girls who were *majime* (earnest or serious) and 'who do not speak too much'.

Like that of prostitutes in magazines, the self-advertising hype employed by pink-salon girls no longer focuses quite so much on corporate pride and company loyalty. These days the emphasis is placed on their skills at fellatio, 'finger service' et al; the *pinsaro* angels now include a little blurb with distinctly autobiographical and more self-centred overtones, even though it does imply a proper degree of dedication. 'I was broke when I first came to Osaka,' says nineteen-year-old Ribon who works in a salon improbably called Bride's School, 'and so I started this kind of work. At first I was afraid, but now "lip service" is my forte. I grew up.'

Many Japanese city suburbs include small entertainment quarters of their own, including drinking spots, restaurants, *pachinko* parlours and, naturally, the odd cabaret or pink salon. Entering a pink salon at random, say the Odoriko (Dancing Girl) in an upmarket and trendy suburb in western Tokyo, the scenario might run as follows. The young man who ushers one in sports the fashions of the underworld but he is always irreproachably polite. 'Ah, this is your first time. You do not have a *shimei* – a regular.' One has by this time crossed the threshold into impenetrable darkness. Just as the doorman becomes invisible, so what he says becomes inaudible above a deafening barrage of disco music.

The customer is led deeper inside by another employee identifiable only by a torch shedding a pool of light on to his designated table, which is number eight. Becoming number eight himself, the customer is left sitting for a few moments, eyes growing used to the gloom and ears almost accustomed to the din. He can just discern that the girl arriving to join him on the bench seat wears a teeny tunic, for its acetate folds catch a dim red glow in which human shapes seem to be writhing like souls in Dante's hell. She says her name is Lemon. 'Hello, how do you do, *yoroshiku* – please be good to me.' Number eight is given beer or whisky and, having paid a fixed fee, is entitled to remain here for exactly forty minutes. During this time, in many salons, he will be allowed to drink as much as is humanly possible; the booze is included in the tab.

The newer, more luxurious cabarets charge a 12,000 yen entrance fee covering everything except for whatever 'special service' the hostesses might provide. Otherwise the usual pricing system starts at 4,000 yen if one visits the *pinsaro* during the afternoon, doubles between eight and nine and reaches 10,000 thereafter. The customer will have been in the place for just over five minutes, by which time Lemon may well have persuaded him to down his first litre of beer. One minute later, she will have ordered another bottle and poured out the first glass. She is now snuggling up to number eight and telling him what a handsome fellow he is, although it is so dark that for all she knows she might just as well be snuggling up to Donald Duck. Nevertheless, her busy little hand is beginning to rub at the front of his trousers. No, not yet. Number eight wants to smoke a cigarette.

As Lemon lights it up for him, the small flame might reveal that she falls rather tragically short of his ideals, and in some cases he will be moved to call for another girl. By now it is probably too late, however, for there are only twenty minutes left and Lemon has anyway unbuckled number eight's belt and unzipped his fly. Number eight may be allowed to slip a hand between her thighs, although that kind of privilege is often strategically reserved for the regular customer. Today, number eight is invited to fondle Lemon's breasts. Meanwhile, the howling music is interrupted at regular intervals by a male voice loudly calling, 'Number fifteen! Time up, number fifteen!' When summoned, the numbers obediently button up, pay up and shuffle for the exit. Number eight, whose pants are around his knees, has fifteen minutes to go.

Glancing beside him, he can now see well enough in the deep red shadows to take in the goings-on at neighbouring tables. There's a man sprawling back supine in his seat with his shirt in disarray and his pants half-down as a woman's head bobs rhythmically over his midriff. Or perhaps two girls fawning over a favoured client: as one lies across his lap in semi-nude abandon, the other may actually be sitting on the table with his head between her thighs. Number eight is thus provided with incentive to become a regular patron.

What the girls advertise as *Ripu sabisu* and *fingaa sabisu* – lip and finger service – are in fact what the *salon* and *kyabare* are really all about. Naturally, if the service is what makes the salon so popular, it is mandatory and also costs extra. Number eight's forty-minute love affair, which is about to reach a conclusion in a paper tissue, will amount altogether to about 15,000 yen. As more than one western investigator has drily remarked, when he comes, he goes. He can, however, pay to remain another forty minutes at a slightly reduced rate. Some may do so if they have come here to have a wild little groping party with friends, but the loner will generally call it a day. What he will have spent in the end could just as well purchase a two-hour full-course session in Soapland.

Predictably, there is often just a bit more to all this than meets the eye. Advertising in specialized weekly and monthly magazines, *pinsaro* angels often say: 'If I have time, I am quite willing to allow the honourable guest to take me out for a drink afterwards, but only if he behaves like a real gentleman.' In the world of pink make-believe, the regular client is that much more likely than the casual visitor to take the hostess out – for a price, of course. In the end the real gentleman, whose evening culminates with the salon girl in a love hotel, will have been persuaded to part with a considerable amount of cash. One foreign reporter aptly summing up the pink-salon scene during the seventies put it rather neatly: 'The pinker it gets, the deeper you go in the red.'

The cabaret/pink salon phenomenon says much about contemporary Japanese society. Random meetings with the opposite sex are not so simple, particularly for the majority of the cabaret crowd, who are men rarely younger than thirty and consequently likely to be husbands. Secondly, none of them have any time. Thus, the kind of fantasy the cabaret or salon is actually providing consists of cramming a scripted sexual affair, starting with a meeting, continuing through drink and conversation and culminating with sexual dalliance into forty minutes. All this again seems to coincide perfectly with the concept summed up in another advertising slogan in fashionable fractured English, which appeared over photographs of bench seats and stools, bars and fixtures in the *mizu-shobai* furniture catalogue quoted earlier:

> A man is a delicate creature.
> At the centre of his disappointment,
> he cannot eat at all.
> Bars are indispensable for his freedom.
> It's the best thing that he is released
> from the depth of his disappointment even for a moment.

The cipher's post-climactic reverie is interrupted. 'Number eight! Time up, number eight!' Before he finally staggers back onto the street, perhaps having consumed four hours' worth of alcohol in forty minutes, number eight awakes in a place in which sexual socializing obeys much the same rules as a boat-hire operation; but then again that's just one of the ways to float along in the *mizu shobai*.

THE HAND JIVE

Good news, bad news: cited as reasons for the decline in old-style coital entertainments are the marked increase in mixed socializing among the young and Aids. The current sex business trends are more towards onanism and voyeurism. One sex-trade operator cites another factor: 'There's no doubt that Aids has frightened a lot of customers away, but the new sex businesses are popular simply because they're cheap. We've been working on low-cost entertainment concepts for some time. Many men find that it's better to get cheaper relief more often, than to spend a lot of money more rarely.'

Still, money and disease are not the only dark facets of the phenomenon. Despite promises aired over the media, the much trumpeted five-day week is still enjoyed only by a privileged few, mostly civil servants and the employees of large corporations. For smaller firms struggling in a ruthlessly competitive market, it is a luxury they can ill afford. For most *salarymen*, catch-words such as 'leisure' and 'lifestyle' are what one reads about in students' and women's magazines. Even if they still have the energy, few can spend the hour or more it takes to work it off in Soapland. Thus just as pink salons symbolically cram a sexual affair into forty minutes, so they have been joined by other, increasingly popular and far more rapid, options for carnal entertainment. The sexual equivalent to fast food, *herusu massagi* and *fashon massagi* – health and fashion massage – are the two rising stars in the field. Although they no doubt owe their inspiration to similar 'massage' parlours in the West, like most novelties in the Japanese flesh trade, they have their place among the branches of a hybrid family tree rooted both in indigenous and western sexual culture.

One of these was the 'nude studio'. By the end of the seventies it had proliferated for over a decade and had all but completed its rapid decline, but one still extant in Shinjuku, for example, was a drab little shack of a place with a stout, slatternly matron loitering unprepossessingly around outside. Glancing through a bead curtain hanging over the open door, one noted a kind of podium which occupied half of a small room bathed in intense red and pink light. The woman was now striking a timeless one-legged pose like a flamingo beneath the perennial streetlamp outside as an ageing prospect sauntered up and whispered to her; then the two were swallowed up by the red gloom inside as the door closed behind them.

The gentleman was a camera enthusiast; the lady was a 'model'. Such studios sometimes entertained dozens of amateur photographers at a time, jostling one another to take the kind of mind's eye pictures that render film superfluous. Depending on the cash flow, the poses would be more or less revealing and, naturally, there was always a price allowing the lone photographer to dispense with the camera altogether and join the model on a mattress. One might argue that the 'photographic model' advertisements one sees alongside doorways in London's Soho amount to much the same thing, but the demands of *tatemae* in Japan often take such subterfuges to more elaborate lengths. It cannot be over-emphasized, however, that in many cases such places are not fronts at all. The writer Ian Buruma summed it up perfectly when referring to the *no-pan kisa* (no-pantie coffee shops) to which it also applies: 'What meets the eye in Japan is often all there is … The fetishist icon is so powerful that the real thing becomes superfluous.'

Things in the *mizu shobai* come and go; one down and two up. By the beginning of the eighties the superannuated nude studio had disappeared, yet other 'nude rooms' appeared again later without requiring any pretence of camerawork whatsoever. Although they refrained from advertising themselves too openly as such at first, they were the precursors of health and fashion massage. One variation on the theme was *nozoki* – a peep show. The perennial spectacle of some bored young woman languidly masturbating behind a pane of glass, as per the western norm, was and is the ostensible fare offered in the majority of places advertised as *nozoki* but not always. No, indeed.

A typical scenario, for instance, would be enacted in a room just a little bit larger than the standard peeping booth. It might contain the usual two-way mirror but where there ought only to be a chair, there is a wide, comfortable couch that doesn't actually face the mirror at all. To his surprise, the customer expecting the peep-show routine finds himself joined by a young lady in a teeny-tiny uniform, perhaps the very pretty Miki-chan. He might point stupidly at the mirror, but Miki-chan would sit down on the couch with a laugh, beckoning to him to join her. No, she would say mischievously, in fact this is *fashon massaaji*. For 10,000 yen, she announces, she will provide a fashion massage. For 15,000 the customer could join her in removing all his clothing and they would do other things. 'And for 20,000,' she might pipe brightly in some places, 'the honourable customer can do what he pleases!' Many massage parlours hang detailed and itemized tariffs on the walls like restaurant menus.

All this in fact goes on a give-'em-an-inch pattern vis-à-vis the law, as sex businesses try their luck at taking a mile. Just as they always have. A popular item in Asakusa at the turn of the century, after all, was the makeshift 'archery stand'. Staffed by young women who took clients for a fling in the back of a sideshow tent, the practice remained in force until the bows and arrows became superfluous and the toxopholite tarts moved indoors in new red-light districts elsewhere. If it had managed the feat of disguising what was at the very least a sex massage parlour for long enough, the spurious *nozoki* could try its luck later in openly calling itself *herusu* or *fashon*. Like all sex businesses here, some of the 'fashion' will offer absolutely nothing more than advertised, and others will provide something that has already been in fashion and likely to remain so for millions of years. Like the archery stands, the *nozoki*, pink salons and cabarets can all be just another front for common-or-garden prostitution.

As it was in its direct ancestor, the meretricious Ginza café of the twenties, the emphasis in the celebrated *no-pan kisa* was more on the charms of the waitresses than on the coffee. In one of his works about Ginza café society's fallen sisterhood, Kafu mentions a real or imagined café in which the waitresses were not allowed to wear underclothes. In the *no-pan kisa*, which is said to have first appeared in the city of Hakata in Kyushu late in 1979, this was initially the obvious rule. Appearing a few months later, the no-pantie pioneer in Tokyo had not the slightest compunction in calling itself Lourdes, but another came to grief following a lawsuit over international copyright violation: it had called itself Chanel. Ian Buruma describes a *no-pan kisa* visited in 1981, in which the walls were festooned with frilly undies and condoms inflated like balloons. 'Don't talk to the waitresses' read a notice in day-glo colours. 'Don't touch them. Don't bother them in any way.' And as he concluded: 'Indeed, nothing seemed further from their [the customers'] minds.' The torpid atmosphere was at last broken, it seems, by a pantie auction – a practice also in vogue in some *nozoki*. The fetishist icon can even be taken home.

As one presenting a novel meld of sex and hi-tech testified, some places could be grimmer still. Here there were none of those cheery icons of fetishistic adolescent fantasy. Minimalist chrome merely succeeded in plunging it into a dour atmosphere midway between the sterile hedonism of *Brave New World* and the steely oppression of *1984*. Serried ranks of grey businessmen lined the walls with blank expressions as android waitresses clad only in teeny miniskirts served them coffee standing on mirrored floors, or hovered close enough to ensure that their pantied bottoms were properly reflected in the mirrored tables. Unlike in the salons, the wallpaper music was kept low. There was no conversation. Looking like masterpieces of taxidermy, the men just sat ogling in silence with glazed eyes; the waitresses took their orders without a word. After half an hour or so of dispassionate reveries, they paid a bill for 2,000 yen for coffee and ambled out into the night.

Having been one of the very few in which the girls actually did not wear panties, Lourdes was eventually forced to close its doors. Shoji Suei, a writer and editor of magazines focusing on the sex trade, fondly remembers an improbable *no-pan kisa* in Osaka. One of the city's pioneers in the field, it had been specially architectured from scratch. A deep hole had first been excavated to make way for the main room, above which was built a second floor entirely made of thick two-way mirrored glass. Customers sitting below rubber-necked up at the girls waitressing on the floor above as they disported themselves in front of floor-level spotlights shining up their skimpy skirts. They wore nothing else.

After a first warning from the police, the manager had no option but to make the girls wear panties. Exemplifying the eternal Japanese genius for compromise, however, he commissioned hundreds of pairs of panties with female genitalia realistically printed on the crotch. Everything worked out fine until one girl, who finally balked at the sheer silliness of the ploy, took the defiant initiative of dispensing with panties altogether. Unfortunately, diligent police officers posing as customers had been squinting up sufficiently hard to note the difference and the place was closed down. Today, the *no-pan kisa* have almost, but not quite, vanished. The few that survive are such only in name: the no-pantie formula is again a front for something rather more tangible.

'In 1985,' Suei remarks, 'what stemmed the flow of novelties wasn't so much the curfew as the law prohibiting building any new shops. I used to spend a lot of time researching around the country, but now the business isn't nearly so inventive; it's pretty well down to health massage.'

When it was still a novelty during those halcyon pre-1985 days, the boom for health massage was given extensive coverage on late-night TV, particularly '11 p.m. – the Wide Show'. Devised with the tired businessman in mind, this was an improbably eclectic magazine programme given to covering items as unrelated as UFOs and Soapland, American lake fishing and the phenomenology of farting – all in one show. As it did with most topics, the programme discussed health massage with a panel of celebrities, venerable sociologists and learned historians of the *mizu shobai*. The camera probed into one dive in Kabuki-cho which the programmers had found representative, albeit with a novel twist.

A former *nozoki*, like many others, it contained mirrored booths arranged around a carpeted central circle. Men riveted to nude girls playing with themselves in a variety of ways had once been seen without being seen as they did similar things to themselves in the dark. The introduction of 'health' changed all that. Three scantily clad girls went from mirror to mirror, below each of which there was a small trap-door. Despite copious blurring-out for the benefit of censorship, the process was quite clear. Interested customers were invited to poke their phalli through the opening and, rather like giraffe feeding-time at the zoo or milking cows on an industrial farm, a girl healthily polished and demolished each member before moving on to the next.

In the *More Report on Male Sexuality*, a transvestite found in these the closest thing to paradise. 'I get an indescribable thrill,' he confided, 'from dressing up in the booth and being serviced by a girl in sexy undies exactly like the ones I'm wearing myself.' On one particularly memorable occasion, he had managed to whisper to the girl about his attire, which she found so exciting herself that she responded by tending to him with unbridled fervour. Many hand-job salons of the genus *Herusu* currently service customers on a conveyor-belt basis. 'The place is like a restaurant,' reported one bewildered American taken there by friends. 'You can see the tops of the customers' heads in all the other booths. A girl comes in, pours one drink, gives head and you go home.'

Health *massagi* can be anything but healthy. One hapless foreigner clipped in an early Shinjuku *herusu massagi* parlour in 1981 recalls being shut up in a tiny room containing a couch with a bony, bedraggled and evil-tempered harridan. 'You get *roshon massaaji* [lotion massage],' she snapped, pushing him back on the couch and cursing as she struggled with his belt buckle. The *roshon* was an evil-looking greenish unguent which she squelched unceremoniously into one hand from a plastic bottle, and it had an ominously painful reek of menthol. No, said the wary foreign visitor: not lotion. The mood was anyway no longer upon him. Either way, the masseuse suddenly and shrilly claimed a right to another 10,000 yen.

Since the customer spoke Japanese, the doorman had gone to some trouble beforehand to brief him in detail about the joys to come, relieving him moreover of 10,000 yen in advance. The reality fell short of the enticing programme, which was anyway not supposed to cost a single yen more. 'I've been ripped off,' the customer said, buttoning up and putting on his jacket. The would-be masseuse's gaunt face dropped further as her eyes lit up in affliction and disbelief. She left the room. '*Masutaa*, oh, master,' she shrieked as she ran down the corridor, 'he says we're thieves!' To the customer, this was beginning to look like nothing particularly beneficial to *herusu* at all; he was obviously about to be beaten up.

When two solid thugs finally came into the room, their faces only showed genuine dismay. 'Could it be that the honourable guest is dissatisfied?' It wasn't a good day, confided the other. Yuki-chan was having another one of her moods. There had been a misunderstanding. She was asking for 10,000 yen because she thought the esteemed guest wanted a *special roshon massaaji*. She's not used to foreigners, you see. If the honourable customer were to come back in a couple of hours there would always be Azusa – the *numbaa wan fureshu gyaru*. No, he appreciated their trouble. Not even fresh girls or number ones; 10,000 yen or not, he thought he'd just call it a day. The assiduous purveyors of pleasure were perplexed. The customer must get his money's worth. At last, with a confidential air, they told him that they had something else that they were positive would not disappoint.

So they led him with some pomp and circumstance down a corridor to a thick velveteen curtain apparently covering a booth, and proudly swished it back. The customer's mouth dropped open. Turning on his heels and leaving them puzzled and standing there, he dashed upstairs and out. Obviously, they were demented. What he had seen in the empty booth, behind a pane of glass, standing regally on a kind of dais and revealing a series of flickering, barely discernible images of things pornographic, was a single large TV set. In 1981, this was in all senses a shape of things to come.

Currently the penchant for screen-induced do-it-yourself is amply catered for with what is known as 'video box' and every amusement district has at least one. In Kabuki-cho, there are multi-storeyed porno centres set out like department stores. Beginning with a pink salon of sorts in the basement, moving up to *herusu* and *fashon* on the upper storeys, the video box will always be somewhere tucked away near the sex-aid shops, beyond the shelves of vinyl-wrapped magazines, the dildos and the Dutch wives. It consists of a narrow corridor with booths on both sides, each containing a monitor screen, a chair and a small shelf bearing a box of tissues. For as little as 1,000 yen, the august guest can honourably entertain himself for half an hour.

The many sex establishments in the *mizu shobai* wax and wane with the tide. Recently there was even a vogue for baby salons, in which businessmen could be dressed up in nappies and suckle at the breasts of whores playing mummy. Written in 1986, Shusaku Endo's *Scandal* was about a staunch old writer in a quandary forcing him to investigate the dark world of the flesh trade. The reference to the baby dives is well documented. As one Mommie-dear explains, 'Our clients dress up like babies ... They play with rattles and baby toys. A lot of men wish they could be babies again ... That's the kind of client who comes to our parlour ... A lot of famous men. Doctors, lawyers – gentlemen like that.' The sessions in these places progressed to a bizarre, ritualized form of surrogate incest, but this was reportedly not the general rule. The infantilizing customer would be bathed, dried off with loving care and, once he had had talcum powder gently patted on his backside, treated to oral or manual relief.

The rattles have fallen silent; the baby boom is over. Whatever next? Currently, the answer lies in sado-masochist clubs. An unprecedented boom catering to a sempiternal predilection, it is now enjoying greater success than ever. As far as the police are concerned, as the mass-circulation *Shukan Shincho* weekly put it in 1988, 'The assumption is that these services do not include sexual intercourse, and they thus evade the legal strictures against prostitution.' Once again, the overwhelming majority are not quite what they seem. Since oversights in the 1985 amendments to the Morals Act overlooked SM, a very large number of the leather ladies in the clubs in question are perfectly painlessly providing services of a rather more ordinary nature.

In the welter of options, one wonders which might be chosen by a young *salaryman* like Takashi Yamashita, whose career we looked at earlier. Being just thirty, some of the entertainments of the *mizu shobai* might hold little appeal for him. Despite his hard schedule, current social mores might just open the door for freer and healthier relations with the opposite sex. Still, there will be times when the pull of sex-for-sale will be strong enough to find him sampling the occasional spot of 'health' and 'fashion' in more ways than belonging to a fitness club or wearing designer suits.

Japan views masturbatory and voyeuristic pursuits in the same light as sexual gratification of any other kind. Even if sex is granted a much lower priority in the order of social activity than in the West, voyeurism and masturbation are as entirely free from taboos as anything else. The paradoxical persistence of antiquated social restrictions makes them in every sense handy substitutes for the more awkward real-life encounter with the opposite sex. In a world in which the price for coital sex-for-sale is rising steeply and which moreover hardly leaves time for it, more purely masturbatory alternatives obviously thrive.

Sex, belonging to the soft world of *ninjo* and part of the sphere of mere human feelings as it is, is not very important. The old ways might be abandoned or cloaked in new words and substitutes, but the *salaryman* remains subject to codes of obligation of a stringency similar to those of the samurai. When frivolous feelings come upon him when much of his twelve-hour working day still lies ahead, that he is expected to take himself in hand is more than just a pun.

Takashi might not be sold on the salons or even on the world of prostitution, but the staggeringly large and ever-changing supply of porno videos in his local rental outlet looms large; for a few hundred yen he can have his 'video box' at home. There is still one aspect of the *mizu shobai* left open to him, however, which combines virtually all the options of the pink trade rolled into a single package. He might not be a regular devotee, but, like his brother-in-law Hiroshi Murakami, there is every chance that at some time or other he will have visited what is called a *nudo gekijo* – a nude theatre.

15

Stripping Japan Style: The Genital Circus

JUN SAYAMA – THE MAN WHO WOULD BE STRING

Tokyo's Asakusa district may still enjoy a reputation as the last to retain the flavour of plebeian Edo, but only the smaller and more recent vestiges of its past as the prime amusement district survive. Rokku avenue boasts the area's last bastions of old-time burlesque: the Rokku-za and Fransu-za theatres. Yellowing photographs of buxom sirens grinning beneath beehive hairdos and inches of false eyelashes in bygone strip extravaganzas evoking the Moulin Rouge, the Yoshiwara and Bath Time hang on the walls of the inner staircases of the Fransu, which is in fact the sole genuine survivor. Partly as a misguided move to replace Ginza's defunct Nichigeki theatre, the former home of Tokyo's most glittering revues from the late twenties, the Rokku-za was rebuilt in 1985. Newly dressed in steel and glass without, it undresses to emulate the *Folies Bergère* within. Notwithstanding an additional zest of raunch, it has not succeeded in bringing back the crowds. Out of the twenty-odd theatres still active in Asakusa at the beginning of the sixties, only these two remain.

The road to hell is paved with good intentions. The police, so often self-appointed champions of morality, have contributed to the area's overall decline. Adhering zealously to what has become a repressive tradition ever since the official closure of the Yoshiwara three decades ago, they strictly patrolled Asakusa and virtually paralysed Rokku avenue's once-prevalent racy entertainments. If they looked aside in nearby red-light districts, Rokku was a kind of scapegoat, a showcase for moral crusading which was not to enjoy the same privilege. Deprived of its traditionally ribald heart, the district died.

Up in the Fransu-za's dank, decrepit auditorium, renovated stage lighting was the electrical equivalent to the layers of greasepaint cracking on the face of an ageing stripper. In a hall able to accommodate hundreds more, she flaunted a sagging, marbled anatomy before a crowd of exactly seven sleepy old men. Illuminated in green and magenta on-stage and looking like a grotesque fauvist painting, Off-White towered improbably over the seven dwarfs. A habit for a handful of wizened nostalgics, Asakusa's dated Fransu-za was fading before fresher flesh and harder core elsewhere.

After managing other theatres and a period of semi-retirement, however, a new manager recently came back to the Fransu-za to liven things up. One of the great patriarchs of the *demi-monde*, he is the indomitable 66-year-old Jun Sayama, alias 'Himo'. Literally meaning string, the word colloquially denotes men who have a female in tow whom they exploit; in short, a pimp. Far from being ashamed of this epithet, Sayama actually presented me with a copy of a book simply called *Himo*, a best-selling biography written by writer Tsubura En who, as befits the Sayama mystique, is a woman. The book pulls no punches, freely mentioning intimate facts that most would prefer to hide including an injury sustained as a child which, although it put a permanent kink in Sayama's privates, hardly seems to have cramped his style. En chronicles the life of Japan's most famous striptease theatre operator, a seducer *extra-ordinaire* who has made his living exclusively from the countless women he has held in his uncanny spell. When I met him at the Fransu in 1988, the theatre building had been redecorated inside and the dingy walls painted white. He is very proud of what he calls his 'coffee shop corner' just outside the auditorium, which is managed by his wife.

Just as modern Japan reserves the kimono only for special occasions, most of the country's 680-odd strip-tease theatres significantly stage one – and only one – act performed by a woman so attired. Some might crown their performance with a dildo demonstration, others portray the victim in SM acts and a few dispense live sex. More usually, what is called a 'kimono show' involves nothing more than unwinding sashes, starting with the brocade obi, going on with the removal of outer and inner silken robes and culminating with a rousing, perennial and explicit nude display – in short, the classic Japanese ecdysiast routine.

Emulating the fashion of the former *oiran*, the kimono-show exponent's outsize obi sash is often tied in front. Such acts tend to be somewhat old-fashioned as can be some of their performers, a fact frequently echoed in an accompaniment of sentimental Enka popular music with a touch of old-time samisen. With her whitened face small beneath a towering wig decorated with elaborate hairpins and lips like a tiny red heart, the woman cuts a phantasmagorical figure in garish finery scintillating in the coloured spotlights. As often as not, being an out-of-work performer of some other persuasion (as many strippers are), she has had some training in traditional dance. As she strikes elegant postures in space and dexterously wields a fan, it shows. Her fluid movements culminate in calculated freezes, which the audience applauds as it did in the traditional theatre.

Of all living kimono-style strippers, the most famous

is Asakusa Koma Daiyu, who happens to be Mrs Sayama. His most successful charge, in her prime she reigned for an unusually long time as the highest paid stripper in Japan. During a career entirely devoted to peeling off layers of traditional silks, she accumulated 240,000,000 yen. Now in her late forties, Koma Daiyu retired from the strip scene ten years ago. The Sayamas still maintain their professional partnership, driving every day to the Fransu-za theatre from a comfortable outlying *shitamachi* home in a luxuriously appointed van.

Lean and wiry, the bantam Sayama reigns from a cramped, cluttered office along the corridor from the dressing room. A fast talker delivering his points in staccato bursts, he fixes you with serious, gimlet eyes behind his glasses and cracks outrageous jokes with the same deadpan, truculent expression. For a pimp, he is certainly highly endearing. Some would call him exploitative but he takes this in his stride. All his life, he has done only what comes naturally.

Sayama was precocious. Born of desperately poor parents in what was then a squalid village in the Arakawa district in Tokyo's *shitamachi*, he was in every way an urchin. Street-wise and thirteen, he took up with a masseuse capable of rubbing men up in all kinds of wonderful ways. This was his first sexual encounter and, as young as he was, the couple warmed to each other. He was enterprising too. Assisting her in finding customers, he persuaded her to hike her price and gleaned a commission from the deal. The discovery that this woman was entertaining a liaison with a mere boy was considered beyond the pale even in morally lax prewar *shitamachi*, however, and she was expelled from the community. Tired of living with a family squabbling in one narrow room in a rundown wooden tenement house anyway, young Sayama went with her.

A sen is a prewar coin and there were one hundred to a yen. The earnings were meagre, but the twenty he took from his girlfriend's one yen fee added up. 'I thought this was a really comfortable arrangement,' Sayama recalls, 'and an absolutely ideal job for a man.'

Indeed, when the couple finally fell out after living some months together, he wasted no time in finding someone to take his masseuse's place. Still regarding his profession as ideal for a man as he grew up, he tended to latch on to any woman, especially a loose one with a big heart, who could take care of him. As the urchin matured, so his companions became less like nannies, although one suspects that most of the women in Sayama's cute little pink world tend to mother him. The majority of his successive amorous and business partnerships involved a variety of *demi-mondaines*, until he focused at last entirely on strippers.

Sayama was nineteen when the Pacific War broke out in 1941, and was drafted into the air force. 'Lose a sock,' he recalls, 'and you got savagely beaten up. It was hell. Many of the friends I made were kamikaze pilots, and those going on missions never came back.' And of course, to the highly sexed Sayama's protracted misery, there were no women. Some would see it as flippant or cowardly, but Sayama's subsequent desertion was a dangerous and daring act in wartime Japan. A staunch practitioner rather than theorist of make-love-not-war, he stole an officer's uniform and was pleased to note that the guards stiffly saluted him as he marched out of the gate of the barracks. Instead of going into hiding, he had the nerve to join an itinerant theatre troupe, among whom only the director knew that he was a deserter.

In 1947, while still with the same troupe, Sayama chanced to see *gakubuchi sho*, one of the early precursors of striptease. Epitomizing the artistic alibi, the *gakubuchi* medium found semi-nude women posing in tableaux vivants staged behind enormous picture frames. Sayama's enthusiasm won over his boss, and the troupe began peeling the clothes from its actresses, starting with his erstwhile girlfriend. His innovations went a step further. Taking *Kunisada Chuji*, a well-known period *yakuza* melodrama and a staple in the popular theatre for years, Sayama turned it into a parody enacted by a cast of semi-naked women. It was a rousing success.

When it was found that Sayama had been dating young Ayako, who was assistant to Mari Akagi, a haughty prima donna of the early striptease stage, he was expelled from the troupe and Ayako took him home to live with her parents. Her father owned a garage and Sayama was not exactly partial to his new job as a grease monkey. As he puts it, 'My kind of work has always consisted of making women work.' As Ayako's father put it, if he wasn't going to work in the garage, he could get out. When he did, Ayako went with him.

They married, but their connubial life was not exactly blissful – especially not for Ayako. Sayama had accumulated an entire harem of strippers in the meantime and was busily farming them out to theatres in Asakusa and elsewhere, and he slept with all of them. 'We established a rota,' he stated quite candidly on a recent TV programme, 'Monday was for Kyoko, Tuesday for Yoko and so on. On Sundays, I used to rest.' As Sayama's marriage floundered, so his peculiar blend of love and business thrived. By now there were eight girls living in the apartment, and he had devised a system whereby half remained while the others toured around the striptease theatres burgeoning in other parts of the country; the rota had by now reached a national scale. In the early sixties he took up with the young woman who was to become Asakusa Koma Daiyu, and his personal and professional focus narrowed down to her.

'I try to keep the old standards,' Sayama explains in his office, 'while always looking out for something new.' His is perhaps the only remaining theatre of its kind to bother with rudimentary scenery. He hands me a pile of papers and scrapbooks showing his sources of inspiration, singling out a British book of cut-out cardboard models of Victorian buildings and interiors. He points to the page depicting the inside of a church. 'This is going to be the backdrop for our next show,' he explains. 'I'm calling it Happy Wedding.'

He puts the strippers through their routines and watches comedians rehearse with an eagle eye. He presides over his world as a kind of father figure and seems well liked by most of the strippers, who will accost him in the corridor with problems about costumes and changing the order of their stage appearances. He seems offhand and relaxed, giving the odd foreign stripper a jocular peck on the lips by way of praising her performance. An ageing fawn, he is at once gruff, amiable and spontaneous, but theatre underlings treat him without exception with traditional reserve; his immediate assistant never fails to enter and exit from his office with a deferential bow.

Occasionally, Asakusa Koma Daiyu still performs. 'Some striptease theatres revive old names,' Sayama explains. 'For instance, there is a young stripper called Sayuri Ichijo II. We thought we'd bring back Koma Daiyu as she is. The real thing. She may not be so young, but she turned striptease into an art and she is still a great artist. If the public goes for it, so much the better. If it doesn't, then Koma Daiyu is dead and so be it.'

Attired like a Yoshiwara *oiran*, she enters the stage in a gaudy kimono glittering with sequins and with a halo of long pins adorning her high coiffure. No longer in her prime and rather amply proportioned, she goes unfazed through the classic kimono-show routine down to the inevitable nude finale. Although still a handsome woman, Koma Daiyu is obviously no longer adulated for her charms alone and her ability to exploit them as seductively as she might have done years ago. As a phenomenon, her routine is analogous to the kabuki theatre, in which old men playing romantic young leads and beauteous maidens are appraised not for their ability to recreate reality, but for their consummate mastery of an established technique. Similarly, Koma Daiyu's performance is a series of perfected gestures, a repertory of established and endlessly repeated signs and ciphers devised to suggest the charm the passing years have begun to erode.

There are no – heaven forbid – live sex shows in the Fransu-za theatre. Old-time vaudeville comedians still come on between the acts; Sayama laments that these days male dancers, once an essential characteristic of the genre and a foil to the women in a great many choreographed acts, are now very hard to come by. 'Burlesque theatre was once an end in itself,' says Sayama. 'It was an art. Anyone can do live sex as they do in the theatres now.' But doesn't this drive a public eager for greater thrills away to pinker pastures elsewhere? Sayama faces the facts: the audience is much smaller than it used to be. 'On the other hand, we get the older regulars and the people who hanker for the good old days. A lot of students and younger men come here too. They don't only come to get turned on, they come to see Asakusa as it was.'

The ageing Himo doesn't think much about the future, except with poignant matter-of-factness and a whimsical touch of fantasy. He admits to being none too fond of his job as theatre manager; he would rather go on the road with an itinerant striptease troupe he would drive around the theatres nationwide. As he put it in a TV documentary programme recounting his extraordinary life and off-beat profession: 'I want my gravestone to have a giant stylized statue of a woman on top, with enormous tits. When people visiting it press one of the nipples, the legs widen, her thing opens up and out comes a recorded message of my voice. "How are you doing?" it would say. "Thank you so very much for coming."'

THE NAKED THEATRE

> For it is to be noted that, though all modesty and reserve were banished, in the transaction of these pleasures good manners and politeness were inviolably observed: here was no gross ribaldry, no offensive or rude behaviour, or ungenerous reproaches to the girls for their compliance with the humours and desires of the men.
>
> John Cleland, *Fanny Hill, or Memoirs of a Woman of Pleasure* (1749)

In today's other *sutorippu gekijo* – striptease theatres – the stripping is gone and even the tease is virtually superfluous. The terminology is changing accordingly. Current striptease parlours are becoming more generally known and advertised as *nudo gekijo*. Beginning with chorus girl revues and bumping and grinding over the years in places like the Fransu-za to culminate in live sex, Japanese striptease not only has a history almost as long as anywhere, but superimposes far older voyeuristic entertainments.

Until shortly after the Meiji period, *misemono* (show-things) were popular at fairs and festivals. Many such sideshows focused on freaks and geeks but, where archery stands once curtained prostitution in a circus atmosphere, another popular item among the *misemono* was genital display. Set in the turbulent days preceding the Meiji restoration, Shohei Imamura's 1981 film *Eejya-naika* showed its impecunious heroine doing a *misemono* stint, hoisting her kimono as men blow between her parted thighs with a feathered tickler. The *nudo gekijo* is plainly a hybrid born of a marriage between western striptease and older precedents. There were after all the old burlesque dances performed in the brothels such as the seventeenth-century 'Naked Islanders' mentioned by Ihara Saikaku and 'Chonkina', the musical strip routine which is said to have been popular with foreign sailors in Yokohama whorehouses in the nineteenth century.

Western striptease made inroads in Japan during the Occupation. The Gakubuchi had been devised to circumvent censorship: although semi-nude, the protagonists did not move. A more animated and daring variant was a show called Baranko (from the French balançoire), with seated, motionless girls swaying on swings suspended from the theatre ceiling. Another development of the early postwar found strippers emerging from a waiting car. Dropping overcoats concealing only a few strategic sequins, they danced between the tables of a club. Once an accomplice had passed around a hat, they scampered off to the car and drove on somewhere else. Peeling off first before the wealthy occupying forces, they soon devoted their new art form to a domestic audience making gradual economic recovery. Within twenty years, their ecdysiastic routines would take on a colour which was very much more Japanese, and which would deepen with time. Today's frankly 'pink' performances would not only have made many a uniformed good ol' boy of the Occupation blush, but turn pale.

Despite far greater overall permissiveness, with the exception of venerable Parisian Folies and Las Vegas chorus-girl spectaculars, a pervasive sense of shame generally taints striptease and current live sex shows in the West with nastiness. Where erotic spectacle is seen as degrading, degrading it is. If it is to be provided contemptuously by exponents despised by the rest of society, it renders its spectators similarly hideous. Since the majority of such businesses are run by thugs, even as he ogles, the western spectator is often haunted by the spectre of violence. The sex trade may be governed by the gangs in Japan too, but even the *yakuza* have a certain ethic: they may break or bend the law to provide the show, but under no circumstances would they do the same to the spectator. Pointing to a relatively innocent sexuality lost in the West during the prudish nineteenth century, the quotation above from *Fanny Hill*, which refers to a brothel in which couples watch each other perform, could just as well have been written about the *nudo gekijo* in modern Japan.

In the Japanese *demi-monde*, where both sojourning sexual practitioners and visiting customers enter a limbo traditionally outside social norms, there is no room for contempt. It is rather interesting to note that the TV documentary about Jun Sayama mentioned above interviewed several *mizu shobai* figures, male and female, about what the word *himo*, or pimp, conjured up for them. In one way or another, the general consensus was that a pimp was absolutely no different from managers in other walks of life. If the official Japanese view is markedly different, in practice the world of sex is seen more as a parallel universe than as a sore festering on polite society's pompous bottom.

Featuring live sex shows, the *nudo gekijo* is a theatre of voyeurism. To the Japanese, this is as apparent a facet of sexuality as those giveaway third-party penises seen bursting through paper doors in countless old *shunga* prints. Associated consequentially in the West with the taboo of masturbation, voyeurism is considered a 'perversion'. The Japanese consider both perfectly natural aspects of sex.

Not that the *nudo* theatre spectator would dream of masturbating in his seat. This is prohibited not by a western taboo, but by a sense of decorum at least as strong. Besides, he has other options. He may queue up quietly for a hand-job administered by a stripper behind a curtain in the corner of the theatre, or publicly hump her on-stage. During the mid-seventies, increasing permissiveness gave strip theatres in Osaka (ever the trailblazer in the field of commercial erotica) the inch they needed to take a mile and striptease theatres all over Japan began offering live sex shows with audience participation. Even here, convention is inviolate. A strict pattern permits only *programmed* licentiousness; at all costs, no outbreaks of spontaneous behaviour.

In Japanese, the word *sukebe* is reserved for men finding themselves haplessly pulled along by the unruly beast between their legs; the implication is often humorous and certainly more tolerant than in the equivalent English word 'lecher'. Provided they confine the satisfaction of their urges to the proper time and place, *sukebe* are perfectly acceptable; never could they collectively be embodied by that mythical western figure of loathing clad in a grimy fawn raincoat: the Dirty Old Man. Horny Japanese don't have to be old, they are of all ages and walks of life, wear raincoats when it rains, and in a country in which cleanliness is closer than close to godliness, they are very unlikely to be dirty.

At the *nudo gekijo*, the proper place for voyeuristic indulgences, prices marked up at the door include reductions for students and pensioners. Rather than surreptitiously shuffling in shifty-eyed with their collars turned up, men breeze in off the street at their own particular proper time and are politely welcomed by well-behaved gangster punks as they purchase tickets from little old ladies at the box office. Clad in barely more than short happi tunics emblazoned with the theatre name, show girls sometimes relax over tea and cigarettes in the foyer with the theatre staff, and greet clients with radiant smiles.

Although some towns offer multiple stage extravaganzas, the auditoriums in the 680 theatres in Japan vary little from place to place. Some older theatres still have a single conventional stage but most feature a small, circular additional one in front, which starts to rotate when the action heats up. Up on the circular stage and bathed in pink light, sexual protagonists look about as wicked as dancing figurines on a rococo plastic gondola. Connecting the two stages, or merely extending from the rear stage and up between the rows of seats, is a raised platform suggesting at once the kind one sees in the American burlesque show and the Hanamichi walkway in the kabuki theatre.

The auditorium is none too prepossessing. Ceilings are festooned with dusty clusters of garish plastic flowers; antiquated seats – often mere benches – are covered in torn vinyl or frayed plush. Where they are not mirrored, the walls are painted black and papered with posters crudely calligraphed in Da-Glo colours luridly shrieking out coming attractions under black light. '10/1 – 10/31: Honey Love, Lucy Satan and *aidoru tarento* [idol talent] show. Plus live *gaijin* sex and hardboiled SM show.' The shows change every ten days, with strippers often journeying between theatres dotted about Japan with suitcases filled with sequined, feathered finery designed only to be removed.

Like high-ranking courtesans in the pleasure quarters of yore, some of these women are stars. Working their way up a rigorous hierarchy, they become *aidoru suto-rippa* (idol stripper) when they reach the zenith of their profession. They receive deluges of fan mail; magazines and jumbo-size glossy paperbacks devoted every so often to the stripper élite give their vital statistics, astrological signs, blood groups, likes, dislikes and aspirations. Not to mention their comments: 'No, I don't really like sex much,' confesses Aoyama Miyo, whereas Honey Love finds that 'When I feel that the august guest on-stage is really doing his utmost, I get wet.'

Between nude pinups, pages carry learned texts penned either by figures from the entertainment world or priapic professors well versed in the field of fleshly pleasure. Being outside of the 'serious' run of things in Japan, writers are freer to step into the stripper's world than the workaday average. Where culturally orientated intellectuals are anyway rarely considered important, literature is often regarded as belonging to the world of pleasure; many writers devote themselves quite seriously to recording its pursuit. Illustrated with a profusion of photographs of the area's vanished theatres between the postwar years and the mid-sixties, a recent book called *Strip Asakusa* has commentaries by figures from the entertainment and literary worlds, including Tanaka Komimasa, the celebrated and prize-winning essayist who started his career as a comedian in a postwar striptease theatre housed in what is now a department store in Tokyo's Shibuya station.

When not spending all those consecutive days in red-light districts for inspirational and other purposes, writer Nagai Kafu (1879–1959) was a familiar figure in the Asakusa strip joints. After the war, when the old pleasure quarters faded altogether, the elderly and increasingly voyeuristic Kafu spent many of his final days inspiring himself among the girls in the theatre dressing rooms. Far from being titillating, Kafu's works are generally given to a peculiar kind of nostalgia, which tends to equate the brevity of youth and beauty with the pleasures of a vanishing Japan. The brief pieces he wrote about strip theatre girls during the postwar period were no exception. In between his ogling in the dressing rooms and nostalgic writings, the ageing Kafu not only scripted spicy little skits for the Rokku-za stage, but also performed in them himself.

Many famous Japanese comedians, including TV superstar Beat Takeshi, began careers in striptease theatres. In Japan, where fun and licentiousness go hand in hand, this is virtually a tradition. No matter how outrageous, if something survives long enough to become a tradition in Japan, it always seems to be exalted with age and provides a focus for learned discussion. The same applies to striptease, which is frequently pondered by panellists and amply illustrated on late-night TV shows.

Like Japan's prostitutes, strippers often capture the popular imagination as romantic figures to men and women alike. Men find prostitutes arousing and, confined to an ordered, narrow little world, many women are reassured to find that someone else's racy life is even worse than theirs. For meretricious pathos, the sad tale of Sayuri Ichijo can hardly be bettered. One of the pioneers of the frank 'open stage' style which is said to have originated in Osaka, Sayuri Ichijo's role as an originator was typically less admired by the authorities. Charged with public obscenity, she was jailed in 1970.

Defiant in court, she had thrown 'Tell me why I shouldn't show my sex organ to men who want to see it?' at a visibly nonplussed judge and thereby earned boundless esteem from the radical intellectual fringe. Two years later she starred in *Nureta Yokujo* (*Wet Desire*), a soft-porn biopic which earned accolades among champions of individual freedom and turned Sayuri into something of a folk heroine. Having fallen into obscurity and hard times towards the end of the decade, Sayuri put the little money she had into a small bar that burned to the ground. Hearts bled all over Japan in 1988, when a weekly magazine discovered Sayuri in a flophouse, penniless, bedraggled and aged beyond her years.

Outside porno-movie contexts, strippers have been heroines in a whole gamut of mass-audience films from *Carmen's Pure Love* in the fifties to Shun Nakahara's *Makeup* in 1986. Reflecting a prevailingly sentimental Japanese view of the frail sisterhood, this sees Mami the stripper striking up a heartwarming, asexual and (more significantly) motherly relationship with a young simpleton she drags around on her travels. Although it shows a good deal of documentary accuracy, dramatizes vicious backstage rivalries and clearly evidences poverty underlying the calling, *Makeup* tugs at the heartstrings and rather typically disregards many of the harsher realities. The theatre manager is a kindly figure (as some are) ruling reassuringly over a friendly, if sleazy, world unsullied by the destitute foreign women herded around striptease parlours in the real Japan.

'Ah,' a stripper's impoverished ex-gangster husband muses sadly, 'it's no good for a woman, letting men fiddle with her and opening everything up in public.' Then again, that's life. Not just for this indolent stereotype, but also in the broader sense of ingrained Japanese fatalism. Earlier on, the heroine Mami and the theatre manager have discussed the stripper's role towards men. 'They're really like nurses,' the manager says and she emphatically agrees, as well she might.

The *nudo gekijo*'s linoleum stage is polished until it gleams, but in what is a tiny haven of do-as-you-please for men living in a society as rigorously ordered as an old-style British public school the bare concrete floor is littered with torn papers, cigarette butts and flattened beercans oozing their last contents. It is not a pretty sight. Both before and during the three-hour shows, men sip drinks from vending machines, fill the air around no-smoking signs with smoke, read newspapers and comic magazines and snooze. Except during the intervals, no one speaks a word. As the prurient samurai sit bathed in pink light before the round table of the stage, the atmosphere suggests all the camaraderie of a Boy Scouts' meeting. The theatre context has typically united these men in a group; not even remotely threatening, the place feels warm and secure. Should a mild squabble occur or a drunk talk too loudly, the compère merely chides gently over the PA system, and the erring parties shrink immediately into repentant silence.

Shows succeed each other from mid-morning to 11.30 P.M. Until the midnight curfew imposed on sex businesses in 1985, *nudo* theatres staged *oru naito* all-night specials on Saturdays until the rolling of the first trains. Like the pink cabarets often adjoining them, the *nudo gekijo* are frequently to be found close to stations.

Some real addicts stay all day. As the sexual extravaganzas writhing on-stage before them are reflected and distorted in cheap mirrors like the agonized flesh of a Francis Bacon painting, they sporadically keep their noses buried in their *obento* lunchboxes. Like porno film theatres, the *nudo gekijo* is a good place to sleep off a hangover; some soporific *aficionados* half-open their drowsy lids to contemplate female flesh spread before them at intervals, before lapsing back into a coma. Not infrequently, a third of the audience is fast asleep.

OPEN STAGE

> Her Augustness the Heavenly Alarming Female, hanging the heavenly clubmoss of Mount Kagu as a sash, making the heavenly spindle-tree her head-dress and binding the leaves of bamboo grass in a posy for her hands, laid a tub before the door of the heavenly rock dwelling and stamped till she made it resound. Doing as if possessed by a deity and pulling out the nipples of her breasts, she pushed her skirt-string beneath her private parts. Then the Plain of High Heaven shook and the eight hundred myriad deities laughed together.
>
> *Kojiki* (A.D. 712)

It's showtime. Through a window high up in the back of the theatre, you can see a rather bored-looking man enter the control booth. He flicks switches darkening things down to an ultraviolet horror-house gloom and picks up a microphone. 'Welcome to today's first [to fourth] show. We would remind you not to harass the dancers. Please, no photographs and no tape recording. Take your time and enjoy yourselves. Now here's Miss Emi – let's have a nice round of applause!'

Prompted like children at a pantomime, the spectators clap obediently, if a bit listlessly. In some places, claques liven the end of performances with all the fever of a baseball match, blowing whistles, banging on tambourines and hurling paper streamers out over the stripper as her act nears the finale. As the lights come up, a deafening barrage of disco sound crashes out over the stage. 'Like a virgin,' improbably howls pop idol Madonna, 'touched for the very first time.' When you can't understand the lyrics, what's in a song?

The curtains swish back to reveal a mirror ball sending beams from coloured spotlights darting out in all directions. Arms outstretched beneath it, Miss Emi sails on like a plastic replica of Scarlett O'Hara in a long, spangled and diaphanous white gown. She might also wear black to emulate Liza Minnelli in *Cabaret*, or come flouncing on in a short flared shocking-pink party dress with mutton-chop sleeves, echoing Japan's mawkish *Kawaii-ko-chan* – little cutie pie – singing stars. Performers' sartorial preferences often reflect their age; in the seedier theatres, portly matrons strive to emulate bygone screen sex-pots to the syncopations of cha-cha-cha. But whether she is over the hill or in her prime, one thing is painfully clear: Miss Emi's dancing skills are virtually nil.

Odoriko, dancing girl, traditionally has the same *risqué* overtones in Japan as anywhere else. Moreover, classifying the *nudo* theatre ladies as 'dancers' is not so much a euphemism as a front to please the authorities, and strip shows had better pay lip service to these by staging cursory dancing – or else. In the case of foreign strippers, 'dancer' is also the term which enables them to enter Japan with a visa in the 'entertainment' category in the first place.

Contrary to that in most countries, Japanese dancing traditionally regards movement not as an end in itself but a means to an end. In geisha entertainments and the kabuki theatre alike, choreography is simply a trajectory on the way to culminating freezes – a matter of striking poses. The technique makes a tragic marriage with disco. Not that anyone cares. At this point the audience is hardly watching. Compensating for her rambunctious, arhythmical bouncing, Miss Emi cocks her head prettily and pouts as her gesturing hands and arms go through a daintified semaphore, which is modelled on the drill animating Japan's insipid singing dollies. Behind the hand jive is the gradual transmogrification of a long cultural heritage.

After shedding her gown to reveal her bosom (which older strippers often bolster with silicone), she clutches the scintillating garment to her naked frontage and exits stage with a little bow as the compère bellows 'Let's have a round of applause!' Except outside Tokyo, where decorum is less compelling and the *nudo gekijo* can be a rowdy affair, the audience, taking no initiative of its own whatsoever unless emboldened with alcohol, must be goaded. After another announcement, the music turns to syrupy soul, and Miss Emi re-enters looking demure. In every *nudo* theatre from northern Hokkaido to southern Kyushu, the show's first act is almost invariably the same and contrived to warm things up.

With pride akin to a connoisseur describing a kabuki stage artifact, a man sitting next to me once explained: 'In Japan, the dildo is traditional.' Indeed, Edo-period carved polished wood and painted porcelain *harigata* fetch high prices with collectors. Today's version keeps the traditional flag flying: the rubber is moulded into an effigy of the Shinto goddess Benten. On the circular stage, Miss Emi first goes through a typical Suzy's Bedtime routine, caressing herself and tantalizing to the conventions of bump-and-grind. Bathed in coloured light, the woman who looked ridiculous dancing a moment ago is stretching, twisting and posturing to emulate every imaginable icon from decades of girly calendars and magazines. She is doing something at which she truly excels: posing.

As the stage starts trundling round, it is apparent that her graphic auto-erotic manipulations, if not for all tastes like everything here, are the product of a certain skill. 'It's amazing,' said an incredulous American stripper.

'Some of those women are over the hill, you'd never look at them in the street. Yet on stage they have real style: something as dumb as using a dildo becomes incredibly erotic.' In Japan, even the gestures of the sex theatre must be learned.

The audience dutifully claps as Miss Emi exits again with a bow. As she re-enters after a costume change leaving her nude from the waist down, the applause is altogether more thunderous. As she prances about the stage, a forest of eager right arms shoots up as before a schoolteacher and she hands the dildo successively around. Squatting down with thighs agape, she allows stageside spectators a small indulgence as torrid as a push-button working model in a science museum. 'Thank you very much,' she says sweetly as she removes the dildo and proffers it to each stretching hand in turn.

Once Miss Emi has exited after this, one might be forgiven for thinking that one has now seen the last of her: not so. The culmination of every single performance here is its very *raison d'être*. What follows is what the spectators have really been waiting for. '*Opeeen suteeeeegi!*' roars the compère: Open stage.

Sigmund Freud once outraged the prim turn-of-the-century West by stating what has always been obvious to the East: the human male is excited by the sight of the female genitals. Nowhere is this biological fact more taken for granted than in Japan. Not only did erotic *shunga* woodblock prints invariably contort their writhing figures the better to expose their enlarged genitalia but many of the genre's masters simply homed straight in on the nitty-gritty with explicitly detailed closeups of the vagina.

Male Japan's unabashed passion for the female genitals is also rooted in the earth-mother worship underlying animistic Shinto, as evidenced in fertility festivals. Beneath its dominative male dressing, matriarchal Japan puts woman on a pedestal as the progenitive focus of the all-important family; she is the demure goddess of the home. Men traditionally seek their pleasure elsewhere, out in the entertainment world, the entirely separate realm of passion. The dichotomy between woman as mother and whore – by no means unique to Japan – progresses symbiotically in the *nudo gekijo*, until it climaxes as a synthesis. In what is as much a brothel for group sex as a temple, motherly priestesses double as Jezebels and male worshippers gaze raptly upon the most obvious symbol of womanhood as both the ultimate turn-on and the origin of the species.

So when it's *open steegi*, lights blaze on all over the auditorium and white neons flash on beneath the glass edges of the central walkway. Miss Emi prances around in front of the men in the audience, clapping her hands in time to the ear-shattering music and entreating them to join in like a nanny at a children's tea-party. At intervals, she squats or lies down inches away from them and spreads her thighs to the utmost. As a beam of harsh light homes in to make Miss Emi's privates public, she draws them apart with her fingers. 'Can you see?' she asks improbably. 'Do you like it?' The men peer intently at the brilliantly illuminated holy of holies; its rosy glow is reflected in their glasses.

All this is inevitably reminiscent of the old myth about Ama-no-Uzume, the Heavenly Alarming Female in the quotation above. Intrigued by the laughter she hears erupting from the deities as they contemplate the latter's genital display, the sun goddess is enticed from her cave to shed light again on the world. Seated around the stage and bathed in pink spotlights, the children of the gods are considerably more staid than their ancestors, who told the old stories long before anyone had thought about Confucianism, let alone the heavy outer armour of nineteenth-century western propriety protecting it.

Some may exchange wisecracks with the stripper, a few wear rapt grins, but the dominant facial expression is about as transported as that of a quality control inspector testing printed circuits. Nevertheless, if ingrained decorum decrees shielding the emotions even here, the excitement seething behind these blank faces makes itself felt like electricity in the air. Sometimes even being handed a magnifying glass, the devotees have no compunction about peering deep into the lady's proffered penetralia. As she exits, admirers sometimes present a stripper with a small token, usually a drink from a vending machine. When one enamoured young man presented a stripper with a large bouquet of roses, however, he blushed to the hair-roots. He had betrayed his emotions, and he was conspicuous.

HONBAN MANAITA SHOW: LIVE ON THE CHOPPING BOARD

The priapic mass continues, interspersed with some four fertility rites, which for instance might begin with a performance by Izumi Honda. The young *salaryman* wears a dark blue suit; hoodlums and workmen have cropped 'punch-perm' hairstyles; older artists and intellectuals have long grey hair; photographers wear army surplus anoraks. The predilection for uniforms is reflected as much among the audience as it is in Izumi's sexy undies and black stockings: they clearly announce her to be a live sex performer as soon as she hits the stage for her prelusive dance. After her exit, a theatre employee unrolls a futon mattress on the stage with a flourish and the compère bellows, '*Honban manaita* show!' (*honban*, the real thing; *manaita*, a chopping board for preparing raw fish). With an alacrity akin to a disaster drill, the soporific audience is galvanized into action. Bespectacled old men, swarthy workmen, gangster punks, shirking *salarymen*, long-haired professorial types and students leap to their feet. Like death and opium, sex makes no distinctions. Izumi Honda offers the additional attraction of being a star in her profession – albeit a minor one, for in this racket stardom can be an ephemeral matter of weeks. She might climb up to the summit; in all probability she will drop out from this calling in a couple of years. A few of her sisters rise to nationwide fame; others like the unfortunate Sayuri Ichijo sink into oblivion with advancing years.

Carrying a small lace-trimmed basket better befitting Little Red Riding Hood, she enters the stage in a revealingly flimsy négligé of white tulle. For all her frilly black underthings and fishnet stockings, she kneels back on her heels atop the circular stage as sedately as a tea ceremony exponent. It is this demureness, blended with a cultivated *kawaii* cuteness that have won Izumi her fame. Young, and of undeniable beauty, she has the oval face and lissom body of a willowy courtesan in a woodblock print; traditional red and blue snake tattoos glow through the silken black network on both pure white thighs.

Men standing around her extend fists to each other, heatedly playing *janken-pon* – the ancient oriental paper-scissors-stone elimination game to win her favours. Coming with a group crowning a raucous office drinking session, one man might coyly fend off jesting colleagues trying to push him on-stage. Unless travelling from elsewhere and accordingly 'leaving their shame at home', however, they know that coming as a corporate group precludes any participation – it might cost them their job. For the most part, the men have come alone or in twos and show no signs of embarrassment.

'These are rather special people,' a Japanese journalist met in a *nudo* theatre once explained, as though counting himself out. 'They're kind of lonely and they go for a special kind of sex.' Then his number was called up for a privilege he had won in a lottery, and he disappeared into a little room curtained off at the side of the auditorium to collect his prize. Many theatres have an adjoining *pinku rumu* (pink room), where strippers offer either masturbatory relief or what they do publicly on-stage in private. Aspirants queue up before the curtain like paupers at a charity soup kitchen.

Nudo theatres have many avid devotees. On Sundays, a computer engineer travels two hours on the bullet train to his favourite Tokyo strip haunt. A young representative from a chemical firm prefers rainy weekday nights: 'It's less crowded; with luck, you can get up on-stage several times.' One, a rather distinguished-looking businessman who spoke perfect English, had no qualms about explaining his own particular predicament. 'I come here a lot,' he said with a sad smile. 'But just to watch. You see, I'm impotent.'

For the most part, the audience comprises a very mixed bunch indeed. During bar-room talk of striptease, a young *salaryman* will often simply tell you: 'It's the cheapest fuck in town.' At 3,000 yen, costing almost ten times less than the average private trick, this may be true. On the other hand, for young office workers on low salaries, who commute to distant dormitories with strict 10 P.M. curfews and who habitually work hours long enough to preclude any association with the opposite sex, the *nudo gekijo* is all too often the only fuck there is.

While reflecting an overall mundanity inconceivable in the West, the audience sometimes comprises a freak contingent unlikely to show its face around sleaze spots anywhere else. The girls on-stage are free to refuse a client and sometimes do, especially if their ritualized inspection detects any signs of dirt, disease or small pubic inhabitants. But never even having the bad manners to balk at servicing a man congenitally or accidentally deformed, they are also sisters of mercy.

The audience will yield the occasional burn victim or perhaps a hunchback. Like some elf imagined by Luis Buñuel, one tiny, wizened dwarf kept his artist's beret on throughout the proceedings. Equally tragi-comical and more frequent is the sight of a very old man finding the dying embers of his amorous inclinations suddenly ignited by a pretty stripper. If he should express the desire to clamber up on-stage, the younger contingent will ignore *janken-pon* out of deference. Conceding gentle touchings and treating him with touching gentleness, the woman addresses her grizzled paramour as *otōsan* – father. If dad's energy flags, the audience breaks its usual silence to encourage him. Managing to the finish, he will be treated to a thunderous round of applause. Staunch Confucianism, it is well known, has made Japan into a paradise for old men. Taking advantage of his venerable age and surprisingly youthful ardour, more than one wily old roué breaks rules to clamber up on-stage more than once during a show.

The last two competitors raise their fists, their voices breathless and tinged with urgency: '*Janken-PON!*' A V-sign versus an open palm: scissors cut paper. Paper sits down with a loser's shrug and a wistful smile; there's always next time. He is an ardent fan who follows Izumi around the Tokyo-Yokohama area as she moves from one theatre to the next. The winning scissors clambers up and kneels reverently down on a mattress on-stage opposite her. After polite greetings, the ensuing ritual is perpetually the same. First, taking a moist tissue from her basket, she carefully washes the guest's extended hands. Then she applies them to her breast as they both get to their knees. Performing exaggeratedly stylized caresses in time to the music, Izumi concedes certain fondlings, but most strippers finding hands groping a little too boldly gently pressure them elsewhere. With less amenable ladies, they are sometimes perfunctorily slapped away. Then she tells the man to undress her, which he does rather as he might a store-window mannikin. The stage starts to revolve.

Now she taps the mattress by her side, and the man obediently lies down. Mother Izumi, hardly more than twenty years old, removes her middle-aged little boy's trousers and underpants, neatly folding both and placing them to one side. She then takes more moist tissues from the basket and busies herself with his pubic ablutions. With its head now poking through a hole torn out of a white tissue, the penis makes a plausible caricature of a surpliced choirboy. Becoming a whore again, Izumi delves into her basket for a condom, which some strippers apply with meticulously practised oral skill. As she fusses over the motionless man with craftswomanly professionalism, she occasionally throws dispassionate glances around the rapt, silent audience. When and if the organ rises to the occasion, the show is on the road. If it doesn't, Izumi might waggle the guilty party and shake her head, after which its owner will dress and leave the stage with an apologetic smile. Being frequent, this and other more literal shortcomings never prompt any contempt. Whether the man makes it or not, each *honban* stripper entertains two successively at each performance.

She now either straddles her guest like a female spider about to devour the male, or signals him to clamber on top of her with a wave of the hand. Forbidden to fondle, kiss or touch, he is conceded absolutely nothing other than copulation. Izumi and her charge are beginning to lose their identity: she is a tool for demonstration; he a mere dildo. Symbols for male and female, they are accessories to a rite.

As her feet flail the air to the copulatory rhythm, she gradually straightens her legs and spreads her tattooed thighs to trace an arc in the air like an opening fan, a gesture quite consciously devised to satisfy enduring curiosity: this is what genitals look like when they're interconnected. Everything is explicit; nothing here is to be left to the imagination. Not a face in the audience betrays the slightest shadow of emotion. The air is charged with erotic electricity, but were there no loud disco music, you could hear a pin drop. The fog of voyeuristic arousal disperses as naturally as clouds in sunshine. Far too blatant for obscenity, the act of copulation is suddenly transformed into an ideogram. Beneath tufted testicles and the branches of a human form trembling with the generative power of orgasm, the trunk of gristle stands rooted in vaginal mother earth like the tree of life. In the bright light of the phenomenon, the protagonists, having become genital organs, no longer exist.

THE GENITAL CIRCUS

Izumi's subsequent 'open stage' arouses uncommon enthusiasm; between her parted thighs she offers vistas of places just visited by the lucky few and an enticing little pink travel brochure for those who hope to go there next time. In between non-coital numbers, the programme might yield another *honban* show theme-conceived to evoke a Soapland massage session on an air mattress, as well as a bizarre variety of acts including perennially popular demonstrations of SM. The average show also yields the tortuous sexual acrobatics of professional *Shiro-kuro* (black and white, meaning male and female) couples and *tachi sho* (touch show), in which men take turns in fondling the girls as a theatrical equivalent to playing doctors. At some point there will always be a nude nymphet, an *aidoru* mawkishly prancing around Kawaii-ko-chan style and handing the men a polaroid camera to snap take-home spread-shots for a small fee. Contributions are placed in a box often edifyingly inscribed with characters informing participants that the proceeds go to charity.

The vaudevillians providing bona fide stand-up comic relief now perform in only a tiny handful of theatres, the majority of which are either revivalist like the Fransu-za or nearly derelict, although some sporadically revive the custom to stay on the right side of stricter laws. Today's laughs come otherwise from a primitive, bawdy clowning akin to ancient Roman Bacchanalia: the genital circus.

A certain Wako might erupt rambunctiously on-stage wearing a fluorescent orange and black PVC corset and sharp cones of gold lamé over her breasts. Her round, hugely grinning face is framed by an unruly mane of permed hair topped with a vast floppy witch's hat. Well shaped but a trifle on the squat side, she has a body as rock hard as one of Japan's lither female wrestlers. Dissimilar striped woollen stockings complete the picture; looking like something out of an X-rated *Wizard of Oz*, she is clearly a clown. After the mandatory *dansu*, Wako re-emerges bottomless on-stage and starts up the show Bangkok-style, puffing at a long *Breakfast at Tiffany's* cigarette-holder clenched firmly between alternative lips.

From a bright red tin prop-box portraited with Felix the Cat, Wako takes out a tampon trailing a length of strong string, rams it inside her with the delicatesse of priming a cannon and hands the loose end to a sheepishly beaming member of the audience. Squatting down before him, she wraps the string several times around his fist, grits her teeth and backs away from him until it is as taut as wire. Taking an apple from the box, she uses the string to quarter, peel and core it. To a spirited round of applause, she hands the segments around to other spectators. '*Oishii deshoo*,' she beams. 'Doesn't it taste great?'

While they're still munching, Wako produces a beer can and hands it to another volunteer. 'Hold it tight, now!' she warns. Squatting, she ties the string to the tab and stands up suddenly to rip the can open, sending an ejaculatory jet of foam hissing into the air. Her prop-box yields a cornucopia of accessories for her subsequent stunts: she tootles improbably on an inserted plastic trumpet, and follows this by sending clouds of soap bubbles floating into the air over her bare backside.

Wako's sleight-of-snatch calls for a great deal of skill. Taking aim with a measured jerk of the pelvis, she blow-pipes cigarettes at selected spectators with astonishing accuracy. In Japan, if a job's worth doing, it's worth doing properly. Incredulous, one tries to imagine Wako practising these skills at home, which she probably does diligently and humourlessly. No doubt she will have been drilled through the *Kata* (the Way-to-Do applied to anything from aikido to pottery) by an older colleague, perhaps a veritable *sensei* – a sage – of cunt stunts.

The unlit cigarettes now point expectantly at Wako from faces around the stage like spokes in a carriage wheel. The lights dim. The prop-box yields a combined bunch of twenty candles, which she sets afire and holds aloft like Liberty's torch. Moving around the stage, she gives her waiting admirers a light. As they sit contentedly savouring the smoke, she hands the waxen torch to a man in the front row and positions herself carefully before him. His amused face glows before her gaping thighs in the candlelight as in a rather special La Tour nativity painting. With one single devastating genital blast, Wako plunges the theatre into darkness.

Such pelvic musclewomen are a frequent feature of the *nudo gekijo*. If they never become stars like *honban* strippers, they certainly acquire a certain measure of renown. Having stuffed herself with a wad attached to a length of rope, one matronly geek's act consists of selecting the heftiest member of the audience and, crawling backwards like a crab, trundling him around the stage aboard a small trolley. Another crams herself with live eels. Apparently of the vegetarian persuasion, another gluts her vitals with a white *daikon* radish as big as a baby. Popular some years ago was the amazing American Goldie, a genitalistic equivalent to Uri Geller who could use her formidable privates to bend a dessert spoon in half.

A more traditional kind of genital circus act sees girls squatting over sheets of paper and calligraphing messages of good luck with writing brushes gripped in their vitals. Others daub their inbetweenies with black Chinese ink, allowing members of the audience to pat on pieces of white paper in order to obtain a variant of the angler's traditional *giyotaku* fish print which they would be rather less eager to show their wives. Finalizing her act with fanfare and a concealed surprise, one internationally minded *nudo* clown's capacious privates at last yielded a long string festooned with the flags of the world.

Crowning their already wholly unlikely demonstrations with a vulvar variant of the farting Petomane famous in Paris in 1900, some of these genital comediennes flex muscles during *open steegi* with loud, undignified expulsions of air to the unrestrained delight of the giggling audience. As difficult as it is to imagine anything more grotesque, an underlying innocence renders the act's outlandishness silly rather than obscene. Anything but arousing, it is defused by its extreme puerility. The most striking thing about this and most performances here, as many an initially inhibited westerner has found, is not just their improbably decorous reception, but their sheer harmlessness.

ENTER THE LAW – KIND OF

> An assistant police inspector was arrested and dismissed for engaging in an indecent act with a striptease dancer on the stage of a theatre in Yamato, Kanagawa prefecture ... He was quoted as telling investigators that he visited the theatre on an off-duty day and got on the stage in response to an invitation from a dancer, overwhelmed by the 'atmosphere' there.
>
> *The Japan Times* (July 1981)

Their sheer prevalence might lead one to assume otherwise, but live sex shows are illegal in Japan. Although rarely prosecuted, those caught humping on-stage are still arrested as the newspaper report above suggests. Subjected to the same humiliating treatment as *Chikan* perverts caught flashing or molesting women on trains, they are hauled down to the public prosecutor's office or even to a mere police station, where an officer simply makes phone calls to inform wives and employers of the outrage. Although a source of pain and embarrassment for the parties concerned, this is unlikely to herald the demise of a marriage in Japan, where women would either view it as a puerile male peccadillo or anyway prefer silence to a humiliating scandal. Should such a misdemeanour reach corporate ears, on the other hand, it would certainly mean the end of a career. Poor 'overwhelmed' policeman! Being dismissed and disgraced may seem a relatively light punishment, but in Japan life imprisonment would only be marginally worse.

If the strippers are prosecuted at all, it is for indecent exposure rather than prostitution, as Sayuri Ichijo found out to her chagrin. Like some other countries, Japan ostensibly puts the heat on strip-show agents and organizers, who frequently have *yakuza* connections, rather than on the prostitutes themselves. Foreign *nudo* performers, however, are invariably deported for visa violations.

In a perpetual and ludicrous cycle, *nudo gekijo* are forever being busted and reopening months later for business *sans* sex, before reverting to the raunchy norm and being closed down again. There are rumours of kickbacks, but equally likely is the tacitly accepted 'safety valve' theory, which sees police preferring to look the other way. Before a 'raid', they often give strip theatre managers advance notice. The worm turns with schizophrenic regularity, however, and cops in plain clothes (on-duty ones, that is) mingle at intervals with the *nudo* audience to wait until they can catch participants *in flagrante delicto*.

If live sex is becoming rather sporadic in closely watched and self-consciously 'international' central Tokyo, it is still the regular stuff of the less inhibited suburbs and countryside. In some *onsen* (hot-spring) resorts, theatres stage strip shows to order – constituting a colourful and literal climax to a bibulous, all-male office bash. The same applies to *onsen* hotels, in which one or two strippers can be invited to spice private parties, with *zashiki sutorippu* – room stripping – performed before revellers in the hotel room.

Like prostitution in Japan generally, *nudo* theatres thrive provided they keep their profile within the tacitly accepted norms. Some, confining themselves to just the odd *honban* act surreptitiously slipped into one of the tri-monthly programmes, have managed to keep their doors open for years. Others, like the DX in Tokyo's Kabuki-cho, go too far over the top too blatantly. The DX went all out to celebrate its opening in 1982, staging Babylonian orgies beyond the wildest dreams of prewar Berlin: not only were there couples undulating both on the front and back stages, but there was also a suspended glass-bottomed gondola which cruised sedately around the ceiling to provide the most amazing vistas of genital interconnections. Meanwhile other tarts relayed each other in an adjacent booth to provide continuous service for the lucky winners of a lottery. Becoming something of a habit, the DX's bombastic initial celebrations outstayed their welcome with the police. One sudden, widely televised fell swoop in 1983 sent bevies of foreign strippers back to their countries of origin, and the bust heralded a clampdown in the whole of Shinjuku. Like other theatres in central Tokyo, however, it soon reopened for business with no *honban* acts at all, before going hard core on a more modest scale. In this particular cloud, one erstwhile DX manager found a silver lining. 'It's fine that way, really,' he confided. 'It's nice and quiet and the atmosphere is warmer.'

'Warmer' holds overtones of huddling reassuringly

together in a group. Although it refers to shame in a more global context, a passage from psychologist Takeo Doi's *The Anatomy of Dependence* about *Amae*, the pattern of parent-child interdependence underlying Japan's predilection for group-orientated behaviour, finds some relevance here: 'The man who feels shame must suffer from the feeling of finding himself, his *amae* unsatisfied, exposed to the eyes of those about him when all he wants is to be wrapped warm in his surroundings.'

As the *nudo* theatre manager's view implies, how much easier it is for a smaller audience to strike up reassuring group contact and a parent-child relationship with the strippers. And even if the crowd is big, how much better it is to have everyone huddled around a single stage than scattered about in a pornodrome containing three. The atmosphere in the *nudo gekijo*, with its celebrants participating in a sexual ceremony staged in a mollifying pink-lit womb, could only exist in a groupist society.

One could contend that its less savoury aspects are much the same as in the West, but this argument loses force in the context of a radically different society with radically different perceptions. At worst, the *nudo gekijo* exhibits gladiatorial cruelty and outlandish ugliness, for undeniably it can sometimes deploy exploited women barely able to hide their revulsion, entertaining desperate men with too few alternative sexual outlets. At best, it is a world where voyeuristic sybarites disport themselves in a disarmingly innocent, ritualized milieu with *demi-mondaines* of a rather special kind. By turns entertaining, repulsive, arousing, poignant, hilarious and sometimes even beautiful, while it is fundamentally only about sex, by definition the *nudo gekijo* remains theatre even more than its female performers and male participants probably realize. Writing about his Theatre of

Cruelty, Antonin Artaud said, 'If theatre is to find any purpose, it must offer us everything which is to be found in love, in crime, in war or in madness.'

LIFE BACKSTAGE

> Revue costumes upon revue costumes, one did not know how many layers of them, blocked the narrow windows even in the hottest of the summer ... Such was the dressing room of the dancers in the Opera House. It was given over to clutter, such a clutter that you wondered how anything more could possibly be added. An indescribable disorder – it might be likened to a laundry or a used-clothes house on moving day. What first caught the eye, however, was not the violent jumble of the colours, or even the faces of the girls as they sprawled about the floor and then sat up again. It was the powerful flesh of their arms and legs. The effect was therefore wholly different from the dirt and clutter of a tenement house. One might say that it called to mind the earthen hallway of a florist's shop, where a litter of torn-off petals and withering leaves is left unswept and trampled into shapelessness.
>
> A mixed odour overwhelmed the nostrils, an odour compounded of cheap perfume and oil and skin and dust.
>
> Nagai Kafu (1942)

Add stale tobacco and beer, and this would be a good olfactory description of the auditorium rather than the dressing room for, although similar, the latter is no longer quite the same as Nagai Kafu evoked it in 1942. In those days, Asakusa's Opera-za was several years and the rest of the war away from turning to striptease, which it did before its demise during the late fifties. Until the end of the war, the boisterous high-kicking of chorines was about as far as the theatres dared to go. Today's dressing rooms smell of soap and shampoo and the perfumes are French and no longer quite so cheap, especially when emanating from 'idol strippers' who make about 50,000 yen per day. The chaos of costumes remains. Gowns of gaudy tulles and taffetas, sequined bodices and costumes in acetate silks and satins are suspended in profusion from hangers on the walls. Rows of mirrors surrounded by bulbs stand on low tables.

There is no longer 'one mirror for each girl', for cities no longer have that kind of space. The good news is that the entire building is air-conditioned, but the bad is that the dressing room is cramped. On the tables before four mirrors, one for three girls, the make-up essentials and brushes are no longer kept in tatty cigar boxes, but in bright plastic cutlery baskets. These are flanked by boxes of tissues and primary school lunchboxes bearing pictures of cutesy animal characters and which contain the requisites for the stage. Alongside these are one-cup instant *ramen* noodles and *bento* lunchboxes too; although girls generally perform only once in three hours, many prefer to spend the day in the dressing room, especially if they are from out of town. Lack of space precludes the 'indescribable disorder' of half a century ago, but the clutter remains, often less colourfully comprising lipstick-stained paper cups, tissues smeared with make-up and ashtrays piled with butts.

The girls nevertheless take turns in clearing up the wreckage and in the majority of theatres, although it is untidy, the dressing room is kept spotlessly clean. As they to and fro from the stage, they are forever taking showers in an adjoining bathroom, both before and after their acts.

In Kafu's time the strains of live orchestras wafted up the stairs; today the canned disco music thundering in the auditorium is muffled but distinctly audible as it pounds through the walls, but the dressing room is peaceful to the point of lethargy. Some women are stretched out on futon mattresses fast asleep; others lounge around on the tatami matting in pyjamas in pastel pinky-blues that look like children's tracksuits, with their hair in garish plastic curlers waving it to look like Seiko Matsuda. These days their husbands and boyfriends might well be in the dressing rooms with them. Mothers occasionally bring along the kids and, until only very recently, one often saw small fry peeking from the wings at mama's performance on-stage. It can be a tough world in which spats between both its male and female inhabitants are not unusual, but a powerful sense of decorum tends to ban squabbles from the torpid dressing room.

Dependent on his thirtyish stripper girlfriend, a seedy little man in a garish black and red shirt whiles away the time in a corner with imaginary partners at a beeping electronic mah-jong game. Another, a pot-bellied ne'er-do-well, whose wife is a sexual clown who has long ceased to find anything very amusing about her job, snores gently in an alcoholic stupor in his pyjamas on a futon mattress. Cups of green tea and instant coffee change hands endlessly. Having finished making up her face at the table, one plump young stripper sits on the tatami mats with a shaving mirror set between her parted legs as she combs her pubic hair. Another talks about going upcountry next week. Most of these girls travel the strip circuit nationwide. 'Mako-chan says in one place she was in in Hokkaido last year,' remarks one as she paints her toenails, 'they had a woman fucking a horse.' 'Heeehhh?' incredulously exhales her companion in cigarette smoke. 'Uso! You're kidding me!'

'So do *honban*, he says to me,' remarks a seasoned

dildo manipulator about a rejected job offer. 'But I've never done *honban*. I couldn't.'

A hulking young man, unusually tall at over six feet, adoringly holds the hand of a petite, winsome Filipina as she applies mascara with the other before the mirror. Crude self-tattoos on his arms and a mop of hair teased into an exaggerated greaser quiff imply membership of a Bosozoku biker gang, but he is soft spoken and impeccably polite. He says he's nineteen and of Korean descent, which, in 'homogenous' Japan, often implies being a victim of discrimination; the world of the *nudo gekijo* has no shortage of social outcasts.

By now his girl has changed into a black leotard and fishnet tights, and sits on his lap. Forgivably carried away, he embraces her. 'Hey!' shrilly snaps an older stripper. 'Cut that out. None of that in here!' This is a universal house rule: sex is kept for the stage or outside, and there is to be absolutely no hanky-panky in the dressing room. Minutes later, some Miss Emi or other enters the room flushed, breathless and bottomless in a silver lamé mini tunic from her boisterous *open steegi* presentation, and it's the Filipina's turn to go on. As his girlfriend lies on-stage being mounted by perfect strangers, the young Korean absently smokes cigarettes and muses about breaking a Japanese taboo: kissing in public.

Meanwhile, the Japanese strippers admire American Vanilla Cream's professional finery, exclaiming, 'Waahh – *suteki*!' Aren't those sexy little black-frilled nothings something? Vanilla ordered them by mail from Frederick's of Hollywood. She comes from a punk background in Los Angeles, where she lived with a junky rock musician in a sort of voidoid squatter commune in a large abandoned car repair shop. Tired of the reek and grime of axle grease and the company of mainline heroin freaks, she decided to head for the East Coast. 'I was broke but I travelled around with a wad of stolen train tickets.' Vanilla Cream, nineteen at the time, got caught. Managing to bolt from the station master's office while awaiting the arrival of the police, she made her way straight to Japan through the shady talent-agent circuit in 1980. 'I can't go back to the States now,' she says, firmly convinced that in a country with a waiting list for the jails, they can find the time to comb the countryside for a waif guilty of stealing a few train tickets.

By now, Vanilla Cream's *honban* shows may have made enough to pay that figure back hundreds of times over. She has no visa problem. As is the case with many foreign strippers, in a country in which matrimonial bonds can be made and broken very easily provided there are no children, she simply paid a flat fee for a blank wedding to a partner she has only seen once, perhaps a taxi driver or a student. Drifting out of the *nudo* circuit, Vanilla landed herself a respectable job and then, after a divorce, an equally respectable Japanese husband. When in Rome; when in Tokyo. Vanilla in fact did exactly what many Japanese *demi-mondaines* do: after accumulating a nice little nest egg, she buried the sleazy past and moved on.

An adept skier, Big Ruby had been thrilled when her brother offered her a job at a winter sports resort in Oregon. Despite his promises of ski instructorship, however, it transpired that all she did was to operate a chair lift. 'I was so mad that I told him I'd go to Japan and do fuck shows,' she laughs. 'And I did.'

Linda was another making her way from her native LA quite wittingly through a spurious talent agency. One night as she sat among a group of strip theatre folk in a large and perfectly ordinary Shinjuku bar, everyone held up open umbrellas to shield her as she insisted on unzipping her bright fuchsia-coloured jump suit and stepping out of it only in her panties. She was very proud of the Japanese peony tattoo gracing the whole of one thigh which, of course, everyone wanted to see. Japanese and otherwise, these girls could well opt for prostitution of a more conventional kind, but they are nearly always given to exhibitionism. 'I'd never dream of doing this in America,' said Linda on the other hand. 'Somehow, Japan is so far away it just doesn't matter.'

According to most strippers who come from more sexually inhibited cultures than Japan, the worst aspect is the peculiar ritual of 'open stage'. 'It's weird, it feels like going to the doctor's,' said one, 'but you soon get used to it like the Japanese girls. In the end, it just seems incredibly silly.' Besides, as Vanilla put it, 'I'd rather do this than turn tricks anyday. It's a lot safer, even in Japan. In the theatre, the guy can't do anything dangerous. There's something else that makes it all easier too: sex on-stage is not like having real sex at all.'

Like everyone else, prostitutes have standards and there is always a point at which they draw the line. Although 'talent agencies' generally recruit girls already on the game, they can be very skimpy on the details. As one American stripper recalled, 'There was this girl from Colombia. She came over here to dance and to do tricks on the side, which was fine. But she always wore a gold crucifix around her neck because she was like, you know, a Catholic. So when she got here and they told her what she'd have to do on-stage, she just burst into tears.'

16
On the Dark Side

HARD FACTS AND VAGUE FIGURES

The police are aware that *toruko* are just a front for prostitution, but contend that they find it difficult to find evidence that would stand up in court. They cannot raid such establishments on mere suspicion that a law is being broken.

Moreover, the lawyers' federation calling for the abolition of *toruko* is against having police barge in 'where people are naked', as this would constitute a violation of individual rights.

Shukan Shincho (22 January 1981)

Called the Committee for Measures Against Bathing Establishments with Private Rooms, the federation mentioned above attracted the attention of the weeklies through its sheer resolve to eradicate carnal excesses from behind closed bathroom doors. As curious as it seems that it should baulk at the prospect of raids which might discover anyone naked in a massage parlour, this is an outlook widely shared by the police. Perhaps as a sign of the times in 1981, however, this venerable committee of two men and two women soon sank into oblivion, but there are always others.

Illegal to be sure, the oldest profession thrives in Japan. Once again, after sporadic periods of conflict between those on both sides of the law, contradictions eventually enter a grudging state of harmony in which logic hardly even enters the picture. Dating back to 1948, the Law for the Regulation of Businesses Affecting

Public Morals predates the Prostitution Prevention Law by eight years. As part of a legacy handed down from the old *ukiyo*, all the shades of pleasure tend to be concentrated in one area, an ingrained concept which also explains why Japanese moral legislation should cover quite so many categories. Although the provisions are vague, the scope clearly covers not only sex concerns, but also *pachinko* parlours, discos and a multitude of different bars. Ever since the more specific prostitution law was passed, the Diet has been regularly exhorted by the usual prim female stalwarts and Christian crusaders, and the Act has been amended no less than twelve times. In one way and another, it prohibits public soliciting, ownership of a house of prostitution or managing a group of prostitutes, but rather magnanimously provides no punishment for either prostitutes or their customers.

Nevertheless, for those over-indulging in things 'pink', the picture is not quite as rosy as it sounds. A law unto itself, when the National Police Agency is not joining officialdom in those protracted periods of looking the other way, it sporadically takes virulent initiatives of its own to curtail the fun and games. Whenever a bawdy-house is raided, prostitutes and clients find themselves arrested and hauled along to the police station for inquisitorial questioning. As a Kawasaki elementary school teacher found to his chagrin in 1987, hanky-panky can be a harbinger of disaster. Fifty-eight years old and married to a woman reportedly 'suffering from an unspecified injury' precluding sex, he told police interrogators that his seven visits to prostitutes over a period of ten months were because he 'felt lonely'. The director of the local education affairs department took the usual hard line. 'This man's behaviour is irresponsible and unforgivable,' he declared before a specially convened committee of local dignitaries. 'Even though he may not be punished by law, the municipal government will take appropriate disciplinary action against him.'

The man had been singled out from among the many entries in an address book seized from a 'hostess' during a raid on one of Kawasaki's shadier cabarets. Reported to moralizing officials, the hapless and perfectly harmless schoolteacher made the best scapegoat, and they went to the lengths of subjecting him to public exposure and ending his career.

The many and widely differing figures put forward by different and often conflicting interests make the true extent of prostitution in Japan impossible to measure. The licensed brothels of the Meiji period may have been corrupt and have fallen far short of their lofty legal ideals, but ever since their closure the supervision of what can only too easily become an exploitative profession has gone backwards and into the shade. If things have immeasurably improved for the majority of native daughters pursuing meretricious trades, there is still a less fortunate minority, especially among the hordes of *Japayuki* girls from South-East Asia.

Police statistics are based on arrests and on the number of establishments providing or likely to provide sexual services. Under the circumstances, a census of the ladies of the evening could hardly be anything but conjectural. Arrests reached an annual peak of 10,000 in 1985 and again in 1987. Seventeen per cent of those arrested were gangsters, but this figure is too nebulous to assess either the number of prostitutes or the degree of *yakuza* involvement in the trade. At the end of 1983 police statistics established that all late-night bars – good, bad and ugly – had increased by more than 5,000 to total a staggering 451,859, with pink salons, cabarets and other more carnal dives accounting for about one third of the total. There were 542 *mantoru*, representing an increase of 80 per cent in twelve months, and the newer 'date' clubs and coffee shops multiplied nearly three times during the same period to total 696. If this new trend boded no good for the parlours of Soapland, there were still nearly 1,700 left, which is about a third more than there were in 1975. Add on live sex in striptease parlours, and even a conservative estimate might find well over 250,000 prostitutes operating in Japan.

Figures like these implied that the sex industry was too brazenly flouting the law; it was obviously time for the National Police Agency to squeeze it. The ostensible bone of contention, however, was not so much priapic as a matter of juvenile delinquency. With nearly 200,000 minors arrested in 1983, the figure marked a record. Although 'moral' offences were still low on a list of misdemeanours dominated by petty theft, sex always makes a handy scapegoat for other social evils. Split into seven categories, the Businesses Affecting Public Morals did not yet cover the newer video-game centres, which allegedly constitute a favourite hang-out for delinquents.

The haunt of sex and many other amusements besides, the raucous district of Kabuki-cho in Tokyo's Shinjuku is also a mecca for video games. Thus to the consternation of officialdom, as juveniles – delinquents and otherwise – twiddled knobs and absorbed themselves in bleeping electronic recreation, the presence of signs screaming sex-for-sale in garish neon nearby might give them ideas; the influence of the area could only be bad and the girls among them were easy prey for pimps. The revisions to the law were inspired almost entirely by conditions in Kabuki-cho, and came as the result of the findings of the grim-faced police officers who had patrolled around assessing the area's status quo for several months.

Drafted in 1984, the new revisions of the public morals law stipulated a minimum age limit of eighteen for women working in bars and cabarets, a ban on new sex businesses in the country's pleasure districts and made it all but impossible to launch new enterprises elsewhere. All sex businesses, including love hotels, would henceforth be barred from operating within 200 metres of government buildings and schools, a measure which immediately prompted influential moralists to erect a new public library on the boundary of Kabuki-cho. The revisions went into effect on 13 February 1985, which many wrily noted was the eve of St Valentine's day. One of the greatest dampers on the *mizu shobai* came from the imposition of a midnight curfew, which found many innocent discos and bars formerly catering perfectly respectably to a late-night (and not a juvenile) clientele either closing up or closed down. Typically, this aspect of the law is full of loopholes. Some discos pose as bars; many obey the rules only sporadically, although those who do never know when they will be the arbitrary targets of the police.

Both before and after the new law, however, the operation of sex-orientated businesses was and is subject to obtaining 'prior permission' from the police and local authorities. This at once casts doubt upon how illegal such things actually are and just what kind of arrangements operators are expected to make in order to open shop. The fact is that bars, cabarets and other concerns employing hostesses are free to operate, provided their services abide by officialdom's favourite old unofficial (and sometimes highly coercive) chestnut of 'voluntary self-restraint'. 'Most of the sex industry is illegal, yet it goes on just the same,' the editor of a Tokyo magazine focusing on the *mizu shobai* recently affirmed. 'As in the strip theatres, people usually know when the police are coming to raid them. In businesses like these, there's a lot of money changing hands under the table.'

The Metropolitan Police Department and National Police Agency trumpeted the success of their endeavours during the first year of the new law, citing that sex shops (which sell sex solely in the form of graphics and playthings anyway) were down by 12.5 per cent and that love hotels (in which sex operates only on a bring-your-own basis) declined by 6.6 per cent. Arrests for prostitution reportedly went up by some 15 per cent, although whether this was due in fact to greater police vigilance or to an increase in the volume of the trade is rather hard to fathom. The police were pleased to report that legal violations in the sex industry had declined by as much as half. While the heat was on for bars and cabarets, however, the number of striptease theatres increased by nearly 14 per cent and massage parlours rose by a whopping 38 per cent.

In fact, the police are reduced to playing a game very like *Mogura tataki* (mole-bashing), an electronic toy popular in game centres: armed with a mallet, the player scores by bashing as many moles emerging from holes set in a table as possible. The trouble is, it's one mole down and two up – with increasing speed. If Shinjuku is currently showing signs of gradual decline, it is not only because increased surveillance has made it too hot; the area has anyway passed its prime. Tokyo's trendies have moved on – to Shibuya and Roppongi. Similarly dominated by a large commuter train station, Shibuya is both a fashionable shopping haunt and an amusement district long peppered with bars, love hotels and other more shady alternatives around the back streets. Until recently a gilded foreign residential ghetto with amusements of a

western kind, Roppongi has risen as a showcase entertainment district befitting a new 'international' image.
The sex businesses, as usual, have wasted no time in
following in the wake of fashion. Behind Shibuya's
fashionable face, it has arguably risen to rival Shinjuku
as Tokyo's capital for the new quickie 'health' massage
setups, telephone date clubs and emergent if surreptitious teenage streetwalkers. Roppongi too, in between
the trendy discos and the plush restaurants, is sprouting
a profusion of little salons with fairy-fingered hostesses
in teeny-weeny gowns.

As the press pointed out, the revisions to the law
merely succeeded in sending the sex industry deeper
underground. Commenting on the latest trends noted
by the Metropolitan Police Department in a new, separate report in 1985, a *Japan Times* editorial stated: 'The
most lurid graphics of the Kabuki-cho scene may have
toned down since 13 February last year, but the game
shops and discos are all the more conspicuous. It is in
these places that the new prostitutes hang out.'

The editorial concluded: 'They are juveniles. They
don't have to solicit for their purpose is apparent, and so
far they have no pimping agents, for the gangsters who
used to run the sex industry are temporarily lying low.
Now here's a real challenge, and not only to the police.
Where are the parents of these young girls? And their
teachers? The eternal task of controlling prostitution has
fallen to the homes and schools.'

Too often shy of sex education in general, homes and
schools are among the last places to provide young
people with much information about prostitution, let
alone to be in a position to take on the task of controlling it. The article's rather less optimistic remark
about the gangsters who do and who are 'temporarily
lying low' reflects a widespread resignation to *yakuza*

control – something the country has by now come to live with.

The degree of respectability that gangsters enjoy in Japan is surprising. The ceremonies inaugurating new bosses for the giant Yamaguchi-gumi gang receive wide, uncritical pictorial media coverage and, in the Senzoku-Yoshiwara Soapland, to give only one example, the headquarters of a local crime syndicate stands not three doors away from the local police box with the gang emblem proudly hanging up outside. Many Japanese argue that having each side knowing what the other is up to, good-neighbour fashion, fosters harmony in the community. Yet few are aware that the illegality of prostitution is as good for the corrupt officials as it is for the crime syndicates. Maintaining prices high enough to make it a profitable monopoly for thugs as well as a lucrative profession for its more fortunate female employees, it also keeps a contingent in a shadow world in which they can be coerced into continuing their careers. As in most places, alas, among those who exploit prostitutes, those who enjoy them and those who condemn them, too few stop to think that it is only bigotry that has turned the profession into the social evil it is.

Still, the prostitute is viewed with an enviable degree of tolerance in Japan. For better or worse, this is another good reason why the laws should be so nebulous. Donning ever more complex and ineffectual moral masks, government officials join the police in doing no more than fronting reality with *tatemae*. With the exception of inveterate prigs, from the loftiest official to the humblest policeman, the *honne* they keep in their hearts is that they find nothing particularly wrong about prostitution at all. What Tokugawa Ieyasu saw quite lucidly as a necessary evil without which 'men of small virtue will become like ravelled thread', officials commonly describe these days as a 'safety valve'. Unfortunately, such enduring Confucian patterns also mean that not a few men, particularly among the *yakuza*, see nothing wrong with exploiting women either.

The old notion of the whore elevated by self-sacrifice is gradually fading from films and TV dramas, but not always in the minds of the harlots themselves. This seems substantiated by the survey on prostitution conducted by the Prime Minister's Office in 1986 on some 680 women apprehended by the police. Nearly 10 per cent were housewives, an equal number were office employees and 4 per cent were students. When asked why they were engaged in prostitution, half said that it was 'to make a living' and 11 per cent because they were in debt. In addition to a miscellaneous remainder after 'money for clothes, travel and leisure', 14 per cent were doing it 'for the sake of the family', a reason both they and their surveyors apparently saw as setting them quite apart from those merely making a living.

Attempting to wipe out prostitution is utopian. As long as there are haves and have-nots and as long as genital organs have an unruly way of deciding that love and procreation are not the sole prerequisites for their interconnection, some women will continue to conclude that they can be readily connected for profit. The prospect of losing votes from what they imagine to be the moral majority makes most governments baulk at what they see as 'becoming pimps'. In Thailand, for instance, one government official's sensible idea of setting up properly regulated pleasure centres was overruled both by his more priggish and his more corrupt peers in March 1989. Whether pimping is best left to the government or not may be debatable to many but, in this era of Aids, not to mention a worldwide increase in sexual slave trading, the proper licensing, legislation, medical supervision and control of prostitution ought to constitute a more urgent priority.

THE CLAP TRAP

As many other countries have discovered, driving prostitution underground not only provides a bonanza for pimps, but also promotes a culture medium for venereal disease. Despite an enduring myth that Soapland is somehow 'safe', the same applies in Japan. In June 1984, a questionnaire was sent out to 230 hospitals dealing with urology and epidemiology by the Institute of Public Health. From the hundred-odd troubling to respond at all, the survey showed that there were 15,667 male VD patients in 1983 and 5,920 females, both figures which had risen by a third from the year before.

With groups of frustrated *salarymen* carousing endlessly around the flesh-pots of East Asia, 'sex tourism' is often cited as one of the causes behind the rising incidence of venereal disease. Most common is gonorrhoea, including the recent strains that have come to thrive on penicillin, followed by venereal diseases relatively new to Japan such as herpes and NSU. Syphilis patients totalled 2,000 in the hospitals covered by the 1984 survey alone, an increase of 44 per cent over the year before. Seven out of ten male patients contracted VD from massage-parlour girls, and half of the females had been infected by their husbands.

In 1988 two dermatologists testing 100 Soap ladies in the Senzoku (Yoshiwara) area of Tokyo revealed that 80 suffered from chlamydia, 21 had been treated but no longer had syphilis, 30 had antibodies to hepatitis B, 85 had type I herpes (labial) and 20 had the genital type II.

As a wily old White-Russian doctor practising in Tokyo ever since 1949, when his former duties in Shanghai came to an end, once warned me about VD in Japan, 'European whores are cleaner inside than out; Japanese whores are the other way around.' Applied to a country in which cleanliness and godliness are synonymous, it struck me as an odd and rather callous remark. However, as an official of the Ministry of Health and Welfare pointed out after the marked increase in VD in 1984, 'Massage girls take birth control pills instead of having their customers wear condoms.'

Despite basic sexual frankness, the dearth of education about the more practical and medical side of things results in widespread ignorance about sexual matters in Japan, even in the areas where it matters most. Meanwhile, if it has been mercifully slower in gaining ground than elsewhere, the shadow of Aids is lengthening. The incidence is very small, but it doubles at regular intervals. Like most things impure to the Japanese, it is seen as coming from overseas. Unfortunately, in the case of Aids, it did. Even as it began making serious inroads in other countries, however, the Japanese felt that it was something that simply didn't concern them. The first cases were haemophiliacs infected with contaminated plasma imported from the US and homosexuals contracting it abroad.

Although some are tardily beginning to sing the praises of the condom and safe sex, features in men's magazines often make Aids into something of a joke. One, for instance, ran a feature with parts humorously written in broken English, a sure-fire way of implying the un-Japaneseness of the disease. 'Aids-panic shot all Japanese *sukebe* [lecher] man!' ran the headline, and photographs showed two young Japanese comedians with their faces peppered with black blotches.

'Recently,' announces a balloon over the fat one, 'I am healthy, become very slender.' 'Recently,' adds the thinner one next to him, 'I am very like Rock Hudson.'

The incidence of Aids is still very low in Japan, as it still seems to be around the Pacific rim. Just as there is substantial evidence that some South-East Asian countries depending on prostitution for income are cooking their books, so it is often said that Japanese officialdom is underplaying the realities to avoid a panic among the population. Fifteen people had reportedly died of Aids in Japan in 1986 which, in a country with a population of about 120,000,000, is very few indeed. Nonetheless, by the middle of 1988, the total was up to forty-six, an additional thirty-four confirmed cases were hospitalized and a total of 1,038 had tested sero-positive. Professor Bin Takeda of China University, chairman of the newly formed Japan Society for Aids Education, lamented: 'A lack of systematic sex education, questions on the subject during entrance examinations and specialist teachers compounds the problem of Aids education in Japan.'

The Aids panic makes itself felt most of all with obdurate racism. Foreign homosexuals report that many former gay paradises, particularly the no-holds-barred male sauna, have closed their doors to non-Japanese. In Soapland, cabarets, date clubs and all the rest, *gaijin* (outside-persons: foreigners) are increasingly and systematically turned away – especially in Shinjuku. Not that the phenomenon is uniquely Japanese; gangland regulations in Paris's rue St Denis long forced whores, including those of other races, to refuse non-white customers. 'It's not that we have anything against *gaijin* personally,' one Shinjuku Soapland tout explained. 'It's bad for business. If Japanese customers see foreigners in here, they won't come any more.'

Apart from the shades of racism and ultra-nationalism

enduring in a segment of society not exactly renowned for its sophistication, the implications are also that the Japanese are ignorant and reluctant about the pursuit of safe sex. The condom is the most widespread form of birth control, indeed it is even sold by the crateful to housewives by door-to-door 'skin ladies' and recently triggered a furore among moralists when a firm wisely targeted a teenage market after a marked increase in youthful abortions. When biology and not morality decides that they are old enough, they're old enough. Condoms for teens bear pictures of two cute little pigs or other animal characters hand in hand on the package and have names like 'Bubu Friend'.

Yet grown men who ought to know better prefer their Soapland forays without it, and its prophylactic function seems unknown. To these, debarring foreigners should suffice; sex is pleasure and, according to all those ancient sex manuals imported from China a thousand years ago, sex is healthy. That it should now be marred by a deadly disease is too awful to contemplate. As with a cat crossing the road with its eyes closed, there seems to be a childish idea that if *gaijin* are excluded from Japan's warm, comfortable womb of mercantile sex, Aids will simply go away. The enviable innocence attached to sexual matters in Japan has gradually been eroded over the years and, unless the practitioners and customers of the sex trade resign themselves to safer habits, the shock that Aids is gaining ground as an epidemic just might deliver the *coup de grâce*.

ZEGEN – THE MEN WHO CONNED THE PROS

In tailoring his petition to please the authorities, Shoji Jinyemon, the pimping reformist who opened the Yoshiwara in the seventeenth century, had been careful to deplore the practice of kidnapping. In those days, the abduction of female children was so common that not even the ostensible threat of decapitation deterred it, but Jinyemon countered that it would end with proper supervision. Throughout the 340 subsequent years of licensed prostitution, the stringency of the laws forestalling this common aberration was to wax and wane several times.

During the aftermath of the seventeenth-century civil wars, prostitution meant survival to multitudes of wretched young widows and kinless girls. At intervals during the eighteenth and above all during the early nineteenth centuries, disastrous crop yields caused famine to fall over much of Japan. In times such as these, the practice of *mabiki*, or thinning out rice shoots, did not refer to plants. As common among the poor of old Japan as it was in China, infanticide was similarly reserved for girls. If not weeded out with *mabiki*, they survived only as additional mouths to feed. Where extreme privation was a fact of life, the tendency was to turn to the flesh trade out of pragmatism. Few lamented much over poverty's practice of putting daughters up for sale and, in point of fact, since it was frequently the only future the poor could give their daughters at all, it was not always as heartless as it sounds. Precedents such as these turned the Edo period into a bonanza for brothel-procurers – the *zegen*.

Keeping their predatory eyes on the countryside and taking advantage of climatic and geophysical inclemencies, the *zegen* were quick to strike when disaster left an abundance of prey. In times of plenty too, they simply prowled around to grab hapless girls crossing their paths, dragging them off to their headquarters on the more desolate fringes of the pleasure quarters in the big cities as the authorities looked aside. Locked in rooms like prison cells, the girls were stripped of their clothing to forestall any ideas about escape. Although they were often partial to gang-rape, the *zegen* refrained to some degree from spoiling the merchandise while they haggled over the prices with the brothels. Virgins could always earn high fees from those eager for the first taste of fresh fruit.

Following reforms in 1872, a girl's subsequent contract had to be ratified by civil servants and the police. As they supervised the signature, they moreover treated incipient brothel inmates to edifying pep talks about serving the emperor and the country. Rather than alleviating conditions as purported, the red tape merely institutionalized sexual slavery with an aura of condescending respectability. No longer officially called such, the *zegen* operated from offices euphemistically known as 'employment bureaux' and sent their agents around the countryside like travelling salesmen. From the 1900s, *zegen* operations moved with the export of women to Manchuria. By 1904 Tsientsin's Taku road was renowned for picturesque little Japanese brothels adjoining bars, tea-houses and even airgun shooting ranges. Until the Russo-Japanese war, *zegen* supplied popular *musume* in Vladivostock. Remaining overt until the late 1920s, all this was tacitly sanctioned by the government. The trade spread around South-East Asian ports meanwhile, and the girls shipped to the brothels in these became known as *karayuki* – outward bound. No one really minded, of course, for the girls were either the daughters of slave labourers sent from the Japanese 'annexe' of Korea, or *burakumin* (village people), a euphemism for the descendants of the Edo-period *Eta* pariahs, the social outcasts who engaged in animal slaughter, tanning and other professions proscribed by

Buddhist law. Like those of Korean descent, the *buraku-min* are heirs to a long legacy of discrimination still felt to a lesser degree today.

Lured from their hamlets with promises of respectable urban employment or abducted from the fields, these women were pushed into vans, crammed into the darkened holds of small cargo vessels and shipped to ports in Malaya and South China, in many cases under conditions not much better than aboard the old slave ships of Europe. In 1970, film director Shohei Imamura made a devastating documentary simply called *Karayuki-san*, which was about one such woman. A septuagenarian living in Kuala Lumpur and the widow of an Indian shopkeeper, the old lady's family hardly seemed to notice her. Imamura took her back to what had been a Japanese brothel, as well as to visit some of her former colleagues in an old folk's home. For about one hour, she serenely describes her abduction and transportation as livestock, and speaking in a mild, dispassionate voice, relates the most appalling life imaginable. It was the way of the world. Perfectly lucid and yet uttering neither a word of resentment nor complaint, she peppered her narrative with earthy good humour and bore no one any grudges.

In 1986, Imamura got into the spirit of more flippant times with a film called *Zegen*. Glossily treated as a flighty *retro* comedy, this true case history of a Japanese pimp in Singapore and Malaya earlier this century almost seemed to belie his eloquent indictment of fifteen years before. Although the facts, from the tacit government approval down to the hardships endured, were accurate enough, life in the brothels was almost made to look like fun. Then again, being more of a realist than a moralist, Imamura's depiction of the other side of the coin may not be so far-fetched. Given the expectancies of the poor in those days, perhaps it some-times was.

Today the term *zegen* has vanished, but the profession is alive and well in the hands of *yakuza* gangs. Rackets battening on teenage runaways and female debtors are uncovered at fairly regular intervals but, with a very large volume of voluntary prostitution, Japan's sex trade involves comparatively little slavery among its native daughters. Would that the same could be said of the hordes of girls from overseas imported in a burgeoning white-slave trade, which constitutes one of the darkest facets of prostitution in Japan.

JAPAYUKI

The Economic Planning Agency has just released its annual report ... health, security and education in the nation have reached the highest ever levels, it says. Japan now stands on the threshold of an 'age of maturity'. It is inexcusable that Japan should cross that threshold on the trampled bodies of the *Japayuki*.

Betty Sisk Swain, 'Guest Forum', *The Japan Times* (December 1985)

Evie is twenty-three. She is a university graduate and she speaks good English. Nevertheless, she found the career opportunities open to her in Manila discouraging. She didn't like being a secretary; it was boring and poorly paid. This isn't always fun either, but the money she earns during a year's stay in Japan will go a long way in the Philippines. Her parents think she's away on a protracted modelling tour, and she looks the part. Anyway, it's not really all that bad. They have great discos; lots of nice clothes. As we talk in a small bar near a *nudo* theatre in a Kawasaki suburb, one of its more unpolished male employees saunters past the door. He doesn't actually enter the place, but he pauses just long enough to make it likely that we have been spotted. Evie's smile freezes on her face. She grabs her handbag and gasps: 'I have to go. They don't like me talking to other men.' Leaping to her feet, she bounds through the door like a frightened rabbit.

Months before in a plush disco in Manila's upmarket Makati district, she ran into flashy young Manuel, who was making a small fortune with a theatrical talent agency. He admired her dancing abilities and he was also a pimp. Having the looks and polish enabling her to enter the profession at the top, as Manuel pointed out, Evie had no compunction about going on the game. Through his agency's connections with Japanese 'show business', Evie landed herself a job on the striptease circuit in the Tokyo-Yokohama area and entertained no illusions about what it entailed. Having gone to Japan almost entirely on her own initiative, Evie is a naughty girl. She is what they call a *Japayuki* – 'Japan-bound' – and whatever the hardships she endures may be, she is still luckier than some of her less-educated sisters.

Until the 1970s, the majority of *Japayuki* came from Korea and Taiwan, but now that these countries have joined the ranks of the NICs, they hail mainly from Thailand and the Philippines. Unlike Evie, most of them were born into the slums of Manila or come from poverty-stricken villages in other areas of the Philippine archipelago. The same applies in Thailand, from whence most of the *Japayuki* comprise urban slum dwellers and girls from hill-tribe villages in the north. Many of them have illegitimate children to support; their careers both at home and abroad are clearly motivated by necessity. Whatever their backgrounds, they are invariably recruited by 'talent agencies' such as Manuel's which, generally run by crime syndicates in the countries concerned, have close ties with *yakuza* gangs.

The toughs of the domestic and *yakuza* persuasions tell the girls how to get visas as 'tourists' and 'entertainers', often lounging around pressing the bricks outside the Japanese embassies in Bangkok or Manila while the would-be *Japayuki* make their applications within. The girls are then flown over in small accompanied groups of up to half a dozen at a time. At Narita airport, one often sees dusky, pathetically ebullient young things in T-shirts and denim miniskirts being openly herded past immigration control by gentlemen with close-cropped 'punch-perms', white leather moccasins and RayBan sunglasses – virtually a *yakuza* uniform.

Having been on the game in their countries of origin (under conditions strikingly similar to those prevailing in Japan until thirty years ago), most of the *Japayuki* are aware of the duties they will be expected to perform. Nonetheless, a smaller but substantial number is consistently lured with promises of dancing, fashion-modelling, singing and bona fide hostessing jobs in 'élite' Tokyo clubs. Instead, as soon as they are outside the airport, it's no more Mr Nice Guy: their passports are taken away from them by their 'manager', who places them under lock and key. The old *zegen* are very much alive.

They are then put up for auction in virtual slave markets in sleazy back-street cabarets near Tokyo's Ueno station, among other places, and sold off to pimps around Japan like sides of meat. One piece costs about a million yen and pays its way handsomely in only a month. Now that self-interest has prompted the insular *yakuza* to overcome their aversion to international cooperation, they are working more closely with South-East Asian crime syndicates than ever before.

Operating from an apartment situated conveniently close to Narita airport, a procuring racket for Thai prostitutes was raided in 1988. What made the operation unusual was that it was one hundred per cent run by Thais. Having brought the girls in directly through their own network in Bangkok, they conducted the venture Japanese style: before putting the girls up for sale, they snatched their passports and kept them under lock and key. The *yakuza* find such arrangements convenient; recruitment and export are being undertaken more cheaply by organized crime in target countries and they are given preferential rates on the imported crop in exchange. Not all of them went to Japanese pimps, however, for the Thais were running a 'hostess club' of their own in Shinjuku, which police raided almost simultaneously. With Filipino crime syndicates striking up very similar deals, these days such operations are growing increasingly common.

Creating a furore in 1985, an NHK documentary put the spotlight on a racket largely mentioned hitherto only in the press. The focus was on a certain 'Jennie', whose dire predicament prompted her to write to the Immigration Department despite her illegal status. The letter was leaked to the press, and a video crew set out to interview club owners, gangsters and other *Japayuki* girls in Japan, eventually tracing her through an entire network of sleaze right back to the flesh-brokers in the Philippines. Jennie, it seemed, had somehow already found her way to Manila before the letter prompted any action; she was back on the game.

Evie says she earns 250,000 yen a month. As only a fraction of the earnings of a Japanese counterpart it isn't much, but it is still more than the South-East Asian stripper's average, which is about one-third less than the lowest official wage for an unskilled worker and ten times less than the amount paid the stripper élite. 'Idol Strippers' and Japanese *honban* ladies make 50,000 yen a day; in a month on the strip circuit, they can make 1,500,000 yen.

Since *honban* strippers often turn tricks on the side, what goes for them goes for prostitutes in general. In the final analysis, foreign prostitutes are paid commensurate with the exchange rate on the currency of their country of origin. Underpaid for doing exactly the same thing as the others, most South-East Asian strippers earn 5,000 yen daily; at night they sleep backstage in the dressing room to save on rent and send back that much more money home to their families. An editor of *mizu shobai* related magazines recently told me that he believed that there were nearly 3,000 *Japayuki* girls working in various flesh-pots in Shinjuku alone. 'One guy I know has an apartment in which he keeps ten in one room,' he confided. 'They're stacked in bunks like in a flophouse.' Despite their meagre earnings, their savings convert handsomely into the currencies of their home countries, so that droves of *Japayuki* find it all worthwhile to enter Japan for six-month stints.

'Whatever the moralists claim, what the *Japayuki* are really complaining about is that they're being ripped off,' says the magazine editor. 'Managers take 90 per cent of their earnings.' Naturally, this triggers less public concern than the perspectives of forced prostitution. If this is understandable on the one hand, on the other it also provides polite society with a good excuse for turning its back on a profession which is denied the status it deserves. That the girls are swindled justifies itself with a righteous 'serves-you-right' attitude towards women opting for such a calling in the first place, regardless of the fact that the majority have no other means of survival. If they inspire pity in some, the

Japanese ideal of the noble whore is seldom extended to those coming from abroad. That a girl who is hardly able to afford a ticket home is in pretty much the same boat as the most abject sexual slave never enters anyone's mind. Although many are willing to work as prostitutes, none are prepared to be locked up and brutalized in the process. Often cheated of their wages altogether, they find themselves penniless and dumped either when no longer serviceable through illness or through their persistent – and courageous – refusal to play the game with a good grace. No one wants a bad whore. Speaking not a word of Japanese, they have precious little hope of tracing their tormentors.

TV Tokyo provided a poignant update on the problem in 1987, focusing on a group of Filipinas who had been screwed in every sense of the word and finally abandoned. 'I address the Philippine embassy,' one nineteen-year-old said in English as she faced the camera in tears. 'Please help us to go home.' Apparently they did; they were lucky. Given the state of the South-East Asian economies most likely to produce *Japayuki*, distributing free tickets home is a luxury they can ill afford. Various Japanese women's organizations agree that there are some 100,000 *Japayuki* in Japan at any one time, out of which they say a substantial portion has been lured on false pretences.

Being more conspicuous by definition, most strippers tend not to be exploited quite as ruthlessly as some of their less fortunate sisters in the network of sleazier bars and clubs – but not all. The pious Colombian hooker mentioned earlier, after all, balked at performing publicly on-stage and one striptease entrepreneur in the Yokohama area was recently busted for forcing about a hundred unwilling Filipinas on-stage as *honban* performers over a period of seven years.

A raid on a Shinjuku club engaging *Japayuki* as prostitutes in 1988 yielded some twelve Thai girls all forced on the game following the confiscation of their passports. An enterprising young woman from their ranks tipped off the police, which was no mean feat: the only words she had been taught to say in Japanese were *irrashaimase* (welcome), *shacho* (company director) and *hai* (yes). She had been fortunate in being able to turn to an association founded in 1986 by the Women's Christian Temperance Union, but the chances are that the task ahead for such organizations is daunting. As in most countries, pimps can yield information on the activities of organized crime, so unless those warring against prostitution can produce the most glaring and indisputable evidence of abuse (always so conveniently difficult to prove), they can count on little cooperation from the police.

In 1989, however, four Filipinas decided for the first time that enough was enough. Despite the certainty of their getting into trouble for overstaying their original two-week visas by over a year, they decided to haul the brutish manager of Le Lapin club in Nagoya over the coals. Although they had all been locked in a small room for two months and repeatedly raped and beaten, prosecutors at first only charged the men with 'detaining' them. A newspaper reporter and a Buddhist monk investigating the club were meanwhile beaten up for their pains, which did not sufficiently frighten the women to stop them protesting about the Nagoya prosecutor's lax decision. Following a grand-scale scandal revealing that some of the police involved had been bribed, the goons were properly charged with a number of more serious offences, including kidnapping, rape and ownership of handguns.

Yakuza ploys to delude the law include seeking less stringent entry points and falsifying *Japayuki* nationalities with forged passports. New legislation in June 1990 made the employment of illegal immigrants an offence, and the impact on the *mizu shobai* was instantaneous. Dives hitherto boasting exotic hostesses either sought new staff or closed down. Within weeks, however, South-East Asian and Colombian *sutoreeto gyaru* were proliferating in Shinjuku back alleys closest to love hotels, and the trade simply moved into the streets.

RIDING ON THE VALKYRIES

Japan's tremendous affluence is attractive not only to meretricious gold-diggers from East Asia, but from around the world. One day I interviewed a strip theatre owner who, after quipping that I might like a job as a sexual acrobat, added perfectly seriously: 'You can choose your partner. These days with the high yen, they come from all over. How about a nice English girl?'

Following clampdowns on spurious 'talent agencies' in the US during the mid-eighties, *yakuza* after fodder for the Japanese sex trade found the much-prized American stripper becoming a rarity. Earning something in between, Caucasians recruited from Latin America, notably Colombia, currently make a handy and cheaper substitute. Although the happy-hooker contingent among the western *Japayuki* is larger than among their Asian sisters, some have been similarly pushed to do tricks after having been signed up as singers and dancers. When it comes to attacking their exploiters, however, those coming from countries which are more affluent and/or in which women enjoy greater emancipation not only tend to be a good deal more aggressive than their Asian counterparts, but also benefit from greater –

if not always overwhelming – cooperation from their embassies.

The prevalence of blondes among the foreign contingent is striking; the prospect of mounting some very large and very blonde Caucasian woman triggers unbridled enthusiasm at the strip theatre. Yet very few are the genuine article. Striving to meet Japanese fantasy ideals in the striptease parlour, even Afro-Hispanic beauties have been known to bleach their heads and peroxide their pubic hair. Thus equipped, they become protagonists in a peculiar picture compounded of aggressive, obdurate feelings of superiority and racism on the one hand, and deference and abject inferiority complexes on the other. Inculcated by die-hard ultra-nationalism, xenophobia rubs shoulders with an awkward inferiority complex towards westerners, both of which are relics of the nineteenth century and equally slow to subside. Although Japanese cities are safer than most, foreign women have been known to complain about being pawed on trains and crudely propositioned in the street by some men who apparently see them as push-overs, if not downright whores.

Be this as it may, the foreign stripper generally triggers a more innocent kind of fascination with exotica: other people's grass is always greener. Red-light districts in western capitals, after all, often deploy South-East Asian women imported according to very similar methods as in Japan and, even though the tendency is to do so on a far larger scale, the sexploitation of South-East Asian women is not entirely a Japanese preserve. An overseas marriage market is another growing phenomenon in Japan. Young farmers living in remote areas with an ever-decreasing female population turn to countries such as the Philippines and Sri Lanka to seek nubile brides, for they are unable to find someone to share their lives among today's urban-minded Japanese women. By and large, the beauty-and-the-beast marriages commonly finding young Asian women pining away with an elderly mate in the bleak industrial towns of Europe are not the pattern in Japan, where most marry virtually mandatorily in their prime. Such women are hampered by having to face dire cultural and language problems nevertheless, and despite efforts social workers have made to help them, not a few of such marriages have gone on the rocks.

'Because they debase their own women as house slaves or prostitutes,' one Asahi newspaper reporter put it in 1985, 'Japanese men feel no compunction about raping foreign women with their money.' How much truer this is of the crime syndicates. Adhering to antiquated traditional machismo, precious few *yakuza* have any respect for women and, even though many are of foreign origin themselves, most harbour even less for *gaijin*. Japanese xenophobia is particularly obvious in the sex trade, in which Aids makes a convenient excuse for turning people of other colours away. To many sex traders, a foreign woman is a very low form of animal life. In short, this is the background for the entire *Japayuki* phenomenon: women can be had cheaply in South-East Asia and exotic Caucasians fetch even higher prices in Japan. Both are mere commodities. Regardless of their countries of origin, not being Japanese makes them all *gaijin* which, to some, still means that they are not descended from the gods. As such, they are not even quite human beings.

GANGSTERS AND THE LABOUR MARKET

The total number of *Japayuki* apprehended in 1978 stood at just over 400; in 1988 it was well over 5,000. Those actually arrested in connection with prostitution in 1988 numbered 930, which police acknowledged was a 150 per cent increase over the year before. The problem is growing and becoming more complex, mainly because it is evolving in parallel with an expanding and highly organized market for illegal foreign labour.

Prospering at a prodigious rate, Japan has joined the ranks of wealthy industrial nations looking abroad for cheap labour to undertake jobs that nationals no longer wish to do. They call these the *ki* jobs: *kitanai* – dirty; *kitsui* – hard; *kiken* – dangerous. In view of the number of years that Japan has enjoyed greater affluence, the process seems long overdue. Meanwhile, Asian migrant workers facing a slump in the job scene in the Middle East are currently turning towards a Japan facing a labour shortage.

Even as untold hordes of them pour in, mostly as 'students', the ruling Liberal Democrats put forward all the usual arguments about the unique nature of Japanese society and the difficulty foreigners would thus find in fitting in. Having observed the problems spawned by immigrant populations elsewhere, Japan would rather not share them. Like it or not, however, the current labour shortage renders the immigrant well-nigh indispensable. Consequently, brokers open the back-door floodgates to underpaid factory workers from South-East and Central Asia. The majority of the workers are divided fairly equally between small factories and the runaway construction industry; underpaid, overworked and contributing towards the Japanese economy, if caught they can expect punishment rather than count on sympathy from the government. According to an estimate in 1989, there were about 100,000 people working illegally in Japan.

Fewer by far in the mid-eighties, illegal male immigrants now outnumber the female. In 1988, the number of women caught totalled 5,385, but there were nearly 9,000 men. The difference is that while the men work at *ki* jobs in insalubrious sweat shops, very nearly 90 per cent of the women work in what can be even more dirty, hard and dangerous conditions in the *mizu shobai*. In its coverage of illegal foreign labour, the press never fails to mention male factory workers and 'hostesses' in the same breath. What these slave markets for both sexes additionally have in common is that they are overwhelmingly under the control of brokers, and these belong to the realm of organized crime.

Whatever they are, the statistics are based only on those who got caught: the tip of the iceberg. Officials found tergiversation more convenient than action, until they drafted a new law in December 1989 making those employing illegal immigrants liable to punishment. Many consider this unfair; the ubiquitous back-street sweatshops manufacturing parts for larger companies turn to cheap labour to remain competitive, and these are recognized as the backbone of the Japanese economy. In many cases since it's just blind eyes and business as usual. *Yakuza* brokers continue to supply firms prepared to take the risk, just as they trade in women for the samurai of the great corporate treadmills.

RAPE YOUR NEIGHBOUR – MONSTERS IN PARADISE

Bangkok or Manila, the scene in the girly bar is exactly the same. Beneath the whirling coloured spotlights big-bellied western brawn lolls hippopotamine in the gloom on stools alongside other Caucasian crocodiles leering at the lissom gazelles dancing and posturing in leotards behind the counter. These days even package tourists in Bangkok respond to the come-ons from touts presenting them with cards for sex shows reading like a menu: '1. Pussy smoke cigarette 2. Pussy open bottle 3. Real fuck show' to name a few. Japan is not the only country in which pussy is liable to develop remarkable talents, although even the most skilled Bangkok vulvar artiste has a long way to go to catch up with her Japanese counterpart.

A middle-aged shopkeeper or a fitter-joiner and his wife from Birmingham, Bari or Bergen stare at fornicatory oriental young things with glazed eyes; the husband's betray a glint of wistfulness. Travel widens one's horizons. Strangely enough, package tourists would never even think of doing this at home. No doubt more fortunate for wandering in here alone, few men can resist the temptation of so much delightfully compliant, readily available and perfectly lovely flesh.

Slave marketing in these countries may be pervasive but, concealed behind a charming demeanour, it is far from being immediately apparent. Moreover, to the consternation of moral crusaders, repeated surveys taken among the prostitute population in Thailand show that the overwhelming majority find life in the bright lights, bars and even bedrooms more fun, lucrative and fulfilling than in the slums or remote and backward native villages. The corollary of this outlook and abusive exploitation is the same as that prevailing in the licensed quarters in Japan until their official closure. As lamentable as it is, it should by now be obvious to the world that the proliferation of subsistence prostitution is a phenomenon unavoidable given its economic precedents. What is most sad is not that these girls are prostitutes, but that they are neither sufficiently protected from pimps nor, while making substantial and vital contributions to struggling economies, given their due respect. As long as moral bigotry and prejudice relegate the whore everywhere to her allotted social nadir, her lot is unlikely to improve.

Cordially welcomed for currency and otherwise abhorred in countries around East Asia, sex tourism is by now well established. There is no reason to berate the Japanese any more than others, for organized, slavering planeloads arrive also from Europe – if much less systematically. The issue seems to be quantitative; the more socio-sexually benighted the culture, the greater the number of men seeking one-track-minded holidays in the South-East Asian flesh-pots. Some hotels in Bangkok renowned for their veritable armies of hostesses and masseuses, for instance, look oddly like harems from a supermarket Arabian Nights. The majority of men from more liberal countries look for their kicks alone or in small groups, often merely slumming during the course of bona fide sightseeing packages, whereas the Japanese come in large tour groups, exclusively monopolize bars and brothels and, according to their own critics, conduct their sexual forays with the arrogance of an invading army on R & R.

'When you leave home,' an old Japanese proverb goes, 'you leave your shame behind.' This occurs very shortly after take-off. Raucously laughing groups of *salarymen* high on duty-free whisky bellow barrack-room songs, run up and down the aisles like unruly little boys to converse with other party members and continually pester flight attendants, addressing them in curt, arrogant tones. In 1988, one man's sex tour proved to be short-lived. After having squeezed an air hostess's bottom *en route* and notwithstanding apologies and pleas that he had been 'carried away', he was arrested by immigration police in Manila and sent back to Japan.

On hearing this, one bona fide Japanese tour operator of my acquaintance was unimpressed: 'It happens all the time,' he said. 'They sometimes even behave like that on flights to Europe and the States. I've had problems between tour members and air hostesses, whom they address as "Ne-san!" [literally "elder sister", a loose male way of addressing a waitress or bar hostess] more times than I care to remember.'

Much publicized during the early seventies, the culminating event during a corporate 'golfing tour' in Manila, which was organized by the trillionaire Japanese shipping magnate and renowned philanthropist Riyuichi Sasakawa, found one specially contrived wall of a banqueting hall coming down as some two hundred 'hospitality girls' burst in to cater to the golfers' drives of the other kind. In the wake of adverse publicity, the tycoon kept subsequent trips down to golf but, rightly or wrongly, this incident is often said to have set the precedent in the Philippines. Today sex tour operations are so well organized and widespread that the golf clubs have almost become superfluous. Travel agencies setting up corporate sex tours keep their charges well besotted with booze and girls, although, in view of the Japanese workers' holiday, the duration of the spree rarely lasts longer than three days including the journey.

As with the *Japayuki* trade, the driving force behind the sex tour phenomenon is organized crime. Often running shady travel agencies, *yakuza* gangs strike up partnerships with local pimping syndicates to create a lucrative priapic co-prosperity sphere, a trend which began in South Korea. The *kisaeng* is the direct Korean equivalent to the Japanese geisha. Described as 'professional unmarried ladies' and revered for their similarly varied accomplishments which may or may not include the obvious, they were reduced to a commodity when Japan occupied Korea from the end of the nineteenth century. Many were shipped over to Japan wholesale in the less refined capacity of prostitute. In those days, the expression *Japayuki* had yet to be coined from its *kara-yuki* predecessor, despite the fact that so many of the 'outward bound' women shuttled around Japanese brothels in South-East Asian ports were actually Korean. Either way, the precursors of the *Japayuki* were certainly Korean; there are still scores of none-too-refined expat *kisaeng* houses in Osaka alone.

Taking advantage of the economic upswing during the mid-sixties and of their unloved capacity as ex-colonials, Japanese businessmen began invading Seoul in their tens of thousands when the gangs and the travel agencies offered them '*kisaeng* tours'. Identical packages were arranged in Taipei according to the same precedents and at about the same time; both are now long-standing traditions. As the economies in these countries gradually became more dynamic, however, the prices in the red-light districts began to rise and the Philippines became a cheaper alternative. Although further away, the flesh-pots of Thailand are similarly inexpensive enough to present Japanese sex tour operators with a bonanza.

Ever since Saigon fell in 1975, the droves of GIs lounging in Bangkok girly bars and massage parlours on R & R from Vietnam are long gone, although the picture may be much the same around the US bases in the Philippines. If American soldiers in such bars obviously outnumber everyone else, they are most unlikely to regard them as their exclusive preserve. Entering a bar at random in Manila, on the other hand, one might find a bespectacled gentleman wearing a Japanese happitunic over his clothes wallowing ecstatically with some five compatriots on a large sofa surrounded by bevies of bored-looking girls. Although he is just a customer, he leaps to his feet as one enters, beaming as though he owns the place. 'Welcome!' he bellows. 'I am Japanese!' A few yards further down, there will be one of several places from which even Filipinos will be rejected by the Filipino doorman. As the notice on the door makes clear, the place is for 'Japanese Only', a measure unlikely to be quite so officially adopted by any bar preponderantly frequented by other foreign nationals during the post-colonial era.

Part of Bangkok's Patpong, a downtown area where top-rank hotels, luxury shops and flesh-pots rub shoulders, is now known as Little Ginza. Alongside Japanese shops and restaurants, the hostess bars have Japanese names. Since Japan is Thailand's number one foreign investor, of course by no means all of these establishments are peddling sex. The management policy for Japanese representatives of large firms working overseas often actively discourages over-fraternizing with the natives and, to encourage compliance, reps are generally posted abroad for no more than two years. Children returning to Japanese schools after two or three years abroad, after all, are often bullied in the classroom and generally have trouble 'fitting in'. Like personnel on military bases, Japanese expat representatives have their own housing estates, their own shops and their own designated havens of entertainment in the city. In one of these, only a tiny ancestor-shelf high up in a corner which burns a small red lamp betrays that the ownership of the club is Thai-Chinese.

The manager speaks Japanese, *mama-san* speaks Japanese and the hostesses speak Japanese, among them 22-year-old Noi, who managed the remarkable feat of learning very adequate Japanese in only eight months. She took lessons during the daytime, she explained, and she practised in the club. 'Some of the patrons have been very helpful. They tell me how to say things properly and correct my mistakes.' No puerile sex tourists, the men in here are expat executives quietly relaxing in their regular bar and, if priced to be a little mercenary when compared to the Thai norm, it is no flesh-pot, even though the chances are that men with a yen can persuade the hostesses to go beyond the call of duty more easily than they can in Japan. Pleasant but businesslike, the bar is comfortable but a bit aloof. To the western observer, it would be a little staid; to the Japanese executive, it is home from home.

There is a low-key band playing Japanese standards, and every now and again one of the expat *salarymen* gets up from one of the plush sofas around the walls to join in a duet with a hostess. Notwithstanding the dictates of professionalism, the girls here still actually seem to like their patrons. Giggling, bantering and doing absolutely nothing untoward, they put the men completely at ease by cajoling them like hostesses at home. They do go just one little bit further, however, by draping an arm around a man's shoulders, or perhaps tickling him around the nape. There is one thing, however, which makes all this distinctly unlike home. The men, who are almost purring, are visibly basking in something once common in the Japanese *demi-monde* and that they would no longer even entertain in today's steely *mizu shobai*: the illusion of affection.

Less than dreams or promises of sex, what is being suggested however artificially is the old pipe-dream of love again, the forbidden fruit of the floating world of yore. The effect is almost poignant. Caught up back home between corporate and family duties and the stylized ministrations of prostitutes, they now find themselves in a realm that has vanished from Japan. It seems significant that among Japanese men spending some time in Thailand or the Philippines, not a few strike up lasting relationships. For better and sometimes much worse, the concept of the *nigo*, the number two, has gone international as some men commute between families in Japan and abroad, the latter sometimes being cherished and sometimes callously dumped.

Out in the street meanwhile, whether in Bangkok or Manila, the packs of lean and hungry sex predators slouch from bars to bedrooms rented by the hour, from massage parlour and back to the four-star tourist hotel. Bed, breakfast and sex come as part of a package deal including air fares: 150,000 yen all told with a cut for Japanese and local crime syndicates and the rest for boosting local economies. The ways in which the corporate samurai are exploited at home predetermines how they are to be exploited abroad. Misbehaving on the plane, pushing bar girls around, yelling at hotel and catering staff – all these are painfully obvious symptoms of acute frustration. More than behaving like arrogant armies as many Japanese critics contend, the sex tourists seem like bands of prisoners of war suddenly released and treated to revels in wine, women and song after years of deprivation.

The smaller firms forcing their employees to work hardest condone the warrior's rest, but large corporations are rather more hesitant to sully their reputations. Sentient Japan is not happy about sex tourism at all. As usual, women's groups – moralizing battleaxes and otherwise – were the first to denounce the phenomenon. But while they lambast the sex tourists, they hardly mention the system producing them, which at once fosters male sexual deprivation and sanctions the predatory infrastructures to palliate it. The tendency to single out scapegoats and ignore the wood for the trees is all too typical.

The Ajia no Baishun ni Hantaisuru Otokotachi no Kai, the Association of Men Against Prostitution in South-East Asia, comprises neither churchmen nor prigs and has recently been attacking sex tourism with its own particular brand of rather grim humour, a new weapon they see as more effective than moralistic whining. Their contention is that sex tourism is seriously undermining Japan's image abroad. Specifically, this applies to its closest neighbours. The invading male armies who so arrogantly regard other countries as nothing other than gigantic brothels, they have it, are spawning increasingly bitter contempt.

In a Japanese TV documentary devoted to sex tourism some years ago, prostitutes in Manila consistently referred to the brutishly behaving Japanese customers foisted on them as 'pigs'. These days, according to the Association of Men Against Prostitution in South-East Asia, the girls have gone a step further and call the Japanese 'monsters'. This prompted the Association to launch a magazine called *Monsutaa Tsushin* (*Monster Press*). The cover shows a cartoon of a hideous suited *salaryman* waving a Japanese flag; he is in such a ruttish state that he has forgotten to put on his trousers. Distributed around companies and handed out to passing potential monsters on city streets, the *Monster Press* was followed by a record. The aircraft caricatured on the sleeve bears Japanese flags and is shaped like a winged penis with a dopey face and a dripping nose. The lyrics of the '*Monsutaa no Uta*' inside, the Monster Song, go something like this:

Father, when you weren't burning houses and killing people during the war, you were screwing women called 'army comfort ladies'. Brother, now you go to Asia and use your big bucks to buy lots of women. You began with what they called *kisaeng* sightseeing, just another way of saying sex-invasion. Do you understand the meaning of embarrassment and shame? Do you know who those they call the Sex Animals are? They wear ordinary civilian *salaryman* suits but they behave like soldiers. The time passes fast and the generations succeed one another, yet still when I walk on South-East Asian streets, as the women pass by me, they just say: sex and money – that's Japan.

Why do we so hurt Asian women's feelings? There must be something wrong with our sex life.

PART V

A Quirk for All Seasons

17

The Cruel World

TOILET TUNES

> Our forebears, making poetry of everything in their lives,
> transformed what by rights should be the most unsanitary
> room in the house into a place of unsurpassed elegance,
> replete with fond associations with the beauties of nature.
> Compared to westerners, who regard the toilet as utterly
> unclean and avoid even the mention of it in polite conver-
> sation, we are far more sensible and certainly in better
> taste.
>
> Junichiro Tanizaki, *In Praise of Shadows* (1934)

Swingers, scatologists and sadomasochists: in Japan too
a lot of very weird things go on in private clubs. In
Tokyo, the kinky sex scene is generally confined to
Shinjuku like everything else, but the kinkiest, being
rendered rather exclusive by dint of inclination, accessibility and price, often finds itself discreetly tucked away
in private 'mansion' apartments in residential areas.
Then there are the swinging 'Orange People', a wife-
swapping association staging wild parties in city homes
and love hotels. Photographs in their sporadically
published contact-magazine show paunchy celebrants
wearing only black masks and matching genital patches
stencilled in to appease the censors. Grinning at the
camera in minimal costume and small groups, the
voluptuaries look more like guests in fancy dress at a
naturists' convention.

A features editor for the trendy *Brutus* magazine told
me of a bizarre ritual periodically staged in a plush

apartment on the residential side of Roppongi. In a spacious room entirely hung with black velvet, wealthy scatologists congregate around a long lacquered table bearing only a large, polished silver tray in the centre, which reflects a single spotlight. Having paid substantial sums of money for an occasion lasting some ten minutes, the guests sit in high-backed chairs as though attending a banquet.

A hush falls as a breathtaking beauty in a dark silk kimono glides across the room and steps noiselessly up on to the table, gradually lifting the hem as she walks like one in a trance towards the gleaming platter. Pausing a moment and gazing into space, she raises the garment over her hips to reveal complete nakedness beneath. As all eyes become riveted to the intimacies reflected in the tray, she defecates. Slowly getting to her feet, she gradually drops the kimono again, steps regally from the table and disappears.

The deposit on the tray is ceremoniously divided with a silver cake knife, the little portions being placed on silver saucers and handed round. 'It had an aroma like incense,' the editor said. 'She'd been fed certain foods perfumed with aromatic herbs.' And the guests, after appreciating the bouquet, partook of the delicacy with dainty silver spoons. Hardly inclined to become a devotee, however, the editor decided to pass. 'Nevertheless,' he said, 'as strange as it was, it wasn't horrifying at all. The whole thing was really rather funny – and quite beautiful.' Beauty, they say, is in the eyes of the beholder.

The concept is echoed in homosexual lore too, notably in old stories of monks consuming offerings from beauteous young novices exclusively fed similar diets. Most of the writer Junichiro Tanizaki's ineffectual heroes are trampled underfoot by heartless heroines, and some have been similarly given coprophilic attributes. In one instance, a jilted medieval lover finds consolation in a small box containing his lady's wastes. Beside himself with elation when his nostrils are filled only with the fragrance of cloves, he ecstatically consumes them.

A famous apocryphal anecdote about the courtesan Kaoru (Fragrance), that most beloved of Edo-period *ingénues*, holds similar undertones. Braggadocio gets the better of a young man carousing with friends in a Yoshiwara brothel and, after swallowing a bowlful of hot-pepper sauce, he is taken ill. The physician is adamant: the only remedy is the equivalent amount of human excrement. 'I would rather die,' the young man groans, 'but if I must partake of this, then let it come from Kaoru!'

Belonging to the realm of filth and putrefaction, faecal matter is an unwelcome reminder of the biological scheme of things – hence death – and constitutes a strong taboo. According to Freudians, however, before the taboo is inculcated during early childhood, the odour of excrement is linked to the mother during toilet training, and retains pleasurable associations to the adult coprophiliac. By extension, coprophilia and masochism share shades of immaturity in common. In pointedly violating the taboo, the coprophiliac debases himself and, deriving pleasure from the knowledge that what he is doing is regarded as repulsive, betrays his masochistic inclinations. By gulping the wastes voided from the object of his desire, he signifies his utter submission.

When not concluding with coitus, SM shows in the *nudo* theatre sometimes culminate more outlandishly with a communally administered enema. As an outsized syringe full of water is presented around the audience,

aspiring hands shoot upwards to receive it and spectators go uncharacteristically overboard: 'Oh, me, please,
me!' The prospect of squirting water up the stripper's
rectum fills them with unbridled excitement. Meanwhile
she crawls around the stage backwards, proffering her
posterior to ritual postulants like a cat on heat. Once the
syringe has been emptied and refilled dozens of times
over from an aquarium hauled on-stage by the pantomime torturer, the bursting stripper squats over it to
relieve herself of gallons of water. In order to ensure that
no scatologist should be disappointed by the production
of only a jet of clear water, some strippers send dozens of
rectally concealed marbles clattering down into the
aquarium.

To those not of the persuasion, such manifestations
are about as sexually arousing as bad breath. Though
such predilections fill most people with repugnance, the
Japanese take bodily functions in their stride; scatology
and coprophilia elicit disgust, but not shock and indignation. Jokes about farts are at least as old as the famous
Hōhigassen, the Farting Competition, a twelfth-century
scroll painted by the great comic artist Toba, who was
not only renowned for the equally famous *Yōbutsu
Kurabe* (Penis Competition) scroll, but also as a Buddhist
bishop. Abroad, Toba is better known for his charming
and more innocuous *Animal Frolic*.

Notwithstanding enduring Rabelaisian currents, not
even western humour harbours much relish for coprophilia. On the other hand, the counter-culture of the
late sixties put many taboos up against the wall. Europe
spawned Marco Ferreri's film *La Grande Bouffe* in which,
among the jaded sybarites feasting themselves to death,
one dies of acute flatulence. France howled over the
corrosive cartoons of the late, lamented Reiser and
America produced the inimitable R. Crumb, whose

vitriolic comics similarly vehicled scatology as a medium for provocation, notably in *Hi-Tone Comics* ('A Toilet Tune Presentation: Weird Sex Fantasies with the Behind in Mind'). Dressed as dissent, however, such fare was justified with an alibi and targeted adults, not children. Highly popular a decade ago in Japan was little Makoto-chan, a suburban brat with a runny nose and nasty habits, whose comic-book adventures abounded with scatological jokes and episodes in the toilet. This kind of thing constitutes a genre in itself, known to children as *unko manga*: turd comics.

In his riveting book on Japanese *manga* comic books, Frederick Schodt mentions the popular serial *Toiretto Hakase* (Professor Toilet) and its scientific hero:

> After being trapped in an elevator, the passengers all finally overcome their inhibitions and defecate on the floor. Professor Toilet and his assistant pontificate on the fundamental equality of man. Japan's cities have been notoriously slow in installing flush toilets, so in 1970 when Kazuyoshi Torii's *Toiretto Hakase* began in *Shonen Jump* (a mass-circulation comic) many young readers confronted powerful smells and the sight of maggots every day. Perhaps this had something to do with the comic's popularity.

Perhaps as a sign of the times and of the installation of improved domestic pipework, the genre has markedly declined. Not necessarily in the country, though, where among the souvenirs in a remote hot-spring hotel (*sans* flush toilet) in mountainous Nagano, I was confronted with a miniature lavatory with a tiny pile of brown ceramic staring up from the bowl with wide, appealing eyes. The *objet* was mounted on a little wooden plaque bearing the words 'Phew, what a stink! Greetings from Unko-san – Mr Turd.'

BLOOD FEAST

> 'You see, the fact that a nation could torture artistically
> instead of physically, and sacrifice truth for art, proves
> that we Japanese are not really barbarians, despite what
> your War Crimes Trials try to prove.'
>
> Kabuki theatre producer Shirai quoted in
> Faubion Bowers, *The Japanese Theater* (1947)

Like samurai dramas on TV, as if harking back to days
when the country was harsher than the protective
present, the SM shows staged in the *nudo gekijo* are often
given to historical flavouring. In those lost lamented
days, men were men and women were property. The
shows spare neither the smothering mother, the tyranni-
cal spouse nor the fiendish hussy who drags men from
the righteous path of duty and obligation. All are
thoroughly and vicariously punished, and when they
bill SM, strip theatres are tellingly more crowded than
when they don't.

Occasionally there is a skit about a wicked doctor
abusing his patient; sometimes the theme is sapphic,
with dominatrix and slave reflecting fetishistic bondage
fantasies like John Wylie's *Gwendoline*. The endlessly
repeated norm, however, is apt to find a lost, classically
kimonoed maiden wringing her hands through blue
semi-darkness resounding with the tempestuous sound
effects of wind and rain. There enters either a ruffianly
swordsman or an evil character from a Noh play,
wearing a mane of crimson hair and a leering demon
mask. In all probability he will be carrying a cheap zipper
bag full of accessories which, clashing incongruously
with his samurai costume, might well also be emblazoned with the words 'NCAA – Let's Sports'.

'Hah-hah-hah!' the demon roars, lunging for the lost

princess. Having tied her hands, he flogs her viciously with a rubber cat-o'-nine-tails, and the thongs send resounding thwacks from the floor near her bared, untouched bottom. The tormentor then goes behind the curtain in the wings and re-emerges armed with a plastic samurai sword; the princess is in real trouble. As he cuts and slices her about, crimson ink concealed in the hilt streams impressively over her breasts and stomach. Taking lengths of rope from the sports bag and working with astonishing speed, the leering devil dextrously trusses up the moaning princess's torso into a tight corset of elaborate boy-scout's knots squeezing her flesh like meat through the strings of a salami sausage. Often explained step-by-step like knitting diagrams in specialized SM magazines, the complex techniques have been perfectly learned. The demon is a master of his craft.

As the spectators lean exophthalmically forward, the roped princess is suspended from hooks on the ceiling. She shrieks long and lustily as the demon leaps up to stand on top of her, using her as a human swing. Once lowered to the ground again she is treated to a bit of extra flogging punctuated with kabukiesque 'Hah-hah-hahs', and perhaps the application of clothes-pegs to nipples. There follows the lighting of the perennial bouquet of candles and the wailing princess is spattered with streams of molten wax. After brief outrages with a mandatory dildo from the prop-bag, the demon removes his mask and everything else to copulate with her, frequently revealing a body covered with a tracery of traditional tattoos perhaps signifying his offstage affiliation with a *yakuza* gang. Like gangsters and prostitutes in Japan from the Edo period, his victim may similarly sport tattoos, which also occupy a privileged place in Japanese SM iconography.

Strangely enough, after the show's lurid grand finale,

the cruel hero may become maudlin. Putting his arms around his brutalized partner, stroking her hair and wrapping her kimono tenderly around her, he leads her offstage as he would a cherished bride. Reflecting a facet universally typical of sadism, he is filled with remorse. But perhaps more typically Japanese, this may also express symbolic atonement for trampling on woman's alter ego – as the progenitive idol of the home.

Cruelty is a feral instinct shared by predators which like to play with prey before the kill, as well as by man, a creature proud of his larger brain. Our species also holds the debatable distinction as the only one capable of deriving sexual pleasure from giving and receiving pain, as well of institutionalizing cruelty in war and cloaking its ferocity in lofty ideals. Naturally, the Japanese are no exception. Whereas contrition over the Nazi past allowed West Germany to enjoy cordial relations with neighbouring countries, Japan's official refusal to acknowledge wartime atrocities still fills many East Asians with mistrust and resentment. The Japanese too young even to remember the war – the vast majority – still bear the burden of a cruel reputation inflicted on them not by propaganda overseas as they have often been led to believe, but by a stubborn, aged handful of corporate, bureaucratic and political autocrats given to dry-cleaning social history textbooks at regular intervals.

In fact, few people could be milder or more gracious. As Buddhists they are committed to non-violence, even if in practice this has deterred warfare in the past about as much as the Judaeo-Christian doctrines of Thou-Shalt-Not-Kill. Abiding by strict Confucian social codes, they are moreover bound to suppress their emotions. The combination helps to avoid turning the city streets into the jungles they can be elsewhere, but this has not been achieved without paying a certain price. As in most Far Eastern societies, betraying one's true emotions is considered extremely rude; regardless of aggravation and misfortune, there is no going around upsetting group harmony with a long face. Hence the legendary smiles visible throughout South-East Asia and culminating in Japan, where the mandatory mask of *tatemae* shields the *honne* from view.

The Malay word *amok* describes a phenomenon such countries share in common, although its prevalence in the West too made the word handy enough for adoption. As rare as it is in the East, it follows a recurring pattern more readily identifiable than the multitude of possible causes triggering homicidal mania in individualistic western societies. In gentle, sleepy little villages in which everyone is perpetually forced to think and do alike, come the hot season and times of personal distress, some individuals run amok and go on a murder spree. With no escape route, the pressure building up in an iron-clad social tank can explode. In Japan, those running amok are called *torima* – passing devils. Since they loom as a constant – however remote – the country's very apparent leanings towards violent entertainment are widely seen as a vicarious substitute – a safety valve.

Even in advanced industrial nations in which institutionalized cruelty has been proscribed, the fantasies lurk beneath the surface. The lasting fascination for the twisted and the dark has earned the Marquis de Sade a much wider readership (irrespective of his seminal theorizing about the relativity of good and evil) than untold hosts of forgotten writers of comparable literary merit. Still, the pose affected by most occidentals, especially the adherents of a religion that once subjected non-believers to agonizingly protracted deaths for the edification of ogling crowds, is that sadism is beyond the pale. The Japanese take sadistic fantasy – provided it remains only fantasy – in their stride. Since there is no absolute sense of right and wrong in the Christian sense, there is no reason why the darker sides of human nature cannot be perused beneath the bright lights shed on a comic book aboard a commuter train.

Shirai, the kabuki producer quoted above, was referring to a famous scene in an eighteenth-century kabuki play, which finds a beautiful courtesan, captured by samurai eager to know the whereabouts of her lover (who is an enemy), on the verge of being tortured. Everyone knows that she is lying when she claims ignorance but, although she is shown the instruments of torture, she is merely requested to play upon the musical ones at which she excels. Greatly moved, the commander pretends to believe her and sets her free.

Shirai's comment about sacrificing truth for art also reflects a facet of *honne-tatemae* that induces a marked cultural preference for the artificial. SM performances in *nudo* theatres, for instance, even if sexually highly uninhibited, tend otherwise to be innocuously sham and hammy. From samurai dramas to SM soft porn, violence in the cinema mainstream is carefully choreographed and the flow of blood is generally of an improbable magenta hue. The painstakingly contrived and endlessly repeated icons of sadism (i.e. 'torturing artistically rather than physically') suffice. In the old kabuki play mentioned in this connection, the mere suggestion of torturing a pretty courtesan let imaginations run wild; there was absolutely no need to torture her on-stage.

Oniroku (Six Devils) Dan, the most celebrated writer of popular SM novels in Japan, speaks of his tastes with disarming frankness. 'There is something absolutely delicious about seizing a beautiful woman and pushing her around. Those who, like me, write about it do so because they get a kick out of it.' Coming out of the closet with a boom during the postwar period after years underground, the SM novel is by now a staple generating ten new titles a month. 'Statistics on book sales', says Dan, who has written over two hundred, 'imply that this penchant is shared by 10 per cent of the male population.'

Dan thinks that the underlying reasons have less to do with circumstances, childhood and vengeance against mothers than is generally believed. 'Some sadists, like me, are just like some homosexuals: we're born that way. I always got on well with women and enjoyed their company. I have absolutely no reason to seek revenge. I even liked this kind of thing in kindergarten. I remember we had a lovely young teacher in her early twenties. More than anything in the world, I wanted to tie her up.'

Dan's best-sellers include the nine-volume *Serpent and the Flower* series and have spawned several films of the *Roman poruno* (porno romance) kind. On the other hand, a Dan novel has arguably the same relationship to hard-core sadism as the Harlequin or Mills & Boon romances have to sex. Preferring the oblique, Dan is emphatically not a pornographer and his themes of damsels in dire distress stop short of explicit description. His own particular leanings lie more in bondage, in which the scout's knots, fetishism and the aesthetics rather than the realities of sadism harmlessly substitute torture with ritual. However, born in 1931 and a family man with a genuine aura of rather tweedy, comfortable professorship, Dan has the knack of making sadism respectable; his tastes probably belong to an older generation.

Although there were jubilant depictions of the torments of Buddhist hells (Hieronymus Bosch makes a good Christian equivalent) as long as a millennium ago, and notwithstanding the graphically sexual and gory subject matter of some woodblock prints, Japanese culture generally prefers the vague to the explicit. In this age of sharp focus, however, the violence of comic books in Japan is legendary, and readily visible upon glancing over shoulders on trains and coffee shops. With brutalities routinely reserved for women, and a repertoire of gang rape, scatology and mutilation, sex comics parallel photographic porno magazines and videos of the SM persuasion in going to extremes. They line the shelves in book shops, newsagents and even convenience stores. Many such magazines are sold in vending machines, less because of the ostensible 'embarrassment' over buying them than to make them accessible to *salarymen* returning home after the stores are closed.

'*Ero-manga* (erotic comics) really only underscore sadism because ordinary sex episodes would be too repetitive,' Dan says. 'Like photographers, *manga* artists must pander to the market by coming up with sensational subject matter.' In a welter of *ero-manga* such as *Erotopia*, *Utopia* or *Chest*, one discovers outrages suffered on the gynaecologist's couch, graphic gropings in swimming pools, gangsters poking guns up blanked-out vulvas or perhaps an old lecher raping a schoolgirl as he pushes her face into a bowl of hot noodle soup. Combinations can be highly bizarre, as a currently popular trend for comics combining sex and golf suggests. After peeking at lady players' crotches on the green, an elderly golfing politician lures them home to rape them. A series so popular that it has gone through over twelve book anthologies is *Rape Man*. A downtrodden Japanese Clark Kent, the protagonist changes into a superhero whose mask and cloak costume leaves him rather uncharacteristically naked from the waist down. Trussing up female employees in dark office corridors and/or schoolgirls in toilets, Rape Man sometimes even suspends himself from high-rises and swings through windows – *in erectio* – to perpetrate his misdeeds.

As in the cinema, unless they are killed first, victims either fall in love with their rapists or swoon with ecstasy. Although the incidence of rape in Japan is statistically low, women's groups contend that the overwhelming majority of victims prefer silence to the embarrassment of reporting their cases. These groups are forever crusading against the ubiquitous depiction of rape in comics and videos and, certainly, comparing pornography in Japan and elsewhere, the violent abuse of women seems disquietingly popular.

'Men are constantly exposed to visions of pretty girls in the media, but few can ever hope to make love to one,' Dan believes. 'Nor do many have a chance to court a beauty from a good family. Wives and girlfriends mostly fall short of the desirable media image. So the majority come to believe that rape is the only chance to bed a beauty there is. As such it becomes a latent male desire; the rape fantasy rules supreme.'

Widely sold in 1985, a book called *Utsukushiki Kossetsu* (*Beauty Refracted*) was a rare feast of unmitigated atrocity by the *manga* artist Jun Hayami. The favoured victim is the perennial schoolgirl; the tormentor is usually a shabby loner or a demented hoodlum. The entire process of mutilation is depicted with every imaginable detail, and some plots, such as they are, are enhanced rather than defused by winding up as mere figments of the protagonist's imagination. A seedy school science teacher, for instance, rapes a pretty pupil. After showing him blinding and eviscerating her with a scalpel, pouring acid over and leaving her explicitly mangled body in a vacant lot, the comic's final frame finds him dead in the corner of the school lab. A victim of his fantasies, he lies with his face burned with vitriol and his erect penis penetrating a gash he has torn in his own stomach.

Citing the brutality of many a hard-boiled *yakuza* or samurai film, Dan surmises that the Japanese are merely fond of violent entertainment. 'Torture was used invariably and routinely for exacting confessions throughout Japanese history,' he says. 'With such precedents, the association in the popular imagination has spawned patterns of sado-masochism quite different from Europe and the United States.' In addition to a variety of tortures, Dan argues, official *keibatsu* (police punishment) dictated scores of different ways of painfully roping up a victim. The trussing styles indicated the type of crime committed and the technique was required learning for Edo-period policemen. Yet the practices of olden Japan are hardly different from, say, the Inquisition; they are merely more recent. Perhaps the collective imagination is hence shadowed still by a hereditary resignation to terror.

Even in bona fide comic books, violence and splatter are ubiquitous. In contexts as wide apart as science fiction, sports, crime and detection, high-school delinquent sagas and samurai themes, bullets blow faces across double-page spreads, eyes are gouged out, severed heads spin from shoulders and entrails are sent flying. In the arena of violent fantasy, the grimacing protagonists are most likely to be towering hulks of musclebound flesh, presenting the more diffident majority of readers with wish-fulfilment as an antidote to their constant submission to social order.

Launching the genre for the nasty travelogue in 1963, Gualtiero Giacopetti's *Mondo Cane* was a runaway success in Japan, where the enduring fascination for violence still makes the shockumentary particularly lucrative. Often produced by hole-in-the-wall American and Italian film companies for the Japanese market, and sometimes by Japanese companies hiding behind American names, popular series such as *Junk* and *The Shock* offer compendia of choice, genuine full-colour footage of gory plane and car crashes, violent murders and autopsies. The shortage of action in the midst of so much dead meat prompts producers to add specially contrived sham footage, including gourmets feasting on live monkey brains or smugglers sewing dope into the carcasses of dead babies. There might also be 'real' executions showing a beheading by 'Arabs' wearing towels over their heads on some beach in southern Italy, or a victim frying in an electric chair until the blood boils and spatters from his face.

Teenagers and even pre-teens lick ice-creams and munch popcorn as they contemplate blood feasts on-screen, all the girls shrieking 'yadaah!', the proper expletive for ladylike revulsion. Or so they used to, until video sent the craze indoors and the splatter feasts came to line the shelves in rental shops. Does this really do any harm? Like the hand-wringing psychologists who began bowdlerizing animated cartoons in the fond belief that it would eradicate delinquency from the USA, some say it does. The horror-comic furore in America during the mid-1950s saw hundreds of largely innocuous comic books banned, forming a comfortable scapegoat for a youthful crimewave welling up both from nascent rebellion against stifling *petit bourgeois* values on the one hand and, on the other, from social substrata too godforsaken to worry much about values anyway. Nowadays Sylvester is no longer properly flattened behind the door by Tweety Pie, even as lady joggers in American urban parkland are increasingly likely to be gang-raped and beaten with lead pipes.

As with a sex industry tacitly tolerated provided it

obeys certain rules, Japanese officialdom sees fictional violence, sexual and otherwise, as a safety valve. That crime – and juvenile crime particularly – is gradually rising has nothing to do with sadism and comic books. Japanese conservatives put it down to a loss of 'values'. With full official support, these values have bolstered a strict system applied not to the oft-lauded old-style loyalty and harmony for its own sake, but to fan the more lucrative fires of materialism. Officials carp about youth in an 'ethical vacuum', but the hole is of their own making. Rarely motivated by lust, often by greed and only by rebellion of the unpondered kind, violent crime shows a proportionately higher rise above an overall increase dominated by petty theft. The conservatives blaming it all on the erosion of the old values never ask themselves whether it is not simply because the values are socially archaic and not vanishing fast enough.

For the land of low crime figures, 1989 was a bad year. The prelude came in early summer, when a schoolgirl kidnapped by a group of juvenile thugs expired after a three-day ordeal of rape and torture. Rocking Japan, the crescendo came in mid-August with the arrest of a retiring, bespectacled and unprepossessing young man named Tsutomu Miyazaki. Impotent and a paedophile, he turned out to be the vampire stalking the distant Tokyo suburbs and responsible for the gruesome mutilation murders of four little girls.

Even the slaughter of the schoolgirl was quickly forgotten in the wake of the Miyazaki case, which was the object of weeks of repetitive news coverage on TV. Gradually the focus of morbid fascination became less on the deeds and more on the perpetrator. Psychotics like Miyazaki exert the same fascination on the popular imagination as the odious fifteenth-century Frenchman Gilles de Rais, whose homo-sadistic murders of children earned him (albeit highly circumspect) immortalization in the fairy-tale 'Bluebeard'. In the West, where the macabre practices of a more recent mass-murderer eventually inspired *The Texas Chain-Saw Massacre* on-screen, the process of becoming a fairy-tale ogre is a long one. In Japan it is virtually instantaneous. The maniac Sagawa, for instance, who murdered and ate parts of a Dutch woman student in Paris in 1981 was photographed in stylish poses in weekly magazines upon his return to Japan (where he was also made a free man) and treated by a leading theatre exponent to a spurious 'biography' slanting towards the pathos of the Japanese at odds with the threatening foreigner.

No such apologias greeted Miyazaki, but the media and the press had a field day. One weekly even published a sensational letter of reproach from Sagawa to the latter, and all went into elaborate details not just about the macabre but about Miyazaki's likes and dislikes. Shortly after his arrest few failed to mention rather poignantly that 21 August was his twenty-seventh birthday. Miyazaki has birthdays like everyone else, yet he is not like the rest of the tribe. Having strayed that far from the straight and narrow, such people are no longer real. So far beyond the pale that they have become inconceivable, they turn into comic-book characters themselves and their gory exploits offer welcome diversions in countless humdrum lives. Condemned to remain forever outside the tribe, they also become figures to be pitied: victims of fate.

The police hastened to point out that Miyazaki was an avid collector of videos. In fact he had nearly 6,000 of them. Having viewed all at the rate of 250 cassettes per day, in between the thousands that were ordinary animated cartoons the police found four that were step-by-step recordings of his own murders. Not a few others, one inspector said, focused on mutilation and bondage, including one from the *Guinea Pig* sex-and-splatter series, showing a woman having her hands severed before being decapitated; much the same treatment that the demented Miyazaki had reserved for one of his small victims. Clearly, out of the hundreds of thousands of men watching sadistic videos and keeping their morbid prurience to themselves, one might be sick enough to find them inspiring. Japan is divided between those who believe more maniacs might come crawling out of the woodwork should they be deprived of a safety valve, and those who counter that if banning sadistic videos could save one life out of odds of scores of millions, so be it. The debate goes on.

In the wake of the case, measures were nevertheless taken to restrict more extreme videos to audiences over eighteen years of age. As strange as it seems, violent screen fare had hitherto been accessible to all, despite a law passed to restrict it in 1964. Enforcement of the law had largely been neglected by the authorities, who were much too busy with the task of preventing any depiction of pubic hair, something seen as far more depraved than graphic splatter and the violent degradation of women. Although the worst comic-book and screen fare may well contribute to the numbing of sensibilities, extreme fantasy is an antidote to the pressures of the treadmill routine, and the catharsis is so powerful that real violence evaporates for most in the harmless clouds of daydreams. More than anything else, the tolerated cathartic role of violence and sadism in the theatre, comics, magazines, films and videos in Japan ultimately joins more ordinary pornography as an equivalent to the 'Feelies' in Aldous Huxley's chilling *Brave New World*.

ENDURING THE UNENDURABLE
FOR PLEASURE

SM clubs proliferate today more than ever before. Prompted by yet another wave of sexual repression, some are mere fronts offering fairly mundane activities in chained and leathered disguise, but sado-masochism is in fact one of the great staples of the Japanese sex scene. One of Tokyo's more notorious love hotels is the Alpha, which currently puts the lash behind the swish in the Roppongi district with theme-conceived rooms with names like Marquis de Sade, Doctor's Office and Insane Crucifix. Japanese SM takes the universal form of the ritualized rape fantasy, the Black Mass with dripping red wax candles, the ropes and straps, whips, stiletto-heeled boots, masks and constricting rubber and leather underwear. Give or take more intrinsically national traits such as the kimono, the sword and the diversions they can be made to provide, the symbolism of pleasurable pain is much the same as anywhere else.

There is one thing, however, which one never, but absolutely never, sees in an SM show in the *nudo gekijo* and that is a man being pushed around by a woman. That kind of nonsense is reserved for the private club. In here, customers on their hands and knees with their spectacles awry play horsy as they are humiliatingly and delectably ridden around the room by disciplinarian hostesses in leather corsets, black stockings and triumphant leers framed in black lipstick. The lady smacks her company-director charge's rump with a riding crop and insists on being called Ojo-ō-sama – August Queen. Much in vogue too is the blonde dominatrix, the big foreign Valkyrie meting out discipline to her Japanese charge.

Save for black candles casting a dim glow over the iron and oaken fixtures of the medieval castle (European or Japanese), such a place might be like any other hostess bar, with the pain of an extortionate bill perhaps offering an additional thrill. Here the usual innocent little party games might take a novel twist according to the whims of Our Lady of Pain, who ensures that the heavily paying customer cries or comes. Many a company director strapped down to a black leather vaulting horse may quiver with bliss beneath the lash of a dominatrix trampling him with spiky heels, but such delectations are shrouded in greater secrecy than the reverse. In the advertisements one sees for SM clubs, the emphasis is more on inflicting pain than receiving it.

Out of the thirty-odd SM clubs in Tokyo, some publicize their rates in evening sports newspapers; 18,000 yen will allow the interested party to inflict 'mild pain', progressing up to twice this figure for 'violent suffering'. Catering to both persuasions, the clubs not only often comprise a stage and private rooms, but can be divided both ways. A session in the sadist department can be bought for 50,000 yen. At 30,000 for masochists, it's cheaper when the hobnail boot is on the other foot. According to Oniroku Dan, although masochists constitute a high proportion of the club clientele, many also find solace in Soapland. Sadistic tastes are gratified almost exclusively in clubs, since most ordinary prostitutes refuse to provide such services.

'Most Japanese men,' Dan believes, 'think that women are all masochists.' On the other hand, he contends that for most, a visit to an SM club suffices to set the record straight. 'Among the women in the clubs, only two out of ten are the real thing. The rest are doing *arubeito*. Since the customers all know that real masochists are as rare as the real sadists, they never complain.'

Ironically, in the whole sex industry, those coming closest to the real McCoy tend to lurk amidst the welter of sham displayed in the SM shows on the strip theatre circuit. 'Some women have faked it on-stage for so long that they end up getting a real kick out of it,' says Dan. 'Also, there are a lot of married couples joining in because they really lean in the SM direction. The husband "trains" his wife and they get a job on the strip theatre circuit as a team. In one way or another, amateur sado-masochists often turn professional.'

Behind the tinsel sadistic fantasies and the ubiquitous iconography of violent cruelty, however, the shadow of masochism hovers like a soul in purgatory and often hardly finds physical expression at all.

The Japanese word *gaman* (endurance) implies much more than its literal meaning. One of the country's most prized virtues, *gaman* is a philosophical concept and one of the prerequisites of bushido – the way of the warrior as resurrected by nationalistic Meiji-period reformers. The art of grinning and bearing is perfected by real and imagined heroes, from teeth-gritting samurai and kamikaze pilots through woeful mothers to the inwardly suffering protagonists of *yakuza* gangster movies. *Gaman* is a prerequisite for enduring long working hours and selfless corporate dedication – the single-minded tenacity behind today's affluence. As the stoically miserable female protagonists of TV soap operas imply, *gaman* permeates every aspect of Japanese life from education, through corporate drudgery to unhappy arranged marriages. In a society in which group harmony is attained at the expense of individual inclination and where a paramount virtue is made of suffering in silence, endurance is a tendency so widespread that turning it into fun on a TV programme surprised no one.

Here was a spectacle in which young contestants were

paraded around the countries of the world, alternately being starved, force-fed with unpalatable foods, confronted with wild beasts, reptiles and noxious insects and suffering a whole gamut of bizarre torments specially devised in between. Not a new episode of *Indiana Jones*, this was the stuff of '*Za* [The] *Gaman*', a spectacular primetime TV game show, and the protagonists were a select group of students from Japan's most prestigious universities. As they struggled through some two years of far-fetched ordeals from 1984, they were avidly followed on TV screens all over Japan and choice highlights were reshown by incredulous commentators in many countries overseas.

Having imbibed a demijohn full of water, for instance, contestants were prevailed upon to refrain from urinating for over twelve hours. The no-peeing ordeals climaxed in wintertime in Holland, where they sat in a tubful of ice-cubes and quaffed chilled beer before stamping around in sub-zero temperatures in their swimming trunks. In Thailand, they tore away the seats of their shorts as they were dragged over rough ground by elephants; they were trundled face-downwards aboard a cable drum through the sands of the Nevada desert; in Jakarta they were treated to facefuls of pepper. Contests were conducted according to a process of elimination: only those enduring one event long enough could qualify to travel on to the next.

The programme's apparent streak of cruelty was not just palliated by its comical presentation, but virtually belied by the eagerness of the 'victims' themselves. Culminating each time in a gruelling struggle with some specially constructed instrument of torture, the formula was invariably the same. Raucous MCs on location goaded, teased and shouted ironic encouragement with a deafening, uninterrupted barrage of words. The volun-

teer victims of *Za Gaman* made their way through painful
slapstick routines with ear-to-ear grins, which re-emerged
as soon as any intermittent tears of rage, pain and
frustration had been wiped away. When the ordeals were
over, hysterically sobbing contestants often embraced
their relenting tormentors with stirring gratitude.

Back in the studio, the presenter energetically commented on the playback action and interviewed the
well-scrubbed returnees with deferential good humour.
The usual TV audience of scores of young women
giggled effusively behind dainty hands but, as soon as
the laughter went overboard, he was quick to remon-
strate. 'This is not just a laughing matter. It is a real-life
youth drama, complete with genuine tears and
emotion.'

Minor incidents of frayed tempers during the course of
the programme went unconcealed. Occasional lapses,
after all, served to remind TV viewers of what *gaman* is all
about. Neither the professors accompanying the
students (including a Zen Buddhist monk) nor anyone
else seemed to find the programme in the least bit
questionable. *Za Gaman* reported no casualties. In fact,
except for the genuine and dangerous starving/stuffing
and extreme temperature routines, most of the worst-
seeming trials of *Za Gaman*, the ones involving the
torture contraptions, were sham.

Or almost. *Za Gaman* was still not exactly a picnic. That
would betray the spirit of the thing. Dave Spector, an
American programme scout based in Japan, also saw it
as a reflection of the ruthless competitiveness of Japanese society. 'At no time,' he said, 'were any of those kids
tied or strapped on to those machines; they hung or
clutched on. *Za Gaman* exploited the fact that, being
Japanese, they would let go and quit only once they had
reached the very limit of their endurance.'

Underlying the games, one detects a rite of passage. French anthropologist Claude Levi-Strauss was referring to American Indian tribes in the following, but it rings a bell:

> They perceive customs and institutions as a single machine whose monotonous operation leaves nothing to chance, luck or talent. The only way to dominate fate is to venture out on a perilous fringe where social norms start losing their meaning as the safeguards and obligations of the group evaporate. This means going to the outermost boundaries of supervised territory, to the very limits of physiological endurance or of physical and mental suffering.

In Amerindian tribes eager young warriors once had to endure the agonies of the sun dance; modern technological Japan subjects its future executives to an unconscious spoof of the same phenomenon. Other executives, and salesmen especially, sometimes attend special 'self-improvement' training schools. Lying at the foot of Mount Fuji, one of the more famous of these was the object of a TV documentary shown in Japan in 1988. It is revealing that the programme was in fact American and dubbed into Japanese, for it not only reflects an obsession with the perception of Japan abroad, but also that only Americans would find such a school sufficiently unusual to be worthy of comment.

'It's very tough,' said the school's director, 'to break the pupil's own conception of himself.' Run according to the same training systems as used for kamikaze pilots and in prewar naval academies, the school is for the benefit of *salarymen* aged mostly from their mid-twenties to late thirties sent by their companies. They are subjected to a memorable two weeks earning the place the nickname 'hell camp'. The routine begins at dawn with callisthenics and cold showers, then about an hour kneeling on one's heels as though for za-zen meditation, with the spine bolt upright.

Some ten hours of various exercises follow, all of which must be accompanied by screaming as loud and unremittingly as the trainees can manage. As they line up outside for roll-call, they scream 'good morning' in unison, before going on to scream into receivers during telephone practice, and then screaming out slogans such as 'The Ten Golden Rules for Doing Business'. The harsh programme is interspersed with long-distance marathons with slogans bellowed out the entire way, and some collapse before the end. Next comes the ordeal of the 'Sales Song', which takes three days to perfect. The song must be delivered at the top of one's lungs. Tears stream down the faces of the sobbing, exhausted singers who must go on and on until they 'pass'. 'With the sweat of our brows, we sell products made by others from the sweat from their brows.' The essence of the song must come from the heart. The words must be believed.

Trainees also throw tantrums like babies, rolling and kicking all over the floor and howling at the top of their lungs – just to let off steam, to break down inhibitions and perhaps work off the rigours of the rest of the training. The quest for more aggressive sales techniques is paradoxically conducted through extreme submission to authority. Those who pass each stage sob hysterically, clasping their comrades around the neck and grovelling in thanks before instructors, in exactly the same way as the contestants did at the end of their ordeals in *Za Gaman*.

Military trainees thrashed black and blue from head to foot with wooden kendo swords for trivial offences during the Second World War had to shout 'thank you very much' after every blow. In Britain, where schoolboys were until very recently punished with canings by older pupils, the mark left on the recipient once the other kind had been healed often took the homoerotic turn exemplified by the nineteenth-century poet Swinburne, a noted sado-masochist who was forever lyrically reminiscing over the 'flogging block' at Eton. In both cases, the chastisements taught the sufferer stoically to bear pain. The similarity ends there. The Japanese military beating, a legacy both of the samurai and the ardours of the master–pupil relationship, was designed to induce conformity and subservience; conversely, the equally barbaric British caning had stalwarts bristling with pride and touting its more individualistic capacity for 'building character'.

Masochism is also said to be rooted in the infantile erotic thrill of punishment administered by a mother, a nanny or a schoolteacher, which gives rise to a recurring fantasy in adulthood. Although beatings were an intrinsic part of military training, corporal punishment is happily rare in the Japanese home if not in some reformatories and stricter private schools. The masochist is also said to be perpetually seeking punishment for the inadequacies he was made to feel by failing to come up to his mother's expectations. In Japan, this option would seem particularly applicable. Where the mother traditionally sacrifices herself utterly for the sake of her children, especially her sons, she can instil feelings of guilt in them by implying that their failures are tantamount to spurning her love. Given such factors as these, Japanese society could hardly be more fertile ground for masochistic predilections which, ultimately, become the sexual expression of the various obligations and restrictions endured and responded to in other ways every day.

DEADLIER THAN THE MALE

In one way or another the Cruel Woman, the queen of pain who never needs to wield a whip, dominates the Japanese masochistic imagination. Despite and because of the ironclad veneer of machismo, it is that much easier for a woman to be cruel. Married by arrangement to a partner she may not love, she can take it out on him in the home, where tradition relegates her to an apparently subservient role on the one hand, while paradoxically granting her absolute power on the other. Perpetually in the office and a barely visible shadow at home, the husband is conceded only pocket money out of a hard-earned salary which is virtually managed by his wife. The tendency is evidenced in *manga* comics, such as the immensely popular serial *Dame Oyaji* (No-Good Daddy), in which the whole family would join a caricatural *mamagon* (a monster mother) in trampling and beating up hapless and ineffectual *salaryman* dad. That the *salaryman* is a corporate slave caught up in a depersonalizing routine is brought home in the welter of *salaryman manga* too, in which the jokes frequently reside in the humiliation to which the protagonist is subjected by his superiors.

The cruel woman finds her counterpart even among ostensibly more liberated youth with the *sukeban*, the 'boss girl' lording it up over high-school gangs in films and comics as she joins the fray in leather dominatrix attire; young male imaginations seem haunted by a cruel, authoritarian female image. Psychological as opposed to physical masochism permeates a recurring porno movie theme, which presents the vicarious thrill of a man tied up and forced to watch his wife repeatedly raped by lusty thugs. The sadistic implications of the rape pale before the delicious torments experienced by the hapless voyeur, who is invariably the main character and conceived solely as a vehicle for audience empathy. A consistent twist in the rape fantasy finds the victim reaching heights of sexual ecstasy that she has never attained with her inadequate husband.

Few have described the mechanics of masochism more eloquently than the novelist Junichiro Tanizaki, starting with *Naomi* (also called *A Fool's Love*) in the twenties. Counting several masterpieces among them, Tanizaki's many tragi-comical tales rely upon the power of understatement to build up a vivid climate of erotic obsession. *Naomi* concerns Jōji, a young *salaryman* who believes that he is saving a virginal teenage girl picked up in a disreputable Ginza café from a fate worse than death. He is struck by her un-Japanese beauty; she looks like a juvenile Mary Pickford. He takes her home and under his wing with her parents' blessing and, give or take suppressed desires, he lives chastely with her until they marry.

Naomi's beauty increases as she grows up. Becoming the ultimate *moga* – the modern girl, the Japanese flapper – she likes dancing, expensive clothes and the gay life, all at her husband's expense. Although Jōji soon learns that he is a cuckold who has married a prostitute from a family of prostitutes, the more she sleeps around and the more she taunts and torments him, the more besotted he is. A prisoner of his suffering, he revels in it as it worsens. Jōji half-heartedly throws her out, but Naomi comes back sporadically to tease him, spurning him each time after calculatedly driving him wild with desire.

Both the book and later the film climax as she rides on his back, playing horsy. This is their reconciliation. In exchange for the privilege of keeping her, Naomi is to be permitted to indulge her expensive whims and to entertain lovers. In the end, to make the hero's humiliation complete, Naomi's favoured paramours are foreigners. Our Lady of Pain dispenses no whips: she doesn't need to. Subjected to her psychological cruelty, her adoring victim suffers happily ever after.

The Key tells of an ugly professor's obsessive relationship with his beautiful middle-aged wife, Ikuko. Married by arrangement, she is physically repelled by her spouse and such as it is, their sex life is marred by his kinky leanings and the fact that she is ostensibly a prude. Since alcohol apparently makes her fall unconscious, however, the husband soon takes liberties by encouraging her to tipple. Having orchestrated an affair between Ikuko and a younger man meanwhile, the ageing professor takes even greater pleasure with his semi-comatose wife in the knowledge that she has just been doing it both consciously and more satisfactorily with someone else. His mounting erotic frenzy is such that he finally dies of a stroke. The twist in the tale comes not from the professor's harmless deviations, but from his more perverse wife, who was leading the dance all along. For all her apparent primness, Ikuko is a calculating monster of insatiable sexual appetites. Black comedy is even more evident in Tanizaki's *Diary of a Mad Old Man*, in which death similarly comes to a goatish dotard obsessed with his devious daughter-in-law. As she wheedles expensive gifts in exchange for the climactic concession of allowing him to suck her toes in the shower, the old man gets so steamed up that his excitement ultimately proves fatal. Before this turn of events, however, he reflects upon the feminine ideal:

> Above all, it's essential for her to have white, slender legs and delicate feet. Assuming that these and all other points of beauty are equal, I would be more susceptible to the woman with bad character. Occasionally there are women

whose faces reveal a streak of cruelty – they are the ones I like best. When I see a woman with a face like that, I feel her innermost nature may be cruel, indeed I hope it is.

Tanizaki put his own predilections into the mouth of his characters. His foot fetishism and occasional excursions into the realm of coprophilia may be quirks he held in common with comparatively few, but there is no doubt that his obsession with the cruel woman is shared by millions of others. That the 'Miss Caine: strict discipline' personal ads posted in British newsagents' windows would be superfluous in Japan, where the ultimate thrill lies less in the cane and more in the discipline, is perhaps best illustrated in one of Tanizaki's strangest short stories, 'Shunkin-Cho'. Set in the mid-nineteenth century, the 'Portrait of Shunkin' focuses on its namesake, a little girl as hauntingly beautiful as she is spoiled and temperamental. A consummate prodigy on the samisen, Shunkin is blind. Sasuke, a teenage houseboy in her parents' employ, secretly practises the instrument himself until he becomes a promising musician, mostly out of love for her. Shunkin haughtily agrees to take him on as a pupil, then later as a guide and manservant for whom she seems to reserve special contempt. As they grow up, the relationship develops into a weird love affair.

Revered as a samisen teacher, Shunkin is ill-tempered and miserly, a monster of egotism with the beauty and evil character of a wicked queen from a fairy-tale. Tanizaki stresses her lack of feelings by dwelling much on the care she lavishes on her cherished song-birds, even as she callously mistreats her pupils and relentlessly domineers the long-suffering Sasuke. Although he eventually becomes her constant companion and an eminent teacher himself, Shunkin never treats him as anything more than an abject servant. His infatuation is constantly exacerbated as he tends to her every whim, assuming more intimate duties such as bathing her and taking her to the toilet, but it is years before it is requited in other ways.

Knowing that he is suffering from toothache one day, Shunkin kicks him on the cheek. The incident sees Tanizaki's foot-fetishism and masochism at work to be sure but, as the only physical manifestation of her cruelty in the tale, it seems designed more to stress her callousness; Sasuke's masochism, after all, is of the more sublimated kind. Shunkin acted out of jealousy: Sasuke had just been giving music lessons – quite innocently – to young girls.

One night an unknown avenger douses the sleeping Shunkin's face with boiling water. Disfigured, she is not only as cruel as ever to the devoted and heartbroken Sasuke, but also forbids him to come near lest he see her face. So Sasuke takes a sewing needle and pokes out his eyes. Once he is blind, he finally earns Shunkin's esteem. 'I admire your courage,' she says. 'You have made me very happy. I don't know who hated me enough to do this to me, but I must confess that I couldn't stand to have you, of all people, see me as I am now. I am grateful to you for realizing it.' And Sasuke is beside himself. 'Ah,' he cries, 'blindness is a small price to pay for the joy of hearing you say that!'

And, as Tanizaki wrote, 'the blind lovers embraced, weeping.'

To the Japanese, if not to Tanizaki, the masochism inherent in 'The Portrait of Shunkin' hardly matters. More important is the dominant concept of *shitei-kanke* – the master–pupil relationship – in which self-abnegation and complete surrender to the teacher comes as a matter of course. No abject masochist, Sasuke is in all senses an admirable model of blind perseverance along the hard road to mastery of technique, and Shunkin's cruelty and quirks are excused respectively by her blindness and as part of her privilege as a *sensei*. Repaying Shunkin for deigning to teach him, Sasuke's unwavering submission belongs to the realm of *gaman*.

Anything but perverted, his self-sacrifice is seen as an extremely moving token of love. Sasuke's self-mutilation causes Shunkin's icy armour to melt, and the couple go on perpetuating their mistress–servant relationship until they die. 'Shunkin-Cho' has been filmed twice. The most recent version, made just under ten years ago, was a mass-audience hit. Tanizaki's perverse premises were waived aside in what was a very sentimental and edifying tear-jerker tailored as a vehicle for a couple of youthful pop idols.

THE PHANTOM SEDUCTRESS

> Kill a woman and back she'll come
> to haunt you – just you see.
> She really is a fearful thing,
> But supposing there were none
> Now what a problem that would be.
> Everybody watch out – haha!
> Woman is a fearful thing,
> Such a fearful thing.
>
> *Hebiyama (Snake Mountain)* –
> an old Geisha song

A favourite piece in the repertoire of Kirara, an 'idol' stripper also given to fringe theatre performances before mixed audiences, is simply called 'Kamakiri' – praying mantis. Surrounded by her agile troupe of two female and two male bodies, all exquisite, Kirara reigns as the Mantis Queen in diaphanous green robes. Following a balletic mime of dinner and erotic dalliance with a large gold paper effigy of a male mantis, the Queen finally devours it for dessert. Then she gives birth to mantis offspring. The child is all-important; the male a vital accessory jettisoned once it has served its purpose. Has this, one wonders, anything to do with women's lib? Kirara is quite emphatic: 'No. The female mantis is a favourite Japanese allegory. Like the *jorōgumo*, it is a demon of traditional folklore.'

The *jorōgumo*, the spider-woman, is another name for the arachnid known in the West as the black widow. Tanizaki, again, uses the symbol in his famous short story 'Shisei' ('The Tattooer'). Set in the Edo period, it concerns a master tattoo artist who is much taken with a very young and unusually beautiful apprentice geisha. After showing her prints of the sadistic Chinese Emperor Chou's favourite concubine delighting at the sight of victims chained to a red-hot pillar, he makes the girl share his conviction that she is similarly a creature of rare cruelty. Seeing her at once excited by the pictures and ashamed of having her secret nature exposed, the tattooer is already snared.

First a word about the Japanese tattoo. Customarily maligned in polite society, it often decorates the skins of those on the lower rungs of the social ladder, where it survives as a traditional folk art. Reputed as gangsters even when not, those with tattoos are even barred from public swimming pools. Few unprejudiced people who have seen such tattoos could deny that they are the most beautiful in the world. There is a temptation to associate tattooing with masochism, but the painfully illustrated genitals, infibulation and other practices common in the West are, according to Donald Richie in his *Japanese*

Tattoo, invariably shunned by Japanese practitioners of the art. The process is hardly comfortable but, as Richie points out: 'Certainly the piercing pain and writhing agony described by popular literature on the subject is the creation of the writer and not the tattoo master.'

Tattooing is not torture unless, of course, the larger body tattoo normally executed over a year or more should be reduced, as in Tanizaki's story, to a single session. After drugging her, the craftsman etches a huge spider on the whole of the geisha's beautiful white back. He works all night; in it he has put his very soul. She awakes and stoically takes a bath 'to bring out the colours', an agonizing process which would make any man weep. Refusing all sympathy from the tattooer as she writhes in pain, the girl eventually comes back calmly to join him in the studio.

'All my fears have been swept away,' she announces, 'and you are my first victim!' The fact the tattoo master is immediately reduced to imploring her to drop her kimono and give him just one more glimpse of his masterpiece leaves us in no doubt.

The spider-woman is celebrated in porno movies too, even in the more recent and usually plotless hard-core videos. One belonging to the *Bakuretsu fakku Seerisu* (*The Bombshell Fuck Series*), for instance, was simply called *Jorōgumo* and about a young entomologist's encounter with the female of the species. Pursuing a rare spider in the mountains, he runs into a sultry beauty who invites him to stay in an isolated house in which she lives alone with her 'brother', with whom she regularly has sex, a favour soon extended to her house guest too. After a night of explicit pleasures, he watches her misbehaving herself in imaginative ways with fruit spread upon the breakfast table but, far from being turned on, the entomologist is worried by her 'brother's' absence.

Concluding that the girl is in reality a spider and that she has devoured her victim, he bolts from the house.

Obsessions underlie the weird tales of Edogawa Rampo, whose name is a homonym for Edgar Allan Poe, whom he much admired. Shades of sado-masochism tint the story of the stunted, hideously ugly furniture maker who hides inside a special armchair of his own deviant design. When the human chair enters the home of a beauteous woman writer, its jubilant secret occupant resigns himself to months in the same painfully cramped position. Remaining in a state of permanent erotic rapture, he can actually paw her through the cushioned fabric without her really feeling it.

A horror story crowning the genre of the demoness is Rampo's story of a man returning from the war a hero, but being limbless, deaf and dumb, the distinction is as lost on him as it is on his wife. She gradually equates him with a monstrous caterpillar, and her revulsion spurs her to torment him. Delighting first in his angered eyes then annoyed when they plead, she finally pokes them out.

Each summer, when muggy evening mists hang over Japan like a pall, the Cruel Woman comes into her own in her most ancient and fearful form. For a sultry month from mid-July, which marks the 'Bon' festival for the dead, the spirits of the departed are said to return to earth. Among the benign host, a variety of *bake-mono*, assorted monsters and goblins, jump on the ghostly bandwagon. Of all the species in this macabre pantheon, however, the one unquestionably inspiring the greatest dread is the female.

Confucianism proscribes jealousy, which if she feels it at all, the virtuous woman is rigorously bound to conceal. In practice, however, few do. Japanese women are tolerant of dalliances with prostitutes, but when threatened emotionally by a full-blown affair, they react exactly the same as women everywhere else. The western cuckold is traditionally represented as the disgruntled and ridiculous wearer of a pair of horns or antlers; Japanese folklore reserves the privilege for the wife. When her jealous rage gets the better of her upon confronting a philandering husband or one lavishing too much affection on a concubine, she sprouts the devil horns one finds crowning the terrifying countenance of the female demon of the Noh and *kagura* stage.

The vengeful female phantom reigns as queen in the rich array of phantasmagoria evoked both in kabuki plays and the old woodblock prints. Tsuruya Namboku, the early nineteenth-century master of 'decadent' kabuki, is perhaps most famous for his chilling 'Yotsuya Kaidan' ('The Yotsuya Ghost Story'). This concerns the beautiful Oiwa, the wife of the devious and impecunious Iyemon, a young samurai who conspires to marry the daughter of a rich old doctor eager to get a foot in the door of the samurai class. One day when Oiwa lies abed with a chill, the doctor gives her a poison in the guise of medicine, which disfigures her so frightfully that she commits suicide. Later, when he lifts the bridal veil during the wedding ceremony, Iyemon sees only the horrible face of his dead wife and, running the apparition through with his sword, kills his new bride. Haunted by the ghastly spirit of Oiwa as he runs away, demented Iyemon drowns himself in a river.

Another great favourite is *Botan dōrō* (*The Peony Lantern*), an old tale of Chinese origin. One of many stories of men in love with a ghost, it has similarly been celebrated in woodblock prints, on the kabuki stage and several times on screen. Prevented from keeping a tryst with the fair Otsuyu, the enamoured young samurai Shinzaburo remains estranged from her. When the girl pines and dies, she is joined in death soon afterwards by her devoted maidservant. A famous late nineteenth-century print by Yoshitoshi depicts the two shades carrying peony-shaped paper lanterns on their way to see Shinzaburo, who believes them both to be still alive. Spying on Shinzaburo's dalliance with a spectral corpse, a terrified neighbour tries to persuade him to stay in the land of the living, but too late. The theme has been treated less poetically in erotic *shunga* prints, with shades of necrophilia emerging from the graphic depiction of a man copulating with a skeleton.

Not so macabre but no less significant is the famous 'Ugetsu Monogatari' which, being also the subject for Kenji Mizoguchi's great film masterpiece of 1953, is an old tale of a potter's dalliance with a ghostly princess. Unaware of the passage of time, he returns contritely to his wife years later and spends the night with her, only to awake the next morning to find himself lying alone in a house long in ruins. The mood here is one of great poignancy. The ghostly princess symbolizes a love affair more exciting than the more dutiful connubial life at home, but the potter has realized the value of his wife too late. Denied the debatable privilege of following a ghostly lover into the afterlife as he might in many other tales, the chastened potter must live out his life in this vale of tears.

Being procreational and pleasurable, sex should fundamentally be about life but, forever and everywhere shrouded in taboos, it tends to have one foot in the grave. At face value, such tales tell of a man facing mortal danger from the folly of a love affair with a spirit – a theme universally bringing home the irrevocability of death. In Japan, most ghost stories are cautionary parables. Unlike the pure male, woman is sullied by episodes of ritual uncleanliness like menstruation and childbirth and has a demonic side to her nature. When not warning against temptresses, ghost stories are also allegories for the sexual jealousy women are forbidden by Confucianism to express.

In the Yotsuya tale, for example, notwithstanding her husband's wickedness, having been spurned, the woman comes back in demon form to torment him. Although Tanizaki would have been the last to spin cautionary Confucian tales, his Shunkin is portrayed to join the ranks of classic demonesses; her kicking Sasuke's face when she suspects his secret delight in teaching young girls is a pivotal point in the tale: she is jealous. Confucian parables too, ghost stories such as 'Ugetsu Monogatari' or 'The Peony Lantern' are about weak-willed men lured from the righteous path of duty into the realm of passion by woman, and the consequences are dire. It seems significant that so many stories involve disfigurement: boiling water for Shunkin, poison for Oiwa and decomposition both for Otsuyu and the seminal goddess Izanami. Betraying her jealousy or luring the male as a temptress, the female is transmogrified.

In the West, the horror of death is similarly expressed in themes of the dead threatening the living. As is the case with the centuries-old allegory of 'Death and the Maiden', these can similarly be cautionary parables about the consequences of seduction. In Japan, however, the genders of the haunters and the haunted are reversed; the macabre dances to a different tune. Unlike in 'The Peony Lantern', Bram Stoker's *Dracula* finds the pure female falling under the spell of a male fiend whose spectral overtures she can resist no more than can Shinzaburo his phantom girlfriend's. The good Count is perhaps western fiction's greatest demon lover, but, notwithstanding a measure of renown from his screen performances, he has scarcely made a dent in Japanese culture.

In the West it is always the male who leads the female astray, but in Confucian countries, although men generally seduce women too, allegories are aimed not at the maiden but the immaculate young man. The womanizer might be a bit of a lad in Europe, but Japanese culture sees him more as a weakling. Confronted with the dangerously attractive female, the great macho heroes of samurai and *yakuza* screen sagas tend to nod awkwardly, and timidly scratch the backs of their heads. The genetic myth of Izanami and Izanagi finds the seminal goddess's and god's initial procreation discarded because the woman made the first move. For all her demureness, which can be either inculcated and real as well as attributed and fondly imagined, the woman is very often the true initiator of an affair in the real as well as in the mythical Japan. The poet Akiko Yosano, whose lusty feminism rocked Meiji-period conventions, made the point most eloquently:

> 'Oh, why
> So timid now?'
> I cried,
> Clinging to his hand,
> My eyes closed.

For the diffident male and the Confucian tough-guy alike, there is only a small step between the female's dominant initiative and turning her into an imaginary sexual predator. In a country in which women have been relegated to brothels or rigorously confined to the home for centuries, it seems odd that men should find the female so threatening. Perhaps the male concept of the demonic female also resides in their being haunted by the ghosts of their own bad conscience. On the other hand, if men have limited woman's scope for as long as they have, it is according to the dictates of a system which ultimately makes victims of them too.

If Japan has relegated women to subservient roles, it has never seen them as the 'gentle sex'; on the contrary. Films and literature are forever celebrating her hardy resilience and legendary strength which, in the ghost story, sometimes seems to transcend death. Akiko Yosano, again, put canny words into the demoness's mouth:

> 'To punish
> Men for their endless sins,
> God gave me
> This fair skin,
> This long black hair!'

And droves of men, some delighting in the demoness's cruelty and others fearful of a formidable mother or spouse, look steadily to SM shows and videos to see her punished right back.

Occurring in the late 1930s and perfectly true, the case of Sada Abe deserves mention among the vengeful demonesses of fiction and folklore. A low-class geisha in love with a man who is likely to have been a philandering pimp, she is also the heroine of Nagisa Oshima's celebrated hard-core porn film masterpiece, *The Realm of the Senses*. Having strangled him during their lovemaking, Sada was picked up by the police as she wandered the streets in a state of elated distraction and carrying a *furoshiki* (a cloth for wrapping gifts) containing his severed penis. That way, she explained, he would remain faithful to her for ever. Sada's crime was judged to be one of passion; after serving a light sentence she was released.

As relatively recent as it is, the occurrence has entered folk legend and the fanciful details cladding the homicidal and amputatory core of truth vary a great deal. Many people affirm that Sada Abe is still alive today and that, now in her eighties, she is still working as a maid in a Japanese inn in the seaside town of Atami. While she sends shivers down the spines and other things of every male in Japan, women see Sada Abe rather differently. The drastic equation between male infidelity and the kitchen cleaver is a very old one and, although all would concede that she went a little far, she hit back against male dominance where it hurts most. To women she is less of a demoness and more of a folk heroine. If Sada Abe still haunts male nightmares, there is good reason. In 1982, a middle-aged bar hostess in Nagoya perpetrated a crime in every way identical except for a more contemporary twist: the police found the severed organ in her deep freeze.

18

Naked Dissent

DEFIANCE AND DISSIMULATION

In its sheer attention to detail, the item in the possession of a Mr Murano, a Tokyo collector of rather special curios and *objets d'art*, at first sight recalls those kitsch porcelain figures of ragged children or Pierrots and Columbines sold in airport souvenir shops. Especially popular earlier this century, it is a meticulously crafted polychrome statuette of a geisha or courtesan decorously embracing (but – heaven forbid – not kissing) a gallant. The theme is a common one, and variations dress the young man as a samurai or an Edo-period townsman, as well as in the old-time trappings of the student, soldier or office worker in a stiff collar and a three-piece suit. Turning it upside down, however, makes all the difference. The primness of the lovers' faces is belied, for they are now caught *in flagrante delicto*. Their interconnected genitals are garishly painted with minute clinical accuracy, if on a rather fanciful scale. A labial ring of bright strawberry-pink greedily devours a pillar of milk-chocolate brown, the point of connection being tastefully decorated with a confectionary ring of foaming white effluvia. It's all explicitly pornographic and, in its choice of cheerful birthday-cake colours, perfectly innocent.

Although such curios are supposedly illegal, their scope is vast and Murano modestly dismisses his own substantial assortment in comparison with collections hoarded by others, some of which are so large that they have constituted various 'Sex Museums' dotted about the country, notably in hot-spring resorts. The museums often display the figurines alongside veiled waxwork models of performing couples, and always with their offending portions concealed. Typically fashioned to look like their ordinary gift-shop counterparts, they generally conceal an assortment of X-rated gimmicks and features behind, inside or underneath.

Perennial icons of folk art, these objects are generally the erotic relatives of a large family of charming, often comical, figurines representing divinities, animals and ordinary human beings. Singly or severally, paramount among them are the pleasure-loving seven gods of good luck, the whole crew or even just a painting of their empty 'treasure boat' auguring prosperity on its own. Made of painted terracotta, china, wood or bronze and always benign, the figurines serve as they have for over a millennium to ward off evil and augur prosperity and happiness. Like Pan and Priapus in ancient Rome, they belong to a pantheon of small, ribald deities closely connected to phallicism and fertility. Whether their intimate attributes were revealed, concealed or merely implicit, they were propitiously placed on shelves in the home, geisha houses, brothels, shops and miscellaneous eating and drinking establishments and they often still are.

Typical of the more suggestive figurine is a seated Heian beauty with long tresses embracing a monumental stylized phallus. A more elegant form of the legendary Otafuku (also called Okame), the girl with a redoubtable sexual appetite, she has over the centuries and in the hands of humorous folk art more commonly become a grotesque, often with her arms wrapped around the trunk of an impressively virile mushroom. Grinning hugely from a tiny mouth and with eyes mere slits in her outsize, dimpled cheeks, she has her voluminous bulk clad in a kimono, and commonly sits on a cushion. Turned upside down, the traditional kneeling posture barefacedly reveals a detailed view of the attributes of her sex.

Another classic is a painted clay statuette of a urinating couple. The man clutches his penis with his head held high with conceit; the woman squatting beside him looks on in rapt admiration. Beneath her raised kimono her ample buttocks are painted pristine white with bright red lips in the centre, surrounded by an exclamatory halo of emphatic little black brushstrokes. A variant depicts a row of three squatting girls and, here again, although the urinary theme is a more modern ploy to defuse the erotic, it nevertheless provides an excuse to expose the genitals – still not so much for titillation as magical organs of protection. For all their comic ribaldry, these talismans still reflect the simple piety of ancient folk religion.

Alcohol is if anything a more frequent prelude to sex in Japan than anywhere else. Measuring only some five centimetres across as though to beg frequent refills from a charming companion, sake cups are much given to suggestiveness. Erotic cups were brazenly decorated with copulating couples of *shunga* inspiration on the inside during the Edo period and, in the Meiji era, they often came to be covered with lids. Although the adoption of western propriety commanded discretion, the cups were used only where they were least likely to offend – in brothels and in 'teahouses' that never served tea. Hence the lids were spawned less by the injunctions of propriety than a time-honoured love of dissimulation. Mass-produced today with the genital areas concealed, erotic sake cups are also sometimes shaped like a phallic mushroom with a hole pierced in the glans, allowing the liquid to be lasciviously sucked from the contiguous cup.

Sold freely in souvenir shops, they come in sets dominated by a flask representing the eternally horny
Otafuku, this time with ambiguity sculpted on her face:
her fat cheeks look more like those she would normally
be sitting on, and the minute smile between them is of a
distinctly longitudinal turn.

Attached to the kimono sashes of both sexes during
the Edo period, the little tiered medicine boxes called *inro*
often bore erotic images painted on the inside or the
back. The cord holding the *inro* was toggled with a
netsuke, a small piece of ivory carved with consummate
skill and often similarly given to erotic themes. Clothed
on one side, the netsuke could sometimes be turned
round to reveal nudity on the other and the minute
genitalia, single or interconnected, could sometimes
actually move. Faces of male and female deities and tiny
Noh masks swivel to reveal genitalia behind and, emulating the statuary of fertility worship, scores of others
can be viewed from angles revealing hidden phallo-
vulvar profiles.

Noh and *kagura* masks are also a favoured medium for
dissimulated erotica. Most common is the face of the
winged and hirsute goblin Tenggu, whose outsize nose
can sometimes be detached for more practical applications, although most are designed solely for hanging on
the wall. Masks concealing erotica are preponderantly
female, notably the skittish Otafuku, though one often
finds Ko-omote, a Noh mask portraying a pretty young
woman, with a placidly smiling face fronting all manner
of hidden sculptural outrages. From the Noh too are
masks of the leering *hannya* demoness, and the frequency with which she is the elected medium for erotic
dissimulation betrays the misogynistic concept of
woman as temptress and fiend.

Murano's collection yielded examples of that 1920s

Shanghai souvenir: a nude invisible beneath a bubble of glass inside until the cup is full. Among several Japanese variants is a teacup decorated with a dainty geisha standing beneath a cherry tree. Add the hot tea, hey presto: the kimono gradually fades into blushing nudity and reappears as the liquid cools. Early this century, there were geisha photographs chemically treated to make the kimono similarly vanish when the card was warmed. On the underside of a tiny cushion full of scented spices in a little box there lies an active pair of lilliputian lovers. Open a fan and discover a mundane scene; half close it again and, as in nineteenth-century Chinese counterparts, the subject matter becomes explicitly erotic. Other drawers in the *tansu* chests in Murano's home contain not only reams of *shunga* prints, but also a wealth of dissimulated pornographic imagery from the twenties and thirties. Looking like children's Advent calendars, cardboard pictures of rooms and houses have doors and windows that open or slide aside, revealing that the cheerful characters visible without are in fact clinched in a startling array of erotic embraces within. Such is the joy of dissimulation.

During the Edo period, when sumptuary laws prohibited townsmen from wearing fancy clothes, they merely turned their ostentatious leanings to rich linings and elaborate under-kimonos, an effect that was soon regarded as more subtle and distinctive than the blatant showiness of the clothing proscribed before. Just as censorship drove erotica underground in the West, so too in Japan. Having had their more explicit votive imagery banned, however, the phallic cults resorted quite happily to subtler camouflage – a welcome cloak of esotericism. A guardian of infant souls, the Buddhist *jizō* figure conjured greater occult power as a preventive deity as a phallic symbol when viewed from behind; the stone *dosōjin* couples were frequently considered all the finer once dressed. With the man's rigid fist thrust deep into the yielding folds of the woman's sleeve, what had at first only been provoked by repression came to be highly appreciated as a poetic metaphor made concrete.

Apart from relegating erotic imagery to the universal clandestine realm of under-the-counter and postcards arrayed on overcoat linings, the Japanese dichotomy between the primitive ritual awe of nudity and official regulations no more led to unconditional acceptance of morality than it did to open defiance. Although flouting proscriptions openly could be very dangerous, the unquenchable desire to flout them remained. Consequently it found expression among the populace in a kind of measured rebellion. The propensity for adaptation and compromise fostered a genius for circumventing proscriptions and dissimulation became an end in itself.

HIDDEN IS BEAUTIFUL

The vague has been preferred over the blatant in erotic artistic expression in Japan for over a thousand years. The celebration of the hidden was obviously a trait more common among the aristocracy, which has forever had to abide by a stricter moral code than commoners. Indeed, the *Manyoshu*, or *Collection of Myriad Leaves*, a book of over four thousand poems compiled during the seventh and eighth centuries, contains a substantial number with a veiled erotic content, as do some of the tenth-century poems in *Tales of Ise*. The thirty-seventh, for instance, finds a young man addressing his faithless love:

> 'Unless it is for me
> Do not unbind your lower sash,
> Although the morning glory
> Never awaits the evening
> To open.'

To which she replies:

> 'The knot
> Which together we two have tied
> Before we meet again
> I shall assuredly not unbind alone.'

Even though such poems were composed during relatively permissive times, allusions to loosening sashes and opening flowers were about as explicit as they came. Morning dew was a metaphor both for the tears perpetually soaking kimono sleeves and dawn, when pre- and extramarital lovers were customarily supposed to part. As another poem from *Tales of Ise* suggests, however, the dew could also stand for something more intimate, as it has in erotic literature in Europe. The poem here is a woman's response to some verses from an old flame pained through his suddenly rekindled desire. The two remain attracted although their mutual infidelities have estranged them, but thinking back on their affair, she owns that even if her ardour has cooled, her physical passion has not entirely dried up. But she does have reservations:

> 'From the morning dew
> Which has evaporated there may always remain
> A few drops.
> But who could rely
> Upon a relationship with you?'

It has often been pointed out that the Japanese are fond of darkness, a trait variously interpreted as a desire to crawl back into the reassuring obscurity of the womb and a manifestation of a fondness for melancholy. Either way, there is little doubt that the aesthetics of dissimulation are also rooted in this fondness for the dark. Junichiro Tanizaki, after all, wrote *In Praise of Shadows* in 1934, a delightful essay on Japanese aesthetics dealing with nothing else. How telling his nostalgic comparison between Bunraku puppets and the lost, lamented women of old:

> The female puppets consist only of a head and a pair of hands. The body, legs and feet are concealed within a long kimono, and so the operators need only work their hands within the costume to suggest movements. To me this is the very epitome of reality, for a woman of the past did indeed exist only from the collar up and the sleeves out; the rest of her remained hidden in darkness.

What began as an obligation to hide erotica evolved into an aesthetic concept in line with the Japanese preference for the artificial over the real. Ultimately, the practice and skill involved with erotic dissimulation came to be seen in the same light. To Ken Ikuta, an editor of sexually orientated features in *Brutus*, an influential young man's fashion magazine with a wide female following: 'Hiding has nothing to do with shame. Dissimulation is more beautiful. And it is also more fun. This is one of the primordial bases of Japanese aesthetics.'

He was referring to a feature he had written about the versatile Gaikotsu Miyatake, a late Meiji-period sociologist, satirist, essayist and artist perhaps best known as the editor of a pioneering satire magazine called *Kokkei Shimbun* (comical newspaper). Although he usually had them executed by others, the illustrations were of his own design and rank highly in the realm of Japanese innuendo.

'We wanted to do something on humorous erotica,' Ikuta explained. 'But everything recent was so westernized. As the last exponent of the old comical sexual metaphor, Miyatake was perfect.' Executed mostly in a style midway between the European seaside postcard and the classic woodblock print, his illustrations subtly veiled outlandish licentiousness with apparent mundanity and daringly mocked Japan's wholesale adoption of 'modern' Victorian morality. The scene of a blushing soubrette buying tissue paper in a shop discovers the mere shadow of a waiting gentleman, implying the imminence of its use. Another shows a class of demure girls and a prim young natural science mistress pointing to a chart full of ludicrously phallic mushrooms. Then there is the bar girl wearing the Japanese flag as an apron with the blood-red sun just over her pubis; she is hanging up a sign: 'Today we're closed for a holiday.'

As outrageous as using the Japanese flag as a humorous allusion to menstruation might have been during an age of dawning ultra-nationalism, he got away with it. His cartoons exposed no genitals and steered clear of identifiable politics. Like the sculptors disguising phalli as deities and vice versa, Miyatake turned restrictions to his advantage to deploy something deliciously subversive without breaking the law.

What also makes dissimulation that much easier and more attractive is the tendency to disguise nature, to tame it, to reduce it to human terms. Although a real tree, the dwarf bonsai is so unnaturally trained that it almost becomes only a symbol and, as such, is often preferred. With its rocks carefully placed like islands in a sea of raked gravel, the Zen garden is less a garden than the emblem of a garden. In a land of typhoons and earthquakes, famine, floods and volcanic eruptions, the apparent love of nature is conditioned by an innate fear of the uncontrollable and the resulting circumspection is extended to the indomitable passion of sex. Although the preference for stylization is embodied by male actors playing female roles in the traditional theatre, these emerged only from the moment actresses were forbidden. Necessity is the mother of invention and the Japanese have a genius for turning adversity into assets. Ploys initially spawned to circumvent repression are elevated in comical, contentious or purely aesthetic contexts to become signs, ciphers and symbols of a quality setting the Japanese soul apart.

LOW-CITY LAUGHTER

Dressed in the blue denim *hanten* tunics of the Edo-period blue-collar worker, feasting on *bento* picnic-boxes and drinking sake, the *mikoshi* shrine-bearers at the Kawasaki phallic festival sit to one side on straw mats after the parade, just as they would have done centuries ago. The atmosphere is boisterous, and swarthy workmen's faces erupt in bursts of unrestrained laughter prompted by quick, animated repartee founded on the subject matter proper to this phallic occasion. These days, however, the time-honoured team of artisans, tradesmen, workmen and shopkeepers might include locals from all walks of life and both sexes. And, as the conspicuous presence of the drag queens of the Elizabeth Club suggests, even the sex in between.

One burly, inebriated labourer, his headcloth awry and tunic flapping loose over beer-bellied nakedness concealed only by a *fundoshi* (the very basic loincloth that had so horrified Victorian visitors to Japan), put his arm around one of the Elizabethans: 'Give us a kiss!' This was no derisive taunt to assert macho normality while calling attention to the other's ostensible freakishness. Both drunk and cawing with laughter, the Elizabethan with blue cheeks beneath the layers of make-up and the dishevelled labourer, despite their outrageously contrasting appearances, looked for all the world like the good drinking companions they were. Echoing the liberating anarchy of the Eejyanaika all over again, this exuberance epitomizes the spirit of *shitamachi*, the 'low city' that was the home of the common people living outside the walls of the feudal lords. Once referring more specifically to an area in north-eastern Edo (now Asakusa), the term has come to be used for a large number of urban working-class areas in which tradition and entertainment rub shoulders.

Since the face it turns officially on the world is notoriously solemn and sedate, many people are unaware that Japan has a sense of humour. The puritanical po-face is typical of Japanese officialdom, a monolith promulgating centuries of samurai stoicism and neo-Confucian bureaucracy. Despite the abolition of the old samurai order during the Meiji period, the ruling classes merely redefined themselves. Living on among those in power, archaic stoicism was nurtured by ultra-nationalists, flared with militarism and smoulders today in sporadic reactionism and a stubborn resistance to all but pragmatic change.

Shitamachi is certainly conservative, but its conservatism is a far cry from its official counterpart. It may be true everywhere that the lower orders tend to be more permissive than the higher ones, but there are not many places in which the dichotomy is as clearly defined as in Japan. Here it is neither a matter of class nor even wealth, but of the diverging outlooks of the authorities and the ordinary people. Far older than the precepts of officialdom and in sharp contrast to them is the humour of the populace, which thoroughly colours Shinto festivals and reverberates in the easy, earthy laughter of *shitamachi*, which French journalist Philippe Pons explains in *D'Edo à Tokyo*, about the history and culture of the Tokyo populace:

> The primary characteristic of this folk humour, which has its source in the low city, lies in the emphasis it places on physical life, especially on the body. Eating and drinking, the fulfilment of natural urges and, above all, sex are high on the list of priorities. Frequently ribald, this popular comedy is marked by a grotesque realism which rails against whatever is considered as elevated, spiritual and abstract. In keeping with the trend, popular humour becomes intentionally irreverent towards the government, if not actively dissident.

Ronald Bell, a gestalt therapist who has studied Japanese phallicism for thirty years, tells of a *kagura* performance he saw at a rural fertility festival, which involved two men costumed as horse and mare. After hamming their way through a spirited copulative pantomime, the lights went out as the two men bared their backsides. To the delighted howls of the crowd, they were joined by others and danced around in the dark together with lighted cigarettes protruding from their nether ends. In the West, the baring of the backside is a very ancient gesture of contempt. Although uncommon in polite Japan, which has neither swear words nor even a gestural repertoire of 'fuck you', the derisive overtones in this curious conclusion to a festival performance, by rights about fertility and not bottoms, seem quite clear. Far from being a slight on the audience, it is a defiant affront to authority on their behalf.

Today, irreverent humour bubbles up from legions of comedians on screen and stage, many of whom significantly began their careers in striptease theatres. They are variants of the extant traditional *manzai* and *rakugo* comedians, who are distant descendants of mendicant Buddhist monks spreading the good word around the countryside in the form of parables – a form that peasants could most readily understand. These ancient storytellers inspired secular offshoots. The shoguns initially patronized them as the reciters of medieval epic tales until, when not even they could stay awake, their role became akin to that of European court jesters. Outside the castle walls, meanwhile, storytellers emulating their courtly counterparts began to appear in the streets. As the townspeople grew more prosperous, these *rakugo* gradually drew crowds into plebeian theatres known as *yose*, a dwindling handful of which still exists.

The *manzai* are a different branch growing out of ancient roots similar to the *rakugo*, and they operate in pairs. Said to have come originally from the Nagoya area, the *manzai* would go from house to house around New Year like mountebanks, telling comical stories which they enlivened with clowning and repartee. Like many costumed Shinto festival celebrants doing similar rounds, including the revellers of phallic festivals, they were also sought for driving evil from the house. These days, the *manzai* are contrasting comical duos of a more vaudevillian kind. Appearing in theatres and on TV, theirs is mostly the universal repartee between smart and stupid clowns, the former underscoring his wisecracks by clobbering his denser companion over the head with a rolled-up newspaper. As amply evidenced in the cinema, in these increasingly permissive times the trend is significantly towards satire; TV comedians such as Beat Takeshi stage acidic skits pointedly parodying institutions in a manner unthinkable only a decade ago.

A large amount of the material both comedians and

comic storytellers exploit revolves around sex. Kneeling on-stage in a smart grey kimono and very ingeniously punctuating their stories with a fan, the *rakugo* often retell old tales revolving around such perennial favourite stock characters as the nagging wife, the insatiable farm girl, the sly seducer and the cuckold, all of whom find their equivalents in Rabelais, Boccaccio or Chaucer. Other stories tell of enchanted animals: the Lothario who finds that the maid he bedded on the eve was really a fox-spirit; the townswoman whose lazy husband is changed into a horse by a magic potion. Starting with the head, the animal rubs on the potion to change back into a man but just as he reaches his midriff, the insatiable woman stops him: 'That's far enough.' Handed down through the generations from a rural past, many tales are set in an agricultural context. Although everyone has heard the story countless times before, a good *rakugo* has his own special way of miming, nuancing and mimicking the voices to bring down the house.

ART, DISSENT AND SELF-LIBERATION

Sex, a pleasure principle forever in opposition to the work ethic in Japan as everywhere, is one of the areas in which authority is most wonted to impose its presence. Japanese Confucianism sees sex as a diversion from the straight and narrow of social duty and, when not a conjugal obligation with procreation in mind, it is grudgingly conceded as a diversion only and should not be allowed to go too far. In a country where open protest is rare at the best of times and could sometimes be severely punished in the past, licentiousness becomes all the more easily a substitute for subversion. From its very beginnings, the kabuki was not only a theatre of innuendo but physical licentiousness; as government repression increased, so the genre took a more oblique – and refined – turn.

Theatre forms openly melding provocation and titillation became more common after the Second World War. The 1947 play *Gates of Flesh* elevated its episodic semi-nudity and prostitute heroines with edifying implications of self-sacrifice, launching an entire genre less given to saving graces. As in most places, a variety of sins can be covered by an artistic alibi in Japan. During the sixties, the shockwaves of violent student dissent spread through the theatre scene and resulted in the *an-gura* – the underground, or the avant-garde theatre movement. Some troupes became internationally famous, such as that of Kara Juro and even more particularly that of the late Shuji Terayama, whose weird oedipal themes and bizarre *retro*-surrealist props and costumes included the trappings of bondage and SM. Initially, pure provocation was part of the Terayama picture, and his famous Tenjo Sajiki troupe's first performances were often raided by police. 'All life', Terayama used to contend, 'is scandalous.'

Today, the old troupe keeps the flag flying with its Banyuin-Ryoku successor, which has earned critical accolades around Europe. Dai San Erotica is another major and much-travelled current exponent of the provocative Japanese avant-garde, although it has now similarly entered the respectable mainstream. Hundreds of struggling troupes performing in tiny basement theatres, especially in areas near universities, are still the provocative mainstay of the movement. In this more flippant age, activist messages are out of fashion but, if the emphasis is more heavily on form than content than it ever was, the tendency to challenge authority with outrageous subject matter is alive and well. The flavour and props might be very Japanese, but the *an-gura* runs often along the lines of the western 'happening' theatre-forms of the sixties. One is reminded of the on-stage hash-smoking and stripping provocations of America's Living Theatre; although the merest whiff of the former is the swiftest way to jail in Japan, the question of removing clothing belongs to a nebulous welter of rules in which the artistic alibi can work wonders for a small theatre, provided it takes care to keep a low profile. G-strings ensure a play a longer run, although many fringe-theatre events are anyway staged little more than twice.

Genqui Numata, thirty-five years old, is the Bonsai Kid. A well-known performance artist on the Tokyo avant-garde scene, he has earned some admirers abroad, including the late Andy Warhol. Genqui's career began with a diploma from a traditional bonsai school, but whether his green-thumbed professors approve of this conceptualist approach to their ancient potted art is debatable. Wearing his hair in a samurai top-knot and dressed up as a bonsai with a giant plastic flowerpot around his midriff, the Kid took off along the Tokaido road pushing a cart, planting a miniature tree at each of the fifty-three stations between Tokyo and Kyoto. On-stage in the same bonsai attire, Genqui sings early sixties Japanese pop songs with subverted and abrasive lyrics. The vocal backing is provided by leggy Bonsai-ettes wearing teeny-tiny flowerpots.

'What irks me', Genqui explains, 'is the intense, for-malized way the Japanese look at art, when art is above all a matter of self-expression.' A born cultural *agent provocateur*, Genqui recently pushed his leanings a step further with a caustic striptease event he called 'Harenchi [shamelessness] a Go-Go' incorporating the Momokira avant-garde theatre duo comprising the strippers Momoko and Kirara. As they danced around nude through a variety of parodies in 'Harenchi', clowning Genqui presided over the event as the Art Angel. A ridiculous figure painted white with matching fluffy wings wired to his back, the Angel sported a Dali moustache and wore only a *fundoshi* loincloth. A long-haired wig and an artist's beret completed the picture. Genqui's art is much given to outrageous practical jokes. To its chagrin, a large camera firm backed one of his shows in a noted Shinjuku theatre in 1988, without first checking overmuch on the content. There may be a little nudity, Genqui had warned but, deferring to the dictates of art, they gave their consent. Called 'X-Day', the event mocked the emperor system and was brazenly staged during the months that Emperor Hirohito lay on his deathbed. Momoko danced in a mourning kimono around a coffin, but the choreography grew increasingly frenzied until she wound up contorting herself in the altogether with a white fan printed with a black sun. Wearing a gilt paper crown, the Art Angel emerged at last from the imperial coffin to make the outrage complete.

Having half-anticipated that the theatre would be raided by the police, Genqui had taken pains to relay the entire event on large video screens, so that the bust was at once presented in detail before the uproarious audience, and recorded in its entirety. As the naked Momoko was dragged off indignantly kicking and screaming by bewildered policemen, the half-naked Art Angel sneaked surreptitiously out of the second-floor window where a waiting video cameraman followed him as he tiptoed through the Shinjuku streets to the amazement of passing crowds. At the bidding of the embarrassed and powerful camera company, known for its official photographs of the imperial family, no charges were pressed. After coverage of the event in a lurid weekly, however, Genqui hardly dared leave his house for a fortnight, during which ultra-rightist thugs paraded outside shaking their fists.

The correlation between sex and the theatre can be due to more than just provocation, particularly where actresses are concerned. In Tokyo's Shibuya, for instance, there is a small striptease theatre which, after an undistinguished beginning, has for some years specialized in bizarre erotic shows by a steady stream of small female troupes from the lunatic fringe. The list of film actresses who started life after drama school in porno films and striptease would not only be a very long one, but would also include some of Japan's most famous film stars. For all the negative connotations of resorting to porno to survive, the aversion is clearly not nearly so strong as in the West. Kirara for one, the dancer of the Momokira troupe sometimes collaborating with Genqui Numata, has no regrets about the turn of her career.

Erotic performances mean provocation to some, but to others, like Kirara, they also mean self-liberation. Studying the dramatic arts at university, she worked first of all with puppets, because she 'liked working with dolls more than with people'. She was nevertheless attracted to *butoh*, a form holding a prominent place in the Japanese avant-garde but generally more highly regarded overseas. For a young woman now working primarily as a glamorous stripper, opting for the grimacing and contortionist mime of *butoh* seems a strange one. 'Actually, it's the grotesque side of *butoh* that attracted me. I've never wanted to do straight plays and drama. I liked the idea of becoming something not entirely human.'

Offered a job as a *butoh* dancer during a drama festival in the late seventies, Kirara found that there was a catch: she had to bare all. 'I was very shy, and I still am. I have no self-confidence. As I was having trouble with self-expression at the time, I thought it might be good for me and I gave it a try.' The experience marked the beginning of a career. The real Kirara can barely hide her timidity. Taciturn until she feels sufficiently at ease to be more talkative, she is pretty in a rather self-effacing way, wearing an elegant, sombre dress and no make-up. On-stage, on the other hand, she presents all the difference between Lana Lang and Supergirl. Appearing in dance drama events of her own creation as the flamboyant and sinister Mantis Queen, she is the ultimate female predator and sovereign of provocation. But this is not her main role. If it seems slightly wasteful that this talented, imaginative performer should settle for second best as a showgirl, Kirara doesn't see it that way.

'At first I thought the cabaret scene was sleazy, performing before ogling male tourists – *ya-na kimochi* [ugh]! But now I get a big kick out of it; it's absurd.' In the end the nude shows were not only more lucrative than *butoh* but they were more fun. 'Show dancing is much easier, more comfortable. It has no meaning. Performance art has messages, which makes it much more difficult. I knew that I couldn't get married with a career like mine anyway and I had doubts about whether I'd ever make it as a serious actress if I took off my clothes. But it had other advantages. It was self-liberating.' Besides, Kirara never felt that what she represented on-stage was a real human being.

'Now I'm a *shoo-dansaa no onna* – a show-dancing-woman,' she says, and you can almost hear her putting quotation marks around the term. If the cabaret audiences see her only as a *femme-objet*, so be it. The Showgirl is a character of her own making – a doll, an artificial alter ego and a conscious effort to create a human work of art, which she perfects in the same way as would a geisha or a kabuki actor. On tour through the strip and cabaret circuit, Kirara also photographs her glamorous super-self in dressing-room mirrors, less through narcissism than as a conscious ploy to detach herself more critically from her creation. The living doll featured in the photographs, which were recently shown in a gallery and in weekly magazines, is a provocative monument of make-believe so far removed from its creator that she is unrecognizable. Diffident, retiring but nevertheless a rebel at heart, as the nude dancer – the Showgirl – Kirara finds fulfilment. Coming from a conservative background in a conservative country, it is her most powerful statement.

It can, however, have pitfalls. Kirara's parents have no idea about her alter ego. On one occasion, as she danced wearing only a tiara and a feather boa in a large Tokyo cabaret, her heart shot up into her mouth. Sitting at a table near the stage with a group of colleagues was her father. 'I couldn't stop dancing, of course, I had to go on,' the reluctant Salome recalls. 'It was agonizing. I was praying that I wouldn't faint halfway.' Kirara's dramatis persona passed the ultimate test. 'Luckily,' she concludes with a triumphant smile, 'he didn't even recognize me.'

BLEATING ABOUT THE BUSH: CENSORSHIP IN JAPAN

There's nothing surprising about the government hanging on so bitterly to article 175 of the penal code: it exists solely to let them tell the people: 'Don't even think of doing as you like.' It is in fact their only means of showing their power to repress the people's self-expression ... Those who are accused of 'obscenity' today are being falsely accused. The government is flexing its muscles, and those accused under article 175 are not, in fact, being tried for the crime of 'obscenity', but as opponents of authority. In my opinion, I am summoned here today in the same capacity. Sooner or later, was this summons not inevitable?

Nagisa Oshima, from his plea during his obscenity trial
(January 1976)

The man with the well-groomed pepper-and-salt hair and a stylish tweed sports jacket is Shoji Suei, a writer specializing in Japanese sexual customs and the *mizu shobai*. He is best known for *Dynamite Mama*, a sad and in every sense explosive book about his mother, who blew herself up with her apartment out of hopelessness over an illicit love affair. Mild and soft-spoken, Suei hardly seems a rebel – let alone a prominent pornographer. As a graphic design student during the late sixties, he leapt energetically into political activism and dissent and, dropping out from the orthodox design scene, he began devising gaudy posters and promotional pamphlets for cabarets. As he came to direct shows and sexy dance routines, he drifted into the cabaret scene itself. But it got a bit stagnant, Suei recalls: 'Wanting to do something of my own, I moved into magazines, starting up with a crew of dissenters who felt the same way.'

Today Suei heads his group of like-souls in running Byakuyōsha, a small but significant publishing empire producing some twenty glossy monthly magazines, all but two of which are erotic. Not entirely a matter of exploiting nudie pictorials, the initial idea was rooted in the time-honoured notion of using licentiousness as a weapon for undermining authority. 'We set out to produce sex magazines with political overtones,' Suei explains, 'but although we didn't carry things too far with nudity, we found that the police showed up just as fast if we got too frankly political. Naturally, sex easily becomes an excuse for things which upset the authorities even more.'

Times have changed since the early seventies. Political dissent has gone out of fashion and the focus narrows down more exclusively on pornography. Independently of legal, provocative and dissenting aspects, the traditional idea of hiding and disguising things is, according to Suei, beginning to die out. 'Now it's just a question of circumventing restrictions; the bottom line is business.'

Against rather considerable odds, greater permissiveness has inched its way into the media, mostly carried step by step by the producers of porno films, videos and magazines. Those involved in the erotic media are constantly engaged in a bizarre game of brinkmanship vis-à-vis the authorities by going as far as they dare. Like beauty, it seems, obscenity is in the eyes of the beholder. Regarding representations of the naked human form, it took the West centuries of quibbling to define what was 'art' and what was 'pornography'. The legal dividing line is narrowing, but the debate goes on. In Japan, it doesn't. Or precious little. Basically, current Japanese ruling amounts to an all-out war on the depiction of one single, unruly little black anatomical detail: pubic hair. If unchecked, it seems, the very fabric of society would be severely eroded and the nation cast into untold depths of depravity.

In 1985, differences between French cultural mores and the Japanese Customs created a minor diplomatic uproar. Typically, the crux of the matter revolved around the crotch. Scheduled for a Tokyo exhibition, nudes taken by the master surrealist photographer Man Ray during the thirties were impounded by the Customs and Tariff Bureau of the Finance Ministry. The pictures, they insisted, would first have to have their offending portions blacked out: they 'failed to comply with local standards'. With French diplomatic ire and pressure from the Foreign Ministry, however, the exhibition was held at last with the pictures intact.

This is the exception rather than the rule. Among countless similar incidents, a 1986 ban on uncensored Tokyo screenings of celebrated Italian *auteur* films incensed Italy's national press. Several angry Japanese individuals have elected to fight customs (in both senses of the term) over anything from artworks to the odd copy of *Playboy* ferreted from luggage at Narita airport. Without diplomatic clout, however, such detractors find themselves caught in a web of bureaucracy revolving around subparagraph 3, paragraph 1, Article 21 of the Customs Tariff Law. They have a right to protest according to the Constitution, for such censorship arguably amounts to a denial of the right to freedom of expression, but protesting involves complex, long and dauntingly expensive legal procedures with little hope of a successful outcome. Japanese officialdom spares no effort to 'safeguard public morals'.

As innocent as nudity may be in ordinary, non-erotic foreign films, nude is rude to the obdurate upholders of the Customs Tariff Law. Kazuko Kawakita of France Eiga-sha, a prestigious importer of quality foreign films known abroad as the Shibata Organization, explains: 'You have to declare films containing nude scenes to the Finance Ministry and censor them yourself. So you scratch out pubic hair frame by frame, or blur it with blobs of glycerine. Then you take the print down to the customs and they check it on a Moviola.'

Riveted to the screen, tut-tutting officials point out any naughty bits that got away. 'They're pretty finicky,' she says. 'They measure censorship in millimetres and it drives one crazy.' Indeed. These officials were recently very miffed when France Eiga-sha overlooked a wisp of pubic hair in a recent French *auteur* film. While turning her back to the camera, a woman taking a shower had revealed her shadowy frontage, a fact which neither the importers nor anyone else with better things to do had even noticed: the outrage amounted to four frames of film – one-sixth of a second.

Having been defaced, countless prominent foreign films shown in Japan display a salacious element where none was intended; similarly blurred, the naked dead in war documentaries seem tainted with repellent shades of necrophilia. Incredibly, zealous Japanese censors managed to find and blur highly unlikely nudity deep in the background of Milos Forman's *Amadeus*. The list of examples is endless, but the censorship saga around Tinto Brass's Roman porn epic *Caligula* in 1980 was a gem. Although made in both hard and soft-core versions, Japanese importers opted for the former. Many distributors prefer the compromise of blurring to overt scissoring, and not a few claim audiences find films that have been blurred more titillating than those censored with cuts. Finally *Caligula* transpired to contain so much nudity that censorship became a daunting task. To the tune of several million yen, a special computer was programmed to detect and electronically blank out the beaver with blobs of light. Thus processed, the many nude crowd scenes improbably resulted in a hilarious galaxy of little dancing stars.

In 1985, a serious ruckus jeopardized the future of the first Tokyo International Film Festival. Among English speakers, the furore almost made the initials TIFF into a standing joke. Brazilian director Hector Babenco (*Kiss of the Spider Woman*) and British director Michael Radford (*1984*) threatened to withdraw their entries if the customs defaced a single frame of film. Japan's international yearnings overrode compliance with 'local standards' and the films were finally shown intact. To safeguard public morals later on, however, they would have to be censored for general release. As Radford's bleak *1984* unfolded, appropriately with its miserably naked protagonists arrested by the forces of Big Brother, the scene set a precedent for subsequent festivals and found news photographers avid for Japan's first public cinematic muff shots clicking away in the darkened auditorium.

As bizarre, violent and extreme as permitted printed sex fantasies can be, minus pubic hair and visible genitalia anything goes. In comics, visual metaphors are the norm. The symbolic vocabulary for the male organ includes flutes, elongated horses' heads, snakes and steam locomotives and these home in on the female equivalents in flowers, ponds, tunnels and assorted molluscs. A highly suggestive and popular alternative consists of familiarly shaped and highly evocative blank spaces. Ploys to circumvent censorship attain ludicrous extremes: the Japanese edition of *Penthouse* magazine recently featured plaster casts of the inbetweenies of nude female models. Sold under sealed plastic covers, explicit *biniru bon* (vinyl books) literally outstripped the bounds of tacit tolerance. Following a police crackdown in 1980, *biniru-bon* publishers briefly got away with violation of the laws dictating the cladding of the crotch by using nude models in transparent panties.

One lurid, mass-circulation candid photo magazine a few years later featured montages of scantily clad young women, grotesquely arranged around only the innermost details of their intimate anatomies. Too close for adjacent hairs, gross surgical focusing resulted in abstractions apparently appeasing the authorities. Another magazine recently got away with a photo-spread of enlarged female genitalia simply by partially covering them with thick gobs of bright yellow paint. Such enlarged genital abstractions have been publicly shown in photographic exhibitions in galleries, but a handsome, bona fide art book published in 1986 by the Mainichi newspaper group containing nude studies by top international photographers met a less fortunate fate: police seized the copies as soon as they hit the stands.

Although Japan subjects photographs, films and videos to strict censorship, art exhibitions featuring graphically erotic works are not unusual – provided they consist of drawings or paintings and no interconnected genitals. Many of the wizened exponents of Japan's enduring post-impressionist school, for instance, seem rather partial to painting bushy bar-room nudes. Although they are recognized as treasures of world art, erotic *shunga* woodblock prints by great Edo-period artists are invariably censored in Japan. Thousands of books about *shunga* have been published, but the merest hint of genitalia is masked during printing. In more lavish and expensive editions, the printed mask is coloured silver or gold, rather like repair work conducted on valuable dynastic porcelain bowls. As to why Japanese classical prints should be censored more than equally explicit contemporary art, one can only surmise that over the years, censoring traditional art has itself become a tradition. Nevertheless the pubic mask is showing signs of lifting at the corners. The change is tacit, making itself evident with suddenly uncensored *shunga* piled high and unpenalized on bookshop shelves. Judging by these, female genitalia are acceptable but, if connected with the male, the outrage must be masked, as must representations of the male genitals, unless in the form of a disembodied votive phallus.

Paradoxically, censorship tends to be far stricter for imported items than for domestic ones. If Japanese publications sometimes sport unretouched, albeit very discreet nudes, the same does not apply to material from overseas. A 1985 'Japan Special' of the famed French art magazine *Zoom* featured female nudes by hyper-realist painter Ikuo Ikeda. Although centred graphically between navel and mid-thigh, these have been exhibited around Japanese galleries and published in domestic magazines.

'A drawing is a drawing,' reads a gleeful French text, 'so Ikeda has blown rice flour into the eyes of the Japanese state inspectors.' Perhaps. But when it came to importing the same works in a foreign magazine, where state censors could have had the last laugh, they merely succeeded in deepening their fatuousness in foreign eyes. One of *Zoom*'s Ikeda nudes bordered frankly on the pornographic, while another revealed the merest pubic fuzz just peeping over a concealing cluster of soap bubbles. When it came to censorship, they scratched the pubic hair from the latter, leaving its bald counterpart to deride their ludicrous oversights with a triumphant vertical smile.

Every month, a flood of over 30,000 copies of foreign girlie magazines is subjected to grotesque Orwellian processing at the customs office in Yokohama. With public morals uppermost in its collective mind, a caucus of customs officials bravely subjects itself to a meticulous scrutiny of a given magazine and red-pencils the offending portions. The master copy is then handed on to the next department. Significantly, the task of eradicating pubic hair from this virtuous man's world is assigned to a group of some two dozen women.

Arming themselves with brushes and indelible ink exhaustively tested for its resistance to solvents, these worthy ladies proceed to black out tens of thousands of anatomical no-nos. An alternative technique involves scratching just the printing ink from the surface of the paper. There's never an idle moment. After the usual monthly batch of magazines such as *Playboy*, *Lui*, *Penthouse* et al have been through the mill, bona fide artistic and fashion publications from abroad are subjected to rigorous scrutiny pending the same treatment; and the importers foot the bill. It seems incredible that anyone should go to such absurd lengths over such a trivial issue. Surely, it would be simpler to ban the importation of such publications and films altogether?

'Those dealing with censorship are the *madogiwa-zoku* [the tribe that looks out of the window: i.e. supernumeraries] of the National Police Agency,' says Suei. 'It's as though they had nothing better to do. Not that they're in any way hateful or unreasonable. They've called me forty times. They give stern warnings, but they can be sympathetic about it too. They're doing their job; we're doing ours. Both sides know it.'

During the 1971 Sapporo Winter Olympics, overseas participants' embarrassing remarks about Japan's disfigurement of foreign magazines caught the attention of the press. This prompted an influential Socialist Party representative to denounce the matter before the Diet in 1972 as an infringement of the constitutional right of freedom of expression. After two parliamentary sessions and eight years of dithering in between, the Finance Ministry finally reached a remarkable decision in 1981. According to an article in *Shukan Shincho* magazine, there would be 'about a 5 per cent reduction in the number of squares and black dots censoring imported magazines that the authorities consider to be harmful to public morals'. In other words, the Finance Ministry and the National Pub(l)ic Safety Commission distinguished

Japan not only as the only country officially tallying pubic hair, but doing so in percentages.

To support this nebulous measuring system, Finance Ministry officials came up with characteristically vacuous arguments in the press. Restrictions would be eased on photographs and films containing full frontal nudity, unless 'they are considered to arouse sexual desire excessively'. If this seemed to read as a concession for all things in moderation in 1981, the negligible resulting changes since imply that officials are still excessively aroused by depictions of nakedness – alive or dead. Above all, the famous local standards must not be jeopardized.

'Full frontal nudity may be shown in films and publications that do not offend established sexual mores in Japanese society ... and which do not feature obscenity.' In nearly all industrialized countries, 'obscenity' requires and gets at least some concrete definition; pornography is either banned outright or sensibly relegated to places in which it can't offend its opponents. But not in Japan. One statement summed up the Finance Ministry's 'more flexible attitude' of 1981 most eloquently of all. 'The new ruling also applies to photographs which use shadows to obscure genital areas.' In other words, pubic hair is fine in photographs that show no pubic hair.

As always, the staunch upholding of 'local standards' reflects the virtuous ideals of ruling entities rather than the realities of the street and defies all logic. Of what conceivable importance, one might be forgiven for arguing, could be the odd tuft of pubic hair, or indeed even a few exposed genitals, compared to the violent splatter in videos and comic books and the denigrating and humiliating image given women in the same? The notion that the censorship of sexual iconography is inconsistent with other mores never even enters the picture, for logic is neither seen as a virtue nor granted a priority as high as in the West, where it is paramount. How and where else, after all, could a body such as the Finance Ministry be entrusted with defining and upholding public morals?

As though still laid down by Confucian tribal elders, the letter of the law is doggedly obeyed and accepted with wary fatalism. Now as always, governmental rulings in moral areas tend to be arbitrary, a relic of the nineteenth century and far behind the times. But until ousted with unexpected suddenness, which is generally how change comes about in Japan, the established letter of the law is beyond question, no matter how irrational it is or ridiculous it becomes over the years.

That there has in fact been relatively little protest about censorship among intellectuals in Japan, even in this democratic age, Suei puts down to a perennial acceptance of the status quo. 'Censorship is illogical,' Suei reflects, 'but it has something about it that is typically Japanese – the hidden is not only more titillating, but more powerful. For example, you only get to see the Emperor on his balcony a couple of times a year. In that way the Emperor and porno are almost the same! Also, even in daily contexts, the Japanese are vague at the best of times. They never say anything straight.'

The notable exception to the rule and the most famous recent battle against censorship waged by Japanese intellectuals was that surrounding film director Nagisa Oshima in 1976. Arguably one of world cinema's only erotic masterpieces and shown uncensored abroad, *Ai no Korida* (*The Realm of the Senses*) made even hard core respectable. Audaciously flouting the censorship laws, Oshima shot the film in Japan and had it developed in Paris, where he edited it. But it was not the film itself, which was heavily censored in Japan, that got Oshima into trouble; it was a glossy Japanese book about the film. Although it included the unexpurgated script and was copiously illustrated with stills, it showed not a wisp of pubic hair. It was seized nevertheless and the subsequent obscenity trial dragged on through 1978.

'In court cases such as these,' Suei maintains, 'to try to make whatever the issue is pass as art is a fatal mistake. The point is to try to force the court to define obscenity.' And this is exactly what Oshima had done. Through his eloquent argument and with wide public support, he eventually won his case.

Although the Oshima incident made great waves in the press, it heralded only minimal changes. If the domestic book paved the way for a modicum of greater tolerance, the cosmetic amendments of 1981 only succeeded in making the import situation even sillier. Japanese intellectuals certainly continue to deplore censorship, but most have given up active campaigning. Up against a brick wall of obdurate officialdom, they are by now resigned to irrational censorship as a fact of life; the system the authorities like to term 'voluntary self-restraint' is effective indeed. What Kazuko Kawakita points out regarding the cinema applies as much to anything else: 'No one wastes time with trials, which take years. Withholding the release of a film would lose you more money in the meantime. You just can't win.'

One worried about winning is Shoji Suei, who has been steadily pushing his luck with censorship over the years. 'Pubic hair was out,' he says, recalling the early days of a magazine called *Shashin Jidai* (*Photo Generation*), 'so for our photographs, we hit upon the idea of shaving them. That worked for a brief spell, until the authorities busted us on the grounds that pubic hair was "supposed" to be there. So in subsequent issues I kept the shaved pubis and put the hairs back on with a magic marker. Naturally, that wouldn't do either. So to show up the silliness of the whole thing, we did a series of naked girls with fake pubic hair reaching all the way up to their necks. Even the police laughed.' But the joke wore off. In March 1988, Byakuyōsha was raided and *Shashin Jidai* was banned.

'For a long time I'd played the whole thing almost like a game. This time I'm afraid I lost. I made a big mistake.' Suei had pushed his luck too far. The size of the black masks had been gradually shrinking, until at last they were mere specks too small to meet police approval.

Censorship showed signs of easing for a while and in some contexts still is, but the revisions to the morals law in 1985 were a setback. 'Come the Tokyo summit in 1986,' Suei believes, as was the case during the 1964 Olympics, 'things got tighter still. After the furore over the censorship of an Antonioni movie during an Italian film festival, things have gone backwards.'

BYE-BYE PINK CINEMA, HELLO ADULT VIDEO

> Naturally, the eroduction is, like all pornographic productions, masturbatory cinema. The audience is not thinking about women, it is thinking about itself. The most elemental of fantasies being enacted before it, it is caught, trapped in its own elemental and hence infantile nature. In Japan the eroduction seems to be like a habit, like smoking, drinking, biting the nails. Its gratifications are instant, meaningless, and necessary.
>
> Donald Richie, *The Japanese Eroduction* (1972)

The American Occupation combed its way through aspects of Japanese culture in a bid to eradicate the bugs of what it termed feudalism, but it also opened up vast new avenues of freedom in other directions. Even as it imposed strict censorship on feudally orientated fare in the cinema, it lifted it elsewhere. In 1946, the screen's first kiss was as big a sensation as the appearance of the first female film stars in the early twenties. Even though this momentous osculation was partially concealed behind an umbrella, it set a precedent for all time. The lighter and darker sides of sex crept gradually into the cinema during the fifties, from Mizoguchi's stark dramas of exploited prostitutes to flighty comedies about strippers.

A popular genre of the early sixties, *taiyo-zokku* (sun tribe) films focused on rich, dissolute beachside teenage delinquents. Many eminent directors had a provocative stab at the genre, and in his famous *Cruel Tale of Youth*, Nagisa Oshima took it off the beach and out of the sun to use it for exposing sociopathies. For the majority, however, it was just a vehicle for plentiful sexual high jinks. The sun tribe films were immensely popular, but some soon fell foul of the authorities and were instrumental in tightening the *Eirin* self-censorship system in the cinema.

Japan's mass-movie audience dwindled under the onslaught of television during the sixties. Faced with bankruptcy in 1971 after nearly sixty years of operation, the venerable Nikkatsu film company launched a new genre: *roman poruno* (porno romance), an offshoot of what was already becoming known as *pinkku eiga* – pink cinema. Meanwhile after overboiling over the renewal of the Security Treaty with the US in 1960, student activism had been simmering in Japan for a decade. Like the producers of porno agitprop magazines, many pink directors were radicals using the sexual medium as a weapon for dissent. Messages lay notably beneath the often very gory and hysterical rape and torture fantasies of Koji Wakamatsu, as they did in the blend of sexual liberation, social realism and grotesquerie characterizing the films of Noboru Tanaka.

Since the exponents of both haunted the same Shinjuku bars and challenged a common enemy, many pink films presented the same cathartic outbursts of violent abandon as the theatrical fringe. The situation was nevertheless ambiguous and muddled. Some directors used porno as socio-political provocation, others touted the lofty ideals of art and dissent merely as an alibi. However reluctantly and whether they could tell the one from the other or not, the bastions of law and morality had to swallow a certain dose of dissent; such is democracy. Censorship nevertheless remained severe, especially when it came to nudity, and many 'pink directors' found their films banned.

Notwithstanding their staunch if rarely productive opposition to censorship, many former sixties radicals engaged in the current sex media look back on the heyday of *roman poruno* with some regret. As one put it very typically: 'Directors had to look for ways to circumvent stricter censorship. Since they were working more with suggestiveness and using sex for socio-political messages, they made more interesting films.'

Monopolizing the *roman poruno* genre, Nikkatsu churned out nothing else at a rate of three pictures a month for over fifteen years, during which time soft porn accounted for a whopping two-fifths of Japan's entire domestic film output. The company was reputed to be a breeding ground for future cinematic talent; in a few of the films, it showed. Protracted shorts rarely lasting more than an hour, they were geared for the now rapidly vanishing porno cinema, which men would drift into indiscriminately in the middle of one film and out halfway through the next, or sleep off a hangover. If a few pink films really stood out from the welter of insignificance, the last place to see them today is Japan, where popular culture dictates rapid change and rarely harbours much enthusiasm for the recent past. Recognized for their cinematic merits abroad and forgotten at home, the best of *roman poruno* and *pinkku eiga* join countless Japanese films of other kinds in drawing a steady public of buffs in America and Europe.

The cinema is ailing everywhere, but in Japan, in which it receives no government support, it looks qualitatively if not yet quite quantitatively close to its last gasp. As revealing about sexual mores and fantasies as they are, and as interesting as some of the films may be, there would be little point in going into pink cinema here except as history. Faced with the proliferation of video, a novel medium affording an armchair porno audience indulgences unthinkable in the theatre, the Nikkatsu company joined in the fray it could not beat. In 1987 the soft-porn cinema came to a very abrupt end. Nagisa Oshima wrote a long diatribe in the press: the demise of the pink film was a symptom of the decline of the Japanese cinema in general. It was an eloquent obituary, but the public hardly even noticed.

Proliferating in their thousands around Japan, video rental outlets now stand several to a neighbourhood in large cities. Representing about a quarter of their total shelf space, *adaruto* (adult) video also amounts to a third of their income. Open until midnight, they do a brisk trade with single men moved to grab the latest *honban* hard-core cassette on their way home. In view of Japan's stringent and arbitrary censorship laws, one might well wonder about the appropriateness of the term 'hard core'. Following a trend that began during the twilight of the pink film, however, directors have had members of the cast diligently performing *honban* (for real), which made a novel departure from the former practice of rubbing tummies together with handkerchiefs taped over privates. The *honban* was then masked on-screen, often by superimposing a flowerpot or the arm of a chair on the negative. Video is more versatile. Today the answer lies either in a mosaic screen masking the genital areas or a solarizing effect dressing them up in the most amazing colour schemes, but the surreal greens and yellows have been gradually giving way to more daring pinks and purples, browns and flesh-tones. The mosaic is currently getting finer, the genitals appearing only about as blurred as they might in some pornographic impressionist painting. Another technique finds them framed in a circle, with the female mollusc and whichever male organ happens to be exploring it appearing in sharp detail in mono-chrome against the surrounding coloured back-ground.

That anyone could get away with this despite stringent laws is typically Japanese; a matter of respecting the law to the letter while bending it outside its provisions: *tatemae* hiding *honne*. It is also a matter of luck. Turning their eyes away from the phenomenon for the time being, the guardians of morality must anyway be overwrought. More than 4,000 porno videos are made annually between over seventy companies, many of which are shady concerns changing names overnight. Last week's hard-core videos are regularly replaced by a fresh batch, which also goes for the *honban* porno actresses who, exalted as superstars in men's magazines and celebrated in late-night TV rundowns on the latest porn videos, are here today and gone tomorrow. On the backs and lids of the serried ranks of cassette boxes shelved in the video stores, elfin schoolgirls or more seasoned little tarts grin coyly in sexy undies and soft focus or look pleadingly out at the browser from the black leather trappings of bondage and SM.

One might be surprised to find that the shelves also contain animated cartoons. Animation accounts for a tenth of Japan's entire film output, which is the highest ratio in the world. In a country given to prizing symbols over reality, in which females are incarnated by actors and in which puppets once made an acceptable substitute for human beings, cartoons are not necessarily aimed at children at all. In the 'Cream Lemon' porno cartoon series, cute little nymphets with big Bambi eyes and squeaky voices do the most amazing sado-masochistic things within the confines of a girl's convent; in another, an adolescent boy gazes at the effluvia of desire running down his sister's thighs, before they embark graphically on an incestuous relationship. According to the manager of one local video outlet, pornographic cartoons are mostly popular with young women, which is why they tend to be discreetly shelved alongside more modest subjects.

Picking up a handful at random, one discovers that the average video targets students and young *salarymen* and goes something like this: boy stalks girl in street to a feeble disco backing maintained throughout, and the camera slithers along the pavement for high-angle pantie shots as she minces along. Porno film heroes seem most at ease in more sadistic contexts, perhaps as a door-to-door rapist specializing in students and housewives. Here, since the boy turns shy at the last moment, the girl entices him and betrays herself as a perfect slut. Next they ogle each other over drinks in a trendy café-bar, before spending the remaining thirty minutes of video time doing all manner of variations on the theme in a hotel/apartment/seaside cottage. Then they part company as the music subsides after the climactic crescendo: the end.

An alternative for the working generation provides fantasy in an office setting: beside herself with excitement after being molested in the lift by a man masturbating behind his briefcase, the Office Lady allows an ugly, acned and thickly bespectacled *bucho* (section chief) to have sex with her. First in a chair, next on the carpet and then even up on the roof of the building. At last they climax on his desk. With a rock-bottom budget and protagonists rivalling the locations for tackiness, the camerawork is as poor as the lighting. Plots and subtleties are generally superfluous. This is going back fifty years to the old blue movie: the forty-minute video equivalent to the ten-minute stag film.

Shooting on bigger budgets, some video productions sandwich the porno bedroom activity between scenes shot in exotic locations, or even in fantasy and horror contexts calling upon fancy special effects. Camerawork in some of the more elaborate videos shows a very high degree of proficiency. Notwithstanding all this, few videos bother with much of a plot. Often representing whopping returns for minimal investment, videos are shot cheaply in love hotels and sometimes even in the production offices. Nevertheless, many exploit their very limitations with a conscious effort at documentary realism: the *cinéma-vérité* of pornography. Protagonists, cameramen and directors talk throughout the proceedings even as they are taped. In between the sex episodes, the actors discuss what they feel about what they've just done or are about to do. As his wary female partner listens wide eyed, 'There is nothing', affirms one male protagonist to another, 'like applying Tiger Balm on the clitoris.' The gasps and screams during the subsequent sex seem to have rather less to do with orgasm than the application of the balm.

The couples performing in hotels are often filmed with the clinical detachment of guinea-pigs experimentally mated in a laboratory. On the other hand, the unrehearsed live action and spontaneous dialogues are strongly reminiscent of the Warholian underground cinema of the sixties, albeit with the interminable talking livened with a welcome quota of sex. 'Aya-chan,' asks the director out of shot, as the post-coitally sweating protagonists lie breathless on the mattress, 'did you come?'

'Oh, yes,' gushes Aya-chan.

'Really, really came?'

'Yes, really.'

'That's great. August congratulations to you both and my reverent thanks for dispensing your energies.' Fade-out.

Sometimes the documentary is faked, predictably with sadistic themes, which nonetheless strive to maintain a spontaneous veneer. In one, for instance, an extraordinarily dense young lady turns up at the production office looking for work. She is vain and supercilious; the interview conversation grows aggressive as the would-be-actress looks more and more nervous and less cut out for the job. Eventually she is pinned down by lusty members of the entourage, who take turns in coercive cunnilingus before raping her on the office floor.

Regarded as an innovator, the man behind the ubiquitously emulated documentary technique is Tōru Muranishi, a former porno actor turned director. Muranishi was one of several recently busted and even briefly jailed for using an underage actress. Not that it was his fault. They don't have to do much talent-scouting for runaways around the train stations these days, the girls come knocking at the office door and have ample incentives to lie about their ages. The biggest single cash outlay in the business goes to the porno actress, who earns 250,000 yen per day on average, a figure which can admittedly be an empty promise among some more unscrupulous concerns, but which doubles at the top of the profession. Meanwhile, the young men are paid only about a tenth of the girl's earnings, for nearly all of them join in the fray merely for kicks.

Muranishi's *Face Shower* series, so-called because the culmination finds the heroine's countenance bespattered with the hero's amorous outpourings, consists of compendia of very basic sequences condensed from his other videos. Each of the girls represents a perennial Japanese fantasy stereotype: the prim Office Lady, the virgin-next-door, the randy farm girl, the leotarded aerobics enthusiast, the sexy predator in the hot-spring resort and, last but not least, the self-assertive slut who is put in her place by being gang-banged on the floor of the cutting room.

As in most of such videos, of the sadistic persuasion or not, the male is a nonentity. Part vehicle for vicarious thrills and part dildo, his face is usually invisible. The focus is preponderantly on the girl, the *femme-objet*, an object of worship and a signifier for masturbatory fantasies. Most adult videos have the simplicity of the old woodblock print, and an inactive third party, the *shunga*'s perennial voyeur, is also nearly always in evidence. While one or two disport themselves with the star on the mattress, a frustrated third representing the spectator sometimes jiggles around in his underpants, either contorting himself in an agony of anticipation or looking on and languidly masturbating.

Muranishi is renowned also for strange, telling little gimmicks which are virtual leitmotivs of sex as social provocation. Actresses attaining orgasm are bidden to blow into a conch shell, rather like the one used as a trumpet in lofty Buddhist rituals. The pornography is not quite enough in itself, there are subtle little asides designed to attack the genteel fabric of conservative society. The current *gurume bumu* (gourmet boom), for instance, finds endless TV food-orientated programmes lensing mindlessly around Japan and abroad. Prim and beauteous young commentators taste dishes *ad nauseam*, invariably coming up with an ecstatic, beaming '*Oishiiiii!*' (delicious). One of Muranishi's videos winds up with an angelically pretty and thoroughly fucked porno actress licking her lips after having just had her face spattered with sperm. After a moment's gustatory reflection she pipes up '*Oishiiii!*' and beams sweetly at the camera.

Muranishi's more famous videos begin often with a sedate and impeccably dressed young woman boldly facing camera and delivering a curious lecture about sexual liberation. She might then be shown aboard a speedboat, the camera panning lovingly over the curves of her revealing swimsuit, before focusing on the generous bushes beneath her arms. Cut to a hotel room: the girl lies naked on a mattress with bespectacled boys staging alarums and excursions in various stages of undress.

'I told you the orgasm had to be real!' threatens the director's angry voice. 'You faked that last one didn't you?'

The heroine is distraught.

'No, I promise you.'

'You're lying aren't you? You faked it!'

She starts to cry. 'Only a little bit. Oh, *director-san*, I'm so sorry!'

'Why, I'll teach you to tell lies!' roars Muranishi, and his foot comes into shot to kick her as his minions dash about the tatami floor, grabbing the pleading heroine and slapping her repeatedly. They swing her around in the air by one foot, as her long hair flails about her head. They knock the slut down onto the mattress and rape her again and again, as she howls lustily.

'That one was real,' wrily enquires Muranishi's voice, 'wasn't it?'

Her face puffy with self-induced crying, porno queen Kaoru Kuroki faces camera with a beatific smile.

'You bet,' she sighs. 'That one was real!'

OUT OF THE ARMPIT, IF IT SHOULD HONOURABLY PLEASE YOU

Porno video, thinks Kaoru Kuroki, cannot be compared to film. Being new and in a category of its own, it might well mark a new direction for Japanese erotica but not the cinema. 'Adult video', she believes, 'has a different atmosphere. It's not very sophisticated, in fact it's primitive.' Not about art, porno video is for satisfying basic desires. 'It's a bit like eating and menus in restaurants: you're hungry and you have a sudden craving for noodles, so you go and eat noodles. Your appetite is towards a porno video, so you go and rent whatever turns you on. And as with food, viewers can use basic ingredients to "cook" the desired stimulation from the video themselves.'

Arguably video is to real sex as junk food is to gourmet cuisine, but then again there are always good and bad hamburgers. No doubt the gourmet does his cooking by manipulating the VTR's fast forward and slow motion knobs as he manipulates his own. 'The best food calls for the freshest ingredients,' Kuroki explains, and as the queen of rude food, she knows what she's talking about. 'What is important to the viewer is how *baajin* [virgin] I appear on camera. He can make a delicious dish out of me!'

And as this most militant of dishes has often been quoted as saying, 'Porno video actresses are the soldiers of the sexual revolution.' In the plush new office of Diamond Productions, Kaoru Kuroki wears an expensive black chiffon dress with white polka dots and thin red piping. She's just a trifle heavy on the make-up, but quite the drawing-room lady. She talks with elegant, expressive little hands with an indefinable hardness about them and from a full red mouth that looks as sensual as it is ruthlessly determined. She is as cute as a pussycat, but the scarlet claws are real. She smiles often, but laughs rarely. She pursues her career with deadly seriousness, which is perhaps why she is not just another porno video queen, but a media superstar. She can be brutally frank, but one of her hallmarks is speaking the most refined, urbane and educated Japanese. She peppers her statements with the formal *de-gozaimasu* (if it should honourably please you), the post-positional condition for the most polite form of address.

Far more bizarre, Kuroki's other hallmark is the unprecedented little gimmick that really boosted her career: she flatly refused to shave the hair under her arms. 'I hate censorship,' she explains. 'On my first day at art school, the model was the first naked woman I had ever seen in public and her nudity left quite an impression on me. I realized how brainwashed I was to be shocked at something as completely natural as pubic hair.'

Hence the rebellious decision to leave her underarms unshaven, although she acknowledges that it was also a 'sales point' in the adult video business. 'More importantly, it was an affirmation of femininity and an assertion of my own identity.'

Her exposure in the media began with the ordinary round of video-sex and other girly magazines, but her novel underarm jibe at censorship attracted the weeklies. When they began to interview her, they were knocked out. Kuroki caught the attention of the mass media. After a first TV appearance, which was predictably on a late-night programme promoting adult videos, her extraordinary blend of outspokenness and polite phrasing made waves: Kuroki had the gift for making the unmentionable seem perfectly banal. She now appears regularly on a great many TV chat shows, not to mention in afternoon programmes for housewives. 'I talk about life as a woman,' she says, 'but with my background, obviously the focus is on sex. I seem to have become a spokeswoman for the too many women who are embarrassed to talk about it.' She deplores the fact that Japanese women, who should by rights have the same sexual freedom as men, see only TV programmes in which male interviewers' childishly titillating questions are always met by giggling girls shrieking '*Yadaa!*'

Becoming a commentator and panellist on TV was something she never expected. 'At first it even made me feel guilty. It wasn't what I was supposed to be doing,' she maintains, for it meant turning away from what she saw as a crusade. 'Obviously, there was some kind of social need for me to be heard.'

And she is. A renowned TV panellist appearing also in commercials and used as a campaign girl for a prestigious department store, the highly articulate Ms Kuroki reaches heights that few female TV personalities in Japan, let alone a porno actress, have achieved at the tender age of twenty-two. Her blend of sex and social rebellion liken her to Italy's La Cicciolina; she is a media counsellor like America's Doctor Ruth.

Finding no outlets for her precocious creative talents at
school, Kuroki left to enter an art college at only fifteen.
She wanted to be a painter herself and in 1988 was still
studying Renaissance art history at Yokohama national
university. She loves cinema too: 'Especially films by
Nagisa Oshima, Ingmar Bergman and Bernardo Berto-
lucci. To me their works suggest an inner struggle – a
kind of yearning for freedom. Sexual freedom was only
part of it, of course, but for me you might say it's a
philosophy, a way of looking at life.'

Kaoru Kuroki (Fragrance Blacktree) is the pseudonym
of the only child of a well-to-do, middle-class family. Her
father is an engineer. 'Like so much of society, life at
home was typically conservative and stifling. Rebellion
is what got me started and why I continue. People are
pretty uptight, even the young. When I started videos, I
found I had far fewer friends at university.' She was still
living at home when she embarked on her new career,
until parental ire prompted her to move out. When her
fame and notoriety increased, it also created problems at
university. 'Although they sent me formal warnings,
they could still find no reason to revoke my student's
card: I guess my kind of case wasn't written in the
books.'

Her distraught mother once warned her that if she
didn't mend her ways, her father would finally be forced
to resign from his job. 'I countered that his company
wouldn't dare; if they forced him to quit,' she said
defiantly, 'I would use it as an example.' She mentioned
a well-known incident during the seventies, when the
father of a political activist committed suicide to atone for
his son's terrorist acts. 'Why should this society continue
to expect others to assume responsibility for actions in
which they have no involvement at all?'

Kuroki believes that because Japanese society precludes personal thinking and opinions, it stifles the creative and even metaphysical side of life. 'You can't escape politics. All human existence is a political statement of some kind or other, especially in a societal context. Whether I talk as a porno star or a student, my political viewpoint is exactly the same. Either way I'm dedicating my life to love and freedom. Attaining ecstasy and sharing it: only sex can do this. Sex makes people happy; sex is pure.'

Be this as it may, is it not strange that in a Kaoru Kuroki video, the woman representing an ideal for liberation is invariably depicted as being humiliatingly slapped around and gang raped? Kuroki doesn't think so. 'As a porno actress people come to expect you to be professionally versed in all the facets of sex, so I have to cater to all tastes. Out of the options, however, I realized that if I'm accepting all this violence, it's because I get a kick out of it.'

As fond as she was of a former boyfriend, Kuroki found, 'I had secret masochistic longings; sex with him was too conventional. I wanted to ask him to do outrageous things, but I was afraid that I'd lose him. In front of the camera, on the other hand, I found myself immediately releasing and fulfilling hidden sexual desires. It was an important revelation to me.' Kuroki anyway feels that her profession is no medium just for depicting conventional sex. 'Porno video shouldn't reflect traditional roles: it should destroy them.'

While in Italy in 1988, Kuroki was pleased to find that she and La Cicciolina (whom she greatly admires and refers to as *sensei*) shared the same views about video as a medium for transcending inhibitions. 'On the other hand, I was amazed at her reticence over SM. We have no Christian morality over here, of course, so we don't really have barriers like that at all.' In the West, however, where there is much greater equality between the sexes, women's lib and SM generally make poor bedmates.

'I don't think her dislike of SM has anything to do with women's lib,' Kuroki says, 'in fact, maybe not even with a system of morals at all. In the end, it's probably just a matter of personal taste. Cicciolina-*sensei* doesn't have any masochistic tendencies; I do.'

Kuroki vehemently refutes the notion that SM scenes are a sign of submission. Neither do they represent a loss in the battle of the sexes nor a betrayal of women's quest for liberation. 'On-screen and off,' she affirms, 'the winning side is the one that gets the orgasm!'

KUROKI ON CAMERA

'I first saw what I do as a kind of performance art,' Kuroki says, 'using my own body as others use paint. And I still see it as a mission.' In fact, in the five years since Kuroki became a media star, around the outlets, one sees fewer of her videos on the shelves. Her career has taken her in other directions, in some ways more than she realizes. She still insists that she is first and foremost a porno actress, and gives quite a different reason for her dwindling erotic appearances: 'Most porno actresses do as many as ten videos a month. I used to, too, but now I do less than that in a year. I find that if you do too many, you finally wind up with a routine and you're faking it.'

As she sees it, the great thing about adult video is realism. She shares the same outlook as Tōru Muranishi in supporting the documentary approach; the best of the genre is what comes closest to a real sexual adventure. It must be spontaneous; it must be 'fresh'. She believes that the idea is to create an encounter between herself and the viewer which, ideally, should stimulate thinking as well as sexual arousal. Because censorship precludes visible genitalia, the sexual stimulus has to be derived from the video in its entirety and not from the details. Independently from the blurred hard core, the peripherals in a Kuroki video are fairly violent stuff. She oscillates between abused sexual slave and the epitome of self-assertion with schizophrenic rapidity. To some, the documentary makes for a jarring experience; the feedback she gets from viewers can be surprising. Some say they almost find her frightening; that they can't get a hard-on. Her videos are no good for masturbation. Kuroki explains that the best are those categorized in the trade jargon as *nukeru* – which means to unsheathe a sword. 'My videos don't let them get their swords out, so to speak, so they're what we call *nukenai* – cannot unsheathe.' Even so, her videos topped the charts by selling some 17,000 cassettes on average which, in this business, represents not only a very big hit but well over a million American dollars.

The maverick Kuroki actively resents being called an actress. The rise of the conventional Japanese actress – from TV through the cinema and up to the theatrical summit – involves a rigorous hierarchy, and she likes to go against it. Adult video requires neither acting ability nor talent, which is exactly what she likes about it. 'I'm just a model,' she contends. 'The point is to get right away from acting and that what you're doing should be for real. Ultimately, what counts most is to be true to yourself. I take pride in being the performer of a primitive art.'

The appropriateness of the word 'model', she says, also lies in its other sense; Kuroki sees herself as a model for women in general. She maintains that if a lot of them support her, it is because she is a revelation to them: she draws out their desires and helps them to discover themselves.

'The men who find my videos frightening often recognize the wilder, more uninhibited side of their own girlfriends. In order to liberate themselves, they must first take off their armour. If a man recognizes Kuroki in his wife or girlfriend, he is forced to strip it off in order to deal with her. That's how I liberate both sexes. I don't really see myself as a feminist at all. It's just that there are a lot of silent women out there and I'm a mouth for them.'

While he agrees, Shoji Suei, who has interviewed her several times for features on her in his magazines, paints a rather more ambivalent portrait:

> As outspoken as she is, one of Kaoru Kuroki's favourite axioms is that woman is man's servant. The social trend is towards equality, but underneath men mostly still disagree. Kuroki panders to this at the same time. Women don't like her just because they agree with her statements on talk shows. If she's a figurehead to some, it's because she's a good talker; she's intelligent. She likes to talk about what whets men's appetites and in her videos she looks as though she's pandering to it. But the point is that she's playing a double game: it's an act, a put-on. They'll invite her to a TV panel discussion focusing on no nukes, for instance, and during the course of the show she can visibly upset the men participating. She represents the absurd.

Kuroki says that she started porno video by way of a personal challenge. 'I wanted to approach it purely as a performance art form, but it turned out to be a lot crazier than that. In fact, if I'd continued to see porno video as art without also acknowledging it as just a fuck film, I wouldn't have gone this far. Initially I thought, "What am I doing here?" I was trying to rationalize but, once I was in front of the camera, it didn't make any sense.' When she found herself lying nude on the mattress before the camera for the first time, it was a memorable experience. 'Censorship has no relevance here, for obviously during recording everything is in the raw. I spread my legs good and wide and watched my pussy being fucked on a video monitor right next to me. It gave me proof of my identity – all of it.'

What she first experienced was a confrontation between the rational and the irrational in which: 'I saw that there was a wall between the controllable and uncontrollable stages of sex. In fact it's the wall of shame.' In other words, the old mask of *tatemae* put up in front of the *honne* of the suppressed self. 'I discovered that if you break it – it's tremendously liberating.'

Lovers are for making love with, she says, porno video actors are something else. The quality she extols as 'freshness' also emerges from the unexpected, because an actress seldom knows who her partner is beforehand. It's a spontaneous encounter, sometimes with an actor or the director. Kuroki works mostly with Muranishi, with whom she started when he was an actor himself. 'I never choose my video partners; that would be too real and too private.' But she enthuses about the alternative: 'I love the adventure, finding out how someone fucks.'

The candidate is often recruited from among the droves of video fans who come to the production office to ask for parts. The director assembles the chosen few together with the video girls, and everyone just sits around talking and drinking beer. Watching them for body language, he suddenly says, 'You and you – go take a bath!' And they're on. The videos are made on locations around Japan and sometimes abroad, with the actors outnumbering the actresses three or four to one.

A forty-minute video, Kuroki says, is shot to a tight schedule and requires three hours' worth of solid humping. A single actor's battery would run down before the end.

Even as we're talking, editors and directors are sitting in the cutting room next door, tanned dark from a recent location trip to Singapore. All the sex scenes, however, have to be shot in Japan with Japanese actresses, otherwise the customs out there impound the videos before they're flown out. In Japan they have to be self-censored on the same basis of 'voluntary restraint' as in the cinema. Tōru Muranishi keeps an ironical eye on his technicians as they create blurs, mosaics and solarizations on the console, leaving as much of the hard-core antics on-screen as they dare.

Kuroki believes that the function of the ubiquitous inactive male third party has a lot to do with censorship. 'Obviously, most viewers are male, so the focus is entirely on the woman. The function of the peeping Tom you get in all these videos is vicarious. His facial expressions put across that the fucking is *honban* – for real. Nikkatsu's *roman poruno* films used artistic disguises, tricks and simulation to stimulate arousal. The video business is much the same.'

Unlike in those days, however, the contention with censorship here revolves around a patch so tiny that it barely conceals the genital areas at all. In any event, the good pornographers are trying to make these smaller still. 'What excites the viewer is the atmosphere – the ambience of sex,' Kuroki believes. 'That's how censorship can work to one's own advantage.'

The directors and technicians, meanwhile, not to mention book and magazine publishers, unanimously echo exactly the same premise, and it sends the corollary of the traditional reaction to repression and the eternal celebration of dissimulation into another dimension. Forming an intrinsic and vital part of the entire picture, it is that of self-deception.

19

The Realm of the Sexless

OKAMA – THE POTTED PERSUASION

Peccatum illud horribile, inter Christianos non nominandum:
the subject is so horribly repulsive and distasteful that the
writer would have preferred to close his eyes to the
existence of this awful phase of human depravity and pass
it by in silence, but friends, in whose judgement he places
entire confidence, have pointed out that the very nature of
this work demands at least a passing allusion to one
terrible form of venery which prevailed in Japan in the
later Middle Ages.

J. E. DeBecker, *The Nightless City* (1894)

On the bill of fare alongside the bottles up behind the bar
the tariffs are standard, except for the one zero too many
on the beer: *mama-san* charges almost ten times the
running price per bottle. She isn't too fond of beer
drinkers; she likes a better class of people. It might well
be a strategic error, for the little Asakusa bar isn't exactly
crowded, but mama is entitled to her idiosyncrasies.
Satisfied that one wouldn't even dream of drinking beer,
she smooths her immaculate apron over her floral silk
kimono and pours whisky on the rocks. The layers of
thick foundation cream barely hide the furrows of the
passing years, and also hardly conceal the fact that
mama has a weatherbeaten face which could well belong
to a fisherman. Since she says she was born in a seaside
town in Kyushu, hereditarily speaking, perhaps it does.
Mama-san is Yuji, and he is sixty-one years old.

'You might say that our whole family was weird,' he

explains, using feminine figures of speech. 'I was a pretty kid and my cousin took a fancy to me. I got seduced.' The experience seems to have left a lasting impression. 'When I was sixteen I had an affair with my sister's fiancé. Don't marry him, I told her, he comes too fast.' His sister stuck her nose haughtily in the air and came up with a withering retort: 'No doubt the excitement over his first gay love affair was too much for him.' Yuji chuckles as he tells the tale. 'She married him anyway, and I came up to Tokyo as a sister-boy.' In 1946, waiters were still called 'boy', and those in specialized establishments took the prefix 'sister'. Along with the mass female exodus from the countryside to staff the burgeoning *mizu shobai*, the eighteen-year-old Yuji joined the tide of gay boys flooding into the cities to cater to the other persuasion.

Assuming, and not always entirely incorrectly, that straight male westerners have an innate horror of homosexuality, Japanese men will often assure foreigners that Japan is devoid of such a perversion and, by the same token, some of them may well be truly convinced. Until the spectre of Aids began to haunt the country during the mid-eighties, however, many foreign gays found Japan, which has a very long, colourful and even venerable history in the field, to be a paradise.

Where many of the founders of Shinjuku's Golden Gai drinking haunt happened to be transvestites, a *mama-san* in drag surprises no one. In a country in which drag queens host TV shows, no one jeers or tosses bricks, and the popular British and Australian sport of queer-bashing is happily unknown. The glamorous Peter, an androgynous pop star of the late sixties, is now not only the owner and exquisitely dressed mama of a renowned and expensive Shinjuku club, but also frequently the 'hostess' interviewing famous faces on popular chat

shows on TV. The twins Osugi and Piko, both caricatur-
ally effete and punctuating their repartee with flicks of
the wrist, similarly attend chat shows both singly and
together, particularly those revolving around films.
They got a great deal of mileage out of *Birds of a Feather*
which, called *Mr Lady and Mr Madam*, was a tremendous
hit in Japan. To the spectators, the majority of whom
happened to be female, far from being seen as outlandish or freakish, it was extremely cute.

None of the larger urban amusement districts in Japan
is without its quota of gay bars and clubs. Situated near
Ueno, some of Tokyo's oldest are shrouded in an aura of
venerability, a legacy of olden days when frustrated
monks came down from nearby temples to engage the
services of male geisha and youthful catamites. Nowhere
do gay bars proliferate more today than in the 2-Chome
section of Shinjuku, which counts some three hundred
such establishments in all. One of Tokyo's unofficially
tolerated red-light districts until prostitution was outlawed in 1957, the area saw the gay brotherhood move in
when the fallen sisterhood moved out. Laws about
prostitution are fairly nebulous at the best of times, and
those covering the alternative side of it tend to be vaguer
still. Every now and again, however, the weeklies home
in on the odd bust of a homosexual host club, which
generally comes to grief either through employing boys
under the legal age of consent or through hiring exotic
Siegfrieds and Adonises working beyond the provisions
of their visas.

Generally disparaging, the popular imagination
prefers the caricatural effeminate stereotype and,
despite its relative tolerance of homosexuality, modern
Japan is no exception. Gays are called *okama*, meaning
'august pots', a metaphor equating the common cooking
appliance with the human rear. Whether one looks at

homosexuality as a deviation or an alternative, its practitioners are not just those corresponding to the fey popular caricature, but also ultra-machos whose preference for male company extends even to their sex lives.

Masculinity was exalted in old Japan not only by the samurai and by the many shoguns who kept legions of pretty pages, but was also rooted in far older religious precepts which may have helped prepare the ground for the way of the warrior to grow. Indeed, the ancient celebration of virility is inherent in certain Shinto rituals. Generally held in winter, and closely associated with purification, the *hadaka matsuri* or naked festivals are exhilarating, exalting and sometimes dangerous. After an icy dip in mountain springs and waterfalls (not to mention the liberal consumption of purifying sake), scores of men and youths wearing only *fundoshi* loincloths leap on top of each other within the confines of a narrow shrine building to form a compact human pyramid. In what is a veritable claustrophobe's nightmare, the individual is fused with hundreds of sweating brothers into a seething mass exaltation of manhood. Although obviously not homosexual *per se*, the body contact and physical rejoicing in maleness leave plenty of scope for the latent and potential.

Homosexuality was reported as being practised by about 6 per cent of male college students, and latent among a third of high-school boys in 1981. In a similar survey in 1987, both figures declined to 4.5 and 20 per cent respectively in proportion to an increase in earlier heterosexual activity. Said to be more common in Japan than popularly believed, homosexuality permeates the most macho strata of society, including among gangsters and the men with tattooed skins. Women, who present the risk of ritual impurity, still occupy a low position in their esteem. The *aficionados* of rough trade are not only as partial to toughs and tattooees as Japanese homo-sexual iconography testifies, but cruise around the country's few slum districts, such as Tokyo's Sanya, where some day-labourers are known to dispense favours both out of financial considerations and in line with their own inclinations. Besides, in a country where a sensible marriage lurks at the back of most single women's minds and prostitutes command high prices, men with no yen of the paper kind often find other avenues of sexuality closed to them.

Down among the lower and less inhibited social strata, homosexuality is often a matter of the rough and ready administration of mutual relief. I once observed this phenomenon in action in a spontaneous and curious occurrence one day in a *nudo* theatre, in which a stripper was busily entertaining a couple of ruffianly young spectators to dual masturbatory relief on-stage. 'You are a long time coming, aren't you?' she admonished after some time. 'I might just as well not be here.' Taking the hand of one and placing it on the member of the other and vice versa, she walked offstage leaving the two quite contentedly jerking each other off until they climaxed to the unrestrained merriment of the audience.

Although the Heian period was an extremely epicene age, there is very little mention of homosexuality in the chronicles and romances of the time. A famous and oft-quoted exception is found in *The Tale of Genji* where, failing to seduce the beauty of his designs, Genji beds her pretty younger brother instead. As refined as the repartee is, the gist is simply what might be less elegantly transcribed as 'You'll do.' The anecdote from Murasaki's tale is often seen as suggesting that homo-eroticism was largely only a stand-by in a society quite as promiscuous as the Heian. Yet it is just as likely that homosexuality was taken for granted, for it was certainly by then a widely accepted practice among the Buddhist priesthood. The injunctions of chastity forbade all contact with women, but homosexuality was considered an acceptable substitute in Japan as in China, indeed as it tacitly still is in many Buddhist monasteries throughout the Far East. According to a system not unlike the mentor/pupil relationship of ancient Greece, the novice pledged himself officially to an older monk for a number of years. In exchange for tuition, he had the status of 'sworn friend' and became his mentor's property, body and soul.

There were not always enough *chigo* novices to go round, however, so that monks frequently resorted to forays outside. From the seventeenth century, some disguised themselves to sneak into heterosexual brothels, but for those more afraid of getting caught, there were even groups of specialized female prostitutes who disguised themselves as young monks. For those either too shy of violating the proscriptions on female contact or whose inclinations lay exclusively in the other direction, there was a lively commerce in boys outside the monastery walls. This is why, when not situated near amusement areas, homosexual brothels proliferated most during the Edo period near Buddhist temples. Pretty male 'incense sellers' in effeminate clothing moreover plied their trade on a door-to-door basis among clerics and aristocrats; in one way and another the avenues of mercantile pederasty were thoroughly pervaded with the odour of sanctity.

The relationship between monk and novice is also the grass roots of the master–pupil pattern in all fields of religion and culture in Japan. The word *chigo* is given in Kenkyusha's Japanese-English dictionary both as 'child in a festive procession' and 'catamite'. Time was when the novice's function was often twofold, which explains the surviving clerical and secular nuances of the same term. Having no religious standing at all beyond their occasional engagement by clerics, the young catamites in homosexual brothels of the Edo period were sometimes also called *chigo* – no doubt an expression coined by pimps to give their charges an exalted aura of divinity. Their ambiguously religious and homoerotic roles may be largely ignored if not entirely forgotten today, but the *chigo*, now small local boys decked out in gorgeous costumes and wearing make-up, are still to be seen in a purely innocent context evoking only their religious standing in Kyoto's famous annual Gion festival parade.

During the long civil wars, centuries of violence increasingly saw the zealous exaltation of the warrior ethic, and women were nothing. As they were in the eyes of the military fanatics of Sparta or Prussia, they were even viewed with scorn. *Onna no ana wa, kari mono* – a woman's hole is a thing for borrowing – so ran a proverb popular in martial circles, in which the hole's only saving grace lay in its capacity as an incubator. Homosexuality was extolled as the ne plus ultra of virility and masculine sexual chic. It was as much the norm in military camps as in the monasteries keeping legions of pretty boys. Sex was necessary to produce sons, but over-indulgence, especially if fired by love, was seen as a weakness which had no place among the rapidly crystallizing concepts of bushido, the stoic way of the warrior and the code of the samurai. *Nanshoku* – male passion – was not a perversion but a lofty ideal. Nevertheless, strict conventions dictated that the passive feminine role was proper only to youths and boys. The predilection was elevated with a proper name, and both professional catamites and their patrons announced themselves to be the followers of *shudo* – the way of the youth.

In power during one of the great lulls in the storm of civil-war brutality, the shogun Ashikaga Yoshimitsu (1358–1408) was one of history's greatest aesthetes. His love for young men found expression not only among his harem of pages, but also in his deep love of the theatre. Passionately fond of the Noh masked drama, Yoshimitsu was captivated by the great beauty of the talented twelve-year-old son of one of the principal actors of the day. Under Yoshimitsu's patronage during the 1370s, the boy Zeami was able to develop his genius and, before he died in 1443, he refined and redefined the Noh into what still survives as one of the greatest traditional theatre forms in the world. The theatre was a male preserve, and an established current of homosexuality was to flow through it for centuries.

As soon as the female precursors of kabuki had been banished from the stage early on in the seventeenth century, the overwhelming majority of their male replacements had been beauteous catamites and followers of Shudo. Until subsequent government bans cramped their style too, albeit without succeeding in eliminating them entirely, the ranks of *onnagata*, the 'female forms', popularly comprised boys in their teens. Decked out in the most elegant feminine fashions of the day, they not only sported feminine hairstyles, but also blackened their teeth with *haguro* like wives and courtesans. In an age in which pederasty was seen as a perfectly acceptable alternative and even extolled by many as the most desirable, the *onnagata* naturally had many admirers.

Describing the high jinks of a group of handsome, wealthy young Kyoto profligates, Ihara Saikaku evoked the spirit of the times: 'One night, till dawn, they amuse themselves in Shimabara with Chinagirl, Fragrance, Florapoint and Highbridge. Next day they might make love to Takenaka Kichisaburo, Karamatsu Kasen, Fujita Kichisaburo and Mitsuse Sakon in the Shijo-Gawara section.' In other words, first the courtesans, then the *onnagata*. Saikaku's satirical tales were often inspired by real occurrences, and the names he used in this case were those of renowned *onnagata* of the contemporary kabuki stage.

The *onnagata* were not just dedicated followers of feminine fashion, they set the trends. Women eagerly took note of the famous late seventeenth-century Kichiya's attire and dressed themselves accordingly in the fashionable 'Kichiya style'. One of the greatest was Yoshizawa Ayame (1653–1729), whose prescriptions for stage-craft stated that 'An *onnagata* should act like an *onnagata* even in the dressing room. When he eats his meals, he should turn away from other people [as was until recently the case with women also] ... Unless an actor lives like a woman even in daily life, he will probably never be considered a successful *onnagata*.' Indeed, in the world of the kabuki theatre until quite recently *onnagata* also wore female attire offstage. No matter of vulgar imitation, female impersonation is an exalted art calling upon painstakingly acquired skills and finding its apotheosis in the synthetic female, who is in every way preferable to the real thing on-stage and – to some – offstage too.

Many an *onnagata*'s theatrical career was short-lived, if indeed he ever reached the stage at all. So popular was kabuki that many pederastic brothels dubbed their charges *wakashu*, the term for youths favoured in the theatre. Some brothels staged playlets as part of their entertainment, for catamites were expected to have accomplishments in line with courtesans. In *The Life of an Amorous Man*, the lament Saikaku puts into the mouth of a young catamite implies that many boys endured exactly the same contractual bondage as girls: 'In this profession ... we cannot refuse any man, no matter if his body is covered with sores or if he has never used a toothpick in his life ... More than once I have felt mortified or chagrined and shed many a bitter tear. But time flies quickly and in the fourth month next year I shall be a free man again.' The predilection for pre-pubescent boys produced male prostitutes who could be pathetically young and not a few specialized brothels called themselves *kodomoya* – child brothels.

Forever reflecting the times, Saikaku's heroes were not only AC/DC, but some were dyed-in-the-wool peder-asts. In a famous book he devoted entirely to pederasty, *Nanshoku no Okagami* (*The Mirror of Manly Love*), he focused on love affairs between the samurai. 'Male love is essentially different from the ordinary love of man and woman,' he remarked in the opening sentences of one story, 'and that is why a prince, even when he has married a beautiful princess, cannot forget his pages. Woman is a creature of absolutely no importance; but sincere pederastic love is true love.'

These days such ideals have been relegated to the closet. Except those in the worlds of show business and the *mizu shobai*, the born homosexual must, like Oscar Wilde, go through the social charade of marriage. For many close and happy male relationships, this is often a harbinger of disaster. In artistic and cultural fields particularly, many younger men entertain homosexual relationships today with an older man, on the basis of the ancient master–pupil ideal. If not a born homosexual, the younger party might swing both ways. What he learns from his older companion and the respect he harbours for him amounts to love strong enough to find physical expression. The Confucian equation between age and wisdom is still extremely powerful. Glad for the years spent learning from his mentor, the acolyte will bid him a fond and poignant farewell either when he marries or if he decides to pursue his stronger inclination towards the opposite sex.

Pederasty has been superficially proscribed through the western opprobrium adopted during the nineteenth century, although Japan's awareness of the occidental disapproval may go back as far as the early Christian missionaries: St Francis Xavier used much ink in chronicling the many Japanese virtues he admired, but he deplored the widespread practice of sodomy, which he equated with conduct more becoming in pigs and dogs. Like everything else, homosexuality was fine as long as it never came to interfere with the accepted daily routine. Nowadays, unlike dalliances with ordinary prostitutes or keeping mistresses, it must be kept in the closet.

In Yukio Mishima's *Forbidden Colours*, when the beautiful young hero's homosexual affairs are revealed to his wife and mother by a blackmailer, their reaction says much for prevailing attitudes. What appals the mother most is nothing in the least related to sin, but that her son's exposure as a catamite would bring shame and scandal on the family. As for his long-suffering wife, the revelation more poignantly and irrefutably demonstrates how little he loves her. In a land in which marriage is virtually a commandment and often arranged, her predicament is fairly common, but perhaps even more so for the woman with a husband whose true inclinations lie elsewhere.

Men forming mutual attachments are known facetiously as *homodachi* (from the word *tomodachi*: friend), and the more promiscuous in the gay fast lane find the usual scope for spontaneous rendezvous in Japan in haunts such as parks, public toilets and specialized saunas. Certain homosexual love hotels too are renowned for their racy free-for-alls, but the fuck trucks plying the streets of some American cities during the permanent coming-out ball of the seventies are far too blatant for Japan. Unless the listings in his international *Spartacus Guide* have been kept scrupulously up to date, the foreigner seeking Graeco-Roman pleasures may find a lot of the doors, even bars, closing in his face. Aids has cramped the style of gay activities in Japan, but rather more for foreigners than for the Japanese. The orgiastic sauna and hotel scene is reportedly alive and well, but rigorously out of bounds to *gaijin*. Perhaps it is just as well. Despite the increasing risk, the lifesaving condom, it seems, is unpopular. Japanese Aids victims may be comparatively few, but although the gay quota among them is high, reportedly even fewer have been persuaded into the practice of safe sex than have the *aficionados* of Soapland.

As one foreign observer lamented some years ago in the English-language *Tokyo Journal*, apart from a recently formed gay support group with an overwhelmingly foreign membership, there are no organizations uniting homosexuals in a bid to break out of the closet in Japan. Magazines such as the famous *Bara zoku* (*The Rose Tribe*) are sold everywhere, but as with other erotic publications, the emphasis is more on titillation than information, let alone socio-political revolt. 'Gay lib' parties on the political fringe do, however, appear regularly at every election. When all's said, even in specialized films and publications, despite claims to use sex as socio-political subversion, provocation residing in the imagery is about as far as it goes. Grouping together for socio-political causes is rare enough in Japan and deadly serious when it occurs; it is not within the scope of a magazine targeting a readership thoroughly resigned to life in the closet and perusing gay magazines in secret to be much given to the conspicuousness of radicalism.

BEAUTIFUL DEATH

The Edo period was the era during which the samurai warriors ruled at last but, having no war to fight, for many it was like abiding by the strict laws of a martial jungle in a genteel landscape garden. Beneath the codified and florid aesthetic refinements, the warrior code was still at work. Actors, a caste beneath contempt, were free to indulge in effeminacy but the samurai were bidden to abide by a code exalting manhood. Even if his lifestyle and sartorial tastes were effeminate, the gay samurai still had to pay lip service to the virile spiritual values of old.

Like their heterosexual equivalent, Ihara Saikaku's pederastic tales generally ended in tragedy, but the culminating suicides tended to dwell on gory, soldierly details. The samurai love stories show chivalry of a kind akin to the romantic European epics of knights and damsels, but abide by radically different rules. The pining, suffering and derring-do characterizing the European knight is never wasted on the unworthy female. Nor did the doomed protagonists die as victims of fate and society like heterosexual lovers, but as one sacrificing himself for the sake of the other. There is to be no comfortable escaping together into the next world as in the stories of double suicides; the protagonists must prove their courage by suffering singly.

Such tales often involve love between pages of incomparable beauty, the one dying through taking some action on the other's behalf. A good example is Saikaku's tale of the love between the beautiful Korin and his fellow page Sohachiro. When the feudal lord finds out that his favourite Korin has been dispensing his favours elsewhere, Korin is shown no mercy. 'I myself will execute you, Korin,' his lord announces, 'as a warning to my courtiers not to deceive me.'

As the lord picks up his halberd, Korin only smiles sweetly, politely expressing his gratitude that his lord, perhaps out of deference to their relationship, should deign to take his life himself. As he stands up to meet his end, the lord begins by slicing off his hand. Saikaku's ensuing dialogue is as extremely bizarre as its context:

'How do you feel, Korin?'
    Korin held out his right hand to be cut off also and said: 'With this hand I caressed and loved my lover. You should hate this hand a great deal also.'
    The lord at once cut that hand off. Then Korin turned his back to his master and said: 'My back is very beautiful. No other page was as attractive as I am. Look at my beauty before I die.' His voice was weak and low through the mortal pain he was enduring. Then the lord cut off his head and, holding it in his hands, wept bitter tears for the death of his favourite.

Although first depicted as a coward going into hiding, the other page, Sohachiro, emerges months later to show his true mettle for the edifying ending of the tale. Catching the rascal who had betrayed Korin to the feudal lord, he chops off his hands and head, before committing *seppuku* on Korin's grave. 'As he opened his belly,' Saikaku concludes, 'he traced upon it the armorial bearings of his Korin with the knife. For seven days after his death his friends and admirers loaded his tomb with flowers. Korin and Sohachiro became an illustrious example of the love of comrades.'

Worthy of Gilles de Rais, the homoerotic sadism implicit in the tale runs down as far as the tormentor's typical outpourings of grief and remorse over the beloved and mutilated victim, and also finds an equivalent in the writings of the Marquis de Sade. The romantic equation between youth and violent death, however, is nowhere so exalted as in Japan. 'Beauty in this world cannot endure for long,' says another of Saikaku's handsome young samurai before slitting his belly. 'I am glad to die while I am young and beautiful, and before my countenance fades like a flower.'

The melancholic aesthetics of *mono-no-aware*, the poignant beauty of the fleeting world, reached a culmination in the real one with the ethos of the young kamikaze pilot, and moreover also finds ample expression in homoerotic sadism. The themes of youth and death thoroughly pervade the work of the late Yukio Mishima who, hailed around the world as one of the century's greatest Japanese writers, is now seldom similarly acknowledged as such in Japan. Ever since the 45-year-old author led his private army, the ultra-nationalist Tatenokai (Shield Society), in taking over the Self-Defence Force headquarters one day in 1970 and committing ritual suicide, Mishima has been something of a closed book. When all is said, it was a rather sordid and gruesome affair. Mishima and two members of the Shield Society planned to commit ritual *seppuku* in the grand old manner, but when it took three chops of the sword to sever the horribly wounded Mishima's head from his body, Grand Guignol ruled the day. Modern Japan was confronted with the irrefutable evidence that the glorious death of old samurai romance was not so beautiful after all.

Smothered by an awesome *mamagon* (monster mother), the frail, sickly Mishima emerged from cloistered childhood into adolescence characterized at once by precocious literary skill and sadistic fantasies of cannibalism and beautiful youths in torment. His first masturbatory climax had been triggered by a reproduction of Guido Reni's young Saint Sebastian languidly agonizing from the arrows piercing his youthful flesh. With *Confessions of a Mask*, Mishima gave a poignant account of a young man who grows up to become aware of his homosexuality and who resigns himself to life in the closet; few readers could be unaware of the autobiographical content.

Enjoying better health as well as fame in later life, Mishima became an avid physical culturist with a he-man torso. A staunch practitioner of martial arts, he was the bizarre star of the odd *yakuza* or samurai movie and developed a taste for the same kind of obsession as inferred in Visconti's *The Damned*. His ultra-nationalism was as much spawned by genuine bitterness over what he saw as a country that had lost its dignity to the West as a sublimation of a homosexual obsession with young men in uniforms. While they exult blemishless purity and love for the emperor, Mishima's descriptions of suicides by ultra-patriotic heroes are given to loving details about warm entrails spilling into strong young laps.

Although it may well owe more to Radiguet than Choderlos de Laclos, the deliciously perverse *Forbidden Colours* was a dark tragi-comedy and a homoerotic Japanese equivalent to *Les Liaisons Dangereuses*. Embittered by years of rejection by the opposite sex, an ugly old writer uses a youth of consummate beauty as a weapon to ruin the lives of the women who spurned him. Sighting the beautiful youth's nakedness and comparing him to Endymion, the old man is haunted by the vision thereafter, and realizes that he has himself fallen under the spell he would cast upon others. As his youthful hero brings misery to the men and women in his dazzling wake, Mishima takes the reader on a trip through the shadow world of Japanese homosexuality, of gay bars and wild parties, a world he knew by heart. An evil spirit and depicted as exaltingly superficial, the boy, his hero, is ultimately hollow; his great beauty is at once everything and all there is. In the end, that Mishima's ultra-nationalism was more a matter of homoerotic fixation than anything else is betrayed by the deep-rooted nihilism pervading his work.

Anyone familiar with the underlying ordeals facing American director Paul Schrader when he made the film *Mishima* in 1984 in Japan (where it was not released) could only be more indulgent than many critics were. Schrader laboured heroically against tremendous odds. Hampered by the widow's contractual proscription of any mention of her late husband's homosexuality, he was shunned by the entire Japanese film community and received a sufficient number of threatening calls from rightist extremists to finish shooting the film in a bullet-proof vest. Despite its obvious literary merits, Mishima's work is avoided in school curricula and the author lives on as an embarrassment in Japan, where he is all but swept under the carpet by the literary community and exalted by rightist extremists. The former look upon his grand finale as a grotesque reversion to prewar ideals; despite the overwhelming evidence to the contrary, most of which is provided by the late author's own frank admissions, the latter obdurately dismiss Mishima's homosexuality as a leftist fabrication. Typically, neither side and precious few people in between care to admit that genius and a degree of madness make fine partners, and that Mishima's eccentricities in no way undermine his literary merit. But this would be all about reality, which is of no importance; having dispensed with his mask, the real Mishima fell short of the elevating fantasies entertained by both parties, so it was much better to bury him.

THE CONGRESS OF SHELLFISH

That lesbian relationships formed between the neglected ladies of the *o-oku*, the shogun's great harem, is well known. Unlike with male homosexuality, however, Japan has neither particularly condemned, celebrated nor spent much ink on reporting sapphic relations. Lesbians are sometimes called *onabe* (stew-pot) as a counterpart to *okama*, but more usually by the Japlish word *resu*. They generally come in two persuasions: the *otachi* (an actress playing male roles: butch) and *neko* or *nenne* (cat or *ingénue*: *femme*). Although by no means unknown and frequently featured in erotic print anthologies, *shunga* with lesbian themes were relatively rare. That lesbianism was even quite practically catered to during the Edo period is evidenced by contemporary sex manual illustrations of the relatively common *ryochidori*, which literally translates as 'dual plover' and more simply refers to a double dildo. Sexually performing females constitute a sempiternal turn-on for men everywhere, but the *resubian sho* (lesbian show) which is now a perennial staple in the modern striptease parlour is, as its name suggests, a foreign import. Lesbianism remains otherwise shrouded in comparative obscurity in Japan.

Confucianism forced all well-to-do women to lead extremely sheltered lives at home until offered as brides. There was thus almost as little scope for homosexuality as there was for affairs with the opposite sex. Besides, since sexual indulgence is so staunchly considered a male preserve, the fact that demure women can adopt a dominating male role in a relationship with a member of her own sex seems outlandish enough as to be more happily ignored. Nevertheless, female homosexual relations are described with the suggestive and taboo slang term *kai awase* – the congress of shellfish. In Junnosuke Yoshiyuki's prize-winning popular novel *Anshitsu* (*The Dark Room*) of 1970, the profligate middle-aged bachelor hero is intrigued by one of his several mistresses, who swings both ways. Badgering her with questions, he asks her whether any of her friends dress up as men, a notion which she emphatically and scathingly denies. The man's retort, 'You prefer the subtle play of the senses, eh?' betrays a mixture of prurient curiosity and typical prepossession.

Yoshiyuki's hero concludes:

> She spoke as though it should be perfectly obvious, but my understanding of the world of lesbianism was still inadequate. Or rather was still full of prejudices.
>
> There was a lingering furtiveness in Maki's face that evening, like the silvery trail left by a slug. It made me want to question her, and I asked her all kinds of things about female homosexuality.

Much spoken about as Tokyo's only bar for female gays, Space Dyke sank into oblivion after blossoming only briefly during the first half of the eighties. Developers eyed the building housing it and, besides, the number of women coming brazenly out of the closet were too few to warrant opening it again elsewhere. Although many male gay bars exclude women altogether, some are known to cater to females on certain days, usually on a women-only basis lasting for only one or two hours.

An international lesbian conference was rather courageously hosted in Japan in 1985, but the turn-out was not exactly overwhelming. As the feminist American writer Kittredge Cherry pointed out in her book about Japanese women, lesbians are deep in the closet, 'a state so expected that there is no Japanese phrase for hiding one's homosexuality'. Although Japanese lesbians have no word for coming out of it, Cherry nevertheless acknowledges that 'a few, modifying the English phrase, do say *kamu auto suru*'.

All things being relative, the fact that male homosexuals enjoy greater freedom than females says much about the secondary status of women in Japan. Many an old ribald tale concerns lesbianism between Buddhist nuns, but whereas the male equivalent is exalted in poignant tragedies, the female is rarely granted more dignity than as a theme for *shunga* or grotesque caricatures. It is not surprising that the incentives lesbians have to *kamu auto* are small indeed.

DREAMS OF YOUNG GIRLS

> Every year the trees are covered with blossom as in the years before; but man cannot keep the blossom of his youth ... The love of boys is, therefore, but a passing dream.

> Ihara Saikaku, *The Great Mirror of Manly Love*

The aesthetic reverence for the ephemeral has long induced an obsession with youth, and such stuff of passing dreams is often imbued with homosexual overtones. Take, for example, the heavy leather phenomenon. Except in one or two dives in Tokyo haunted by a handful of genuine enthusiasts and private practitioners, conspicuous heavy leather attire does not go down well in Japan. The 1980 film *Cruising*, about a straight cop donning gay apparel to track a killer through New York's homosexual underworld, was insulting to

gays and panned everywhere. It was a big hit in Tokyo.
If it left Japanese gays cold too, it launched a vogue
among the disco crowd. Black leather jackets, chains,
biker boots and caps were all the rage, and adorning the
back pocket of jeans with paisley handkerchiefs became
a must. Marketed in cinema foyers and now long forgotten, the 'look' was packaged like cowboy outfits pandering to the dreams of little boys.

The gay comic book obviously sets itself apart from
other porno productions with buggery beneath the
blank-outs and an all-male cast of he-men with rosy
cheeks and optional tattoos embracing elfin boys with
foal-like, adoring eyes, but the stylistic conventions it
obeys are almost exactly the same as in the straight
equivalent. Like the Edo-period artists given to *shunga*
themes, some of today's *manga* comic-book illustrators
cater to both persuasions. Finding an accepted place in
popular culture too, more subtle homoeroticism often
pervades more innocent fare and sometimes quite
unconsciously, above all in the incarnation of *bishonen*
and *binan* – beautiful boys and men. Nowhere are these
characters drawn with greater androgyny or effeminacy
than in comics for women and girls. The gender of the
long-lashed youths in some can be determined from
their virile physiques; other more willowy styles make it
hard to tell the sexes apart.

Gender definition in Japan can transcend the anatomical; masculine and feminine attributes can fade or fuse
through conventions. During the course of the *daijosai*
enthronement ceremony, the emperor ritually becomes
female – an incarnation of the sun goddess Amaterasu.
Nor need the *bishonen* be a weakling, for beauty precludes neither courage nor fighting skills to the Japanese. Although described as stunted and ugly in reliable
contemporary accounts, the great twelfth-century

military hero Miyamoto Yoshitsune died young and, as such, was virtually canonized in a pantheon of beautiful tragic youths, being invariably portrayed later on the kabuki stage by the most beauteous of *onnagata*, mincing exquisitely and making deliveries in a high falsetto voice. He is depicted as an archetypal *bishonen* with rosy cheeks and ruby lips, especially by children's illustrators such as Kasho Takabatake, who enjoyed a veritable cult following from the 1920s. Melding traditional Japanalia with chocolate-box art, Takabatake's demure maidens and pretty boys share the same improbably sweet faces. As innocent as they both are, a uniformly languid, heavy-lidded look seems to load them with unconscious sexuality. The *bishonen* even occasionally graces the TV samurai drama. To emphasize one lad's beauty in a recent serial, for instance, albeit with tongue in cheek, the character was portrayed by the transvestite Peter who, in drag twice over, looked for all the world like a principal boy in a pantomime.

Like transvestites everywhere, the members of Tokyo's Elizabeth Club are not all homosexual. For some, the thrill of cross-dressing is an end in itself. Providing the wherewithal with an extensive wardrobe of hundreds of costumes and kimonos, not to mention a team of half a dozen beauticians, the club has a membership of about 700 and grosses annual profits nearing 300,000,000 yen. Most of the members are married and sneak away on some evenings to dress up as their favourite fantasy female. The hefty middle-aged 'Candy', dressed always as a renowned heroine from a little girls' comic book, heads the team at the annual Kawasaki phallic festival parade, during which he was once accosted by a bewildered little girl finding him not altogether like her comic-book favourite. 'Are you a man or a woman?' she asked point-blank. Candy laughed:

'Sometimes I'm a man, and sometimes I'm a woman.' The little girl seemed quite satisfied: some people are like that.

One of Ihara Saikaku's most famous satirical tales, the seventeenth-century 'Oman and Gengobei', takes a novel slant on the universal theme of cross-dressing. Gengobei is a handsome, staunchly pederastic priest who tries to forget the death of his favourite *chigo* by seducing as many others as he possibly can. Lovestruck as soon as she sets eyes on him, the beauty Oman swears to herself that she will have him in spite of himself. Disguised as a boy priest, she works her way into Gengobei's hermitage and finally into bed with him. Gengobei discovers the subterfuge at the last moment, but has already taken a fancy to her for what she really is. Concluding with a cynical little twist implying that their marriage will be blissful mostly thanks to Oman's sudden, huge inheritance (which Gengobei hints will buy him a covey of actors), the fantasy reflects a persistent tendency to confuse gender in the no man's land of pleasure.

At the two extremes of male and female in popular culture, one finds the geisha and the sumo wrestler: the dainty living doll standing for femininity and the mountainous icon of macho flesh with the little porcine eyes. Between the two bookends plenty of scope lies in a nebulous heaven of make-believe far from the constrictions of daily routine. Segregating the sexes during childhood and defining the contexts and nature of their encounters later on, Japanese society defines gender roles with adamantine rules. In the realm of the imaginary, the strict roles encapsulating male and female are broken, being transgressed in fantasies which can be singly and variously violent, sadistic, maudlin, sentimental or comical. Transcending the laws of society, authority and even gender, these fantasies reach an apotheosis in the popular imagination with ethereal creatures as blessedly sexless as occidental angels. Beyond categorization and gender, the fancy-free ideal ultimately seems to imply release from the body itself – rather like death.

A great hit in 1983, Nobuhiko Obayashi's film *Tenkosei* (*Exchange Students*) was an offbeat youth comedy about junior high-school lovers suffering a freak accident, which causes the girl's soul to enter the boy's body and vice versa. The theme revolves around awakening sexuality and its further complication through reversal, for the protagonists are forced to adopt the physical and social gender roles of the other. The boy turns into a wallflower using feminine figures of speech, and the girl struts around saying things that would make the most aggressive tomboy blush. Deeply Japanese, the film is thoroughly imbued with frank physicality and at the same time extremely chaste; the lovers never exchange so much as a kiss.

Between the jokes about genital differences, the mortified male faced with menstruation and the girl aghast at having to stand and hold that thing to urinate, what is most persuasive is a peculiar exaltation of adolescence, which seems rooted in the homoeroticism preceding the time when physical, chemical and physiological changes properly come into focus. Returning to normal, the two are definitely separated, the girl's parents move house and the strange romance is over. *Tenkosei* was certainly funny, but being permeated with an odd transsexual sentimentality, its overall flavour was melancholic and bittersweet, betraying both the director's and other adults' nostalgia for the carefree sexual limbo of adolescence.

Made in 1988 and set in a parallel universe in which

retro and futurism combine in the décor, Shusuke Kaneko's engaging *1999 no Natsuyasumi* (*The Summer of 1999*) stands at the apex of the epicene genre. Staying on at their élite boarding school in the lush green countryside when the other pupils have gone on holiday, four lovely adolescent boys perpetually attired in short trousers and immaculate white shirts live an idyll cramming together before their computer screens, quite alone in a sun-dappled classroom. The setting is romantic, and it moves the young protagonists. Pining with unrequited love for one of the other boys, one pupil drowns himself in a nearby lake. A mysterious look-alike appears some days later, and the drama recurs with a slight alteration of affective focus. The culmination comes again by the lakeside, but this time the lovers are together and enter a suicide pact. An *éternal retour* with variations, the cycle of love and death brings the film repeatedly back to its starting point, which all the more effectively prevents the protagonists from growing up. Just before they throw themselves into the lake, what the lovers finally chant in unison goes to the very heart of Japanese androgynous fantasy: 'Let us die together, you and I. Die together and be born again. Childhood is the loveliest of times, so let us die together as children.'

Intense and bewitching, *The Summer of 1999* is charged with the same idealized male homoeroticism as girls' comic books. When the enchanting protagonists at last exchange an exalting kiss, the love of boys is truly beautiful to behold. As it happens, all four roles were entirely portrayed by young girls. Touching, sexless and ethereally pretty, they are as bittersweet and immaculate as little angels of death. To Ian Buruma, this is a quintessential aspect of popular culture: 'The emphasis in so many Japanese stories, including those on the Takarazuka stage, is on the ending of youth, on the destruction of it, rather than its flowering. The alternative is to remain an eternal youth or virgin, neither man nor woman, which is the same as not growing up at all.'

Bidden to live in chastity as befits the Confucian ideal of purity, the women employed in the famed Takarazuka theatre troupe inhabit a small town of the same name near Osaka. Part of a virtuous theme-paradise called Family Land and likewise owned by the Hankyu Electric Railway Company, the theatre village is open to the public, but the troupe's living quarters are as unsullied as a convent and rigorously out of bounds to males. It is a florid world of Tinseltown baroque in pink, a feminine Disneyland with rose-coloured bridges spanning artificial water courses. To the foreign observer, the setting would be as outrageously kitsch as the Takarazuka theatre form itself. In 1987, seventy-three years after its foundation, the Takarazuka troupe unsuccessfully pushed to have itself recognized as a 'traditional Japanese art form'. The weekly press rather cynically pointed out that this blessed state would exempt it from taxes, but the cultural argument nevertheless holds its own. The kabuki theatre, after all, has long found a female equivalent in certain geisha theatricals comprising dances and playlets in which some of the cast adopt male roles.

The Takarazuka Young Girls Opera embraces many older male-role superstars with short, slicked-back hair and years of experience at swaggering about the stage in braided pantomime military uniforms, tuxedos, cowboy suits and samurai armour – complete with blue cheeks and moustaches. The Takarazuka has an enormous following of young girls. Given to frilly confectionery décors in soft pastels, the repertoire favours Jazz Age musicals, operettas such as Messager's *Véronique* and a variety of spectacularly fanciful revues. One of the most famous is *The Rose of Versailles*, which is based on a phenomenally popular serial in a girls' comic book, about young Marie Antoinette's infatuation with the heroine Oscar, an androgynous captain of the guards. Staging it again to commemorate the bicentennial of the French Revolution in 1989, the Takarazuka sold all tickets months in advance.

Speculative rumours fly about the offstage predilections of some of the Takarazuka male-role superstars, but the phenomenon has precious little to do with lesbianism *per se*. Primness is inculcated in girls, and the vicarious thrills to be derived from seeing a heroine in a long, scintillating pink gown trembling in the arms of a crop-haired principal male in a sequined tuxedo is irreproachable. The glitzy never-never land is one of reassurance, offering all the shades of romance without ever darkening them with the threatening shadow of a penis. The most avid followers are young girls, but longings to banish the male seem shared by droves of ardent fans in middle age, many of whom personally patronize their Takarazuka favourites and shower them with expensive gifts.

The Japanese would never use a term as rude as 'fag hag', but there is always *okoge* which, meaning burned rice stuck to the bottom of the *okama* cooking pot, is a metaphor for the same thing. *Okoge* are numerous in Japan, where many women adore homosexuals for the same reasons as they do the Takarazuka theatre. The fascination for gays finds expression in night clubs staging glitzy entertainments for the benefit of a preponderantly female clientele. One such was the Swan Lake in Shinjuku, in which a stage emerging at intervals from the circular bar bore an enormous fat man simpering in a tutu as he led a cast in drag through a balletic parody inspiring the club's name. Gay Filipino boys in glittering costumes stage go-go dance spectaculars in ordinary urban discos with Babylonian regularity. Among scores of others, Shibuya's Aun celebrates the body beautiful with imaginative and colourful shows vehicling young Apollos, exquisite transvestites and transsexuals – all in costumes costing many millions of yen. In Mandy's in Roppongi, mascara-laden Mandy wears a spiky punk hairstyle atop a traditional kimono, screaming out a welcome at the shrill top of his lungs, flapping his wrists as a flurry of 'waitresses' in similarly feminine attire overwhelm bewildered then delighted customers as they enter the door. Whether they are practising homosexuals or not is quite irrelevant; more important is that they should appear as such in the eyes of the public. Hence the affectation of exaggerated whoops and limp-wristed posturing, for the act is perfected around the clock in much the same way as with the old *onnagata* in the floating world.

Travelling up to Tokyo from the gilded suburbs, prim young things queue up to gape wide-eyed at John Waters movies, fascinated with the grotesque, late and much lamented Divine flaunting his ersatz feminine bulk as a jilted housewife in *Polyester* or devouring poodle droppings from the gutter in *Pink Flamingoes*. This is in fact the lunatic fringe of a widespread obsession for films dealing with male homosexuality. The very different subjects, messages and treatment of films such as the British *Another Country* and *Prick Up Your Ears* are as lost on the majority of their audiences as they were on the droves of girls swooning over Helmut Berger in *Blue Angel* drag in Visconti's *The Damned*, which triggered the craze during the seventies. Many serious Japanese directors lament the flippancy of national audiences, citing their inability to empathize meaningfully with what they see on-screen, as well as their marked distaste for any messages or didacticism marring a quest for superficial entertainment. If the real merits of such films are thus mostly cast to the wind anyway, the feminine penchant for boys-kiss-boys films may, in addition to perspectives of vicarious thrills-without-threat, reside in that they rule out empathy by definition.

How strange the dreams of young girls. Abroad, female pro wrestling implies shapely Amazons in teeny bikinis contemplated by bug-eyed males. *Joshi-puro*, Japanese women's pro wrestling, however, presents a very different picture. Some exponents, such as the idol Chigusa, with her boyish hairstyle and the features of a young male TV *talento*, prelude their matches by sweetly singing popular songs, which serves to endear them all the more to their droves of fans. As they contemplate formidable female heavies in garish leotards savagely twisting, gouging, pummelling and dragging each other around the ring by the hair, the fans of *joshi-puro* squirm around in their seats squealing with excitement – they are overwhelmingly made up of teenage and pre-teen girls.

For starters the diminutive male referee is frequently hurled straight from the ring, and the Amazons often proceed by stepping out themselves, perhaps grabbing hastily vacated folding chairs from the front row to clobber each other mightily over the head. A rainbow cockatoo crest towering over a head shaved bald, Dump Matsumoto had a swastika devil mask painted on her face and was over 200 pounds of awesome female flesh. An idol *extraordinaire* to young girls, her wild eyes and twisted black mouth would scare the hell out of Mad Max and are character-merchandised to adorn teeny T-shirts, bags and candy. Retiring in 1988 at twenty-eight and predictably moving in among the zany plethora of TV characters in quizzes and chat shows, she is replaced by rising heavyweight Bull Nakano.

Sponsors argue that young girls see *joshi-puro* as a way of wrestling with the problem of growing up. In a 1989 interview, Rossy Ogawa, director of the All-Japan Women's Pro Wrestling Association, put the popularity of *joshi-puro* down to the fact that young girls, having been kept apart from boys at school, find them mysterious, unapproachable and even frightening. 'Women pro wrestlers are very strong,' he said. 'I think that young girls see them as a substitute for boyfriends. They see women pro wrestlers as ideal men. They feel safer in getting close to them because they're the same sex. Thus while they're idols in one sense, they're vicarious boyfriends in another.' Young women may also see *joshi-puro* exponents not only as a source of vicarious thrills but also as aggressive champions of self-assertiveness.

In the Japanese fantasy world of genderless sex, the grotesque is never far away. Indeed, the female wrestler joins the late Divine in a pantheon of fantasies in which the *bishonen* and the outsize club host are antidotes as proportionately far-fetched as the extreme humdrum of day-to-day reality demands. As Ian Buruma remarked in a context referring mainly to comic books, 'Possibly many young girls – and to a lesser extent young boys – feeling that their natural inclinations are being slowly crushed by an adult world that forces them to be calculating and conformist, find an outlet in homosexual fantasies too remote from their own lives to be threatening: a far-away romantic ideal like the "Paris of our dreams". *Bishonen*, homosexual or not, are treated in a similar way to vampires and creatures from outer space.'

Between their pastel pinky-blue floral covers, the pages of many *shojo manga* (comics for young girls) were increasingly given to male homosexual adventures during the seventies. Driving his admirers to distraction at the time both in his boys' boarding school and among the tender young things following his adventures in the pages of a comic book called *Shojo* (*Young Girl*), the languid Gilbert Cocteau was always late for class, emerging from crumpled sheets and the arms of a friend, with his long forelock tousled over his huge watery eyes. Notorious for more outrageous homoerotic fantasies was the girls' comic *June*, which has now strayed more into the male homosexual camp, with some most unladylike illustrations of lissom *bishonen* boys being heartily buggered by leering beefcakes. With an increase in permissiveness during the past decade, however, male homoeroticism is fading increasingly from women's comic books, which are now given to frank and surprisingly graphic explorations of other avenues of sex.

With this kind of fare in vogue, young girls' comics gained a wide readership among the not so little. During the past few years, more explicit offshoots have been packaged in a marked breakaway from the traditional *shojo* mainstream in the form of *reedisu komikku*. With names such as *Morelove*, *Belove* and *Loving*, ubiquitous ladies' comics make their bias clear and are currently enjoying a huge boom. Like the rest, *Morelove* puts a more carnal edge on its sentimental romances, advertising its features on commuter trains with Japlish adjectives such as *sekkushiaru roman* (sexual romance) and the *chienji rabu* (change-love) adventures of Kawasaki Michiko who, one is promised, is the same heroine as in 'Sexy Boys', a popular serial battening on long-lashed hunks. The more adult *shojo manga* had a readership from high-school age, but the more licentious fantasies of the *reedisu komikku* target the OL, the Office Lady, and the *sekkushiaru* highlights can be quite as graphic as in the male equivalent.

The *manga* artist Yumiko Igarashi's work in *Morelove* has a cult following, and summer 1988 saw the publication of a special issue entirely devoted to a tale she called '*La Nuit Magic*', which is 320 pages long. Like many other people in Japan, *manga* artists work dauntingly hard. Based on a novel, the plot concerns an ideally pretty and downtrodden office flower called Yoriko Koganei. She hates her job, is pushed around by her superiors, lives at home and respects a strict 10 P.M. curfew. Indeed, only the fact that she has been brought up by her aunt and uncle instead of her parents sets her apart.

The many subsequent departures, however, begin as Yoriko is molested in a cinema and go a very long way. She burns the man's hand with a cigarette, but not before he has also filched her wallet, so that she is unable to pay the bill in a coffee shop afterwards. Allowing a mysterious young man in sunglasses who introduces himself as her *jujo* (imperial servant) to pay for her, she accepts his invitation to go to a disco. Here the *jujo*, who pops up thenceforth with the regularity of a genie, introduces her to a beautiful go-go dancer with whom she has a fleeting sapphic affair. Yoriko eventually works as a hostess in a lesbian club and leaves home to live with a colleague as woman and wife.

One day the *jujo* takes her to an exclusive SM club, where Yoriko dons a leather corset and black stockings to become a dominatrix joining an *ojo-ō-sama* (august queen) to form a twosome flogging a middle-aged gentleman pilloried in the trappings of bondage. '*Otōsan!*' she suddenly exclaims, believing him to be her long-lost father. Not only is he indeed her father, but Yoriko soon meets a mysterious and lovely customer at the lesbian club, who happens to be his mistress. The lady is a lesbian, which is fine, because Yoriko's father happens to be homosexual into the bargain. Yoriko is in heaven.

A recurring fantasy among comic-book heroines in the land of raven hair finds Yoriko blessed with long blonde tresses, which she cuts off short as she comes right out of the closet in a man's business suit as a full-fledged dike. Her many affairs climax in a double-page spread festooned with flowers, showing her ecstatically clinched in the nude in the arms of female playmates or those somewhere in between, but almost never male. Dreams and reality mingle confusingly as Yoriko has sex with a hermaphrodite and learns that her dissimilar and lost twin brother/sister was of the same persuasion. At last, as she blissfully allows herself to be tortured by her father's mistress down in the dungeon of the family mansion, Yoriko is finally fulfilled. In the knowledge that she is a fully liberated bisexual sadomasochist, that she comes from a background rather like a kinky-sex answer to the Adams Family (indeed, in most Japanese fantasies the omnipotent family is never far away) she goes back to work in an office a new woman.

The catharsis for the Office Lady is clear. Yoriko jabs her knee into the groin of a *frotteur* on the subway, repels the advances of her gross, bloated boss, leaves uncle and auntie and the 10 P.M. curfew behind, quits her job and takes to life in a fast lane unsullied by the persecuting male. The *shojo manga* has come a long way. The vicarious thrill of male homosexuality is washed away on the tides of sapphic fantasies finally banishing the male altogether. Not that the appeal of all this lies in real lesbianism. Since her males are either gross caricatures like Yoriko's boss, ambiguous shadows like the *jujo*, or completely androgynous, Igarashi ultimately offers her readers escape into a feminine universe in which males are not only superfluous, but have barely more substance than phantoms.

HOST CLUBS

Men dally with geisha but women, even if they wanted to, could hardly do the same with sumo wrestlers, who are confined to stables and subjected to a regimen removed only from the monastic by training bouts and gargantuan portions of food. The West likes its hunks with the accent more on visible muscle than spare tyres, so it may seem odd that a body quite as bloated as the sumo wrestler's could constitute any canon of beauty. Although the sport has nothing to do with sex appeal anyway, some women nevertheless succumb to the hippopotamine charm. The currently reigning *yokozuna* or grand champion Chiyonofuji is a departure from the norm for being built more of visible muscle and less like one of the fatter gods of fortune, but the same hardly applies to the overweight norm. It did not apply, for instance, to the monumental Bambi, a retired sumo wrestler and the reigning star at Heracles, a host club in Asakusa.

Strutting around between the tables in only a Spartacus loincloth secured by a belt as thick as a boxing champ's, Bambi would kneel before starry-eyed matrons and pour drinks as deferentially as the meekest bar hostess from paws as big as hams. Interviewed on TV some years ago, he proudly displayed a solid gold, diamond-studded Cartier watch dwarfed around his massive wrist, as well as the white Rolls he drove to work. Heracles met its demise a few years ago, the story goes, precisely and typically because such media overkill drove its regular clientele away.

Gokudo no Onnatachi (*Women of the Underworld*), a quirky recent *yakuza* film by the popular director Hideo Gosha, targets a female audience. The opening scene is set in a host club with a bibulous hen party every bit as boisterous as its stag equivalent, showing the inebriated wives of gang bosses carousing beneath crystal chandeliers with legions of somewhat effete males in tuxedos and sharp, fashionable suits. In Tokyo, host clubs range from sleazy dives in Ikebukuro haunted by pathetically frustrated females vying for the favours of young weasels in garish striped jackets to fabulously plush male harems for tycoons' wives after a bit of the other in Akasaka or Shinjuku. Gosha's film accurately implies that the clubs attract underworld spouses, but the clientele also includes those of club and cabaret owners, real estate dealers, top corporate executives and politicians.

Like the male equivalent, the host club deploys fantasy stereotypes of various kinds. Suave middle-aged smoothies with the looks of macho film stars click Dunhill lighters beneath the customers' trembling cigarettes, miscellaneous hunks flex oiled muscles Heracles-fashion in slave costumes, and others in business suits emulate shy young office workers. Coveys of young men also evoke the image of *nimaime* – the romantic leads of song, stage and screen currently epitomized by Go Hiromi or the frankly effeminate *bishonen*, the pretty boy. Like hostesses, hosts dispense favours optionally, but the perks they wear around wrists, drive to work or even sometimes live in have been earned from something more than just good tableside manners.

The Japanese word for gigolo is *tsubame*, or swallow. Like gigolos everywhere, many of the hosts in clubs catering to a female clientele swing both ways. Precedents abounded during the Edo period, when sedate ladies from the shogun's court and women of wealth slumming in the amusement quarters would dally with kabuki actors, often paying them for their services in cash. They sometimes rubbed shoulders with pederasts in selecting beautiful boys in specialized teahouses and, for those fond of aquatic pleasures, there were also bath-houses staffed with understanding young attendants. All of these things exist in modern guises and equivalents today, a phenomenon showing a revival of an older pattern forced to lie dormant from the late Edo 'modernization' drives until the relative emancipation of women during the postwar period.

An old *onsen* geisha in Izu once confided to me that she made regular monthly trips up to Tokyo – the purpose being exclusively to visit gay bars, because she always had such a wonderful time. Not a few gay bars are favourite after-hour haunts for women from the *mizu shobai*, and some virtually double as host clubs. Late at night in a club in Roppongi fairly recently, for instance, hostesses joined kimonoed mamas in contemplating transsexuals smoking cigarettes through their backsides; popular some years ago with young women was a bizarre cabaret called Banana Power, in which the evening highlight found them hurling cream cakes at transvestites and effeminates performing on-stage. Women perhaps like to put the shoe on the other foot: over and above holding the appeal of desexed male company, host clubs and certain gay bars allow the oppressed female to have a crack at the subservient male.

During a bibulous evening some years ago, one of the company was a young woman unhappily married into one of Japan's wealthiest industrial families. For all her jet-set sophistication and education abroad, she was still a prisoner of the old system. Living with her husband in deep-frozen cordiality on the understanding that they would maintain appearances while leading separate lives, there would – could – never be a divorce. During the day she was a model of dutiful motherhood to her two children; at night she cast tradition to the wind as she parked them with a baby-sitter and drowned her sorrows in élite bars. As attractive as she was, she surrounded herself with flunkies in tuxedos and bow-ties. They were students, she explained, whom she kept to entertain her and paid them salaries. How far this went was something one naturally refrained from asking, but many wealthy women trapped in bleak *mariages de convenance* find the flighty company of gigolos a much less dangerous alternative to the full-blown affair.

She took everyone to a fairly small but very plush bar looking essentially like scores of others, except for a pervasive aroma of perfume. Being situated in Shinjuku 2-Chome, its persuasion was obvious. The hosts wore much the same attire as her minions, except that they wore make-up and their physical attributes ranged from the merely pleasing to the disconcertingly lovely. Not just pretty faces, some could spice a lively couple of hours' tippling with fast talking and a lively sense of humour. This was during the early eighties, when even some straight men with broader minds often owned that they found the conversation with hosts more interesting than the established and formalized banter of the hostess club. The boom for gay bars peaked to the extent that, faced with male customers seeking gayer pastures elsewhere, some of them closed their doors to women.

Because Japanese grow up from childhood freedom into the constraints of adulthood, the *mizu shobai* offers an escape into a world affording frequent reversions to early adolescence. Always true of men, now that women are beginning to assert themselves socially, the escapist fantasies not only loom as large for them but can also be strikingly similar. If it gives women a footing in a more physical fantasy world, equality may also have a darker side: after struggling so long to join the work force in the same capacity as men, many may find themselves caught in an office routine just as time-consuming, taxing and ultimately sterile as the *salaryman*'s.

PART VI

A New Era

20

The Hard Road to Equality

BECAUSE THEY'RE WOMEN

Although in reality Japanese tradition has never frowned on working women, and today the majority of working married women are obliged to help make ends meet in their families, the officially sponsored portrait of 'wholesome' family life invariably shows that the proper place for women is at home. In a country where stereotypes are treasured, emphasis on the established proper roles of women is especially noticeable. It extends to demurely polite deportment, a studied innocent cuteness, a 'gentle' voice one octave above the natural voice and always a nurturing, motherly disposition. The model woman in the world of the *salaryman* is a cross between Florence Nightingale and the minister of finance (as women are always totally responsible for household finances). Superior intelligence is a liability for girls and women, and must be disguised.

Karel Van Wolferen, *The Enigma of Japanese Power* (1989)

Not too far from the Yamashita family home is the Orwellian empire of the automotive Toyota company, which holds a town of the same name in a grip of steel. At the company's decree, the Toyota town takes its day off on Friday instead of Sunday. Since local residents are nearly all Toyota employees, corporate holidays have become school and shopkeepers' holidays too. On many of these, the company stages community celebrations, and the streets are filled with cheerful corporate martial music and the motor equivalent to the totalitarian parade. The management is firmly convinced that a 'relaxed family atmosphere' is quintessential to productivity, so Toyota house rules prohibit workers' wives from undertaking even part-time jobs. According to one 27-year-old ex-employee, if female staff members should surpass the *tekireiki* marriage age without actually tying the knot, perhaps in deference to the Equal Employment Opportunity Law adopted in 1986, they are not exactly fired but squeezed in other ways: 'Both male and female colleagues kept asking me how come I still wasn't married. The atmosphere got increasingly strained; you might say that I finally got the message. I left.'

Implementing medieval principles to build cars, the Toyota company indeed seems fantastic. Yet this particular practice is by no means unique to Toyota, but a general, unwritten rule in the majority of companies in Japan. Otherwise female employees would cost too much; one would have to raise their salaries commensurate with their slow, unwelcome climb up the ladder. *Onna dakara*: because I'm a woman. It's a line often heard in those perennially popular and unabashedly sentimental Enka folk songs. Indeed, in a conservative country in which Confucian samurai ethics were resuscitated in the 1880s and fomented lucratively ever since in industrial disguise, being a woman can be tough. Obligatory marriage and motherhood, and subservience to her husband and his family would seem to have no place in a technopolitan economic supergiant in which nearly half of the work force is female. A Welfare Ministry campaign in early 1989 stressed that the differences between male and female are only physiological with a poster campaign showing two bespattered toddlers gleefully romping in the mud. '*Tamatama otokonoko, tamatama onnanoko*' read the caption: 'He just happens to be a boy; she just happens to be a girl.' Such notions, however, gain little support from the ministries more closely allied to business and industry, who join ruling politicians in upholding traditional values as a means of continually exploiting the diligence of the populace.

The Equal Employment Opportunity Law seems purely devised as a smoke screen constituting part of the stagecraft of 'internationalism'. Even if it were not quite so ineffectual, large corporations have standing with the government, making any measures against sexual discrimination very unlikely. From the largest to the smallest firms, besides, the widespread view is that such practices are unethical only according to concepts adopted a mere forty-odd years ago and which, to some, remain foreign. The law entitles women to complain but this merely prompts 'counselling' rather than action and, so far, few have. Most women would have nothing to gain. Even if it could theoretically win them higher wages and guard them from dismissal, their action would be tantamount to a degree of disloyalty earning them complete ostracism by their colleagues.

Some major firms, including several banks, have nonetheless recently moved to put ability before traditional hierarchical promotion and greater sexual equality in the office. According to the British president of a noted Tokyo advertising agency co-directed with a Japanese counterpart, however, implementing the system is not always so easy: 'We have a brilliant young woman executive, but putting her on some accounts would be like banging our heads against the wall. Some clients would never accept her. Women are emerging as brighter and more creative, and the signs are that they're coming to the fore in a big way. But as long as certain types of men remain in the seat on the client side, you're going to have a problem.'

An opinion poll conducted among women in Japan and five other countries by the Prime Minister's Office in

1982, however, suggested that 'Japanese women still believe a woman's place is in the home and that little girls should be brought up to be "ladylike"'. Supported by only a small fraction of those questioned in Europe and the US, such role definitions were upheld by 70 per cent of their Japanese counterparts. 'Disappointingly for feminists', concluded an article in *The Japan Times*, 'the women's awareness of the UN International Women's Decade and its efforts to improve women's standing was strikingly low.'

In another multinational survey on the theme 'Men should work and women should stay at home' by the same agency in 1989, the number of women actively disagreeing was well over a third both in Britain and the US; in Japan it was only 6 per cent. Once again, adding together the Japanese women who agreed either completely or 'somewhat' with the premise, one reaches a figure of 71 per cent. In the wake of all the exaltation of equality and the working woman in the media during those seven years, not to mention recent political events, it seems incredible that the survey should have arrived at almost exactly the same conclusions.

It is often said that the replies to surveys conducted in Japan, especially on a direct interview basis like these, tend to be more what the respondents think the interlocutor wants to hear, and that official research is anyway biased towards perpetuating the status quo. Notwithstanding, marriage is a durable social imperative and many women remain amenable to tradition, whereby they assume temporary, subordinate roles in the office, marry and join the work force again in middle age. Surveys from the private sector, however, often set things in a rather different perspective. One recently conducted by a noted cosmetics firm, for instance, found four-fifths of the women asked whether they found working mothers admirable replying in the affirmative, and 70 per cent refuting the notion of quitting employment after marriage. The arguments in favour of supporting the status quo, however, are highly persuasive: so far only two out of ten firms concede a year's maternity leave, in most cases without pay, and day-care facilities remain woefully inadequate. Although the 23 per cent who disagreed (either fully or 'somewhat') with the postulates of the government survey no doubt aspire to an equal footing in the workplace, women accounted for 3.5 per cent of managerial staff in 1987, a figure more than double the total a decade before but still paltry by western standards. The signs are that an authentic rise in the status of women comparable to the West is only just dawning in Japan.

THE MEN IN THE SEAT

If they sometimes manifest a fondness for geisha, the ruling politicians have generally had a rather low opinion of woman, except in her exalted capacity in the home, a place in which they spend as little time as other men. As it happens, however, women have meanwhile been gaining clout faster than they gave them credit for. Ironically, this came about partly as the result of an exploitative ploy. During the early eighties, increasing criticism of Japan's trade surplus overseas prompted a slight decline in exports and, as the yen rose steeply during the middle of the decade, the prices of Japanese products rose proportionately on foreign markets. As the attentions of commerce and industry turned more to the home front, the government backed the launching of an all-out domestic spending drive. Handy for alleviating a growing labour shortage on one hand, women represented a huge, untapped market on the other. Young OLs living with parents earn salaries but pay no rent; many housewives complement the household budget with full or part-time work. Employed according to the mixed blessing of mandatory shorter hours, working women have far more time and money to spare than their male colleagues.

The gold rush roared ahead in the wake of a barrage of media publicity addressing a mythical 'new' woman, and floodgates opened to booming new businesses in the service, consumer and media sectors. Covering retailing, fashion, culture and entertainment and preponderantly targeting the female consumer, the drive greatly expanded her horizons. Even as the majority merely duly and dutifully consumed, others entered an expanding job market and a precious few, again greatly magnified by the media cultivating illusions of change, emerged as female entrepreneurs. One given extensive press coverage, for instance, was 23-year-old Nagisa Araki, who dropped out of music college to found a pop concert planning and discount fashion store empire chalking up 300,000,000 yen in sales in 1988. Men hardly even entered the picture of Araki's success: 'We used to have several male employees,' she said in a newspaper interview, 'but young men mature slowly and often can't take the bold steps the job requires. Besides, the best male employees prefer to move to bigger corporations. When we look for the most capable and suitable people among applicants, we find that they are women.' Many men resent being ordered around by a woman but, as some women rise to prominence in a growing and diversifying labour force, some are having to eat humble pie.

One who found the taste bitter indeed was Prime Minister Sousuke Uno, who was forced to resign in summer 1989 after less than three months in office. He hardly knew what hit him. His dalliance with a geisha, which ran according to a time-honoured and perfectly respectable scenario only slightly tainted by the shadow of sex for cash, helped to rock a ruling Liberal Democratic Party already weakened by the Recruit scandal preceding it. Arguably, that was a time-honoured activity too. Some might call it bribery, but mutual gift-giving to curry political favour and seal business relationships is perfectly fitting according to the canons of tradition.

Propelled by mutual back-scratching ever since its creation in 1955 from a merger between two tottering prewar conservative political parties – the one 'Liberal' and the other 'Democratic' – the LDP has always encouraged big business to stalk the corridors of power. The dominant figure pulling the strings behind the scenes during the undertaking was the shady Yoshio Kodama, a noted ultra-nationalist and former gangster who had directed extortionate industrial operations and a vast spy network in China during the war. Initially a patchwork hastily stitched together from prewar remnants, the Japanese government is an oligarchical amalgam abiding by no particular political ideology, atop of which the LDP dances to the tunes called by industry, commerce, real estate development and bureaucracy as it holds hands under the table with its old friends on the far right and among the *yakuza* gangs. Beneath the spiritual father-figure of the emperor, it's all one big happy family, over which the prime minister presides as an embellishment and in which there are no true villains. This tends to turn Japanese officialdom into what Karel van Wolferen aptly calls the 'System', and it indeed has no focus of accountable power. Political party members join bureaucrats and industrialists as mere cogs in an unbreakable machine.

If it can be credited with raising Japan from the bottom of the heap of the third world to the richest nation in only four decades, the gerontocratic system staunchly advocates prewar ethics: the gung-ho solidarity and the stoicism, blind self-sacrifice, ruthless single-mindedness and antiquated Meiji-period patriotism. Such tenets triggered the catastrophe of the Second World War, even as they spurred the economic miracle later on. The miracle has by now been a reality for twenty years and too few Japanese are enjoying the fruits.

Outward signs are there for the world to behold and are promulgated through glitzy media images at home. Behind the democratic *tatemae*, the *honne* is rather different. Triggering a rapacious building spree, runaway speculation has sent real estate values so far through the roof that too many Japanese can no longer afford to buy one of their own. The costs of imports have dropped through the rising yen, but consumer prices largely remain the same. The labour shortage makes immigrant workers inevitable yet, ferried in by the same gangsters who shuttle about the *Japayuki* prostitutes, these can similarly expect to be punished by the law. Trade and industry feed politicians substantial cash contributions for party campaigns; legal and otherwise, pork-barrelling has everything to do with why government policies have so largely presented much greater benefits for trade and industry than for public welfare.

The war effort goes on. The new lifestyle cosmetically pervading the media is a reality only for the young; to the majority of the toiling corporate armies, the five-day work week remains a distant dream. Because individuals are constantly checking and controlling themselves to conform to the norm and to swim with the stream, Japan is not unlike Orwell's *1984* might be hundreds of years on. Oppression has worked its way so far inwards that overt repression is quite superfluous. Oblivious, obedient and unflinchingly industrious, a resigned population is only rarely given to complaints about substandard conditions.

Or so it was. Recent polls increasingly paint a rather different picture. One conducted internationally on workers of both sexes between the ages of twenty-five and thirty-five in 1989 showed that whereas only two out of ten were dissatisfied with their working conditions in Britain and the USA, the number in Japan amounted to nearly half. Another comparing Tokyo with cities of the West showed that, unlike the majority in these, Tokyoites felt that the rewards of their labours were as meagre as their leisure time. Another conducted among workers selected at random from top corporations by the Fukoku Life Insurance Company in 1989 was revealing too. Citing reasons as diverse as poor working relations at the office, colds and even hangovers, nearly eight out of ten often dreaded going to work. Despite wanting to stay at home for legitimate reasons such as illness, about the same number said that they felt obliged to go to the office anyway. Eighty-two per cent thought about work even when commuting, two-fifths dreamed about work at night, one-third said that worries over work caused them loss of sleep and, finally, nearly half were afraid of *karoshi* – dying from overwork. Their fears are not ungrounded; recent statistics show that the incidence of *pokkuribyoo*, the redoubtable dropping-dead sickness, is on the rise.

LYSISTRATA COMES TO TOKYO

I was born in 1928, and women of my day were taught to defer to masculine pride and authority. Thus I was all the more disappointed to discover the truth: the giants were actually pygmies ... What happens when women, unable to tolerate male vanity and immaturity any longer, lose respect for their husbands and abandon the role of mother and homemaker? Many unloved women will end the charade and walk out. The shock reverberating from that is potentially more traumatic than Japan's defeat in World War II.

Feminist writer Seiko Tanabe, *Chuo Koron* magazine,
June 1987

No one is particularly enamoured of taxation, but the first to be inconvenienced by the government's clumsily conceived 3 per cent consumption tax were women. Everything was priced in odd figures, causing irksome pile-ups of tinny one-yen coins in handbags and before the cash registers in the supermarkets. Never exactly loved either, the LDP made itself markedly more unpopular. Months later, coming as the crowning achievement to decades of corrupt practices about which few any longer entertained any doubts, the Recruit insider-trading scandal brought down several cabinet ministers and caused Prime Minister Takeshita to resign in 1989. A mountain of corruption involving so many ruling politicians, it even turned the earlier Lockheed bribery uproar into a molehill. The credibility of the LDP plummeted in the eyes of the people. Just before the upper house elections in July 1989, Agriculture Minister Hisao Horinouchi followed in a grand tradition for political ineptness. Putting his foot firmly in his mouth during a campaign speech, he announced that 'Women are useless in politics.'

The timing of this particular statement could hardly have been worse. Who would have imagined ten years ago that the Japan Socialist Party would now be headed by a woman? That the honour befell the former law professor Takako Doi in 1986 should have been ample proof of the spirit of the times, but the LDP waited for the local elections for a well-honed feminine axe to fall on them out of the blue. As the seats they lost in the Diet went whizzing past their stunned heads, they found themselves in a position comparable to the shogunate during the years before the Meiji restoration. Hardly had the eruption of the Recruit scandal ousted Prime Minister Takeshita when Sousuke Uno, pushed on-stage as his successor, was unseated through his geisha affair.

Before the lower and upper house elections, the Japan Socialist Party launched what it called 'Operation Madonna', which involved persuading women with a good record for community activity but no political experience to run in local elections. The object of the drive was 'clean' politics, *sans* sex and corruption, and its success was phenomenal. Even Niigata, the fort held by the veteran Kakue Tanaka, former prime minister and LDP 'king-maker', fell to a woman from the JSP; Takako Doi's radiant countenance graced *Time* magazine as 'Woman of the Hour'. The LDP may be a monolith, but even in Japan, where opposition parties tend to rest more on the laurels of opposition than to come up with concrete alternative policies, monoliths eventually have a way of toppling.

Joshi mondai – woman problems – thoroughly haunted politics at the end of the eighties. Hardly had the ruling party drawn up a new 'clean' cabinet under Prime Minister Kaifu, when it was hit by another carnal bomb-shell: female trouble struck Chief Cabinet Minister Tokuo Yamashita too. Salving his conscience upon finding himself in high office in a freshly laundered cabinet, the 69-year-old Yamashita had promptly bidden goodbye to a 24-year-old Akasaka bar hostess with whom he had enjoyed an extramarital affair for three years, and wrote her off with a cheque for three million yen. As the marriage ceremony's three-times-three drinking cup ritual suggests, three is a portentous figure. Sousuke Uno had paid for his sexual favours with a three million downpayment and monthly instalments of 300,000 yen.

Although she showed no compunction in tattling in a weekly magazine, the story goes that Yamashita's hostess was so deeply hurt that she sent the cheque back. Yamashita confessed all during a televised press conference, but staunchly denied that his gesture had anything to do with hush money. She had been in financial difficulties; this had been what he saw as a decent way of ending the affair. If the more arrogant Uno had raised female hackles even higher by patly refusing all comment, the humbly apologizing Yamashita resigned as a pathetic picture of contrition. To err is human, to forgive is female. *Joshi-mondai*, it was said, was turning into a witch hunt. Mutual product emulation is a basis for competition in Japan; keeping up with the Socialists and hastily whitewashing its image, the LDP appointed a woman, Mayumi Moriyama, as an immaculate new chief cabinet minister to replace the tarnished Yamashita.

As the 'madonnas' gained ground, male politicians were increasingly gripped by the short and curlies. In 1989, Japan paralleled the ancient Greek tale of Lysistrata, the Athenian lady who goaded all female citizens into a mass sexual strike until the belligerent menfolk mended their ways. What most women were objecting to was not, in fact, just sexual dalliance. The bone of contention was less about morals and more about money being traditionally used to reduce women who are not even professional prostitutes to the virtual status of slot machines. Whether or not it had been on his own initiative, as the geisha selling the story to a magazine had claimed, Uno had paid for her in cash. She was roundly spurned by the geisha sisterhood thereafter, but few women cared to denounce the woman's treachery. In the magazine article, she had posed as a victim of the chauvinistic Uno's ill-treatment and the spirit of the times incited women to swallow the premise whole.

Either way, *joshi mondai* clearly symptomized the fact that women were no longer prepared to put up with the age-old socially sanctioned privilege of keeping mistresses. If some were still prepared to forgive a *nigo* scenario in the classic tradition, the fact that many saw Yamashita's golden handshake as a more dignified way of ending an affair than Uno's merely infuriated other women all the more. 'Many LDP politicians', remarked Teruko Yoshitake, a female political commentator, 'live with the misunderstanding that lots of money and lots of women make them greater politicians.'

If many resigned to a one-party system for too long don't bother to vote at all, women voters outnumber men – albeit by a narrow margin. Whereas men find their horizons confined to a routine of work and compulsory after-hours play, women have more time to widen theirs. As a result, they tend to have more flexible ideas. Some women's magazines formerly given exclusively to things 'feminine' now include extensive social, economic and political features. Many housewives are involved with community work which, as trite and suburban as it often may be, at least encourages some exchange with other people in society.

The worm turns. The signs were all there but too many men were hardly even able to take note of them. Television, for instance, is a medium increasingly orientated towards females, and increasing numbers of programmes seem overpowered by assertive female journalists.

The downtrodden housewives and mothers of classic soap operas dwindle in the wake of self-possessed corporate ladies and women detectives; even the samurai drama is given to steely heroines handy with *ninja* techniques behind their silken, doll-like façades. Not that the fighting female is anything new. Tai Kato's famed *Hibotan Bakuto* (*Red Peony Gambler*) series in the late sixties starred Junko Fuji as card shark and gang boss, almost by way of a hysterical metaphor for the hardy woman fighting heroically in a violent universe while still respecting a subordinate role. Emancipation was about as far removed from here as from the old samurai custom dictating that a woman raped should commit suicide for the sake of her own and her husband's honour.

Today film producers too cater to a majority female audience. Even the staunch Toei company recently dressed up the dwindling *yakuza* movie genre with a new breed of beauteous bloody mamas. In Gosha's *Women of the Underworld* and *Sister* alike, for instance, the violent *yakuza* males are accessories in a theatre in which the dominant female assumes functions once exclusively reserved for the male. Between the idealizations and dramatizations, the syrup, cooking programmes and the soaps on TV meanwhile, one gains a picture not so much of the predicaments passively endured by women, but their true, active aspirations.

Even Seiko Matsuda, the meek queen of the Kawaii-ko-chan, those eternally simpering cute-little-girl singing stars, recently earned droves of additional female admirers. Not because she married, had a child and allowed her career to be edifyingly switched off by conservative producers according to the accepted pattern, but because she not only went on pursuing it but also launched her own fashion business. Such women are very rarely militant feminists; they hardly need to be. No one thought petticoat talk was of any importance; over the years women have turned the affliction of being ignored into an asset building them quietly up into a force to be reckoned with.

To some women the changing TV image is deceptive. Since men dominate overwhelmingly on the programming side, it is arguably a façade, a superficial fashion merely pandering to a feminine target. The feminist author Kuniko Uemura nonetheless sees what she calls 'an era of androgyny' around the corner. 'In Japanese TV dramas, women are often depicted as dynamos at work and devoted housewives and good mothers at home,' she noted in a press interview. 'That's supposed to be the role model for scores of aspiring career women today.' Uemura believes that this in fact only adds to the psychological pressure upon them. Women have by now broken into hitherto exclusively male domains but, like the gangland heroines of *The Peony Gambler* series, they are expected to conform to traditional role models at the same time. If society is to attain the desirable state she described as 'androgyny' in a recent book, Uemura says that to be truly liberated, women must first become psychologically and economically independent from men.

In the meantime, the battle between the sexes and the political parties goes on. Deeming that the Chief Cabinet Minister had served her purpose as a public relations puppet for the lower house elections in February 1990, the winning LDP simply booted Mayumi Moriyama out of office. With the house Madonna out of the way, it was business as usual for the men in the seat.

THE NEW MORAL ORDER

Whether it is due to biology or social conditioning is a universal chicken-and-egg debate but, even in the most egalitarian societies, men are still more likely than women to indulge in casual, promiscuous sex. One foreigner reports that his Japanese wife once asked him whether he had ever visited Soapland. When he replied that he hadn't, her reaction amazed him. 'Oh, you should! They say that it's ever such fun and the techniques are peerless.' No Japanese wife would iron her husband's shirts and press his suit prior to his forays into the Yoshiwara as she did not so long ago, but even among today's most emancipated women, a comparatively marked degree of indifference to flings with prostitutes remains; they are too fleeting to endanger a relationship. Not that men in Japan can take the mandatory fidelity of their wives any more for granted than in any relatively democratic society. Female adultery is as widespread as the existence of host clubs, housewife-prostitutes, neglected spouses turning to lovers and the growing legions of women divorcing testify.

Despite a pragmatic view of prostitution, however, even more liberal women have recently come to look upon the carnal side of the *mizu shobai* as a blight on the landscape and, even if many of its inhabitants might not share their opinion, more militant women see it both rightly and wrongly as an area in which their sisters are degraded as slaves. Their animosity stems also from its still having much the same relationship to the home as its *ukiyo* ancestor, which was the result of the rarity of sexual entente between man and wife.

Scrounging on the incontrovertible uprising of women against centuries of relegation to the kitchen or the cat-house, a chilly new moral order, a wave of sancti-moniousness resuscitating Meiji-period priggery, is sweeping a Japan in which philandering politicians can now expect to go the way of Gary Hart. This naturally entails the occident's calculated use of hypocrisy as a weapon for political gain, but the old sword of Confucian propriety is poised and may well come slashing down – but not fatally – on prostitution too.

It will no doubt continue to be tacitly tolerated and sporadically repressed to placate its opponents, but there may no longer be any innovations. Peep shows and cabarets will not be donning any fanciful new disguises to turn old tricks and, if there is still scope for adult video critiques in the wee small hours of the morning, there will be no more 'Tissue Time' on late-night TV. The modifications to the Public Morals law in 1985 put the freeze on the flesh-pots, caused the sun to set on carnal novelties and ushered in a wave of moral rearmament. Patrolling bookstores in the Yokohama area, women's groups succeeded in forcing a lot of them to remove the more explicit sex mags and comics from the shelves, but no one even suggested relegating them more practically to the porno shops, far from offended eyes. Knowing that the lady is the one who ultimately does the choosing and that a fashion for primness governs her tastes, love hotels are redecorating, replacing interiors conducive to fantasy with discreet, impersonal blandness. Primness is even visible in fitness clubs, where men over thirty-five converse naked in the sauna, while the younger set huddles modestly in its trendy swimming trunks.

Like the famous 'mascot girls' on *11 p.m.*, one used to see a lot of simpering nymphets smiling wanly and waving at the camera in bikinis on TV. In the wake of both the TV clean-up campaign in 1985 and the rising

tides of feminism, like other programmes, *11 p.m.*
eventually either clad them in designer dresses or elimi-
nated them altogether. After more than twenty years on
screen three times a week, besides, the anyway out-
moded *11 p.m.* died early in 1990. The fun on the
salacious side of the *mizu shobai*, on which the programme had formerly concentrated, had resided precisely in its changing, colourful and often improbable
presentation. The absurd dimension that attracted so
many social rebels into the world of raunch gurgled
down the drain as drab uniformity on the one hand and
mindless pornography on the other.

Sensing the zeitgeist, Shinya Yamamoto, for one, put
away his image-friendly Raybans and even removed his
baseball cap – the crown that once adorned his head as
TV's king of sleaze. Things ain't what they used to be. A
former film director from the pink heyday who moved
long ago onto the tube, Yamamoto used to guffaw and
whoop his way through the flesh-pots, giving the
lowdown on the erogenic highspots and refinements of
Soapland and health massage. His public face was calculatedly obnoxious, another case of a stereotype contrived
and assiduously perfected. Nowadays, however, Yamamoto hosts and researches programmes on issues such
as deforestation and pollution and has turned from
pussy talk to interviews in cat-fanciers' magazines. The
reason he gives is that the sex scene is no longer such fun
but, as one of the old radical set, the chances are that he
is also aware that there are other, ultimately more adult
ways to jolt social consciousness than sexual provocation. A legacy of the Edo period, coming into its own
again after the Second World War and going overboard
during the late sixties, sex-as-dissent is now entering its
twilight.

Despite the sexual frankness of the Japanese, the

virtue of primness impressed upon them both by Confucianism and nineteenth-century European morality has led not a few women to believe that sex is as dirty and degrading as do an albeit dwindling number of their western sisters. Others counter that this is just an outward pose. 'Don't you believe it,' the popular woman novelist 'Angel' Ui once confided to me: 'Underneath it all, Japanese women are completely *sukebe* [lechers] – just like men!' Formulated by men, imposed by men and implanted in their minds by men, the seeds of prudery have nevertheless borne fruit in some. As ye sow, so shall ye reap. And as it was in Victorian England, that the yield is not to every male taste is yet another incentive driving some to seek bigger thrills in the red-light districts than their prim wives would concede at home.

Making a convenient marriage with resentment, primness has also produced numerous and vociferous women's groups constantly launching crusades to have prostitution outlawed altogether. Once they superficially succeeded during the fifties, the leagues of decency turned their attentions to striptease. The ranks of Christian soldiers counted female student recruits enjoined to protest in the very places of perdition. Alongside the po-faced moralists of both genders who stoically mixed with the priapic crowd, the tender young things were frequently photographed nobly sacrificing themselves as they averted their eyes from the outlandish celebrations of the female form on-stage. Myopic and irrational, few ever stop to think that tolerance and legislation make better sense than greater repression, which only drives the sex industry even deeper underground and causes women to suffer much greater injustices in the hands of exploitative thugs.

The wave of the sexual revolution (real and fondly imagined) flooding the West in the sixties and seventies has yet to break but, as the droves of young couples beetling freely in and out of the love hotels over the weekend suggest, the backwash looms large. Chauvinists and conservatives watch the process with a wary eye; during the past half century they have had to put up with women's emancipation and suffrage, a rising career woman and now even female politicians. They have seen a marriage pattern swing increasingly from centuries-old arrangement to love matches. Divorce laws introduced in 1946 moreover precluded the old three-line letter of dismissal, which explains why prewar Japan had one of the highest rates in the world. Today the divorce rate has risen sharply after an all-time postwar low, and most of the suits are filed by women. If subsequent legal amendments still leave things rather skimpy on alimony, they have nonetheless put child-custody in favour of the mother, instead of mandatorily placing children in the husband's family once she had been summarily dumped.

Many *mizu shobai* commentators, including Shinya Yamamoto, lament the mercenary nature of its new breed of female denizens. 'These days', they lament, 'they're only in it for the money.' Why anyone would dispense professional sexual favours for less, one might think, is beyond imagining, but like scores of others of his generation, Yamamoto was recently quoted in an interview as regretting the 'old days' before the banning of official brothels in 1957, when girls became prostitutes to support their parents and graciously conducted their profession to the utmost of their abilities. That prostitutes were sold into the profession willy-nilly never enters their heads; more important is the fantasy of their being fired by filial piety rather than crass personal gain. There can be little doubt that the gap in perception between Japanese men, who are fettered to the past, and women, who live more with practical current realities, is an awesome chasm.

Many Japanese Don Juans affirm that conquest comes easiest among women between the ages of seventeen and twenty-five – the group with the roundest heels. Some are bound to parental curfews, but many others, granted greater freedom both in and outside the home during the past two decades, make the most of the years before marriage, which for some may still be 'the cemetery of life'. Conservative pundits lament that the youthful sowers of wild oats in the amusement districts are going over the top. A few certainly may wind up scattered by the wayside too tanked up to move, and a minute fraction may resort to amphetamines and solvents. A small contingent of young females may discreetly solicit male prospects to earn the wherewithal to buy expensive clothing in the nearby boutiques. Nobody's perfect.

Shoji Yamashita, our earlier high-school hero, is now at university in Tokyo. Although he's doing pretty well with his economic studies (i.e. attending class), he's not thinking too much about the future. He goes to the discos in Roppongi, and hangs out in Shibuya, a rather deceptive showcase of the freewheeling youthful lifestyle often called *yangu taun* – young town. Out of all the teenagers flocking to Tokyo for the sheer joy of a day's pullulation between the fast-food outlets and the boutiques, more than half come from neighbouring prefectures or even further out in the country where things are much slower to change. Those slightly older, and preponderantly female, cram restaurants and café-bars, watch foreign films in increasing numbers of specialized cinemas or wander round an abundance of miscellaneous art exhibitions held in the area's prominent department stores.

Among the hordes relaying each other in the love hotels, some of the younger couples, to whom no one troubled to give a sex education, may find themselves praying later for a crop failure. Most tend anyway to view abortion as a minor inconvenience and there are still those contraceptives called Bubu Friend, with the two little pigs dancing on the package. Shibuya abounds with *herusu massagi* too, but Shoji, who reached manhood through the good offices of a more experienced young lady met at a party, has neither been there nor to Soapland – which had been the theatre of initiation for both his elder brothers. Places like that aren't sordid, they're old fashioned. But if Shoji should marry more out of a sense of duty than inclination, will he still uphold this opinion by the time he's greying on his way up the rungs of the corporate ladder? Tomorrow is another day.

The years of affluence have worked wonders. The new generations are taller, more elegantly dressed and better fed. Women no longer have legs with shapes inspiring the formerly oft-heard and despondent comparison with *daikon* radishes. As many foreign males point out, there are more beauties per square metre in Tokyo than anywhere else on earth. Today's Japanese are a handsome people to be sure, and they can afford to have more fun than most of the world can dream of. Yet do they?

Hyped in the media, the city settings for new, mixed socializing are not what they seem. The in-spots are overwhelmed by groups of young women, while young men with comparable attributes and assets go out in groups of their own. Each sex prefers its own company. There are always the exceptions which, by conspicuously daring to have more fun, set examples filtering slowly through the rest of society, without which the future would look bleak indeed. Used to segregation from childhood, the sexes do not understand one another. It's 'menu for lady' in many restaurants and ladies' cars, ladies' drinks, ladies' vitamins, ladies' station kiosks, ladies' tour packages et al – the discriminatory overtones pale before women's readiness to go along with lucrative commercial sexual stereotyping and segregation.

As though striving for an exclusive feminine universe, female emancipation Japan-style veers towards a peculiar self-possession rendering the male just as superfluous as the rosy, sapphic and vindictive fantasies in 'ladies' comics' suggest. If the macho is becoming a dinosaur, the female view of his replacement merely seems to make Kurt Singer's comment about men as 'mere protuberances' much truer than it was in the 1930s. Comfortable only in the company of his own sex too, the conservative male's worst fears are being realized: completely emancipated, the spiderwoman will soon be able to eat him up.

Nowhere is the old epithet 'battle of the sexes' more apt than in Japan, where the two seem engaged in a cold war. Reacting to centuries of male chauvinism, females dig in their heels and are perpetually on their guard. Launched by lawyers associations in Tokyo and Osaka in 1988, sexual harassment 'hotlines' immediately prompted deluges of phone calls, including two from diffident men. More seriously, one in five of some fifty women in Tokyo had been raped by a boss, and the rest included those fondled by superiors, offered promotion for sex or simply fired for rebuttals. No one could deny that the extent of the phenomenon and the fact that its victims had hitherto had no recourse were outrageous; the countermeasures were long overdue. Within weeks, however, *sekishiaru harasumento* became a grossly amplified national feminine obsession. Alarmed at a mere curtain to protect her in mixed railway sleeper cars, one woman wrote to the press of the imminence of sexual harassment. 'What about providing a buzzer in each sleeper in case of an emergency?'

To one young woman office worker of my acquaintance, *sekku-hara* is often a choice topic of malicious office gossip and has gone too far. During corporate resort parties, she says, some see even the custom of women pouring sake for men as *sekku-hara*; the issues of discrimination and harassment are being confused. 'These days during such mixed parties,' she told me, 'when men carouse in their *nemaki* sleeping kimonos, some women take offense: *sekku-hara*.' Men sometimes emerge from their dormitory bedrooms later to rouse the women to share midnight bowls of noodles; yesterday's schoolboy pranks are *sekku-hara* today. Matching the vituperousness of recent feminist media rhetoric, such attitudes make it clear: the enemy, omnipresent, is simply male.

In the eyes of too many Japanese women, men are merely to be put up with and unwelcome. They go to bed with men and they marry them, the one being considered sometimes much too arbitrarily as a prelude to the other, but too few really like them. Man is an absentee, a creature perfunctorily fulfilling supportive financial duties and the dictates of procreation at home, and seeking kicks between the legs of prostitutes after his long office hours on the morrow. For sixteen hours a day, six days a week and thirty years, she can get along perfectly well without him.

Aspiring to greater freedom than ever before, the young rally to the cry of *kojin seikatsu* – the individual life – so the generation gap is a chasm too. Some might see greater freedom as a harbinger of decadence, but it means that the sexes can enjoy a richer social life and select their mates themselves. Greater permissiveness may well involve the sowing of wild oats for some, but it is the hallmark of an individualistic society which Japan, if not its exploitative corporate giants and monolithic authorities, manifestly aspires to become. Ironically enough, however, if this is truly to be achieved, it will have to begin with the social liberation of men.

PARADISE LOST

Milestones of social realism during the more politicized sixties and seventies and focusing on the lower depths, the films of Shohei Imamura depict an amoral world in which ethics and conduct wax and wane according to the vagaries of fate and necessity. The battle between the sexes is set against a hardboiled backdrop of poverty in which the heroine is typically a bar woman, a prostitute or a neglected urban or rural housewife. Sensual and cunning, she is a hardy survivor outwitting, turning the tables on and sometimes outliving the exploitative male. Epitomized in the 1964 *Intentions of Murder* by a martinet husband snuggling against his wife in bed and crooning 'Mummy', Imamura's men hide their weakness behind a strong façade. As the noted film critic Tadao Sato said: 'For Imamura, sex is the act of the child seeking to nestle in the security of the womb. It symbolizes the lost sense of communalism that existed in the villages of old.'

Among the castes beneath the stoic samurai and far from the official urban curtailments, the mixed bath was a social occasion, sex was guiltlessly regarded as one of the pleasures of life and free love was a more frequent prelude to parenthood than an arranged marriage. So it was in parts of the countryside until the mid-fifties, when the old rustic ways were abandoned as villages were depopulated or vanished with the exodus to the towns. The past is idealized as a paradise full of good neighbours; everyone was kind; everyone lived as one big happy family. As reassuring as a womb, it was 'warm' and it was 'wet', both adjectives incessantly bandied about and forming a virtual triumvirate with the word *'yasashii'* – gentle. Chauvinist cultural critics never fail to underscore such 'unique' qualities in contradistinction to the West, which is cold, dry and insensitive. The modern townsman looks back on halcyon rural and *shitamachi* urban pasts with unmitigated nostalgia, even though the quality of farm life depended precariously upon crop yields, and the inhabitants of sprawling city slums toiled for pittances. Too much of both in summer, life was otherwise warm if you could afford fuel and wet when the rain leaked through the roof.

Urbanization, industrialization and progress have been pushed too far; also blamed correctly and sometimes xenophobically on the Second World War, paradise lost is viewed as a tragedy. Permeating the ever-changing *mizu shobai* in which things are anyway never what they were, nostalgia colours the male popular imagination with poignant visions of the vanished prostitute's quarters and the good old agapeic rural life. It characterizes the universal view of the village household – the *furusato* – the mythical rural 'sweet home' that few have ever really known except as a favourite name for thousands of homely little urban restaurants. Wet, warm or otherwise, the patterns of life among the rural and urban populations were similar: hard new buildings change the face of residential Tokyo, but they have only superficially transformed what was in fact a haphazard amalgam of autonomous villages until only three decades ago.

Thus one thinks of Tora-san, the lovable itinerant *tekiya* pedlar and hero of some forty nearly identically plotted films: wandering the countryside as a loner, he keeps his *furusato* in his heart. It is a place in a real *shitamachi* area of Tokyo, idealized on film as a working-class heaven far from factories and cold concrete high-rises, in which everyone is close, kind and gentle. As lovable as he is, lazy Tora-san is too far beyond the social pale to marry: without exception, his rejection by the beauteous leading damsel he assists in distress constitutes the sentimental climax of every single film. A tubby figure with his hat askance above an amiable face and embodying all that is noble in the traditional common man, the unhurried, unharried and Chaplinesque Tora-san is a bewildered anachronism.

He also stands as a gentle warning to those who would stray beyond the safe confines of conformity. Those who haven't empathize with his sister's family, which forever awaits his news and visits in their confectioner's shop as they lead sweet, uneventful little lives. Nevertheless, condemned to bumble aimlessly along the roads of modern Japan, Tora-san draws as many laughs as he does uncontrolled sniffling from the audience. In this, many men conscious of having lost the comforting security of their *furusatos* and who feel a loss of identity and lead alienated lives in the workaday world see in Tora-san a hypothetical, if not a symbolic self. It is certainly no coincidence that this figure is phenomenally popular above all among the older generation and has little following among the young. The title of the entire series, *Otokowa tsurai-yo*, is telling too: *It's Tough Being a Man*.

Tora-san films are chaste and ennobling. He confines his perpetual sexual frustration strictly to his heart. Yet Tora-san comes from a stratum of society which not only had freer and easier attitudes to sex than most, but which until the late fifties was among the most likely to be providing fodder for the brothels only a short trip over the Sumida river. When the girls in the Yoshiwara were not from the countryside, they were obviously recruited from among the equally exploited urban poor. The plight of the unwilling slave is well known and still a reality but, like the heroines of Shohei Imamura's films, women from the lower orders were not, as the feminist journalist Asahi Shimbun pointed out earlier, 'especially demure'. Their attitude to sex was often sufficiently freewheeling to present them with no compunction to offer it for sale.

The licensing of prostitution was perfectly sensible, but in practice it was beyond the pale. That the modern Japanese sex industry should still be officially sanctioned as a kind of concentration camp for pleasure is lamentable enough; that it retains too many aspects fuelling the arguments of its opponents is worse. But where they house women having no qualms, as they often do, the Streets of Shame are enviably shameless when compared to their occidental equivalents. The ideal would be to keep them that way but, if sex should come to be viewed at last as degrading and shameful in Japan, the chances look slim.

The complete acceptance of the human body and its sexual functions was once upon a time one of the lessons that Japan could have taught the West, but the first western visitors were far too immured in their 'civilized' morality to notice. The moral legacy they left behind has entered the mainstream of social custom so long ago and so completely that it is now far too late. That reams of male magazines should now be devoted to surreptitious pantie shots of women on trains and tennis courts and that the sex trade is overrun with outlets for more furtive, purely masturbatory relief make what has been so often said before clearer than ever; Japan has lost its innocence.

Yet supposing that the welcome new political winds further emancipating women have in fact blown in the mixed blessing of a new moral order, how real is it? Japan, as it always has been, is a land of irrational contradictions. TV is said to be 'cleaner' than it used to be. And yet, recently focusing on SM and taking a professional female masochist in frilly black undies, 11 p.m. trussed her up and had her interviewed by a panel as she swung upside-down like a bat before them, suspended from a chain. The TV nymphets are back with a vengeance. Even comedy and variety programmes, which play to a majority female audience both in and outside the studio, often deploy whole armies of shapely young things in tight and teeny leotards. The difference is that although their function is purely decorative, they are now – albeit only slightly – less given to simpering and giggling coyly behind their hands.

In some of the comedy programmes devised by the indomitable and often acerbically satirical Beat Takeshi, for instance, they merely add a note of innuendo and join in a kind of zany, spontaneous overall boisterousness inconceivable on carefully rehearsed and generally prerecorded western TV. In the end, the implication is that neither sex sees anything intrinsically wrong with young girls in skimpy attire; they are simply there for fun. As the populace sees it and as officialdom buttresses with laws covering brothels and game parlours simultaneously, fun is a realm embracing sex by definition – and no longer a male preserve.

Yet that women could go topless as they do on the beaches of the occident is unthinkable in a country in which youths have taken to modest concealment in the showers in the sports club. Arguably this is merely a matter of fashion, although fashion too is a reflection of a social climate. Officialdom's obdurate aversion to pubic hair remains, but permissiveness is at last beginning to be viewed in a much more sophisticated light than either arbitrary official proscriptions or the old-time licentiousness of the populace. The irrational acceptance of the coercive and communally perceived *idée reçue* is gradually receding in the wake of more individualistic reason and logic.

Ubiquitous in the subways in mid-1989 was an advertisement showing a voluptuous blonde lying beside a bottle of Nikka whisky in a Wild West décor. Her blouse was torn, she was besmirched with sand and the picture raised a feminist furore. Not because it was overtly suggestive. Except for those upholding the arbitrary western equation with degradation, most Japanese women see little wrong with the ubiquitous practice of selling with sex; indeed, some of TV's sexiest commercials target women. The trouble with the Nikka advertisement lay in what it was suggesting. Part of a campaign, it complemented a TV commercial revealing that its thirty-second heroine had just been raped by a bunch of cowboys. The reaction came this time not just from the league of decency, but from women usually less given to sharing their views. In the end the commercial was cancelled and the subway ads removed. As it is with mascot girls on TV, a degree of sexual allure is fine, but pandering to antiquated macho values exalting rape fantasies: no. Japan has not entirely lost its innocence; it is beginning to mature.

A NEW ERA FOR THE YAMASHITAS

O-share: the word in front of the honorific *O* means witticism and joke, but it also means stylishness, dandyism and, as sometimes evidenced by misconstrued

T-shirt English, foppery. Buoying the consumer boom, the media currently hurl the word around in commercials targeting both sexes. It is not applied just to clothing and cosmetics, but also to beverages soft and alcoholic, cars, houses, bathroom fixtures, credit cards, noodles and even pink salons. Equated with that other great catch-word, 'lifestyle', *o-share* stands for the quest for greater individualism and it is forever on the lips and in the minds of young Japan.

Yesterday's youthful rebellion and glandular political activism both have a universal way of becoming today's fossils; the pendulum swings back and forth. Having caroused through the late sixties, occidental Flower Children engendered a more sedate generation with upwardly mobile aspirations. Having similarly donned the trappings of hippiedom, punk and heavy-metal and counting few true tearaways, young Japan now equally studiedly affects a yuppie pose but, as usual, there are variations on the theme. Chances are that in her office, the young woman you see with briefcase and designer suit, talking assertively with her girlfriends over glasses of wine in a café-bar, will be serving her male colleagues cups of tea. Where competition is collective and ambition tends to be quelled by the routine, the turn-on resides less in business acumen than in the accumulation of consumer status symbols. Fashion spawns the age of androgyny, the market for cosmetics for young men is brisk and a welter of male fashion magazines, catalogue-fashion, bring home the imperatives of buying. But is all this really new?

Observing fast-changing fads, an obsession with fashion, a mercantile culture fuelled by conspicuous spending and a comparable surge in cultural activities patronized by commerce, social commentators often equate the late twentieth century with Genroku – the

Edo-period zenith of fashion and style. As similarly mercantile and superficial as it is, the quest for individualism nevertheless sets the new Heisei era apart. Dressing up and dating, young Japan is searching for a new identity.

Although it would have assured his climb up the ladder, let us suppose that Takashi Yamashita, now thirty-three, is still a bachelor. Lured by a higher salary and a better job in a rising young advertising agency, he quit life employment and left the corporate straight and narrow behind. Driven by personal ambition, he is a *shinjinrui*, a new human being. This makes him an epitome of *o-share* and a darling of the films, TV dramas and commercials which plug him as a widespread phenomenon. He joins a newer feminine counterpart insofar as they do both exist and are slowly multiplying, but they are still only a tiny handful standing out from among the silent, conforming millions.

Having lost its glitter, the word *salaryman* is having its tarnish glossed over by a media bandying around the term *bijinesu-man*, which it matches with an image forever reassuring the public that everyone beneath the age of forty is running around socializing in mixed company. Fashionable fantasy would concede Takashi *ipso facto* relations with the opposite sex, implying that sexual desegregation does indeed present an alternative to *omiai* introductions and perhaps setting a welcome example to the many diffident, lonely males glued to rape comics and videos. However gradually, the ubiquitous imaginings of liberalism are making themselves felt in real life. Young office employees go out more and more often, yet the phenomenon will probably take as long to become the rule as it takes for the young to go grey. More ominously, those who frolicked in the bars of Shinjuku and waved banners in the demos of the sixties and seventies, and now in their forties, are the ones most likely to endure the worst of the corporate treadmill today.

If Takashi works in a smaller company, no matter how progressive, it will saddle him with a formidable workload to remain competitive. Years ago he would have saved money, but now that he knows that he will not be able to afford to buy a home when he marries, he spends most of his salary on designer suits and perhaps a European car. Such trappings confirm his aspirations towards an individual lifestyle, which is bludgeoned home by a media image serving a system striving unrelentingly to create a population of perfect consumers. He may also look forward to a trip abroad. Although it is well within his means, his sluggishly lengthening summer holiday time depends more upon his company's latitude than anything approaching legislation, and he is still much less likely to enjoy such a privilege than his female colleagues.

Next year he's nevertheless planning to go to Europe with his new girlfriend. His parents' anxious enquiries might have made the thought of marriage cross his mind, but if she's a *shinjinrui* too, she might be doing nicely in a job quite as taxing as his and it is very far from hers. Marriage is almost synonymous with producing offspring, a condition that would force her to quit. Takashi introduced her to his parents when they once visited Tokyo, but when they asked her about her work, she allowed her career-orientated enthusiasm to go a bit over the top. They gently said 'Is that so?' and politely smiled with annoyance.

People like Takashi may no longer work late every night, but company loyalty would still make their colleagues the prime option for after-hours companionship. The difference is that the horizons of younger employees are widening. Office friendships are becoming more a matter of spontaneity and personal inclination; the tight corporate drinking circle occasionally expands with nights on the town with acquaintances of both sexes and from more varied backgrounds. That deep change is in the air in Japan is clearer at the end of the twentieth century than ever before. Whether it is again a superficial matter of *plus ça change, plus c'est la même chose* depends entirely upon the Japanese themselves and how much they are prepared to swing things as a whole by shaping their destinies in their own, individual hands.

Meanwhile, out in the quiet of the countryside, Mayumi gave birth to a baby girl in June 1989. This seemed to fit the spirit of the times, which was auspiciously reconfirmed on 31 December, when the annual *Kohaku* TV song contest was won by the Reds. Like her husband and both their families, she had hoped rather more for a son – but never mind. Hirohito, the Emperor Showa, died on 7 January, following a grim six months clouded by his illness, during which taxis tuned in to European classical music aired over radio stations late at night and hardly anyone dared throw any parties, as much as through respect as from fear of reprisals from rightist thugs. Obaa-san, poor dear, suddenly succumbed to pneumonia in late November.

When Kimiko Yamashita cleaned out her room and opened the *tansu* chest, she took various belongings from the drawers and put them in a storage box. Among them were two small cases, one containing the medal grandpa received from the Emperor Meiji and the other the engraved silver pocket-watch presented him by a Kobe hospital. There was also an oval frame containing a faded sepia photograph of a man in a formal kimono complete with swords and a topknot. No one remembered seeing it before, but because it had been placed alongside grandpa's medals and slightly resembled him, the Yamashitas later surmised that it might be his father, but they would never know for sure. Turning out another small item, wrapped in a square of silk, Kimiko was shocked.

Fancy! What if the children saw it? But the children were grown up. They have left home, she reflected despondently: what would she and Shigeru do when they got too old to cope? Will one of their sons bring his bride back to care for them? Fat chance. Like daycare, facilities for the elderly are lamentable. She decided to throw the object away, but as it caught the rays of the setting sun through the window, she had second thoughts. Rewrapping it carefully in the square of silk, she put it back in the box with a sigh of annoyance. Wasn't that just like grandpa?

Following the Showa emperor's demise, Shigeru took down his portrait but did not replace it with the Heisei successor. It was not that he did not respect the sovereign, but it somehow no longer seemed necessary. Modern and telegenic, the Emperor had suddenly become too down to earth to hang on the wall. His son Prince Aya would soon be marrying a university classmate of his own choice – a commoner. Shigeru surmised that old Hirohito's portrait had perhaps been to honour his father's spirit, but most of all to please his mother.

During the celebrations on New Year's Day 1990, Shigeru's nephew and niece were too taken by his new granddaughter to roll quite so boisterously over the floor. Perhaps Kimiko had meanwhile had just one too many; she suddenly decided to show everyone the thing she had found in grandma's drawer. Handed round and much admired once the children had safely gone to play outside, the new family heirloom also triggered a great deal of merriment. Glazed a delicate cherry-blossom pink outside, it was a little sake cup. Inside, painted in pretty colours and with minute anatomical detail, was a picture of a geisha and a samurai ecstatically clasped in a graphic erotic embrace.

References and Notes

Opening quotations

W. E. Curtis in *The Truth About Japan*, ed. Andrew Watt, Yenbooks/Charles E. Tuttle Co., 1988.

Poem by Akiko Yosano, from *Tangled Hair (Midaregami)*, tr. Stanford Goldstein and Seishi Shinoda, Charles E. Tuttle Co., 1987.

Part I – New Year

p. 29: Quotation from Lafcadio Hearn, *Japan: An Interpretation*, Charles E. Tuttle Co., 1959.

p. 30–43: The creation myths, the *Kojiki*, tr. Basil Hall Chamberlain, and *Nihongi*, tr. W. G. Aston, Charles E. Tuttle Co., 1981 and 1972.

p. 36: Quotation from Théo Lésoualc'h, *Erotique du Japon*, Jean Jacques Pauvert, 1968, and Henri Veyrier, 1987.

p. 39–40: Quotation from Kurt Singer, *Mirror, Sword and Jewel*, Croom Helm, London, 1973.

p. 45: Love hotel figures: *The Japan Times*, 16 May 1984.

p. 67: Akiko Yosano's poem from *Tangled Hair*, Charles E. Tuttle Co., 1987.

p. 76: Quotations from *Salaryman in Japan*, The Japan Travel Bureau Inc., 1986.

p. 78: Mainichi letter from *The Japan Times*, November 1987.

p. 82: Quotation from James Trager, *Letters from Sachiko*, Abacus, Sphere Books Ltd., 1984.

p. 83–4: Tokyo Metropolitan Government survey on discrimination, *The Japan Times*, 6 June 1987.

p. 87: Quote from Harumi Befu, *Japan: An Anthropological Introduction*, Harper & Row Publishers Inc., New York, 1971.

p. 103: Quotation from Ogai Mori, *Vita Sexualis*, tr. Kazuji Ninomiya and Stanford Goldstein, Charles E. Tuttle Co., 1972.

p. 107: Quotation by Ejima Kiseki from *The Floating World in Japanese Fiction*, Howard Hibbett, Oxford University Press, 1959.

p. 113: Teacher on sex education, *The Japan Times*, 27 October 1988.

p. 114–17: Figures from the Japan Sex Education Association and Prof. A. Fukushima's remarks,

The Japan Times, 18 December 1988.

p. 122–6, Japanese child rearing: Ruth Benedict, *The Chrysanthemum and the Sword – Patterns of Japanese Culture*, Charles E. Tuttle Co., 1954.

p. 125: *The Anatomy of Dependence*, Takeo Doi, tr. John Bester, Kodansha International Ltd, Tokyo, New York and San Francisco, 1973.

p. 127: Murasaki Shikibu's remark as in *The World of the Shining Prince*, Ivan Morris, Alfred A. Knopf, Inc., 1964.

p. 128–30: Genital terminology: Donald Richie and Kenkichi Ito, *The Erotic Gods*, Zufushinsha, Tokyo, 1967.

p. 130: Feminists on genital terminology: Kittredge Cherry, *Womansword*, Kodansha International Ltd.

p. 132: Quotation, *ibid*.

Part II – The Rites of Spring

p. 147: Fertility festivals: D. Richie and K. Ito, *op. cit.*

p. 148: Quotation from *Sexual Life in Ancient Rome*, Otto Kiefer, Routledge & Kegan Paul Ltd, 1934.

p. 148: Inuyama and Tagata shrine festivals: *see* K. Cherry, *op. cit.* and T. Lésoualc'h, *op. cit.*

p. 152–4: Tachikawa Ryu and Fuji-Kō, D. Richie and K. Ito, *op. cit.*

p. 158: Quotation from L. Hearn, *op. cit.*

p. 160: The God of Speedy Ball: *see* H. Befu, *op. cit.*

p. 160: Silk worms: *see* D. Richie and K. Ito, *op. cit.*

p. 161: *De Civitate Dei* quotation, O. Kiefer, *op. cit.*

p. 161: The Holy Light: *see* I. Morris, *op. cit.*

p. 163: 8th-cent. festivals edict: *see* T. Lésoualc'h, *op. cit.*

p. 163–4: Yami Matsuri: *see* D. Richie and K. Ito, *op. cit.*

p. 165: Plea to Emperor Saga, 9th cent: *see* T. Lésoualc'h, *op. cit.*

p. 167: *Dosojin: see* D. Richie and K. Ito, *op. cit.*

p. 174: Poem from *L'Expression poétique dans le folklore japonais*, Georges Bonneat, Librairie Orientaliste Paul Geuthner, Paris, 1934.

p. 176: Urinating in the grooves of sliding doors: *see* T. Lésoualc'h, *op. cit.*

p. 177: Sei Shonagon, *The Pillow Book of Sei Shonagon*, tr. Ivan Morris, Columbia University Press, 1967.

p. 178–9: Quotation from Georges Bataille, *L'Erotisme*, Editions de Minuit, Paris, 1957.

p. 184: *Kuruma arasoi*: I. Morris, *The World of the Shining Prince*.

p. 185: Sei Shonagon quotation from I. Morris, *The Pillow Book of Sei Shonagon*.

p. 192–3: Quotation on *mono no aware: see* I. Morris, *The World of the Shining Prince*.

p. 195: Quotation from *The Tale of Genji*, tr. Edward G. Seidensticker, Alfred A. Knopf, New York, 1976.

p. 196: *The Tale of the Lady*

Ochikubo, tr. Wilfred Whitehouse and Eizo Yanagisawa, Peter Owen Ltd, London, 1970.

p. 198: Quotation, *The Tale of Genji*, tr. E. G. Seidensticker.

p. 199: T. Lésoualc'h, *op. cit.*

p. 201–3: *The Tale of Genji*, tr. E. G. Seidensticker.

p. 205–13: Quotations from R. H. Van Gulick, *Sexual Life in Ancient China*, E. J. Brill, Leiden, 1974.

p. 215: Koshibaki-zoshi: T. Lésoualc'h, *op. cit.*

p. 216: 'Women of Pleasure' quotation from E. G. Seidensticker, *op. cit.*

p. 217–19: Exercises in seduction: *see* I. Morris, *The World of the Shining Prince.*

Part III – The Venereal Equinox

p. 233–40: *Re* the shogun's sex life, Kiyoyuki Higuchi, *Edo Sei Fuzoku Yobanashi*, Kawade Bunko, Tokyo, 1988.

p. 240: Ihara Saikaku quotation from *The Woman Who Spent Her Life in Love*: *see* Howard Hibbett, *op. cit.*

p. 242: Quotation from *Le Chant de l'Oreiller – l'art d'aimer au Japon*, Bibliothèque des Arts, Paris, 1973.

p. 243–4: Sex aids, etc: *see* T. Lésoualc'h, *op. cit.*

p. 244: *Rin-no-tama*: *see* R. H. Van Gulik, *op. cit.*

p. 247: Shoji Jinyemon: *see* J. E. DeBecker, *The Nightless City*, Charles E. Tuttle Co., 1971.

p. 253–4: Okuni and the kabuki: *see* Faubion Bowers, *The Japanese Theater*, Hermitage House, New York, 1952.

p. 258: Yoyoda Tatsugoro: *see* H. Hibbett, *op. cit.*

p. 262: Chikamatsu Monzaemon: *see* F. Bowers, *op. cit.*

p. 268: Ihara Saikaku: *see* H. Hibbett, *op. cit.*

p. 269–70: Edicts quoted from Richard Lane's essay, *Saikaku's Five Women* as in *Five Women Who Loved Love*, tr. Wm Theodore De Bary, Charles E. Tuttle Co., 1963.

p. 270: The story of Oshichi, *see* W. T. De Bary, *op. cit.*

p. 271: Kiseki's quotations: *see* H. Hibbett, *op. cit.*

p. 271: *The Woman Who Spent Her Life in Love, idem.*

p. 273: Quotation from Saikaku's *The Life of an Amorous Man*, tr. Kengi Hamada, Charles Tuttle Co., 1964.

p. 273–85: *Ukiyo-e* prints: Richard Lane, *Images from the Floating World: The Japanese Print*, New York, 1978; *The Japanese Print*, Hugo Munsterberg, John Weatherhill Inc., 1982; T. Lésoualc'h, *op. cit.*; *Le Chant de l'Oreiller*, Paris, 1973; Bernard Soulie, *L'Erotisme Japonais*, Productions Liber S.A. Geneva, 1981.

p. 286: Quotation from J. E. DeBecker, *op. cit.*

p. 286–91: Ranks of prostitutes and brothels: *ibid.*

p. 291: Higuchi Ichiyo: Robert Lyons Danly, *In the Shade of Spring Leaves*, Yale University Press, 1981.

p. 294–6: Fujimoto Kizan: Donald Keene, *Landscapes and Portraits/Appreciations of Japanese Culture*, Kodansha International Ltd, Tokyo, New York and San Francisco, 1971.

p. 297: Trade in hair and fingernails: Ihara Saikaku, *The Life of an Amorous Man*, tr. Kengi Hamada.

p. 298–300: Famous courtesans, and quotation: J. E. DeBecker, *op. cit.*

p. 298–9: Quotation from *The Real Japan*, Henry Norman, in J. E. DeBecker, *op. cit.*

p. 305: *Chonkina*: T. Lésoualc'h, *op. cit.*

p. 306: Quotations from *The Woman Who Spent Her Life in Love*, Howard Hibbett, *op. cit.*

p. 307–8: *Eejyanai-ka*: *see* Shohei Imamura's film of the same name, Shochiku Productions, 1981.

p. 309: 'The British Grenadiers': Richard Storry, *A History of Modern Japan*, Pelican/Penguin Books, 1960.

p. 310: Nipponese girls: Dr Tresmain-Trémolières, *La Cité d'Amour au Japon*, Librairie Universelle, Paris, 1908.

p. 312: J. E. DeBecker: *op. cit.*

p. 312–16: Meiji figures on prostitution: *see* J. E. DeBecker, *op. cit.*

p. 318: Saito Shinichi, *Meiji Yoshiwara Saikenki*, Kawaide Shobo Shinsha, 1985.

p. 321: Quotations from Ogai Mori, *Vita Sexualis*, tr. Kazuji Ninomiya and Stanford Goldstein, Charles E. Tuttle Co., 1972.

p. 322: Shinagawa and Meishimori, Paul Waley, *Tokyo Now and Then*, John Weatherhill Inc., New York and Tokyo, 1984.

p. 323–4: References to Nagai Kafu: *see* Edward G. Seidensticker, *Kafu the Scribbler*, Stanford University Press, 1965.

p. 326: Police ban on sexual relations with foreigners: Robert Guillain, *Orient Extreme*, Arléa/Le Seuil, Paris, 1986.

p. 327: 1944 restrictions on geisha: *see* Robert Guillain, *Les Geishas*, Arléa, Paris, 1988.

p. 329: The 'six-inch' barrier: Donald Richie, 'Tokyo Remembered', article in *Winds* magazine, 1988.

p. 331–2: Toshio Kanai's comments from *Nikutai no Mon* programme pamphlet, Toei Productions, 1988.

Part IV – Heatwaves in the Water Trade

p. 340–41: Quotation from *Nihongi*, *op. cit.*

p. 344: Quotation from Harumi Befu, *Japan: An Anthropological Introduction*, Harper & Row, New York, 1971.

p. 344–5: 'Tiger box' statistics from *Shukan Gendai* magazine, Nov. 1980, as quoted in *The Japan Times*, 3 Nov. 1980. Quotation, *ibid.*

p. 347–8: Shinjuku: *see* Philippe Pons, *D'Edo à Tokyo*, Gallimard, Paris, 1988.

p. 355: Quotation from Kurt Singer, *Mirror, Sword and Jewel*, Croom Helm, London, 1973.

p. 368–9: Quotation from Liza Dalby, *Geisha*, University of California Press, 1983/Vintage Books, New York, 1985.

p. 370: 40% statistic – from the Japanese Green Cross Society survey, May 1988.

p. 375: Quotation from Robert Guillain, *Les Geishas*, Arléa, Paris, 1988.

p. 377: Quotation from Nagai Kafu, *Geisha in Rivalry (Udekurabe)*, tr. K. Meissner and R. Friedrich, Charles E. Tuttle Co., 1963.

p. 377: 'Foreign Girls Invade Geisha's Turf', from *Shukan Bunshun* magazine, quoted in *The Japan Times*, 14 December 1982.

p. 377–81: Geisha statistics (1980), Liza Dalby, *op. cit.*

p. 379: Shukan Sankei *re* Niigata Geisha Co., *The Japan Times*, 13 December 1987.

p. 382: Junichi Mita's remark quoted from Robert Guillan, *Les Geishas*.

p. 395: Quotation from Akiyuki Nozaka, *The Pornographers (Erogotoshi-tachi)*, tr. Michael Gallagher, Alfred A. Knopf Inc., New York, 1968.

p. 395: Remark from Boye DeMente, *Bachelor's Japan*, Charles E. Tuttle Co., 1967.

p. 408: Quotation from Akiyuki Nozaka, *op. cit.*

p. 408: Quotation: Junichiro Tanizaki, *Naomi (Chijin no ai)*, tr. Anthony H. Chambers, Alfred A. Knopf Inc., New York, 1985.

p. 409: Survey ('81): *Shukan Shincho* magazine, 22 January 1981; Tokyo Metropolitan Taito Hospital report ('88), *The Japan Times*, 23 February 1988.

p. 411: 'Morals officer': *Shukan Shincho* magazine, 22 January 1981.

p. 413: Kofu girl students and sex: *The Japan Times*, 15 May 1975.

p. 421: Osaka's 'Family Aoyama', *The Japan Times*, 11 September 1987.

p. 422: Prime Minister's Office survey on prostitution, released on 7 March 1986.

p. 422: *More Report on Male Sexuality*, Shueisha, Tokyo, 1984.

p. 424–5: Statistics from *More Report on Female Sexuality*, Shueisha, Tokyo, 1983.

p. 431–2: References to Nagai Kafu and quotation: *see* Edward G. Seidensticker, *Kafu the Scribbler*, Stanford University Press, 1965.

p. 446: Shusaku Endo, *Scandal*, tr. Van C. Gessel, Charles E. Tuttle Co., 1988.

p. 447: The SM club as subterfuge, *Shukan Shincho* magazine, November 1988.

p. 452–3: Jun Sayama *see* Tsubura En, *Himo*, Kobunsha Bunko, 1987.

p. 458: *Baranko*: Tanaka Komimasa, *Komimasa sinema tsua*, Hayakawa Publishing, 1989.

p. 463–4: Sayuri Ichijo: *see* Max Tessier, 'L'Exutoire du roman-porno', *Cinéma d'Aujourd'hui*, Paris, Winter 1979–80.

p. 466: Quotation from *The*

Kojiki, tr. Basil Hall
Chamberlain, Charles E.
Tuttle Co., 1981.

p. 483: Quotation from *Takeo
Doi*, *op. cit.*

p. 483–4: Theatre of cruelty: *see*
Antonin Artaud, 'Le Théâtre
et son double', *Collection Idées*,
Gallimard, Paris, 1964.

p. 484: Kafu quotation: *see* E. G.
Seidensticker, *op. cit.*

p. 490: Quotation and references
from *Shukan Shincho* magazine,
The Japan Times, 19 January
1981.

p. 491: Elementary schoolteacher: *The Japan Times*, 5
September 1987.

p. 492–3: Figures: National Police
Agency (NPA) white paper on
Businesses Affecting Public
Morals, December 1983.

p. 493: NPA and Metropolitan
Police Department (MPD)
figures as in *The Japan Times*,
23 February 1986.

p. 496: Quotation, *ibid.*

p. 498: Prime Minister's Office
survey on prostitution, March
1986.

p. 498: Thailand: *The Bangkok
Post*, 15 March 1989.

p. 499: VD figures from Health
and Welfare Ministry survey,
November 1983–January 1984.

p. 499: Senzoku area survey, *The
Japan Times*, 23 February 1988.

p. 500–501: Aids: Prof. Bin Takeda,
The Japan Times, 21 May 1988.

p. 508: Slave markets: *see* Alec
Dubro & David E. Kaplan,
Yakuza, Addison-Wesley
Publishing Co. Inc., USA,
1986.

p. 509: Thai prostitution racket,
Asahi Shimbun, 5 July 1988.

p. 512: Filipina's lawsuit: Asahi
Shimbun, 21 June 1989; *The
Japan Times*, 6 June, 8 and 14
July.

p. 516–17: Illegal immigrant
figures: Ministry of Justice,
quoted in *The Japan Times*,
14 June 1989.

Part V – A Quirk for All Seasons

p. 529: Quotation from Junichiro
Tanizaki, *In Praise of Shadows*,
tr. Thomas J. Harper and
Edward G. Seidensticker,
Leete's Island Books, Inc.,
1977.

p. 533: *Toiretto Hakase*: *see*
Frederik L. Schodt, *Manga!
Manga! The World of Japanese
Comics*, Kodansha
International, 1983.

p. 534: Quotation from Faubion
Bowers, *op. cit.*

p. 552: Quotation from Claude
Levi-Strauss, *Tristes Tropiques*,
Librairie Plon, Paris, 1955.

p. 555: *Dame Oyaji*: *see* Frederik
Schodt, *op. cit.*

p. 556–7: Junichiro Tanizaki,
Naomi (Chijin no Ai), tr.
Anthony H. Chambers, Alfred
A. Knopf, New York, 1985.

p. 557: Junichiro Tanizaki, *The
Key (Kagi)*, tr. Howard
Hibbett, Alfred A. Knopf,
1960.

p. 557–8: Junichiro Tanizaki,
*Diary of a Mad Old Man (Futen
Rojin Nikki)*, tr. H. Hibbett,
Alfred A. Knopf, 1965.

p. 558–60: Portrait of Shunkin
(Shunkincho) from Junichiro

Tanizaki, *Seven Japanese Tales*, tr. H. Hibbett, Alfred A. Knopf, 1958.

p. 560: Junichiro Tanizaki, *ibid.*

p. 561–2: Donald Richie, *The Japanese Tattoo*, John Weatherhill, New York & Tokyo, 1980.

p. 563: Edogawa Rampo, *Japanese Tales of Mystery and Imagination*, tr. James B. Harris, Charles E. Tuttle Co., 1956.

p. 564: *The Peony Lantern* (*Botan Doro*): Lafcadio Hearn, *Kwaidan: Stories and Studies of Strange Things*, Charles E. Tuttle Co., 1960.

p. 567–8: Poems by Akiko Yosano, *op. cit.*

p. 569: Nagoya bar hostess: *The Japan Times*, 29 June 1982.

p. 575–6: Ise poems: *Les Contes d'Isé*, tr. G. Renondeau, Gallimard-Unesco, Paris, 1969.

p. 577: Tanizaki, *In Praise of Shadows*.

p. 581: Philippe Pons, *op. cit.*

p. 588: Nagisa Oshima quoted from *Oshima: Ecrits 1956–1978*, Gallimard, Paris, 1980.

p. 589–601: Bleating about the Bush: parts of this section are taken from the author's article in *Intersect* magazine; facts and official remarks from *The Japan Times*, November 1980.

p. 601: Quotation from *The Japanese Eroduction* in *A Lateral View*, Donald Richie, *The Japan Times*, 1987.

p. 622: Quotation from J. E. DeBecker, *op. cit.*

p. 629–30: Ihara Saikaku quoted from *Five Women Who Loved Love*, tr. Wm. T. De Bary, *op. cit.*; reference to 'Kichiya', *ibid.*

p. 630: Yoshizawa Ayame quoted from Donald Keene, *op. cit.*

p. 635: Quotations from Ihara Saikaku, *Comrade Loves of the Samurai*, tr. E. Powys Mathers (from French, Ken Sato), London, 1928 and Charles E. Tuttle Co., 1972.

p. 639–41: Lesbian terminology: Kittredge Cherry, *op. cit.*

p. 640: Quotation from Junnosuke Yoshiyuki, *The Dark Room* (*Anshitsu*), tr. John Bester, Kodansha International, 1975.

p. 643: Bishonen: *A Japanese Mirror*, Ian Buruma, Jonathan Cape, London, 1983.

p. 644: 'Oman and Gengobei', from *Five Women Who Loved Love*.

p. 646–7: Takarazuka: *see* Ian Buruma, *op. cit.*

p. 651: *Joshi-puro* interview: Don Morton, 'Bubblegum and Blood', *The Tokyo Journal*, July 1989.

p. 651: Quotation from Ian Buruma, *op. cit.*

Part VI – A New Era

p. 663: Quotations from Karel Van Wolferen, *The Enigma of Japanese Power*, Macmillan, 1989.

p. 666: 1982 survey figures and quotation: *The Japan Times*, 5 April 1983; 1989 survey: *The Japan Times*, 3 January 1990.

p. 668: Nagisa Araki: *The Japan Times*, 16 July 1989.

p. 671: March 1989 comparative survey between New York, Los Angeles and Tokyo conducted by Dentsu Soken Co.; workers' attitudes by Fukoku Mutual Life Insurance Co., 29 August 1989.

p. 671–2: Seiko Tanabe in *Chuo Koron* magazine, June 1987, as in *The Japan Times*, 9 June 1987.

p. 677: Kuniko Uemura: *The Japan Times*, 27 September 1988.

p. 685: Kurt Singer, *op. cit.*

p. 685–6: Harassment hot line: *The Japan Times*, 9 October 1989, 3 December 1989.

p. 687: Tadao Sato's quotation from *Currents in Japanese Cinema*, tr. Gregory Barrett, Kodansha International, 1982.

p. 688–9: Tora-san: *ibid; see* also Ian Buruma, *op. cit.*

(*Note*: all translations from French by the author.)

Index